Early Childhood Experiences in

Language Arts

Early Literacy

Eighth Edition

Join us on the web at

EarlyChildEd.delmar.com

Early Childhood Experiences in Language Arts

Language Arts

Early Literacy

Eighth Edition

Jeanne M. Machado
Emerita, San Jose City College

THOMSON

DELMAR LEARNING

Australia   Canada   Mexico   Singapore   Spain   United Kingdom

THOMSON

DELMAR LEARNING

Early Childhood Experiences in Language Arts: Early Literacy, Eighth Edition

Jeanne M. Machado

Vice President, Career Education SBU:
Dawn Gerrain

Director of Learning Solutions:
Sherry Dickinson

Managing Editor:
Robert L. Serenka, Jr.

Senior Acquisitions Editor:
Erin O'Connor

Editorial Assistant:
Stephanie Kelly

Director of Production:
Wendy A. Troeger

Production Manager:
J.P. Henkel

Production Editor:
Joy Kocsis

Production Assistant:
Angela Iula

Director of Marketing:
Wendy E. Mapstone

Channel Manager:
Kristin McNary

Marketing Coordinator:
Scott Chrysler

Composition:
Graphic World Inc.

Cover Design and Illustration:
Chris Watkins

Library of Congress Cataloging-in-Publication Data

Machado, Jeanne M.
  Early childhood experiences in language arts : early literacy / Jeanne M. Machado.—8th ed.
    p. cm.
  Includes bibliographical references and index.
  ISBN-10: 1-4180-0026-4
  ISBN-13: 978-1-4180-0026-4
    1. Language arts (Early childhood)
  2. Language acquisition—Parent participation. 3. Literacy. I. Title.

  LB1139.5.L35M335 2005
  372.6—dc22

                                    2005054670

NOTICE TO THE READER

CONTENTS

v

Early Childhood Experiences in Language Arts: Early Literacy is a state-of-the-art teacher-training text designed to help those working in the early childhood education field provide an opportunity-rich program full of interesting, appropriate, and developmental language arts activities. As new terms are encountered, definitions are provided, and a running glossary reinforces comprehension of key concepts. It is both a practical "how-to" manual and a collection of resources that includes a large number of classic, tried-and-true activities. The No Child Left Behind Act and its influence and impact on early childhood education are also given comprehensive coverage.

The first few chapters present a detailed account of language acquisition, young children's early communicative capacities, growth milestones, and age-level characteristics (infancy through preschool), along with suggested professional techniques to promote each child's self-esteem and potential. Because a comprehensive, dynamically planned early childhood language arts curriculum consists of four broad interrelated areas—speaking (oral), listening, writing, and reading—each is fully explored and described in a separate text section. Visual literacy, a new language arts focus, is given textual coverage due to young children's growing interactions with visual technologies. It is hoped that confidence and skill gained by the reader will help provide young children with an enthusiastic, knowledgeable teacher-companion who enjoys and encourages them in their discovery of the language arts.

Infant and toddler chapters are intended to increase the reader's understanding of infant and toddler communication abilities and the role of adult behavior in promoting language growth. Because the number of children with special needs enrolled in early education programs has dramatically increased, discussion and recommended teacher techniques are provided. Special attention has been given to ways of providing the child with language-rich environments and enthusiastic, supportive teachers who are dynamic, observant companions and collaborators. The influence of Vygotsky's theories has been given attention. Scaffolding and webbing techniques are included. Fine literature and classics appropriate to the child's age level are recommended. Activity ideas and patterns for storytelling and flannel board sets provide the student with resource ideas to try out in early child classrooms. A current view of young children's progress in the understanding and use of print in daily life has been updated. Children's curiosity and their natural ability to become communicators are described to give the reader increased confidence in children's ability to learn. A discussion concerning children's intelligent pursuit of knowledge and skill helps teachers recognize and provide growth-producing comments in verbal exchanges. Parent tips to extend language and provide literacy-enriched home environments are also present.

The eighth edition has noted current public and legislative interest in those prekindergarten experiences that equip young children with the necessary background to master with ease the task of beginning reading. Research and activities promoting phonological and phonemic awareness are discussed in detail, as is the alphabetic principle. Sections concerned with developmentally appropriate instruction in these areas outline the current concern regarding curricula and relating it to children's activities, interests, and life experiences.

The diversity in preschool classrooms is addressed, in particular the fact that non-native English-speaking children are abundantly present in many geographical areas of the United States. Cultural differences are increasingly common, and this new edition, as in former editions, urges teachers to respect, understand, and dignify each child's uniqueness as they promote the English language arts.

Educators are concerned with discoveries made by neurolinguistic researchers regarding young children's brain capacities and development and how these new findings affect their planned curricula. This is addressed, and text discussion reflects current thinking and research reviewed by the National Literacy Panel.

The text emphasizes the importance of adult and parental attitudes about young children's communicative abilities from birth onward. It alerts adults to act in ways that promote, rather than impede, growth in children's language arts skills and abilities. Home-school partnership goals for children's literacy development are reviewed. The everyday and special opportunities families have to develop growth in language arts skills and to promote school success receive additional attention in this edition.

NEW FEATURES

The eighth edition includes a number of new and former features to aid the student's mastery of each chapter's content.

- *Discussion Vignettes*—a new feature, these short vignettes introduce chapters, add real-life situations, and pique student interest. The *Questions to Ponder* promote reflection and discussion.

- *Key Terms*—important terms to know are listed in alphabetical order at the beginning of each chapter, in color where they appear within the chapter, in a running glossary at the bottom of the page on which they appear, and again in the glossary at the back of the book. Reinforcement and cross-referencing enhance comprehension for the student.

- *Helpful Web Sites*—Web sites to professional organizations, associations, public entities, and colleges or universities are identified at the end of each chapter. A brief description of a chapter-related item accompanies many provided listings or suggestions that will narrow the student's search.

- *Activities*—this feature ends chapters in which ideas for child or adult activities have been presented. This allows for uninterrupted reading of theory and later examination of activities suggested by the author.

- *Additional Resources*—this section follows each chapter's summary. It presents readings for students wanting further depth, reinforcement of chapter topics, and/or pursuit of special interests. Resources such as commercial educational materials suppliers and professional organizations where further information can be obtained are also included.

- *Online Companion*™—the Online Companion™ to accompany the eighth edition of *Early Childhood Experiences in Language Arts: Early Literacy* is your link to early childhood education on the Internet. The Online Companion™ contains many features to help focus your understanding of language arts for young children.

Addtional *Review Questions* for each chapter will allow students to gauge their understanding of presented material.

Additional *Student Activities* and a *Discussion Forum* are available to promote the sharing and exhange of ideas and outcomes with classmates and instructors on-line,

or they can be used for a training group's classroom discussions.

Additional classic or "tried-and-true" *Language Arts Activity Ideas,* finger plays, stories, and directions for teaching visuals provide a wider range of items than found in the text. These can be downloaded and printed, increasing or supplementing students' collections.

Rating Forms included on-line will permit assessment of teaching behaviors and promote the student's assessment of children's progress.

Opportunities for the student's creation of children's language arts activities and experiences are plentiful. Authorship of literary works to share with young children is stimulated through on-line suggestions and exercises.

 Additional readings, Web sites, and views about legislation affecting children with disabilities are found in the Online Companion™. Presented material promotes sharing your ideas with peers. The criteria for the selection of Afrocentric books and their key elements, identified by C. W. Hudson, is available. You may wish to take part in a discussion forum examining the issue of authors who can best depict African-Americans in preschool picture books.

ANCILLARIES

Instructor's Manual

The *Instructor's Manual* includes suggested training session discussion topics and classroom exercises promoting the exchange of ideas and active student participation and application of each chapter's content. Answers to review questions, test items, multimedia resources, and suggested student assignment sheets are part of the manual.

Computerized Test Bank

eResource The new e-Resource component is geared to provide instructors with all the tools they need on one convenient CD-ROM. Instructors will find that this resource provides them with a turnkey solution to help them teach by making available PowerPoint® slides for each book chapter, the Computerized Test Bank, an electronic version of the Instructor's Manual, and other text-specific resources.

PROFESSIONAL ENHANCEMENT BOOK

A new supplement to accompany this text is the *Language Arts and Literacy Professional Enhancement* booklet for students. This book, which is part of Thomson Delmar Learning's Early Childhood Education Professional Enhancement series, focuses on key topics of interest to future early childhood teachers and caregivers. Students will keep this informational supplement and use it for years to come in their early childhood practices.

WEBTUTOR™

The WebTutor™ to accompany *Early Childhood Experiences in Language Arts: Early Literacy,* eighth edition, allows you to take learning beyond the classroom. This Online Courseware is designed to complement the text and benefit students by helping them better manage their time, prepare for exams, organize their notes, and more. Special features include:

◆ Chapter Learning Objectives—is correlated with textbook chapter objectives.

◆ Online Course Preparation—lists what students should have read or done before using on-line content.

◆ Study Sheets—outline the content of each chapter and contain notes. Study Sheets can be printed to help students learn and remember important points.

◆ Glossary—provides definitions for terms in each chapter or in the course as a whole.

◆ Flash Cards—allow students to test themselves on word definitions.

◆ Discussion Topics—are posted to encourage use as a threaded bulletin board and as assignments to develop critical thinking skills.

♦ FAQs—provide questions and answers that students may have about specific content.

♦ Online Class Notes—provide additional information about the chapter content.

♦ Online Chapter Quizzes—are given in various formats, including matching exercises, true/false quizzes, short-answer questions, and multiple-choice questions, and provide immediate feedback for correct and incorrect answers. Multiple-choice questions also include rationales for right and wrong choices.

♦ Web Links—provide students with practice searching the Web for information. Learners choose from a variety of Web links and report findings to their instructor through e-mail.

A benefit for instructors as well as students, the WebTutor™ allows for on-line discussion with the instructor and other class members, real-time chat to enable virtual office hours and encourage collaborative learning environments, a calendar of syllabus information for easy reference, e-mail connections to facilitate communication among classmates and between students and instructors, and customization tools that help instructors tailor their course to fit their needs by adding or changing content.

WebTutor™ allows you to extend your reach beyond the classroom and is available on either WebCT or Blackboard platforms.

ONLINE COMPANION™

The Online Companion™ to accompany the eighth edition of *Early Childhood Experiences in Language Arts: Early Literacy* is your link to additional Early Childhood Education resources on the Internet. This informative supplement includes Case Studies with Critical Thinking Questions, Student Activities, a Discussion Forum, Practice Test Questions, Observation Forms, and Helpful Web Links, culled from each chapter. You can find the Online Companion™ at http://www.earlychilded.delmar.com.

ABOUT THE AUTHOR

The author's experience in the early childhood education field has included full-time assignment as community college instructor and department chairperson. Her duties included supervision of early childhood education students at two on-campus laboratory child development centers at San Jose City College and Evergreen Valley College, as well as child centers in the local community. Her teaching responsibilities encompassed early childhood education, child development, and parenting courses.

She received her MA from San Jose State University and her vocational community college life credential with coursework from the University of California at Berkeley. Her experience includes working as a teacher and director in public early childhood programs, parent cooperative programs, and a self-owned and operated private preschool. Ms. Machado is an active participant in several professional organizations that relate to the education and well-being of young children and their families. She is a past president of CCCECE (California Community College Early Childhood Educators) and Peninsula Chapter of the California Association for the Education of Young Children. Her authoring efforts, with Dr. Helen Meyer-Botnarescue of the University of California at Hayward, produced a text for student teachers entitled *Student Teaching: Early Childhood Practicum Guide,* fifth edition, Thomson Delmar Learning, 2005.

Currently, Ms. Machado consults with teachers and interacts with young children in Cascade, Idaho.

ACKNOWLEDGMENTS

The author wishes to express her appreciation to the following individuals and agencies.

The students at San Jose City College, AA Degree Program in Early Childhood Education

Arbor Hill Day Care Center, Albany, NY

San Jose City College Child Development Center staff

Evergreen Valley College Child Development Center personnel, San Jose, CA

James Lick Children's Center, Eastside High School District, San Jose, CA

Kiddie Academy, Albany, NY

Piedmont Hills Preschool, San Jose, CA

Pineview Preschool, Albany, NY

St. Elizabeth's Day Home, San Jose, CA

W.I.C.A.P. Headstart, Donnelly, ID

Cascade Elementary School-Preschool, Cascade, ID

Erin O'Connor and the staff at Thomson Delmar Learning

In addition, special appreciation is due the reviewers involved in the development of this edition:

Julia Beyeler, PhD
University of Akron Wayne
Akron, OH

Martha Dever, PhD
Utah State University
Logan, UT

Kerry Holmes, MA
University of Mississippi
University, MS

Leanna Manna, MA
Villa Maria College
Buffalo, NY

Dawn Murrell, MA
Baker College of Jackson
Jackson, MI

Sharon Radebaugh, MEd
Middle Georgia Technical College
Warner Robins, GA

Timothy Rasinski, PhD
Kent State University
Kent, OH

Debbie Stoll, MEd
Cameron University
Lawton, OK

Ann Watts, MEd
Forsyth Technical Community College
Winston-Salem, NC

TO THE STUDENT

Because you are a unique, caring individual who has chosen an early childhood teaching career or who is currently working with children, this text is intended to help you discover and share your developing language arts gifts and talents. Create your own activities; author, when possible, your own "quality" literary, oral, and writing opportunities for young children. Design and base your activities on a knowledge of current research and theory found in the text. Consider the wisdom you have gained through your past experiences with children. Share your specialness and those language arts–related experiences that excite you now and delighted you when you were a child.

In this text, I urge you to become a skilled interactor, collaborator, and conversationalist, "a subtle opportunist," getting the most possible out of each child-adult situation while also enjoying these daily exchanges yourself. Your joy in language arts becomes their joy.

A file box and/or binder collection of ideas, completed sets, patterns, games, and so on, carefully made and stored for present and future use, is suggested. Filling young children's days with developmental, worthwhile experiences will prove a challenge, and your collection of ideas and teaching visual aids will grow and be adapted over the years.

In this text, I attempt to help you become increasingly skilled at what you may already do well, and I also urge you to become the kind of teacher Greenberg (1998) describes as one "who seems to create atmospheric miracles in which light is cast on each child in such a way as to make him/her shine." Suggested activities and review sections at the end of chapters give immediate feedback on your grasp of the chapter's main ideas and techniques. Because I am growing too, I invite your suggestions and comments so that in future revisions I can refine and improve this text's value.

You can make a difference in young children's lives. Ideally, this text will help you become the kind of teacher who does.

SECTION 1

Language Development:
Emerging Literacy
in the Young Child

CHAPTER 1

Beginnings of Communication

OBJECTIVES

After reading this chapter, you should be able to:

◆ Describe one theory of human language emergence.

◆ Identify factors that influence language development.

◆ Discuss the reciprocal behaviors of infants, parents, and caregivers.

◆ List suggested child-adult play activities for infants one to six months and infants six to twelve months.

◆ Explain the significance of infant signaling.

KEY TERMS

acuity	echolalia	responsive
affective sphere	equilibrium	mothers
articulation	gaze coupling	rhythm
attachment	holophrases	sensory-motor
auditory	language	development
babbling	moderation level	signing
communication	neurolinguistics	spatial-temporal
cognition	parentese	reasoning
cooing	perception	synapses
cues	phonation	
dual coding	resonation	

A NEW SIGN

Noah, ten months, had a new sign for "cracker" that he had used a few times during the day at the infant center. He was very pleased when his "sign" resulted in someone bringing him a cracker. At pick-up time, one of the staff believed it important to talk to Noah's dad. Mr. Soares did not really understand what the teacher, Miss Washington, was talking about when she said "signing." Miss Washington gave Mr. Soares a quick explanation. He smiled proudly and then said, "That's great. I'll talk to his mom and let her know."

QUESTIONS TO PONDER

1. Miss Washington had a new language-related topic for the next staff meeting. What would you suspect it was?

2. Did this episode tell you something about the language-developing quality of the infant center?

3. What do you know about male infants and their signing ability compared with that of female infants? Could you describe infant signing behavior?

(If you are hesitating, this chapter supplies answers.)

In this chapter the reader is acquainted with those elements in an infant's life that facilitate optimal growth in communication and language development. Socioemotional, physical, cognitive, and environmental factors that influence, promote, or deter growth are noted. Recommended interaction techniques and strategies are supported by research and reflect accepted appropriate practices and standards.

Each child is a unique combination of inherited traits and environmental influences. From birth, infants can be described as communicators interested in their surroundings.

Researchers confirm that newborns seem to assimilate information immediately. Some suggest an infant possesses "the greatest mind" in existence and the most powerful learning machine in the universe. Cowley (2000) describes exposure to language before birth.

> During the third trimester of pregnancy, many mothers notice that their babies kick and wiggle in response to music or loud noises. The sound of speech may draw a less spirited reaction, but there is little question that fetuses hear it.

Technology can now monitor the slightest physical changes in breathing, heartbeat, eye movement, and sucking rhythm and rates. Tronick (1987) suggests that babies begin learning how to carry on conversations quickly and sucking patterns produce a **rhythm** that mimics give-and-take dialogues. He notes that infants respond to very specific maternal signals, including tone of voice, looks, and head movements.

Greenspan (1999) suggests what may happen when interacting with a one- or two-month-old baby at a relaxed time after a nap or feeding.

> . . . when you hold him at arm's length and look directly into his eyes with a broad smile on your face, watch his lips part as if he's trying to imitate your smile.

Babies gesture and make sounds and seem to hold up their ends of conversations. Infants often appear to suppress and channel their energy into seeing and hearing.

Young infants' eye contact with their mothers is believed to be one of their first steps in establishing communication and is called **gaze coupling**. Infants can shut off background noises and pay attention to slight changes in adult voice sounds.

The qualities a child inherits from parents and the events that occur in the child's life help shape the child's language development. Genetic givens include gender, temperament, and a timetable for the emergence of intellectual, emotional, and physical capabilities (Villarruel, Imig, & Kostelnik, 1995). In the short 4 to 5 years after birth, the child's speech becomes purposeful and adultlike. This growing language skill is a useful tool for satisfying needs and exchanging thoughts, hopes, and dreams with others. As ability grows, the child understands and uses more of the resources of oral and recorded human knowledge and is well on the way to becoming a literate being.

The natural capacity to categorize, invent, and remember information aids the child's language acquisition. Although unique among the species because of the ability to speak, human beings are not the only ones who can communicate. Birds and animals imitate sounds and signals and are believed to communicate. For instance, chimpanzees exposed to experimental language techniques (American Sign Language, specially equipped machines, and plastic tokens) have surprised researchers with their language abilities. Some have learned to use symbols and follow linguistic rules with a sophistication that rivals that of some two-year-olds (de Villiers & de Villiers, 1979). Researchers continue to probe the limits of their capabilities. However, a basic difference between human beings and other species exists.

It is the development of the cerebral cortex that sets humans apart from less intelligent animals. Our advanced mental capabilities, such as thought, memory, language, mathematics,

---

rhythm — uniform or patterned recurrence of a beat, accent, or melody in speech.
gaze coupling — infant-mother extended eye contact.

and complex problem solving, are unique to human beings.

Humans have the unique species-specific ability to test hypotheses about the structure of language. They can also develop rules for a particular language and remember and use them to generate appropriate language. Within a few days after birth, human babies recognize familiar faces, voices, and even smells and prefer them to unfamiliar ones.

Over the past two decades, infant research has advanced by leaps and bounds to reveal amazing newborn abilities. Long before they can talk, for example, babies remember events and solve problems. They can recognize faces, see colors, hear voices, discriminate speech sounds, and distinguish basic tastes. If you combine the psychological and neurological evidence, it is hard not to conclude that babies are just plain smarter than adults, at least if being smart means being able to learn something new (Gopnik, Meltzoff, & Kuhl, 1999).

The human face becomes the most significantly important communication factor for the infant, and the facial expressions, which are varied and complex, eventually will be linked to infant body reactions (interior and exterior). Emotional reactions often involve the cardiovascular and gastrointestinal systems (Ornstein & Sobel, 1987). Parents and caregivers strive to understand the infant's state of well-being by interpreting the infant's face and postures, as infants also search faces in the world around them.

Figure 1–1 identifies a number of signals infants use and their probable meanings. Response and intentional behavior become apparent as infants age and gain experience.

> The infant ... will respond initially with various pre-programmed ... gestures like smiling, intent and interested looking, crying, satisfied sucking or snuggling, soon to be followed by active demanding and attention-seeking patterns in which attempts to attract and solicit caregiver attention rapidly become unmistakable, deliberate, and intentional. (Newson, 1979)

Researchers are studying the roles of facial expressions, gestures, and body movements in

INFANT ACTS	PROBABLE MEANING
turning head and opening mouth	feeling hungry
quivering lips	adjusting to stimuli
sucking on hand, fist, thumb	calming self, feeling overstimulated
averting eyes	tuning out for a while
turning away	needing to calm down
yawning	feeling tired/stressed
looking wide-eyed	feeling happy
cooing	feeling happy
appearing dull with unfocused eyes	feeling overloaded, needing rest
waving hands	feeling excited
moving tongue in and out	feeling upset/imitating

FIGURE 1–1 Born communicators.

human social communication (Figure 1–2). Early smilelike expressions may occur minutes after birth and are apparent in the faces of sleeping babies, whose facial expressions seem to constantly change. Infants with total blindness have been observed smiling as young as two months of age in response to a voice or tickling.

Speech is much more complex than simple parroting or primitive social functioning. The power of language enables humans to dominate

FIGURE 1–2 "Wow, that is interesting!"

other life forms. The ability to use language creatively secured our survival by giving us a vehicle to both understand and transmit knowledge and to work cooperatively with others. Language facilitates peaceful solutions between people.

DEFINITIONS

Language, as used in this text, refers to a system of intentional communication and self-expression through sounds, signs (gestures), or symbols that are understandable to others. The language-development process includes both sending and receiving information. *Input* (receiving) comes before *output* (sending); input is organized mentally by an individual long before there is decipherable output.

Communication is a broader term, defined as giving and receiving information, signals, or messages. A person can communicate with or receive communications from animals, infants, or foreign speakers in a variety of ways. Even a whistling teakettle sends a message that someone can understand. Infants appear to be "in tune," focused on the human voice, hours after birth.

INFLUENCES ON DEVELOPMENT

A child's ability to communicate involves an integration of body parts and systems allowing hearing, understanding, organizing, learning, and using language. Most children accomplish the task quickly and easily, but many factors influence the learning of language.

Klaus and Klaus (1985) describe an infant's life within the womb, based on ultrasound studies, as

> . . . floating in his private island . . . after sleeping he opens his eyes, yawns, kicks and rolls to his other side . . . brings his fin-

gers to his face and sucks his thumb . . . he can hear his mother's voice . . . he stops to listen . . . ever present is the lullaby of his mother's heartbeat. . . .

Immediately after birth

> Hands are stroking and cradling him . . . He can hear his mother's soothing familiar heartbeat . . . voices are much clearer and closer . . . he relaxes . . . he mouths his fists making small sucking sounds.

Research suggests that babies instinctively turn their heads to face the source of sound and can remember sounds heard in utero. This has promoted mothers talking to, singing to, and reading classic literature and poetry to the unborn. Research has yet to document evidence of the benefits of these activities.

Of all sounds, nothing attracts and holds the attention of infants as well as the human voice—especially the higher-pitched female voice. "Motherese," a distinct caregiver speech, is discussed later in this chapter. Rhythmic sounds and continuous, steady tones soothe some infants. A variety of sound-making soothers are now marketed and designed to attach to cribs or are placed within plush stuffed animals. Most emit a staticlike or heartbeat sound or combination of the two. Too much sound in the infant's environment, especially loud, excessive, or high-volume sounds, may have the opposite effect. Excessive household noise can come from television sets, radios, and stereos. Some mothers report that at about age five to eight months their children have an interest in lively, colorful television programs, such as *Sesame Street*, and seem to watch for reasonably long periods, sitting quietly and focused while doing so. Many have described sensory-overload situations when infants try to turn off sensory input by turning away and somehow blocking that which is at the moment overwhelming, whether the stimulus is mechanical or human.

---

language — the systematic, conventional use of sounds, signs, or written symbols in a human society for communication and self-expression. It conveys meaning that is mutually understood.
communication — the giving (sending) and receiving of information, signals, or messages.

FIGURE 1–3 Sound-making toys attract attention.

AGE	APPROPRIATE HEARING BEHAVIORS
birth	awakens to loud sounds
	startles, cries, or reacts to noise
	makes sounds
	looks toward then looks away from environmental sounds
0–3 months	turns head to hear parent's or others' speech
	reacts to speech by smiling
	opens mouth as if to imitate adult's speech
	coos and goos
	seems to recognize a familiar voice
	calms down when adult's voice is soothing
	repeats own vocalizations
	seems to listen to and focus on familiar adults' voices
4–6 months	looks toward environmental noise (e.g., barking, vacuum, doorbell, radio, TV)
	attracted to noise-making toys
	babbles consonant-like sounds
	makes wants known with voice
	seems to understand "no"
	reacts to speaker's change of tone of voice
7–12 months	responds to own name
	may say one or more understandable but not clearly articulated words
	babbles repeated syllables or consonant- and vowel-like sounds
	responds to simple requests
	enjoys playful word games like Peak-a-boo, Pat-a-cake, etc.
	imitates speech sounds frequently
	uses sound making to gain others' attention

FIGURE 1–4 Auditory perception in infancy.

Although hearing ability is not fully developed at birth, newborns can hear moderately loud sounds and can distinguish different pitches. **Auditory acuity** develops swiftly. Infants inhibit motor activity in response to strong auditory stimuli or when listening to the human voice and attempt to turn toward it. This is seen by some researchers as an indication that infants are geared to orient their whole bodies toward any signal that arouses interest (Figure 1–3). Infants' body responses to human verbalizations are a rudimentary form of speech development (Figure 1–4).

Sensory-motor development, which involves the use of sense organs and the coordination of motor systems (body muscles and

auditory — relating to or experienced through hearing.
acuity — how well or clearly one uses senses; the degree of perceptual sharpness.
sensory-motor development — the control and use of sense organs and the body's muscle structure.

parts), is vital to language acquisition. Sense organs gather information through seeing, hearing, smelling, tasting, and touching. These sense-organ impressions of people, objects, and life encounters are sent to the brain, and each **perception** (impression received through the senses) is recorded and stored, serving as a base for future oral and written language.

Newborns and infants are no longer viewed as passive, unresponsive "mini" humans. Instead, infants are seen as dynamic individuals, preprogrammed to learn, with functioning sensory capacities, motor abilities, and a wondrous built-in curiosity. Parents and caregivers can be described as guides who open opportunity and act *with* newborns rather than *on* them.

A child's social and emotional environments play a leading role in both the quality and quantity of beginning language. Brazelton (1979) describes communicative neonatal behaviors that evoke tender feelings in adults.

> When the stimulus is the human voice, the neonate not only searches for the observer's face but, when he finds it, his face and eyes become wide, soft and eager, and he may crane his neck, lifting his chin gently toward the source of the voice. As he does so, his body tension gradually increases, but he is quietly inactive. A nurturing adult feels impelled to respond to these signals by picking the baby up to cuddle him.

Human children have the longest infancy among animals. Our social dependency is crucial to our individual survival and growth. Much learning occurs through contact and interaction with others in family and social settings. Basic attitudes toward life, self, and other people form early, as life's pleasures and pains are experienced. The young child depends on parents and other caregivers to provide what is

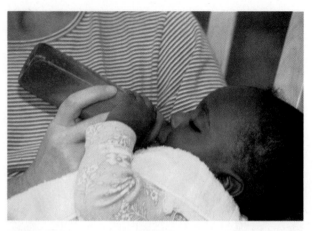

FIGURE 1–5 Care and attention in the early years influence language development.

needed for growth and **equilibrium** (a balance achieved when consistent care is given and needs are satisfied). This side of a child's development has been called the **affective sphere**, referring to the affectionate feelings—or lack of them—shaped through experience with others (Figure 1–5). Greenspan (1999) believes that each time a baby takes in information through the senses, the experience is *double-coded* as both a physical/cognitive reaction and as an emotional reaction to those sensations.

Textbooks often speak indirectly about the infant's need to feel loved consistently, using words like *nurturance, closeness, caring,* and *commitment*. The primary goal of parents and caregivers should be handling the infant and satisfying the child's physical needs in a way that leads to mutual love and a bond of trust (Figure 1–6). This bond, often called **attachment**, is an event of utmost importance to the infant's progress. A developmental milestone is reached when a baby responds with an emotional reaction of his own by indicating *obvious pleasure* or *joy* in the company of a parent or caregiver. Attachment is formed through mutual gratification of

---

perception — mental awareness of objects and other data gathered through the five senses.
equilibrium — a balance attained with consistent care and satisfaction of needs that leads to a sense of security and lessens anxiety.
affective sphere — the affectionate feelings (or lack of them) shaped through experience with others.
attachment — a two-way process formed through mutual gratification of needs and reciprocal communication influenced by the infant's growing cognitive abilities. Sometimes referred to as bonding or a "love affair" relationship.

FIGURE 1–6 An infant who feels comfortable and whose needs are satisfied is alert to the world around him.

FIGURE 1–7 With tears still wet, this infant has moved on to observing another feature of his environment.

needs and reciprocal communication influenced by the infant's growing cognitive ability. The two-way nature of the attachment process is also referred to as bonding.

> A new idea about attachment, or bonding, is that babies and young children develop "internalized working models" that are systematic pictures of how people relate to one another—theories of love. (Gopnik, Meltzoff, & Kuhl, 1999)

The specialness an infant feels for the main caregiver later spreads to include a group of beloved family members. If an attachment bond is evident and consistent care continues, the child thrives.

Newborns seem to have an individual preferred level of arousal, a **moderation level**, neither too excited nor too bored. They seek change and stimulation and seem to search out newness. Each human may possess an optimal level of arousal—a state when learning is enhanced and pleasure peaks. Mothers and experienced caregivers try to keep infants at moderate levels of arousal, neither too high nor too low (Kaye, 1979). One can perceive three states during an older infant's waking hours: (1) a state in which everything is all right and life is interesting; (2) a reactive state to something familiar or unfamiliar, when an observer can see an alert "what's that?" or "who's that?" response; and (3) a crying or agitated state. One can observe a switch from feeling safe or happy to unsafe or unhappy in a matter of seconds (Figure 1–7). Loud noises can startle the infant and elicit distressed crying. Infants control input and turn away or turn off by moving their eyes and head

---

moderation level — an individual preferred state of arousal between bored and excited when learning and pleasure peak.

or body and by becoming fussy or falling asleep.

Greenspan (1999) urges parents and caregivers of infants to improve their observational skills.

> As you sharpen your observational skills and pay attention to the times when your baby seems to have more trouble becoming calm and sharing attention with you, you'll begin to assemble a truly revealing developmental profile of your child. You'll start recognizing whether an unpleasant smell, an unexpected hug or cuddle, or a piercing noise overwhelms your child. Don't forget, though, that even a crying, finicky baby is capable of a lot of looking and listening. You may receive some very expressive looks from your three-month-old when he's got a gas bubble in his stomach! If you rub his back while murmuring sympathetically, he may be encouraged to keep his looking and listening skills even when he's not feeling so good. He may be able to use your soothing sounds and touches to calm himself. Practicing under slightly stressful conditions will make him into a stronger looker and listener later on.

Recent research indicates that parent's and caregiver's *attitudes* and *expectations* about infants' awareness and sensory abilities may be predictive of developmental growth.

> Certainly there are many possible explanations for developmental differences. But the fact remains: The earlier a mother thought her baby would be aware of the world, the more competent her baby grew to be.

> Why was this so? Because the mothers treated the babies according to their expectations. In home visits, researchers observed that mothers who knew more about their infants' abilities were more emotionally and verbally responsive to their babies. They talked to them more. They provided them with more appropriate play materials and initiated more stimulating experiences. And they were more likely to allow their babies to actively explore the world around them. (Acredolo & Goodwyn, 2000)

Other important factors related to the child's mental maturity or ability to think are ages, stages, and sequences of increased mental capacity that are closely related to language development. Language skill and intellect seem to be growing independently, at times, with one or the other developing at a faster rate. The relationship of intelligence and language has been a subject of debate for a long time. Most scholars, however, agree that these two areas are closely associated. Links between emotions and intellect are also being given new attention by early childhood educators. Researchers suspect the mind's most important faculties are rooted in emotional experiences from very early in life.

The natural curiosity of humans requires discussion here. Curiosity can be defined as a compulsion (drive) to make sense of life's happenings. Over time, exploring, searching, groping, and probing by infants shift from random to controlled movements. The period starting at about eight months of age is an age when infants possess insatiable appetites for new things—touching, manipulating, and trying to become familiar with everything that attracts them. Increasing motor skill allows greater possibilities for exploration. Skilled caregivers of infants are kept busy trying to provide novelty, variety, and companionship while monitoring safety. The curiosity of infants seems to wane only when they are tired, hungry, or ill.

Cultural and social forces touch young lives with group attitudes, values, and beliefs. These have a great impact on a child's language development. Some cultures, for instance, expect children to look downward when adults speak, showing respect by this action. Other cultures make extensive use of gestures and signaling. Still others seem to have limited vocabularies. Cultural values and factors can indeed affect language acquisition.

THEORIES OF LANGUAGE EMERGENCE

Many scholars, philosophers, linguists, and researchers have tried to pinpoint exactly how language is learned. People in major fields of study—human development, linguistics, sociology, psychology, anthropology, speech-language pathology, and animal study (zoology)—have contributed to current theory. The following are major theoretical positions.

Behaviorist/Environmentalist (or Stimulus-Response) Theory

As parents and main caregivers reward, correct, ignore, or punish the young child's communication, they exert considerable influence over both the quantity and quality of language usage and the child's attitudes toward communicating. Under this theory, the reactions of the people in a child's environment have an important effect on a child's language development. In other words, positive, neutral, and/or negative reinforcement plays a key role in the emergence of communicational behaviors.

The child's sounds and sound combinations are thought to be uttered partly as imitation and partly at random or on impulse, without pattern or meaning. The child's utterances may grow, seem to stand still, or become stifled, depending on feedback from others (Figure 1–8). This theory is attributed to the work of B. F. Skinner, a pioneer researcher in the field of learning theory.

FIGURE 1–8 Enjoyable conversational interactions occur early in life.

Maturational (Normative) Theory

The writings of Arnold Gesell and his colleagues represent the position that children are primarily a product of genetic inheritance and that environmental influences are secondary. Children are seen as moving from one predictable stage to another, with "readiness" the precursor of actual learning. This position was widely accepted in the 1960s, when linguists studied children in less-than-desirable circumstances and discovered consistent patterns of language development. Using this theory as a basis for planning instruction for young children includes (1) identifying predictable stages of growth in language abilities and (2) offering appropriate readiness activities to aid children's graduation to the next higher level.

Predetermined/Innatist Theory

Under this theory, language acquisition is considered innate (a predetermined human capacity). Each new being is believed to possess a mental ability that enables that being to master any language to which he has been exposed from infancy. Chomsky (1968), a linguistic researcher, theorizes that each person has an individual language acquisition device (LAD). Chomsky also theorizes that this device (capacity) has several sets of language system rules (grammar) common to all known languages. As the child lives within a favorable family climate, his perceptions spark a natural and unconscious device, and the child learns the "mother tongue." Imitation and reinforcement are not ruled out as additional influences.

Chomsky notes two- and three-year-olds can utter understandable, complicated sentences that they have never heard. Current researchers supporting similar theory believe young children are equipped with an implicit set of internal rules that allows them to transform the sequences of sounds they hear into sequences of ideas (Gopnik, Meltzoff, & Kuhl, 1999). The child has to possess either remarkable thinking skills to do so or very special skills as a language learner. Chomsky favors the latter explanation. Theorists who support this position note the infant's ability to babble sounds and noises used in languages the child has never heard.

Cognitive-Transactional/ Interactionist Theory

Under a fourth theory, language acquisition develops from basic social and emotional drives. Children are naturally active, curious, and adaptive and are shaped by transactions with the people in their environment. Language is learned as a means of relating to people. Others provide social and psychological supports that enable the child to be an effective communicator. L. S. Vygotsky's major work, *Thought and Language* (1986), suggests children's meaningful social exchanges prepare them for uniting thought and speech into "verbal thought." This inner speech development, he theorizes, promotes oral communication and is the basis for written language. Drives stem from a need for love and care, and the need prompts language acquisition.

Children are described as reactors to the human social contact that is so crucial to their survival and well-being. They are natural explorers and investigators. The adult's role is to prepare, create, and provide environments and events. Children's views of the world consist of their mental impressions, which are built as new life events are fit into existing ones or as categories are created for new events. Language is an integral part of living; consequently, children seek to fit language into some pattern that allows understanding. With enough exposure and with functioning sensory receiving systems, children slowly crack the "code" and eventually become fluent speakers. The works of Jean Piaget, Jerome Bruner, and J. McVicker Hunt have promoted a wide acceptance of this theory by early childhood professionals.

Vygotsky (1980) argued that language learning is, in part, biological but that children need instruction in the zone between their independent language level and the level at which they can operate with adult guidance. Bodrova and Leong (1996) list four basic principles underlying the Vygotskian framework.

1. Children construct knowledge.
2. Development cannot be separated from its social context.
3. Learning can lead development.
4. Language plays a central role in mental development.

The early childhood practitioner adopting Vygotsky's ideas would believe both teacher behaviors and the child's active physical manipulation of the environment influence and mediate what and how a young child learns or "constructs" mentally.

> If one teacher points out that the blocks are distinct sizes, that student will construct a different concept than the student whose teacher points out the blocks' color.
> (Bodrova & Leong, 1996)

In other words, without the teacher's social interaction, a child does not learn which characteristics are most important or what to notice and act upon. The teacher's role is to find out through thoughtful conversation, observation, and collaboration what concept a child holds during a jointly experienced happening and to aid the child to further mental construction(s). Consequently, under Vygotskian theory teachers can affect young children's cognitive processes—the way they think and use language. Other individual and societal features that affect children's thinking are family, other children and people in their lives, and society at large, including language, numerical systems, and technology.

Children learn or acquire a mental process by sharing or using it when interacting with others (Bodrova & Leong, 1996). Once gained, the child's learning (the acquired mental tool) is used by the child in an independent manner.

Constructivist Theory

Proponents of constructivist theory propose that children acquire knowledge by constructing it mentally in interaction with the environment. Children are believed to construct theories (hypothesize) about what they experience and then put happenings into relationships. Later, with more life experiences, revisions occur and more adequate explanations are possible. Constructivists point to young children's speech errors in grammar. Internal rules have been constructed and used for a period of time, but with more exposure to adult speech, these rules change to more adultlike forms. The rules young children used previously were their own construct and never modeled by adult speakers. Clay (1991a), in *Becoming Literate,* points out

> We know that children operate on some kind of language rules to form plurals and the past tense of verbs and negatives, and we know that many of the rules they seem to use could not have emerged from anything they have heard adults use. They must have been constructed by children themselves.

Planning for language development and early literacy using a constructivist perspective would entail offering wide and varied activities while emphasizing their interrelatedness. Teachers and parents are viewed as being involved jointly with children in literacy activities from birth onward. The overall objective of a constructivist's approach is to promote children's involvement with interesting ideas, problems, and questions. Teachers would also help children put their findings and discoveries into words, notice relationships, and contemplate similarities and differences. Children's hands-on activity is believed to be paired with mental action.

Epstein, Schweinhart, and McAdoo (1996) describe the socioeconomic settings constructivists deem necessary for realizing cognitive objectives.

> A secure and noncoercive environment allows children to decenter and cooperate, develop respect for one another, exercise curiosity, gain confidence in their ability to figure things out on their own, and become autonomous.

OTHER THEORIES

There is no all-inclusive theory of language acquisition substantiated by research. Many relationships and mysteries are still under study.

Gopnik, Meltzoff, and Kuhl (1999) discuss the challenges theorists face today.

> We need to develop detailed, specific theories that define what children know at each point and how they learn more. That will mean hard scientific work. And no single scientist can attack more than a tiny piece of the problem. Whole careers may be devoted to understanding just what six-month-olds know about sounds or what one-year-olds know about objects.

In addition, they state

> The first basic idea is that babies can solve the ancient problem (learning language) because the human brain is like a biological computer designed by evolution.

Current teaching practices involve many different styles and approaches to language arts activities. Some teachers may prefer using techniques in accord with one particular theory. One goal common among educators is to provide instruction that encourages social and emotional development while also offering activities and opportunities in a warm, language-rich, supportive classroom, center, or home. Educators believe children should be included in talk and treated as competent language partners. Eveloff (1977) identified three major prerequisites for a child's development and language acquisition: (1) thinking ability, (2) a central nervous system allowing sophisticated perception, and (3) loving care. These all are present if children are healthy and in quality child care at home or school.

This text promotes many challenging activities that go beyond simple rote memorization or passive participation. It offers an enriched program of literary experience that encourages children to think and use their abilities to relate and share their thoughts.

This text is based on the premise that children's innate curiosity, desire to understand and give meaning to their world, and their predisposition equips them to learn language. Language growth occurs simultaneously in different yet connected language arts areas. Children continually form, modify, rearrange, and revise internal knowledge as experiences, activities, opportunities, and social interactions are encountered.

Because language arts areas are interlinked, co-occurring, overlapping, and interacting, children's inner unconscious mental structuring of experience proceeds in growth spurts and seeming regressions, with development in one area influencing another.

RESEARCH ON INFANT'S BRAIN GROWTH

Rich early experience and time with caring and loving parents or early childhood educators has become even more important as researchers of **neurolinguistics** make new discoveries about infants' and young children's brain growth. Although awed by the brain's exceptional malleability, flexibility, and plasticity during early years and its ability to "explode" with new **synapses** (connections), scientists also warn of the effects of abuse or neglect on the child's future brain function (Nash, 1997).

It is estimated that at birth each neuron in the cerebral cortex has approximately 2,500 synapses, and the number of synapses reaches its peak at two to three years of age, when there are about 15,000 synapses per neuron.

A new discipline called cognitive science has appeared, uniting psychology, philosophy, linguistics, computer science, and neuroscience.

New technology gives researchers additional tools to study brain energy, volume, blood flow, oxygenation, and cross-sectional images. Neuroscientists have found that throughout the entire process of development, beginning even before birth, the brain is affected by environmental conditions, including the kind of nourishment, care, surroundings, and stimulation an individual receives (Shore, 1997). The brain is profoundly flexible, sensitive, and plastic and

is deeply influenced by events in the outside world. The new developmental research suggests that humans' unique evolutionary trick, their central adaption, their greatest weapon in the struggle for survival, is precisely their dazzling ability to learn while they are babies and to teach when grown-ups (Gopnik, Meltzoff, & Kuhl, 1999).

Early experience has gained additional importance and attention. New scientific research does not direct parents to provide special "enriching" experiences to children over and above what they experience in everyday life. It does suggest, however, that a radically deprived environment could cause damage. Gould (2002) states that various types of unpredictable, traumatic, chaotic, or neglectful environments can physically change the infant's brain by overactivating the neural pathways. According to Gould, these changes may include a change in the child's muscle tone, profound sleep difficulties, an increased startle response, and significant anxiety. Life experiences are now believed to control both how the infant's brain is "architecturally formed" and how intricate brain circuitry is wired. Infant sight and hearing acuity need to be assessed as early as possible given this new information. If a newborn's hearing disability is diagnosed and treated within 6 months, the child usually develops normal speech and language on schedule (Spivak, 2000).

With new technology, hearing tests are far more accurate and can pinpoint the level of hearing loss in babies who are only a few hours old. (Check Internet Web sites at the end of this chapter for further information.) The American Academy of Pediatrics recommends that all infants be examined by six months of age and have regular checkups after age three.

Older debates about nature (genetic givens) versus nurture (care, experiential stimulations, parental teaching, and so on) are outdated (Figure 1–9). Nature and nurture are inseparably in-

---

neurolinguistics — a branch of linguistics that studies the structure and function of the brain in relation to language acquisition, learning, and use.

synapses — gaplike structures over which the axon of one neuron beams a signal to the dendrites of another, forming a connection in the human brain. Concerns memory and learning.

OLD THINKING . . .	NEW THINKING . . .
How a brain develops depends on the genes you are born with.	How a brain develops hinges on a complex interplay between the genes you are born with and the experiences you have.
The experiences you have before age three have a limited architecture impact on later development.	Early experiences have a decisive impact on the architecture of the brain and on the nature and extent of adult capacities.
A secure relationship with a primary caregiver creates a directly favorable context for early development and learning.	Early interactions do not just create a context; they affect the way the brain is "wired."
Brain development is linear: the brain's capacity to learn and change grows steadily as an infant progresses toward adulthood.	Brain development is nonlinear: there are prime times for acquiring different kinds of knowledge and skills.
A toddler's brain is much less active than the brain of a college student.	By the time children reach age three, their brains are twice as active as those of adults. Activity levels drop during adolescence.

FIGURE 1–9 Rethinking the brain. (From Shore, R. [1997]. *Rethinking the brain.* New York: Families and Work Institute. Reprinted with permission.)

tertwined, and innate endowments enable babies to use their powerful learning mechanisms to take advantage of the information they receive from grown-ups (Gopnik, Meltzoff, & Kuhl, 1999). The interaction and interplay between both is now viewed as critical in determining brain development and which neural pathways and circuitry will diminish, possibly disappear, or grow stronger and become permanent.

Nash (1997) describes a growth spurt that occurs in the infant's brain shortly after birth.

> After birth, the brain experiences a second growth spurt, as the axons (which send signals) and the dendrites (which receive them) explode with new connections. Electrical activity, triggered by a flood of sensory experiences, fine-tunes the brain's circuitry—determining which connections will be retained and which will be pruned . . . Each time a baby tries to touch a tantalizing object or gazes intently at a face or listens to a lullaby, tiny bursts of electricity shoot through the brain, knitting neurons into circuits as well defined as those etched onto silicon chips. The results are those behavioral mileposts that never cease to delight and awe parents.

Many scientists believe that in the first few years of childhood there are a number of critical or sensitive periods, or "windows," when the brain demands certain types of input to create or stabilize certain long-lasting structures (Nash, 1997). Acredolo and Goodwyn (2000) posit that if a child's brain is not stimulated during a specific window of time, consequences occur.

> For example, the critical window for visual development is very narrow, the first six months of life. If by around six months a baby is not seeing things in the world around her, her vision will never be normal.

> With a series of critical and sensitive periods clustered from birth to around age ten or twelve, some windows of opportunity open early, while others open relatively late.

In the neurobiological literature, these special periods are described as "critical periods" or "plastic periods" (Shore, 1997). Chugani (1997) believes this is an opportunity, one of nature's provisions for us to be able to use environmental exposure to change the anatomy of the brain and to make it more efficient.

Kantrowitz (1997) points out

Every lullaby, every giggle and peek-a-boo, triggers a crackling along his neural pathways, laying the groundwork for what could someday be a love of art or a talent for soccer or a gift for making and keeping friends.

Other scientists, such as Bialystok and Hakuta (1994), are skeptical and observe clear evidence of differential abilities to learn language during certain time periods is not easily forthcoming. Gopnik, Meltzoff, and Kuhl (1999) are uncertain, in the case of language learning, whether critical periods exist or only seem to exist because brain structures have already developed through early experiences, affecting the way in which one perceives and interprets the world. These neuroscientists note that the subject of critical periods is hotly debated. One thing is clear—children who learn a second language between three and seven years of age perform like native speakers on various tests, whereas children learning a second language after puberty speak it with a foreign accent. Wardle (2003) believes brain research also supports early *second* language learning, for it suggests that young children have the brain capacity and neural flexibility to undertake the challenging task. She observes that second language learning creates new neural networks that increase the brain's capacity for all sorts of future learning, not just language learning.

What specific courses of action do brain researchers recommend?

◆ providing excellent child care for working parents

◆ talking to babies frequently

◆ cuddling babies and using hands-on parenting

◆ using "parentese," the high-pitched, vowel-rich, singsong speech style most adults readily undertake when interacting with babies that helps babies connect objects with words

◆ giving babies freedom to explore within safe limits

◆ providing safe objects to explore and manipulate

◆ giving babies regular eye examinations and interesting visual opportunities

◆ providing loving, stress-reduced care for the child's emotional development

Cowley (1997) describes "red flag behaviors" that should alert parents to possible child learning difficulties.

◆ *0–3 months:* Does not turn when you speak or repeat sounds like coos.

◆ *4–6 months:* Does not respond to the word *no* or changes in tone of voice; does not look around for sources of sound like a doorbell, or babble in speechlike sounds such as *p*, *b*, and *m*.

◆ *7–12 months:* Does not recognize words for common items, turn when you call his name, imitate speech sounds, or use sounds other than crying to get your attention.

The idea that electrical activity in brain cells changes the physical structure of the brain during the early years tips the scales in the longstanding debate about the importance of nature or nurture in child development. Increasing focus and importance is bound to be attached to quality care in infancy and preschool years (Figure 1–10). Care should be provided by knowledgeable adults who realize that early experiences and opportunities may have long-term developmental consequences and who provide rich, language-filled experiences and opportunities.

Healy (1987) worries that "excess pressure" for inappropriate skills at early ages may cause problems for the child during later schooling. Parents' or other adults' enthusiasm for creating "superbabies" may motivate them to offer meaningless age-inappropriate activities. She suggests

Most babies give explicit clues about what kind of input is needed and let you know when it's overpowering or not interesting anymore. Explaining things to children won't do the job; they must have a chance to experience, wonder, experiment, and act it out for themselves. It is this process throughout life that enables the growth of intelligence.

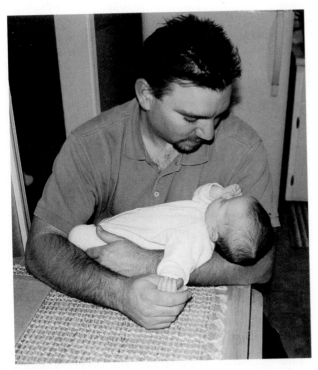

FIGURE 1–10 Emotional health is built from nurturing contact with others.

tion of both **cognition** and emotion (feelings, desires, enthusiasms, antipathies, etc.).

Interactive emotional exchanges with caregivers and their reciprocal quality are increasingly viewed as critical to human infants' growth and development, including language development.

With new appreciation of the importance of the quality and quantity of caregiver nurturing, early childhood caregivers realize

> . . . the adult a baby will someday become is the end result of the thousands of times a parent or caregiver comforted her when she cried, helped her to play well with others in the sandbox and sang just one more lullaby before she finally closed her eyes for the night. Each of these seemingly simple acts gently shapes a child's growing sense of self. (Kantrowitz, 2000)

Raymond (2000) describes the importance of environmental feedback.

> One especially powerful synaptic glue is the feedback, in the form of emotional satisfaction and praise, that a child receives from successfully crawling across a room to retrieve an errant ball. The feedback serves to strengthen the web of brain synapses that encodes the "crawl" program.

> Perhaps the most powerful reinforcement a child can get is the feeling that he is an independent little being.

Babies come equipped with the "need to know"; our job is to give them love, acceptance, and the raw material of appropriate stimulation at each level of development.

Greenspan (1997) believes his observations make clear that certain kinds of emotional nurturing propel infants and young children to intellectual and emotional health and that affective experience helps them master a variety of cognitive tasks. He states

> As a baby's experience grows, sensory impressions become increasingly tied to feelings. It is the **dual coding** of experience that is the key to understanding how emotions organize intellectual capacities and indeed create the sense of self.

Coles (2004), a reviewer of current brain research, also points out that growing evidence suggests that thinking is an inseparable interac-

Some developers of infant materials, equipment, books, and services suggest they can speed brain development, "lock-in a baby's smarts," and promote emotional well-being. Gopnik (1999) believes teachers and parents are under considerable pressure to find ways to accelerate early childhood experiences needlessly. In Gopnik's view, babies are already born with their brains programmed to learn. They think, observe, reason from birth, and explore and experiment with new information that changes their perceptions of the world. Early in

---

dual coding — the belief that infants' experience and emotions influence cognition.
cognition — the process that creates mental images, concepts, and operations.

life they begin to draw conclusions about faces, language, and objects.

Gopnik's critics point out that really good infant and toddler products and services are available and that it is up to parents to find them. Gopnik (1999) counters that the real missing piece in modern child rearing is spending time with babies and providing natural parenting, such as playing, engaging in baby talk, and simply putting plastic mixing bowls on the floor.

COMMUNICATIVE BEGINNINGS IN INFANCY

Development of the ability to communicate begins even before the child's birth. Prenatal environment plays an important role, and factors such as the mother's emotional and physical health and nutrition can affect the development and health of the unborn. These factors may also lead to complications later in the child's language-learning capabilities.

Newborns quickly make their needs known. They cry and their parents respond. The parents feed, hold, and keep their children warm and dry. The sounds of parents' footsteps or voices and their caring touch often stop the babies' crying. Babies learn to anticipate. The sense perceptions they receive begin to be connected to stored impressions of the past.

Infants are very powerful in shaping relationships with significant caregivers. Newborns are a wonderful combination of development, potential development, and cognitive flexibility.

An infant can perceive from maternal behavior a willingness to learn from the infant and respond to his patterns of behavior and rhythms of hunger. This is accomplished by close observation of infant vocal and body clues, which indicate the child's state of being.

At some point, the mother notes her infant's gaze. This usually triggers a type of brief conversation.

> . . . once a pattern of mutual gazing is established, the mother tends to behave in a given way within mutual gaze episodes. This would seem to be the case with proto-conversation: mutual gazing sets the stage for maternal vocalizations which set up the possibility of an unfolding process of learning, probably strengthened by selective attention. (Bateson, 1979)

Curry and Johnson (1990) describe two developmental tasks that confront infants. They

1. regulate themselves with others. Babies begin to establish "islands of consistency" as adults soothe, hold, feed, and otherwise nurture them.

2. interact with others. Playful encounters first occur around caregiving functions (diapering, dressing, playing This Little Piggy) and later through play with toys.

The infant is a noisemaker from birth. The child's repertoire includes sucking noises, lip smacking, sneezes, coughs, hiccups, and, of course, different types of cries. As an infant grows, he makes vocal noises, such as **cooing** after feeding. During feeding, slurping and guzzling sounds indicate eagerness and pleasure. Cooing seems to be related to a child's comfort and satisfaction. During cooing, sounds are relaxed, lowpitched, and gurgly vowel sounds that are made in an open-mouthed way; for example, e (as in see), e (get), a (at), ah, and o, oo, ooo. The infant appears to be in control of this sound making. Discomfort, by comparison, produces consonant sounds, made in a tense manner with the lips partly closed and the tongue and the ridge of the upper or lower jaw constricting air flow.

Parents who attend to infant crying promptly and who believe that crying stems from legitimate needs rather than attempts to control tend to produce contented, trusting infants. Advice for parents of colicky babies consists of holding and carrying the infant more frequently in an effort to soothe.

---

cooing — an early stage during the prelinguistic period in which vowel sounds are repeated, particularly the *u-u-u* sound.

Infants differ in numerous ways from the moment of birth. In speaking to parents about the unique differences in infants, Greenspan (1999) notes the following:

> For most babies, swaddling (gently but firmly bundling the baby's arms and legs in a receiving blanket wrapped around their bodies) is soothing. Other babies enjoy a body massage in which their limbs are gently flexed and extended.

> Up until recently, scientists assumed that all human beings experienced sensations in similar ways. We now know that individuals perceive the same stimulus very differently. Your feathery touch could feel tickly and irritating on your newborn's skin, while another baby might take delight in the same caress.

Raymond (2000) points out that the individual pace of development varies.

> The development of the brain pathways that fire up nerve endings and muscle groups to perform specific tasks occurs at a pace as individual as a fingerprint.

Whether a baby reaches developmental milestones on the early or late side of normal seems to bear little relation to either cognitive skills or future proficiency (Raymond, 2000). However, in most cases, milestones in language development are reached at about the same age and in a recognizable sequence (Figures 1–11 and 1–12).

Babies learn quickly that communicating is worthwhile because it results in action on the part of another. Have you ever watched a baby

AGE	RESPONSES
newborn	is startled by a loud noise
	turns head to look in the direction of sound
	is calmed by the sound of a voice
	prefers mother's voice to a stranger's
	discriminates many of the sounds used in speech
1–2 months	smiles when spoken to
3–7 months	responds differently to different intonations (e.g., friendly, angry)
8–12 months	responds to name
	responds to "no"
	recognizes phrases from games (e.g., "Peak-a-boo," "How big is baby?")
	recognizes words from routines (e.g., waves to "bye-bye")
	recognizes some words

FIGURE 1–11 Examples of the typical order of emergence of responses to sounds and speech in the first year, with approximate ages. (From Berko Gleason, J. [1997]. *The development of language* [4th ed.]. Boston: Allyn and Bacon. © 1997 by Allyn and Bacon, Boston, MA. Copyright © 1997 by Pearson Education. Reprinted by permission of the publisher.)

AGE	NONWORD VOCALIZATIONS
newborn	cries
1–3 months	makes cooing sounds in response to speech (*oo, goo*)
	laughs
	cries in different ways when hungry, angry, or hurt
	makes more speechlike sounds in response to speech
4–6 months	plays with some sounds, usually single syllables (e.g., *ba, ga*)
6–8 months	babbles with duplicated sounds (e.g., *bababa*)
	attempts to imitate some sounds
8–12 months	babbles with consonant or vowel changes (e.g., *badaga, babu*)
	babbles with sentencelike intonation (expressive jargon/conversational babble)
	produces protowords

FIGURE 1–12 Examples of the typical order of emergence of types of nonword vocalizations in the first year, with approximate ages. (From Berko Gleason, J. [1997]. *The development of language* [4th ed.]. Boston: Allyn and Bacon. © 1997 by Allyn and Bacon, Boston, MA. Copyright © 1997 by Pearson Education. Reprinted by permission of the publisher.)

gaze intently into his parent's eyes? Somehow, the child knows that this is a form of communication and is avidly looking for clues. If the parent speaks, the baby's entire body seems to respond to the rhythm of the human voice. The reciprocal nature of the interactions aids development. Greenspan (1997) warns that unless a child masters the level we call two-way intentional communication, normally achieved by an eight-month-old infant, the child's language, cognitive, and social patterns ultimately develop in an idiosyncratic, piecemeal, disorganized manner. There is a high degree of relationship between a mother's responsiveness and her child's language competence. By 9 to 18 months of age, the more responsive mothers promoted greater language facility and growth.

Infants quickly recognize subtle differences in sounds. As Shore (1997) points out

> Children learn in the context of important relationships. The best way to help very young children into curious, confident, able learners is to give them warm consistent care so that they can form secure attachments to those who care for them.

A parent's talk and touch increase sound making. Greenspan (1999) suggests speaking in low, soothing tones while tending to an infant's needs. He believes this helps babies calm down and pay attention, in other words, listen. Infants move their arms and legs in synchrony to the rhythms of human speech. Random noises, tappings, and disconnected vowel sounds do not produce this behavior.

There is a difference between people in an infant's life. Some talk and touch. Others show delight. Some pause after speaking and seem to wait for a response. The child either "locks on" to the conversationalist, focusing totally, or breaks eye contact and looks away. It is almost as though the infant controls what he wants to receive. Of course, hunger, tiredness, and other factors also influence this behavior and may stop the child's interest in being social.

Research continues to uncover previously overlooked response capabilities in both infants and their parents. In one experiment, newborns learned to suck on an artificial nipple hooked to a switch that turned on a brief portion of recorded speech or music. They did not suck as readily when they heard instrumental music as when they heard a human voice (de Villiers & de Villiers, 1979). Neuman and Roskos (1993) believe that lacking speech, babies use a form of protolanguage—gestures, expressions, and voice tones—to communicate.

The special people in the infant's life adopt observable behaviors when "speaking" to the child, just as the child seems to react in special ways to their attention. Talking to babies differs from other adult speech in that the lyric or musical quality of speech seems more important than words. Honig (1999) points out that infants listening to these long, drawn-out vowels experience an increase in heart rate. At the same time it speeds up the brain's ability to recognize connections between words and objects. Ingram (1995) suggests that "baby-talk" speech modifications may reflect social conventions and can vary among cultures. The attention-holding ability of this type of adult speech may help the infant become aware of the linguistic function of vocalizations (Sachs, 1997). Mothers sometimes raise their voice pitch to a falsetto, shorten sentences, simplify their syntax and vocabulary, use nonsense sounds, and maintain prolonged eye contact during playful interchanges. Masataka's study (1992) of mothers found their speech with infants characterized by higher overall pitch, wider pitch exclusions, more distinctive pitch contours, slower tempo, and longer pauses than in their normal adult conversations. Most infants are attracted to high-pitched voices, but a few infants seem to overreact and prefer lower speech sounds. Infants can pick up higher-pitched sounds better than lower-frequency ones, which may be why they are entranced by the high-pitched coos and singsong nature of **parentese**. Parents' voices when talking to their infants can be described as playful, animated, warm, and perhaps giddy. Falk (2004) proposes that "motherese" forms a scaffold for infants' language acquisition, and human mothers often

parentese — a high-pitched, rhythmic, singsong, crooning style of speech. Also known as motherese or baby talk.

use vocal means to placate and reassure their infants. They attempt to control their infant's state of well-being. Falk notes vowels are lingered over, phrases are repeated, and questions carry exaggerated inflections.

A mutual readiness to respond to each other appears built-in to warm relationships. The infant learns that eye contact can hold and maintain attention and that looking away usually terminates both verbal and nonverbal episodes.

Gopnik, Meltzoff, and Kuhl (1999) point out

> Babies know important things about language literally from the time they are born, and they learn a great deal about language before they ever say a word. Most of what they learn at that early age involves the sound system of language. We decode the sound cryptogram, and solve many of the problems that still baffle computers, before we can actually talk at all.
>
> Newborn babies already go well beyond the actual physical sounds they hear, dividing them into more abstract categories. And they can make all the distinctions that are used in all the world's languages.

CRYING

Crying is one of the infant's primary methods of communication. Cries can be weak or hardy, and they provide clues to the infant's general health. Crying is the only way an infant can affect his situation of need or discomfort. Infants begin early in life to control the emotional content of their cries. Many parents believe they can recognize different types of crying, such as sleepy, frightened, hungry, and so on, especially if infant body movements are observed concurrently. Researchers have discovered that parents do indeed accurately infer the intensity of an infant's emotional state from the sound of the cry itself, even if the baby is not visually observed. Even adults inexperienced with infants seem to possess this ability (Hostetler, 1988).

Child development specialists advise adult alertness and responsiveness to minimize crying. Crying will take place in the best of circumstances, and research has indicated that there are some positive aspects of crying, including stress reduction, elimination of toxin in tears, and reestablishment of physical and emotional balance (Ornstein & Sobel, 1987). However, although crying may have its benefits, it is not recommended that infants be left to cry, but rather that adults continue to attempt to soothe and satisfy infant's needs.

A baby's crying may cause strong feelings in some adults, including anger, frustration, irritation, guilt, and rejection. Successful attempts at soothing the infant and stopping the crying give both the infant and the caregiver satisfaction, feelings of competence, and a possible sense of pleasure. When out-of-sorts infants cease crying, alertness, attentiveness, and visual scanning usually happen and/or the infants fall asleep (Figure 1–13). Infant-parent interaction

FIGURE 1–13 A child may fall asleep while being soothed.

has been described as "a rhythmic drama," "a reciprocal ballet," and "a finely tuned symphony." All of these touch on the beauty and coordination of sound-filled moments between the parent and child. Crying is a helpful mechanism that promotes maintenance of physical satisfaction and comfort. It releases energy and tension.

Emotions are expressed frequently in crying as the infant nears his first birthday. Fear, frustration, uneasiness with novelty or newness, separation from loved ones, and other strong emotions can provoke crying through childhood and beyond.

Infant care providers in group programs engage in frank staff discussions concerning infant crying. Normal and natural staff feelings concerning crying need open discussion so that strategies can be devised in the best interests of both the infants and staff members. Many techniques exist to minimize crying and also to monitor the crying levels of individual infants so that health or developmental problems can be spotted quickly.

SMILING AND LAUGHING

Smiling is seen in some babies who are only a few days old. Some smile in their sleep. This type of smiling seems to be tied to inner stimuli. True smiling can occur before six months of age and is usually associated with a caretaker's facial, auditory, or motor stimuli. Laughter may occur as early as four months of age and is thought to be a good predictor of cognitive growth and the child's level of involvement in what he is doing (Spieker, 1987). Spieker suggests that the earlier the baby laughs, the higher the developmental level. In the second half of the first year, infants smile at more complex social and visual items. Laughter at this age may be full of squeals, howls, hoots, giggles, and grins. Incongruity may be noticed by the infant, and laughter follows. If an infant laughs when he sees the family dog in the driver's seat

FIGURE 1–14 A quick parental response to crying is appropriate and recommended.

with its paws on the wheel, the child may be showing recognition of incongruity—the child has learned something about car drivers.

Responsive mothers promote infant smiling. Ainsworth and Bell (1972) concluded that **responsive mothers**, those who are alert in caring for the infant's needs, had babies who cried less frequently and had a wider range of different modes of communication (Figure 1–14). These responsive mothers created a balance between showing attention and affording the infant autonomy (offering a choice of action within safe bounds) when the infant became mobile. They also provided body contact and involved themselves playfully at times.

Infant Imitation

Acredolo and Goodwyn (2000) suggest infants as young as one or two days old may imitate parent head movements and facial behaviors; they explain

> This inborn push to mimic others gets babies into a problem-solving mode from the very beginning. And as we mentioned ear-

---

responsive mothers — mothers who are alert and timely in responding to and giving attention to infants' needs and communications.

lier, babies thrive on problem solving. The payoff is such a pleasant one—Dad sticks around to interact some more, and baby is amused. Imitation is such an important developmental component that Mother Nature has not left it up to chance. She has made sure that each of us begins life's journey with a necessary tool in hand.

BABBLING

Early random sound making is often called **babbling**. Infants the world over babble sounds they have not heard and will not use in their native language. This has been taken to mean that each infant has the potential to master any world language. Gopnik, Meltzoff, and Kuhl (1999) explain

> At birth the baby's citizen-of-the-world brain recognizes the subtle differences among all sounds of all languages. But in order to acquire a specific language, the infant brain has to develop a structure that emphasizes the distinctions in the child's own language and ignore others.

> By six to twelve months of age, the baby is no longer a citizen of the world but a culture-bound language specialist, like you and me.

Close inspection shows repetitive sounds and "practice sessions" present. Babbling starts at about the fourth to sixth month and continues in some children through the toddler period. However, a peak in babbling is usually reached between 9 and 12 months. Periods before the first words are spoken are marked by a type of babbling that repeats syllables, as in *dadadadadada*. This is called **echolalia**. Infants seem to echo themselves and others. Babbling behavior overlaps the stages of making one and two or more words, which ends for some children at about 18 months of age.

Infants who are deaf also babble. In play sessions, they will babble for longer periods without hearing either adult sound or their own sounds, as long as they can see the adult responding. However, these children stop babbling at an earlier age than do hearing children. It is not clearly understood why babbling occurs, either in hearing or nonhearing children, but it is thought that babbling gives the child the opportunity to use and control the mouth, throat, and lung muscles. Researchers trying to explain babbling suggest that infants are not just exercising or playing with their vocal apparatus. Instead, they may be trying out and attempting to control their lips, tongues, mouths, and jaws to produce certain sounds. A child's babbling amuses and motivates the child, acting as a stimulus that adds variety to the child's existence.

In time, the child increasingly articulates clear, distinct vowel-like, consonant-like, and syllabic sounds. *Ba* and *da* are acquired early because they are easy to produce, whereas *el* and *ar* are acquired late because sophisticated articulatory control is required. Although babbling includes a wide range of sounds, as children grow older they narrow the range and begin to focus on the familiar, much-heard language of the family. Other sounds are gradually discarded.

There is a point when an infant's eyes search and follow sound in his environment and when the infant can easily turn his head toward the speaker. Toys are visually examined and reached for and sometimes talked to. Almost any feature of environment may promote verbalness.

Physical contact continues to be important. Touching, holding, rocking, and engaging in other types of physical contact bring a sense of security and a chance to respond through sound making. The cooing and babbling sounds infants make also draw caregivers into "conversations" with them (Sachs, 1997). Babies learn to wait for the adult's response after they have vo-

babbling — an early language stage in sound production in which an infant engages in vocal play with vowel and consonant sounds, including some sounds not found in his or her language environment.
echolalia — a characteristic of the babbling period. The child repeats (echoes) the same sounds over and over.

FIGURE 1–15 Infants' vocal and playful interactions with caregivers are the precursors of true conversations.

calized, and both infants and adults are constantly influencing one another in establishing conversation-like vocal interactions (Masataka, 1993; Sachs, 1997). See Figure 1–15. The active receiving of perceptions is encouraged by warm, loving parents who share a close relationship. Secure children respond more readily to the world around them. Children who lack social and physical contact or those who live in insecure home environments fall behind in both the number and range of sounds made; differences start showing at about six months of age.

Simple imitation of language sounds begins early. Nonverbal imitated behavior, such as tongue protrusion, also occurs. Sound imitation becomes syllable imitation, and short words are spoken near the end of the child's first year.

Stages of Vocalization

Stoel-Gammon (1997) outlines stages in infants' production of sounds and notes that vocalization types typically overlap from one stage to another.

>   Stage 1 (birth to 2 months): *Reflexive vocalization*. Characterized by crying, fussing, vegetative sounds like coughing, burping, sneezing, and some vowel-like sounds.

>   Stage 2 (2–4 months): *Cooing and laughter*. Characterized by comfort-state vocalizations, laughter, and chuckles.

>   Stage 3 (4–6 months): *Vocal play*. Characterized by very loud and very soft sounds, yells and whispers, very high and low sounds—squeals and growls, raspberries (bilabial trills), and sustained vowels.

>   Stage 4 (6 months and older): *Canonical babbling*. The appearance of sequences of consonant-vowel syllables with adultlike timing, wordlike utterances, reduplicated babbles (bababa), and variegated babbles (bagidabu). The infant's hearing of his own and others' vocalization takes on increased importance. The vocalization of babies with deafness decreases.

>   Stage 5 (10 months and older): *Jargon stage*. Babbling overlaps the early period of meaningful speech and is characterized by strings of sounds and syllables uttered with a rich variety of stress and intonational patterns. Sound play, containing recurring favorite sequences, or even words, may occur.

A Shared Prelanguage Milestone

By the last half of the first year, children begin to take part in a new interactional pattern with their caretakers. They share attention given to objects with another person by following that individual's gaze or pointing, responding to the individual's emotional reaction to an event, and imitating that person's object-directed actions (Nelson & Shaw, 2002). This gives adults who notice this behavior a chance to pair words with objects. First words or sounds are usually simple associates of objects or situations. The infant simply voices a shared reference. Nelson and Shaw note that the leap from shared reference associations to meaningful language requires the child to integrate these prespeech skills with prespeech communicative patterns and conceptual knowledge. The child is then standing on a first communicative step.

INFANT SIGNALING/SIGNING

During the latter part of the first year, alert caregivers notice hand and body positions that suggest the child is attempting to communicate (Figure 1–16). Fackelmann (2000), reviewing Acredolo and Goodwyn's book *Baby Minds* (2000), notes that the researchers suggest parents pair words with easy-to-do gestures. At age one, children cannot gain enough mastery over their tongues to form many words. Gesturing with their fingers and hands is simpler. For example, infants as young as seven months may bang on a window to get a family cat's attention or reach out, motion, or crawl toward something or someone they want. The use of signs continues until the child's ability to talk takes off, and the re-

searchers believe **signing** may spark other critical thinking skills and better intelligence quotient (IQ) scores when testing begins.

Toward the end of the child's first year, pointing becomes goal-oriented—the infant may want a specific object. As time progresses, more and more infant body signaling takes place. Signals are used over and over, and a type of sign-language communication emerges. Research suggests that infants use a "signal and sound system" understood by caregivers. Halliday (1979) believes a "child tongue" develops before "mother tongue." When responded to appropriately, the infant easily progresses to word use and verbal aptitude.

Acredolo and Goodwyn (2000) believe baby signs stimulate brain development, particularly in areas involved in language, memory, and concept development.

> Every time a child successfully communicates with a "baby sign" connections get made or strengthened that make it easier for subsequent efforts to succeed. Without baby signs, these changes would have to wait until the child could actually say the words, often months down the line.

> Baby signs turn babies onto the notion of language as a way to connect with people, enabling them for the first time to become active partners in conversations and get their needs met.

Some studies of gestural communication note that infants with more advanced gestures had larger vocabularies and that girls seem slightly more advanced in gesturing than boys. (This paragraph offered an answer to one of the questions in this chapter's beginning vignette. The next paragraph answers another.)

Well-meaning parents may choose not to respond to infant gestures and signals, thinking this will accelerate or force the use of words. The opposite is thought to be true. Lapinski

GESTURE	POSSIBLE MEANING
allows food to run out of mouth	satisfied or not hungry
pouts	displeased
pushes nipple from mouth with tongue	satisfied or not hungry
pushes object away	does not want it
reaches out for object	wants to have it handed to him
reaches out to person	wants to be picked up
smacks lips or ejects tongue	hungry
smiles and holds out arms	wants to be picked up
sneezes excessively	wet and cold
squirms and trembles	cold
squirms, wiggles, and cries during dressing or bathing	resents restriction on activities
turns head from nipple	satisfied or not hungry

FIGURE 1–16 Some common gestures of babyhood. (From Hurlock, E. B. [1972]. *Child development.* New York: McGraw-Hill. Copyright 1972. Reproduced with permission of The McGraw-Hill Companies.)

signing — a body positioning, sound, action, or gesture or combination of these undertaken by an infant that represents an effort to communicate a need, desire, or message.

(1996) suggests aware parents may acquire early insights into their baby's thinking.

> . . . signing and the eye contact it requires helps your baby learn that communication is a satisfying, back-and-forth process. And signing can provide parents with an early window into your baby's mind.

Alert parents who try to read and receive signals give their infant the message that communication leads to fulfillment of wishes. Successful signaling becomes a form of language—a precursor of verbal signals (words). Lapinski (1996) believes baby signers by age two are better at both expressing themselves and understanding others' speech and, on average, have slightly larger vocabularies than their nonsigning peers. Sitting down at the child's level at times when the infant is crawling from one piece of furniture to another may facilitate the adult's ability to pick up on signaling. Watching the infant's eyes and the direction the infant's head turns gives clues. Infants about eight months old seem fascinated with the adult's sound-making ability. They often turn to look at the adult's lips or want to touch the adult's mouth. Early childhood educators employed by infant-toddler centers need to know their center's position regarding expected educator behaviors. Most centers expect educators to actively pair words with adult or child signs, encourage child use of signs, and learn and respond to each child's individual sign language.

UNDERSTANDING

Most babies get some idea of the meaning of a few words at about six to nine months. At about ten months of age, some infants start to respond to spoken word clues. Somewhere between eight and thirteen months, the child's communication, whether vocal or gestural, becomes intentional as the child makes a connection between responses, his behavior, and parent or early childhood educator responses (Figure 1–17). A game such as Pat-a-cake may start the baby clapping, and "bye-bye" or Peek-a-boo brings about other imitations of earlier play activities

FIGURE 1–17 This adult is watching to see if a conversational moment is possible with this young infant.

with the parents. The child's language is called passive at this stage, for he primarily receives (or is receptive). Speaking attempts will later become active (or expressive). Vocabulary provides a small portal through which adults can gauge a little of what the child knows. There is a point at which children expand nonverbal signals to true language.

Older infants communicate with their parents through many nonverbal actions; one common way is by holding up their arms, which most often means, "I want to be picked up." Other actions include facial expression, voice tone, voice volume, posture, and gestures such as "locking in" by pointing fingers and toes at attention-getting people and events.

Although infants at this stage can respond to words, speaking does not automatically follow, because, at this early age, there is much more for infants to understand. For example, Bornstein's studies (1991–1992) point out that infants have the capacity to distinguish phonemes, the smallest significant units of sounds in words, and to understand that speech pauses indicate a "my turn–your turn" situation. When mothers used longer speech pauses, their babies did also. Changes in parents' facial expressions, voice tone and volume, and actions and gestures carry feelings and messages important to infants' well-being. Understanding the tone of parents' speech comes before understanding parents' words.

Gopnik, Meltzoff, and Kuhl (1999) describe what happens when babies are about one year old.

> One-year-old babies know that they will see something by looking where other people point; they know what they should do to something by watching what other people do; they know how they should feel about something by seeing how other people feel.

FIRST WORDS

Before an understandable, close approximation of a word is uttered, the child's physical organs need to function in a delicate unison and the child must reach a certain level of mental maturity. At approximately 12 months of age, the speech centers of the brain are poised to produce what is perhaps the most magical moment of childhood: the first word, which marks the flowering of language (Nash, 1997). The child's respiratory system supplies the necessary energy. As the breath is exhaled, sounds and speech are formed with the upward movement of air. The larynx's vibrating folds produce voice (called **phonation**). The larynx, mouth, and nose influence the child's voice quality (termed **resonation**). A last modification of the breath stream is **articulation**—a final formation done through molding, shaping, stopping, and releasing voiced and nonvoiced sounds that reflect language heard in the child's environment.

Repetition of syllables such as *ma, da,* and *ba* in a child's babbling occurs toward the end of the first year. If *mama* or *dada* or a close copy is said, parents show attention and joy. Language, especially in the area of speech development, is a two-way process; reaction is an important feedback to action.

The term *protoword* is often used for the invented words a child may use during the transition from prespeech to speech. During this transition, a child has acquired the difficult concept that sounds have meaning and is unclear only about the fact that one is supposed to find out what words exist instead of making them up.

Generally, first words are nouns or proper names of foods, animals, or toys; words may also include "gone," "there," "uh-oh," "more," and "dat" (what's that?). Greetings, farewells, or other social phrases, such as "peek-a-boo," are also among first recognizable words.

Monolingual (one language) children utter their first words at approximately 11 months of age; the range is from about 9 months to about 16 months. Gleitman (1998) estimates that until about age 18 months, babies learn roughly one word every 3 days. Reznick (1996) believes that talking alone shows no link to mental development at age 2, but a child's *comprehension* of words is paramount. Cowley (1997) points out there is no evidence that late talkers end up less fluent than early talkers. Some children acquire large numbers of object names in their first 50 to 100 words. The first spoken words usually contain *p, b, t, d, m,* and *n* (front of the mouth consonants), which require the least use of the tongue and air control. They are shortened versions, such as *da* for "daddy," *beh* for "bed," and *up* for "cup." When two-syllable words are attempted, they are often strung together using the same syllable sound, as in *dada, beebee.* If the second syllable is voiced, the child's reproduction of the sound may come out as *dodee* for "doggy" or *papee* for "potty."

At this stage, words tend to be segments of wider happenings in the child's life. A child's word *ba* may represent a favorite, often-used toy (such as a ball). As the child grows in experience, any round object seen in the grocery, for instance, will also be recognized and called *ba.* This phenomenon has been termed overexten-

phonation — exhaled air passes the larynx's vibrating folds and produces "voice."
resonation — amplification of laryngeal sounds using cavities of the mouth, nose, sinuses, and pharynx.
articulation — the adjustments and movements of the muscles of the mouth and jaw involved in producing clear oral communication.

sion. The child has embraced "everything round," which is a much broader meaning for ball than the adult definition of the word. Gopnik, Meltzoff, and Kuhl (1999) state language is as much invented as learned.

> Babies don't simply soak up associations between names and things or mimic adults' use of words. Instead, they actively restructure language to suit their own purposes. If they need a word for disappearance or failure, they'll happily press *all gone* or *uh-oh* into service. If they need a word for all animals, they'll make *doggie* fit the bill.

Lee (1970) describes the child's development from early situation-tied first words to a broader usage.

> All words in the beginning vocabulary are on the same level of abstraction. They are labels of developing categories of experiences.

Following is a list of words frequently understood between 8 and 12 months of age: mommy, daddy, bye-bye, baby, shoe, ball, cookie, juice, bottle, no-no, and the child's own name and names of family members.

A child finds that words can open many doors. They help the child get things and cause caregivers to act in many ways. Vocabulary quickly grows from the names of objects to words that refer to actions. This slowly decreases the child's dependence on context (a specific location and situation) for communication and gradually increases the child's reliance on words—the tools of abstract thought. Children learn very quickly that words not only name things and elicit action on another's part but also convey comments and express individual attitudes and feelings.

TODDLER SPEECH

Toddlerhood begins, and the child eagerly names things and seeks names for others. As if playing an enjoyable game, the child echoes and repeats to the best of his ability. At times, the words are not recognizable as the same words the parents offered. When interacting with young speakers, an adult must listen closely, watch for nonverbal signs, scan the situation, and use a good deal of guessing to understand the child and respond appropriately. The child's single words accompanied by gestures, motions, and intonations are called **holophrases**. They usually represent a whole idea or sentence.

While the child is learning to walk, speech may briefly take a back seat to developing motor skill. At this time, the child may listen more intently to what others are saying.

The slow-paced learning of new words (Figure 1–18) is followed by a period of rapid growth. The child pauses briefly, listening, digesting, and gathering forces to embark on the great adventure of becoming a fluent speaker.

IMPLICATIONS FOR INFANT-CENTER STAFF MEMBERS

The importance of understanding the responsive, reciprocal nature of optimal caregiving in group infant centers cannot be overestimated. The soothing, calming, swaddling, rocking, sympathizing, and responding behaviors of infant care specialists help infants maintain a sense of security and a relaxed state, calmness, and equilibrium.

Weissbourd (1996) describes the type of adult a child needs.

> All children should have a continuous relationship with a consistently attentive and caring adult who treats them as special— and not just another inhabitant of this world—who is able to stimulate and engage.

> Responsive mothers—those who ignore few episodes and respond with little delay—have infants with more variety, subtlety, and clarity of noncrying communication . . . . Mothers who vocalize and smile frequently

---

holophrases — the expression of a whole idea in a single word. They are characteristic of the child's language from about 12 to 18 months.

FIGURE 1–18 "You can do it. Just take one small step."

have been found to have infants who vocalize and smile frequently.

Greenspan (1997), discussing the emotional base needed for intellectual growth, describes a developmental consequence.

> Our observations of children suggest that even the capacities generally considered to be innate, such as the ability to learn language, require an emotional base in order to acquire purpose and function. Unless a child masters the capacity for reciprocal emotional and social signaling, her ability to use language (as well as her cognitive and social patterns) develops poorly, often in a fragmented manner.

At about four months, babies begin to gaze in the direction in which caregivers are looking. Caregivers are able to follow the line of vision of babies as well. Well-trained caregivers naturally comment on what the babies are looking at, providing them with language labels. This process is known as "joint attentional focus" and is thought to provide the framework for language development (McMullen, 1998). When the adult knows the infant does not yet understand language, most adults behave as if a child's response is *a turn* in the conversation.

As Honig (1981) points out, "caregivers who boost language are giving the gift of a great power to babies"; consequently, infants benefit from sensitive, alert, skilled adults. Adult caregivers need to read both nonverbal and vocalized cues and react appropriately (Figure 1–19). They need to be attentive and loving. Learning to read each other's signals is basic to the quality of the relationship. Liberal amounts of touching, holding, smiling, and looking promote language and the child's overall sense that the world around him is both safe and fascinating. Recognizing the child's individuality, reading nonverbal behaviors, and reacting with purposeful actions are all expected of professional infant specialists, as is noticing activity level, moods, distress threshold, rhythmicity, intensity, ad-

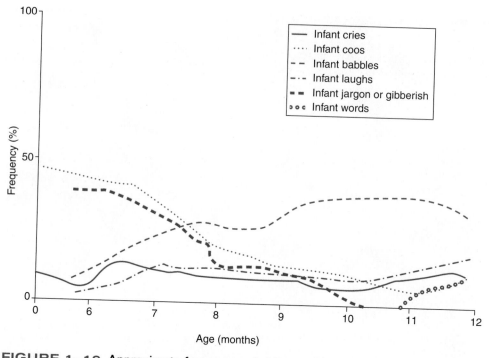

FIGURE 1–19 Approximate frequency of child utterances from 6 to 12 months.

venturesomeness, distractibility, adaptability, and attention span. The following are suggestions that can be used to promote the infant's sound making and subsequent first spoken words.

DURING EARLY INFANCY

- Hold the infant firmly yet gently, and make soft, gentle sounds while moving smoothly and holding the infant close.
- Talk in a pleasant, soothing voice; use simple language; and make frequent eye contact.
- Emphasize and expect two-way "conversation." Hesitate. Pause for an infant response.
- Make a game out of the infant's smiles, sounds, and movements when the infant is responsive.
- Imitate the infant's babbling, cooing, or other sound making between four and six months of age (playfully echo). Make new sounds for infant imitation.

- Whisper in the infant's ear to soothe him.
- Be watchful for signs that the infant may need a less stimulating setting and is emitting "escape signals."
- Use the infant's name—for example, "Scott's toes" instead of "baby's toes."

ESPECIALLY DURING LATE INFANCY

- Speak clearly.
- Explain what is happening and what will happen next.
- Encourage the infant to look at you while you speak.
- Do not interrupt vocal play, jargon, or self-communication.
- Engage in word play, rhyme, chants, and fun-to-say short expressions.
- Be an animated speaker and a responsive companion.
- Try simple finger plays.
- Plan concrete, participatory activities with textures, sights, and sounds.

- Encourage sound making and provide noise-making and musical toys.
- Talk about sounds when you hear them—"Knock, knock, there's daddy at the door."
- Remember to pause and wait for the child's response.
- Label objects, happenings, actions, and emotions.
- Use highly intonated speech (Cowley, 2000).
- Use a high pitch.
- Use *slow* pace and musicality in speech (Cowley, 2000).
- Speak distinctly with clear enunciation to help children identify phonemes.
- Emphasize one word in a sentence to rivet the child's attention (Cowley, 2000).
- Use repetition but do not make it drill-like (Cowley, 2000).
- Take *conversational* turns.
- Speak *face to face*.
- Give feedback by responding with both words and actions. Example: Respond to child's "Bot, Bot, Bot" with "Yes, here's your bottle" (Cowley, 2000).

Weiser (1982) suggests occasionally using "singing conversations" with infants and also urges change of pitch with expressions like "up comes the spoon." This lays the basis for both speech and later music education. Both recorded and live musical sounds are part of an auditory-rich environment for infants. For identified adult goals and caregiver activities, see Figure 1–20.

How does a caregiver go about establishing a dialogue with an infant? First, consider the infant to be intentional by communicating from day one and expecting many face-to-face opportunities. Newson (1979) provides an example of a caregiver's attempt to establish dialogue.

The child suddenly arrests the ongoing pattern of his play activity in response to a new noise such as a car passing outside.

His mother takes her cue from this shift in his attention to mark or "comment" on his reaction by indicating that she too has noticed the intrusive noise. Perhaps she picks up the child to let him look out of the window and see the car as it disappears down the road. The maintenance of communication in an incident of this kind is only accomplished by the fact that one of the two communicating persons is socially sensitive to the effect of what is happening to the other, moment by moment.

Remember that infants are alike yet uniquely different. Some sensitive infants may appear overwhelmed and require little stimuli to maintain equilibrium. Others will thrive in an environment that provides a multitude of people, sights, sounds, and new activities. Each infant provides a challenge one must "puzzle out" to decide best courses of action—what works, what does not work, and what is best.

The individualism of infants has been described by Greenspan (1997) as follows:

Another aspect of this new understanding of thought and emotion is a recently discovered fact: a given sensation does not necessarily produce the same response in every individual. Inborn differences in sensory makeup can make a sound of a given frequency and loudness—say, a high-pitched voice—strike one person as exciting and invigorating while it impresses another as piercing and shrill, rather like a siren. A light of a certain brightness might seem cheerful to one person but glaring and irritating to another. A gentle caress may soothe one but painfully startle another, like a touch on sunburned skin. . . .
A given sensation can thus produce quite different emotional effects in different individuals—in one case pleasure, for example, but in another anxiety.

Because infants' first sensory experiences are part of emotional relationships with caregivers, caregivers' efforts to provide developmental care go hand in hand with providing

AGE	ADULT GOALS	ADULT ACTIVITY
birth to 2 months	1. to create a trusting, intimate relationship 2. to take pleasure in the reciprocal infant-adult interactions 3. to help infant calm and regulate himself 4. to verbally communicate and promote a two-way pattern of responses 5. to maintain eye contact and spend time face to face 6. to seek to create an appropriate environmental moderation level	1. anticipate and satisfy infant needs 2. show interest and provide positive reactions and joy in the infant's presence and communicative attempts 3. provide sights, sounds, touches, and playful companionship 4. talk, croon, whisper, sing, and mimic infant gesture 5. repeat infant sounds 6. provide a comfortable environment that satisfies the child's needs
2–6 months	1. to keep alert to infant attempts to communicate distress or needs 2. to strengthen growing bond of enjoyment in adult-infant "together time" and explorations 3. to recognize child individuality, moods, likes and dislikes, uniqueness 4. to encourage "you talk" and "I talk" behaviors 5. to see infant gestures as possibly purposeful 6. to hold child's eye contact when speaking and gain child's attention with animated speech 7. to use clear and simple speech	1. provide adult-infant play time and joint new experiences 2. provide infant exploring of sights, sounds, music, and play materials and indoor and outdoor environments 3. offer "talking" opportunities with others 4. name child's actions, toys, happenings while changing, bathing, and feeding 5. play baby games such as Pat-a-cake 6. use talk and touch as a reward for the child's communication attempts 7. repeat child sounds and gestures
6–12 months	1. to pursue infant interests, tailoring your talk to child focus 2. to promote the idea that language is used for naming and describing 3. to play with rhythm and rhyme in adult-infant communications 4. to speak clearly, emphasizing new words when appropriate 5. to show delight in child's verbal and physical accomplishments 6. to pair your words with actions, happenings, and objects 7. to recognize and respond appropriately to child signaling and words 8. to make sure sound level and noise is appropriate 9. to listen for intent, not perfection 10. to provide safe environment conducive to child exploring and action	1. expand the child's world with neighborhood trips, people, playthings, and experiences 2. name and describe happenings, emotions, actions, and environments as things take place 3. introduce and read board books to the child, letting child explore them himself 4. sing songs, perform finger plays, play word games with visual and touching actions 5. listen and pause for infant response 6. name body parts, colors, and objects 7. tell simple stories 8. delight in the world and its joyful pursuits with the child

FIGURE 1–20 Adult goals and activities for language development during infancy.

positive emotional support in daily reciprocal exchanges between the child and adult. The terms *child-centered* and *child-focused* need to be coupled with reactive, observant, playful, nuturant adult-sending behaviors. This type of infant care is nearly impossible when adult-infant ratios in out-of-home care are inadequate.

Generally, the types of adults who promote language are those who are alert to the child's achievements, notice them, and enjoy interacting, as well as adults who can offer novelty, assistance, and enthusiasm in addition to focusing on the child's interests. Language competence at age three is related to maternal (or caregiver) emotional and verbal responsiveness.

Threats to early language development include:

- ◆ hearing loss.
- ◆ lack of sharing experiences with caring adults.
- ◆ failure of adults to talk frequently to preverbal infants.
- ◆ stifling baby's curiosity (White, 1986a).

BABY GAMES AND EXPLORATIONS

Almost daily, infants seem to increase the ways they can explore and enjoy verbal-physical games. Most mothers or infant educators create their own games and activities that are enjoyable to both infants and caregivers. They become aware of their infants' focus and reactions to people, toys, and other environmental features; they then build activities and child-adult interactions on child interest. Games that deal with child anticipation often elicit smiles or giggles. Playing classics such as Peek-a-boo or Johnny Jump Up or hiding an object under a cloth has delighted generations of children. Tying a soft tinkling bell to the wrist or leg of an infant or connecting a soft ribbon from an infant's ankle to an overhead mobile (under adult supervision) are more newly devised activities.

Acredolo and Goodwyn (2000) recommend that, from a baby's earliest days, parents play simple imitation games during face-to-face interaction, making sure to pause long enough for the infant to take in the information and mount a response. According to the researchers, the best distance for these games is 8 to 12 inches away from the child's face. Parent imitation of the baby's movement is also suggested, as is rewarding the baby's efforts with smiles and verbal encouragement.

A few favorite infant play pursuits and examples of adult comment follow.

COMMON ACTIVITIES	POSSIBLE ADULT REMARKS
look and watch	"See the kitty."
touch it	"Grandpa's nose."
mouth it	"Eat the cracker."
make a sound	"Ring goes the bell."
pick it up	"A rock! You found a rock."
push it or pull it	"Push the box."
drop it off	"Down goes the block."
empty it, fill it	"Out come the dish towels."
climb it	"Foot goes up."
carry it	"Robert's holding the car."
roll it	"The ball's rolling on the rug."

Curry and Johnson (1990) suggest that adult interaction with older infants helps develop a joint feeling of exploration.

Display an attitude about the environment that nourishes children's curiosity and sense of wonder about themselves and objects. Think about what you are saying and how it affects baby's feelings about exploration.

Because caregivers spend considerable time supervising active infants, it usually takes little effort to supply brief running remarks. Pausing is as important as talking. Coexplorers must give the infant time to send signals and then must issue approving nods or words or reactions. Infants quickly catch on that conversation is a two-way process. An infant's caregiver, who has primarily a policing orientation that is full of "no-no's" and little else, misses tremendous language opportunities.

A more knowledgeable and interactive adult talks about objects and events in the immediate surroundings. Children benefit when adult contributions are meaningful and related to children's own utterances. This might be done by direct imitation or expansion of the child's utterance into a phrase or sentence that captures the child's intention by providing a novel feature or by recasting the child's meaning into a more precise form.

SOCIAL PLAY

It is obvious that infants six months and older watch, imitate, and attempt physical and verbal contact with other infants and children. There is a strong attraction to other small people and animals. Most young infants prefer to be in the same room with a favored caregiver. Only as they become mobile and older do they explore adjacent rooms and areas on their own.

The following classic language and body-action play has brought delight to generations of infants. The most enjoyed play activities include tickling, bouncing, and lifting with accompanying words and rhymes.

THIS LITTLE PIGGY
(Each line is recited while holding a toe, moving toward the pinkie.)

> *This little pig went to market,*
> *This little pig stayed home,*
> *This little pig had roast beef,*
> *This little pig had none,*
> *This little piggy cried, "Wee, wee, wee, wee!"*
>   *all the way home.*

PAT-A-CAKE
(Recited while helping the child imitate hand clapping.)

> *Pat-a-cake, pat-a-cake, baker's man,*
> *Bake me a cake as fast as you can.*
> *Pat it and prick it and mark it with a "B,"*
> *And put it in the oven for baby and me.*

SO BIG

> *Say, "Look at you—so big!" Slowly raise both infant's arms up, extending them over the child's head while saying "[child's name] is so-o-oh big" and then slowly bring the arms down.*

> *Repeat. Say the child's name slowly as you raise the infant close to your face at eye level; say, "So-o-oh big." Then gently say, "Wow, wow, wow—what a baby. A so-o-oh big baby." Smile.*

Other play games are found in the Activities section.

MUSIC

Rock, Trainor, and Addison (1999) believe music (along with singing and musical speech) appears to be a central part of the crucial interaction that occurs between caregivers and infants as infants develop over the first year of life. They identify two types of musical and/or singing interactions by adults and others: (1) "lullaby-style," a soothing or go-to-sleep variety, and (2) "play-song" style, described as playful, brilliant, rhythmic, and smiling behaviors. The first style is seen as caregiver attempts to regulate or promote a particular infant state (such as relaxation, contentment, sleep), and the second style, the communication of emotional information (such as mutual enjoyment, love, specialness, playfulness).

Common sense tells us certain musical experiences enrich infants' lives and may soothe both infants and caregivers. Pick (1986) believes babies as young as three months can distinguish between certain melodies. Musical infant babbling described by Gordon (1986) includes both "tonal babble and rhythm babble." *Tonal babble* is babbling in a single pitch, the babble sounding like a monotone singer. In *rhythmic babble* the child's body or voice displays a rhythmic beat or quality.

Much of the music offered to infants may be accompanied by the mother's singing. Nursery, cultural, and folk tunes shared by caregivers can introduce language in intimate, pleasant settings. Simple, safe musical instruments can be explored, and moving to music is natural to young children. Wolf (2000) suggests educators start with songs they love, ones sung to them as children. Others suggest investigating children's music publishers, recorded children's music, and well-known performers and producers of young children's music. Names like Raffi, Ella Jenkins, Hap Palmer, Tom Hunter, and many others are well known to most early childhood educators.

Garcia-Barrio (1986) suggests Bach preludes and Vivaldi's "Springtime Symphony" as good infant-listening selections.

One benefit of musical activities for older preschoolers and primary children is enhanced abstract and **spatial-temporal reasoning** (Singhal, 1999). Early childhood infant and toddler educators now give added priority to planned musical experiences during a child's first years of life, hoping to promote possible intellectual advantages and developmental growth not yet identified by researchers.

Begley (2000) explains scientists are finding that the human brain is "prewired" for music and suspects that some forms of intelligence are enhanced by music. She cites the work of S. Trehub, University of Toronto, who discovered that infants six to nine months old could recognize a melody whose pitch or tempo had changed as being the same melody heard previously. Begley (2000) states Trehub has found the following:

> Infants smile when the air is filled with perfect fourths and perfect fifths—chords or sequences separated by five half steps, like C and F, or even half steps, like C and G, respectively. But babies hate the ugly tritone, in which two notes are separated by six half steps, like C and F sharp.

Although controversial at present, many educators believe learning musical skills in childhood can help children do better at mathematics. The fact that it can make infant and preschool care more enjoyable is not disputed by early childhood educators.

Campbell (1997) believes that music can strengthen children's minds and serve as a fundamental skill in learning. He believes music has the ability to build neuropathways in the brain that can increase memory and help children's language development. Hodges (1996) claims every infant is born with a "musical brain" that is capable of tracking musical elements such as melody, harmony, rhythm, and form. What will most early educators do with the new ideas about music and infants? They will continue to offer musical experience and hope that, in addition to improving the quality of the care they provide, it is developmentally appropriate, with perhaps "hidden" and yet to be discovered benefits. Rauscher (2003), on the other hand, who examined a wide range of research on the subject, declares that no scientific evidence supports the claim that listening to music improves children's intelligence; however, he also notes that the relationship between music and spatial-temporal reasoning is particularly compelling. Only more studies with more children will prove whether music produces lasting benefits in cognition.

See Additional Resources at the end of this chapter for favorite musical and movement activities and song books.

READING TO INFANTS

Some parents read books during a mother's later stages of pregnancy believing the practice will affect some positive results. Few experts recommend this activity. Studies, such as Fifer and Moon's (1995), have intrigued parents and educators. Their research findings suggest that infants remember and give greater attention to stories read to them before their birth. Conclusive research evidence is yet to verify Fifer and Moon's conclusions, but some parents are still eager to adopt the practice.

Between 6 and 12 months, some infants will sit and look at a picture book with an adult. Kupetz and Green (1997) alert teachers to

---

spatial-temporal reasoning — the mental arrangement of ideas and/or images in a graphic pattern indicating their relationships over time.

what attracts and encourages infants and toddlers to join a caregiver reading a book.

> It is the sound of the reader's voice that gets the young child's attention even before he can focus on the pictures. The warmth and security of being held and the reader's voice make for a very pleasurable combination.

The child will want to grab pages and test the book in his mouth or try to turn pages. The child's head may swivel to look at the adult's mouth. If the child has brought a book to the adult, he will usually want to sit on the adult's lap as both go through the book. The child gets ever more adept at turning pages as his first birthday nears. Familiar objects in colorful illustration set on white or plain backgrounds and large faces seem to be particularly fascinating. Infants seem to respond well to and enjoy the rhyme they hear.

Adult reading to infants younger than 12 months of age is increasingly recommended by researchers investigating this practice. P. W. Jusczyk (1997) of Johns Hopkins University states

> As you are sitting there reading, the child is learning something about sound patterns of words. That is important because they learn how words are formed and it helps them to segment sound patterns out of speech.

Book-reading techniques include reading something the adult enjoys with average volume and expression, using gesturing or pointing when called for, promoting child imitation, letting the child turn sturdy pages, and making animal or sound noises. A good rule of thumb is to stop before the child's interest wanes. Adults may find that many infants enjoy repeated reading of the same book during the same sitting. A study by Jones (1996) shows that some parents are very adept in engaging infants in picture books. They find **cues** in book features such as objects, events depicted, sounds, colors, and so on, that give the infant pleasure:

> More successful parents identify a large number of pictorial details, their visual and linguistic coding both carrying a high emotional charge for the infant.

> A disproportionate amount of time may be devoted to details of the pictures that often have little to do with the story text. The parent may adapt the story to include pictorial details more salient to his/her child.

Skilled parents, as well as infant educators, realize it is often the colorful illustrations that attract, so they name and point to features. They attempt to make illustrations relevant to the child's past experience.

Simple, colorful, sturdy-paged or cardboard books are plentiful. Reading them regularly can become a pleasant activity. Books of cotton fabric, heavy plastic, canvas, or cardboard, and ones with flaps to lift and peek under, soft furry patches to feel, rough sandpaper to touch, and holes to look through or stick a finger through are books that include sensory experiences. Homemade collections of family photographs have delighted many young children. The ideal book for babies, according to Schickedanz (1986), has simple, large pictures or designs set against a contrasting background and is constructed to stand on its own when opened.

There are a number of literary classics (although not all experts agree to the same titles) that most children in our culture experience. Many of these involve rhyme, rhythm, touching, motions, or hand gestures. They have, over time, become polished gems passed onto succeeding generations. Some are shared as songs, and include:

"Here We Go Round the Mulberry Bush"

"One, Two, Buckle My Shoe"

"Hush-a-Bye Baby"

"Twinkle, Twinkle, Little Star"

"Rock-a-Bye Baby"

"Ba Ba Black Sheep"

---

cues — prompts or hints that aid recognition, such as a parent pointing to and/or saying "teddy bear" when sharing a picture book illustraton. This is done because the infant is familiar with his own teddy bear.

RECORDINGS

Growing numbers of CDs, tapes, and videos are being produced for infants. Infants listen and sometimes move their bodies rhythmically. Environmental and animal sound recordings are available. Caregivers find that certain recordings are soothing and promote sleep. Infants are definitely attracted to musical sounds, and researchers are studying whether listening to music during infancy promotes listening abilities and speech production.

EARLY EXPERIENCE WITH WRITING TOOLS

As early as 10 to 12 months, infants will watch intently as someone makes marks on a surface or paper. They will reach and attempt to do the marking themselves. Chalk and thick crayons or crayon "chunks" are recommended for exploring. Large-sized paper (torn apart grocery brown bags) taped at the edges to surfaces and chalkboards work well. These activities require constant, close supervision to prevent infants from biting or chewing writing tools. The child may not realize the writing tool is making marks but may imitate and gleefully move the whole arm. Many believe it is simply not worth the effort to supervise very young children during this activity and save this activity until the children are older. Healy (1990) speculates awkward hand positions in writing may become habitual and difficult to change at a later time. She suggests waiting. Adult help with large, blunt pencil-holding or nontoxic marker-holding technique after the child has developed an interest in making marks is another course of action.

IMPLICATIONS FOR PARENTS

Parental attitudes about their infant's communicating abilities may influence the infant's progress.

> Mothers who believe their babies are potential communicative partners talk to them in ways which serve both to strengthen that belief and to make it come true. (Snow, De Blauw, & Van Roosmalen, 1979)

The highly simplified and repetitive "mother talk" typical of many American mothers and verbal conversations with preverbal infants are not typical in some cultures. Some cultures do not view the infant as a legitimate conversational partner.

Parents' expectations and feelings shape their responses to their children. These attitudes are the early roots of the critical partnership between adult and child, and the child's sense of feeling lovable and powerful. Consequently, they influence the child's assessment of self.

Special infant projects that have promoted later school success have provided information in this area. Home factors mentioned include:

- a lot of attention by socially responsive caregivers
- little or no disruption of bonding attachment between the infant and his primary caregiver during the first year
- availability of space and objects to explore
- good nutrition
- active and interactive exchanges and play time
- parent knowledge of developmental milestones and the child's emerging skills
- parent confidence in infant handling
- maintenance of the child's physical robustness
- positive attention and touching in play exchange

Parent (or family) stress and less-than-desirable quality in child-parent interactions seem to hinder children's language development. Because most families face stress, a family's reaction to stress, rather than stress itself, is the determining factor. In today's busy two-parent-worker families and single-parent-worker families, parent *time* spent with babies and young children needs to remain a family priority.

It is good practice to talk through the routines of dressing, feeding, and bathing the infant in simple sentences. Also, statements such as "push the switch on" and "lights off" while these actions are being performed are recorded in the child's memory. Pausing in conversations for the infant to make his own noises and acknowledging these with a smile or look of recognition will encourage the infant to continue making sounds.

Fischer (1986) has good advice for parents.

> Don't worry about teaching as much as providing a rich and emotionally supportive atmosphere.

The richness to which he refers is a richness of opportunity, rather than expensive toys and surroundings. Parents may get the idea that a parent has to talk constantly and that early infant "talkers" have parents with more competency in parenting skills. However, current research indicates that parents who spontaneously speak about what the child is interested in and who zoom in and out of the child's play as they go about their daily work are responsive and effective parents. Also, early and late "talkers" usually show little difference in speaking ability by age three. The variation between children with respect to the onset and accomplishment of most human characteristics covers a wide range when considering what is normal and expected.

Infants and Children Living in Poverty

Vernon-Feagans, Hammer, Miccio, and Manlove (2003) posit the largest group of children at risk for school failure and learning disabilities are the children of the poor. A disproportionate percentage of poverty's children reside in black and Hispanic families who may have limited access to health care. Premature birth, poor nutrition, poor health, lack of immunizations, and chronic ear infections may damage neural organization, brain development, and physical capacity. Other environmental factors, such as crowded living conditions, less-than-abundant home language usage, absence of play objects and books, limited parent vocabulary, limited verbal interaction, and meager parent understanding of factors influencing language development, can contribute to children's problems acquiring language and literacy.

Poor families, whose children may escape at-risk status, share the following commonalities. They are large, extended families who provide supportive language-stimulation and encouragement; no other social/biological risks are present; and they manage to safeguard their infants' and older children's health (Vernon-Feagans et al., 2003). Intervention and social service programs may also have been accessible. It is the isolated poor families with multiple risk factors, including abusive home environments, whose children are the most negatively affected.

SUMMARY

Each child grows in language ability in a unique way. The process starts before birth with the development of sensory organs. Parents play an important role in a child's growth and mastery of language.

Perceptions gained through life experiences serve as the base for future learning of words and speech. Babbling, sound making, and imitation occur, and first words appear.

A number of environmental factors, including poverty, may influence a child's language acquisition. Adults' attitudes concerning infants' intellectual and communication abilities are important also. Most children progress through a series of language ability stages and milestones at about the same ages (Figure 1–21) and become adultlike speakers during the preschool period. The way children learn language is not clearly understood, hence the numerous differing theories of language acquisition.

Technology has permitted neuroscientists to research infant abilities in greater depth than ever before. Research has enlightened educators who are awed by discoveries concerning infants'

INFANT'S AGE	STAGES OF LANGUAGE DEVELOPMENT
before birth	Listens to sounds. Reacts to loud sounds.
at birth	Birth cry is primal, yet individual—vowel-like. Cries to express desires (for food, attention, and so on) or displeasure (pain or discomfort). Makes eating, sucking, and small throaty sounds. Hiccups. Crying becomes more rhythmic and resonant during first days. Shows changes in posture—tense, active, or relaxed.
first days	Half cries become vigorous; whole cries begin to take on depth and range. Coughs and sneezes.
1 month	Three to four vowel sounds apparent. Seems to quiet movements and attend to mother's voice. Eating sounds mirror eagerness. Sighs and gasps. Smiles in sleep.
2–3 months	Coos and makes pleasurable noises (babbling) and blowing and smacking sounds. Most vowel sounds are present. Open vowel-like babbles may begin. Consonant sounds begin, usually the following—*b, d, g, h, l, m, n, p, t*. Markedly less crying. Smiles and squeals and may coo for half a minute. Peers into faces. Adults may recognize distinct variations in cries (i.e., cries that signal fear, tiredness, hunger, pain, and so on). Focuses on mother's face and turns head to her voice. May be frightened by loud or unfamiliar noise. May blow bubbles and move tongue in and out.
4–5 months	Sound play is frequent. Social smiling more pronounced. Can whine to signal boredom. May laugh. Reacts to tone of voice. Seems to listen and enjoy music. Likes adult vocal play and mimicking. Favorite people seem to induce verbalness. Babbles several sounds in one breath. Body gestures signal state of comfort or discomfort. Attracted to sounds. Approaching 6 months of age, may start to show understanding of words often used in household. Turns head and looks at speaking family members. Consonant sounds more pronounced and frequent.
6–8 months	Increased babbling and sound making; repeats syllables; imitates motions and gestures; uses nonverbal signals; vocalizes all vowel sounds; reduplication of utterances; more distinct intonation. Increases understanding of simple words. Enjoys making noise with toys and household objects. Repeats actions to hear sounds again. May blow toy horn. Delights in rhythmic vocal play interchange, especially those that combine touching and speaking. Twists and protrudes tongue, smacks, and watches mother's mouth and lips intently. May look at picture books for short period or watch children's television programs.
9–10 months	May make kiss sounds. Increasing understanding of words like *no-no, mommy, daddy, ball, hat,* and *shoe*. May play Pat-a-cake and wave bye-bye. May hand books to adults for sharing. Uses many body signals and gestures. May start jargonlike strings of sounds, grunts, gurgles, and whines. Listens intently to new sounds. Imitates.
11–14 months	Reacts to an increasing number of words. Speaks first word(s) (usually words with one syllable or repeated syllable). Points to named objects or looks toward named word. Makes sounds and noises with whatever is available. Imitates breathing noises, animal noises (like dog's bark or cat's meow), or environmental noises (like "boom" or train toot). Uses many body signals, especially "pick me up" with arms outstretched and reaching for another's hand, meaning "come with me." May understand as many as 40 to 50 words. At close to 15 months, one word has multiple meanings. Jargonlike strings of verbalness continue. The child's direction of looking gives clues to what the child understands, and the child may have a speaking vocabulary of 10 or more words. Uses first pretend play gestures such as combing hair with a spoon-shaped object, drinking from a pretend cup, pretending to eat an object, and pretending to talk with another on a toy telephone.

FIGURE 1–21 Milestones in developing language behavior.

learning capacities and abilities to sort and categorize human speech sounds. Deprivation, abuse, and neglect can affect infants' future brain function, as can sight and hearing acuity.

Early in life, infants and parents form a reciprocal relationship, reacting in special ways to each other. The quality and quantity of parental attention becomes an important factor in language development.

The child progresses from receiving to sending language, which is accompanied by gestures and nonverbal communication. From infancy, the child is an active participant, edging closer to the two-way process required in language usage and verbal communication.

Staff members in infant care programs can possess interaction skills that offer infants optimal opportunities for speech development.

ADDITIONAL RESOURCES

Readings

Acredolo, L., & Goodwyn, S. (2000). *Baby minds: Brain-building games your baby will love to play.* New York: Bantam Books.

Bowlby, J. (1988). *A secure base: Parent-child attachment and healthy human development.* New York: Basic.

Gonzales-Mena, J., & Eyer, D. W. (1997). *Infants, toddlers, and caregivers* (4th ed.). Mountain View, CA: Mayfield.

Kinney, M., & Ahrens, P. (2001). *Beginning with babies.* St. Paul, MN: Redleaf Press.

Kupetz, B. N., & Green, E. J. (1997). Sharing books with infants and toddlers: Facing the challenges. *Young Children, 52*(2), 22–27.

Raikes, H. (1996). A secure base for babies: Applying attachment concepts to the infant care setting. *Young Children, 51*(5), 59–67.

Rhodes, C. S., & Ringler, L. H. (2004). *Born to learn: Developing a child's reading and writing.* Toronto: Pippin Publishing Corporation.

Snow, C. E. (1997). The development of conversation between mothers and babies. *Journal of Child Language, 4,* 1–22.

Infant Books

Boyton, S. (2004). *Moo baa, la la la!* New York: Simon & Schuster.

Capucilli, A. (1994). *Peek-a-boo bunny.* New York: Scholastic.

Carter, N. (1991). *Where's my fuzzy blanket?* New York: Scholastic.

DK Publishing Inc. (1998). *Touch and feel farm* [sensory board book]. New York: Author.

Dunn, P. (1987). *I'm a baby.* New York: Random House.

Fujikawa, G. (1963). *Babies.* New York: Putnam.

Hoban, T. (1984). *What is it?* New York: Greenwillow.

MacDonald, A. (1992). *Let's play.* New York: Candlewick.

Oxenbury, H. (1981). *Dressing.* New York: Little Simon.

Oxenbury, H. (1995). *I hear.* New York: Candlewick.

Ra, C. F. (1987). *Trot trot to Boston, play rhymes for baby.* New York: Lothrop, Lee, and Shepard Books.

Shott, S. (1996). *Baby's world.* New York: Dutton.

Tafuri, N. (1987). *My friends,* New York: Greenwillow Books.

Watanabe, K. (2003). *My first Taggies book: Sweet dreams.* New York: Scholastic.

Ziefert, H. (1987). *Where's the dog?* New York: Harper & Row.

Infant Play Games

Lansky, V. (2001). *Games babies play: From birth to twelve months.* New York: Book Peddlers.

Rowley, B. (2000). *Baby days: Activities, ideas, and games.* New York: Hyperion.

Wilner, I. (2000). *Baby's game book.* New York: Greenwillow.

Infant Music, Movement Activities, and Song Books

Beall, P. C., & Nipp, S. (1996). *Wee sing for baby.* New York: G.P. Putnam Publishing.

Brown, M. (Ed.). (1985). *Play rhymes.* New York: Dutton.

Burton, M. (1989). *Tail, toes, eyes, ears, nose.* New York: Harper and Row.

Engvick, W. (Ed.). (1985). *Lullabies and night songs.* New York: HarperCollins.

Long, S. (2002). *Hush little baby.* San Francisco: Chronicle Books.

Manning, J. (1998). *My first songs.* New York: Harper-Collins.

Nursery songs. (1997). New York: McClanahan Book Co.

Palmer, H. (1984). *Babysong* [audio CD]. Kiddo Music.

Raffi. (1996). *Singable songs for the very young: Great with a peanut butter sandwich* [audio CD]. Rounder.

Shore, R. (1998). *Bach and baby bedtime* [cassette or CD]. Huntington Beach, CA: Youngheart Music.

HELPFUL WEB SITES

High/Scope Educational Research Foundation
http://www.highscope.org
Reading to infants and toddlers is suggested.

KidSource Online
http://www.kidsource.com
Search for the Infant's Language Growth Chart.

National Child Care Information Center
http://nccic.org
Select *Popular Topics* and then choose the appropriate child-related topic.

National Parent Information Network
http://npin.org
Check library for readings.

U.S. Department of Education
http://www.ed.gov
Reading research about children from birth through age six is presented. Select *Publications.*

Zero to Three
http://www.zerotothree.org
Offers information on helping parent-child bonding during daily activities.

Read about "Educator Behaviors and Actions That Really Matter during an Infant's First Year." Additional infant-adult interaction games, readings, and Web sites are included, along with an annotated infant book list. A review on early recognition of autistic behaviors is also presented for those who are interested.

STUDENT ACTIVITIES

1. What parental expectations of infants might interfere with the infant's ability to develop the idea he is an effective communicator? List three or four. Give examples from your own experience if possible. Compare your list with that of a classmate.

2. Observe two infants (birth to 12 months). Note situations in which the infants make sounds and how adults (parents or teachers) react to the sound making.

3. Sit with a young infant facing you. Have a notepad handy. Remain speechless and motionless. Try to determine what moment-to-moment needs the child has, and try to fulfill each need you recognize. Try not to add anything new; just respond to what you think the child needs. Write a description of the needs observed and your feelings.

4. Visit an infant-toddler center. Focus on an infant older than six months of age. What behaviors can you pinpoint in the infant's early childhood teachers that promote future language?

5. Try sharing a colorful, simple book with an 8- to 12-month-old. What behaviors did you observe?

6. Create a new game, rhyme, or movement word play, and test it on an infant 6 to 12 months of age.

7. Locate three books you think would be appropriate for older infants, and share them with the class.

8. Observe three children younger than one year of age each interacting with an adult for one 10- to 30-minute period. Try parks, family homes, doctors' waiting rooms. Take notes concerning their verbalness and interactions. What language-developing techniques were present? Which child would you choose to be if you could change places with one of the observed children and why?

9. What tips or strategies would you suggest to a relative who is attempting to share a simple picture book with an infant? List.

CHAPTER REVIEW

A. Write your own theory of language acquisition. (A child learns language . . .) Compare and contrast your theory with those on pages 11–14.

B. Finish the following: Early childhood educators working in group infant care programs who wish to give infants opportunities to acquire language should carefully monitor their ability to . . . (list specific techniques).

C. Write definitions for:

articulation	echolalia	moderation level
bonding	infant signing	phonation
critical brain growth periods	larynx	resonation

D. Explain the difference between *cooing* and *babbling*.

E. Finish the following: Language is a kind of game infants learn—a game played with precise recognizable rules. To learn the game, it's best to have adults in your life who . . .

F. Select the best answer.

1. Environmental factors that can affect future language development start
   a. at birth.
   b. before birth.
   c. during infancy.
   d. during toddlerhood.

2. The tone of a parent's voice is
   a. understood when a child learns to speak in sentences.
   b. less important than the parent's words.
   c. understood before actual words are understood.
   d. less important than the parent's actions.

3. In acquiring language, the child
   a. learns only through imitation.
   b. is one participant in a two-part process.
   c. learns best when parents ignore the child's unclear sounds.
   d. does not learn by imitating.

4. Select the true statement about babbling.
   a. Why babbling occurs is not clearly understood.
   b. Babbling is unimportant.
   c. Babbling predicts how early a child will start talking.
   d. Babbling rarely lasts beyond one year of age.

5. How a child acquires language is
   a. clearly understood.
   b. not important.
   c. only partly understood.
   d. rarely a subject for study.

G. With a partner create a parent billboard drawing or other pictorial artwork, and relate it to infant language development. Write a clever caption (slogan). Share with the group. (Example: Picture of an infant and father. Caption: "Hey big daddy, that sweet talk and hug is just what I needed." [Not very clever? You can do better.])

H. What is the significance for early childhood educators of current discoveries concerning young children's brain growth?

INFANT-ADULT PLAY GAMES

WHAT HAVE WE HERE?

> Here's two little eyes big and round
> And two little ears to hear all sounds,
> One little nose smells a flower sweet,
> One little mouth likes food to eat.
> Here's ten little fingers to grasp and
> wiggle,
> Tickle ten toes and there's a giggle.
> Here's a button on a tiny tummy
> Around and around—that feels funny!

ROUND AND ROUND

(This is a frequently used tickling verse of English mothers.)

> Round and round the garden (said
> slowly while circling the baby's
> palm)
> One step, two steps (walking fingers
> toward a tickling spot at neck,
> stomach, or underarms, and said a
> little faster)
> Tickle you there! (said very fast)

TWO LITTLE EYES

> Two little eyes that open and close.
> Two little ears and one little nose.
> Two little cheeks and one little chin.
> Two little lips that open and grin.

BABY RIDES

> This is the way baby rides, (bounce
> infant on knees; with each new
> verse, bounce a little faster)
> The baby rides, the baby rides.
> This is the way baby rides,
> So early in the morning.
> This is the way the farmer rides . . .
> This is the way the jockey rides . . .

LITTLE MOUSE

> Hurry scurry little mouse
> Starts down your toes. (touch child's
> toes)
> Hurry scurry little mouse
> Past you knees he goes. (touch child's
> knees)
> Hurry scurry little mouse
> Past where your tummy is. (touch
> child's tummy)
> Hurry scurry little mouse
> Gives you a mousy kiss. (give child a
> loud kiss)

HERE WE GO

> Here we go up, up, up (lift child's legs
> up)
> Here we go down, down, down (lower
> child's legs down)
> Here we go backward and forward
> (sway child backward and forward)
> And here we go round and round
> (move child's legs in air)

WHAT HAVE WE HERE?

> These are baby's fingers, (touch child's
> fingers)
> These are baby's toes, (touch child's
> toes)
> This is baby's belly button, (touch
> child's tummy)
> Round and round it goes! (tickle child's
> tummy button)

WHOA HORSE

> Giddy-up, giddy-up, giddy-up horsey
> (bounce child on knees—last line,
> let child slip through knees)
> Giddy-up, giddy-up, go, go, go.
> Giddy-up, giddy-up, Whoa!

CHAPTER 2

The Tasks of the Toddler

OBJECTIVES

After reading this chapter, you should be able to:

◆ Discuss phonology, grammar, and the toddler's understanding of semantics.

◆ List three characteristics of toddler language.

◆ Identify adult attitudes and behaviors that aid the toddler's speech development.

KEY TERMS

concept
grammar
inflections
inner speech
joint attention
modifiers
morpheme

morphology
over-
    regularization
phoneme
phonetics
phonology
pragmatics

prosodic
    speech
semantics
symbols
syntax
telegraphic
    speech

THE TODDLER TEACHER

Kelsa (26 months) and her grandfather entered the classroom. He drew me aside after his granddaughter had run off to the housekeeping area. With a smile he shared what Kelsa had done and said to him. "We were watching TV, and I commented on something," he said. "She got up and stood right in front of me. Next, she cupped my cheeks with her hands and said, 'Look at me when you say words.'" He laughed. I explained, "Sometimes with toddlers we can understand their words only if they speak right into our face."

QUESTIONS TO PONDER

1. Is this a teacher strategy that helps toddlers?

2. Was the teacher's explanation to Kelsa's grandfather sufficient, or would a longer explanation have been better?

3. Is Kelsa's language acquisition advanced or about average for her age?

If you were amazed at the infant's and one-year-old's ability, wait until you meet the toddler! Toddlerhood marks the beginning of a critical language-growth period. Never again will words enter the vocabulary at the same rate; abilities emerge in giant spurts almost daily. When children stop and focus on things, from specks on the floor to something very large, concentration is total—every sense organ seems to probe for data.

Toddlerhood begins with the onset of toddling (walking), a little before or after the child's first birthday. The toddler is perched at the gateway of a great adventure, eager to proceed, investigating as she goes, and attempting to communicate what she discovers and experiences (Figure 2–1). "The bags are packed" with what has been learned in infancy. The child will both monologue and dialogue as she ages, always knowing much more than can be verbally expressed. As Harris (1990) points out

> Communication is well established *before* children begin to use words, and it seems that children's first word meanings are created by the very fact that the words they use are embedded in social acts which already have communicative significance.

FIGURE 2–1 This toddler is exploring how it feels to paint his hand.

Toddlers are action-oriented. McMullen (1998) points out that they act on and simultaneously perceive the world around them. She believes one can see toddlers thinking because their thought is a sensorimotor activity; only at a later age does higher-level thinking happen, allowing them to think first and then act.

By the age of two, toddlers' brains are as active as those of adults. The metabolic rate keeps rising, and by the age of three, toddlers' brains are two and a half times more active than the brains of adults—and they stay that way throughout the first decade of life (Shore, 1997). Quindlen (2001) compares the working rate of a toddler's mind to an adult's mind as that of a race car to a lawn tractor.

Greenspan (1997) describes an important happening during the toddler period when the child switches from communicating primarily through motor or gesture action to using symbolic (speech) communication. He believes this happens through the maturing possibilities of the child's neurology combined with the richness of the child's affective experiences. The key, Greenspan believes, is a warm, close relationship with an adult, one in which communication becomes important enough to provide satisfaction in itself. Lloyd-Jones (2002) notes that experts agree that the primary need of toddlers (and infants) is *emotional connection.*

From a few spoken words, the toddler will move to purposeful speech that gains what is desired, controls others, allows personal comments, and accompanies play. It becomes evident that the toddler realizes the give and take of true conversation and also realizes what it is to be the speaker or the one who listens and reacts—the one who persuades or is persuaded, the one who questions or is questioned. Toddlers become aware that everything has a name and that playfully trying out new sounds is an enjoyable pursuit. The child's meanings for the few words she uses at the start of the toddler period may or may not be the same as common public usage (Dopyera & Lay-Dopyera, 1992):

> The task of gradually modifying the private meanings of words to coincide with public meanings continues throughout the life span.

Cambourne (1988) describes the enormous complexity of learning to talk.

> When one has learned to control the oral version of one's language, one has learned literally countless thousands of conventions. Early language spoken on the Earth today (some three or four thousand) comprises a unique, arbitrary set of signs, and rules for combining those signs to create meaning. These conventions have no inherent "rightness" or "logic" to them, just as driving on the right or left side of the road has no intrinsic rightness or logic to it. Yet each language is an amazingly complex, cultural artifact, comprising incredibly complex sets of sounds, words, and rules for combining them, with equally numerous and complex systems for using them for different social, personal, and cognitive purposes.

Even though toddlers have an innate predisposition for learning to communicate, they face four major tasks in learning the rule systems of language: (1) understanding *phonology* (the sound system of a language); (2) learning *syntax* (a system of rules governing word order and combinations that give sense to short utterances and sentences, often referred to as grammar); (3) learning *semantics* (word meanings); and (4) learning *pragmatics* (varying speech patterns depending on social circumstances and the context of situations). The understanding of these rule systems takes place concurrently—one area complementing and promoting the other. Rule systems form without direct instruction as toddlers grope to understand the speech of others, express themselves, and influence others both verbally and nonverbally. We can think of the toddler as a "hypothesis tester," a thinker who over time can unconsciously formulate the rules of language (Genishi, 1985).

Language emergence is but one of the toddler's achievements. Intellectually, toddlers process, test, and remember language input.

They develop their own rules, which change as they recognize what are and are not permissible structures in their native language. Other important developmental achievements intersect during late toddlerhood as children increasingly shift to symbolic thinking and language use. Gains in social, emotional, and physical development are apparent, as are issues of power and autonomy.

PHONOLOGY

Toddlers learn the **phonology** of their native language—its phonetic units and its particular and sometimes peculiar sounds. This is no easy job! The young language learner must sort sounds into identifiable groups and categories while she is possibly experiencing the speech of a variety of people in various settings. Because spoken language is characterized by a continuous flow of word sounds, this makes the task even more difficult.

After sounds are learned, sound combinations are learned. A **phoneme** is the smallest unit of sound that distinguishes one utterance from another—implying a difference in meaning. English has 46 to 50 phonemes, depending on what expert is consulted. Harris (1990) defines language from a phonetic perspective in the following.

> ... language might be characterized as a continuous sequence of sounds produced by the expulsion of air through the throat and mouth ... Structures in the ear are sensitive to the airwave vibrations produced in this way and make the detection of speech sounds possible.

Languages are divided into vowels and consonants. When pronouncing vowels, the breath stream flows freely from the vocal cords; when pronouncing consonants, the breath stream is blocked and molded in the mouth and throat area by soft tissue, muscle tissue, and bone, with the tongue and jaw often working to-

---

phonology — the sound system of a language and how it is represented with an alphabetic code.
phoneme — one of the smallest units of speech that distinguishes one utterance from another.

gether. The child focuses on those sounds heard most often. The toddler's speech is full of repetitions and rhythmic speech play. Toddler babbling of this type continues and remains pleasurable during early toddlerhood. Sounds that are combinations of vowels and consonants increase. Vowels are acquired early, and most studies suggest that vowel production is reasonably accurate by age three (Donegan, 2002). Low, nonrounded vowels are favored during infancy (that is, i, o, u). Consonant sounds that are difficult to form will continue to be spoken without being close approximations of adult sounds until the child reaches five or six years of age or is even slightly older (Figure 2–2). Early childhood teachers realize that, in many instances, they will have to listen closely and watch for nonverbal clues to understand child speech.

It is a difficult task for the child to make recognizable sounds with mouth, throat, and

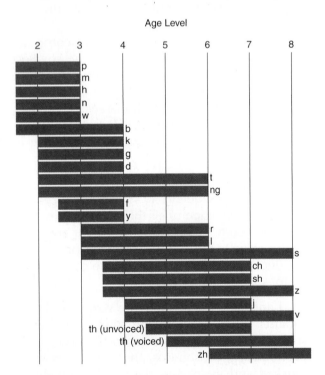

FIGURE 2–2 Consonants—age of acquisition. (Reprinted with permission from Sander, E. K. [1972]. When are speech sounds learned? *Journal of Speech and Hearing, 37,* 55–63. Copyright American Speech-Language-Hearing Association. All rights reserved.)

breath control working in unison. Lenneberg (1971) comments on the difficulties of perfecting motor control of speech-producing muscles, noting that this sophisticated skill comes ahead of many other physical skills.

> Speech, which requires infinitely precise and swift movements of tongue and lips . . . is all but fully developed when most other mechanical skills are far below levels of their future accomplishment.

Much of early speech has been described as unintelligible or gibberish. The toddler seems to realize that conversations come in long strings of sound. Rising to the occasion, the child imitates the rhythm of the sound but utters only a few understandable words.

Toddlers hear a word as an adult hears it. Sometimes, they know the proper pronunciation but are unable to reproduce it. The child may say "pway" for *play.* If the parent says "pway," the child objects, showing confusion and perhaps frustration. Toddler talk represents the child's best imitation, given present ability. Parents and teachers are urged to look at toddlers' speech mistakes as evidence that children are learning in an intelligent way.

Baron (1989) defines adult-child talk as "special language" or "child-directed speech," that is, a set of speech modifications commonly found in the language adults use to address young children. She goes on to divide adult-child language into five main categories: pedagogy, control, affection, social exchange, and information.

The pedagogy mode is characterized by slow adult speech that overenunciates or overemphasizes one or two words. This type of adult speech is "tailor-made" for one- or two-year-olds trying to segment the speech stream into comprehensible units.

Parents tend to label happenings and objects with easy-to-learn, catchy variations, such as *choo-choo, bow-wow,* and so forth. Other parental language techniques include:

1. labeling themselves as "Mommy" or "Daddy," instead of "I" or "me" in speech.

2. limiting topics in sentences.

3. using short and simple sentences.

4. using repetition.

5. expanding or recasting children's one-word or unfinished utterances. If toddler says "kitty," parent offers "Kitty's name is Fluff."

6. using a wide range of voice frequencies to gain child's attention and initiate a communication exchange.

7. carrying both sides of an adult-child conversation. Parents ask questions, then answer. This technique is most often used with infants but is also common during the toddler period. The parent is modeling a social exchange.

8. echoing a child's invented word. Many toddlers adopt a special word for a certain object. The whole family may use the child's word in conversational exchanges also.

When parents feel their infants and toddlers can communicate, parental actions and speech can increase children's communicative abilities and opportunities.

Early childhood educators believe caregivers should treat toddlers as communicating children, avoiding childlike or cutesy expressions. They offer simple forms of speech and easy-to-pronounce words whenever possible.

Views on adult use of baby talk include the idea that the practice may limit more mature word forms and emphasize dependency. On the other hand, parents may offer simplified, easily pronounced forms like *bow-wow* for a barking poodle. They later quickly switch to adult, harder-to-pronounce forms when the child seems ready. In the beginning, though, most adults automatically modify their speech when speaking with toddlers by using short sentences and stressing key words.

Children progress with language at their individual rates and with varying degrees of clarity. Some children speak relatively clearly from their first tries. Other children, who are also progressing normally, take a longer time before their speech is easily understood. All basic sounds (50 including diphthongs) are perfected by most children by age seven or eight.

Morphology

A **morpheme** is the smallest unit of language standing by itself with recognized meaning. It can be a word or part of a word. Many prefixes (un-, ill-) and suffixes (-s, -ness, -ed, -ing) are morphemes with their own distinct meaning. The study of morphemes is called **morphology**. There are wide individual differences in the rates toddlers utter morphemes (Figure 2–3). It is unfortunate if early childhood teachers or parents attempt to compare the emerging speech of toddlers or equate greater speech usage with higher ability, thus giving the quiet toddler(s) perhaps less of their time.

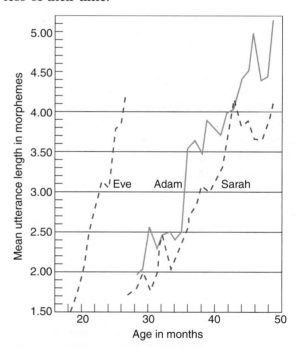

FIGURE 2–3 Individual rates in morpheme usage. (From Brown, R., Cazden, C., & Bellugi-Kilma, U. [1969]. The child's grammar from I to III. In J. P. Hill [Ed.], *Minnesota Symposium on Child Psychology* [vol. 2]. Minneapolis: University of Minnesota Press. Reprinted with permission of the University of Minnesota Press.)

---

morpheme — the smallest unit in a language that by itself has a recognizable meaning.
morphology — the study of the units of meaning in a language.

Between the ages of two and four years, children gradually include a variety of different morphemes in their spontaneous utterances. There seems to be a common sequence in their appearance (Brown, 1973).

SYNTAX

Languages have word orders and rules, and young children speak in word order and follow the rules of their native tongue. Children typically acquire the rules of grammar in their native language with little difficulty from normal communicative interactions with adults.

Harris (1990) points out

> The rules for ordering words in sentences do not operate on specific words, but on classes of words such as nouns, verbs, and adjectives. This has the advantage that a relatively small number of syntactical rules can account for the production of a very large number of sentences.

In one language, the subject of a sentence follows the verb; in other languages, it precedes the verb. **Modifiers** (descriptive words) in some languages have gender (male and female forms), but in others they do not. Plurals and possessive forms are unique to each language. Young speakers will make mistakes, but adults marvel at the grammar the child does use correctly, having learned the rules without direct instruction. Donoghue (1985) compares children's mastery of **phonetics** to their mastery of **syntax**.

> In contrast to the gradual mastery of phonology, children use syntax correctly (though incompletely of course) from the very beginning. By age two, and sometimes as early as 18 months, children begin to string together two or more holophrases and have thereby arrived at telegraphic stage.

All telegraphic speech consists of acceptable grammatical sequences which are the precursors of the sentence.

From all the perceptions received and the words spoken to and about the child, the child has noted regularities and has unconsciously formed rules, which are continually revised. Chukovsky (1963) describes this task.

> It is frightening to think what an enormous number of grammatical forms are poured over the poor head of the young child. And he, as if it were nothing at all, adjusts to all the chaos, constantly sorting out in rubrics the disorderly elements of words he hears, without noticing as he does this, his gigantic effort. If an adult had to master so many grammatical rules within so short a time, his head would surely burst.

Grammar involves the way sounds are organized to communicate meaning. With grammatical knowledge the young child can produce and understand a wide range of new, novel, grammatically correct, and meaningful sentences.

Clay (1993) notes that as the child learns to talk during preschool years, she produces many ungrammatical sentences and uses words in unusual ways. The errors of the two-year-old disappear as the child gains more control over language, but new kinds of errors appear in three-year-olds, who are trying new forms of expression. An understanding of the general rules of grammar develops before an understanding of the exceptions to the rules. Correct grammar forms may change to incorrect forms as the child learns new rules. Slobin (1971) has an interesting example of this phenomenon.

> In all of the cases which have been studied . . . the first past tenses used are the correct forms of irregular verbs—came, broke, went, and so on. Apparently these irregular

---

modifiers — words that give a special characteristic to a noun (for example, a large ball).
phonetics — pertaining to representing the sounds of speech with a set of distinct symbols, each denoting a single sound.
syntax — the arrangement of words as elements in a sentence to show their relationship.
grammar — the rules of a specific language that include both written and spoken utterances and describe how that specific language works and the forms of speech that conform to the rules that well-schooled speakers and writers observe in any given language.

verbs in the past tense—which are the most frequent past tense forms in adult speech—are learned as separate vocabulary items at a very early age.

Then, as soon as the child learns only one or two regular past tense forms—like helped and walked—he immediately replaces the correct irregular past tense forms with their incorrect over-generalizations from the regular forms. Thus children say "it came off," "it broke," and "he did it" before they say "it comed off," "it breaked," and "he doed it." Even though the correct forms may have been practiced for several months, they are driven out of the child's speech by the **overregularization**, and may not return for years.

In later years, during elementary school, the child will formally learn the grammar rules of the native language. What the child has accomplished before that time, however, is monumental. The amount of speech that already conforms to the particular syntactical and grammatical rules of language is amazing. The child has done this through careful listening and by mentally reorganizing the common elements in language that have been perceived.

The toddler's growing use of intonation and **inflections** (changes in loudness of voice) adds clarity, as do nonverbal gestures. The child is often insistent that adults listen.

The toddler's system of nonverbal signals, body postures, and motions that she used in late infancy has continued and expanded, becoming part of the toddler's communication style (Figure 2–4). Many signals translated by mothers to strangers leave strangers bewildered as to how the mother could possibly know what the child wants from what the stranger and the mother have both observed and heard.

English sentences follow a subject-verb-object sequence. Bruner (1966) notes three fundamental properties of sentences—verb-

FIGURE 2–4 Teachers try to identify each child's individual communication style.

object, subject-predicate, and modification—and he explains their universal use.

> There are no human languages whose sentences do not contain rules for these three basic sentential structures, and there are no nonhuman languages that have them.

Learning grammar rules helps the toddler express ideas (Bellugi, 1977). Understanding syntax helps the child to be understood.

> It is our knowledge of the rules of combination that governs how we construct and understand an infinite number of sentences from a finite vocabulary. Syntax gives language its power.

overregularization — the tendency on the part of children to make the language regular, such as using past tenses like -ed on verb endings.
inflections — the grammatical "markers" such as plurals. Also, a change in pitch or loudness of the voice.

If one listens closely to the older toddler, sometimes self-correction of speech errors takes place. Toddlers talk to themselves and to their toys often. It seems to aid storage and memory. The toddler understands adult sentences because she has internalized a set of finite rules or combinations of words.

SEMANTICS

Semantics is the study of meanings and acquisition of vocabulary. It probes how the sounds of language are related to the real world and life experiences. The toddler absorbs meanings from both verbal and nonverbal communication sent and received. The nonverbal refers to expressive associations of words: rhythm, stress, pitch, gesture, body position, facial change, and so on. Adults perform important functions in the child's labeling and concept formation by giving words meaning in conversations.

The toddler who comes from a home that places little emphasis on expressing ideas in language may be exposed to a relatively restricted range of words for expressing conceptual distinctions (Harris, 1990). Every early childhood center should offer opportunities for children to learn a rich and varied vocabulary to refer to various experiences and to express ideas (Figure 2–5).

In toddler classrooms, teachers have many opportunities to name objects and happenings as the day unfolds. Using teacher gesturing along with words (or pointing to pictures in simple picture books and magazines) helps the toddler form a connection between what she heard and what was said. Repeating words with voice stress can be done in a natural way while monitoring whether the child is still interested.

Word meanings are best learned in active, hands-on experiences rather than "repeat-after-me" situations. Meanings of words are acquired through their connotations, not their denota-

FIGURE 2–5 Play brings toddlers together in social situations.

semantics — the study of meanings associated with words and the acquisition of vocabulary.

tions, that is, in situations that consist of feelings and verbal and nonverbal messages with physical involvement. The word *cold,* for instance, means little until physically experienced. Toddlers assume that labels (words) refer to wholes instead of parts (the creature, not the tail) and to classes instead of items (all dogs, not one dog) (Cowley, 2000).

For a while toddlers may use one sound for a number of meanings.

> When a baby is first learning to talk, the same sound often serves for several words; for instance, "bah" can mean "bottle," "book," "bath," and "bye." And sometimes babies use one sound to name an object and also to express a more complicated thought, for example, a baby may point to the stroller and name it, but later may say the same word and mean, "I want to ride in the stroller." (Sherwin, 1987)

The child's **concept** building is an outgrowth and result of a natural human tendency to try to make sense of the surroundings. Attending to and pondering about the relationships, similarities, and differences in events and happenings, and mentally storing, remembering, and retrieving those ideas and impressions are important aspects of concept development. With young children's innate curiosity, drive, and desire to explore and experience, concepts are continually being formed, reformed, and modified.

Examples of toddler behavior demonstrate that conceptual conclusions happen daily in group and home care settings. When a child blows a whistle-shaped toy, licks and bites a plastic fruit in housekeeping play, tightly clings to an adult when a dog barks, or says "hot" when pointing to a water faucet, one can see past experiences are basic to the child's behavior.

To understand how concept development is individual and based upon life experiences, ask yourself what makes a cup a cup. How many distinguishing features can you list? Ask another adult to do the same. You will both probably list some of the following characteristics.

- has a handle
- holds liquids and substances
- is often round on top, tapering to a smaller round base or can be cylindrical
- is used as a standard measurement in cooking (8 ounces)
- is made from clay, plastic, glass, metal, or other solid substances
- can be used to drink liquids

Adults speaking about cups understand one another because they usually recognize the same distinguishing characteristic(s). If asked to get the cup on the shelf, they won't get a glass. A toddler using the word *cup* often means her personal drinking cup.

A toddler may overuse concepts in new situations. Perhaps a bandage on the tip of a brother's finger will be called a thimble. For a short time, all men are daddies, a cow may be called a big dog, and all people in white are feared. As mental maturity and life experiences increase, concepts change; small details and exceptions are noticed. Toddlers underextend words also by using a word to refer to a smaller category than would adults. An example of this phenomenon is the toddler's use of the word *dog* only in reference to the child's pet rather than all dogs encountered.

Concepts, often paired mentally with words, aid categorizing. Concept words may have full, partial, or little depth of meaning. The toddler's level of thought is reflected in speech. When counting to three, the toddler may or may not know what "three" represents. Words are **symbols**.

Pan and Gleason (1997) explain how young children acquire word meaning and also the symbolic nature of words.

---

concept — a commonly recognized element (or elements) that identifies groups or classes; usually has a given name.
symbols — things that stand for or suggest (such as pictures, models, word symbols, and so forth).

First, it is important to note that the meaning of a word resides in speakers of a common language, not in the world of objects. The word is a sign that signifies a *referent,* but the referent is not the meaning of the word.

Let us assume that a child learns that the word *kitty* refers to her cat; in this case, the actual cat is the referent of the word *kitty.*

There is nothing intrinsic to cats that makes one or another name more appropriate or fitting—the relationship between the name and the thing is thus arbitrary, and it is by social convention in a particular language that speakers agree to call the animal by a particular word. This arbitrary relationship between the referent (the cat) and the sign for it (the word cat) is *symbolic.*

In a few words the relationship between a word and a referent is not arbitrary; an example of this is the word *hiss.* In this case the word resembles the sound; other words, such as *ticktock, tinkle,* and *woof* also fall in this category.

A toddler's firsthand sensory experiences are very important. Stored mental perceptions are attached to words. Spitzer (1977) points out that words are only as rich as the experiences and depth of understanding behind them.

Our society puts tremendous emphasis on the acquisition of a large vocabulary in young children. But few realize that words without experiences are meaningless. . . . The more experiences and meaning that back up words, the more rewarding the communication process will become.

The activities and experiences found in subsequent chapters will help the early childhood teacher enrich the child's concepts by providing deeper meanings in a wide range of language arts. Every activity for young children—a total school program—gives them a language arts background full of opportunities to explore by handling, tasting, smelling, and touching, as well as by seeing and listening.

PRAGMATICS

The subtleties of our language are multifaceted. **Pragmatics** is the study of how language is used effectively in a social context, or the practical aspect of oral communication. It is the study of who can say what, in what way, where and when, by what means, and to whom (Figure 2–6). Language is a tool in questioning, ordering, soothing, ridiculing, and engaging in other social actions. One can request quiet in the form of a question such as, "Can't anyone get a peaceful moment around here?" or talk longingly about the candy in a store for the purpose of obtaining it—as in, "Oh, they have my favorite kind of chocolate bar!"—without making a direct request.

The language that young children use to express desires, wishes, concerns, and interests becomes a reflection of their social selves. When a toddler communicates effectively, the toddler

PRAGMATIC SKILLS

1. taking turns in a conversation with another
2. knowing you are supposed to answer when a question is asked
3. noticing nonverbal body cues, signals, gestures, and signs and then responding
4. introducing a topic in a conversation for the listener to understand
5. having the ability to stay on the subject of a conversation
6. maintaining the right amount of eye contact; not staring or turning away too frequently
7. using different communicative styles that suit different communicative partners
8. learning that in certain situations talking is inappropriate

FIGURE 2–6 Pragmatic skills.

---

pragmatics — the study of how language is used effectively in a social context; varying speech patterns depending on social circumstances and the context of situations.

receives feedback from others. Many times, a sense of well-being elicited by positive events helps the child shape a feeling of competency and self-esteem. Not yet socially subtle in speech, the toddler has not learned the pragmatically useful or appropriate behaviors of older children. Toddlers seem to have one intent: to get messages across by gaining adult attention regardless of who is present and in what situation. The world, from the toddler's perspective, revolves around the toddler and her need to communicate.

ATTACHMENT AND DEVELOPMENT OF LANGUAGE SKILLS

Attachment problems can slow communicative development. Observers describe infants and toddlers in less-than-adequate care situations as fearful, apathetic, disorganized, and distraught. If responsive social interaction and adult feedback exchanges are minimal, limited, frightening, or confusing, the infant or toddler may display a marked lack of interest in holding or obtaining adult attention. During toddlerhood these children can fall behind in speech development. Lally (1997) describes the importance of toddler social interaction:

> . . . infants and toddlers develop their sense of who they are from the adults who care for them. They learn from their caregivers what to fear, what behaviors are appropriate, and how their communications are received and acted upon. They learn how successful they are at getting their needs met by others, what emotions and intensity levels of emotions to safely display, and how interesting others find them.

FIRST WORDS

Any time between 10 and about 22 months is considered within the normal range for first words (Acredolo & Goodwyn, 2000). Lindfors (1985) describes first words as "building blocks" and "content words" (nouns, verbs) that carry a

lot of meaning. They usually consist of names of important people or objects the toddler encounters daily and include functional words such as *up, out, night-night,* and *bye-bye* used in social contexts (Figure 2–7). Pan and Gleason (1997) suggest that words that are easier for children to pronounce are more likely to be included in their early expressive vocabularies.

Single words can frequently go further than naming by representing a meaningful idea (a holophrase). The task of the adult includes both being responsive and guessing the child's complete thought. This may sound simple, but many times it is difficult and frustrating. Many

Sound effects
baa baa, meow, moo, ouch, uh-oh, woof, yum-yum

Food and drink
apple, banana, cookie, cheese, cracker, juice, milk, water

Animals
bear, bird, bunny, dog, cat, cow, duck, fish, kitty, horse, pig, puppy

Body parts and clothing
diaper, ear, eye, foot, hair, hand, hat, mouth, nose, toe, tooth, shoe

House and outdoors
blanket, chair, cup, door, flower, keys, outside, spoon, tree, TV

People
baby, daddy, gramma, grampa, mommy, [child's own name]

Toys and vehicles
ball, balloon, bike, boat, book, bubbles, plane, truck, toy

Actions
down, eat, go, sit, up

Games and routines
bath, bye, hi, night-night, no, peek-a-boo, please, shhh, thank you, yes

Adjectives and descriptives
allgone, cold, dirty, hot

FIGURE 2–7 Children's earliest words: examples from the vocabularies of children younger than 20 months. (From Berko Gleason, J. [1997]. *The development of language* [4th ed.]. Boston: Allyn and Bacon. © 1997 by Allyn and Bacon, Boston, MA. Copyright © 1997 by Pearson Education. Reprinted by permission of the publisher.)

factors influence the degree of adult responsiveness and talkativeness, particularly in child center settings—room arrangements, adult-child ratios, adult job satisfaction, and other emotional and environmental factors. The greatest inhibitor of adults' talking and responding to children seems to be adults' talking to one another. The nature of the work in a group care program can easily be described as emotion packed and demanding, in addition to rewarding and challenging. On the surface, the general public may not see or understand skilled verbal interactions taking place between toddlers and caregivers. What seems to be random, natural playfulness and verbal responsiveness is really very skilled and professionally intentional behavior. The same, of course, is true regarding parent behavior.

Adults sometimes question the practice of responding to toddlers' grunts and "uhs" instead of seeking words first. Many toddlers seem to understand everything said to them and around them but get by and satisfy most of their needs with nonword utterances. The points for adults to consider are that the child is performing and learning a difficult task and that speech will soon follow. The message that responsive adults relay to children when rewarding their early attempts is that children can be successful communicators and that further attempts at speech will get results.

FROM EGOCENTRIC SPEECH TO INNER SPEECH

During the toddler period, observers notice that words or short phrases spoken by adults are remembered and spoken out loud. The toddler's "hot," "no," "kitty," or similar words accompany the child's actions or a simple viewing of objects at hand. Vygotsky (1986) has called this "egocentric" speech, which is ultimately and usefully tied to the toddler's thinking.

As the child matures, this type of speech slowly becomes **inner speech**, part of the child's thinking process. Egocentric speech is regulatory, that is, useful in helping the child regulate (manage) her own behavior. As adults, we see examples of this regulatory function when we talk ourselves through particular perplexing situations. For example, "First the key goes in the lock, then turn the handle, and the bar moves to the left."

SYMBOLIC GESTURING

It is old-fashioned to believe that real communication does not exist before a child's first words (Figure 2–8). Researchers have helped us understand that gestures and signs (signals) occur in tandem with early vocalizing. Young toddlers can possess a rich repertoire of signals, and female infants tend to rely on or produce them with slightly greater frequency. Signs have been defined as nonverbal gestures symbolically representing objects, events, desires, and conditions that are used by toddlers to communicate with those around them. They literally can double a young toddler's vocabulary.

Grey (1996) points out that toddlers' interest in learning hand signals (signing) varies greatly. Conducting an infant-toddler program where signing is a regular part of the curricu-

FIGURE 2–8 Gestures often indicate a child's desire or need.

---

inner speech — mentioned in Vygotsky's theory as private speech that becomes internalized and is useful in organizing ideas.

lum, Grey found some toddlers used 25 baby signs for various objects, feelings, and needs while other toddlers mixed only a few gestures with beginning word usage. Grey believes both displayed normal development.

The use of words and symbols to influence other people in predictable ways requires the child to represent mentally the relationship between the symbol (word or gesture), the mean-ing for which it stands, and the intended effect on the other person (Harris, 1990). A symbol—a word, a picture, a dance—exists because of human intention to infuse some tangible form—a sound, a mark, a *movement*—with meaning and thereby to comment on or take action in the social world (Dyson, 1993).

Gesturing significantly increases children's power to obtain what they are after. It enriches

SIGNS	DESCRIPTION	AGE OF SIGN ACQUISITION (MONTHS)	AGE OF WORD ACQUISITION (MONTHS)
flower	sniff, sniff	12.5	20.0
big	arms raised	13.0	17.25
elephant	finger to nose, lifted	13.5	19.75
anteater	tongue in and out	14.0	24.0
bunny	torso up and down	14.0	19.75
Cookie Monster	palm to mouth plus smack	14.0	20.75
monkey	hands in armpits, up-down	14.25	19.75
skunk	wrinkled nose plus sniff	14.5	24.00
fish	blow through mouth	14.5	20.0
slide	hand waved downward	14.5	17.5
swing	torso back and forth	14.5	18.25
ball	both hands waved	14.5	15.75
alligator	palms together, open-shut	14.75	24.0
bee	finger plus thumb waved	14.75	20.00
butterfly	hands crossed, fingers waved	14.75	24.0
I dunno	shrugs shoulders, hands up	15.0	17.25
hot	waves hand at midline	15.0	19.0
hippo	head back, mouth wide	15.0	24.0
spider	index fingers rubbed	15.0	20.0
bird	arms out, hands flapping	15.0	18.5
turtle	hand around wrist, fist in-out	15.0	20.0
fire	waving of hand	15.0	23.0
night-night	head down on shoulder	15.0	20.0
X-mas tree	fists open-closed	16.0	26.0
mistletoe	kisses	16.0	27.0
scissors	two fingers open-closed	16.0	20.0
berry	"raspberry" motion	16.5	20.0
kiss	kiss (at a distance)	16.5	21.0
caterpillar	index finger wiggled	17.5	23.0

FIGURE 2–9 Symbolic signs, in order of acquisition, produced by case study subject. (From Acredolo, L. P., & Goodwyn, S. W. [1985]. Symbolic gesturing in language development. *Human Development, 28,* 53–58. Reproduced with permission from S. Karger A.G.)

their contacts and communicative competence. Adult recognition and attention to toddler signs enhance, rather than impede, language growth.

Acredolo and Goodwyn (1985) studied a child whose parents recognized that their child was interested in communicating and capable of learning nonverbal as well as verbal labels. The parents informally concocted signs on the spot for new events without any reference to a formal sign-language system. Figure 2–9 describes the signs and gives the age the signs appeared in the child's communicative behaviors and the age the child said the word represented by the sign. The list of signs includes the signs the child learned with and without direct parent teaching.

Gestures are integral companions of toddler verbalizations. Adults may have modeled the gestures in their adult-child interactions. Mothers' signals are "read" by toddlers, and a hand held palm up is usually read as "give it to me." Toddlers show their understanding by behaviors. Toddlers can and do invent new ones; consequently, signing is not simple, imitative behavior. Pointing is probably the most commonly used gesture of toddlers. Eventually, words are preferred, and gesturing remains as an accompaniment of speech. We have all slipped back into a gesturing mode as we search for words in conversation, and hand gestures are used automatically to convey the word(s) that we cannot quite express.

Early childhood educators employed by infant-toddler centers need to know their centers' position regarding expected language-developing behaviors. Most centers expect educators to pair words with adult hand signs, to encourage toddler use of signs, and to learn and respond to each child's individual sign language. To do this, teachers must be alert to children's cues, in particular noticing what in the environment attracts them so that words can be supplied and the children's intentions "read." Teachers' behaviors should reflect their awareness, intentional efforts, and attention to toddlers' efforts to communicate. Their continual goal is to establish a warm, emotionally fulfilling connection to each child in their care.

Toddlers are very interested in exploring. Teachers should "hang back" when toddlers interact with other toddlers and try not to interrupt play. Socialness with peers is given priority and promoted.

Teachers of toddlers do a lot of "word modeling." They attempt to be both calm and fun companions. Some will tell you that after a full day with toddlers they look forward to conversing with adults.

FIRST SENTENCES

The shift from one word to a two-word (or more) stage at approximately 18 months is a milestone. At that time, the toddler has a speaking vocabulary of about 50 words; by 36 months, upwards of 1,000 words. It is crucial in talking about vocabulary to acknowledge that children not only acquire new words as they get older but also expand their understanding of old words.

If one looks closely at two-word utterances, two classes of words become apparent. Braine (1973) termed the smaller group "pivot words." Examples of toddlers' two-word sentences, with pivot words underlined, are shown in Figure 2–10. They are used more often than

TWO-WORD SENTENCES	MEANINGS
<u>Dat</u>* car	nomination
Daddy <u>dare</u>	location
<u>See</u> kitty	identification
<u>More</u> cookie	repetition, recurrence
Milk <u>allgone</u>	nonexistence
<u>Sit</u> chair	action–location
<u>No</u> car, <u>no</u> want dat	negation
<u>Todd</u> shoe, <u>mine</u> toy	possession, possessor
<u>Big</u> cup	attribute description
Jin <u>walk</u>, truck <u>go</u>	agent–action
<u>Kiss</u> you, <u>fix</u> car	action–direct object
<u>Where</u> ball?	question

*Underlined words are pivots.

FIGURE 2–10 Pivot words in toddlers' two-word sentences.

nonpivots but seem to enter the vocabulary more slowly, perhaps because pivot words are stable and fixed in meaning. In analyzing two-word toddler comments, one finds they are both subject-predicate and topic-comment in nature. Frequently stressed syllables in words and word endings are what toddlers first master, filling in other syllables later. At times, toddlers use -um or -ah as place holders for syllables and words and replace these with correct syllables and words as they age.

Understanding grammar rules at this two-word stage is displayed even though many words are missing. Braine (1973) points out the frequency with which toddlers use a simple form and, almost in the same breath, clarify by expansion (by adding another word). The invention of words by toddlers is common. Meers (1976) describes an 18-month-old who had her own private word for "sleep," consistently calling it "ooma." Parents trying to understand their toddler get good at filling in the blanks. They then can confirm the child's statement and can add meaning at a time when the child's interest is focused.

TODDLER-ADULT CONVERSATIONS

Toddlers control attending or turning away in gamelike, playlike episodes, as do infants. At about one year, they understand many words and begin to display turn-taking in conversation, with "you talk, I answer" episodes. Weitzman (1992) believes **joint attention** starts by 10 months of age.

> By 10 months, an infant has developed intentional communication and willingly shares his emotions, his intentions, and his interest in the outside world. To do this, he has to establish joint attention. In other words, he has to be sure that both you and he are focused on the same thing, and he does this by:

> - getting your attention
> - letting you know what he's communicating about (establishing the topic of conversation)
> - keeping his attention on both you and the topic by looking back and forth

> His communication consists of one or more of the following: looking, pointing, showing, giving, making sounds, and changing his facial expression.

Toddlers learn that speech deserves attention and that speech is great for getting adult attention. They seem to revel in the joint-endeavor aspect of conversations.

Toddlers are skillful communicators. They converse and correct adult interpretations, gaining pleasure and satisfaction from language exchanges. The following incident shows more than toddler persistence.

> A first-time visitor to the home of a 20-month-old toddler is approached by the toddler. The visitor eventually rises out of his chair, accompanies the toddler to the kitchen, gets a glass of water, and hands it to the child. The toddler takes a tiny drink, and returns, satisfied, to the living room. Parents were not involved. Thirst, itself, was unimportant. The pleasure gained by the child seemed to motivate his actions.

For the child to accomplish her ends, the following actions occurred.

VISITOR BEHAVIOR

1. focuses attention on child
2. realizes a "talking" situation is occurring
3. listens and maintains a receiver attitude
4. corrects own behavior, guesses at child's meaning, and tries new actions
5. realizes conversation is over

---

joint attention — child's awareness that he or she must gain and hold another's focus during communicational exchanges to get his or her message understood.

CHILD BEHAVIOR

1. stands in front of visitor; searches face to catch eye; makes loud vocalization, dropping volume when eye contact made; observes visitor behavior

2. repeats first sound (parents understand, visitor does not) and observes visitor reaction

3. grabs visitor's hand, vocalizes loudly, and looks in visitor's eyes

4. tugs at hand, uses insistent voice tone, and gestures toward the kitchen

5. pulls visitor to sink and uses new word (visitor does not understand); corrects through gestures when visitor reaches for cookie jar

6. corrects visitor's guess (milk), gestures toward water, and holds out hand

7. drinks and hands back glass, smiles, and walks away

This type of behavior has been called instrumental expression because vocalization and nonverbal behaviors were used to obtain a certain goal.

The toddler seeks out people willing to listen and learns from each encounter. Adults modify and adapt their speech based on the abilities they observe in the child. This is done intuitively by use of shorter and less complex comments, and it changes when adults notice increased capacity (Figure 2–11).

Cawlfield (1992) describes a time in some toddlers' lives she calls "Velcro Time." During this period, the toddler's behavior is characterized by sticking close to a primary caregiver, watching adult lips intently, showing decreased interest in toys or playing independently, frequently bringing objects to the caregiver, and attempting to say words. The duration and appearance of these grouped behaviors is unique to each toddler, Cawlfield believes. Parents, she notes, often worry about spoiling the child with attention during this stage, but Cawlfield urges

FIGURE 2–11 Children seek out people willing to show interest in what they are doing.

parents to feed the child's desire to hear language, for soon the child emerges with a longer attention span and with new ideas and interests.

CHARACTERISTICS OF TODDLER LANGUAGE

The speech of young children speaking in two-word, or longer, sentences is termed **telegraphic** and **prosodic**. It is telegraphic because many words are omitted because of the child's limited ability to express and remember large segments of information; the most important parts of the sentence are usually present. *Prosodic* refers to the child's use of voice modulation and word stress with a particular word or words to give special emphasis and meaning. Donoghue (1985) describes telegraphic speech as follows:

> Their utterances are devoid of function words and resemble messages that adults would send by telegraph, for instance, "Jimmy truck" could represent "That truck belongs to Jimmy" or "Give me my truck."

---

telegraphic speech — a characteristic of young children's sentences in which everything but the crucial word(s) is omitted, as if for a telegram.
prosodic speech — the child's use of voice modulation and word stress to give special emphasis and meaning.

Meanings will often depend upon context and intonation of the utterance.

For additional toddler language characteristics that may appear before the child's third birthday, see Figure 2–12.

TODDLER LANGUAGE CHARACTERISTICS

- Uses two- to five-word sentences.
  "Baby down."
  "Baby boom boom."
  "No like."
  "No like kitty."
  "Me dink all gone."
  "See me dink all gone."

- Uses verbs.
  "Dolly cry."
  "Me going."
  "Wanna cookie."

- Uses prepositions.
  "In car."
  "Up me go."

- Adds plurals.
  "Birdies sing."
  "Gotta big doggies."
  "Bears in dat."

- Uses pronouns.
  "Me big boy."
  "He bad."

- Uses articles.
  "The ball gone."
  "Gimme a candy."

- Uses conjunctions.
  "Me and gamma."

- Uses negatives.
  "Don't wanna."
  "He no go."

- Runs words together.
  "Allgone," "gotta," "gimme," "lookee."

- Asks questions.
  "Wa dat?"
  "Why she sleep?"

- Does not use letter sounds or mispronounces spoken words.
  "Iceam," "choo" (for shoe), "member" (for remember), "canny" (for candy).

- Sings songs.

- Tells simple stories.

- Repeats words and phrases.

- Enjoys word and movement activities.

FIGURE 2–12 Toddler language characteristics.

NEGATIVES

No discussion of older toddlers' language would be complete without mentioning the use of "no." There seems to be an exasperating time when children say "no" to everything—seemingly testing whether there is a choice. Young children first use "no" to indicate nonexistence. Later it is used to indicate rejection and denial. Even when the child can speak in sentences longer than three words, the "no" often remains the first in a sequence of words. A typical example is "No want go bed." Soon, children insert negatives properly between the subject and the verb into longer utterances, as sentence length increases. Of all speech characteristics, toddlers' use of negatives and their avid energetic demands to be "listened to" stick in the memories of their caregivers.

AIDS TO TODDLER SPEECH DEVELOPMENT

The swift rate of new words entering toddlers' vocabularies indicates that educators caring for them should begin to become increasingly specific with descriptive terms in their speech. If a truck is blue, a comment like "The blue truck rolled in the mud" is appropriate. If an object is on the *bottom* shelf, in the *top* drawer, or *under* the table, those words can be stressed. A color, number, or special quality can be inserted in simple comments.

Playing detective to understand toddlers will always be part of adults' conversational style. Teachers may request that toddlers look directly at them when they communicate so that teachers can better hear each word and determine intent.

Holmes and Morrison (1979) offer adults advice for providing an optimal toddler environment for language stimulation.

- Expose the child to language with speech neither too simple nor too complex, but just slightly above the child's current level.

- Stay in tune with the child's actual abilities.

- Omit unreasonable speech demands, yet encourage attempts.

◆ Remember that positive reinforcement is a more effective tool than negative feedback.

◆ Accept the child's own formulation of a language concept.

◆ Channel progress by providing a correct model.

◆ Make a point of being responsive.

◆ Follow the child's interest by naming and simple discussion.

Other suggested pointers follow.

◆ Explain what you are doing as you work. Describe what is happening.

◆ Show excitement for the child's accomplishments (Figure 2–13).

◆ Talk about what the child is doing, wanting, or needing.

◆ Pause and listen with ears and eyes after you have spoken.

◆ Encourage toddler imitation of gestures and sounds.

◆ Imitate the child's sounds.

Language and self-help skills blossom when two-year-olds have opportunities to participate in "real" activities such as cutting bananas (us-ing plastic knife), sponging off the table, and helping sweep the floor (Poole, 1999).

The following adult behaviors are included in appropriate practices identified by the National Association for the Education of Young Children (NAEYC) (Bredekamp & Copple, 1997).

> Adults engage in many one-to-one, face-to-face conversations with toddlers. Adults let toddlers initiate language, and wait for a response, even from children whose language is limited. Adults label or name objects, describe events, and reflect feelings to help children learn new words. Adults simplify their language for toddlers who are just beginning to talk (instead of "It's time to wash our hands and have a snack," the adult says, "Let's wash hands. Snacktime!"). Then, as children acquire their own words, adults expand on the toddler's language.

Toddler-adult activities suggested by the *Parents As Teachers Program Planning and Implementation Guide* (1986) include:

◆ setting out two or three familiar objects and asking the child to get one.

◆ calling attention to interesting things you see, hear, smell, taste, or feel.

FIGURE 2–13 Educators are alert to recognizing and commenting on child accomplishments.

◆ showing and labeling your facial features and the child's in a mirror.

◆ labeling and pointing to objects around a room.

◆ verbally labeling items of clothing as the child is dressing and undressing.

◆ labeling the people in the toddler's world.

Toddler-adult language and movement play are recommended. One classic play activity follows. Others are in the Activities section.

TAKE YOUR LITTLE HANDS

Take your little hands and go clap, clap, clap
Take your little hands and go clap, clap, clap
Take your little hands and go clap, clap, clap
   Clap, clap, clap your hands.
Take your little foot and go tap, tap, tap
Take your little foot and go tap, tap, tap
Take your little foot and go tap, tap, tap
   Tap, tap, tap your foot.
Take your little eyes and go blink, blink, blink
Take your little eyes and go blink, blink, blink
Take your little eyes and go blink, blink, blink
   Blink, blink, blink your eyes.
Take your little mouth and go buzz, buzz, buzz
Take your little mouth and go buzz, buzz, buzz
Take your little mouth and go buzz, buzz, buzz
   Buzz like a bumblebee.
Take your little hand and wave bye, bye, bye
Take your little hand and wave bye, bye, bye
Take your little hand and wave bye, bye, bye
   Wave your hand bye-bye.

LANGUAGE THROUGH MUSIC

Toddlers are music lovers. If a bouncy melody catches their ear, they move. They obtain plenty of joy in swaying, clapping, or singing along. Many can sing short, repeated phrases in songs, and some toddlers will create their own repetitive melodies (Figure 2–14). Words in songs are learned when they are sung repeatedly. Adult correction is not necessary or appropriate. Playful singing and chanting by adults is a recommended language-development technique.

Hildebrandt (1998) urges educators to encourage young children's creativity with music. If teachers always focus on everyone singing the same words and/or doing the same actions, they may not be using music to promote creative expression. Fortunately, with the uninhibited and exuberant toddler this is not a problem; teachers are going to see some fantastic "moves" and hear some unique lyrics and takeoffs on songs and dances. The author enjoys remembering the time a two-year-old composed his own song— "Zipper your do da."

FIGURE 2–14 Toddler teachers sometimes sing nursery songs that include hand motions.

Honig (1995) cites the soothing aspect of many nursery songs and how teacher singing can aid the child's understanding of daily classroom routines. She believes teacher's songs give tots "aesthetic pleasure" as they listen to the lilting notes of richly onomatopoeic poetry found in both rhymes and simple songs.

The social component in musical games is also a language facilitator. Joining the fun with others gradually attracts even the youngest children (Figure 2–15).

A toddler's introduction to new songs, musical listening, and participation experiences adds another avenue for language growth.

Andress (1991) suggests a "tactile modeling" technique with music used along with other teacher techniques, such as verbally describing how a particular child is moving to music. ("Johnny is lifting his knees high up to his tummy.")

Tactile modeling . . . holds great promise as a technique to encourage two-year-old children's movement to music and should be used frequently when appropriate. The adult can extend the two index fingers for the child to grip (thus allowing the child to release at any time) and then begin to gently sway or otherwise guide movements to music.

Wolf (1994) suggests the following criteria for selecting sing-along songs, recorded music, and songbook selections.

1. shortness
2. repetitive phrases
3. reasonable range (C to G or A)
4. simple rhythms

She also urges the inclusion of folk music diversity.

More emphasis on adding music to toddlers' lives is evident because neuroscientists have suggested that musical experiences may increase intellectual abilities.

Suggested music resources are found in the Appendix.

FIGURE 2–15 Making music is a popular preschool activity.

SYMBOLIC PLAY

Somewhere around 12 to 15 months, toddlers who are developing well engage in symbolic (pretend) play. This important developmental leap allows the child to escape the immediate and firsthand happenings in her life and use symbols to represent past experiences and imagine future possibilities (Gowen, 1995). The acts of toddler pretend play observed by adults are widely diverse and depend in part on the child's life experiences. Greenspan (1999) describes a parent observing a young toddler's symbolic play.

> . . . he tenderly puts his teddy bear to be inside an empty shoe box, and the parent recognizes the child is starting to grasp that one thing can stand for, or symbolize, another. Because he can picture what a

bed looks and feels like in his mind, he is able to pretend that a hollow, rectangular box is really a symbol for a bed. When the parent comments that his teddy bear "is sleeping in his bed," he will eventually comprehend that the word "sleeping" stands for the bear's activity in the bed. As soon as he can articulate the sounds, the toddler will himself use the word symbol "sleeping" to describe an elaborate pattern of behaviors that he has observed.

One can always find toddlers who will talk into toy phones, spank dolls, grab the steering wheel of toy vehicles, and accompany motor movements with sounds, speech, and vrooms. Some reenact less common past experiences that are puzzling to their teachers. Gowen (1995) suggests the teacher techniques listed in Figure 2–16.

Comment on what the child is doing.
Examples:
Child pushes truck, saying, "Brummm."
Say, "I hear your truck coming."
Child puts baby bottle to doll's mouth.
Say, "You're feeding your baby. You're such a good mommy!"

Imitate the child's action.
Examples:
Child pushes truck, saying, "Brummm."
Push another vehicle and make motor sound.
Child pretends to drink from toy cup.
Pick up another cup and pretend to drink from it.

Reinforce the child's symbolic play.
Examples:
Child pretends to feed doll.
Say, "You're such a good mommy!"
Child pushes toy across floor.
Say, "Boy, you can really make that car go!"
Child puts toy dishes on table.
Say, "You've got the table all ready!"

Make indirect suggestions.
Examples:
Child is playing with toy beings.
Say, "I think your baby [this horse, this man] is hungry [is sleepy, needs a bath]."
Child fed milk to doll from toy baby bottle.
Say, "Your baby's had her dinner. I bet she's sleepy now."
Child pushes car, then stops it.
Say, "Is your car out of gas?"
Child puts plates on table.
Say, "I'm hungry. May I have a hamburger?"

Make direct suggestions.
Examples:
Pick up round, red paper scrap.
Say, "This can be our pizza, OK?"
Put rectangular block (size of a stick of butter) on the table.
Say, "Let's pretend this is our butter."

Model symbolic-play behaviors.
Examples:
Put undressed doll in box, rub square block on a piece of fabric, and pretend to bathe the doll.
Hop toy person to toy car, put it in, and say in a low voice, "I'm going shopping. See you later."

FIGURE 2–16 Techniques for promoting symbolic play through caregiver-child interaction. (From Gowen, J. [1995]. The early development of symbolic play. *Young Children, 50*[3], 75–84. Reprinted with permission from NAEYC.)

MAKING FRIENDS

Often, toddler play is side-by-side play. A toddler may watch what a neighboring peer is doing and may sometimes imitate the peer's actions. However, two toddlers playing in an organized, shared-goal play situation is infrequent. Toddlers are usually in-their-own-world-of-discovery people, but they do at times pick up play ideas from one another. Social graces may be absent, yet some beginning empathy for others may be apparent when one toddler communicates by patting or hugging a crying peer. Poole (1999) describes the difficulties toddlers face in building peer friendships.

> It's hard work for toddlers to learn how to play with one another. At first, some may examine their playmates as if they were inanimate objects, such as a doll or a ball, pinching and poking without understanding that their actions can hurt. Toddlers also don't always have control over their strong emotions.

> It takes time to learn not to hug too hard or to say "Hello" rather than swipe at a friend's face. Even when toddlers begin to sense that such behavior is frowned upon, they may continue testing the limits.

By 15 to 18 months of age, many toddlers participate in joint physical activities, enjoying others' company. By age 2, children often pair off with a peer and have favorite companions. Their emotions may erupt when sharing classroom playthings is necessary, causing friendships to change quickly. It is then, at age 2, that words can help children attract companions and repel others. Two-year-olds mimic increasingly and use words a friend uses.

LEARNING FROM MOTHERS

Burton White's projects have influenced many early childhood educators. His writings have highlighted the importance of the environment and mothering behaviors during what has been termed "a critical childhood growth stage"—toddlerhood. White (1987), while observing mothers from all economic levels and watching their children's progress, identified maternal skills that he believed accounted for the competence in the observed children. The competence, ingenuity, and energy of this group of mothers, he believed, was commendable. White believed that mothering can be a vastly underrated occupation.

The following describes some of White's identified mother behaviors.

> Mothers talk a great deal to their children, and usually at a level the child can handle. They make them feel as though whatever they are doing is usually interesting. They provide access to many objects and diverse situations. They lead the child to believe that he can expect help and encouragement most, but not all of the time. They demonstrate and explain things to the child, but mostly on the child's instigation rather than their own. They are imaginative, so that they make interesting associations and suggestions to the child when opportunities present themselves. They very skillfully and naturally strengthen the child's intrinsic motivation to learn.

More and more evidence has highlighted the importance of parent and caregiver attitudes and beliefs concerning toddlers' and young childrens' experiences with books and literacy activities. Baker, Scher, and Mackler (1997) point out that parents who believe reading is a source of enjoyment and entertainment have children with more positive views about books and the reading experience. Adults taking to heart this evidence will make "toddler book reading times" times of pleasure and enjoyment rather than times to pass on the information the book contains.

Honig (1999) provides additional advice related to book reading and brain development.

> The more you talk with toddlers, croon to and sing with them, read picture books together, and point out and name objects, the more firmly synaptic connections (brain connections) are reinforced and the less likely they are to disappear.

RECOGNIZING DIFFERENCES IN LANGUAGE GROWTH

Early childhood teachers are better able to identify accelerated, normal (average), and delayed speakers at about 18 months of age (White, 1987). What causes diversity is too complex to mention here, but some factors can be inferred, and others have been previously mentioned. Mothers' and caregivers' responses to children's verbalness toward the end of the children's first year and into the second year can be a determining factor.

> Sooner or later caregivers become aware of [the] child's emerging capacity of language acquisition. Some choose to feed the growth of language by going out of their way to talk a great deal to their children. Some provide language input effectively by careful selection of suitable words and phrases and by exploiting the child's interest of the moment. Others provide a great deal of input but with considerably less skill and effectiveness. Other[s] . . . show minimal attention to the language interest of children or for other reasons provide negligible amounts of language input. (White, 1987)

INTRODUCING TODDLERS TO BOOKS

Toddlers show an interest in simple, colorful books and pictures and enjoy adult closeness and attention. Pointing and naming can become an enjoyable game. Sturdy pages that are easily turned help the toddler. A scrapbook of favorite objects mounted on cardboard individualizes the experience. Clear contact paper and lamination will add life and protection.

Board books (usually stiff, coated, heavy cardboard) for toddlers allow exploratory play and may offer colorful, close-up photographs or illustrations of familiar, everyday objects. These books promote the child's naming of pictures and active participation at book-reading times.

They are both fiction and nonfiction, and the best are simple, direct, inviting, and realistic (Vardell, 1994). With durable, glossy, wipe-clean page coating and smaller-than-average picture-book size, small and sometimes sticky hands can explore but rarely tear covers or pages.

Because a toddler may move on quickly to investigating other aspects of the environment, adults offering initial experiences with books need to remember that when interest has waned, it is time to respect the search for other adventures (Figure 2–17).

Other technique hints from Kupetz and Green (1997) are as follows:

◆ Do not expect to quiet a rambunctious toddler with a book.

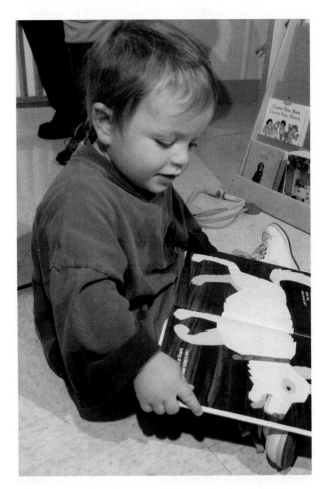

FIGURE 2–17 The "right" book can hold a toddler's attention.

◆ Pick a time when the child seems alert, curious, and interested.

◆ Establish a special reading time (although books can be read anytime).

◆ Use your voice as a tool to create interest.

◆ Be responsive.

◆ React positively to all of the child's attempts in naming objects, turning pages, or attempting any form of verbalization (Figure 2–18).

Toddlers with past experiences with picture books may have certain expectations for adult-child book sharing. They may want to cuddle with a blanket, sit in adult laps, turn pages for themselves, point to and question book features, name objects, watch the adult's mouth during reading, and so on. Exhibiting flexibility and following the child's lead reinforces the child's social enjoyment of the book.

Kupetz and Green (1997) caution that caregivers who require a group of toddlers to sit and listen to a story together are asking for

FIGURE 2–18 Toddlers often name the objects they see in picture-book illustrations.

trouble. The key words are *group* and *require*. Toddler group times are of short duration and planned for active child participation. As toddlers age, they maintain focus for longer periods. Educators of toddlers may share a picture book with a few children. When they do so, they endeavor to keep the experience warm, comfortable, and intimate.

What can toddlers begin to understand during the reading of picture books? Besides knowing that photographs and illustrations are between the covers of books, the toddler gathers ideas about book pleasure. As the child touches pictured objects, the child may grasp the idea that the objects depicted are representations of familiar objects. The toddler can notice that books are not handled as toys.

Holdaway (1979) describes the very young child's reading-like behaviors.

> By far the most surprising and significant aspect of preschool book-experience, however, is the independent activity of these very young children with their favorite books. Almost as soon as the infant becomes familiarized with particular books through repetitive readings, he begins to play with them in reading-like ways. Attracted by the familiar object with which he has such positive associations, the infant picks it up, opens it, and begins attempting to retrieve for himself some of the language and its intonations. Almost unintelligible at first, this reading-like play rapidly becomes picture stimulated, page-matched, and story complete.

Near two years of age, the toddler probably still names what is pictured but may understand stories. The toddler may grasp the idea that book characters and events are make-believe. If a particular book is reread to a child, the child can know that the particular stories in books do not change, and what is to be read is predictable. Sometimes the toddler finds that she can participate in the telling by singing, repeating character lines, and making physical motions to represent actions; for example, "knocking on the door" and saying "moo."

Selecting Toddler Books

It is suggested that books for the toddler age be

- repetitive and predictable.
- rhythmical.
- illustrated with simple, familiar, easy-to-identify colorful objects, animals, toys, and so on.
- filled with feel, touch, and smell opportunities.
- sturdy, with easy-to-turn pages.
- set with few words on each page.
- relatively short, with simple, concise story lines about common, everyday life and environmental experiences.
- formatted with illustrations matched to the text on each page.

Additional desirable features of toddler-appropriate books often include simple, uncomplicated storylines; colorful, uncrowded illustrations or photographs; opportunities for the toddler to point and name familiar objects; sensory features; predictive books (ones allowing the child to guess or predict successfully); and strong, short rhymes or repetitive rhythms. "Touch and feel" books are particularly enjoyed, and sturdy, heavy board pages that can be mouthed but not torn are practical. Novelty books that make noise or pop-up books and books with sturdy moving parts capture a toddler's attention. Weiser (1982) lists "reading-related objects" that can be provided for the exploring toddler.

- catalogs and magazines to look at, touch, finger, mouth, and otherwise investigate
- cloth books
- first books, homemade or center-made on cardboard pages, protected by transparent stick-on coverings
- photographs or books containing photographs of people and objects in the toddler's life (including photos of the toddler)
- homemade sensory books that call for touching or smelling and that use safe materials

Now is the time to also share the strong rhyming rhythms of Mother Goose and introduce two classics: "Mary Had a Little Lamb" and "Pop Goes the Weasel." Recommended toddler books are found in the Additional Resources section at the end of this chapter.

NAEYC (Bredekamp & Copple, 1997) suggests that "adults frequently read to toddlers, individually on laps or in groups of two or three. Adults sing with toddlers, do finger plays, act out simple stories like 'The Three Bears' with children participating actively, or tell stories using a flannelboard or magnetic board, and allow children to manipulate and place figures on the boards."

Electronic Books

Books with electronic features provide another way to engage toddlers with stories and print. Each book differs, but many have colorful illustrations that move, flash, "talk," or make musical sounds and noises. Pressing an area, button, icon, or symbol activates prerecorded features.

Most educators and parents agree that electronic books do attract toddlers but that interest wanes quickly unless the book is shared with a responsive adult.

Scribbling

In most home environments, toddlers see others writing and want to try it themselves. Large, chunky crayons and nontoxic markers are easily manipulated by toddlers around 18 months of age. They usually grasp them in their fist and use a scrubbing motion. They have some difficulty placing marks where they might wish, so it is best to use very large sheets of sturdy paper taped to a tabletop. Brown bags cut flat or untreated shelf paper work well. Crosser (1998) believes that the act of scribbling can serve several useful purposes, including enhancing small muscle coordination, exercising cognitive abilities, promoting social interaction, and allowing emotional release. It can also be seen as a precursor to an interest in symbols and print. Crosser observes that an important point in development is reached when the child converts linear scribbles to enclosed shapes and at a later age begins realistic, representational drawing. Because parents in some cultures (Taiwanese and Chinese American) place more emphasis on opportunities for their children to draw, their children's drawings have been deemed more advanced (Berk, 1994).

BEGINNING LITERACY

During toddlerhood, some children gain general knowledge of books and awareness of print. This is viewed as a natural process, which takes place in a literate home or early learning environment. Toddlers learn through imitation, by reacting and constructing their own ideas, and by internalizing social action as an apprentice to others (loved ones, early childhood educators, and so on). Immersing toddlers in language activities facilitates their literacy development. It is possible to establish a positive early bonding between children and book-sharing times—a first step toward literacy. Some toddlers who show no interest in books will, when exposed to books at a later time, find them as interesting as other children. Parents need to understand that a literary interest can be piqued throughout early childhood. The fact that a toddler may not be particularly enamored with books or book-sharing times at a particular stage is not a matter of concern. It may simply be a matter of the child's natural, individual activity level and her ability to sit and stay focused in an environment that holds an abundance of features to explore.

Musical Activities

Skill-promoting musical play with toddlers can include:

- listening experiences.
- activities focusing on or highlighting discrimination of loud and soft and fast and slow, rhythms, repeated patterns, tones, words, and so on.
- steady beats, catchy melodies or words, clapping, tapping, rocking, galloping, marching, motions, and body actions.
- coordination of movement and music in some way.
- creative and imaginative opportunities.
- experiences with a variety of simple, safe musical instruments.
- the singing of age-appropriate songs.

Singhal (1999) believes that music activities can create an affectionate adult-child bond. She describes toddlers participating in adult and child music activities.

> Toddlers are beings in motion, and music is the perfect vehicle for directing and freeing their movements. They feel and internalize the steady beat of adult motions. Contrary to popular belief, toddlers can also be excellent listeners. They are fascinated by sound, whether it's a bee buzzing or a clarinet melody. The different shapes, feel and sounds of simple rhythm instruments also mesmerize toddlers. Being able to make a steady sound by himself on an instrument such as the drum is very empowering to a young child who wants to "do it myself!"
>
> Even though at this age children may not be willing to echo back chanted tonal and rhythm patterns, it is still important that they hear them. The patterns are being "recorded" in their minds for future reference.
>
> Singing, listening, and music-making are a completely natural and enjoyable part of a tiny child's being.

TOYS

Certain types of toys have a strong connection to toddlers' emerging language development (Figure 2–19). Musical toys, dolls and stuffed animals that make noises or talk, and alphabet toys, including magnetic alphabet letters, can

FIGURE 2–19 Certain types of play objects may encourage child speech.

be described as language-promoting toys. Noise-making toys or recordings, both audio and visual, capture the toddler's attention. Videos for toddlers are becoming increasingly available. Songs and music are also enjoyed by toddlers and offer another language-inputting opportunity; however, some educators are concerned about the quantity, quality, and subject matter of audiovisuals that possibly may be replacing adult-child language interaction.

Greenspan (1999) emphasizes how toddler problem solving develops and describes its relationship to "freedom to explore" (within supervised limits).

> An ability to solve problems rests on the even more basic skill of seeing and deciphering patterns. It is the ability to understand patterns that lets a toddler know if she takes two steps here and two steps there that she'll be able to reach her favorite toy. She becomes a successful navigator not only because her muscles are coordinated, but also because her growing brain now en-

ables her to understand patterns. Toddlers learn to recognize how one room leads to another, and where you are in relation to them. They can meaningfully explore the world long before they are able to express their wishes and thoughts in words.

The Comical Toddler

Acredolo and Goodwyn (2000), citing their own observations and the work of Paul McGhee (1979), believe adults often do not realize children begin honing their own comedic skills at impressively early ages. They point out that a child's reaction to physical stimuli, seen in activities such as tickling and bouncing, takes a new form sometime after the first birthday by becoming visual or oral rather than tactual. Toddler silliness or "joking" behavior can be seen as rudimentary attempts at humor and can be appreciated as child-initiated attempts to get others' reactions to the ridiculous, the unexpected, or their play on words.

ADVICE TO PARENTS OF TODDLERS

Verbally responsive and playful people, and a "toddler-proof" home equipped with objects and toys the toddler can investigate, are positive factors in increasing emerging toddler language. An adult sitting on the floor or on a low chair near a toddler at play can promote toddler communication and also help the adult see things from the child's vantage point.

Objects and toys need not be expensive and can be designed and created at home. Social contact outside the home is important also. Toddlers enjoy branching out from the home on excursions with caring adults. Local libraries may offer toddler story hours, and play groups are increasingly popular and sponsored by a wide number of community groups. Exposing the toddler to supervised toddler play groups gives the child "peer teachers" and promotes social skill. Typically, toddlers play side-by-side rather than cooperatively, but beginning attempts at sharing and short give-and-take interactions take place.

Some toddlers may frequently ask for the names of things and can be insistent and impatient about demands. Words will be learned during real events with concrete (real) objects. Children continue to generate language when their early efforts are accepted and reinforced (Morrow, Burks, & Rand, 1992). Situations that involve positive emotions and those that involve multiple sensory experiences also evoke child language production.

Regularly involving toddlers in educative conversations with educational toys and simple books prompts language growth. Patience and interest—rather than heavy-handed attempts to teach—are best. Getting the most from everyday experiences is a real art that requires an instructive yet relaxed attitude and the ability to talk about what has captured the child's attention. A skilled adult who is with a toddler who is focused on the wrapping paper rather than the birthday present will add comments about the wrapping paper. Or at the zoo, in front of the bear's cage, if the child is staring at a nearby puddle, the adult will discuss the puddle. Providing words and ideas along the child's line of thinking, and having fun while doing so, becomes second nature after a few attempts.

Skilled adults tend to modify their speech according to the child's ability. They speak clearly, slowly enunciate and slightly exaggerate intonation, and pause between utterances. They may end their sentences with the "focused-upon" new word and emphasize it in pitch and stress. They also add to sentence length and complexity, providing that which is just a little beyond the child's level. Parent talk that sensitively and effectively suggests and instructs primes the child's language growth.

Two parent and teacher resource books that contain a number of adult-child interactive games follow.

Silberg, J. (1993). *Games to play with two year olds*. Bettsville, MD: Gryphon House.
Silberg, J. (1996). *More games to play with toddlers*. Bettsville, MD: Gryphon House.

Parents may need to become aware of the consequences that can result from home or center environments where toddlers experience chaos, unpredictability, violence, and frightening experience as a daily reality. Honig (1999) describes these toddlers as quick to be startled, aroused, angry, defiant, fearful, or withdrawn. She describes the chemical activity in their brains as abnormal. Building intimate, warm, trusting relationships is the best way to teach a child's brain that it need not send the body messages to pour high levels of stress into their systems. She recommends that nurturing providers can and must offer each child interpretable, orderly, soothing, and loving experiences daily to support optimal brain development.

SUMMARY

Language ability grows at its fastest rate of development during the toddler period. Young children accomplish difficult language tasks. They learn their native language sounds (phonetics) and successfully produce an increasing number of sounds. Grammar rules form and reform as the child gets closer to reproducing mature speech patterns. The child listens more carefully, noticing regularities and meanings (semantics) of words and gestures.

Concepts develop, serving as categories that help the child organize life's events. Many concepts are paired with words. Word symbols aid communication and language by allowing the child to speak and to be understood. Parents' conversations and the child's firsthand exploration through sense organs give depth to new words.

Toddlers are active in conversations, speaking and listening, sometimes correcting, trying to get the message across to whoever in the family will listen. Toddlers talk to themselves and their toys in one-word and then two-word (or more) sentences. These sentences are barely recognizable at first but gain more and more clarity as children age.

Differences between children's speech output may be noticed, and responsive, sensitive adults are language-promoting companions. Toddler books are enjoyed and plentiful.

ADDITIONAL RESOURCES

Readings

Acredolo, L. P., & Goodwin, S. W. (1986). Symbolic gesturing in language development. *Human Development, 28*, 53–58.

Acredolo, L. P., & Goodwin, S. W. (2000). *Baby mind: Brain-building games your baby will love to play.* New York: Bantam Books.

Baker, L., Scher, D., & Mackler, K. (1997). Home and family influences on motivations for reading. *Educational Psychologist, 32*(2), 69–82.

Bredekamp, S., & Copple, C. (1997). *Developmentally appropriate practice in early childhood programs* (rev. ed.). Washington, DC: National Association for the Education of Young Children.

Fischer, B., & Medvic, E. (2003). *For reading out loud: Planning and practice.* Portsmouth, NH: Heinemann.

Jusozyk, P. (1997). *The discovery of spoken language.* Cambridge, MA: MIT Press.

Nichols, J. (1998). *Storytimes for two-year-olds.* Chicago: American Library Association.

Owens, R. (2001). *Language development.* Boston: Allyn and Bacon.

The National Research Council. (1999). *Starting out right: A guide to promoting children's reading success.* Washington, DC: National Academy Press.

U.S. Department of Education. (1995). *Helping your baby learn to talk.* Washington, DC: U.S. Government Printing Office.

Toddler Books

Ahlberg, J., & Ahlberg, A. (1983). *The baby's catalogue.* Boston: Little, Brown. (Features objects in a toddler's environment.)

Barton, B. (1986). *Trucks.* New York: Crowell. (Vivid color and objects that move.)

Blegvad, L. (1986). *This is me.* New York: Random. (Board book.)

Blonder, E. (1988). *My very first things.* New York: Gossett. (Board book.)

Brown, M. (1985). *Hand rhymes.* New York: E. P. Dutton.

Chorao, K. (1984). *The baby's story book.* New York: E. P. Dutton.

Cousins, L. (1991). *Farm animals.* New York: Tambourine.

Cowley, J. (1999). *Mrs. Wishy-Washy.* East Rutherford, NJ: Philomel Books. (Board book.)

Davenport, Z. (1995). *Mealtime.* New York: Ticknor & Fields. (Large colorful food and food-related illustrations.)

Davenport, Z. (1995). *Toys.* New York: Ticknor & Fields. (Common toys and objects for identification.)

Dyer, J. (1996). *Animal crackers.* New York: Little, Brown. (A delectable collection of pictures, poems, and lullabies for the very young.)

Hoban, T. (1985). *One, two, three.* New York: Greenwillow.

Hoban, T. (1985). *What is it?* New York: Greenwillow.

Kunhardt, D. (1942). *Pat the bunny.* New York: Golden Touch and Feel Books.

Lynn, S. (1987). *Farm animals.* New York: Macmillan.

McCue, L. (1987). *Ten little puppy dogs.* New York: Random. (Board book.)

Oxenbury, H. (1988). *Tickle, tickle.* New York: Macmillan.

Pearson, S. (1987). *The baby and the bear.* New York: Viking.

Prelutsky, J. (Ed.) (1988). *Read-aloud rhymes for the very young.* New York: Alfred Knopf Publishers.

Price, M., & Claverie, J. (1987). *Easy objects.* New York: Tuffy Books Inc.

Price, M., & Claverie, J. (1987). *Show and tell me.* New York: Tuffy Books Inc.

Price, M., & Claverie, J. (1987). *Simple objects.* New York: Tuffy Books Inc.

Price, M., & Claverie, J. (1988). *Happy birthday*. New York: Alfred Knopf Publishers.

Tafuri, N. (1987). *Where we sleep*. New York: Greenwillow.

Wellington, M. (1999). *Bunny's rainbow day*. New York: E. P. Dutton. (Told in rhythmic prose.)

Williams, S. (1989). *I went walking*. New York: Harcourt Brace Jovanovich. (Board book.)

Song Books

Schiller, P., & Moore, T. (1993). *Where is thumbkin?* Beltsville, MD: Gryphon House.

Silberg, J. (1998). *The I can't sing book*. Beltsville, MD: Gryphon House.

HELPFUL WEB SITES

ECRP—Early Childhood Research & Practice
http://ecrp.uiuc.edu
A research article on toddler development can be reviewed.

IbcTech
http://www.thebestkidsbooksite.com
Recommended books on many topics are identified.

Kid Source Online
http://www.kidsource.com
A speech development outline is available.

National Parent Information Network
http://npin.org
To obtain information about stages of toddler language production, select *Library*.

Visit the Online Companion to read about professional toddler teacher behaviors used to develop toddler's language and to learn more about syntax. You will also find out how to tell if toddlers are forming unconscious mental rules concerning language. In addition, you can also join a discussion forum focusing on toddler computer use and exposure to interactive story books; the forum includes an informative question and answer section. Also available are the criteria used for selecting toddler books.

STUDENT ACTIVITIES

1. Make a book for toddlers from magazine illustrations or from photographs of common objects familiar to toddlers. Pages should be sturdy. Cut away any distracting backgrounds. If desired, outline objects with a wide-tip felt pen and protect pages with clear adhesive plastic or slip into page protectors. (An old binder works well to hold the pages.) Test your book on toddlers, and share your results.

2. Using only gestures, get the person sitting next to you to give you a tissue or handkerchief or to tell you that one is not available.

3. Observe three toddlers (15 to 24 months old). Write down consonant sounds you hear. Record the number of minutes for each observation.

4. Using the following scale, rate each of the following statements.

1	2	3	4	5
Strongly Agree	Agree	Can't Decide	Mildly Disagree	Strongly Disagree

   a. Toddlers can be best understood when adults analyze their words instead of their meanings.

   b. Some parents seem to have a knack for talking to young children and probably do not realize they possess this skill.

   c. The labeling stage is a time when children learn concepts rather than words.

   d. Learning language is really simple imitation.

   e. The study of semantics could take a lifetime.

   f. A toddler who does not like books is not progressing properly.

   g. After reading this chapter, I will not react to toddler grunts.

   h. Parents whose toddlers are speaking many words have purposely taught words to their children.

   i. It is a good idea to have a special place in the home where books are enjoyed with a toddler.

   j. It is best to give the toddler specific words for things, such as *pick-ups* instead of *trucks*, or *bonnet* instead of *hat*.

   Talk about your ratings in a group discussion.

5. You notice your sister is ignoring her toddler's sign language attempts. What would you say or do? Be specific.

CHAPTER REVIEW

A. Match each word in Column I with the phrase it relates to in Column II.

COLUMN I	COLUMN II
1. phonology	a. "Allgone cookie."
2. grammar	"Shoe allgone."
3. dis? dat?	b. toddler goes through a naming or labeling stage
4. pivot	c. toddler unconsciously recognizes word order
5. alphabet	d. although they are limited in number, many serve
6. symbol	a double purpose *the sound system of lang*
7. toddler brain	e. each world language has its own
	f. as active as an adult
	g. a word represents something

B. Write a brief description of experiences that could promote a toddler's learning the word *hat*. (Example: Parent points to a picture of a hat in a book and says, "hat.")

C. List five identifying characteristics of the following concepts:
van, rain, needle, giraffe

D. Return to question B. How many of your examples involved the child's sensory exploration of a hat? Why would this aid the child's learning?

E. Why is the toddler period called the prime or critical time for learning language?

F. Select the best answer.

1. Most children clearly articulate all English letter sounds by age
   a. seven or eight.
   b. six.
   c. five.
   d. twenty-four months.

2. Most concept words used correctly by toddlers are
   a. labels and imitative echoing.
   b. fully understood.
   c. used because identifying characteristics have been noticed.
   d. rarely overused.

3. From beginning attempts, children
   a. reverse word order.
   b. use full simple sentences.
   c. use stress, intonation, and inflection in speaking.
   d. are always clearly understood.

4. One should _____ insist that the toddler pronounce "tree" correctly if he or she is saying "twee."
   a. always
   b. usually
   c. never
   d. tactfully

5. A toddler's one-word sentence, "Wawa," may mean
   a. "I want a drink of water."
   b. the child's dog, Waiter, is present.
   c. the child's father's name is Walter.
   d. any one or none of the above.

6. A child's first word is usually spoken between _____, and this is considered within the normal range.
   a. 10 and 22 months
   b. 9 and 20 months
   c. 11 and 25 months
   d. 8 and 18 months

TODDLER FAVORITES

TURTLE

There once was a turtle
who lived in a box
He swam in the puddle
and climbed on the rock

He snapped at a mosquito
He snapped at a flea
He snapped at a minnow
and he snapped at me

He caught the mosquito
He caught the flea
He caught the minnow
But he didn't catch me!

Author Unknown

TEDDY BEAR, TEDDY BEAR

Teddy Bear, Teddy Bear, turn all around,
Teddy Bear, Teddy Bear, touch the
    ground:

Teddy Bear, Teddy Bear, read the news,
Teddy Bear, Teddy Bear, shine your shoes:

Teddy Bear, Teddy Bear, go upstairs,
Teddy Bear, Teddy Bear, say your
    prayers:

Teddy Bear, Teddy Bear, turn out the
    lights,
Teddy Bear, Teddy Bear, say
    GOODNIGHT!

Author Unknown

THE LITTLE WHITE DUCK (SONG)

There's a little white duck sitting in the
    water,
A little white duck doing what he oughter;
He took a bite of a lily pad,
Flapped his wings and he said,
"I'm glad I'm a little white duck
    sitting in the water,"
quack, quack, quack.

There's a little green frog swimming in
    the water,
A little green frog doing what he
    oughter;
He jumped right off the lily pad,
that the little duck bit and he said
"I'm glad I'm a little green frog
    swimming in the water,"
glumph, glumph, glumph.

There's a little black bug floating on
    the water,
A little black bug doing what he oughter,
He tickled the frog on the lily pad
That the litle duck bit and he said,
"I'm glad I'm a little black bug
    floating on the water,"
chirp, chirp, chirp.

There's a little red snake lying in the
    water,
A little red snake doing what he
    oughter,
He frightened the duck and the frog so
    bad
He ate the little bug and he said,
"I'm glad I'm a little red snake lying
    in the water,"
sss, sss, sss.

Now there's nobody left sitting in the
    water,
Nobody left doing what he oughter,
There's nothing left but the lily pad,
The duck and the frog ran away. It's
    sad. . . .
That there's nobody left sitting in the
    water,
boo, hoo, hoo.

Author Unknown

Chapter 3
Preschool Years

OBJECTIVES

After reading this chapter, you should be able to:

◆ Identify characteristics of typical preschool speech.

◆ Describe differences in the language of younger and older preschoolers.

◆ Discuss the preschooler's growth of language skill.

KEY TERMS

consonant

expressive (productive) vocabulary

metalinguistic awareness

overextension

receptive (comprehension) vocabulary

regularization

vowel

ON AND ON AND ON. . .

Wilford is four and eager to speak in groups. He rambles, goes on and on, and both bores and loses his audience. Renee, his teacher, waits, patiently listening, but occasionally interrupts him to say, "Thank you, Wilford, for sharing with us." Sometimes this stops him, but often it does not.

QUESTIONS TO PONDER

1. Is this "stream of consciousness" talking typical of four-year-olds? Some adults?

2. What teacher strategies might help Renee?

3. What program activities might help Wilford?

The preschool child's speech reflects sensory, physical, and social experiences, as well as thinking ability. Parents and teachers accept temporary limitations, knowing that almost all children will reach adult language levels.

During the preschool years, children move rapidly through successive phases of language learning. It is generally agreed that by the time youngsters reach their fifth year, the most challenging hurdles of language learning have been overcome.

Teachers should interact with the children and provide growing opportunities and activities. An understanding of typical preschool speech characteristics can help the teacher do this.

Background experiences with children and child study give a teacher insight into children's language behavior. The beginnings of language, early steps, and factors affecting the infant's and toddler's self-expression were covered in Chapters 1 and 2. This chapter pinpoints language use during preschool years. Although speech abilities are emphasized, growth and change in other areas, as they relate to speech, are also covered.

In addition to the child's home environment, playing with other children is a major factor influencing language development. Finding friends in the child's age group is an important part of attending an early childhood center. In a place where there are fascinating things to explore and talk about, language abilities blossom (Figure 3–1).

It is almost impossible to find a child who has all of the speech characteristics of a given age group, but most children possess some of the characteristics that are typical for their age level. There is a wide range within normal age-level behavior, and each child's individuality is an important consideration.

For simplicity's sake, the preschool period is divided into two age groups: early preschoolers (two- and three-year-olds) and older preschoolers (four- and five-year-olds).

YOUNG PRESCHOOLERS

Preschoolers communicate needs, desires, and feelings through speech and action. Close observation of a child's nonverbal communication can help uncover true meanings. Raising an arm, fiercely clutching playthings, or lying spread-eagle over as many blocks as possible may express more than the child is able to put into words. Stroking a friend's arm, handing a toy to another child who has not asked for it but looks at it longingly, and following the teacher around the room carry other meanings.

One can expect continued fast growth and changing language abilities, and children's understanding of adult statements is surprising. They may acquire 6 to 10 new words a day. Figure 3–2 displays children's stunning word growth from ages one through seven.

Squeals, grunts, and screams are often part of play. Imitating animals, sirens, and environmental noise is common. The child points and pulls to help others understand meanings. Younger preschoolers tend to act as though others can read their thoughts because, in the past,

FIGURE 3–1 Children often share their ideas concerning how or what they might play.

VOCABULARY GROWTH

10–14 months	first word	First words are usually nouns instead of verbs.
12–18 months	two words a week; close to 50 by 18 months	Child looks at something (or someone), points, and then says one or two words. Mispronunciations are common.
18–24 months	200 words	Some toddlers constantly ask "What dat?" or just "Dat?" They want objects named.
2–3 years	500 words	Questions, questions, questions! Mispronunciations still happen, and consonants may be substituted for one another in some words.
3–4 years	800 words	Preschoolers start to use contractions ("won't," "can't") as well as prepositions ("in," "on") and time expressions ("morning," "afternoon"). They may also make up words.
4–5 years	1,500 or more words	Children speak with greater clarity, can construct five- and six-word sentences, and make up stories.
5–7 years	11,000 words	Children retell and discuss stories. They have many words at hand and will know more than 50,000 as adults.

FIGURE 3–2 Vocabulary growth.

adults anticipated what was needed. A few children may have what seems to be a limited vocabulary at school until they feel at home there.

A difference between the child's **receptive** (or **comprehension**) **vocabulary** and his **expressive** (or **productive**) **vocabulary** is apparent, with the productive vocabulary lagging behind the receptive vocabulary. The receptive vocabulary requires that a child hear a word and anticipate or react appropriately; the production of a word means the child speaks the word at an appropriate time and place.

Tabors (1997) notes

> Children also begin to acquire the more complicated forms of grammar during this time period; in English these are past tenses, embedded clauses, and passive constructions. This process frequently results in creative mistakes, like "my mom breakeded the plate," which show that children are noticing consistent patterns and applying them to the language system as they understand it.

The words used most often are nouns and short possessives: my, mine, Rick's. Speech focuses on present events, things are observed in newscaster style, and "no" is used liberally. As preschoolers progress in the ability to hold brief conversations, they must keep conversational topics in mind and connect their thoughts with those of others. This is difficult for two-year-olds, and true conversational exchange with playmates is brief, if it exists at all. Although their speech is filled with pauses and repetitions in which they attempt to correct themselves, preschoolers are adept at conversational turn taking. Garvey (1984) estimates that talking over the speech of another speaker at this age occurs only about 5 percent of the time.

Speech may be loud and high pitched when the child is excited (Figure 3–3), or it may be barely audible and muffled when the child is embarrassed, sad, or shy. Speech of two- and three-year-olds tends to be uneven in rhythm, with comments issued in spurts rather than in an even flow like the speech of older children.

receptive (comprehension) vocabulary — the comprehension vocabulary used by a person in listening (and silent reading).
expressive (productive) vocabulary — the vocabulary a person uses in speaking and writing.

FIGURE 3–3 Children's outside play is often boisterous.

There seems to be an important step forward in the complexity of content in children's speech at age two. They may begin making comments about cause and effect and sometimes use conjunctions, such as 'cause, 'ah, and 'um, between statements. Pines (1983) describes conversational topics identified in a New York research project that monitored two-year-olds' speech.

> The children talked mostly about their own intentions and feeling, why they wanted or did not want to do certain things, or what they wanted other people to do.

Curry and Johnson (1990) point out

> Two-year-olds . . . go through a stage of commenting on their own actions. "I'm painting." "I'm climbing on the steps!"

Much of the time very young preschoolers' play focuses on recreating the work of the home—cooking, eating, sleeping, washing, ironing, infant care, and imitations of family events and pets (Figure 3–4). Play of slightly older preschoolers is more interactive. The child continues self-play but also explores other children, adults, environments, and actions. Eventually, most preschoolers understand that it is usually worth their while to share toys and take turns because when other playmates are around it is more fun. Two-year-olds may believe, as one preschooler remarked to his teacher, that "share means you give it away." When children begin exploring these other play options, "what's happening" in play becomes a speech subject, along with brief verbal reactions to what others are saying and doing.

A desire to organize and make sense of their experiences is often apparent. Colors, counting, and new categories of thought emerge in their speech. There is a tendency for them to live out the action words they speak or hear in the speech of others. An adult who says "We won't run" may

FIGURE 3–4 Teachers encourage the verbalizations of young preschoolers.

motivate a child to run; in contrast, an adult who says "Walk" might be more successful in having the child walk. This is why experienced teachers tell children what they want children to do rather than what they do not want them to do.

The Subdued Two-Year-Old

In any given group of young children, a few may appear subdued and quiet, having a tendency toward what many might call shyness. These children may possess a natural inclination that tends to inhibit spontaneous speech. Strong emotions can cause muscle tension, including tension in the larynx. Some adults asked to speak in front of a group experience this phenomenon. It can also affect speech volume. Most preschool teachers have worked with children whose speech was difficult to hear. Often, these children seem restrained when faced with unfamiliar situations. Older preschoolers may become more outgoing and talkative or may continue to be less talkative and somewhat subdued when compared with their more boisterous counterparts. Teachers respect these children's natural inclinations and tendencies.

Verb Forms

In English, most verbs (regular forms) use -ed to indicate past tense. Unfortunately, many frequently used verbs have irregular past-tense forms, such as came, fell, hit, saw, took, and gave. Because the child begins using often-heard words, early speech contains correct verb forms. With additional exposure to language, children realize that past events are described with -ed verb endings. At that point, children tack the -ed on regular verbs as well as on irregular verbs, creating words such as broked, dranked, and other charming past-tense forms. This beautiful logic often brings inner smiles to the adult listeners. Verbs ending with "ing" are used more than before. Even auxiliary verbs are scattered through speech—"Me have," "Daddy did it." Words such as wanna, gonna, and hafta seem to be learned as one word, and stick in children's vocabulary, being used over and over.

A term for children's speech behavior that indicates they have formed a new internal rule about language and are using it is **regularization**. As children filter what they hear, creating their own rule systems, they begin to apply the new rules. An expected sequence in formed rules for past-tense verb usage follows:

- uses irregular tense endings correctly (e.g., ran, came, drank)
- forms an internal rule when discovering that -ed expresses past events (e.g., danced, called, played)
- overregularizes; for example, adds -ed to all regular and irregular verbs that were formerly spoken correctly (e.g., camed, dided, wented, breaked)
- learns that both regular and irregular verbs express past tense, and uses both

In using plural noun forms, the following sequence is common.

- remembers and uses singular forms of nouns correctly (e.g., ball, dog, mouse, bird)
- uses irregular noun plurals correctly (e.g., men, feet, mice)
- forms an internal rule that plurals have "s" or "z" ending sounds
- applies rule to all nouns (e.g., balls, mens, dogs, feets, birds, mices, or ballsez, dogsez, feetsez)
- achieves flexible internal rules for plurals, memorizes irregular plural forms, and uses plurals correctly

Key-Word Sentences

The two-year-old omits many words in sentences, as does the toddler. The remaining words are shortened versions of adult sentences in which only the essentials are present. These words are key words and convey the essence of the message. Without relating utterances to real occurrences, meaning might be lost to the listener. Sentences at this stage are about four words long. Some pronouns and adjectives,

---

regularization — a child's speech behavior that indicates the formation and internalization of a language rule (regularity).

such as pretty or big, are used. Very few, if any, prepositions (by, on, with) or articles (a, an, the) are spoken. Some words are run together and are spoken as single units, such as "whadat?" or "eatem," as are the verb forms mentioned earlier. The order of words (syntax) may seem jumbled at times, as in "outside going ball," but basic grammar rules are observed in most cases.

Pronouns are often used incorrectly and are confused, as in "Me all finish milk," and "him Mark's." Concepts of male and female, living things, and objects may be only partly understood, as shown in the following example.

> And when a three-year-old says of the ring she cannot find, "Maybe it's hiding!" the listener wonders if she hasn't yet learned that hiding can be done only by an animate object. (Cazden, 1972)

Questions

Wh- questions (where, what, why, who) begin to appear in speech. During the toddler period, rising voice inflection and simple declarative utterances such as "Dolly drink?" are typical. At this stage, questions focus on location, objects, and people, with causation (why), process (how), and time (when). This reflects more mature thinking that probes purposes and intentions in others. Figure 3–5 shows one child's questioning development. Questions are frequent, and the child sometimes asks for an ob-

ject's function or the causes of certain events. It is as if the child sees that things exist for a purpose that in some way relates to him. The answers adults provide stimulate the child's desire to know more.

Vocabularies range from 250 to more than 1,000 words (Figure 3–6). An average of 50 new words enter the child's vocabulary each month.

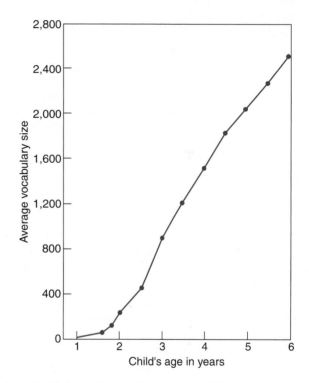

FIGURE 3–6 Growth of vocabulary.

AGE	
age two	raises voice pitch at sentence ending: "Me go?" "All gone?"
	uses short "what" and "where" questions: "Whas dat?" "Where kitty?"
age three	asks yes-no questions
	begins to use "why" questions
	begins to use auxiliary verbs in questions: "Can I have gum?" "Will you get it?"
	begins to use "how" questions: "How you do that?"
age four	adds tag endings: "Those are mine, okay?" "You like it, huh?" "That's good, isn't it?"
	inverts auxiliary verbs in questions: "Why are you sad?" "Why aren't we staying with gramma?"
	begins to use complex and two-part questions and statements: "I will tell him how to do it if you like." "What can I do when he won't come?" "I don't know what to do." "Why does it fall down when the door slams?"

FIGURE 3–5 Question development.

WORD	OBJECT OR EVENT FOR WHICH THE WORD WAS ORIGINALLY USED	OTHER OBJECTS OR EVENTS TO WHICH THE WORD WAS LATER APPLIED
mooi	moon	cakes, round marks on windows, writing on windows and in books, round shapes in books, tooling on leather book covers, round postmarks, letter *O*
buti	ball	toy, radish, stone spheres at park entrance
sch	sound of train	all moving machines
em	worm	flies, ants, all small insects, heads of timothy grass
fafer	sound of trains	steaming coffee pot, anything that hissed or made a noise
va	white plush dog	muffler, cat, father's fur coat

FIGURE 3–7 Some examples of overextensions in the language of one- and two-year-old children. (From Clark, E. V. [1975]. Knowledge, context, and strategy in the acquisition of meaning. In D. P. Dato [Ed.], *Georgetown University Round Table on languages and linguistics, 1975. Developmental psycholinguistics: Theory and applications.* Washington, DC: Georgetown University Press. Copyright 1975 by Georgetown University, Washington, DC.)

CATEGORIES IN CHILDREN'S THINKING

Children organize a tremendous amount of sensory and experiential happenings by forming mental categories. Recent studies point out that children can be quite sophisticated in how they group objects and think about those groupings (Gelman, 1998). Young preschoolers' categories differ from those of older children. The young preschooler tends to focus on superficial properties such as the "look" of something and where it is found. A younger child may focus on the teacher's fuzzy sweater by wanting to touch and rub it and saying "soft." An older preschooler may talk about its number of buttons, or patterns, or its similarity to his own sweater or other sweaters he has seen. Preschoolers often put items together in a scene rather than grouping items that are alike in more fundamental ways (Gelman, 1998).

Overlapping Concepts

Younger preschoolers commonly call all four-footed furry animals "dog," and all large animals "horse." This reflects **overextension**, in which the child has overextended and made a logical conclusion because these animals have many of the same features, can be about the same size, and therefore fit the existing word. This phenomenon is seen in the examples given in Figure 3–7.

Concept development, defined in Chapter 2 as the recognition of one or more distinguishing features or characteristics, proceeds by leaps and bounds during preschool years and is essential to meaningful communication. Details, exceptions, and discrepancies are often discussed in four-year-olds' conversations. The younger preschooler can be described as a "looker and doer" who engages in limited discussion of the features of situations. The excitement of exploration and discovery, particularly of something new and novel, is readily apparent in preschool classrooms. Children typically crowd around to see, touch, experience, and make comments about objects and events. Teachers notice the all-consuming focusing and the long periods of watching or touching, usually followed by verbalizing and questioning an event or experience.

Running Commentaries

As children play, their actions are sometimes accompanied by a running self-commentary or "stream of conciousness" talking concerning

---

overextension — in the early acquisition of words and their meanings, the application of a word to include other objects that share common features, such as "water" being used to describe any liquid.

what they are doing or what is happening (Figure 3–8). It can be described as a kind of verbal thought process, like mentally talking to oneself. It seems to increase in complex play situations as the child problem solves and talks it through.

Brophy (1977) offers reasons for private speech.

> Children talk to themselves to give themselves directions for the same reason that they use their fingers in counting; they need sensorimotor activity as a reinforcement or "crutch" because their cognitive schemes are not yet developed well enough to allow them to think silently.

Self-talk may help children sequence actions, control their own behavior, use flexible modes of thinking, and manipulate the goals they are trying to achieve in their play.

Talking to self and talking to another can occur alternately. Toys, animals, and treasured items still receive a few words. Statements directed to others do not usually need answers. Private speech rarely considers another's point of view. A conversation between young preschoolers may sound like two children talking together about different subjects. Neither child is really listening or reacting to what the other says. When a very young preschooler does wish to talk directly to another child, it is sometimes done through an adult. A child may say, "I want

truck," to an adult, even if the child playing with the truck is standing close by.

Researchers who have examined self-talk suggest a number of possible developmental reasons and benefits. These include:

- practicing newly recognized language forms.
- obtaining pleasure through play with word sounds.
- exploring vocal capacities.
- reliving particular significant events.
- creating dialogue in which the child voices all people's parts, perhaps helping the child later fit into social settings.
- experimenting with fantasy, thereby accommodating the creative urge.
- attending objectively to language.
- facilitating motor behavior in a task or project.

Whatever its benefits, self-talk is natural, common behavior. By the age of five, the child's self-talk is observed infrequently. As children approach the age of three, both dialogue and monologue are apparent. Observers of play conversations find it difficult to determine just how much of each is present.

Teachers, who conduct group times with younger preschoolers and have children who ramble, often develop strategies to encourage

Situation: Four- and five-year-old girls playing with water

	COMMENTARY	CHARACTERISTIC
Debbie:	"Two of those make one of these." (playing with measuring cups)	Talking to self.
Debbie:	"Two cups or three cups . . . whoops it went over."	Talks about what happened.
Tifine:	"Stop it or else I'll beat you up." (said to Debbie)	Does not respond to another's speech.
Debbie:	"This is heavy." (holding the 2-cup measuring container full of water)	Describes perception.
Christine:	"Is it hot?" (Christine just dropped in)	
Debbie:	"Feel it and see." "It's not hot." (feeling the water)	Hears another; answers appropriately. Child talking to self.
Debbie:	"I'm finished now. Oh this is awfully heavy—I'm going to pour it into the bottle."	Talking about what she perceives and what she is doing.

FIGURE 3–8 Conversation during play activity.

"my turn, your turn" behaviors. A kitchen timer, a ping-pong paddle held by each speaker, or a turned on flashlight to signal a child that his speaking turn is over are strategies some teachers have devised. Teachers also try to draw focus back to the subject at hand by saying, "Amy, yes, dogs do use their tongues when they drink. It is Jeremy's turn to tell us about his dog now."

Repetition

Repetition in speech is common. Sometimes it happens randomly at play, and at other times it is done with a special purpose. A young child may repeat almost everything said to him. Most young preschoolers repeat words or parts of sentences regularly. Children's growing language skills allow them to create repetitions that rhyme, as in "oogie, woogie, poogie bear," which greatly please them. They quickly imitate words that they like; sometimes, excitement is the cause. Chukovsky (1963) points out that rhyming words or rhyming syllables may promote enjoyable mimicking and that the younger the child, the greater the child's attraction to word repetition that rhymes. Some reasons for repetition are (1) it helps children remember things (just as adults mentally repeat new telephone numbers), (2) it reduces stress, and (3) it is an enjoyable form of sound making.

Free associations (voiced juggling of sounds and words) occur at play and at rest and may sound like babbling. Many times, it seems as though, having learned a word, the child must savor it or practice it, over and over (Figure 3–9).

Lack of Clarity

About one in every four words of the young preschooler is not readily understandable. This lack of clarity is partially caused by an inability to control the mouth, tongue, and breathing and to hear subtle differences and distinctions in speech. Typically, articulation of all English speech sounds, especially some **consonant** blends, is not accomplished until age seven or

FIGURE 3–9 Elsa Beth calls this "bussing" her teeth.

eight. Young preschoolers are only 40 to 80 percent correct in articulation. This lack of intelligibility in children can be partly attributed to the complexity of the task of mastering the sounds. Although children may be right on target in development, their speech may still be difficult to understand at times.

The young preschooler may have difficulty with the rate of speech, phrasing, inflection, intensity, syntax, and voice stress. Misarticulation and defective sound making can also contribute to the problem. The child who attempts to form the longest utterances is the one who is hardest to understand. The child who omits sounds is less clear than the one who distorts them. As a rule, expect omissions, substitutions, and distortions in the speech of two- and three-year-olds, for they will be plentiful.

Stoel-Gammon (1997) points out that although children's pronunciation patterns are not fully adultlike by three years of age, the basic features of the adult phonological system are present. Most children can produce all of the **vowel** and nearly all of the consonant sounds in at least a few words, but their productions are not 100 percent accurate.

---

consonant — (1) speech sound made by partial or complete closure of the vocal tract, which obstructs air flow. (2) An alphabet letter used in representing any of these sounds.

vowel — a voiced speech sound made without stoppage or friction of air flow as it passes through the vocal tract.

Young children typically omit sounds at the ends of words, saying, for example, "ba" for ball. Middle consonants in longer words are also passed over lightly—"ikeem" for ice cream or "telfone" for telephone. Even beginning sounds may be omitted, as in "ellow" for yellow.

Substitutions of letter sounds are also common, for example, "aminal," and "pasghetti." Until the new sound is mastered, one consonant may even take the place of another; "wabbit," "wun," and "wain" are common examples. Children who cannot yet produce all of the speech sounds accurately can generally hear the differences between *w* and *r*, or *t* and *th* when they are pronounced by others.

Dramatic Play

Short play sequences that involve acting or imitating the behavior of mom or dad begin at home and school. Speech usually accompanies the reenactments. Although young children at this age play side-by-side, most of this type of play starts as solitary activity. Common play themes include mom on the phone, mom caring for baby, or mom or dad cooking (Figure 3–10). Dolls, toys, and dress-up clothes are usually part of the action and may

serve to initiate this type of play. Observers of two- and three-year-olds in classrooms find it hard to determine whether children are engaged in joint planning of play or are simply playing in the same area with the same kinds of playthings. Preschools purposely purchase multiple dolls so that many children can feed and rock "their babies" when they see others doing it.

Advice for Parents and Early Childhood Staff Members

Parents sometimes worry about a child who stops, stammers, or stutters when speaking. Calling attention to this speech and making demands on the child cause tension, making the situation worse. All children hesitate, repeat, stop, and start in speaking—it is typical behavior. Searching for the right word takes time, and thoughts may come faster than words. Adults need to relax and wait. Speech is a complex process of sending and receiving. Maintaining patience and optimism and assuming a casual "I'm listening" stance is the best course of action for the adult. Many schools routinely send home informational material to alert parents to age-level speech characteristics.

FIGURE 3–10 Dress-up play may be enhanced if a mirror is provided.

Cooper's conclusions (1993) about what teachers may feel about children's seemingly illogical speech statements coincide with what many teachers suspect. Child logic is there, but teachers are not privy to young children's inner thought processes or their past experiences. Cooper states

> On the whole, I find that young children *intend* to be intelligible though sometimes they are unable to coordinate their words with their thoughts, which is a very different state of mind than egocentrism. If we could understand their mental references and associations, we could see that most often they are being quite logical.

When working with the young child, the listening teachers will sometimes feel on the edge of understanding what the child is trying to say. This happens with both younger and older preschoolers struggling at times to put into words what they are thinking. Acceptance and interest are appropriate (Figure 3–11).

Attentive interaction with positive feedback is recommended for adults who live or work with two- and three-year-olds. Reacting to the intent of the child's message is more helpful than concentrating on correctness. In other words, focus on what is said rather than the way it is said. A lot of guessing is still necessary to determine what the child is trying to say. The adult's model of speech will override temporary errors as the child hears more and more of it.

By simply naming objects, adults can encourage children to notice how different items are similar and can help children gain new information about the world (Gelman, 1998). Helping children see details and relationships in what they encounter is useful if done in an unpressured manner. Connecting past events to present events may aid their understanding.

Children's hearing should be checked regularly because even a moderate hearing loss may affect speech production. Preschoolers are particularly prone to upper respiratory infections and ear problems.

Books for Younger Preschoolers

Many picture books are available for this age group. Generally, experts suggest books that have

- themes, objects, animals, or people that are familiar and within their range of life experience.
- clarity of content and story line.
- clear, simple illustrations or photographs with backgrounds that do not distract from the intended focus.
- themes concerning everyday tasks and basic human needs.

FIGURE 3–11 "Me eatem!"

FIGURE 3–12 Rene is explaining why she selected a certain puzzle piece.

Most two- and three-year-olds enjoy actively participating in story reading, but they can be very good listeners as well. Participation can include pointing, making noise, repeating dialogue, or performing imitative body actions. Books that are repetitive and predictable offer the enjoyment of anticipating what will come next. For children who are used to being read to at bedtime, the calming effect of listening to the human voice becomes very apparent during story reading. Chapter 9 covers the topic of introducing preschool children to literature.

OLDER PRESCHOOLERS

As younger preschoolers get older, adults can expect the following:

- longer sentences with more words per sentence
- more specificity
- more "ing" endings on verbs
- increased correctness in the forms of the verb "to be"
- use of more auxiliary verbs
- more facility with passive-voice verbs, including "did" and "been"

- changes in negative sentences, from "No want" to "I don't want"
- changes in question forms, from "Car go?" to "Where did the car go?"
- changes in mental categories
- additional clarifications in articulation of speech sounds

Between four and five years of age, most preschoolers approach adultlike speech; their sentences are longer, with almost all words present rather than only key words (Figure 3–12).

Preschoolers' play is active and vocal, and they copy each other's words and manner of speaking. A word such as "monster," or more colorful words, may swiftly become of interest and spread rapidly from child to child. Remember the joy that both younger and older children exhibited with the phrases: "zip-a-dee-doo-dah," "bibbidi-bobbidi-boo," "scoobi-scoobi-do," "blast off," "fuzzy-wuzzy," and "ooey-gooey"? Every generation of preschoolers seems to have its own favorite sayings, and new ones are constantly appearing.

Social speech and conversations of the older preschooler are heard and interpreted to a greater degree by others of the child's age. The child learns and practices the complexities of social conversation, including (1) gaining another's attention by making eye contact, touching, or using words or catch-phrases like "Know what?"; (2) pausing and listening; (3) correcting himself; (4) maintaining attention by not pausing so as not to let another speaker jump in; (5) taking turns in conversing by developing patience and trying to listen while still holding in mind what he wants to say.

Friendships

The young preschooler may develop a new friend or find another he prefers to play near or with. At ages two and three, friendships are usually temporary, changing from day to day. Friendships of older preschoolers are more stable and lasting. By ages four and five, there seems to be a desire to remain compatible and work out differences, therefore creatively maintaining a type of play acceptable to both. Negotiation, clarification, and an open-mindedness flourish during play. A friend's needs and requests are handled with sensitivity, and flexibility characterizes conversations. Needless to say, spats, "blowups," and the crushed feelings accompanying rejection sometimes occur. Verbal interaction between children adds a tremendous amount of verbal input and also promotes output.

Group Play

Joint planning of play activities and active make-believe and role-playing take on new depth. Adults often see themselves in the play of children. The four-year-old's main concern seems to be interacting with age mates. Twosomes and groups of play companions are typical in older preschoolers' classrooms and play yards (Figure 3–13). As speech blossoms, friendships blossom and disintegrate (Figure 3–14). Speech is used to discourage and disallow entrance to play groups when running from newcomers is impossible. Speech is found to be effective in hurting feelings, as in statements such as "I don't like you" or "No girls." Children find that verbal inventiveness may help them join play or initiate play.

In group play, pretending is paramount. Make-believe play appears to be at its zenith.

Many children grow in the ability to (1) verbally suggest new directions and avenues of fantasy, (2) engage in verbal negotiation, (3) compromise, (4) argue, and (5) become a group's leader by using the right words. Popular children seem to be those who use speech creatively and become enjoyable companions to others.

Violent statements such as "I'm going to shoot you" or "cut you up" are sometimes heard, and these tend to reflect television viewing or video drama. The reality-fantasy of some play situations may become temporarily blurred, causing some children considerable anxiety.

Older preschoolers talk "in character" as they elaborate their dramatic play. If a scenario calls for a mother talking to a baby or teenagers talking, preschoolers adopt appropriate speech. Imitations of pop singers or cartoon characters are common. Role-taking is an important skill in mature communication, indicating that social/dramatic play and improvisation are effective means of facilitating growth in communicative competence (Pinnell & Jaggar, 1992).

Four-year-olds seem to boast, brag, and make lots of noise. However, apparently boastful statements such as "Look what I did" may

FIGURE 3–13 Group play encourages social development and social connectiveness.

FIGURE 3–14 "Bosom buddies" enjoy the same play choices.

just be the child's attempt to show that he is capable and to share his accomplishments. Although preschoolers enjoy being with their peers, they quickly and easily engage in quarreling and name-calling. Sometimes, they do battle verbally. Typically, three- to five-year-olds disagree over possession of objects or territory, and verbal reasons or verbal evidence may help them win arguments. Many conflicts are resolved and lead to continued play. Speech helps children settle their affairs with and without adult help.

As a child develops a sense of humor, giggling becomes part of the noise of play. Silliness often reigns. One preschool boy thought it hilarious to go up to a teacher named Alice and say, "What's your name, Alice?" and then run off laughing—quite mature humor for a four-year-old! Honig (1988) cites instances in which preschoolers distort and repeat what a caregiver says, making changes in sounds and gleefully chanting the distorted message. She urges teachers who want to cultivate children's ability to understand and appreciate humor to present materials that challenge children's ability to interpret humor.

Arguing, persuading, and children using statements aimed at controlling others are frequently heard during play. Older preschool children are able to state reasons (Figure 3–15), request information, give explanations, utter justifications for their behavior, and verbally defend themselves. At times, establishing authority in disagreements seems paramount to compromising.

Inner Speech

Much of child speech during early preschool years concerns child comments about what the child is doing as he is doing it or what the child has done. A subtle shift takes place during the later preschool years, when inner speech becomes

FIGURE 3–15 Emily is explaining to her playmates her ideas about why the ground feels cool and soft.

apparent and the child more frequently plans, monitors ideas, and evaluates mentally. The child is still talking about his accomplishments and actions in a look-at-me fashion, but a greater portion of his self-commentary is unspoken.

Exploring the Conventions of Conversation

Children learn language by reinventing it for themselves, not by direct instruction. They crack the code through exposure and opportunities to converse. They actively, although unconsciously, ingest and discover the rules of the system. Their speech errors often alert adults to the inner rules of language being formed.

Conversations have unwritten rules and expectations, "You-talk-I-talk" sequence being the most apparent. Some preschoolers (three- and four-year-olds) may delight in violating or "playing" with the conventions of conversation. Geller (1985) notes that this can be seen in child-child or adult-child conversations when savvy preschoolers deliberately mislead (usually to tease playfully) or use "taboo" bathroom talk, nonsense talk, or tone unexpectedly when capable of verbally responding at a more mature level. Most teachers sense the child may be asserting independence by rejecting conversational convention. One teacher termed this "going into the verbal crazies" to reject what another child or adult is saying, therefore attempting to change or control the situation (Schmidt, 1991). By violating conversational convention, children may clarify how conversational interaction should take place.

Relational Words

More and more relational words appear as the child begins to compare, contrast, and revise stored concepts with new happenings. The following teacher-recorded anecdote during a story-telling activity shows how the child attempts to relate previously learned ethics to a new situation.

> During story telling Michael repeated with increasing vigor, "He not berry nice!" at the parts of the story when the wolf says, "I'm going to blow your house down." Michael seemed to be checking with me the correctness of his thinking based on his internalized rules of proper moral conduct. (Machado, 1989)

Perhaps because adults stress bad and good or because a young child's inner sense of what is and what is not correct is developing, teachers notice that preschoolers often describe feelings and people within narrow limits. One is either pretty or ugly, mean or nice. Shades of meaning or extenuating circumstances seem yet to be understood.

Beck (1982) describes how concepts mature.

> Just as infants use single-word sentences to name and describe objects, and as the two-year-old combines words to describe the nature of a ball or dolly or truck, and three-year-old children continue to specify and describe, four-year-old children are also creatures of their senses. They are concerned with the smell of a thing, the touch of a thing, the look of a thing and the sound of a thing. What is special about four-year-old children, however, is that their sensual awareness begins to take on conceptual dimensions. They begin to notice function or use and they begin to see it comparatively. . . . They come to see relationships between several objects and/or several events, and in comparing one to the other, they are learning the principle of categorization.

Space and size relationships and abstract time relationships rarely are expressed with adult precision. Although the words "big" and "little" are commonly used by preschoolers, they are overused. Many other comparison words give children trouble, and one hears "biggerer," "big-big-big," and "bestus one" to describe size. Time words elicit smiles from adults as children wrestle with present, past, and future, as in "zillion days" or "tomorrower." Number words are difficult for some children to handle, and expressions such as "whole bunches" and "eleventeen" are sometimes heard. The following displays one four-year-old's understanding of "unseen revered beings."

> Grandma and her grandchild are filling plastic Easter eggs for a family hunt.
>
> *Brianna:* "We're doing this for the Easter bunny—huh grandma?"
>
> *Grandma:* "Yes, we are."
>
> *Brianna:* "And, for Santa Claus and God, too—huh grandma?"

Although four-year-olds are able speakers, many of the "plays on words," double meanings, and connotative language subtleties that are important in adult speech are beyond children's understanding. Their creative uses of words at times seem metaphoric and poetic and are valiant attempts to put thoughts into words. Half-heard words and partially or fully learned words are blended together and are, at times, wonderfully descriptive.

Speech and Child Behavior

There is tremendous variety in the ways children can modify their voices, and they may speak in a different pitch or rhythm when speaking to different people. They can whine, whisper, change volume, and distort timing and pronunciation (Garvey, 1984).

Some children discover that by increasing volume or changing tone they can affect others' behavior. They find that speech can show anger or sarcasm and can be used aggressively to hurt others.

Preschoolers may mimic the speech of "bad-guy" television characters. Acts of aggression, clothed in the imitated speech and actions of a TV character, can become part of this type of play.

Purposeful echoing or baby talk can irritate or tease. Excessive talking is sometimes used to get one's way, and "talking back" may occur.

Some children find that silence can get as much attention from adults as loud speech. Tattling on another may simply be a way of checking for correctness, or it can be purposeful.

Through trial and error and feedback, the child finds that words can hurt, gain friends or favor, or satisfy a wide range of needs. Because preschoolers are emotion-packed human be-

ings, their statements range from expressions of "you're my buddy" to "you're my enemy" within a matter of minutes.

What may appear to be violent statements may be just role-playing or make-believe competition. To some adults, the preschooler speech may appear loud and wild. Speech seems overly nasal and full of moisture that sprays out in some words. A young child may have frequent nasal colds and congestion during this period. Preschoolers tend to stand close to others, and their volume increases when they are intense about their subjects.

Impact Words

Not all speech used by older preschoolers is appreciated by adults. Name-calling and offensive words and phrases may be used by active preschoolers to gain attention and reaction from both adults and children. Children discover that some phrases, sentences, and words cause unusual behavior in others. They actively explore these and usually learn which of these are inappropriate and when they can be used. Children learn that most of this type of talk has "impact value." If certain talk makes people laugh or gives the children some kind of positive reward, it is used over and over.

Bathroom words seem to be explored and used as put-downs and attention getters. As every parent and teacher knows, young children experiment with language related to the body, and particularly to the private parts, going to the bathroom, and sexuality (Rothbaum, Grauer, & Rubin, 1997). In fact, children's use of sexual words can make it seem as if they know more than they do. Giggles and uproarious laughter can ensue when these words are used, adding to the child's enjoyment, and new teachers may not know how to handle these situations. The school's policy regarding this matter can be a subject for staff discussion. Generally, newly spoken bathroom talk should be ignored unless it is hurtful, or the child should be told that the place to use the word is in the bathroom. This often remedies the behavior because the child's enjoyment of it is spoiled without an audience. Alternatively, it might suffice to firmly say, "That's a word that hurts. His name is Michael," or in a calm but firm voice, "That kind of talk is unacceptable." Preschoolers love using forbidden words, especially when they play together. What parents and teachers can control is what is said in their presence.

Sound Words

In our culture, children are particularly fond of repeating conventionalized sounds reputedly made by animals ("arf-arf," "meow," "baa") as well as action sounds for toy vehicles ("putt-putt," "beep," "varoom"). When a child is playing the baby in home reenactment dramatic play, "wa-wa" will be heard frequently. Rough-and-tumble outside play may be accompanied by cartoon strip sounds like "pow," "bam," and "zap." In addition, a good number of four-year-olds can distinguish rhyming words.

Created Words

Created words such as "turner-overer" for pancake turner, "mudpudders" for rain boots, or "dirt digger" for spade are wonderfully descriptive and crop up occasionally in child speech, perhaps as a means of filling in gaps in their vocabularies. Many cite young children's fascination with the functions of objects in their environment as the reason such words are created. Children love making up words, including nonsense words and rhymes, and revel in their newly gained abilities to do so.

Word Meanings

During later preschool years children often become focused on what words mean and think and wonder about them. They begin to understand that words are arbitrary symbols with no intrinsic connection to their meaning but rather are representatives of meaning. The young child who says, "Templeton has a big name; my name is small," is displaying a recognition of word length or number of syllables.

Reality and Nonsense

Some preschool children can enjoy the absurd, nonsensical, and ridiculous in their experiences and find humor in the unexpected. Others, at a different stage in their cognitive development with another orientation, insist on knowing the right way—the real, the accepted, the "whys and wherefores"—and will see no humor in what confuses them or contradicts the "usual order of things."

A number of preschoolers view life and surroundings seriously, literally. Others can "play" in speech with the opposite of what they know to be true. We know this is true in some adults also. Some simply do not seem to enjoy what most of us may find humorous.

Calkins (1997) describes the "language play" that many young children display and the possible roots of the ability.

> From nursery rhymes, fairy tales, and familiar stories children discover wonderful, fun ways to say things. They stomp upstairs to bed saying, "Fee fi fo fum, I don't wanna go to my room!" They build bridges over the bathtub and make their rubber duck "trip, trap, trip, trap" across.

Geller (1985) cautions teachers to be aware of the tendency to suppress a child's delight in absurdity by insisting upon exact or literal renditions of things. She urges teachers to encourage nonsense play by appreciating a child's inventions or nonsensical propositions, as in the following example.

> During moments of chanting . . . I would sometimes say, "And the dogs go meow and cats say bow-wow." Through their laughter, my listeners would inwardly shriek, "No!" and then either correct me or join in the game, producing their own inversions. (Geller, 1985)

Myths Concerning Speech and Intelligence

A large and mature vocabulary at this age may tend to lead teachers to think a child has superior intelligence. Making conclusions about children based on language ability at this age has inherent pitfalls considering the many factors that could produce limited or advanced vocabulary, particularly when one considers cultural differences, bilingualism, and the child's access to "language-rich environments." At later ages language usage does seem to be related to school success.

Common Speech Patterns

Four-year-olds often rhyme words in their play speech, and teachers sometimes join the fun. Older preschoolers engage in self-chatter, as do early preschoolers. Older preschoolers continue to make errors in grammar and in the use of the past tense of verbs ("He didn't caught me"), adjectives ("It's biggerer than yours") (Figure 3–16), time words ("The next tomorrow"), and negatives ("I didn't did it"). But preschoolers' skills are increasing at this stage, and their use of forms of the irregular verb "to be" improve: "I am so," or "Mine are hot, and yours are cold." Sentence structure becomes more adultlike, including use of relative clauses and complex and compound sentence forms. Articulation of letter sounds is still developing; about 75 percent of English letter sounds are made correctly. Omissions of letter sounds (*'merca* for *America*) and substitutions (*udder* for *other*) are still present.

The older preschooler may have a vocabulary of more than 1,500 words. Pan and Gleason (1997) point out that not only do children learn new words and new concepts, they also enrich and solidify their knowledge of known words by establishing multiple links among words and

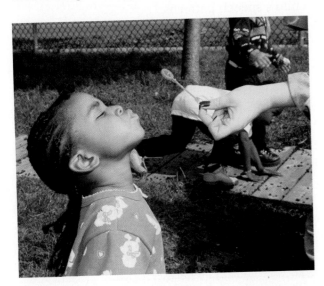

FIGURE 3–16 "Watch teacher. I'm going to make a giganticer one!"

concepts. The child is very concerned about the correct names of things and can find the errors in the speech of others. Because the older preschooler is an active explorer, his questions still probe the "purposefulness" of objects or actions (as in "Why is the moon in the sky?"). The four-year-old becomes an active problem solver and tends to explain things through visually noted attributes; for example, "A cow is called that 'cause of its horns." Elkind (1971) describes preschoolers' inability at times to talk about their solutions.

> Although the preschooler can respond to and solve problems posed verbally, he is not able to verbalize his solutions.

The child can transform questions; for example, if asked to carry a message asking mom whether *she is* ready, the child will correctly ask her, "Are *you* ready?"

Most four-year-old children enjoy books, stories, and activities with words. More and more of their time is spent on these pursuits.

The four-year-old may still stutter and clutter and stop speech when there is stress or excitement. The less-mature speech of a best friend might be copied, and nonverbal expression is always a part of communication. However, most four- and five-year-olds are avid speakers. They are interested in exploring the real world and make-believe worlds. Chukovsky (1963) prizes the child's ability to fantasize and encourages teachers and parents to accept and value it, writing, ". . . it should be diligently nurtured from earliest childhood."

A wide range of individual speech behavior is both normal and possible. Knowing some typical behaviors can help the teacher understand young children. Some younger preschoolers may have the speech characteristics of older preschoolers, whereas some older preschoolers have the characteristics of younger preschoolers. Each child is unique in his progress and rate of acquiring language skills.

Metalinguistic Awareness

Teachers and parents hope that preschool language arts experiences will, when the time comes, help and aid children's learning to read and write with ease. Preschoolers may begin to notice words as objects. **Metalinguistic awareness** can be defined as a knowledge of the nature of language as an object. Pan and Gleason (1997) suggest that children begin to notice words as objects and later become able to manipulate them to learn to read and write and to accomplish a host of nonliteral ends, such as using metaphors, creating puns, and using irony. They observe

> Before children can engage in flexible uses of words, they must have an implicit understanding that words are separate from their referents. Young children often consider the name of an object another of its intrinsic attributes. They believe, for instance, that if you called a horse a cow, it might begin to moo. Later children learn that words themselves are not inherent attributes of objects, which allows them to move beyond literal word use and adopt a metaphoric stance.

The Brain Growth of Four-Year-Olds

Early childhood educators are often awed by the learning abilities of four-year-olds. Through new technology, neuroscientists are able to confirm the validity of educators' observations. Kotulak (1996) reports

> A third critical restructuring of the brain takes place between the ages of four and twelve. Educators suspected that something dramatic was happening during this period because of the surge in learning that takes place then.

> It is a time when the brain is deciding whether to keep or eliminate connections. And in the process of keeping connections, the brain eagerly seeks information from the senses.

> Things that a child experiences becomes part of his mental architecture, laid down in the connections that are retained. There is room for a virtually unlimited number of memories. Connections that are not reinforced by stimuli from the outside world are pruned away, dead branches that no longer flower.

Based on the new discoveries of brain growth and function, many researchers are urging that the nation's educational curricula be changed to allow more emphasis on early childhood education in the key areas of language, music, math, and problem solving.

SUMMARY

Knowing typical and common language development characteristics helps the teacher understand that children are unique individuals. Rapid growth of vocabulary and language skills is part of normal growth. Errors in the speech of young preschoolers (aged two to three) make verbalizations partly understandable. Key words in the correct order give adults clues to what is intended. Self-talk during the child's play usually describes what the child is doing and may alternate with social comments.

Teachers can use their knowledge of early childhood language development in many ways, such as alerting the staff about a child's need for hearing tests or special help and helping parents who are concerned with their child's speech patterns.

Older preschool children (aged four to five) have almost adultlike speech. They explore words and begin to understand their power. Fantasy play peaks and is accompanied by speech. Some newly learned speech may be irritating to school staffs and parents, but it can indicate physical, mental, and social growth. Exploring and enjoying books occupies more of the children's time. Exploring the real and make-believe worlds with words becomes children's active pursuit during the early childhood years.

There is no "average" child when it comes to language development; individual differences exist and are treated with acceptance and optimism (Figure 3–17).

---

metalinguistic awareness — a conscious awareness on the part of a language user of language as an object in itself.

CHILD'S AGE

2–2½ years	joins words in sentences of two or more words knows name has vocabulary of more than three words understands long spoken sentences and simple commands begins using plurals and past tense changes pitch and/or loudness for specific meaning begins using forms of verb "to be" uses a few prepositions uses "I," "me," and "you"	uses about 25 phonemes articulates about 10 to 12 vowel types and about 12 to 15 consonants points to and names objects in pictures names five to eight body parts enjoys rhythm in words, nursery rhymes, finger plays, and simple stories understands and responds to almost all of adult speech generalizes by calling round objects ball, and so on
2½–3 years	begins to use negatives, imperatives, and commands shows variety in question types adds as many as two to three words to vocabulary daily names items in signs and books uses three- or four-word sentences enjoys fun with words	follows simple directions points to body parts when asked names many common objects uses an increasing number of nouns, verbs, and pronouns draws lines and circular forms in artwork knows words or lines from books, songs, and stories
3–4 years	asks why, what, where, how, and when questions loves word play makes closed figures in art begins using auxiliary verbs tells sex and age utters compound sentences with connecting "and . . . er . . . but," and so on engages in imaginary play with dialogue and monologue says full name follows two- and three-part requests relates ideas and experiences uses adverbs, adjectives, and prepositions answers who, what, and where questions names some colors and is interested in counting	looks at books while alone and enjoys reading times talks about relationships memorizes a short song, poem, finger play, or story repeats three digits and two to three nonsense syllables if asked uses adjectives and pronouns correctly can copy a recognizable circle or square well if shown a model can imitate a clapping rhythm starts to talk about the function of objects can find an object in group that is different can find missing parts of wholes can classify using clear, simple distinctions knows names of common shapes
4–5 years	has vocabulary of more than 1,500 words uses sentences of five to six (or more) words may use impact, shock, and forbidden words may use words of violence argues, convinces, and questions correctness shares books with friends acts out story themes or recreates life happenings in play has favorite books likes to dictate words notices signs and print in environment uses etiquette words, such as "please," "thank you," and so on enjoys different writing tools knows many nursery rhymes and stories	may add alphabet letters to artwork creates and tells long stories can verbally express the highlights of the day knows many colors can repeat a sentence with six or more words may pretend to read books or may actually read others' name tags holds writing tools in position that allows fine control traces objects with precision classifies according to function asks what words mean is familiar with many literary classics for children knows address and phone number can retell main facts or happenings in stories uses adultlike speech

FIGURE 3–17 Developmental language-related milestones at ages two through five.

Added interest and emphasis on language fundamentals during preschool years has occurred in light of research on brain growth and function (Shore, 1997).

ADDITIONAL RESOURCES

Readings

Bowman, B. T., Donovan, M. S., & Burns, M. S. (Eds.). (2001). *Eager to learn: Educating our preschoolers*. Washington, DC: National Academy Press.

Christie, J., Enz, B., & Vukelich, C. (1997). *Teaching language and literacy: Preschool through the elementary grades*. Boston: Addison-Wesley.

Clay, M. M. (2001). *Change over time in children's literacy development*. Portsmouth, NH: Heinemann.

Davidson, J. (1996). *Emergent literacy and dramatic play in early education*. Clifton Park, NY: Delmar Learning.

Hart, B., & Risley, T. R. (1999). *The social world of children learning to talk*. Baltimore: Paul H. Brookes.

Morrow, L. M. (1990). Preparing the classroom environment to promote literacy during play. *Early Childhood Research Quarterly, 5*, 537–554.

Ohl, J. (2000, Fall). Linking child care and early literacy. *Child Care Bulletin. 27*, 1–4.

Paley, V. G. (1988). *Bad guys don't have birthdays: Fantasy play at four*. Chicago: University of Chicago Press.

Paley, V. G. (1988). *Mollie is three: Growing up in school*. Chicago: The University of Chicago Press.

Rice, M. (1995). Children's language acquisition. In B. Powers & R. Hubbard (Eds.), *Language development: A reader for teachers*. Upper Saddle River, NJ: Merrill/Prentice Hall.

Roskos, K. A., Christie, J. F., & Richgels, D. J. (2003). The essentials of early literacy instruction. *Young Children, 58*(2), 52–60.

Schickendanz, J. A. (1999). *Much more than the ABCs: The early stages of reading and writing*. Washington, DC: National Association for the Education of Young Children.

Weitzman, E. (1992). *Learning language and loving it*. Toronto: A Hanen Centre Publication.

HELPFUL WEB SITES

ECRP—Early Childhood Research & Practice
http://ecrp.uiuc.edu/
Topics related to growth and learning during preschool years are presented.

National Child Care Information Center (NCCIC)
http://nccic.org
Staff will research your questions and connect you with information on young children's language and literacy. Select *Questions and Answer Services*.

National Network for Child Care
http://www.nncc.org
For the ages and stages of three- and four-year-olds, select *Articles & Resources* and then select *Child Development*.

Vivian Paley's writings have been treasured and extensively read by early childhood educators. One strategy that aided her understanding of the children in her classroom could easily be replicated. Read and discuss her strategy with peers in a discussion forum. The findings of a kindergarten readiness study that involved 700 children in an urban California school district will alert you to the communication abilities the study believed important. It points out how instrumental preschool teachers can be in preparing children for kindergarten.

STUDENT ACTIVITIES

1. Observe a two-, three-, four-, and five-year-old for 15-minute periods. (Omit children's names.) Try to write down what is said and a brief description of the setting and actions. Underline typical characteristics described in this chapter. Make comparisons between older and younger preschool children. Add any new language characteristics you notice.

2. Interview two teachers. Ask if any preschool child within their care seems to have special speech or language problems. Write down the teachers' comments and compare them with typical characteristics mentioned in this chapter.

3. What rules or restrictions concerning the use of inappropriate speech (name-calling, swearing, and screaming) would you expect to find in a preschool center?

4. Write definitions for the following:

consonant	metalinguistic awareness
egocentric speech or private speech	overextension
expressive vocabulary	running commentary
fantasy	vowel
impact words	

CHAPTER REVIEW

A. Associate the following characteristics with the correct age group. Some may seem to fit both categories; choose the most appropriate one. Write the characteristics under the headings "Younger Preschooler" (two- and three-year-olds) and "Older Preschooler" (four- and five-year-olds).

75 to 85 percent perfect articulation	nonverbal communication
"Look, I'm jumping."	vocabulary of more than 1,500 words
telegraphic speech	talking about what one is doing
rhyming and nonsense words	stuttering
name-calling	talking through an adult
repetitions	substitutions
omission of letter sounds	role-playing
adultlike speech	planning play with others
bathroom words	arguing

B. Select the correct answers. Many questions have more than one correct response.

   1. The younger preschool child (two to three years old)
      a. may still grunt and scream while communicating.
      b. always replies to what is said to him by another child.
      c. articulates many sounds without clarity.
      d. speaks in complete sentences at two years of age.

2. A truly typical or average child
   a. would have all the characteristics of his age.
   b. is almost impossible to find.
   c. is one who speaks better than his peers.
   d. sometimes makes up words to fit new situations.

3. Repetition in the speech of the young child
   a. needs careful watching.
   b. is common for children aged two to five.
   c. can be word play.
   d. happens for a variety of reasons.

4. Name-calling and swearing
   a. may take place during preschool years.
   b. can gain attention.
   c. show that children are testing reactions with words.
   d. happen only with poorly behaved children.

5. A word like "blood" or "ghost"
   a. may spread quickly to many children.
   b. has impact value.
   c. can make people listen.
   d. is rarely used in a preschool group.

6. Most younger preschoolers
   a. cannot correctly pronounce all consonants.
   b. omit some letter sounds.
   c. have adultlike speech.
   d. will, when older, reach adult-level speech.

7. Stuttering during preschool years
   a. happens often.
   b. should not be drawn to the child's attention.
   c. may happen when a child is excited.
   d. means the child will need professional help to overcome it.

8. "Me wented" is an example of
   a. pronoun difficulty.
   b. a telegram sentence.
   c. verb incorrectness.
   d. the speech of some two- or three-year-olds.

9. Joint planning in play with two or more children is found more often with
   a. two- to three-year-olds.
   b. four- to five-year-olds.
   c. slowly developing children.
   d. male children.

10. Knowing typical speech characteristics is important because teachers
    a. may need to alert their director's attention to a child's difficulty.
    b. can help individual children.
    c. interact daily with young children.
    d. should be able to recognize typical age-level behavior.

CHAPTER 4

Growth Systems Affecting Early Language Ability

OBJECTIVES

After reading this chapter, you should be able to:

◆ Describe sequential stages of intellectual development.

◆ List three perceptual-motor skills that preschool activities might include.

◆ Discuss the importance of a center's ability to meet young children's social and emotional needs.

KEY TERMS

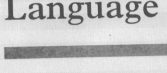

accommodation
assimilation
classify
conceptual
  tempo

impulsive
mental image
metalinguistic
  skills

reflective
social
  connected-
  ness

101

The child is a total being, and language growth cannot be isolated from physical, mental, and social-emotional well-being. All body systems need a minimum level of movement (exercise) to keep the body in good working order and to stimulate brain growth. A proper intake of nutritious foods and living conditions that provide emotional security and balance can affect the child's acquisition of language and her general health and resistance to disease. A preschool, child center, or learning center intent on developing language skills focuses on satisfying both physical and emotional needs while also providing intellectual opportunity and challenge by offering a variety of age-appropriate activities (Figure 4–1).

FIGURE 4–1 Outdoor materials and equipment invite physical activity.

PHYSICAL GROWTH

Physical development limits or aids capabilities, thereby affecting children's perceptions of themselves, as well as the way they are treated by others. Early childhood teachers are aware of these fundamental physical changes that take place in young children. For instance, a slightly taller, physically active, strong, and well-coordinated child who can ride a two-wheel bike and drop-kick a football may be admired by her peers. These two skills are not usually witnessed during preschool years, but occasionally, a child possesses such physical skills. A wide range of physical abilities in individual children exists within preschool groups as in all developmental areas.

Preschoolers grow at the rate of 2 to 3 inches in height and 4 to 6 pounds in weight a year. At about 18 to 24 months, the child's thumb is used in opposition to just one finger. The ability to use tools and drawing markers with a degree of skill emerges. The nutritional quality of the child's diet exerts an influence on both body and neural development. Monitoring nutrient intake, height, weight gain, and emotional well-being can alert parents to possible deficiencies.

Illness during accelerated growth may produce conditions affecting language development if it damages necessary body systems.

Hearing loss and vision difficulties impair the child's ability to receive communications and learn her native language. A brain impairment may hinder the child's ability to sort perceptions, slowing progress.

Preschools and early learning programs plan a wide range of motor activities; much of the children's time is devoted to playing with interesting equipment in both indoor and outdoor areas (Figure 4–2). The well-known bene-

FIGURE 4–2 Outdoor climbing structures can promote development of both large and small muscles.

fits of a healthy mind in a healthy body should be planned for by incorporating daily physical activities that promote well-exercised and well-coordinated muscles into young children's daily programs.

Planned physical movement opportunities and activities prepare children for academic learning. As Pica (1997) points out

> Not only does movement stimulate learning physiologically, but it also helps young children to experience concepts so they can process them cognitively. Teachers must offer children opportunities to solve movement problems, invent their own solutions to challenges, and make abstract concepts (like high and low) concrete by physically experiencing them.

PERCEPTION

An infant's physical actions are the vehicle of knowledge. Seeing and trying to touch or act upon the environment are the work of infancy. This early physical stage precedes and develops into the child's **mental image** of her world, and this makes later verbal labeling and speech possible.

As the child matures, perceptual acuity increases; finer detail is seen. Most children achieve 20/20 vision (adult optimum) at age fourteen. At ages two to five, vision is in the 20/45 to 20/30 range (Weymouth, 1963). It is estimated that 20 percent of preschoolers have some eye problem that, if uncorrected, could delay learning or cause vision loss (Neergaard, 2004). Experts advise parents and teachers to watch for an eye that slightly turns in or out, squinting, eye closing or head turning when the child is focusing, avoidance of coloring activities or books, and clumsiness or frustration during play. Unfortunately, many eye screening tests preformed by school staffs, instead of pediatric eye specialists or professionals, miss an accurate diagnosis.

Hearing acuity increases from birth through ages four and five (Weiss & Lillywhite, 1981). At this point, the hearing mechanisms are essentially mature and will not change greatly except through disease or injury. Ohl (2002) points out that in infancy, before babies can speak, they have already figured out many of the components of language and they know which particular sounds their language uses, what sounds can be combined to create words, and the tempo and rhythm of words and phrases. She also states that this information is important because developmental science has taught educators that there is a strong connection between early language development and reading.

> Both oral language and reading require the same types of sound analysis. The better babies are at distinguishing the building blocks of speech at 6 months of age, the better they will be at other more complex language skills at 2 and 3 years of age, and the easier it will be for them at 4 and 5 years to grasp the idea of how sounds link to letters.

Kotulak (1996) describes what happens to a child who is born deaf.

> In a child who is born deaf, the 50,000 nerve pathways that normally would carry sound messages from the ears to the brain are silent. The sound of the human voice, so essential for brain cells to learn language, can't get through and the cells wait in vain. Finally, as the infant grows older, brain cells can wait no longer and begin looking for other signals to process, such as those from visual stimuli.

Young children are noted for their desire to get their hands on what interests them. If a new child with particularly noticeable hair joins a group, hands and fingers are sure to try to explore its texture. If a teacher wears bright or shiny jewelry, some children will want to touch it. Perceptions are gathered with all sense or-

---

mental image — a "perceptual representation" or mental picture of a perceptual experience, remembered or imagined.

gans. Ornstein and Sobel (1987) believe that the main purpose of receiving, organizing, and interpreting what one encounters perceptually is to achieve constancy—a stable, constant world. Development involves changes or shifts in the way a person organizes experience and copes with the world, generally moving from simpler to more complex, from single to multiple and integrated ways of responding.

Researchers exploring infant visual preferences have pinpointed a series of changes in attention-drawing features from infancy to age five (Gibson, 1969).

Two months—change from having attention captured by movement and edges of people and objects to active search and explore

Age two to five—change from unsystematic exploring to systematically examining each feature carefully

Children get better and better at focusing on one aspect of a complex situation: they become selective in focusing their attention, and they ignore the irrelevant and distracting. Life events that cause tension and anxiety can interfere with children's emerging abilities. In complex situations children do best when perceptual distractions are minimized, allowing deep concentration.

Individual differences have been noted in the way children explore their environment and react to problems. Kagan (1971) has described **conceptual tempo** to contrast the **impulsive** child, who answers quickly and may make mistakes, with the **reflective** child, who spends considerable time examining alternatives. A second difference in perception identifies field-independent and field-dependent styles of perceiving. Field-independent children are those good at ignoring irrelevant context, whereas field-dependents tend to focus on the total context.

Visual Literacy Skill

Educators interested in visual literacy (viewing skill) describe it as a primary basic human capacity that aids learning and problem solving and that is useful across many educational disciplines—math, science, music, art, language, and so on. It is not unlike Gardner's spacial-kinesthetic intellectual theory (Gardner, 2000), which involves relationships and the ability to notice characteristics and details that lead to ideas and conclusions.

The International Visual Literacy Association (IVLA, 2004) defines visual literacy thusly:

> Visual Literacy refers to a group of vision competencies a human being can develop by seeing and at the same time having and integrating other sensory experiences. The development of these competencies is fundamental to normal human learning. When developed, they enable a visually literate person to discriminate and interpret the visible actions, objects, symbols, natural or man made, that he encounters in his environment. Through the creative use of these competencies, he is able to communicate with others. Through the appreciative use of these competencies, he is able to comprehend and enjoy the masterworks of visual communication.

A preschool example of this skill/capacity/ability would be the four-year-old boy who said sadly, "Katrin (a coteacher and gifted storybook reader) won't be here for storytime." "Why?" his teacher asked. "She's all dressed up," the boy answered. Katrin had left school for a series of dental appointments, therefore missing storytime recently.

The process of visual perception involves several basic parts, including the sensing of information along dual pathways. An understanding of this process is essential to realizing the power of visual images to move us emo-

---

conceptual tempo — a term associated with Jerome Kagan's theory of different individual pacing in perceptual exploration of objects.

impulsive — quick to answer or react to either a simple or complex situation or problem.

reflective — taking time to weigh aspects or alternatives in a given situation.

tionally and behaviorally and to influence our conscious thought.

Reggio Emilia influenced educators, who promote children's expression of ideas through graphic arts using diverse media and symbol systems and who attempt to make children's learning visual (Edwards, Gandini, & Forman, 1998). It can then be talked about, reflected upon, and refined. This can lead to a new perspective and/or a new line of child exploration, discovery, and deeper understanding.

Burmark (2002) believes visual literacy is a learned skill and discusses the learning process:

The process of becoming visually literate is not unlike the process of learning to read. When a child first looks at words on a page, the letters and spaces are meaningless. They appear to be nothing but random shapes—little curves and lines that big people keep pointing at all the time. In time, the child begins to associate those shapes with the sounds coming out of parents' mouths, and is soon able to crack the mysterious code of meaning behind the words on the page. Verbal literacy involves a person's ability to interpret and use spoken and written language to decode the world of words. Likewise, visual literacy relates to a person's ability to interpret and create visual information—to understand images of all kinds and use them to communicate more effectively.

The primary literacy of the twenty-first century will be visual—pictures, graphics, images of every kind—and students must learn to process both words and pictures and shift back and forth between them (Burmark, 2002). Glazer (2000) proposes that just as we help children become more knowledgeable and more skilled in their use of verbal communications, so too we can help them gain skill in using and understanding visual images.

Perceptual-Motor Skills

Sensory-motor (or perceptual-motor) intelligence has been defined by Jewell and Zintz (1986) as a kind of action-knowledge that is not to be con-

fused with the intelligence involving thinking and logic. The latter grows during preschool years and beyond, when children can think about and know without acting out in a physical way.

Piaget, the noted Swiss psychologist and researcher, greatly affected early childhood educators' interest in perceptual-motor activities. Piaget and others observed that automatic movements such as crying, sucking, and grasping in infants became controlled, purposeful body movements as the child grew. He speculated that physical movement served as a base for later mental abilities (Figure 4–3). His theory (1952) includes stages in the development of human intelligence, which are condensed in the following:

1. *Sensorimotor period* (birth to 18 to 24 months). Reflex actions become coordinated and perfected by physical movement and exploration of real objects and events.

2. *Preoperational period* (18 to 24 months to 7 to 8 years). Mental symbols represent what is experienced; imitation occurs. As the child matures, meanings attached to symbols grow and become detailed and precise and physical actions combine with mental actions.

FIGURE 4–3 Play structures can challenge a child's ability.

3. *Concrete operations period* (7 to 8 years to 11 to 12 years). Child's thinking now is less dependent on physical involvement or immediate perceptual cues that aid classifying, ordering, grouping, numbering, and "inner" and "cross" subgrouping of concepts.

During the preschool years, the development of motor skills is as important as the development of language skills. Just as there is gradually increasing control over language, movement, and body control in the preschool years, there is also a similar continuing increase in the ability to scan new material, organize one's perception of it, remember it, and perhaps refer to it by some label or assign meaning in some other way (Clay, 1991a). The close ties between motor activities and thought processes indicate that the child needs motor activity involving the five sense organs, as well as large-muscle use. Exactly how much of a child's mental activity is dependent on or promoted by physical activity is unknown. Most educators of young children believe that a definite, strong connection exists.

Motor skill develops in an orderly, predictable, head-to-toe fashion. Head, neck, and upper-body muscles are controlled first (large muscles before small muscles), and center of body muscles are coordinated before extremities (fingers and toes). Handedness (left or right) is usually stable by age five or six (Figure 4–4). Clay (1991a) discusses child limitations if motor experience is limited.

The child who has had limited experience to run around, to climb, to use his body effectively in activities which demand gross motor skill, will not be ready for the finer adjustments that are required in the motor skills of eye movement and hand-eye coordination in school activities.

Montessori's approach (1967a) to educating young children is noted for direct manipulation of real objects presented in sequenced form. This led to her design and construction of many tactile (touching) exploring materials

FIGURE 4–4 When cutting paper, Mario uses both hands.

for the young child. She explains her motives in the following:

The training and sharpening of the senses has the obvious advantage of enlarging the field of perception and of offering an ever more solid foundation for intellectual growth. The intellect builds up its store of practical ideas through contact with, and exploration of, its environment. Without such concepts the intellect would lack precision in its abstract operations.

Preschools are full of appealing equipment and programs that offer a planned approach to the development of sensory-motor skills. They are seen as integral parts of the curricula.

School success in later elementary years may also be influenced by the development of perceptual-motor skill.

There seems to be no clearly accepted or defined separate place within the preschool curriculum for sensory-skill development. Some centers identify a series of sequential activities and label them perceptual or sensory-motor; their main goal is skill development. In other centers, every activity is seen as developing perceptual-motor skill. Commonly, music activities and physical games deal with physical coordination and endurance. Other programs plan for perceptual-motor activities within their language arts curriculum. What remains important is that this type of emphasis be part of every center's program.

This list of objectives designed to refine perceptual-motor skills is drawn from a number of schools' and centers' goal statements.

- awareness of self in space
- awareness of self in relation to objects
- flexibility
- body coordination
- posture and balance
- awareness of spatial relationships
- rhythmic body movements
- ability to identify objects and surfaces with the eyes closed
- awareness of temperatures by touch
- ability to trace form outlines with fingers
- ability to discriminate color, shapes, similar features, different features, sizes, textures, and sounds
- ability to match a wide variety of patterns and symbols
- ability to identify parts of figures or objects when a small part of a whole is presented
- eye-hand coordination
- familiarity with the following terms: same, different, long, longer, longest, small, smaller, smallest, big, little, tall, short, wide, narrow, high, low, above, below, on, in, hard, soft, sweet, salty, sour
- ability to identify food by tasting
- ability to identify smells of various items
- ability to identify common sounds

Activities for Perceptual-Motor Development

It is difficult to think of one piece of preschool equipment or one activity that does not contain some aspect or component of perceptual-motor development. Figure 4–5 lists perceptual-motor development activities and equipment, gathered from a broad range of early childhood books and sources. It can serve as a beginning.

COGNITIVE DEVELOPMENT

There are major, opposing views concerning the link between language and thought. One view is that language is the foundation of thought and vital to a person's awareness of the world. Another view suggests that language is dependent on thinking; as intelligence grows, language grows, reflecting thoughts. Vygotsky (1980) has influenced early childhood educators' beliefs by theorizing that language is an actual mechanism for thinking, a mental tool. Language makes thinking more abstract, flexible, and independent from immediate stimuli (Bodrova & Leong, 1996). It is difficult to determine which of these ideas is closer to the truth. White (1987) states that "It's clear that you can't fully separate the topics." Harris (1990) takes the view that in learning to communicate, the child is also learning to represent experience and learning to think. Most educators will agree that language and thought are closely associated.

Gopnik, a professor of psychology and coauthor of *The Scientist in the Crib* (1999), believes very young children, including preschool children, are much more capable of learning than previously thought. The reason that young children's cognitive development and rapid learning curve may have been underestimated is that young children are learning seemingly ordinary things encountered in everyday activities and play. She suggests that adults should not assume that children will simply soak up needed knowledge from their environment, but rather, adults can provide "gentle lessons," building language skills and basic numerical understandings (Figure 4–6). Some educators may find Gopnik's views controversial and believe because children are capable learners, it is more important for educators to promote and provide for children's self-discovery. Lyons (1999a) presents a review of the importance of the child's early experiences and brain growth in the following:

From the first hour of birth, our brains are getting wired, developing tracks that will last us for a lifetime. Early brain simulation

EXPERIENCES DEALING WITH:	POSSIBLE MATERIALS AND EQUIPMENT
Visual Discrimination	
long, longer, longest	felt or paper strips; sticks; ribbons
small, smaller, smallest	nested boxes; blocks; buttons; measuring cups
big, little	blocks; jars; buttons; balloons; toys
tall, short	felt figures; stuffed toys
wide, narrow	pieces of cloth and paper; scraps of wood; boxes
high, low	jump rope; small ball; see-saw made from small board with tiny block in middle
above, below	felt pieces to place above and below a box with colored stones
Auditory Discrimination	
quiet, noisy	two boxes: one containing something that rattles (such as stones or beads) and one containing cloth or paper
bell sounds	bells of varying shapes and sizes for a variety of tones
falling sounds	feather; leaf; stone; block of wood; cotton
shaking sounds	maracas; baby rattle; pebbles inside coffee can
musical sounds	variety of rhythm instruments
Tactile Discrimination	
textures	sandpaper; tissue; stone; waxed paper; tree bark; velvet; wool; fur; cotton
outline of shapes	thin wooden circle, square, triangle, rectangle; letters cut from sandpaper
recognition of objects	four different-shaped objects, each tied in end of sock—children guess what each is by feeling it (change objects often)
hard, soft	handkerchief; rock; cotton batting; nail; sponge
Taste Discrimination	
identifying food: sweet, salty, sour	small jars: filled with salt, sugar, unsweetened lemonade
trying new foods	variety of vegetables children may not know; samples of fruit juices; honey, molasses, maple syrup
Smell Discrimination	
identifying object by smell	cake of soap; vial of perfume; pine sprig; onion; vials of kitchen spices; orange
Kinesthetic Discrimination	
lifting, racing downhill, swinging, throwing, running, jumping, climbing, bending, stretching, twisting, turning, spinning, balancing	yard and motor play materials

FIGURE 4–5 Perceptual activities.

is critical to learning and emotions play a major role in developing cognitive abilities. The critical time to build neural networks is during the first three years of life. By the time a child is three years old, his or her brain has already reached two-thirds to three-quarters of its adult size. By age five, when a child enters kindergarten, so much of the brain is developed that a child who has not acquired the necessary skills of at-

FIGURE 4-6 The adult's words accompany the child's activity choices at times.

tention, communication, and the ability to participate actively in relationships (give and take with others) is at a disadvantage. The earlier the child is provided opportunities to build this complex electrical and chemical neural network that becomes the mind, the easier it will be for the child to learn.

By age three, the small child's brain is actually twice as active as an adult brain, and this bristling activity remains at twice the level of an adult until the child reaches the age of nine or ten (Gopnik, Meltzoff, & Kuhl, 1999).

As the brain grows, it is reorganized by child experience. Experience changes the brain, but then those very changes alter the way new experience affects the brain. Children who have been passive viewers of life (through television, videos, etc.) rather than active listeners (explorers and conversationalists) may lack practice in both auditory analysis and logical, sequential reasoning skills (Healy, 1990).

Greenspan (1997) suggests that perhaps the most critical role for emotions is to create, organize, and orchestrate many of the mind's most important functions. He states

In fact, intellect, academic abilities, sense of self, consciousness, and morality have com-

mon origins in our earliest and ongoing emotional experiences.

Greenspan (1997) presents educators with what he perceives to be the fundamental sequential building blocks of mental growth based on human beings' capacity to experience emotions. They include the ability to

◆ attend.
◆ engage.
◆ be intentional.
◆ form complex, interactive, intentional patterns.
◆ create images, symbols, and ideas.
◆ connect images and symbols.

The idea that the reciprocal emotionally charged interactions between infants and young children and caregivers influence their cognitive development is not new, but increasingly it is given close attention by anyone caring for the very young.

Snow, Burns, and Griffin (1998) describe children's cognitive development as follows:

Children gain an increasingly complex and decontextualized understanding of the world as their brains develop during their first years of life. As they grow and gain experience, new neural connections are established at irregular rates, with spurts and plateaus (Peterson, 1994). Although this process is orderly, it is variable among individual children due to differences in both biological and experiential influences.

Problem solving has been associated with "literacy behaviors" that come before conventional reading and writing. McMullen (1998) explains that once children become higher-level symbolic thinkers, they are able to piece together the mental processes used in everyday problem solving with the symbols needed for reading and writing.

Classifying Information

Intellect is rooted in each particular child's stored perceptual and sensory-motor experiences. Each child interprets happenings and attempts to connect each to what she already knows. If it fits, the child understands and it all falls together. An example of this might be seen if one watches a nine-month-old learn to make noise come out of a toy plastic horn. At first, the child has no knowledge of how the horn works. When she first blows into it and it makes a toot, the child blows into it repeatedly (and usually happily). After that, the child knows how to toot the horn. Infants, toddlers, and preschoolers can be thought of as having mental groupings (classes and categories). They **classify** what they encounter, including events, people, and objects, before they have words for them. The nine-month-old just described probably has no word associated with what the child knows about the horn. Each mental grouping is distinguished by a set of distinctive features, and objects yet to be classified are examined for the presence of these features. If the horn-blowing infant reacts by trying to blow into a new toy horn of a similar shape, one can be relatively sure the child is forming a class of "horn" mentally. One can expect that this infant will try blowing into any

horn shape that comes her way. Later, a word or language symbol can be attached to a class or category, which makes it possible for the child to communicate about what the class or category means to the child or how the child feels about it. Simple words like *doggie*, *milk*, or *ball* may be among children's earliest categories of the world around them (Gelman, 1998). Gelman notes that researchers have consistently found that even newborns form sensible categories of simple sights, sounds, tastes, and smells.

Preschool teachers readily see differences between the feelings and meanings expressed by each child. For example, the way that a child reacts when meeting a new large animal may demonstrate what she knows and feels about large animals. Another child's reaction might be entirely opposite.

Putting events and experiences into classes and categories is innate—a natural mental process. The motivation to engage actively with the environment—to make contact, to have an impact, and to make sense of experience—is built into human beings. The mind yearns for order, and knowledge is built within from what is experienced. Children construct theories or hypotheses about objects and phenomena by putting things into relationships. A child's knowledge is constantly changing, for children are curious and are constantly searching for a variety of experience, fighting to overcome boredom. A new or novel idea or event may greatly affect a child by adding to or changing all a child knows and feels on a particular subject.

As a child's language ability develops, mental classes, categories, and concepts are represented symbolically by words. Words become an efficient shortcut that eliminates the need to act out by gesturing or signaling to make something known to another. Thoughts can be analyzed and evaluated internally as the child grows older. If there exists a common language system between the child and others, it can be used to reveal the child's unique self (Figure 4–7).

Piaget's (1952) terms **assimilation** and **accommodation** describe what happens when

---

classify — the act of systematically grouping things according to identifiable common characteristics, for example, size.
assimilation — the process that allows new experiences to merge with previously stored mental structures.
accommodation — the process by which new experiences or events change existing ideas or thought patterns.

FIGURE 4–7 Group play exposes children to the ideas of others.

infants and children experience something new. From the time of conception, each individual unconsciously structures (internally builds and organizes) what is perceived. If a new experience or event is perceived, it is assimilated into what already mentally existed. If it changes or modifies those existing structures (ideas or thought patterns), the new is accommodated. In other words, children attend to features that make sense to them, and learning involves adding to what is already known or modifying (changing) what is known.

Smith-Burke (1985) gives an example of a child trying to make sense of her experience in the following:

> . . . after a visit to the hospital to see her dying great-grandmother who was 101, Abby (age 4) commented, "Ya know, Dad, the Brooklyn Bridge is pretty old. It's going to die soon!" In her struggle to understand life and death, Abby had made a connection between the Brooklyn Bridge, the celebrations of its centennial, and her great-grandmother.

Although children use words adults know and recognize, the knowledge behind children's words often carries quite a different meaning and understanding.

Different Levels of Maturity

The human brain's cortex contains two differently specialized hemispheres. Each hemisphere appears designed for unique functions, different abilities, and styles of thought, including verbal and spatial thinking. Different brain areas are well defined and possess a rich concentration of certain abilities that are not equal among children (Ornstein & Sobel, 1987) (Figure 4–8). Naturally, the brain structures of some children may be developing more slowly than those of others, which might affect their ability to learn and may cause teachers to compare them unfairly with children of the same age who have developed more quickly. Consequently, teachers need to pay special attention to how they act when comparing children. Competitive, pressurized lessons can create an unhealthy "I'm not good (smart) enough" attitude that can be self-perpetuating.

Preschool children's statements that seem to be "errors in thinking" on the surface can, on deeper analysis, be seen as quite mature and understandable, not just random guesses. When a child says a camel is a horse with a hump, she should be given credit for seeing the similarity rather than merely corrected.

The child's fantasy world, which appears and is expressed in speech, should be seen as

1. seeking information (focusing)
2. seeking word labels (concept building)
3. naming, classifying, categorizing, and grouping experiences mentally—objects, ideas, etc. (general to specific; revising concepts)
4. responding and remembering (memorizing and recalling)
5. comparing and contrasting information (abstracting)
6. making inferences and predicting in general ways (predicting)
7. generalizing (inductive thinking)
8. applying known information to new situations (transferring)
9. making hypotheses (educated guesses) and predicting in specific ways (deductive thinking)

FIGURE 4–8 The child's emerging intellectual skills.

FIGURE 4–9 "Hurry, the elephants are after us!"

a giant intellectual leap (Figure 4–9). Make-believe is internal intellectual creation and/or recreation. A preschooler may say she is someone else—most often this someone else is a hero of sorts or an admired personage, usually from the movies, videos, television, or real life. There may be days when the child wishes to assume the name and identity of a friend or animal.

Many children during preschool can readily follow story sequences and identify with book characters. An in-depth discussion of preschoolers and books is found in Chapter 9.

Teachers need to realize that there are differences between adult concepts and child concepts. The child's view of the world is usually based on immediate, present happenings and beginning thought processes. A child's speech is full of many unique misconceptions, conclusions, and errors (as judged by adult standards). These errors arise because of each child's unique way of sorting out experiences— a continuous process of trying to make sense and order out of daily events. Errors based on just a few happenings may be quite logical conclusions. For example, a child may conclude that milk comes from the store, or, when looking at an *n*, that it is a "baby *m*."

Teacher's Role

Teachers who work with infants, toddlers, and preschoolers realize sensory-motor experiences and opportunities with people, toys, and room environments are early intellect-building events. Exploring and experimenting are enhanced by adult provision of materials and equipment. At some point, teachers realize some actions look as though the child thought first and then acted. At about 10 months, some infants seem to be majoring in dropping and emptying. They drop things from high-chair trays and watch the objects fall or put things into containers, drawers, or boxes and empty and refill these over and over. One has to smile and think of very young infants as active scientists. The work of Vygotsky (1980) has influenced educators' ideas of how they should verbally interact with young children to increase what children learn from new experiences. When working with two-year-olds and young three-year-olds, teachers notice a good deal of voiced external speech that accompanies play. Vygotsky theorizes that this speech helps the child order and organize thoughts, plan and develop solutions, and come to conclusions. A "zone of proximal development" is what Vygotsky calls the area between what the

FIGURE 4–10 Teachers may act as an interesting "sounding board" that encourages the child's expression of what he has discovered.

child can solve alone when faced with problems and experience and what the child can possibly solve or come to know with the help of adults or more experienced, knowing children. When adults name and explain happenings and talk about relationships, this is seen as a stimulant to both language and mental growth. A teacher trying to put into practice Vygotsky's theories would try to talk with children, becoming a catalyst who names, discusses, and prompts children's exploration and expression of what they have discovered or formulated (Figure 4–10). It also means that adults must know when not to interrupt children's thoughts when they are deeply emerged in play. Dialogue makes much more sense when children seek adult help or when they are companions in activities.

In promoting what children will store (learn and remember), teachers deal with both meaning and feelings. Each intellect-building encounter and interaction with children starts with the adult's supportive acceptance and caring. Purposeful teacher dialogue is often part of child-teacher exchanges. Its goal is to advance further discovery or to help put the discovery or experience into words. A teacher listens and observes closely. This listening may expose aspects of the child's thinking, logic, inner concepts, and feelings.

Working with children daily, teachers strive to understand the logic and correctness behind children's statements. The balance a teacher maintains between gently correcting false impressions and having children discover the misconceptions for themselves is not easy to maintain. Piaget (1952) encourages teachers to concentrate on discovery techniques.

> Each time one prematurely teaches a child something he could have discovered for himself, that child is kept from inventing it and consequently from understanding it completely.

As children try to make sense of happenings and experiences, teachers can expect to be asked questions. Four-year-olds average 300 questions a day (Leads, 2003). Teachers sometimes answer a question with a question. Skillful questioning and sensitive responses from the teacher preserve a child's feelings about expressing worthwhile ideas and makes the child more willing to speak and share. These are some examples.

- ◆ "I can see you want to have a turn talking too, Emma, and I want to hear you."
- ◆ "Would you tell us, Jacob, about the boat you put together this morning?"
- ◆ "You thought of a different way to make a hole in your paper; perhaps your friends would like to hear about it."
- ◆ "Shayne, you wanted to know how our hamster got out of his cage. Can you see an opening he might have squeezed through?"
- ◆ "Did anyone see what happened to Yang's shoe?"
- ◆ "I wonder if there's a way for three people to share two pairs of scissors?"

Teachers can support children as they converse by encouraging them to step outside their own perceptions to become aware of larger, more generalized patterns in the things they observe (Owens, 1999). Owens suggests that the processes of questioning, predicting, and testing possibilities can be learned only firsthand as children solve their own problems. Early childhood educators facilitate children's ability to come to their own conclusions and relate those conclusions to observable evidence, if possible. A teacher may also ask children to compare their ideas with one another in group conversations.

Children may gain **metalinguistic skills** during the preschool years. They are then able to "think about language." Many play with language and words and make comparisons between spoken and written words. Others may be able to analyze words into individual parts and judge what is correct word usage and what is not.

SOCIAL AND EMOTIONAL GROWTH

Interaction with other people is always a major factor in the child's language learning. Children who have positive feelings about themselves—

feelings of self-value and security—speak frequently. New contacts with adults outside the home run smoothly as the child branches out from the home.

Feelings and emotions are part of each human conversation. A child's feelings toward adults are generalized to teachers in early school years. The parent-child bond and its influence on language learning has been described by Douglass (1959).

> The feeling relationships between parents and child appear to be a tremendous factor in the child's learning of language. The child who avoids talking because he fears lack of acceptance, the child whose feelings are not understood, the standards of eating, toilet training, and behaviors which are imposed too soon, and emotional tensions existing in the home, can create surface symptoms produced by a child who attempts to cope with an unsatisfying and hostile world.

During preschool years, children form ideas of self-identity. It becomes difficult for children to believe in themselves—or their language abilities—if self-esteem is constantly undermined. Figure 4–11 suggests teacher behavior and response in communicating with children to promote social growth.

Erikson (1950) identified a series of social-emotional developments in the young child.

- (Infants) *Trust vs. Mistrust.* Trust develops from consistent care, which fulfills basic needs (food, warmth, physical contact, and so on), leading to stable and secure feelings rather than anxiousness. A positive view of life forms.
- (Toddlers and two-year-olds) *Autonomy vs. Shame and Doubt.* Children get to know themselves as separate persons. What they control, decisions they can make, and freedom they may have while still being very dependent become apparent. Awareness of inabilities and helplessness is sensed. Behavior may be testing and full of the word "no."

metalinguistic skills — the ability to think about language as a separate entity.

In communication, the teacher:

- cares and is ready to give of self.
- listens, intent on understanding.
- adds simple words when the child cannot.
- does not correct speech when this might break down willingness to speak further.
- is available for help in clarifying ideas or suggesting new play and exploring possibilities.
- senses child interests and guides to new real experiences.
- is available when problems and conflicts happen.
- enjoys time spent in child activities.
- establishes friendships with each child.
- talks positively about each child's individual uniqueness.
- is an enthusiastic and expressive communicator.
- offers friendly support while redirecting undesirable social behavior or stating rules.
- notices and respects each child's work.

FIGURE 4–11 Teacher behaviors that are helpful to the child's social growth.

- (Preschoolers) *Initiative vs. Guilt Feelings.* Experimentation and active exploration of new skills and directions occur. There are strong emotions at times in resistance to authority figures and rules, yet children are still dependent on adult approval.

Werner and Smith (1982) have studied what they describe as "resilient children," those who thrive and succeed despite what could be termed "at-risk" childhoods. As children, they displayed positive self-concepts and well-developed identities. As adults, they became socially well-integrated, confident, and autonomous adults—people who "worked well, played well, loved well, and expected well" (1982).

Social development must not be ignored in planning and conducting language activities or in trying to manage groups. Structure and rules are necessary for group living. An individual child's status in the eyes of the group can be enhanced through the sharing and appreciation of the child's ideas and accomplishments and by providing frequent opportunities for the child to lead or help lead the group in activities, which is almost always a confidence- and status-building experience.

Teachers should be concerned with a child's **social connectedness**—a term defined by Ornstein and Sobel (1987) as characteristic of people with stable, secure lives; supportive families and friends; and close ties to community and who are accepted as a worthy part of a group and able to weather life's stresses with a sense of individual identity. A teacher is in control of a school's atmosphere and works with the home and community.

Preschoolers begin to learn labels for feelings, such as happy, sad, jealous, fearful, and so on. They begin to think of others' feelings. The conscience is forming, and interest in right and wrong is expressed. Teachers who speak of their own feelings as adults set an example and provide a climate in which children's feelings are also accepted and understood.

Most children explore social actions and reactions. Perry (2000) believes young children have a strong desire to spend time with their peers (Figure 4–12). They want to have friends, and in play, they learn to make plans, negotiate, and communicate. Strong emotions accompany much of children's behavior; their total beings speak. When a child feels left out, life becomes an overwhelming tragedy; on the other hand, a party invitation may be a time to jump for joy.

Berk and Winsler (1995) suggest that it is through *symbolic/pretend play* that young children are most likely to develop both socially and intellectually. Opportunities for spontaneous child-initiated social play need to rate high on the center's agenda. The following activities can help children develop a sense of self.

social connectedness — a term associated with the following human characteristics: is stable and secure, develops close relationships with others, has supportive family and friends, and is deemed a worthy individual by others. Often seen by others as able to transcend stress and possess an individual identity.

FIGURE 4–12 Making a friend is an important step during the preschool years.

These are just a few suggestions; many more are possible.

◆ activities using mirrors

◆ activities using children's photographs and home movies

◆ tracings of the child's outline

◆ activities that involve making name tags and placing names on belongings, drawings, lockers, and projects

◆ activities that identify and discuss feelings

◆ activities concerned with personal opinions

◆ activities that show both similarity to others and individual diversity

◆ activities that build pride or membership in a group

◆ activities that identify favorite pursuits, objects, or individual choices

◆ small group activities involving cooperation

Based on research of outstanding and well-developed two- and three-year-olds (24 to 36 months), White (1986a) identified social abilities that he believes serve as a strong foundation for future schooling. Children should be able to

• get and hold the attention of adults in a variety of socially accepted ways.

• express affection or mild annoyance to adults and peers when appropriate.

• use adults as resources after determining that a task is too difficult to handle alone.

• show pride in achievement.

• lead and follow children of the same age.

• compete with age mates.

White (1986a) goes on to say

If a three-year-old has acquired this pattern of abilities, we believe she has had a "superior education" during her first years. Furthermore, such a foundation probably goes a long way toward ensuring that a child will enter school well-prepared for future development.

Teachers strive to supply a center atmosphere in which a sense of trust and security thrives. Danoff, Breitbart, and Barr (1977) believe this is crucial to each child's opportunity to learn.

Basic to the learning process is children's ability to trust themselves and the adults who teach them. This is totally interactional. Children must trust people in their world, or else they reject all that these people want to teach them. They learn to have faith in those who respect them and accept their feelings. In turn, they learn to trust themselves. In a climate that engenders trust, they want to learn and are able to learn.

Securely attached infants, those who have received responsive and developmentally appropriate care, emerge as confident, energetic toddlers with beginning awareness of self as a person. Imitative play, self-pretending play, and play that models emotions (hugging or spanking dolls) appear during the child's second year. Empathy for others who are hurt or crying may also be displayed.

As children age, self acts can be talked about and judged by the child. The author once met a young three-year-old boy who would sit himself in a chair if he thought he had misbehaved (for example, if he had purposely bumped another with a bike, pushed another, taken another's toy). He would sit only a few moments, then happily resume play. This type of guidance technique was not used by the staff, but at home, sitting in the "thinking chair" was a common occurrence. The center staff respected the child's behavior and watchfully intervened when behavior warranted urging the child's use of words to solve problems. The child's chair-sitting behavior slowly disappeared as he learned to ask for a turn and gained new social skills.

Whether young children see themselves as "valued identities" depends on their interactions with their care providers and families. As Curry and Johnson (1990) point out

> . . . all individuals need a great deal of responsive, supportive adult investment throughout childhood to enable them to construct valued identities in the complex, changing, diverse yet increasingly interactive world in which we live.

The child whose confidence stems from the security of feeling loved, valued, and appreciated as an individual is a child who continues to communicate. Adults contribute greatly to the ever-maturing view the child has of herself.

SUMMARY

Physical, intellectual, and social-emotional growth is proceeding concurrently with the child's speech. Understanding these growth systems allows teachers to use appropriate techniques and behaviors. Child characteristics and teacher-provided growth opportunities are included in Figure 4–13.

Perceptual-motor activities are an integral part of many centers' language arts programs. Many educators believe that there is a strong correlation between physical activity during this period and mental growth. Some educators present visual literacy activities to preschoolers, believing visual literacy is a learned skill (Figure 4–14).

CHILD CHARACTERISTICS	TEACHER-PROVIDED GROWTH OPPORTUNITIES
• curiosity • ability to learn • interest in what affects the child personally • focus on here and now • intellectual activity • social involvement • physical energy • symbolic thinking • language growth • emotionally "charged" • growth is in spurts with parallel and uneven growth possible in different growth areas	• varied, firsthand experience with abundant sensory materials, objects, and media • teacher enthusiasm for learning • time to explore and make own discoveries • language arts activities • planned program with developmentally appropriate activities and age-suitable classrooms and play yards • supportive assistance when pursuing a line of inquiry • an environment that encourages the development of the child's sense of trust • caring adults and a safe, secure environment • activities and routines to satisfy physical, intellectual, social, and emotional needs • cultural respect and dignity • play with peers • knowledgeable adults who take a personal interest in each individual child's welfare and growth • opportunities for child-initiated project work

*Note: This figure is not intended to be complete but rather to offer highlights of chapter text.

FIGURE 4–13 Growth and opportunity.

VISUAL LITERACY ACTIVITIES

- Read Ellen Stoll Walsh's *Mouse paint* (1999, New York: Harcourt/Red Wagon Books [board book]), which discusses how useful color can be.
- Chart color choices. Offer shell pasta that has been colored with yellow, blue, red, and green food coloring. Chart children's choice of the best one to eat. Discuss.
- Display child art with a word in 2- to 3-inch letters that closely connect. Ask children for a word that "talks" for her art. "Does your artwork need a word to go with it?" "If your painting could talk, what would it say?"
- Make graphs. Example: How many came to school in a car or bus, walked, or biked? What kind of pets do we have—dog, cat, bird, turtle?
- Use visual cards as a transition devise. The card selected by the child is the place she chooses to go next. (Book for library area, block for block area, paint can with brush for art area, etc.)
- Find round, square, and triangular objects in illustrations or photos.
- Create a flower garden wall display with a photo of a child's face or child's name in the center of each flower. Children can make flowers using various media.
- Make a "Guess-What-I-Am?" flannel board set using simply shaped objects such as a house, tree, scissors, hat, and so on. Make all shapes with no details and use the same color.
- Line up three photos and have children guess what story they tell.
- Post photographs or images representing honesty, empathy, kindness, helpfulness, beauty, work, responsibility, and so on, that expand children's understanding of human characteristics. Discuss one characteristic daily.
- After a story is read and is familiar, decide how it could be told with pictures, in dance, or with clay instead of using words.
- Collect photos or illustrations of happy, sad, frightened, and so on, multicultural faces. Discuss ones that go together and what emotion is present.

FIGURE 4–14 Visual literacy activities.

Adults need to react to and sense the correctness of what seem to be errors in children's thinking. Guiding the child's discovery of concepts is an integral part of early childhood teaching.

A child who trusts can learn. Teachers must accept children's feelings and concentrate on establishing bonds between themselves and the children. This encourages growth of abilities. The feeling tone that lies beneath each human contact and conversation creates a setting for learning.

ADDITIONAL RESOURCES

Readings

Britz, J., & Richard, N. (1992). *Problem solving in the early childhood classroom.* Washington, DC: National Association for the Education of Young Children.

Burmark, L. (2002). *Visual literacy: Learn to see, see to learn.* Alexandria, VA: Association for Supervision and Curriculum Development.

Christie, J. (Ed.). (1991). *Play and literacy development.* Albany, NY: State University of New York Press.

Elias, M., Zins, J., Weisberg, R., Frey, K., Greenberg, M., Haynes, N., Kessler, K., Schwab-Stone, M., & Shriver, T. (1997). *Promoting social and emotional learning: Guidelines for educators.* Alexandria, VA: Association for Supervision and Curriculum Development.

Honig, A. S., & Wittmer, D. S. (1996, January). Helping children become more prosocial: Ideas for classrooms, families, schools, and communities. *Young Children, 51*(2), 31–39.

Jensen, E. (2000). *Learning with the body in mind.* San Diego: The Brain Store.

Reynolds, C., & Jones, E. (1997). *Master players: Learning from children at play.* New York: Teachers College Press.

Wells, G. (1986). *The meaning makers: Children learning language and using language to learn.* Portsmouth, NH: Heinemann.

HELPFUL WEB SITES

International Visual Literacy Association (IVLA)
http://www.ivla.org
Articles, research, and conferences

National Child Care Information Center
http://www.nncc.org
Ages and stages of growth

National Institute of Mental Health
http://www.nimh.nih.gov
Risk factors affecting social and emotional
development and readiness for school; key word,
GoodStart

The highlights of Gurian and Ballew's (2003) book *The Boys and Girls Learn Differently* are covered in a Online Companion™ book report. This is an interesting volume that impacts teacher's views of how genders may differ in learning styles. Conduct a miniresearch exercise dealing with uncovering how stereotypes of appropriate preschool girls' behaviors are influenced by literature and may be changing.

STUDENT ACTIVITIES

1. Observe young children (two to four years old) in a public place (restaurant, laundromat, grocery store, park, bus, department store). What do the children seem to notice, and how do they investigate what they notice? Write down those environmental objects, people, and so on, and what features capture children's interest (for example, sound, color, texture).

2. Using the chalkboard or a large piece of newsprint (or shelfpaper), list, with a small group of other students, the teacher behaviors that might develop a sense of trust and build children's self-esteem.

3. Plan and conduct two activities with preschool children that concentrate on a perceptual-motor skill. Report your successes and failures to the group.

4. With your eyes closed, identify three objects given to you by another person.

5. Pair with another student. Taking turns, have one person take three personal articles and place them on the table or desk in front of the other person. Try to categorize these articles. How many objects can you put in the same category? Can you find a category that includes all of the items?

CHAPTER REVIEW

A. Write a brief description of Piaget's stages of intellectual development or Erickson's stages of social-emotional development.

B. Choose the category that fits best, and code the following words with the headings (1) perceptual-motor development, (2) social-emotional development, or (3) mental development.

1. trust	6. categorizing	11. security
2. concepts	7. predicting	12. generalizing
3. tasting	8. avoiding people	13. balance
4. self-awareness	9. eye-hand skill	14. conscience
5. self-image	10. body image	15. abstracting

C. Read the following teacher behaviors and verbalizations. Write the numbers of those you think would help a child develop healthy social-emotional skills.

1. Recognizing each child by name as the child enters.

2. Pointing out (to others) a child's inability to sit still.

3. Telling a child it is all right to hate you.

4. Keeping a child's special toy safe.

5. Encouraging a child's saying, "I'm not finished," when another child grabs his or her toy.

6. Saying, "Jerome (child) thinks we should ask the janitor, Mr. Smith, to eat lunch with us."

7. Saying, "Hitting makes me angry. It hurts."

8. Planning activities that are either "girls only" or "boys only."

9. Encouraging children who show kindness to others.

10. Allowing a child to make fun of another child and then neglecting to speak to the first "funmaker" about it.

11. Changing the rules and rewards often.

12. Ignoring an irritating behavior that seems to be happening more frequently.

D. Discuss children's vision and hearing acuity and perception during preschool years.

E. Choose the best answer.

1. Most centers agree that perceptual-skill development belongs
   a. somewhere in the program.
   b. in the language arts area.
   c. in the music and physical education area.
   d. to a separate category of activities.

2. The younger the child, the more the child needs
   a. demonstration activities.
   b. to be told about the properties of objects.
   c. sensory experience.
   d. enriching child conversations.

3. Trust usually _____ being able to risk and explore, when considering early childhood school attendance.
   a. follows
   b. combines
   c. is dependent upon
   d. comes before

4. Young children's thinking is focused on
   a. firsthand current happenings.
   b. abstract symbols.
   c. pleasing adults for rewards.
   d. the consequences of their behavior.

5. There is a _____ relationship between language and thought.
   a. well-understood
   b. well-researched
   c. clear
   d. cloudy

VISUAL DISCRIMINA-TION GAMES

◆ Find hidden objects in illustrations or photographs. Hide cutouts of different shapes made from any adhesive paper in illustrations or photographs. Example: Cut out geometric shapes and simple object shapes (dog, cat, hat, glove, ball, bat, flower, and so on); then stick shapes in a scene cut from a magazine. Ink stamping set shapes or commercial stickers also work. Make a key of duplicate hidden shapes on a blank sheet so that children know what they are looking for. Children can circle or color the object when found.

◆ Find objects in the same category, such as food, clothing, shoes, hats, flowers, bugs, cars, and so forth, in a picture book.

◆ Make a set of index cards onto which you have pasted food items. Make other categories. Mix them up. The task is to sort in box lids with an item in that category already pasted in the lid.

RESOURCES FOR ACTIVITIES AND GAMES

ABB Creations
http://www.itchysalphabet.com
Has sticker sets, game cards, and alphabet strips.
1-877-368-7890

Treetop Publishing
http://www.barebooks.com
Has blank, precut puzzles for making photograph puzzles and also has stickers, blank books, and game boards. Sticker sheets are available in bugs, cats, dogs, fish, and animals. These can be used to make visual matching games.

SECTION 2

Developing Language Arts Programs

CHAPTER 5
Understanding Differences

OBJECTIVES

After reading this chapter, you should be able to:

◆ Discuss Standard and non-Standard English.

◆ Describe the teacher's role with children who speak a dialect.

◆ Discuss early childhood centers' language programs for second-language learners.

◆ Identify common speech problems.

KEY TERMS

accent

auditory
    processing

bilingual

Black English

cluttering

culture

deafness

dialect

Ebonics

hearing
    disorders

otitis media

scaffolding

selective
    (elective)
    mutism

speech and
    language
    disorders

Standard
    English

subculture

✱ defecit perceptie

Excerpts from Hunter, T. (2003, May).
What about Mr. Baker? *Young Children, 58*(3),77.

A PROBLEM SOLVED

It was the first song at circle time.

Good morning, I like the shoes you've got on. / In fact, I like 'em so much, I'm gonna put 'em in a song. / In a song, in a song, / I'm gonna put you and your shoes in a song.

A boy asked if we could put hair in. *Good morning, I like the hair you've got on . . . .* The boy stopped singing. We finished the verse . . . The boy leaned toward me and said quietly, "But what about Mr. Baker?" "Who's Mr. Baker?" I asked. The boy lifted one hand from his lap and pointed to his left. I saw Mr. Baker, one of the father volunteers who came to tell stories. He was totally bald and trying not to laugh. None of the children found it funny. To leave Mr. Baker out was not funny. A girl whispered loudly to the boy, "Say *skin.*" He leaned toward me and said, "Sing skin this time." The cloud left the boy's face . . . and Mr. Baker gave him a thumbs-up, as if to celebrate another problem solved (Hunter, 2003).

QUESTIONS TO PONDER

1. This reading is an example of . . . ?

2. Why do most teachers get a "life in the classroom is like that smile" when reading this vignette?

3. What do you like about this song?

125

The United States is a multicultural society. Kantrowitz (2000) describes young children's families as follows:

> . . . a vast mosaic of race and ethnicity; married, remarried and single; gay and straight; birthparents and adoptive parents. These parents and children have broken almost all the rules for what makes a family and still affirms the most basic definition: a bond reinforced by love and caring.

Experienced teachers throughout the United States report that the children they teach are more diverse in their backgrounds, experiences, and abilities than were those they taught in the past. Census figures suggest that by the year 2025, more than half of the children enrolled in America's school will be members of "minority" groups, not of European American origin (U.S. Bureau of the Census, 1995).

The National Assessment of Education Progress, known as the nation's report card, shows an alarming trend. Between 1996 and 2000, the gap between affluent and poorer students in the United States widened in seven out of nine key indicators, such as reading, math, and science. Seventy percent of children in high-poverty schools scored below even the most basic level of reading (Alexander, 2004).

Early childhood programs at the preschool and elementary levels are experiencing an influx of Spanish-speaking children in areas of the country with little or no history of ethnic or racial diversity—a trend that is expected to continue at an increasing rate (Lundgren & Morrison, 2003).

Roughly 4.6 million English as a second-language learners were in the education system of the United States in 2000–2001 (Kindler, 2002). Thomas and Collier (2002) predict language-minority students will comprise 40 percent of the school-aged population by 2030.

Grant and Murray (1999) believe more children than ever come to school with addictions, diseases, and disorders such as fetal alcohol syndrome, and without having had sufficient sleep, food, or supervision at home. Teachers have found themselves virtually unprepared to deal with the vastly different linguistic experiences and abilities of language-diverse children (Figure 5–1).

Early childhood educators recognize that extra efforts made early in some young children's lives can prevent problems with learning to read. Children who are poor, nonwhite, and nonnative speakers are considered much more likely to fail to learn to read adequately (Snow, Burns, & Griffin, 1998).

FIGURE 5–1 Ethnic and cultural diversity is typical in America's classrooms.

Early childhood programs and elementary schools are examining older, traditional curriculum and teaching techniques. Quite simply, our school populations have changed.

Although speaking primarily about dialect-speaking African-American children, Au (1993) pinpoints the kinds of early childhood literacy programs most early childhood educators would recommend for *all* children in the culturally diverse United States.

> African American children deserve literacy programs that build on and expand their language and culture with a view toward helping them understand and value their heritage and respect the heritage of others. They deserve teachers and administrators who value diversity and recognize its presence in every child.

As with other educators, you will be searching for ways to meet young children's varied educational needs.

For many language-limited or language-diverse young children, play opportunity opens children to expression and is an integral part of any early childhood program. As Wiltz and Fein (1996) explain

> Young children have numerous ways of expressing themselves. Through play, language, movement, and stories, they reveal their feelings and thoughts, usually with ease and spontaneity. Language is one mode of expression, and play is another.

Speech and vocabulary are improved when these children keep talking or trying to communicate, particularly communication in which the child attempts to express his own needs and intentions.

Barrett (2003) has reviewed research concerning preschool enrollment and later reading achievement. His summary of short-term findings follows:

> Preschool programs can have an important short-term impact on general cognitive development and academic abilities including reading achievement. Effects appear to be larger for intensive, high-quality educational programs targeting children in poverty.

Long-term findings included the following comments. School success (primarily grade repetition and special education placement) is dependent on verbal abilities, particularly reading plays an important role in accessing new knowledge from textbook readings and other schoolwork.

Barrett concluded that preschool education in a variety of forms improves general cognitive abilities during early childhood and produces long-term increases in reading achievement. He also notes that additional research on learning and teaching in the early years could provide more guidance for teachers regarding the most productive approaches to the development of abilities and dispositions that facilitate later achievement in reading and other subject-matter areas. The National Early Literacy Panel's research on early literacy education is discussed in Chapter 6.

CHILD-FOCUSED AND CHILD-SENSITIVE APPROACHES

Program planners are experimenting and refining instructional models. These new approaches are described as child-focused and child-sensitive approaches (Figure 5–2).

A safe classroom environment—one that respects differences and uniqueness—energizes

KIDS ARE DIFFERENT

Kids are different
They don't even look the same
Some kids speak different languages
They all have a different name
Kids are different
But if you look *INSIDE* you'll see
The one with brown hair, black hair, red hair or blond hair,
Is just like you and me.

Author Unknown

FIGURE 5–2 Wall chart.

young children's ability to communicate desires, fears, and understandings (Wiltz & Fein, 1996).

The NAEYC (1996) has recommended the following:

> For the optimal development and learning of all children, educators must accept the legitimacy of children's home language, *respect* (hold in high regard) and *value* (esteem, appreciate) the home culture, and *promote* and *encourage* the active involvement and support of all families, including extended and nontraditional family units.

Noori (1996) notes that recent perspectives in education encourage teachers to celebrate diversity and reflect on their own teaching behaviors and practices. Young children explore, question, predict, discover, and interact with their early childhood teachers, who are bent on fostering natural curiosity by serving as coexplorers, feedback agents, providers of opportunity, and facilitators of children's emerging language abilities.

Teachers realize that children whose language skills or patterns are different are just as intelligent and capable as those who speak Standard English. Before discussing language differences, it is important to clarify the intent of this book. The purpose here is to help teachers (1) help the children and (2) help in such a way that it will not actually make matters worse. The teacher's sensitivity to and knowledge of a particular cultural group and different language patterns can aid a particular child's growth. Preserving the child's feelings of adequacy and acceptance is the teacher's prime goal; moving the child toward the eventual learning of standard forms is a secondary goal.

Early childhood educators strive, through professional associations, individual efforts, and attention to standards, to increase program quality. In doing so, each center needs to examine its program to ensure language learning is not seen as occurring only at language time but from the moment teachers greet each child at the beginning of the day. Every child-adult interaction holds potential for child language learning. The key question is whether each child is receiving optimum opportunity during group care to listen and speak with a savvy adult skilled in natural conversation that reinforces, expands, and extends.

Language acquisition is more than learning to speak; it is a process through which a child becomes a competent member of a community by acquiring both the linguistics and sociocultural knowledge needed to learn how to use language in that particular community (Gutierrez, 1993). It is particularly important that every individual have equal access to educational and economic opportunity, especially those from groups who have consistently been found on the bottom of the educational, social, and economic heap—African-American, Latino, Mexican-American, and Native American people (Bartoli, 1995).

STANDARD ENGLISH

Standard English is the language of elementary schools and textbooks. It is the language of the majority of people in the United States. Increasingly, preschool programs are confronted with children whose speech reflects different past experiences and a cultural (or subcultural) outlook that is different from the majority. When attending a preschool or center, these children, by practicing and copying the group's way of speaking, become aware of the group's values, attitudes, food preferences, clothing styles, and so on, and gain acceptance as group members. Some theorize that group membership influences children's manner of thinking about life's experiences.

Standard English usage is advantageous and a unifying force that brings together cultures within cultures, thereby minimizing class differences.

Standard English — substantially uniform formal and informal speech and writing of educated people that is widely recognized as acceptable wherever English is spoken and understood.

Dialect, as used here, refers to language patterns that differ from Standard American English. Dialects exist in all languages and fall into categories: (1) regional and geographical and (2) social and ethnic. Two widely recognized dialects are a Boston accent and a Southern drawl. Diverse dialects include African-American English, Puerto Rican English, Appalachian English, varieties of Native American English, Vietnamese English, and others. Dialects are just as highly structured, logical, expressive, and complex as Standard English.

Washington and Craig's study (1995) of African-American preschoolers who speak **Black English** (African-American English) found the children used advanced syntax such as linking two clauses 12 percent of the time, while their Standard English–speaking peers used complex syntax only 6 percent of the time. Black English is a systematic, rule-governed dialect that can express all levels of thought. African-American English, Black English, and the term **Ebonics** refer to a grammatically consistent speech whose key features include not conjugating the verb "to be" and the dropping of some final consonants from words (Figure 5–3). Debate has occurred concerning whether African-American English is a distinct language or a dialect. Elevating African-American English to the status of a language has evoked emotional reaction nationwide from both African-Americans and others. Early childhood professionals have mixed opinions. Many educators believe the professional teacher's primary task is to preserve children's belief that they are *already* capable speakers and also provide the opportunity for children to hear abundant Standard English speech models in classrooms. Linguists and educators do agree on the desperate need to teach some African-American children Standard English, but there is little agreement on how best to do so (Hale, 1997). Although it has long been suggested that the dialectic features of African-

1. extreme reduction of final consonants ("so" for "sold," "fo" for "four," "fin" for "find," "ba" for "bad")
2. phonological contrasts absent, such as -th versus -f at word endings ("baf" for "bath," "wif" for "with")
3. "l" or "r" deleted in words ("pants" for "parents," "doe" for "door," "he'p" for "help")
4. verb "be" used to indicate extended or continuous time ("I be walkin")
5. deletion of some "to be" verb forms ("He sick" or "She talk funny")
6. deletion of s or z sounds when using third person singular verbs ("He work all the time" or "She say don't go")
7. elimination of s in possessives ("Mama car got crashed")
8. use of two-word subjects ("Ben he be gone")
9. use of "it" in place of "there" ("It ain't none pieces left" for "There are no pieces left")

FIGURE 5–3 Some features of African-American vernacular English.

American vernacular English and its phonology create additional challenges for learning to read English, few efforts to test this hypothesis have been undertaken directly. It should also be pointed out that many African-American children speak Standard English, not African-American English.

Actually, only relatively minor variations in vocabulary, pronunciation, and grammatical forms are apparent in most dialects. As Jaggar (1980) explains

> Most variations occur in pronunciation. For example, nonstandard speakers may not pronounce the "rr" and "l" sounds and the consonant cluster at the ends of words. . . . The pronunciation rules thus produce different homonyms in children's language,

---

dialect — a variety of spoken language unique to a geographical area or social group. Variations in dialect may include phonological or sound variations, syntactical variations, and lexical or vocabulary variations.
Black English — a language usually spoken in some economically depressed African-American homes. A dialect of non-Standard English having its own rules and patterns. Also called African-American English.
Ebonics — a nonstandard form of English, a dialect often called Black English that is characterized by not conjugating the verb "to be" and by dropping some final consonants from words.

just as *their* and *there* and *pail* and *pale* do in standard English. These and other differences are shared by many regional standard dialects and should not interfere with communication. The context should be sufficient to reveal the child's meaning.

Speakers of a particular dialect form a speech community that reflects the members' lifestyles or professional, national, family, or ethnic backgrounds. Certain common features mark the speech of the members, and no two members of a particular community ever speak alike because each person's speech is unique. Unfortunately, to some, the term *dialect* can connote less-than-correct speech. Speech accents differ from one another in a number of ways and are fully formed systems. As Farr (1992) points out, children from nonmainstream groups enter school with a set of linguistic and cultural resources that in some respects differ from, and even conflict with, rather than resemble, those of the school culture.

Dialects evolve naturally over time and possess an element of regularity and systematic usage. Clay (1991a) describes child acquisition of dialectic speech and its importance.

> Some children acquire through parents and neighborhood what has been called a "nonstandard" dialect. It is an intimate possession, understood by loved ones. It reflects their membership in a particular speech group and identifies them with that group. It is personal and valuable and not just an incorrect version of a standard dialect.

Individuals react to dialects with prestige, acceptance, ambivalence, neutral feelings, or rejection based on value judgments. Stoel-Gammon (1997) believes most Americans have but a superficial acquaintance with stereotypes of American Southern or New York varieties of English, which have been experienced while listening to advertisement or entertainment media. People make assumptions about an

individual's ethnicity, socioeconomic status, and competence based on the way he speaks, and unfortunately, discrimination is not uncommon (DeGraw, 1999).

Just as a child who meets another child from a different part of the country with a different **accent** might say, "You sound funny!" so others may think of dialectic speech as crude or reflecting lack of education. Early childhood teachers are urged to remain nonjudgmental.

Dialect-speaking teachers, aides, and volunteers (working with children and families of the same dialect) offer children a special degree of familiarity and understanding (Figure 5–4).

FIGURE 5–4 The bilingual classroom aide is often the easiest adult to approach for the English language–learning child.

---

accent — prominence or emphasis given to a word or syllable through one or more of the following factors: loudness, change of pitch, and longer duration (Harris & Hodges, 1995).

A Standard English–speaking teacher may sound less familiar but affords the child a model for growth in speaking the dominant language of our society, which is important to his life opportunities.

Although a dialect (or accent) may be an advantage in one's community, it may be a disadvantage outside of that community. Farr (1992) believes

> To learn mainstream language and cultural patterns, then, is tantamount to denying one's identity and joining forces with those who are rejecting one's group.

Speaking a nonstandard variety of English can impede the easy acquisition of English literacy by introducing greater deviations in the representation of sounds, making it harder to develop the sound-symbol links needed for beginning reading.

Accented speech, for this discussion, is defined as distinctive, typical speech habits of an individual or group of individuals associated with a geographical location or region.

WORKING WITH DIALECT-SPEAKING FAMILIES

Many centers employ staff members who have dialects that the children can easily understand so that children feel at home. Teachers who speak the children's dialect may be eagerly sought and in short supply. Additional insight into the child's culture and the particular meanings of their words is often an advantage for teachers who have the same dialect as the children. They may be able to react to and expand ideas better than a Standard English–speaking teacher.

It is important for teachers to know whether the children are speaking a dialect and to understand dialectic differences. The four most common dialectic differences between Standard English and some common dialects occur in verb forms. These differences occur in the following areas.

- subject-verb agreement
- use of the verb "to be"
- use of present tense for past tense
- use of "got" for "have"

In some areas where a language other than English is spoken, part of the rules of the second language may blend and combine to form a type of English different from the standard. Examples of this are (1) English spoken by some Native American children and (2) English spoken in communities close to the Mexican-American border.

There are differing opinions about the teaching of preferred Standard English in early childhood centers. In most centers, however, preserving the child's native dialect while moving slowly toward Standard English usage is considered more desirable than immediate, purposeful instruction in standard forms. Joint parent and center discussions can help clarify program goals.

THE TEACHER'S ROLE

Understanding dialectic differences is important to the teacher's understanding of each child. To give young children the best model possible, the early childhood teacher should speak Standard English. Bruno (2003) reminds teachers that every child has been mandated to learn English in American public schools, and instruction in English always begins at some point during the child's elementary school years.

Many successful teachers have speech accents and also possess other characteristics, abilities, and useful techniques that aid young children's development of language and literacy. It matters very little to children whether the teacher speaks a bit differently from the way they speak. The teacher's attitude, warmth, and acceptance of the dialect and the children themselves is a very important consideration (Figure 5–5).

Teachers are in a unique position to build bridges rather than walls between cultures. Teachers' essential task is to create new and shared meanings with the children—new contexts that give meaning to the knowledge and skills being taught. The challenge is to find personally interesting and culturally relevant ways of creating

FIGURE 5–5 Teacher behavior, actions, and conversations can create children's positive feelings of self-value and worth.

new contexts for children, contexts in which school skills are meaningful and rewarding.

Competence is not tied to a particular language, dialect, or culture.

Galda, Cullinan, and Strickland (1993) clarify the correct techniques to encourage the child's use of Standard English.

> Encourage standard English through exposure to a variety of oral and written texts and oral language activities. Keep in mind that while competence in standard English is a worthy goal for all children, it must not mean a rejection or replacement of one language and culture with another. Rather, it should be viewed as language expansion and enrichment of the student's home language to include standard English, giving them the opportunity and the *choice* to communicate with a broader speech community.

Teachers may receive little instruction (teacher training) in the types of language be-

haviors to expect from diverse speakers or may receive little help in how to effect growth in language competencies. Teachers themselves will need to do their own classroom observation and research to identify variations and differences. Young preschoolers have learned the social speech expectations of their homes and possibly their communities. They know when to speak and when to be silent. At school they make inferences about what is appropriate based on what they hear and observe there. When children begin to use a second language or second dialect, they tend to use words in syntactic constructions found in their native speech or dialect. Because many cultures, including Chinese, Vietnamese, and some Native American communities, expect children to learn from listening, these young children may be relatively silent compared with children encouraged to be verbal from birth. Hawaiian children observed by researchers often did not like to be singled out for individual attention and tended to give minimal answers when questioned.

Because impact words and swear words are said with emotion and emphasis, it is not uncommon for these words to be learned first and used at the wrong time. In some cultures children may be encouraged to use "yes" and interrupt adult speech to signify they are in tune with the speaker.

Some facial expressions or gestures acceptable in one culture may be highly insulting in another. Even the acceptable distance between speakers of different languages varies. Teachers may interpret various child language (or lack of it) as disrespectful without considering cultural diversity. Misunderstandings between children, humorous as they may be to teachers, require sensitive handling.

A child may be a very good speaker of his particular dialect or language, or he may be just a beginner. Staff members working with the young child should respect the child's natural speech and not try to stop the child from using it. The goal is to promote the child's use of natural speech in his native dialect. Standard English can be taught by having many good speaking models available at the center for the child to hear. Interested adults, play activities, other children, and a rich language arts program can provide a setting where children listen and talk freely. Teachers refrain from correcting children's oral language errors and look for meaning and intention. They stress cooperation and collaboration and frequent conversation.

The teacher should know what parts of the center's program are designed to increase the child's use of words. Teachers can show a genuine interest in words in their daily conversations with the children. Teachers can also use the correct forms of Standard English in a casual way, using natural conversation. Correcting the children in an obvious way could embarrass them and stop openness and enthusiasm.

Delpit (1995) points out that constant teacher correction and focus on correctness impedes the child's "unconscious acquisition" of a language by raising the child's anxiety level and forcing him to cognitively monitor his every word. She provides an example of one four-year-old's resistance to being taught to answer the teacher's morning greeting with a specific "I'm fine, thank you" response. Delpit's example (1995) follows:

Teacher:	Good morning, Tony. How are you?
Tony:	I be's fine.
Teacher:	Tony, I said, How are you?
Tony:	(with raised voice) I be's fine.
Teacher:	No Tony, I said. How are you?
Tony:	(angrily) I done told you I be's fine. I ain't telling you no more.

Careful listening, skillful response, and appropriate questions during conversations help the child learn to put thoughts into words. The child thinks in terms of his own dialect or language first and, in time, expresses words in Standard English. Delpit (1995) recommends that teachers provide students with exposure to an alternative form and allow children the opportunity to practice that form in contexts that are nonthreatening, have real purpose, and are intrinsically enjoyable.

Preschool teachers must face the idea that children's accents and dialects may affect their attitudes about those children and, consequently, their behaviors. A teacher may tend to seek out and communicate with children whose speech is most similar to the teacher's speech. Extra effort may be necessary to converse and instruct. Staff-parent meetings and additional planning is a must to meet the needs of children with diverse language patterns. Pronunciation guides helping teachers say children's names correctly are gathered from parents at admitting interviews. This is just a small first step.

Working with culturally diverse children means lots of teacher observation ("kid watching"). This may give clues to each child's preferred or learned style of language interaction.

Sensitive, seasoned teachers will not put some children on the spot with direct questions or requests at group times. They may include additional storytelling or demonstration activities with young children whose native cultures use this type of approach. "Rappin," chanting, and words-to-music may appear to a greater extent in some child programs. Drama may be a way to increase language use in other classrooms. To be sure, with the great diversity in today's early childhood classrooms, teachers will be struggling to reach and extend each child's language competence. This is not an easy task.

Farr (1992) urges teachers who work with nonmainstream children to

♦ understand that their own views of the world, or ways of using language in that world, are not necessarily shared by others.

♦ be aware of the extent to which they believe their own cultural and linguistic patterns are natural or logical and realize how they may tend to interpret others' behavior according to their cultural norms.

♦ realize indirectness in language or other behavior can signify respect or politeness in one culture and dishonesty in another.

♦ understand communication between teacher and student is crucial to effective teaching and learning.

Soto's suggestions (1991), based on her own observation and review of research, follow:

1. Accept individual differences with regard to language-learning time frames. Avoid pressures to "rush" and "push" children. Young children need time to acquire, explore, and experience second-language learning.

2. Accept children's attempts to communicate because trial and error are a part of the second-language learning process. Children should be given opportunities to practice both native and newly established language skills. Adults should not dominate the conversations; rather, children should be listened to.

3. Recognize that children need to acquire new language skills instead of replacing existing linguistic skills. Afford young children an opportunity to retain their native language and culture.

4. Provide a stimulating, active, diverse linguistic environment with many opportuni-

ties for language use in meaningful social interactions. Avoid rigid grammatical approaches with young children.

5. Valuing each child's home culture and incorporating meaningful active participation will enhance interpersonal skills and contribute to academic and social success.

6. Use informal observations to guide the planning of activities, interactions, and conversations for speakers of other languages.

7. Provide an accepting classroom climate that values culturally and linguistically diverse young children.

Additional Teacher Tips

A teacher should guard against

♦ correcting children in a way that makes them doubt their own abilities.

♦ giving children the idea that they are not trying hard enough to correct or improve their speech.

♦ discouraging children's speaking.

♦ allowing teasing about individual speech differences.

♦ interrupting children who are trying to express an idea.

♦ hurrying a child who is speaking.

♦ putting children on stage in an anxiety-producing way.

SECOND-LANGUAGE LEARNERS

Many English-language learners are geographically situated in California, Texas, New York, Florida, and Illinois, and more than half have family incomes under $15,000 (August & Hakuta, 1997). Non-English-speaking children, like nonstandard dialect speakers, tend to come from low socioeconomic backgrounds and attend schools with disproportionately high numbers of children in poverty; however, many will not fit this description. A large group of professional, foreign-born technology workers' families reside in some areas. Hispanic children are the largest group of children with limited English proficiency in the United States. Papadaki-D'Onofrio (2003) reminds educators that it is "natural" to grow up speaking more than one language. In today's world, more than 70 percent of the world's population speaks more than one language.

Garcia (1991) defines language-minority children (second-language learners) as children who

1. participate primarily in non-English-speaking social and cultural contexts out of school.
2. have developed the communicative competence required for participation in those sociocultural contexts.
3. are being introduced, in substantive ways, to an English-speaking environment.

Grant (1995) describes the two categories of second-language learners as follows:

> In educational settings, young learners who speak no or very little English fall into two categories. The first includes those children who come to this country at a very young age or are born here to immigrants who have lived in areas of the world where language as well as the culture, systems of government, and social structures are quite unlike those of the United States. The second category comprises learners who are native born, such as Native Americans or Alaskan natives, yet enjoy different languages, personal histories, and cultures.

The following terms may be used in reading and research to describe second-language learners (Grant, 1995).

- **bilingual** learner
- English as a second-language student
- students with limited English proficiency
- language-minority learner
- English-language learner
- linguistically diverse student

Weitzman (1992) defines *simultaneous bilingualism* as a child younger than three years of age who learns two (sometimes more) languages at the same time and *sequential bilingualism* as a child who learns a second language after age three. Sequential acquisition is described as occurring when children begin to learn a second language after the first language is partially established (for example, when a child starts preschool or school and the school's language is different from the one at home) (Papadaki-D'Onofrio, 2003).

Children are just learning and may possess different degrees of proficiency in two or more languages (Figure 5–6). Genesee and Nicoladis (1995) discuss the vocabulary development of young preschoolers in the following:

> That bilingual children initially might have smaller vocabularies when each language is considered separately should not be surprising when one considers a couple of facts. The memory capacity of young children is limited and presumably restricts their rate of vocabulary acquisition, even if only one language is involved. Bilingual children have equally limited memory ca-

FIGURE 5–6 Arianne speaks Spanish, German, and English.

---

bilingual — refers to an individual with a language background other than English who has developed proficiency in the primary language and a degree of proficiency in English.

pacities but two sets of vocabularies to learn. Thus, at any particular point during development, one would expect them to know fewer vocabulary items in each language but approximately the same number when both languages are taken together.

White (1986b) suggests that if more than one language is spoken in the home and both languages are spoken well, the baby should be exposed to both from the beginning. However, if, as is so often the case, the first language is spoken exclusively in the home, research indicates the child should be encouraged to develop expertise in a wide range of language functions in the first language, in the expectation that these will easily transfer to the second language (English). Snow, Burns, and Griffin (1998) urge educators to consider the folly of equating learning English with developing readiness for school.

> Pre-schoolers' experiences with their own language allows, for example, phonemic sensitivity to develop; the child can then experience the alphabetic insight and get the idea needed for learning to read. The undeniable asset of a second language need not be provided at a time or in a way that could create a risk to the child's preparation for reading.

The most immediate question the teacher of a bilingual child must face is deciding how well the child is progressing in all the languages the child is learning. A full language assessment with respect to the child's first language and with respect to the child's knowledge of English will probably show the child's difficulties are limited to the acquisition of English, but testing young children in today's multicultural and economically diverse classrooms is a growing practice. Genishi (1993) points out

> The phrase "culturally sensitive" refers to whether the test is responsive to social and cultural differences among test takers. Because tests of language always reflect aspects of culture and children in early child-

hood settings belong to increasingly diverse cultures, it is impossible to construct a single test that is "culturally sensitive," that incorporates aspects of all cultures to which children belong.

When working with second-language learning preschoolers, Allen (1991) suggests

> . . . it is important that the learner receive input that is not only comprehensible but just slightly beyond his or her current level of competence.

Pressure tactics by overeager teachers that cause young children anxiety actually delay second-language acquisition.

Wong-Fillmore (1976) has identified several strategies that children used to learn English as a second language.

1. They assumed that what people are saying is directly related to the ongoing situation.
2. They learned a few stock expressions or formulaic speech and started to talk.
3. They looked for patterns that recurred in the language.
4. They made the most of the language they had.
5. They spent their major effort on getting across meaning and saved the refinement for later.

She estimates that most second-language learning children will require 4 to 6 years to be competent users of English, and some will take as long as 5 to 8 years.

Garcia and McLaughlin (1995) suggest that effective early childhood curricula should provide

- abundant and diverse opportunities for speaking and listening.
- **scaffolding** to help guide the child through the learning process.
- encouragement to take risks, construct meaning, and reinterpret knowledge within compatible social contexts.

---

scaffolding — a teaching technique helpful in promoting languages, understanding, and child solutions. It includes teacher-responsive conversation, open-ended questioning, and facilitation of children's initiatives.

The dilemma that second-language learners may face in early school experiences is likened to a "double bind" (Tabors, 1997). Tabors explains that to learn a new language, one needs to be socially accepted by those speaking the language; however, to be socially accepted, one has to be able to speak the new language. Young children often hurdle this bind using various strategies, including gestures to invite others to play and accept their company. Crying, whimpering, pointing, miming, and making other nonverbal requests may also be tried. Children collect information by watching, listening, and speculating. They may talk to themselves and experiment with sounds or rehearse what they have heard. Telegraphic and formulaic language develops. This includes naming people and objects (Tabors & Snow, 2002). Catch phrases, such as "Hey!" "Lookit," "No," "Yes," and "Mine," are commonplace. Tabors (1997) believes

> . . . early childhood educators need to be aware that social isolation and linguistic constraints are frequently a feature of young second-language learners' early experience in a setting where their home language is not available to them.

Monolingual and bilingual speakers make inferences about social and linguistic appropriateness based on continued interaction in diverse social settings (Genishi, 1985). Learning a second language includes a number of difficult tasks. The child must

- produce sounds that may not be used in the native language.
- understand that native speech sounds or words may have different meanings in the new (second) language.
- learn and select appropriate responses.
- sort and revise word orders.
- learn different cultural values and attitudes.
- control the flow of air while breathing and speaking.

Tabors (1997) cites four stages when describing the way children pursue learning a second language. She believes researchers have identified these stages as a consistent developmental sequence.

1. There may be a period of time when children continue to use their home language in the second-language situation.
2. When they discover that their home language does not work in this situation, children enter a nonverbal period as they collect information about the new language and perhaps spend some time in sound experimentation.
3. Children begin to go public, using individual words and phrases in the new language.
4. Children begin to develop productive use of the second language.

Tabors also recognizes there can still be individual differences. Researchers have identified at least four factors that may have an impact on how quickly young children acquire a second language: motivation, exposure, age, and personality (Tabors & Snow 2002). Tokuhama-Espinosa (2001) identifies additional factors that can influence second-language acquisition. These are aptitude, consistency, attitude, learning style, opportunity and suppport, and the individual characteristics of the home/family environment.

The following milestones of second-language acquisition are cited by Papadaki-D'Onofrio (2003).

- the silent period stage
- the mixing languages and code-switching stage
- the separation of languages stage
- the dominance of one language over another stage
- the stage of rapid shift in balance when input in the environment changes

Okagaki and Diamond (2000) point out that one of the most useful strategies for second-language learners is observing and following what other children are doing. By combining formulaic phrases and the names of objects, they build unique sentences. They may then make many more language mistakes.

An important technique—admitting and recognizing that a child is a classroom resource when it comes to explaining other ways of naming and describing objects or other ways of satisfying human needs—should be understood by teachers. Printed word cards in both languages can be added to the classroom to reinforce this idea.

The preschooler's language capacity helps the child who learns two languages during the early years. In preschool work, it is common to meet children who can quickly switch fluent conversation between two languages.

Research has promoted the idea that bilingual youngsters are more imaginative, better with abstract notions, and more flexible in their thinking than monolingual children. They also have been described as more creative and better at solving complex problems (Tokuhama-Espinosa, 2001). Compared with monolingual children, bilingual children may develop more awareness about the nature of language and how it works, and there is evidence that being bilingual enhances cognitive development (Genishi, 2002).

Some English-only parents, particularly more affluent ones, are either seeking tutors or early childhood programs that offer their monolingual children the opportunity to become second-language learners. Papadaki-D'Onofrio (2003) believes bilingual programs should be available for all children.

Researchers have noticed that bilingualism improves many children's self-esteem and strengthens family ties. Other researchers state it may cause family distress. Research by Wong-Fillmore (1991) has raised concerns that placing bilingual children in English-only preschools may lead to these children losing their ability to communicate effectively in their native language, which can adversely affect family relationships and conceptual development.

PROGRAM PLANNING FOR SECOND-LANGUAGE LEARNERS

Delpit (1995) urges program planners who provide second-language learning opportunities to realize that the child's exposure, comfort level, motivation, familiarity, and practice in real communicative contexts are all factors to consider.

Curriculum developers in early childhood programs that enroll other-than-English-speaking children will have to decide their position on the best way to instruct. A debate rages. One end of the debate espouses native language use, native cultural instruction, and academic learning in the child's native language before instruction in English as a second language begins. At the other end, advocates would present English on the child's first day of schooling, with minimal use of the child's native language. This view believes the earlier English is introduced and confronted, the greater the child's linguistic advantage.

Educators between these two points of view and those who see themselves as curriculum innovators using other instructional techniques will agree that other-than-English-speaking children need to be perceived as intellectually able and academically advantaged. Their teachers should hold high achievement and academic accomplishment expectations for them as they do for all enrolled children.

Most early childhood centers adopt a variety of plans and methods to help bilingual children. Techniques are often researched and studied by individual staff members and are often part of a center's in-service education. Soto (1991) describes the optimal early childhood bilingual program as supportive and natural, with a language-rich environment affording acceptance and meaningful interactions.

Most programs approach the differences existing between home and school cultures by promoting children's biculturalism. This allows children to have successful experiences in their families, where one set of values and behaviors prevails, and in school, where another set of values and behaviors may be expected (Cohen & Pompa, 1996). Emphasis on children's language development is an important part of increasing children's success at school. Cohen and Pompa suggest that, in a culturally sensitive approach, early childhood professionals would use modeling with culturally diverse children and slowly introduce and increase the practice of teaching via direct inquiry, particularly using verbal questions while they continue to use modeling. They believe this practice would help increase children's verbal skills and their ability to follow directions; they also point out that early childhood programs should strive to be more "adaptable" to the variety of approaches to learning that children bring with them.

Padron, Waxman, and Rivera (2002) define cultural-response teaching as teaching that incorporates the *everyday concerns* of students, such as important family and community issues. The goal of this type of curriculum includes helping children feel more comfortable and confident at school. Planned activities that relate to the experiences of children's everyday lives are relevant and significant. Cooperative learning activities that involve a small group of young children working together can be planned. This is recommended so that social skills and intergroup relations can develop.

What are some of the common characteristics of programs that aim to provide students with dual- or multiple-language proficiency and foster academic success? Papadaki-D'Onofrio (2003) lists the following:

◆ Development of the mother tongue is encouraged to promote cognitive development and as a basis for learning the second language.

◆ Parental and community involvement are essential.

◆ Teachers are able to understand, speak, and use with a high level of proficiency the language of instruction, whether it is their first or second language.

◆ Teachers are well trained, have cultural competence and subject matter knowledge, and continually upgrade their training.

The NAEYC (1996) supports the need for linguistically and culturally aware early childhood educators.

Within the field of early childhood education, there is a need for knowledgeable, trained, competent, and sensitive multilingual/multicultural early childhood educators. Early childhood educators who speak more than one language and are culturally knowledgeable are an invaluable resource in the early childhood setting. In some instances the educator may speak multiple languages or may be able to communicate using various linguistic regionalisms or dialects spoken by the child or family. The educator may have an understanding of sociocultural and economic issues relevant within the local linguistically and culturally diverse community and can help support the family in the use and development of the child's home language and in the acquisition of English.

Cummins (1979) advocates recruiting teacher aides and classroom volunteers who speak the child's native tongue.

The value of exposing second-language learning children to quality books cannot be overlooked (Figure 5–7). Story times and one-to-one, adult-child book readings can supply vocabulary and meaning in a way that conversational models alone cannot accomplish. Songs and music can also present language-learning opportunities. Print use in the center environment can also promote literacy development. Opportunities for abundant play and interaction with English-speaking children is another important aspect of all early childhood programs handling second-language learners.

FIGURE 5–7 The introduction of English picture books benefits second-language learners.

The most successful methods for teaching a second language include the same features mentioned in the child's learning of his first language—warm, responsive, articulate adults involved with children's everyday, firsthand exploration of the environment.

Additional suggested teacher techniques follow:

◆ Provide a safe, accepting classroom environment.

◆ Listen patiently, maintaining eye contact.

◆ Give attention to child attempts.

◆ Respond to meaning rather than speech technicalities or specifics.

◆ Promote sharing and risk taking.

◆ Make classroom activities inviting, interesting, meaningful, and successful.

◆ Emphasize key words in sentences.

◆ Point at objects or touch them while naming them, when possible (Figure 5–8).

◆ Learn how to correctly pronounce the child's name.

◆ Include the child in small groups with other child models to follow (Okagaki & Sternberg, 1993).

◆ Help the child realize he is unique and special, exactly "as is."

Tabors (1997) also suggests the following:

◆ Learn a few useful words in the child's language (for example, bathroom, eat, stop, listen).

◆ Gesture and use objects and pictures that give children additional clues, such as a picture-based daily schedule.

◆ Provide activity choices where the child does not have to interface with others—so-called safe havens.

◆ During activity times, provide enough staff that teachers can work closely with children and materials.

◆ Use a running commentary technique in interactions. "Su-yong is painting with red paint." "I'm pinning a name tag on your sweater."

◆ Choose predictable books to share.

FIGURE 5–8 Objects can be named when the teacher touches them.

◆ Work with a small group at story-reading times.

◆ Use repeated presentations of the same songs at group times.

◆ Link up English-speaking "partners" in noncompetitive games.

When working with second-language learners, a number of sources find that teachers made adjustments similar to parents when talking to their very young children, such as organizing talk around visual references (*real* objects, actions, happenings, people, and so on), using simple syntax, producing many repetitions and paraphrases, speaking slowly and clearly, checking often for comprehension, and expanding and extending topics introduced by the child.

During planned teacher-led instruction, the recognition of the child's presence, his needs, and other children's positive attitude toward and acceptance of the second-language learners in the group is paramount. Children's seating in a group, ability to sit near a "translating friend," and their participation as a comember of the group are also given close attention.

The NAEYC (1996) recommends that teachers faced with many different languages in their classrooms consider grouping together, at specific times during the day, children who speak the same or similar languages so that children can construct knowledge with others who speak their home language. It is usual for children to choose to play with others who use their language. They later branch out to other-than-home-language speakers.

Playmates of second-language learners can be encouraged not only to be aware and accepting of other children but to approach and invite them to play. Through discussion, example, and modeling, children can learn to use gestures, to use simple sentences spoken slowly, and to repeat themselves or use different words when they think their "friends" do not quite understand. Teachers stress that these new classmates may need help. One classroom regularly scheduled a short picture-book reading time when a parent shared a book in another language. Children could choose whether to attend. The book would then be repeated in English by their regular teacher, and a discussion period examined how children both attempted to understand and felt during the first reading.

For any child learning English as a second language, making a friend is an important developmental step. Educators often pair children with an English-speaking partner or ease children into play groups for the inherent social and language benefits. Individual differences always exist in any group of young second-language learners, just as they do with first-language learners.

As mentioned earlier, second-language learners can be ignored and left out of peer play. Even when trying to communicate nonverbally, they can be treated as "babies" or as invisible. They may be cast as the infant in dramatic play situations or be the object of a mothering child's attention—perhaps unwanted attention. Other children may speak to them in high-pitched voices and in shortened and linguistically reduced forms.

Reaching Parents

Home-school instructional programs have provided books, audio tapes, and "borrowed" tape players (recorders) for use in homes with limited access to English-language models and sto-

rybooks (Blum, Koskinen, Tennant, Parker, Straub, & Curry, 1995).

Tabors and Snow (2002) recommend encouraging parents to continue to maintain their first language use at home, to provide first-language literacy activities, to continue and perhaps increase everyday conversation, and to aim for quality verbal interactions with their children. They also recommend that teachers ask parents questions about what types of language exposure a child has had since birth and what literacy experiences had language associated with them. A final recommendation is assessing what each child knows and in which language.

In some cases an interpreter may be necessary. Consultants and parents are invaluable. Bilingual teachers or aides are *required* in a number of centers that serve newly arrived populations. Designing room features and planning curriculum activities that welcome and show acceptance are important staff tasks.

Behaviors Teachers Can Expect

Both teachers and children can be expected to experience some frustration. Preschoolers' language ability is amazing, and teachers will notice more and more understanding of English, then hesitant naming, followed by beginning phrases. If the teacher tries to learn the child's language, the same sequence is apparent.

When young children with a native language other than English are enrolled in an English-speaking preschool, there is usually a period of time in which they will try to use their native language with children and teachers. Eventually, they discover this is not an effective technique unless other children of their native language group are present. A realization that another language different from their own is being used transpires, along with the understanding they will need to learn this new and different language to communicate.

The use of nonverbal communication makes it possible for second-language children to be communicative even before they can use the verbal forms appropriate for situations. Children's nonverbal attempts can consist of

(1) attention getting, (2) requesting, (3) protesting, or (4) joking, but they are effective in only a limited set of circumstances.

Tabors (1997) suggests a stage in which second-language learners seem to repeat words, focusing intently and mouthing words heard in a *rehearsing* fashion. This happens not to communicate but rather to practice through repetition, which is reminiscent of younger preschoolers' private speech or self-talk during play situations. These rehearsing-like behaviors are usually done at a low volume.

The sounds and intonation of English may also be understood, practiced, and copied by the second-language learning child. The first unintelligible utterances that second-language learners often issue may be sound experimentation.

CULTURAL DIFFERENCES

Cultural differences in communicating are important for a teacher to understand because cross-cultural communication abounds in many early childhood classrooms. Diversity represents the richness and uniqueness of human life. It is something we value and share with the children we work with. The word *multidimensional* may best describe today's children.

Multicultural education hopes to prepare children for a diverse society in which differing languages are spoken and customs and values differ. Its goals include communicating despite differences, cooperating for mutual good, fighting bias and discrimination, respecting others' values, and providing for dignity and fair treatment for all.

A study of cultural differences can help teachers receive accurate messages. Gestures and body language of the cultural groups attending a center may differ widely in meaning.

Teachers interested in studying the cultures of enrolled children might use Saville-Troike's (1978) identified components of culture. These components include family structure; definitions of stages, periods, or transitions during a person's life; roles of adults and children; their corresponding behavior in terms of power and politeness; discipline; time and space; religion;

FIGURE 5–9 Teachers studying enrolled children's cultures may find that children's religious observances differ from their own.

food; health and hygiene; history; traditions; holidays; and celebrations (Figure 5–9).

The ways in which language is used in different situations vary from one culture to another. People from different cultural groups transact business in different ways; converse with one another in different ways; praise, criticize, and greet one another in different ways; and have different ideas concerning the value of education for their children. Variations in the ways cultures organize the use of language reflect differences in cultural beliefs, values, and goals concerning social roles and relationships in their group.

Thernstrom and Thernstrom (2003) posit many American-born Hispanic children may, like their foreign-born, newly arrived Hispanic contemporaries, have difficulty communicating in English. Latinos, they point out, are taking three generations to reach the same level of English competence that Asians attain by the second generation. These authors believe the sojourner status of some Mexican parents and their determination to keep alive their non-English mother tongue may account for a lack of enthusiasm to learn English.

In some cultures it is believed that children are not appropriate conversational partners for adults. Children may not be encouraged to initiate conversations about themselves or their interests, and adult talk may not be child-centered. Children may have learned not to look directly at adults when talking. Some children grow up learning that cooperation is more highly valued than competition; others do not.

Cultures are complex and changing, so understanding cultural similarities and differences can be a life's study in itself. **Culture** is defined here as all the activities and achievements of a society that individuals within that society pass from one generation to the next.

Ethnic origin is often a basic ingredient in subcultural groupings. **Subculture** is defined as other than a dominant culture. Class structure also exists in societies consisting of upper, middle, and lower income groups. Often, patterns of child-rearing vary between cultures and classes. Families may express attitudes and values peculiar to their class or culture. Attitudes and feelings of an impoverished group, for instance, often include futility, anger, violence, and loss of trust in anyone or anything.

Teachers try to determine the backgrounds of their attending families, noting the individual nature of children's home communities—housing, income, general numbers, and types of cultural groups—in an attempt to better understand children and provide language-developing experiences. Their ability to respond and relate to what attending children verbalize is enhanced.

What cultural differences can inhibit child speech? Adult models' lengths of sentences or their inability to modify their speech to child levels, neutral or negative environments, family arrangements that require children to be alone for long periods or in which children are expected to be quiet or cannot gain adult attention, and lack of books or early reading experiences are all factors that can affect speech growth. Parents are the primary language teachers in the early years, and language competence grows out of familiar situations such as seeking help or establishing joint attention—situations that provide frameworks in which children learn to make their intentions plain and to interpret the intentions of others.

Okagaki and Diamond (2000) suggest the following teacher strategies.

- Have consistent routines.
- Learn and sing a family song with the total group.
- Encourage children to share their cultural ways.
- Encourage children to share something special in their lives with others.
- Use photographs of the children's and teacher's families on a bulletin board or class book.
- Ask parents about the children's favorite music or stories.
- Invite parents to classroom activities.

PROMOTING ACCEPTANCE

Practitioners may have to field questions from children about another child's speech. Answering in an open, honest fashion with accurate information gives the adult an opportunity to affirm diversity and perhaps correct a child's biased ideas. Negative stereotypes can be diminished or dismissed. Before answering, it is a good idea to clarify what the child is really asking. Examples of teacher statements follow:

> "Yes, Paloma speaks some words you don't understand. Her family comes from Guatemala and they speak the Spanish language. Paloma is learning lots of new words at school in the language of her new country—English."

---

culture — all the activities and achievements of a society that individuals within that society pass from one generation to the next.
subculture — an ethnic, regional, economic, or social group exhibiting characteristic patterns of behavior sufficient to distinguish it from others within an embracing culture or society.

"Quan doesn't talk to you because he doesn't know our words yet. He speaks a different language at his house. He is listening, and one day he will speak. While he is listening and learning words to speak, he wants to play. Show him with your hands and words what you want him to do. He will understand."

Teachers working with culturally diverse children need to watch and listen closely. Children's behavior and movements will give clues to their well-being and feelings of safety in the group. Teachers may need to ease into situations in which unpleasant remarks or actions are directed at a newly enrolled child who speaks a different language and express sadness, such as

"Ricardo has heard some unkind and unfriendly words from you boys in the loft. He is new at school and doesn't know what our school is like. I'm going to try and help Ricardo enjoy his first day in our room."

Working with culturally diverse children also means that educators will guard against alienating children from their own cultural values.

Teachers need to remember that the ability to learn a second language and the syntax of that language is highest between birth and the age of six (Nash, 1997). The same experiences and responsive care that gave rise to language in infancy will work—lots of language activities, labeling activities, listening to picture books, musical activities, play with peers, and the adult's time and confidence in the child's grasp of new-for-him language usage. Just as repetition of experience was needed in infancy, it will again be needed.

CULTURAL AWARENESS ACTIVITIES

In planning language activities of all types, every effort must be made to make children aware of cross-cultural similarities and to explore differences. Genesee and Nicoladis (1995) urge language arts programming to draw on the linguistic, cultural, and personal experiences of language-diverse children when planning instructional activities so that opportunities that are familiar to them are provided. Parents and extended family members can be invited to share family stories and artifacts relating to theme units, learning centers, or other program components.

Young children can be exposed to the idea that people eat, sleep, wear clothing, celebrate, dance, sing, live in groups, and speak to one another in common languages, and that they do these things in ways that may be either the same as or different from the ways their families do these things. Planned activities can make comparisons, treating diversity with the dignity it deserves. Skin color, hairstyles, food preferences, clothing, and music are starting points for study. Modeling friendship and cooperation between cultures and planning activities showing dissimilar individuals and groups living in harmony is a good idea. Stories exist in all languages and in most dialects. Some centers ask children and parents to contribute family photos to use to construct a classroom "My Family" book. Each child is asked to dictate a caption for each family photo. The book is permanently placed in the class library collection. When a new child enrolls, new family photos are added. See also the Additional Resources at the end of this chapter for helpful books.

Identifying quality multicultural and multiethnic picture books is discussed in Chapter 9. Room displays, bulletin boards, and learning centers should also reflect the cultural diversity of attending children.

It is important to plan language arts programs that incorporate different cultural styles of dramatic play, storytelling, and chanting. Librarians can help teachers discover picture books and other materials written in dialects or two-language translations.

Planning for Play

Unfortunately, young children who lack language and social skills may miss out on peer play interactions, which are important in lan-

FIGURE 5–10 When deeply focused, this child prefers to be alone, but soon she will seek one of her friends.

guage learning. Educators need to be aware of those children in their classrooms who are alone (Figure 5–10) and perhaps humming, singing, and/or talking to themselves and should expend extra efforts to help them become skilled play companions (Tabors, 1997). This can have a tremendous impact on both development and social skill growth. Through play and its resultant conversations, peers are teachers. The child who cannot sustain play interactions with peers needs to learn skills associated with maintaining play relationships, which is sometimes tough enough for fluent child speakers. The acts of resolving conflict, sharing, cooperating, collaborating, and negotiating all involve the use of language and are typical parts of preschool peer play.

Planning play opportunity and experiences is an important teacher task in program planning. This involves observing individual children during play periods and promoting play groups for children experiencing difficulties.

Parents as Partners

Translating to parents the school's respect for the culture and language of the parent is not an easy job. Knowledgeable educators realize the child's long-range advantage as a future bilingual and bicultural job seeker. Every effort should be made to support parental efforts to acquaint their children with the parents' native culture and its language, literature, history, beliefs, values, and heritage.

When working in communities with newly arrived immigrant populations, teachers have to devote considerable time and study to understanding the families and lives of attending children. A strong connection between home and school should exist, with parents playing a role in program planning and as assistants or teachers in classrooms. Parents can help teachers understand the many areas of similarity and diversity that possibly exist. When parent literacy rates are less than desirable, teachers have to proceed carefully with suggestions concerning reading to their children. Wordless books and parent storytelling are alternatives. Family literacy programs are discussed in Chapter 19.

PROGRAM TYPES

Controversy exists concerning which type of program is best suited to the child learning English as a second language. Commonly found programs include the following:

Bilingual program. Two languages are used for instruction.

Transitional bilingual program. Children's first language is used as a medium of instruction until they become fluent enough to receive all of their instruction in English.

Newcomer program. Recent immigrant children with no or limited English proficiency, native literacy skills, or formal education are provided a special academic environment for a limited period. Both elementary-level and secondary-level newcomer programs exist. They provide a "welcoming environment." Teachers use instructional strategies to orient children to American life and culture. Bilingual staff familiar with the children's cultures are secured when possible. The aim of this type of intense program is to prepare children for success in English as a second language, bilingual, or mainstream classes.

Developmental bilingual program. Equal status is given to English and another language, promoting full proficiency in both languages. Academic instruction is given in English and the child's first language. Teachers are proficient in both languages. Mixing and translating language is avoided but acceptable at social times.

Two-way immersion program. This type of program provides integrated language and academic instruction for native English speakers and native speakers of another language. Students are together at least 50 percent of the day and communicate in both languages. This enables English speakers to develop second-language proficiency. Both groups' families must have an interest in bilingualism.

Tutor-assisted program. A special tutor (or teacher) works with a child for a portion of the school day.

A full-immersion program offers an age-appropriate curriculum in a language foreign to the child. Some parents, like Wardle (2003), believe the early years are the optimal time to learn a second language and that every child in America should learn an additional language besides English. Wardle notes that most full-immersion programs in the United States start in preschool, kindergarten, or first grade and that students attending these programs are fluent in the foreign language by second or third grade.

Some classrooms combine approaches and program types. The Center for Research on Education, Diversity & Excellence (2001) identi-fied elements common to successful English-language learner programs.

- ongoing and guided parental involvement
- professional development for both specialized and mainstream teachers
- the promotion of proficiency in both first and secondary languages
- the use of assessment methods linked to instructional objectives to inform instructional planning and delivery
- developmentally appropriate curriculum
- high standards for language acquisition and academic achievement
- strong staff leadership
- sheltered instruction, an approach that integrates language and content instruction
- academic instruction in English
- special strategies to make content (in activities) meaningful and comprehensive

Visuals and images (pictorial representations) used while the teacher is talking almost always improve student listening comprehension and reduce recall errors.

The role of peers as teachers in preschool classrooms is important. Teachers are urged to organize programs that encourage children to work together on tasks that involve purposeful talk based on their own interests. Developing a buddy system in classrooms that pairs a newly arrived immigrant child with a long-term second-language resident is suggested.

The second-language child may associate more with other children speaking his native language, while monolingual peers present a better English model. When grouping is planned, teachers need to recognize and be sensitive to non-English-speaking children who work well with other speakers and those who still need the security of a buddy who speaks the native language. Encouraging child friendships among children has extra meaning to teachers working with non-English speakers.

Thernstrom and Thernstrom (2003) point out that bilingual education has been a controversial subject.

For more than two decades, critics have raised questions about these classrooms (bilingual), but until recently the issue remained outside the political arena. In 1998, however, a large majority of the California electorate approved Proposition 227, which mandated the end to bilingual classes (unless parents specifically asked for them) and their replacement with "structured immersion," which means special classes for Spanish-speaking children but taught mostly in English.

Following California's lead, Arizona and Massachusetts enacted similar legislation.

Assessment

Assessment is usually undertaken when teachers suspect that a child has difficulty communicating and could profit from specialized instruction. Schools and programs affected by the federal No Child Left Behind Act or affected by local, regional, or state standards routinely conduct mandated, periodic testing. The teachers in these programs must document each child's progress. Individual learning plans are developed that include systematic instructional strategies when children are not progressing. The goal is to identify whether a child's language is less advanced than that of other children his age (delayed language) or is deficient when compared with performance on social and/or intellectual tasks (language deficit) or whether the child fits both categories. Screening tests should be conducted by trained professionals. Kotulak (1996) discusses the urgency of identification and remedial help.

> Correcting language disorders is vitally important. Children who do not develop normal language at the expected age are at high risk for all kinds of problems—academic, social, behavioral.

In attempting to assess children with suspected language impairment during early childhood years, the staff needs to remember that children learn the language of their particular community.

CHILDREN WITH SPECIAL NEEDS

Special language-development preschool centers with expert personnel are available in most communities for children with easily identifiable communication deficiencies such as hearing loss, visual impairment, and obvious speech impairments. Other children in need of special help may not be identified at the preschool level and may function within the wide range of children considered to be average or typical for preschool ages. In language arts, *learning disability* is a term that refers to a group of disorders manifested by significant difficulties in the acquisition and use of listening, speaking, reading, or writing. Most programs are reticent to label children as having language learning problems because of their lack of expertise to screen and evaluate children in a truly professional manner. Referral to speech-language pathologists or local or college clinics is suggested to parents when a question exists concerning a particular child's progress. Early childhood teachers are not speech or language pathologists and therefore should not be expected to diagnose language problems or prescribe therapy. The National Association for Hearing and Speech Action (NAHSA, 1985) divides communication disorders into two main categories.

Hearing disorders are characterized by an inability to hear sounds clearly. Such disorders may range from hearing speech sounds faintly or in a distorted way, to profound deafness. Hearing loss occurs in 3 of every 1,000 births. Identification of hearing loss and appropriate intervention *before* a baby is six months old can significantly improve language and cognitive development. See Figure 5–11, a parent resource published by the

---

hearing disorders — characterized by an inability to hear sounds clearly. May range from hearing speech sounds faintly or in a distorted way, to profound deafness.

HEARING AND UNDERSTANDING

birth–3 months
- startles to loud sounds
- quiets or smiles when spoken to
- seems to recognize your voice and quiets if crying
- increases or decreases sucking behavior in response to sound

4–6 months
- moves eyes in direction of sounds
- responds to changes in tone of your voice
- notices toys that make sounds
- pays attention to music

7 months–1 year
- enjoys games like Peek-a-boo and Pat-a-cake
- turns and looks in direction of sounds
- listens when spoken to
- recognizes words for common items like "cup," "shoe," "juice"
- begins to respond to requests ("Come here," "Want more?")

1–2 years
- points to a few body parts when asked
- follows simple commands and understands simple questions ("Roll the ball," "Kiss the baby," "Where's your shoe?")
- listens to simple stories, songs, and rhymes
- points to pictures in a book when named

2–3 years
- understands differences in meaning ("go-stop," "in-on," "big-little," "up-down")
- follows two requests ("Get the book and put it on the table")

3–4 years
- hears you when you call from another room
- hears television or radio at the same loudness level as other family members
- answers simple "who?" "what?" "where?" "why?" questions

4–5 years
- pays attention to a short story and answers simple questions about it
- hears and understands most of what is said at home and in school

TALKING

birth–3 months
- makes pleasure sounds (cooing, gooing)
- cries differently for different needs
- smiles when sees you

4–6 months
- babbling sounds more speechlike with *many* different sounds, including *p, b,* and *m*
- vocalizes excitement and displeasure
- makes gurgling sounds when left alone and when playing with you

7 months–1 year
- babbling has both long and short groups of sounds such as "tata upup bibibibi"
- uses speech or noncrying sounds to get and keep attention
- imitates different speech sounds
- has one or two words (bye-bye, dada, mama), although they may not be clear

1–2 years
- says more words every month
- uses some one- to two-word questions ("Where kitty?" "Go bye-bye?" "What's that?")
- puts two words together ("more cookie," "no juice," "mommy book")
- uses many different consonant sounds at the beginning of words

2–3 years
- has a word for almost everything
- uses two to three words to talk about and ask for things
- speech is understood by familiar listeners most of the time
- often asks for or directs attention to objects by naming them

3–4 years
- talks about activities at school or at friends' homes
- people outside family usually understand child's speech
- uses a lot of sentences that have four or more words
- usually talks easily without repeating syllables or words

4–5 years
- voice sounds clear like other children's
- uses sentences that give lots of details (e.g., "I like to read my books")
- tells stories that stick to topic
- communicates easily with other children and adults
- says most sounds correctly except a few like *l, s, r, v, z, j, ch, sh, th*
- uses the same grammar as the rest of the family

FIGURE 5–11 Speech and hearing ages. (From "How Does Your Child Hear and Talk?" Reprinted with permission from the American Speech-Language-Hearing Association.)

American Speech-Language-Hearing Association (ASLHA, 2001).

Speech and language disorders affect the way people talk and understand; these range from simple sound substitutions to not being able to use speech and language at all.

SPEECH-LANGUAGE DISORDERS

More than 13 million people in the United States have some kind of expressive speech disorder, the most common problem involving articulation—affecting an estimated 75 percent. The rest, approximately 25 percent, have language, voice, and fluency disorders, or a combination of these. Most articulation problems not caused by physical, sensory, or neurological damage respond to treatment. Nonorganic causes of problems can include:

- lack of stimulation.
- lack of need to talk.
- poor speech models.
- lack of or low reinforcement.
- insecurity, anxiety, crisis.
- shyness or lack of social confidence.

Language Delay

Language delay may be connected to one or more of the following areas (Taylor, 2002):

- syntax (putting words together to create sentences)
- semantics (using words and understanding their meanings)
- morphology (using word endings, given the language context)
- pragmatics (using social language)
- sequencing (recalling and relating events in the correct order)
- vocabulary (comprehending and using new words)

Language delay is characterized by a marked slowness in the development of the vocabulary and grammar necessary for expressing and understanding thoughts and ideas. It may involve both comprehension and the child's expressive language output and quality. Greenspan (2001) recommends

> If the child has a receptive- and expressive-language problem and is more than six months delayed, it's essential to consult a speech pathologist, and if recommended, to have speech and language therapy.

A complete study of a child includes first looking for physical causes, particularly hearing loss, and other structural (voice-producing) conditions. Neurological limitations come under scrutiny, as do emotional development factors. Home environments and parental communicating styles are examined. Dumtschin (1988) has identified possible noticeable behavior of language-delayed children.

> Language-delayed children may display limited vocabularies, use short, simple sentences, and make many grammatical errors. They may have difficulty maintaining a conversation, talk more about the present and less about the future, and have difficulty in understanding others and in making themselves understood.

> In addition to strictly linguistic problems, language-delayed children may also have difficulty classifying objects and recognizing similarities and differences. They may spend little time in dramatic play with others and may exhibit general difficulties in the classroom. The extent of concern would necessarily differ according to the age of the child.

Other behaviors a teacher might notice include:

- less variety in sentence structure.
- simple two- and three-word sentences.
- less frequent speech.

---

speech and language disorders — communication disorders that affect the way people talk and understand; range from simple sound substitutions to not being able to use speech and language at all.

◆ frequent occurrence of playing alone.

◆ less adept participation in joint planning with classmates.

Early childhood educators concerned about "late talkers'" speech and socialization should discuss their suspicions with their head teacher and directors.

Tabors (1997) points out

> Preschool educators are often called upon to assess whether a child's behavior warrants further investigation for intervention. Because communicative factors related to language affect children's social behavior, it is often difficult for preschool educators to know where certain behaviors in second-language-learning children are indicative of true developmental delay or are merely due to the pressure of the new social environment to which the children are being exposed.

Robertson and Weismer (1999) suggest that language delay may have social growth complications.

> Because of their poor communication skills, these children do not interact effectively with their peers and may be rejected socially by them. This leads to a reduction in the number of social interactions these children experience, reducing opportunities to practice and refine their social skills. In this way, language deficits and social deficiencies interact and intensify one another, potentially resulting in long-term negative social consequences.

Teachers might readily agree with the following description of a language-delayed child: "Speaks markedly less well than other children of the same age and seems to have normal ability in intellectual, motor, sensory, and emotional control areas."

An indication of language delay mentioned by NAHSA (2000) includes a child's not using words by the age of two years or not being able to speak in short sentences by age three. Another indication would be a child's inability to respond to simple requests, such as "sit down" or "come here," by age two.

Okagaki and Diamond's study of differences in the quantity of parent talk to their infants and young children (2000) estimates one child might hear 700 utterances each day while another child might hear 11,000. Children in the first category can seem to possess lower-level language skills not caused by any innate problem but rather an environmental situation.

Teachers working with language-delayed children use the following interactive techniques.

◆ gaining attention with tempting, interest-catching activities

◆ being at eye level, face-to-face, if possible

◆ establishing eye contact

◆ displaying enthusiasm and playfulness

◆ establishing a play activity involving "my turn, your turn" interaction

◆ verbalizing single words, short phrases, or short sentences depending on the child's verbal level

◆ pausing, waiting, and looking expectantly, encouraging the child's turn to talk

◆ repeating teacher statements and pausing expectantly

◆ copying the child's actions or verbalizations

◆ following the child's focus of interest with joint teacher interest

◆ probing the child's interest with logical questions

◆ maintaining close, accepting physical contact and a warm interactive manner

A few children may make a conscious decision not to try to learn Standard English or a new language when they are confronted with a language other than their native language or dialect-dominated preschool experience. A number of reasons for their choice is possible. If others enrolled or teachers speak their native language, they may believe it is not necessary or simply not worth the effort. Families may not give a high priority to learning the new language, or children's enrollment may consist of only a few mornings a week. A strong identification with a "nonstandard" dialect in a particular community may limit a child's desire to talk like an outsider. A child's decision can be temporary or long term.

The Cloistered Child

Some teachers and educators describe children with inadequate language due to lack of human interactive environments (Costa, 1990; Healy, 1990; O'Rourke, 1990). To be "cloistered" connotes isolation, separation, limited experience, meager human contact, a narrow view of the world, small or sparsely furnished living quarters, and a time-consuming devotion to spiritual contemplation and prayer. In the cloistered child the spiritual contemplation and prayer have been replaced with the passive pursuit of hours and hours of undiscussed television and/or video watching.

The cloistered child is thought to display one or many of the following characteristics.

◆ limited attention span
◆ inability to express ideas
◆ limited language and vocabulary
◆ inability to draw on past knowledge
◆ inability to listen
◆ impulsiveness (says first thing that pops into mind)
◆ lack of perseverance ("It's work. It's too hard.")
◆ blunted interest and curiosity
◆ disorganization
◆ impatience, inability to wait
◆ poor conversation skill

The curriculum recommended to develop what is seen as "missing language and missing experience" includes lots of talk, active involvement, time and play with other children, and exposure to literature. Benard (1993) would recommend opportunities to plan, which facilitates seeing oneself in control, and the promotion of child resourcefulness in seeking help from others.

The Overstressed Child

There are many different reasons why some children have stressful living situations. When young children's stress is connected to new adults, new situations, groups of peers, books and book-reading times, or talking with an adult, teachers will notice child anxiety and aversion behavior. O'Leary, Newton, Lundz, Hall, O'Connell, Raby, and Czarnecka (2002) describe degrees of stress and possible causative factors teachers should avoid.

> Mild stress enhances conscious learning, but too much stress, especially for too long a time, prevents it. Stress speaks primarily to the emotional learning system, and there it works primarily in a negative way. Extreme stress, caused by too much different information, unrelated information, or information too rapidly introduced or presented within too short a space of time, adds to a negative emotional reaction and clicks in a fear response. This memory is engraved below the level of awareness and becomes conscious as an attitude toward or feeling about the situation or topic.

Fortunately, when an unpressured, unstressful, and safe school environment is experienced, many children who display an initial aversion to certain school activities, including language arts activities, venture forth slowly and their attitudes change. Most early childhood teachers have been acquainted with children who avoid book-sharing times yet listen from another area in the classroom. After a period, they move closer, and eventually they join the read-aloud group. Their former avoidance and what seemed to be apathy becomes anticipation and enjoyment. These children often do not avoid social contact with peers but rather the newness of the group book-reading experience.

Expressive and Receptive Language Difficulties

Educators begin suspecting problems in language development when they observe attending children in a variety of classroom situations, including group times, play times, adult-child exchanges, and social interactions. In lower elementary school grades, including kindergarten, the following characteristics are cause for concern. They are seen as behaviors indicating *expressive-language difficulties* (Howard, Shaughnessy, Sanger, & Hux, 1998).

1. limited use of language
2. trouble starting and/or responding to conversation
3. heavy reliance on gesture or nonverbal communication
4. limited or nonspecific vocabulary
5. inappropriate grammar
6. difficulty in sequencing rhymes or stories

Teachers handling preschoolers may think many of these characteristics are typical of younger preschoolers and that they will be corrected as the child approaches kindergarten age. Their program planning and teacher-child interactions aim to erase difficulties, and they *would* be concerned if growth in a preschooler's language ability and skill was not observable and apparent over time. *Receptive-language difficulties* in lower elementary school are indicated by the following behavior (Howard et al., 1998).

1. limited comprehension of spoken and/or written language
2. limited understanding of abstract concepts, indirect requests, humor, or multiple word meanings

Preschool teachers, on the other hand, would not feel these characteristics apply to preschool populations. They *would* agree that part of their task is to increase both the comprehension and understanding of words and concepts encountered by attending children during their school day.

Articulation

Articulation disorders involve difficulties with the way sounds are formed and strung together, usually characterized by substituting one sound for another, omitting a sound, or distorting a sound.

If consonant sounds are misarticulated, they may occur in the initial (beginning), medial (middle), or ending positions in words. It is prudent to point out again that normally developing children do not master the articulation of all consonants until age seven or eight.

Most young children (three to five years old) hesitate, repeat, and re-form words as they speak. Imperfections occur for several reasons: (1) a child does not pay attention as closely as an adult, especially to certain high-frequency consonant sounds; (2) the child may not be able to distinguish some sounds; or (3) a child's coordination and control of his articulatory mechanisms may not be perfected. For example, the child may be able to hear the difference between Sue and shoe but cannot pronounce them differently. About 60 percent of all children with diagnosed articulation problems are boys (Rubin & Fisher, 1982).

Articulation characteristics of young children include the following:

- *Substitution.* One sound is substituted for another, as in "wabbit" for "rabbit" or "thun" for "sun."
- *Omission.* The speaker leaves out a sound that should be articulated. He says "at" for "hat," "ca" for "cat," "icky" for "sticky," "probly" for "probably." The left out sound may be at the beginning, middle, or end of a word.
- *Distortion.* A sound is said inaccurately but is similar to the intended sound.
- *Addition.* The speaker adds a sound, as in "li-it-tle" for "little" and "muv-va-ver" for "mother."
- *Transposition.* The position of sounds in words is switched, as in "hangerber" for "hamburger" and "aminal" for "animal."
- *Lisp.* The *s, z, sh, th, ch,* and *j* sounds are distorted. There are 2 to 10 types of lisps noted by speech experts.

Articulation problems may stem from a physical condition such as a cleft palate or hearing loss, or they can be related to problems in the mouth, such as a dental abnormality. Many times, articulation problems occurring without any obvious physical disability may involve the faulty learning of speech sounds.

Some children will require special help and directed training to eliminate all articulation errors, and others seem to mature and correct articulation problems by themselves.

Teacher behavior that aids the situation includes not interrupting or constantly correcting the child and making sure that others do not tease or belittle the child. Modeling misarticulated words correctly is a good course of action. Simply continue your conversation and insert the correctly articulated word in your answering comment.

Voice Disorders

Teachers sometimes notice differences in children's voice quality, which involves pitch, loudness, resonance, and general quality (breathiness, hoarseness, and so on). The intelligibility of a child's speech is determined by how many of the child's words are understandable. One can expect 80 percent of the child's speech to be understandable at age three.

Stuttering and Cluttering

Stuttering and cluttering are categorized as fluency disorders. Stuttering involves the rhythm of speech and is a complicated many-faceted problem. Speech is characterized by abnormal stoppages with no sound, repetitions, or prolonged sounds and syllables. There may also be unusual facial and body movements associated with efforts to speak. This problem involves four times as many males as females and can usually be treated. All young children repeat words and phrases, and this increases with anxiety or stress. It is simply typical for the age and is not true stuttering. A teacher should wait patiently for the child to finish expressing himself and should resist the temptation to say "slow down." An adult talking at a slow, relaxed rate and pausing between sentences can give a child time to reflect and respond with more fluency. Keeping eye contact and not rushing, interrupting, or finishing words is also recommended. Classmates should be prohibited from teasing a stutterer.

Trautman (2003) identifies the following causes of stuttering.

There are four factors most likely to contribute to stuttering, genetics (approximately 59% of all people who stutter have family members who stutter); child development (children with speech, language, cognitive or development delays are more likely to stutter); neurophysiology (research has shown that some people who stutter process speech and language in different areas of the brain than nonstutterers); and family dynamics (fast-paced lifestyles and high expectations can contribute to stuttering).

She notes that most stuttering starts between the ages of two and four and about 20 percent of children in that age group are affected. Many others in this age group go through a temporary period of "disfluency" and outgrow it. She points out that if stuttering lasts longer than 3 months and begins after age three, the child will likely need therapy to correct it.

Bowen (1998) advises

Stuttering is not a normal part of learning to talk; children's voices should not be hoarse unless they have a cold, and if children are disinterested in communicating with other people, have poor eye-contact and are aloof with people outside the family, or usually respond to what you say by echoing all or part of it back to you word-for-word, their communications skills should be assessed.

Teachers need to listen patiently and carefully to what the child is saying, not how he is saying it. A speech-language pathologist is the appropriate person to evaluate and plan improvement activities.

Cluttering is more involved with the rate of speaking and includes errors in articulation, stress, and pausing. Speech seems too fast, with syllables and words running together. Listener reaction and good speech modeling are critical aspects in lack of fluency. Bloodstein (1975) suggests that adults who work with young children

◆ refrain from criticizing, correcting, helping the child speak, or otherwise reacting nega-

---

cluttering — rapid, incomplete speech that is often jerky, slurred, spoken in bursts, and difficult to understand; nervous speech (Harris & Hodges, 1995).

tively or calling a speech problem to the child's attention.

◆ improve parent-child relationships if possible.

◆ eliminate any factors or conditions that increase problems in fluency.

◆ strengthen the child's expectation of normal fluency and self-confidence as a speaker.

Approximately 25 percent of all children go through a stage of development during which they stutter (Kay, 1996). A child who appears to be having a problem may be going through periods of normal disfluency associated with learning to speak.

About 1 in every 13 four-year-olds evaluated by their parents in the U.S. Department of Education's *National Household Education Survey* (1993) stutters, stammers, or speaks in a way not understandable to a stranger.

Yairi and Ambrose (1999) observe that it becomes increasingly evident that only a minority persists in early childhood stuttering, whereas in the majority of cases, stuttering is temporary and an often short-lived disorder that disappears without formal intervention, apparently on its own. Females evidence a higher recovery rate than do males.

Selective (Elective) Mutism

Occasionally, early childhood teachers encounter silent children. Silence may be temporary or lasting and will be a matter for teacher concern. Children with **selective (elective) mutism** are described simply as children who *can* speak but do not. They display functional speech in selected settings (usually at home) and/or choose to speak only with certain individuals (often siblings or same-language speakers). Researchers believe selective mutism, if it happens, commonly occurs between ages three and five years. Because child abuse may promote delayed language development or psychological disorders that interfere with communication, such as selective mutism, teachers need to be

concerned (Angelou, 1969). School referral to speech professionals leads to assessment and individual treatment programs. School directors prefer that parents make appointments and usually provide parents with a description of local resources.

Teachers can help professionals by providing observational data to describe the child's behavior and responses in classroom settings. Many factors can contribute to a particular child's silence or reduced speech. Consequently, teachers are cautioned to avoid a mutism diagnosis. Children's teasing or embarrassment of a child with language or speech diversity should be handled swiftly and firmly by preschool staff members.

At the beginning of the school year or a child's enrollment, some children may prefer to watch and observe rather than interact. Speakers of languages other than English may choose to play and speak only to those children and adults who understand their language. These behaviors change as English usage grows and the child feels comfortable and secure at school.

OTHER CONDITIONS TEACHERS MAY CONSIDER PROBLEMS

Frequent Crying

Occasionally, frustrated children will cry or scream to communicate a need. Crying associated with adjustment to a new situation is handled by providing supportive attention and care. Continual crying and screaming to obtain an object or privilege, on the other hand, calls for the following kinds of teacher statements.

"I don't understand what you want when you scream. Use words so I will know what you want."

"Sara does not know what you want when you cry, Billy. Saying 'Please get off the puzzle piece' with your words tells her."

---

selective (elective) mutism — a behavior that describes child silence or lack of speech in select surroundings and/or with certain individuals.

This lets the child know what is expected and helps the child see that words solve problems.

Avid Talkers and Shouters

Occasionally, children may discover that talking incessantly can get them what they want. In order to quiet children, others give in. This is somewhat different from the common give-and-take in children's daily conversations or children's growing ability to argue and state their cases.

Language becomes a social tool. A child may find that loudness in speech can intimidate others and will outshout the opposition. It is prudent to have the child's hearing checked.

Questioners

At times, children ask many questions, one right after another. This may be a good device to hold or gain adults' attention: "Why isn't it time for lunch?" or "What makes birds sing?" or "Do worms sleep?" The questions may seem endless to adults. Most of the questions are prompted by the child's natural curiosity. Teachers help children find out as much as possible and strive to fulfill the needs of the individual child. Along the way, there will be many questions that may be difficult or even impossible to answer.

Learning Disabilities

In 1996, 2.6 million children (4.36 percent of the nation's students) were in publicly funded learning-disabilities programs. Wingert and Kantrowitz (1997) list the following signs that may indicate a learning disability during preschool years.

- starts talking later than other children
- has pronunciation problems
- has slow vocabulary growth; is often unable to find the right word
- has trouble learning numbers, the alphabet, days of the week

- has difficulty rhyming words
- is extremely restless and distractable
- has trouble with peers
- displays a poor ability to follow directions or routines
- avoids puzzles, drawing, and cutting

Bregman (1997) believes, as do many others, that the sooner a problem can be identified and treated, the better the outcome is likely to be.

HEARING

A screening of young children's auditory acuity may uncover hearing loss. Rones (2004) estimates 2 to 3 infants of every 1,000 are born with significant and/or permanent hearing loss and about 70 percent get their ears checked before leaving the hospital. The seriousness of hearing loss is related both to the degree of loss and the range of sound frequencies that are most affected. The earlier the diagnosis, the more effective the treatment. Because young children develop ear infections frequently, schools alert parents when a child's listening behavior seems newly impaired.

Otitis media is a medical term that refers to any inflammation of the middle ear. There are two types of otitis media: (1) a fluid-filled middle ear without infection and (2) an infected middle ear. Researchers believe that otitis media may affect babbling and interfere with an infant's ability to hold on to a string of utterances in working memory long enough to draw meaning (Mody, Schwartz, Gravel, & Ruben, 1999). Many preschoolers have ear infections during preschool years, and many children have clear fluid in the middle ear that goes undetected. Even though the hearing loss caused by otitis media may be small and temporary, it may have a serious effect on speech and language learning for a preschool child. The common cold outranks child ear infection, and a teacher can expect one child in three to be affected on any given day.

otitis media — inflammation and/or infection of the middle ear.

If undetected hearing distortion or loss lasts for a long period, the child can fall behind. One of three children enrolled in speech and language special treatment therapy is estimated to have a history of middle ear disease (Mody et al., 1999). General inattentiveness, wanting to get close to hear, trouble with directions, irritability, or pulling and rubbing of the ear can be signs a teacher should heed. Other signs to look for include:

◆ difficulty hearing word endings such as -ed, -ing, and -s.

◆ problems interpreting intonation patterns, inflections, and stress.

◆ distractibility.

◆ inattentiveness.

◆ asking adults to repeat.

◆ confusion with adult commands.

◆ difficulty repeating verbally presented material.

◆ inappropriate responses to questions.

◆ watching for cues from other children.

◆ complaints about ears.

◆ persistent breathing through the mouth.

◆ slowness in locating the source of sounds.

◆ softer or "fuzzier" speech than others'.

◆ aggressiveness.

◆ loss of temper.

Barrio-Garcia (1986) estimates that 84,000 children younger than the age of six have hearing impairments. Hearing loss can be temporary or permanent. Early detection and treatment are important, and newborns test with reasonable accuracy.

Preschool staff members who notice children who confuse words with similar sounds may be the first to suspect **auditory processing** difficulties or mild to moderate hearing loss.

Mild hearing impairment may masquerade as

• stubbornness.
• lack of interest.
• a learning disability.

With intermittent **deafness**, children may have difficulty comprehending oral language.

Severe impairment impedes language development and is easier to detect than the far more subtle signs of mild loss. Most infected ears cause considerable pain, and parents are alerted to the need for medical help. However, if the ear is not infected or if the infection does not cause pain, the problem is harder to recognize.

SEEKING HELP

If a child's speech or language lags behind expected development for the child's mental age (mental maturity), school staff members should observe and listen to the child closely to collect additional data. When speech is unusually difficult to understand—rhythmically conspicuous, full of sound distortion, or consistently difficult to hear—this indicates a serious problem. Professional help is available to parents through a number of resources. Most cities have speech and hearing centers and public and private practitioners specializing in speech-language pathology and audiology. Other resources include:

◆ city and county health departments.

◆ universities and medical schools.

◆ state departments of education offices.

◆ the American Speech-Language-Hearing Association Directory (found by checking local medical societies).

A center's director can be alerted to observe a child whom the teacher believes may

---

auditory processing — the full range of mental activity involved in reacting to auditory stimuli, especially speech sounds, and in considering their meanings in relation to past experience and to their future use (Harris & Hodges, 1995).
deafness — hearing is so impaired that the individual is unable to process auditory linguistic information, with or without amplification.

benefit from professional help. It is important to have a referral system in place at a school or center to assist parents in finding appropriate testing and therapy for their children. Directors can establish a relationship with a therapist or agency before a referral is needed. Speech-language pathologists have master's degrees or doctoral degrees in speech-language pathology and, in many states, hold licenses.

Experts give the parents of hearing-impaired children the following advice.

◆ Help the child "tune" into language.

◆ Talk.

◆ Provide stimulation.

◆ Read picture books.

◆ Enroll the child in an infant-stimulation program during infancy.

◆ Schedule frequent doctor examinations for the child.

◆ Join parent organizations with a hearing-impairment focus.

◆ See the child simply as a child rather than "a hearing-impaired child."

ADVANCED LANGUAGE ACHIEVEMENT

Each child is unique. A few children speak clearly and use long, complex, adultlike speech at two, three, or four years of age. They express ideas originally and excitedly, enjoying individual and group discussions. Some may read simple primers (or other books) along with classroom word labels. Activities that are commonly used with kindergarten or first-grade children may interest them. Just as there is no stereotypical average child, language-talented children are also unique individuals. Inferring these language-precocious children are also intellectually gifted is not at issue here. Young children with advanced language development may exhibit many of the following characteristics. They:

◆ attend to tasks in a persistent manner for long periods.

◆ focus deeply or submerge themselves in what they are doing.

◆ speak maturely and use a larger-than-usual vocabulary.

◆ show a searching, exploring curiosity.

◆ ask questions that go beyond immediate happenings.

◆ demonstrate avid interest in words, alphabet letters, numbers, or writing tools.

◆ remember small details of past experiences and compare them with present happenings.

◆ read books (or words) by memorizing pictures or words.

◆ prefer solitary activities at times.

◆ offer ideas often and easily.

◆ rapidly acquire English skills, if bilingual, when exposed to a language-rich environment.

◆ tell elaborate stories.

◆ show a mature or unusual sense of humor for age.

◆ possess an exceptional memory.

◆ exhibit high concentration.

◆ show attention to detail.

◆ exhibit a wide range of interests.

◆ demonstrate a sense of social responsibility.

◆ show a rich imagination.

◆ possess a sense of wonder.

◆ enjoy composing poems or stories.

◆ use richly descriptive expressions in talking.

◆ are highly attentive listeners who remember exceptionally well.

◆ read print in the classroom environment.

◆ write recognizable words or combinations of words.

◆ have sophisticated computer skills.

◆ express feelings and emotions, as in storytelling, movement, and visual arts.

◆ use rich imagery in informal language.

◆ exhibit originality of ideas and persistence in problem solving.

◆ exhibit a high degree of imagination.

Preschoolers may recognize letters early and show an early focus on printed matter. They may be interested in foreign languages and also exhibit correct pronunciation and sentence structure in their native language. Young children may show an advanced vocabulary and may begin reading before they start preschool.

Unfortunately, young children who may be quiet, noncompetitive, and nonassertive; who are slow to openly express feelings; who rarely make direct eye contact, ask questions, or challenge something they know is incorrect; and who are acting appropriately according to their home culture may not be identified as gifted or talented (Hartley, 1991). For indicators of outstanding verbal and linguistic abilities in Native American and Alaskan native children, see Figure 5–12.

Kitano (1982) recommends planning activities within the regular curriculum that promote advanced children's creative thinking. Suggestions include providing the following opportunities.

- *Fluency opportunities.* Promoting many different responses, for example, "What are all the ways you can think of to . . ."
- *Flexibility opportunities.* Having the facility to change a mind-set or see things in a different light, for example, "If you were a Christmas tree, how would you feel . . ."

INDICATORS OF OUTSTANDING VERBAL AND LINGUISTIC ABILITIES

knows signs and symbols of the traditional culture (at an earlier age and beyond the average child)

recalls legends in greater depth and detail after fewer hearings

is more aware of cultural norms and standards at an earlier age

has great auditory memory

remembers details of "everyday" events

makes up elaborate stories, songs, and/or poems

FIGURE 5–12 Identifying outstanding talent in American Indian/Native American (AI/NA) students. (From U.S. Department of Education, Office of Educational Research and Improvement, *Identifying outstanding talent in American Indian and Alaska Native students.* Washington, DC: 1994.)

- *Originality opportunities.* For example, "Make something that no one else will think of."
- *Elaboration opportunities.* Embellishing of an idea or adding detail, for example, presenting a doodle or squiggle and asking, "What could it be?"

Schwartz (1980) notes that teachers can help ward off problems for advanced students and recommends

- grouping children with others of high ability or shared interests.
- arranging situations in which the child's gifts or talents are seen as a group asset.
- using special assignments and varied projects.

If teachers believe as does Gardner (1993) in the theory of multiple intelligences (one of which is linguistic intelligence) and in the occurrence of "crystallizing experiences," those teachers will notice the young children who take particular interest in and react overtly to some attractive quality or feature of a language arts activity. These children will tend to immerse themselves and focus deeply. This may be the child who loves to act roles in dramatic play, collects words, is fascinated with books or alphabet letters, creates daily rhymes, or displays similar behaviors. The child may persist and spend both time and effort on his chosen pursuit and displays a definite intellectual gift.

Renzulli (1986) defines the talented child's behavior as

. . . evident when a child displays three basic characteristics . . . above-average ability, creativity, and "task commitment," that special drive and motivation that causes some individuals to persist at something when others would quit.

SUMMARY

Teachers work with children who may differ greatly in language development. One of the teacher's roles is to carefully work toward increasing the child's use of words while providing a model of Standard English through activities and daily interaction. Teachers are careful not to give children the impression that their speech is less worthy than that of others.

Program goals should be clearly understood, as should the needs and interests of children who have developed a language that differs from the language of the school. Cultural differences exist, and teachers need to be aware of them to understand the young child. The teacher can provide activities that start at the child's present level and help the child grow, know more, and speak in both Standard English and his native speech. Bilingual programs have become a political issue, and some states have eliminated them.

Speech differences require observation and study by a center's staff. Various language behaviors are considered speech and language disorders. Parents can be alerted to whether their children may need further professional help.

ADDITIONAL RESOURCES

Readings

Ballenger, C. (1999). *Teaching other people's children: Literacy and learning in a bilingual classroom.* New York: Teachers College Press.

Beaty, J. J. (1997). *Building bridges with multicultural picture books: For children 3–5.* Upper Saddle River, NJ: Merrill/Prentice Hall.

Dyson, A. H. (1997). *What difference does difference make?* Urbana, IL: National Council of Teachers of English.

Greenspan, S. I., & Wieder, S. (1998). *The child with special needs.* Menlo Park, CA: Addison Wesley.

Herman, R., & Stringfield, S. (1997). *Ten promising programs for educating disadvantaged students: Evidence of impact.* Arlington, VA: Educational Research Service.

Meier, D. R. (2003). *The young child's memory for words: Developing first and second language and literacy.* New York: Teachers College Press.

Miller, J. (2000). Teaching and learning about cultural diversity. *The Reading Teacher, 53*(8), 666–667.

Opitz, M. F. (Ed.). (1998). *Literacy instruction for culturally and linguistically diverse students.* Newark, DE: International Reading Association.

Swick, K. (2004). *Empowering parents, families, schools and communities during the early childhood years.* Champaign, IL: Stipes Publishing.

Vail, P. (1980). *The world of the gifted child.* New York: Penguin.

Wong-Fillmore, L. (1991). When learning a second language means losing the first. *Early Childhood Research Quarterly, 6*(3), 323–346.

HELPFUL WEB SITES

American Educational Research Association (AERA)
http://www.aera.net
Information on the academic achievement of second-language learners (search publicatons)

Council for Exceptional Children
http://www.cec.sped.org
Publications and readings

ERIC Clearinghouse on Disabilities and Gifted Education
http://ericec.org
Gifted recent immigrant children, warning signs in preschoolers' language development

National Association for Bilingual Education
http://www.nabe.org
Teaching bilingual children

National Black Child Development Institute
http://www.nbcdi.org
Issues concerning African-American children

National Center for Children in Poverty
http://cpmcnet.columbia.edu
Investigate articles about child poverty

National Parent Information Center
http://npin.org
Communication disorders, second-language learners

Additional readings, Web sites, and views about legislation affecting children with disabilities are found in the Online Companion™. Presented material promotes sharing your ideas with peers. The criteria for the selection of Afrocentric books and their key elements, identified by C. W. Hudson, is available. You may wish to take part in a discussion forum examining the issue of authors who can best depict African-Americans in preschool picture books.

STUDENT ACTIVITIES

1. List and describe dialects found in your community. Give a few sentence examples of each.

2. In small groups, discuss what you believe are essential factors to language growth that may be missing in a disadvantaged child's background.

3. Interview the director of a center that cares for bilingual and/or economically disadvantaged young children. Ask what techniques are used to increase a child's language ability. If there is no early childhood center in your community, give examples of goals or techniques used to increase a child's language ability that you have found from research at a library.

4. Observe a "silent-at-group-time" child at play and lunch period. Try to assess when or under what circumstances this child is more verbal. Take written notes.

5. Tape record your voice in a 5-minute conversation with a friend. Have the recording analyzed for dialect, accent, and Standard English usage.

6. Consider the following children. Which children would you suggest to the center's director as possibly needing further staff observation and expert assessment and help?

   a. Trinh seems roughly 2 years behind his age mates in vocabulary.

   b. Rashad turns his head toward speakers frequently.

   c. Barbara rubs one ear constantly.

   d. Doan cups his hand behind his ear when spoken to.

   e. Tisha is three, and one cannot understand her words.

   f. Bill says, "Why did his folks call him Rocky, when he can't say it? He says his name is Wocky Weed!"

   g. Maria is always stressed and extremely tense when she has to speak.

   h. Ben has a monotonal quality to his voice.

   i. Becky reads difficult books without help.

7. React to the following concerning Ebonics: Pride and self-respect should be the result of effort and achievement. The issue of providing students who are already at an educational disadvantage with a false sense of pride in the misuse of language is an unwise course of action.

8. Observe a second-language learner during a 30-minute classroom free play period. Record (1) nonverbal attention-getting behaviors, (2) requesting behavior, (3) protesting in a nonverbal way, or (4) joking nonverbally. Briefly describe observed actions such as clever or not-so-clever attempts to gain others' attention by making noises, using a toy in a new way, pointing, seeking help, holding a hand out, threatening, hoarding with body, turning a back to another talking to him, or doing funny things and outrageous actions. Note any other expressions or nonverbal behavior that is present. Share with your training group.

CHAPTER REVIEW

A. Answer the following questions.

1. How can a teacher learn about the cultural background of a child?
2. What should be the teacher's attitude toward children whose speech is different from the teacher's?

B. Define these speech terms.

1. dialect
2. bilingual
3. stuttering
4. auditory
5. cluttering
6. articulation
7. otitis media
8. subculture
9. Standard English

C. Select the correct answer. Some items have more than one correct answer.

1. Standard English is
   a. the language of textbooks.
   b. often taught slowly to non-Standard English speakers.
   c. often different from English spoken in a dialect.
   d. needed for success in any line of work.

2. Early childhood centers try to
   a. teach children Standard English during the first days of school.
   b. make sure each child feels secure.
   c. plan activities in which language-different children have an interest.
   d. provide for each child's development of word use in his own dialect.

3. Teachers should be careful to guard against
   a. correcting children's speech by drawing attention to errors.
   b. thinking that only Standard English is correct and therefore better than English spoken in a dialect.
   c. giving children the idea that they speak differently or "funny."
   d. feeling that children who come from low-income homes are always disadvantaged when compared with children from middle-income homes.

4. Young children with speech errors
   a. rarely outgrow them.
   b. may need special help.
   c. often do not hear as well as adults.
   d. can hear that what they say is different but do not have the ability to say it correctly.

5. Bilingualism in the young child is
   a. always a disadvantage.
   b. sometimes a disadvantage.
   c. a rewarding challenge to the teacher.
   d. a problem when schools make children feel defeated and unaccepted.

D. Explain why designations such as Asian or Hispanic do not accurately describe a child's culture.

E. List teacher techniques appropriate and useful in classrooms enrolling second-language learners.

F. Describe the speech characteristics of children who speak African-American English.

161

CHAPTER 6

Achieving Language and Literacy Goals through Program Planning

OBJECTIVES

After reading this chapter, you should be able to:

◆ Define literacy.

◆ Describe emerging literacy in early childhood.

◆ Discuss program planning for early childhood language arts activities.

◆ Describe assessment's role in program development.

◆ Write an activity plan for a language arts activity.

KEY TERMS

activity plans
assessment
behaviorism
child-initiated
  curricula
constructivist
  theory
cultural literacy
curriculum

curriculum
  models
early literacy
interactionists
literacy
nativists
nurturist
phonological
  awareness

psychosocial
  theory
social
  constructivist
  theory
visual literacy
webbing

BAD LANGUAGE

A group of Asian, second-language learning boys were fast friends and often played only with each other. I was continually attempting to help them branch out and play with other children. It was slowly happening.

At pick-up time, Mrs. Vu, Tan's mother, asked to speak with me. She had brought her neighbor with her as an interpreter. Moving out of children's earshot, her neighbor expressed Mrs. Vu's concern. Some of the Asian boys were using very inappropriate words in their native tongue, laughing and then running away. They had been careful in avoiding the activity when Phan, the bilingual assistant, was near. After assuring Mrs. Vu that we shared her concern and would monitor the children's behavior, I thanked her. Fortunately, we had an impending parent meeting.

QUESTIONS TO PONDER

1. Could some kind of planned child activity be used with this problem?

2. What words would you use if you "caught" the boys in this behavior?

3. Should this be discussed at a parent meeting, or is this a private matter?

This text divides language arts into four interrelated areas—listening, speaking, writing, and reading—and also discusses **visual literacy** (viewing) as a primary, basic human capacity closely related to the other language arts areas. Increasing the child's understanding of how language arts combine and overlap in everyday preschool activities helps increase language use and **literacy**.

Stanchfield (1994) discussed the interrelatedness of literacy skills.

> I believe the most important thing we have learned in the last 30 years about the teaching and learning of reading is dynamically concerned with the interrelatedness of the literacy skills of listening, speaking, thinking, reading, and writing. For the last 15 years, I have been convinced that reading cannot be taught in isolation, but rather as a part of the whole—the "gestalt" of the literacy. Students who can listen, discuss, and think with words are going to learn to read more effectively. Conversely, students who have meager vocabularies, limited sentence structure, short attention spans, and little experience with expressive language may have almost insurmountable difficulties in learning to read. Today, most educators stress the word literacy rather than reading.

To that end, a unified and balanced approach is recommended, one in which the teacher purposefully shows and stresses connections between areas (Figure 6–1).

Past practice and program planning in schools attempted to promote literacy by dividing (segmenting) language arts into separate skills. Educators now believe separate, but integrated, skill activities can be part of a balanced language arts program.

The ages of the children and their past life experiences will decide the literacy activities one plans and presents and the techniques and adult-child interaction one deems appropriate.

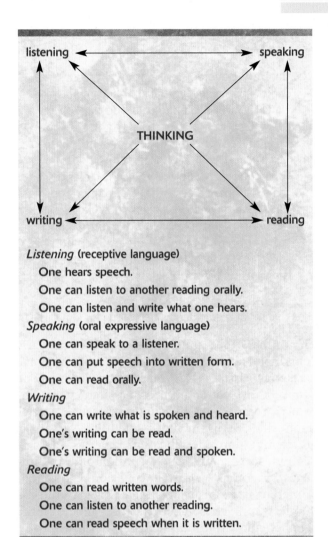

Listening (receptive language)
  One hears speech.
  One can listen to another reading orally.
  One can listen and write what one hears.
Speaking (oral expressive language)
  One can speak to a listener.
  One can put speech into written form.
  One can read orally.
Writing
  One can write what is spoken and heard.
  One's writing can be read.
  One's writing can be read and spoken.
Reading
  One can read written words.
  One can listen to another reading.
  One can read speech when it is written.

FIGURE 6–1 Interrelations of early childhood language arts.

Classes may include children who have been in group settings for 3 or 4 years, children with identified disabilities, children with exceptional abilities, children who are already independent readers, and children just beginning to acquire some basic literacy knowledge (National Association for the Education of Young Children &

---

visual literacy — the ability to interpret and communicate with respect to visual symbols in media other than print.
literacy — involves complex cognitive interactions between readers and their texts and between background knowledge and new information. It involves both skill and knowledge and varies by task and setting. Different types of literacy are described—prose, document, quantitative, academic, workplace, and functional.

the International Reading Association, 1998). MacDonald (1992) observes

> Literary development happens within relationships. When you acknowledge an infant turning the page of a book or a toddler turning a picture book right-side-up, you are encouraging their interest in literacy. When you listen intently as a preschooler reads you the scribbles she carefully made on a sheet of paper, and encourage a school-age child to explain to a friend how he figured out the meaning of an unfamiliar word, you are helping children feel good about themselves as readers and writers.

VISUAL LITERACY

A number of researchers and experts in the early childhood literacy field believe a fifth language arts area exists—visual literacy, or viewing. The goals of instruction in the visual literacy area involve promoting young children's visual perception skills. This includes attending behavior, discrimination, identification, analysis, classification, sorting, and categorization of visual images. In other words, a conscious noting of differences in visual characteristics would be undertaken. These characteristics include line, shape, color, number, texture, movement, and dimension, as well as other features. This area of study can be referred to in professional readings as visual thinking, visual intelligence, visual awareness, visual sensitivity, and visual arts. It specifically relates to a child's perception of the world; how she reacts to viewed images; how she sees, feels, and interprets emotions evoked; and how she arrives at insights concerning visual media (Weismann, 1970).

Visual literacy, based on the idea that visual images are a language, is defined as the ability to understand and produce visual messages. It is believed useful in improving children's cognitive, reading, writing, and creative skills.

Visual literacy is currently a field of educator research and study. It has become increasingly important with young children's growing exposure to television, videos, video games, computers, and other mass media. The ability to think critically and visually about images is a crucial skill.

Stieglitz (1972) points out that the sense of sight is the most important and basic source of information concerning one's surroundings. It involves not only the eye but also the brain. Elements of the visual perception process are light, the visual stimulus and its characteristics, eye receptors, the individual's past experiences, previous knowledge and ideas, and the individual's purposes, interests, and feelings at a particular time. All those who work with young children may easily relate to this discussion if they have observed young children's diverse reactions to a person in a white jacket or a large dog. Piaget (1970) noted that individuals do not simply record reality but rather transform it by operation of the intellect.

Morrow and Asbury (2003) believe the visual literacy area should be integrated with writing, listening, reading, and speaking. They also suggest using instruction that is spontaneous, is authentic, and involves children in problem solving; in addition, they recommend instruction that is direct, explicit, and systematic.

Telling stories using a photograph or drawing, eliciting the children's ideas about story content after viewing a picture book's cover, and discussing children's creative art and the details therein or the emotions they feel give teachers insights into what children are thinking. These activities also reveal children's ability to read visual cues and symbols.

Barry (1999) believes that when children and adults are in the process of viewing an image or living an event, they are not involved in the process of critical analysis. Rather, they are absorbing those images and events and actively seeking meaning. This would account for children's barrage of questions if they are interested in a new classroom animal, and also explains a good number of their other questions.

When children are encouraged to express their learning through the medium of graphic arts, they are "documenting" their understandings. They are encouraged to do this in the Reggio Emilia approach (Edwards, Gandini, & Forman, 1998). Children trace and revisit their discoveries and actions, making them visible.

The exercise is an instrument for reflection and language development as the children discuss their creations. Reflection can lead to a refinement of ideas and further search and discovery. It can be likened to a scientist writing the results of her inquiry, which then leads to further questions.

DeMarie (2001), discussing Reggio Emilia children, believes

> It is only through the process of repeated investigations using many different languages to represent their learning (Edwards, Gandini, & Forman, 1998) that these children begin to see the world differently and to attain higher levels of thinking about the topic.

The primary literacy of the twenty-first century will be visual. Pictures, graphics, and images of every kind will be processed. Children need experience shifting from word to illustration and illustration to word. Visual literacy truly has become the new currency of learning (Burmark, 2002). Burmark points out that good teachers have always known that visual images help learners understand and remember complex information and abstract concepts.

LITERACY GOALS—SKILL AND KNOWLEDGE

Any discussion of literacy begins with a working definition. Hillerich (1976) defines it as a

> ... demonstrated competence in communication skills which enables the individual to function, appropriate to age, independently of society and with a potential for movement in society.

Literacy can be conceptualized as a relatively narrow domain of academic inquiry and educational practice (as in reading), or it can be viewed as an encompassing way of being that involves all forms of communication, including mathematical, scientific, and artistic forms (Graue, 1999). Leu (1997) believes that literacy definitions change and reflect different historical, cultural, and technological development. He sees literacy in our "information age" as essential to enabling individuals access to the best information in the shortest time, which allows them to identify and solve the most important problems and communicate this information to others. Reading and writing, he believes, are but the initial layers of the richer and more complex forms of literacy required in Internet use.

Young children usually progress by developing what Gordon Wells (1981) termed "a knowledge of literacy," which includes oral language skill and an awareness that written (graphic) marks and words carry meaning. Wells believes that early superficial understandings about picture books and being read to lead to a much deeper understanding of the purpose of reading. Psycholinguistic theory focuses on the unique nature of human language—humans' innate search for order, structure, and meaning (Itzkoff, 1986). Using this theory as a basis, one can see how children will initiate their own first steps toward literacy when exposed to language-rich environments in which positive attitudes develop toward language arts activities.

Cambourne's definition of literacy (1988) stresses one's ability to use language in daily life.

> ... literacy is a word which describes a whole collection of behaviours, skills, knowledge, processes and attitudes. It has something to do with our ability to use language in our negotiations with the world. ... Reading and writing are two linguistic ways of conducting these negotiations. So are talking, listening, thinking, reflecting, and a host of other behaviours related to cognition and critical thinking.

Hirsch (1987) describes **cultural literacy** as the possession of the basic information needed to thrive in the modern world and the only sure avenue for culturally disadvantaged children to escape social determinism. He

---

cultural literacy — literacy that reflects a culture's knowledge of significant ideas, events, values, and the essence of that culture's identity.

points out that children from poor and illiterate homes tend to remain poor and illiterate unless educational opportunities "break the cycle." Gutierrez (1992) describes "being socialized to literacy" and consequently developing behaviors such as knowing how and when to ask questions, how to hold a book or listen to a story, and when and how to participate.

WHAT IS EARLY LITERACY?

The term **early literacy** refers to young preschool children's language arts behaviors, concepts, and skills that precede and can develop into a literacy that includes reading, conventional writing, and a larger body of literary knowledge at later ages. It considers change over time in how the child thinks about literacy and the strategies the young child uses in her attempts to comprehend or produce oral or written language (Teale, 1995).

The act of printing shapes with an underlying logic and children's "pretending to read" behaviors are viewed as early forms of reading and writing. Teale (1995) believes additional research is necessary to understand exactly "what clicks into place" when young children make the transition from early reading and writing to conventional reading and writing. Instructional strategies and behavioral techniques based on that knowledge and the identification of what children understand, and which skills aided that transition, enhance a school's planning ability.

Early literacy learning happens best in an atmosphere of social collaboration with peers and others who are more literate (Morrow, Burks, & Rand, 1992). Vygotsky (1978) believes the helpful support of more competent others provides a "scaffolding," which promotes children's learning.

Figure 6–2 shows a set of particular accomplishments that a successful learner is likely to exhibit during preschool years (Snow, Burns, &

Griffin, 1998). The authors state that the list is neither exhaustive nor incontestable, but rather it captures many highlights of the course of literacy acquisition revealed through research.

Early home-life activities start children's literacy development by providing early experiences, including parent models and attitudes. A home environment can be stimulating or drab, rich in literate activities or deficient. Children actively search for meaning, and many have lives in which print surrounds them and picture books are familiar. If children have observed and participated in home reading or writing activities, they often enter group care with interest and a positive attitude and an early head start in literacy. They are able to enjoy symbolic dramatic play and eventually attempt symbolic representation in art, block building, and a variety of other preschool pursuits. They communicate ideas, discuss meanings, and probe adults and other children for information.

Children's growing awareness and "knowledge of literacy" is evident and can include all language arts areas—reading, writing, speaking, listening, and visual representing.

Becoming literate is an extension and companion of language arts skill. Most children acquire spoken language without sit-down instruction; they all become speakers, although at different rates, unless disease, illness, or trauma interferes. Literacy, on the other hand, is not attained unconsciously or by all in our society. Literacy requires a shared body of understanding, much of which involves a common exposure to oral and written material and a level of proficiency in listening, speaking, reading, and writing. Snow, Burns, and Griffin (1998) point out that we are seeing an increasing number of students who are not proficient readers, and surveys show 4 in 10 children experience literacy problems. Literacy acquisition involves a commitment of time and mental energy plus opportunity. At the preschool level, this commitment is a teacher's commitment to presenting a program that both promotes language arts

---

early literacy — speaking, listening, print awareness and writing behaviors, reading of alphabet letters and words, and other skills that evolve and change over time, culminating in conventional literacy.

Birth to Three-Year-Old Accomplishments	Three- and Four-Year-Old Accomplishments
• recognizes specific books by cover • pretends to read books • understands that books are handled in particular ways • enters into a book-sharing routine with primary caregivers • vocalization play in crib gives way to enjoyment of rhyming language, nonsense word play, etc. • labels objects in books • comments on characters in books • looks at a picture in book and realizes it is a symbol for real object • listens to stories • requests/commands adult to read or write • may begin attending to specific print such as letters in names • uses increasingly purposive scribbling • occasionally seems to distinguish between drawing and writing • produces some letterlike forms and scribbles with some features of English writing	• knows that alphabet letters are a special category of visual graphics that can be individually named • recognizes local environmental print • knows that it is the print that is read in stories • understands that different text forms are used for different functions of print (e.g., list for groceries) • pays attention to separable and repeating sounds in language (e.g., Peter, Peter, Pumpkin Eater, Peter Eater) • uses new vocabulary and grammatical constructions in own speech • understands and follows oral directions • is sensitive to some sequences of events in stories • shows an interest in books and reading • when being read a story, connects information and events to life experiences • asks questions and makes comments demonstrating an understanding of literal meaning of story being told • displays reading and writing attempts, calling attention to self: "Look at my story." • can identify 10 alphabet letters, especially those from own name • "writes" (scribbles) message as part of playful activity • may begin to attend to beginning or rhyming sound in salient words

FIGURE 6–2 Developmental accomplishments of literacy acquisition. (Reprinted with permission from *Preventing reading difficulties in young children.* © 1998 by the National Academy of Sciences. Courtesy of the National Academy Press, Washington, DC.)

skills and furnishes a shared body of understandings appropriate to preschoolers.

Elementary school reading textbooks in the early part of the twentieth century were collections of classics. The idea of reading levels was not in vogue, but rather the goal was to have every child learn information and skills that were common to the democratic literate public electorate of the time and necessary to the development of a truly educated man or woman. Literacy today is still seen by some as only referring to reading and writing, but many researchers and early childhood educators are concerned with the taproots of literacy, which may be developed during the preschool period (Figure 6–3).

In the age of electronic information processing, meaningful participation is increasingly dependent on literacy. Few researchers deny that millions of adult Americans are severely hampered by literacy problems and that minorities and the poor are disproportionately affected.

To be considered functionally literate, one must have a knowledge of shared, common information that is neither set down on paper nor explicitly stated in oral communication and that provides the basis for understanding what is heard or read. This idea is well illustrated by a similar phenomenon that occurs when outsiders listen to an in-group whose members have learned a specialized technical vocabulary. For instance, suppose we are having a difficult

FIGURE 6–3 Teachers are trained to encourage child speech during daily interactions and conversations.

time understanding a group of computer buffs. We know they are speaking our language, but we cannot understand the bulk of their conversation. As they chat about bits, vaporware, or TCP/IP, they do not make any sense to us. We then consider ourselves functionally illiterate in computer terminology.

Real access to concepts of cultural heritage comes from extended, personally meaningful conversations with adults, books read aloud at home, and children reading by choice for pleasure.

In programming, an integrated language/literacy approach that emphasizes child comprehension is suggested by current research. It is one of the goals of this textbook.

LANGUAGE ARTS INSTRUCTION—HISTORICAL ROOTS

In examining the historical roots of language arts instruction one could start with the seventeenth-century theorist René Descartes (1637), a French philosopher who theorized God was responsible for the innate knowledge in children's minds, and the English philosopher John Locke (1690), whose contrasting position suggested children's minds at birth were blank and unfilled. Locke (1974) also emphasized the importance of experience in learning.

In the eighteenth century, Johann Pestalozzi (1764), of Switzerland, and Friedrich Froebel (1782), of Germany, presented yet another theory based on their personal interactions with young children. Both Pestalozzi (Rusk & Scotland, 1979) and Frobel (1974) recommend providing "natural environments" in which sensory experiences produced learning and a natural unfolding. Play, they suggested, was the route to learning and intellectual development, along with social, emotional, and physical development. Froebel introduced the notion of treating children with kindness, caring, and compassion. Many schools of the day offered sparse, sterile classroom environments, with young children seated in rows or at desks. Teachers required rote memorization, repetition, imitation, and strict adherence to rules.

The Twentieth Century—The United States

At the turn of the twentieth century in the United States, schools for very young children copied primary school practices, which included memorization and recitation by children, or they simply offered custodial care. Disciples of Froebel began to influence educators along the eastern seaboard. In the Midwest, John Dewey (1916) began experimenting with young children's educational environments. His beliefs promoted a curriculum of teacher-selected topics, themed units of study, and theme-influenced play areas. His ideas affected language arts instructional practices. Dramatic play and book (library) areas are still with us today, and theme instruction has not disappeared. Formal skill-building activities were avoided, but on-the-spot recognized learning moments (teachable moments) were capitalized upon.

Gesell (1940) was also influential. He suggested that developmental "norms" existed, and he believed child growth and development were based on maturation. For teachers to be effective, they needed to determine children's readiness for learning on a child-by-child basis.

Maria Montessori (1967b), a physician-educator who in 1907 started her experiment by bringing education to children in a deprived area of Rome, captured the attention of some American early educators. Ideas concerning children's learning through sequenced manipulative materials and special teacher-child interactions were recognized. Some group lessons were believed necessary, but primarily, children self-selected from offered activities and decided their own pace, followed their own interests, and worked independently. Montessori instruction stressed order and self-contained tasks. Activities (tasks) had definite beginnings and endings, which included returning materials to shelves. Many of Montessori's activities approached learning in a sensory way; some were color-coded.

In the 1930s and 1940s, it was widely believed that early exposure to formal reading instruction should wait until the necessary skills had been achieved, which was believed to be somewhere around the age of six and a half (Morphett & Washburne, 1931). These prerequisite skills included auditory and visual discrimination, visual motor skills, and large motor skills.

A change occurred in early educational practice during the 1960s and the 1970s. Children were beginning to be seen as constructing their own knowledge of language from their experiences. Rather than moving children to higher levels of development, teachers were to match experiences to children's current levels. Piaget (1876–1980), a Swiss psychologist noted for his observations of his own children, studied children's cognitive growth. Piaget (1952) theorized that a child passed through several sequential stages and was unable to move to a higher stage unless she had mastered the stage before it. Learning took place as the child made sense of her environment through exploration and manipulation.

Chomsky (1968), who was concerned with language development, believed that acquiring language was a matter of the child's gaining facility with the rules that govern language. These rules were not learned but rather ingested as the child matured and interfaced with more mature speakers. Chomsky theorized that the human brain was uniquely equipped with a language facilitator that he called the "language acquisition device" (LAD).

Vygotsky (1978), considered a sociocultural theorist, suggested that learning took place through social contact and the development of what he termed "private speech." He emphasized the development of socially shared cognition with adults and peers. Adults (or others) assist the child to move ahead in development by noticing what the next logical step might be.

Morrow and Asbury (2003) have listed how different early constructivist approach theorists and philosophers influenced language arts program planning.

- use of prepared and natural environments for learning
- equal emphasis on social, emotional, physical, and intellectual development
- supportive adults who encourage social interaction to aid learning
- a focus on learning rather than teaching
- awareness that children must be actively involved to learn

Research in the twentieth century provided educators with additional data focusing on oral language, early writing attempts, development of early reading skills, and alphabet letter learning and/or alphabet sound learning. It emphasized early reading behaviors. This supported the idea that literacy began at birth. Educators tended to believe children's natural interests were promoted in a rich literary environment with activities that aided the development of literacy skills rather than direct reading-readiness instruction. The whole-language movement promoted young children's access to quality literature together with listening, discussion, and active participation in dramatizing, storytelling, poetry, and picture-book times. Early writing and print-related language arts activities gained wide acceptance.

With the focus shifting to developmentally appropriate practice in the 1990s (Bredekamp & Copple, 1997) and educators becoming aware of instructional strategies to prevent reading difficulties through the development of early skills during the preschool years (Snow, Burns, & Griffin, 1998), early childhood language arts instruction has changed again. Many programs are working toward a balanced approach to programming, combining a developmental environment and appropriate literacy experiences accompanied by research-based, skill-offering activities that purposely aim at equipping children with skills that aid a smooth transition from nonreader to beginning reader to reader.

In the Present

At no time in our history has the public eye been more intently focused on children's reading and writing achievement and classroom instruction in reading and writing (McGee, 2003a).

The National Reading Panel Report (2000) urges an organized and systematic instructional approach with highly qualified teachers. Morrow and Asbury (2003) describe a comprehensive approach to early childhood literacy.

> . . . grounded in a rich model of literacy learning that encompasses both elegance

and the complexity of reading and language arts processes. Such a model acknowledges the importance of both form (phonemic awareness, phonics, mechanics, etc.) and function (comprehension, purpose, meaning) of the literacy processes, and recognizes that learning occurs most effectively in a whole-part-whole context. This type of instruction is characterized by meaningful literacy activities that provide children with both the skills and the desire to achieve proficiency and lifelong literacy learning (Gambrell & Mazzoni, 1999). Teaching literacy skills and providing opportunities for learning literacy skills are appropriate for young children as long as the teaching methods are appropriate to the child being taught. In such a program, teachers provide numerous literacy experiences that include the integration of reading, writing, listening, speaking, and viewing.

Early childhood instruction may now include the task of assessing developing skills and making instructional plans based on **assessment** data.

In the many early childhood programs that are impacted by the Elementary and Secondary Education Act that includes the No Child Left Behind Act (U.S. Department of Education, 2002), periodic assessment is the rule—not the exception—in kindergartens. Early childhood programs are being asked to be accountable by providing data that show young children's progress in the language arts. They are also asked to work more effectively with children's parents.

The quest to identify the most appropriate and effective means by which to promote children's literacy development has remained elusive for the last half century (New, 2002). New believes the term *emergent literacy* has been replaced by *early literacy*. From this perspective, literacy begins at birth, is ongoing, and is influenced and interpreted by the surrounding sociocultural context. New suggests that as a nation, we are far from common ground on considering the meanings, means, or purposes of early literacy.

Reading educators and early childhood educators in the late 1990s attempted to forge a

---

assessment — a broad repertoire of behaviors involved in noticing, documenting, recording, and interpreting children's behaviors and performances. Testing is a subset of assessment behaviors in which performances are controlled and elicited in standardized conditions (Johnston & Rogers, 2002).

consensus about what literacy is and how best to promote it. Goldenberg (2002) notes that the broad outlines of this consensus suggest that productive early literacy experiences and effective literacy instruction must address distinguishable, yet ultimately interrelated, aspects of literacy.

◆ understanding and use of print functionally (reading and writing for communication, expression, etc.)

◆ understanding and use of the "alphabetic principle" (**phonological awareness**, letter names and sounds, efficient and automatic decoding, i.e., writing)

◆ motivation and interest in using print for a variety of purposes

◆ language, cognitive skills, and knowledge necessary for comprehension and communication

Although there is no consensus about how much of each aspect should be stressed, a successful literacy program addresses each of these in sufficient depth and breadth to promote literacy growth in the earliest and later years.

Goldenberg (2002) points out that although there is wide agreement that phonological awareness is an important aspect of being ready to learn to read, there is less agreement about whether children should receive direct instruction and training or whether phonological awareness should be accomplished in "natural language" activities such as poems, chants, songs, and so on. Proponents of strong phonics and phonological awareness training recommend a different set of practices than do those who emphasize the more contextual uses of literacy. Most early childhood educators search for meaningful and functional literacy activities, but many are introducing phonological skill-developing opportunities that encourage children to generate rhymes and segment phonemes within meaningful activities.

The joint position statement of the International Reading Association and the NAEYC, *Learning to Read and Write* (1998), serves as a guide for early childhood language arts program development. It describes developmentally appropriate language arts activities in infancy through the early primary grades. Recommended teaching practices and activities are categorized according to children's age levels. It promotes nurturing adult-child relationships; print-rich environments; daily reading and discussion of high-quality books; oral opportunities that focus on sounds and meaning; phonemic awareness activities; play that includes play with literacy tools; exposure to print, icons, and words in computer games; and firsthand activities that expand knowledge and vocabulary. No one teaching method or approach is likely to be the most effective for all children, according to the position paper. A variety of teaching strategies suited to child diversity and individuality is recommended.

The National Early Literacy Panel

The National Early Literacy Panel is currently studying literacy research findings. This group recognizes that building young children's literacy skill works and recognizes that the demands on early educators is greater than ever before (Shanahan, 2004). The panel hopes to identify appropriate early childhood language arts curriculum and discover what additional research may be necessary.

The panel is pursuing answers to many questions, including the following:

◆ What literacy skills and abilities in young children (birth to age five) predict later reading, writing, and spelling outcomes?

◆ What environments and settings contribute to or inhibit gains in skills and abilities and are linked to later outcomes in reading, writing, and spelling?

◆ What child characteristics contribute to or inhibit gains in children's skills and abilities and are linked to later outcomes in reading, writing, and spelling?

---

phonological awareness — the whole spectrum from primitive awareness of speech sounds and rhythms to rhyme awareness and sound similarities; at the highest level, awareness of syllables or phonemes (Neuman, Copple, & Bredekamp, 1999).

◆ What programs and interventions contribute to or inhibit gains in children's skills and abilities and are linked to later outcomes in reading, writing, and spelling?

The panel has already identified a number of variables that have strong and consistent relationships with later literacy outcomes. After their review of a relatively large number of research studies with a relatively large number of children, the following variables were found.

STRONG PREDICTORS

◆ alphabet knowledge
◆ concepts about print
◆ phonological awareness
◆ invented spelling
◆ oral language (expressive, receptive, vocabulary)
◆ writing of name
◆ RAN (rapid automatic naming/lexical access) (Strickland, Shanahan, & Escamalia, 2004)

In using the predictors, the panel cautions they reviewed only existing studies. Other predictors may yet be discovered when additional research becomes available.

Putting Theories in Categories

Binding similar theories loosely together may help language arts program planners realize the theoretical basis for their language program decisions.

The **nativists**, those who believe in the natural unfolding of children without direct teaching from adults, include Rousseau, Pestalozzi, and Froebel. These educators can be conceived as thinkers who led later scholars and researchers to propose maturational theories with ages, stages, and normative behaviors.

Psychosocial theory, which stresses stages of human development, is associated with Freud. It can also be seen as a variant of the nativist tradition. Erikson's psychosocial theory stressed specific tasks to be resolved during stages of human development. The major tasks of toddlers and preschoolers were autonomy and initiative. Theory, along this line of thinking, may have evolved into a philosophy of child-directed learning such as traditional Montessori.

Locke's **nuturist** philosophy can be seen as a precursor of highly didactic preschool practices, although he also advocated offering children experiences to promote learning. Program models promote teachers as dispensers of knowledge, but activities might also be presented. These programs are based on the theory of **behaviorism**.

Interactionists view child development and learning as taking place between children and their environment. Program planners promoting this view subscribe to the **constructivist theory,** believing in children's creation of their own internal knowledge as they interact in both social and environmental pursuits. Piaget would describe this interaction as assimilation, accommodation, and equilibration. Vygotsky (Berk & Winsler, 1995) would emphasize the importance of language and socially shared cognition (**social contructivist theory**). He would recommend promoting assisted and scaffolded

---

nativists — those who adhere to the theory that children are born with biological dispositions for learning that unfold or mature in a natural way.

psychosocial theory — the branch of psychology founded by Erik Erikson; development is described in terms of eight stages that span childhood and adulthood.

nurturist — one who adheres to the theory that the minds of children are blank or unformed and need educational input or direct instruction to develop and "output" knowledge and appropriate behavior.

behaviorism — the theoretical viewpoint, espoused by theorists such as B. F. Skinner, that behavior is shaped by environmental forces, specifically in response to reward and punishment.

interactionists — those who adhere to the theory that language develops through a combination of inborn factors and environmental influences.

constructivist theory — a theory such as that of Jean Piaget, based on the belief that children construct knowledge for themselves rather than having it conveyed to them by some external source.

social constructivist theory — such as Vygotsky's emphasis on the importance of language and socially shared cognition, scaffolded exchanges, and the child's private speech.

learning and encouraging children to use private speech to aid them in solving problems.

The National Research Council (2000) points out that although theories differ in important ways, they share an emphasis on considering children as active learners who are able to set goals, plan, and revise. They recognize that children's cognitive development, which is so closely tied to language development, evolves gradually as children acquire strategies for remembering, understanding, and problem solving (Machado & Botnarescue, 2005).

PHILOSOPHIES

A variety of approaches to literacy instruction, representing different philosophical positions, have emerged, resulting in practices using widely diverse teaching techniques, materials, and assessment methods. Miller (1998) believes that contrasting points of view will probably continue to be around for a long time. Currently, educators debate the efficacy of academically oriented versus **child-initiated curricula**. Whole-language versus teacher-directed phonics instruction has also received considerable ongoing attention. Out of these debates the "balanced," "eclectic," "natural," and "centrist" philosophical positions have evolved and become often recommended positions.

Marcon (1999) describes a child-initiated model of instruction in which children's self-directed actions are facilitated by a teacher.

> In this approach a teacher facilitates learning by (a) providing children with a wide variety of experiences, (b) encouraging children to choose and plan their own learning activities, (c) engaging children in active learning by posing problems and asking questions that stimulate and extend learning, (d) guiding children through skill acquisition activities as needed, and (e) encouraging children to reflect on their learning experiences.

The staff of each early childhood center drafts a program based on the unique mesh of their staff's personal theories about what they believe is appropriate and effective. If a language arts program focuses on the correct form(s) of language, such as the planned and sequential learning of letter names, sounds, and so forth, the program could be described as *traditional*, or conventional. This text urges an approach to teaching language arts that is *meaning-based* and *functional* for children, *literature-rich*, and taught in a balanced and interrelated fashion. This type of program approach believes child learnings in language arts are reinforced and made meaningful when the reading, writing, listening, and speaking aspects of daily activities are encountered concurrently. A developmentally appropriate program first considers the unique group of children enrolled, their needs, their abilities, their interests, and their parents' wishes concerning desirable educational outcomes.

Preschools and child care centers have given special attention to *developmentally appropriate* practice guidelines published by the NAEYC in *Developmentally Appropriate Practice in Early Childhood Programs* (Bredekamp & Copple, 1997). In designing programs for young children, developmentally appropriate practice has three recognized components: age appropriateness, individual appropriateness, and knowledge and honor of children's social and cultural contexts (Kasten, Lolli, & Vander Wilt, 1998). Many centers depend on developmentally appropriate practice to form a framework for curriculum and adult interactions with children. Deeply embedded in developmentally appropriate practice is the idea that children have a natural disposition toward learning and actively construct their own knowledge through exploration and interaction with materials, peers, and adults (Kasten, Lolli, & Vander Wilt, 1998). Educators also realize that low-achieving students often need planned and systematic instruction to acquire skills that will enable them to progress and eventually learn to read with ease.

Developmentally appropriate programing may aim to strengthen what a child already knows and can do and/or may promote what a

---

child-initiated curricula — a basic tenet underlying this type of curriculum is the belief that *true* growth occurs when children are free to develop intrinsic interests naturally.

child can potentially discover or knows or can newly accomplish. See the Appendix for NAEYC's widely held expectations for three- to five-year-olds.

Some research supports the belief that developmentally appropriate practice programs have been associated with improved language outcomes (Dunn, Beach, & Kontos, 1994; Marcon, 1992).

Dunn and Kontos (1998), researching the effect of developmentally appropriate practice on children's cognitive development, conclude that children's receptive language was better in programs with higher-quality literacy environments and when developmentally appropriate activities were more abundant.

Neuman, Copple, and Bredekamp (1999) believe that outdated views, including extensive whole-group instruction and intensive drill and practice of isolated language arts skills, are not suitable or effective with preschoolers.

Hand and Nourot (1999) discuss the outcomes that programs based on development-based education can expect.

> In terms of cognitive development, the use of developmentally appropriate instructional strategies appears to facilitate children's creativity, is associated with better verbal skills and receptive language, and contributes to higher levels of cognitive functioning.

Weaver (1998b), an expert in reading methods, outlines what she believes a quality preschool language arts program encompasses.

> Ensure that all children receive quality preschool experiences, which include being read to, reading together in shared book experiences, writing collaboratively with guidance, reading and writing themselves as best they can, and using oral language in various ways. Attention can be given to developing phonics knowledge and phonemic awareness through oral language, but such teaching may be most effective and/or efficient when done in conjunction with written texts. Such experiences will give less advantaged children a chance to

start kindergarten more in step with their relatively advantaged peers.

Figure 6–4 offers a possible sequence of children's language learning in both planned and unplanned classroom activities.

Child has experiential background observing and participating in a rich language arts school environment.

↓

Child gives attention to classroom activities, demonstrations, behaviors modeled by others, new happenings, teacher presentations, or other classroom events. Child perceives activity to be useful, interesting, or worthwhile.

↓

Child feels comfortable and safe in this situation and feels capable and likely successful. Child understands that teacher expects appropriate classroom behavior.

↓

Child continues focus and concentration on activity that is unfolding and progressing.

↓

Child gathers and selects information and data; develops beginning ideas; may ask questions; and looks, listens, touches as if investigating or trying to find out.

↓

Child may see or state relationships and form hypotheses or conclusions and may discuss points of view.

↓

Child may test ideas or check ideas with teacher or others present.

↓

Child may receive feedback from teacher and/or other children. Child may be uncertain or puzzled.

↓

Child may develop a definite idea and "fit" the newness experienced in the activity into what she already knows. Learning occurs.

FIGURE 6–4 Possible sequence in language learning.

FEDERAL INTEREST AND LEGISLATION AFFECTS LANGUAGE ARTS CURRICULUM

In July 2001, The White House Summit on Early Childhood Cognitive Development met and focused on the chain of negative educational events that can result when children are unable to master reading in the lower grades of elementary school. An increased federal emphasis exists on not only reading instruction but also what prepares young children and precedes their kindergarten enrollment (Love, 2003). McGee (2003b) points out that teaching reading at all levels, from preschool through high school, is headline news.

The federal No Child Left Behind Act (U.S. Department of Education, 2002a) sections dealing with guidelines for reading are designed to improve children's reading in publicly funded schools from kindergarten through third grade. *Early Reading First,* the portion of the law aimed at improving prekindergartener's reading achievement, specifies that preschool teachers at publicly funded schools must deliver systematic and explicit instruction to increase children's oral language development, print awareness, alphabet knowledge, and phonological awareness (McGee, 2003a). Pushing formal reading instruction into preschool classrooms was not recommended and was not the legislation's intent. The idea that literacy experiences during preschool years are critical for successful learning during elementary school years was a central concern.

Muenchow (2003) states that the No Child Left Behind Act has led to discussions of accountability. Policy makers, she notes, often use terms such as *assessment* and *screening* interchangeably as a means "to evaluate programs." She believes

> The interest in readiness assessment can be viewed as just a first step in the broader effort to hold publicly funded education for all age groups accountable. More specifically, the call for readiness assessments arises from the ongoing debate in the United States regarding whether it should

be a national priority to invest in early childhood programs and if so, for which children and at what level of expense.

The assessment of preschool children is a "hot button" topic for many early childhood educators. They worry that testing will label very young children, and they are concerned about assessment validity and unfair judgments of programs working with disadvantaged children or second-language learners.

A draft position statement created by the NAEYC and the National Association of Early Childhood Specialists in State Departments of Education (NAECS/SDE) lists both (1) a general description of responsibilities of educators concerning assessment and (2) the indicators of assessment effectiveness.

- Make ethical, appropriate, valid, and reliable assessment a central part of all early childhood programs. To assess young children's strengths, progress, and needs use methods that are developmentally appropriate, culturally and linguistically responsive, tied to children's daily activities, supported by professional development, inclusive of families, and connected to specific, beneficial purposes: (a) making sound decisions about teaching and learning. (b) identifying significant concerns that may require focused intervention for individual children, and (c) helping programs improve their educational and developmental interventions.
- Ethical principles guide assessment practices.
- Assessment instruments are used for their intended purpose.
- Assessments are appropriate for ages and other characteristics of children being assessed.
- Assessment instruments are in compliance with professional criteria for quality.
- What is assessed is developmentally and educationally significant.
- Assessment evidence is used to understand and improve learning.
- Assessment evidence is gathered from realistic settings and situations that reflect children's actual performance.

- Assessments use multiple sources of evidence gathered over time.
- Screening is always linked to follow-up.
- Use of individually administered, norm-referenced tests is limited.
- Staff and families are knowledgeable about assessment. (NAEYC & NAECS/SDE, 2003)

Standardized testing tends to lead to standardized teaching—one approach fits all—the opposite of the kind of individualized diagnosis and teaching that is needed to help young children continue to progress in reading and writing (IRA & NAEYC, 1999).

More about the No Child Left Behind Act

The No Child Left Behind Act's provision that federal grants be contingent on the fact that all enrolled children at primary schools make "adequate yearly progress" in reading created shock waves throughout public educational systems (Hirsch, 2004).

As a result, regional areas, states, cities, local communities, school districts, and professional organizations and groups have made attempts to identify age-level literacy characteristics. They have also developed standards and goal statements, pinpointing the literacy skills gained in the early years that may ease children's learning to read. Written standards statements and prescribed curricula can include mandating the time children are to spend in daily classroom literacy-promoting activities. They have also developed, refined, or examined testing alternatives; initiated teacher training and retraining; and pursued various additional efforts. Hirsch (2004), after examining the results of these efforts (only 3 years at this time), believes test scores for elementary-aged children have risen only modestly or not at all, and the reading gap remains large. He attributes U.S. schools' failure to remediate children's reading deficiencies not to instructional time spent on literacy activities but to children's lack of exposure to background information in history, science, literature, and art. Children instead are offered "bland stories about Jose at the supermarket" or "Janice and her new friend." He urges *content-rich* reading selections that build up the broad knowledge and varied vocabulary required for true reading comprehension along with the introduction and promotion of decoding skills and activities that sound out words.

Early childhood centers reflecting Hirsch's view will attempt to design curricula that are culturally relevant, introduce content and promote varied vocabulary development, instill an enthusiasm for learning, and introduce activities with phonological and phonemic awareness elements.

Child observation and documentation activities are now part of the teacher's responsibility in many preschools as well as elementary schools. Child journals, child portfolios, teacher checklists, testing sessions, recording, and observations are commonplace as teachers struggle to identify the literacy growth of each child.

Many educators are involved in debates concerning the wisdom of some or all of the practices that are a result of this federal legislation. Most commonly, they expressed fears and frustrations involving "pushed down" curriculum formerly introduced in higher grades, literacy or academic activities "crowding out" playtime or other curricular activities, bilingual instructional techniques, and "fairness" in testing.

Schickendanz (2003) points out that the beliefs of some early childhood educators concerning the code-related aspect of literacy development may create a barrier to their offering literacy instruction (either formal or informal). Code-related components of early literacy consists of phonological awareness, letter name knowledge, knowledge of sound-letter associations, and the insight that letters function to represent sounds in words (that is, the alphabetic principle) (Schickendanz, 2003). Some factors that may influence teachers' behaviors include:

- sticking to older, well-known language arts programming activities that ignore new research-based instructional models.
- giving a higher priority to other favored daily language arts activities, such as picture-book reading, and so on.
- receiving teacher training that does not address code-related language development issues.
- feeling negative about any "skill" development lessons, whether informal or formal.

She goes on to point out that among the revisions and clarifications of the original developmentally appropriate practice philosophy (Bredekamp & Copple, 1997), there is a caution against taking *to the extreme* such things as the importance of children's play and self-selection of activities and relying on developmental categories as the basis for curriculum and assessment, causing the exclusion of subject-matter content considerations (Schickedanz, 2003). Early childhood educators are as worried as some parents are about skill-and-drill sessions, work sheets, and lessons that have no connection to children's backgrounds or interests. Many early childhood educators realize that they may be failing the children who need them the most. Stipek (2004) believes studies show many children from low-income families enter kindergarten a year to a year and a half, on average, behind middle-class children in their language development, as well as other cognitive skills. This is a gigantic lag that dramatically affects children's success in the first grades of primary school and perhaps their entire educational future.

The field is searching for palatable techniques and strategies to incorporate code-related components of literacy mentioned in the No Child Left Behind Act into language arts programing, particularly for children most in need. The easy part may be intentionally incorporating skill building into daily conversations and daily activities. The hard part may be overcoming teachers' reticence concerning systematic planned skill-based instruction and effectively identifying at-risk children. Stipek (2004) points out teachers do not need to *make* children ready for learning; most are quite eager learners.

Criticism and Positive Comments Concerning the No Child Left Behind Act

Some superintendents of urban elementary school districts with large minority and disadvantaged child populations are calling the No Child Left Behind Act the No Teacher Left Standing Act. Because these districts include public schools that have been labeled "in need of im-

provement," their teachers are struggling and under pressure to show accountable improvement.

Other teachers are angry with the "high standards" and believe the standard equates perfection and is consequently unattainable (Toppo, 2004). Yet others criticize the federal government's amount of funding, saying it is inadequate. After reviewing research undertaken after 2002, Coles (2004) questions what he calls the "meager" research data underpinning the legislation.

Parents, on the other hand, seem to be quite supportive of the No Child Left Behind Act. They are now being told more clearly how much their children are learning at school and whether the school is rated well or poorly.

Dean (2004), an elementary school principal, views the No Child Left Behind Act as providing a "tough love" approach that works. Dean's formula for doubling children's reading and math scores in her school follows.

> Use curriculums proven by research and embrace unpopular testing that prods all students to learn.

She credits the strategies of the No Child Left Behind Act for the success of her students.

What Is Happening Now with the No Child Left Behind Act. The 2003–2004 school year saw the first widespread public school implementation of the No Child Left Behind Act's accountability measures. These measures, Howell and Casserly (2004) point out, were intended to stimulate competition, provide students with better alternatives, and punish underperforming schools. School districts worried about losing federal dollars are designing supplemental services and tutoring programs.

Two later stages of sanctions dictated in the No Child Left Behind Act include "corrective action" and "restructuring." These sanctions apply to public elementary schools that register 3 consecutive years of inadequate gains. These consequences can range from firing staff to closing a school. If school districts have not yet focused on the years before kindergarten, especially children's language arts activities, they cannot afford to ignore them much longer.

The "highly qualified" teacher requirement in the No Child Left Behind Act is aimed at ensuring teacher quality in elementary schools (Section 1119). It mandates that teachers have the content knowledge and teaching skills necessary to enable children to succeed. A "highly qualified" teacher of reading must hold a bachelor's degree by the end of the 2005–2006 school year. Subject-matter competency tests and/or teacher competency demonstration on a state's standard evaluation may determine whether a teacher keeps her job.

Casserly (2004) foresees the following happenings.

> Eventually, No Child Left Behind and the paradigm shift it represents are likely to give the nation exactly what it wants urban schools to deliver—more choice and higher achievement. Once that happens, urban schools will have succeeded in meeting a challenge as ambitious as any nation has set for its schools.

Reading Today (2004) states that a new report by the Education Trust, a nonprofit, nonpartisan organization, shows that student achievement in reading and math is rising in the elementary grades in most states and that achievement gaps are narrowning.

State Standards, Head Start Performance Standards, the Head Start Child Outcomes Framework, and the McREL Framework

Many states have enacted state initiatives and standards aimed at preparing preschoolers for kindergarten. Head Start is funded by federal and state funds. Under President George W. Bush's 2003 proposal for improving preschool programs in general and Head Start in particular, states are offered the opportunity to coordinate all preschool programs, including Head Start, in exchange for meeting certain accountability requirements.

> States must develop an accountability program that will indicate how well children in individual programs are performing relative to the skills and behaviors identified by the state as prerequisites for effective kindergarten performance.

> The skills and behaviors should include: pre-reading skills including phonological awareness, letter knowledge, and vocabulary; numeracy; and social-emotional competence.

Curriculum planners and developers in early childhood schools and centers keep standards in mind while preparing a school's program of activities if they receive public funds. Standards adopted at a particular school represent what that school and its teachers expect children to recall, replicate, manipulate, understand, or demonstrate at some point in time—in this case, prior to kindergarten entry.

Early childhood programs nationwide, depending on their state's decision to mandate or recommend their standards, may not be able to design their program of activities, for they may be spelled out in law. Some written standard statements provide examples of child behaviors teachers can observe that indicate child accomplishment or progress toward mastering a particular standard statement. Many state standard statements are in draft or final written form and are available on the Internet or available by contacting a state's Department of Education. The National Institute for Early Childhood Research (NIEER) has a directory of states that have downloadable early childhood (preschool) language and literacy standards *(http://www.nieer.org)*. Another source is *http://www.educationworld.com*.

Head Start, reauthorized by Congress in 1998, augmented its *Head Start Performance Standards,* a document that guided language arts program planning along with other curricular areas. In 2000, the Administration for Children and Families (ACF) issued guidelines for devising and implementing outcome-based education plans. Consequently, *The Head Start Child Outcomes Framework* (U.S. Department of Health and Human Services, 2003) was released. The framework involves eight basic learning and development "domains." Two domains are identified as *language development* and *literacy*. Each domain is composed of 27 domain elements and 100 examples of specific indicators of ability. Head Start has shifted from its original focus on social competence and play to literacy and discrete academic outcomes (Snow, 2003).

The framework gives definition to learning objectives for Head Start and Head Start teachers and could be used to guide curriculum planning and assessment. The objectives include five federally mandated indicators of learning achievement that were set as requirements for Head Start children graduating their programs and entering kindergarten.

The framework also emphasizes the importance of parents' understanding of their vital out-of-school function in promoting language and literacy development. It promotes parents' understanding that children's cumulative life experiences and adult-child interactions from birth on affect language and literacy growth.

All early childhood educators who wish to can use the Head Start framework as a research-based guide and design program activities that work toward the identified outcomes. Individual states may choose to adopt or recognize the *Head Start Performance Standards* and *The Head Start Child Outcomes Framework,* in whole or in part, as they endeavor to better coordinate their early childhood programs and also create preschool programs of excellence.

To obtain a copy of *Head Start Performance Standards* or *The Head Start Child Outcomes Framework,* go to: *http://www.hsnrc.org/*.

To obtain a copy of the Mid-continent Research for Education's *Framework for Early Literacy Instruction,* search online at *http://www.mcrel.org.* The framework outlines standards, benchmarks, developmental accomplishments, and child behaviors for pre-K through kindergarten.

Stott (2003) has noted the uncertain feelings and fears about accepting standards, either state, federal, association, or center created. She has attempted to list both standards' advantages and "downsides."

ADVANTAGES

◆ Standards may help all entering kindergartners start school with similar knowledge and skills.

◆ Preschool standards align with K–12 education standards.

◆ The same learning expectations are set for all students.

◆ Early childhood teachers are provided with guidelines concerning what children need to learn before beginning kindergarten.

◆ The same high standards are used for all children, regardless of geographical area, consequently smoothing child transfer adjustment from school to school.

◆ Standards help preschool teachers put meaningful content into their curricula.

◆ As universal standards, they could guide early childhood educators in curriculum development, including complex grammatical structure and vocabulary.

◆ Standards could specify the knowledge, skills, and competencies.

◆ Greater professionalism may be brought to the early childhood career field.

DOWNSIDES

◆ The specificity of standards may be too broad or too inflexible.

◆ Assessment and accountability could lead to the identification of narrowly defined skills or facts.

◆ Standards could lead to high-stakes testing.

◆ Curriculum may be constructed to match test items.

◆ Children's social-psychological development or cognitive and creative thought may be ignored.

◆ Less mature children may be labeled failures.

◆ Standards may affect children's self-confidence and motivation.

◆ Teachers may know what to teach but may not know how to teach it.

◆ Parents or caregivers may be affected by academic pressures exerted through their children's teachers.

Stott believes standards in the field of early education are an essential first step for designing a more effective preschool curriculum.

LANGUAGE USE IN ALL CURRICULUM AREAS

Every planned preschool activity uses language in some way. Past experience is basic to all language arts because a child's success often depends on her understanding of what is happening. Language helps children learn, retain, recall, and transmit information. Messages are received through words and nonverbal means. The teacher's speech, behavior, and use of words in planned activities are discussed in the following chapters.

In addition to the center's planned program, daily routines, play with peers, and unplanned happenings also stimulate language. Teachers use every opportunity to add meanings in a natural, conversational way during the preschool day. This generally begins with the teacher's personal greeting or affectionate physical contact as the child enters the early childhood center. The "hello" and comments are part of the rituals in preschools that aim to recognize each child's presence each arrival time.

Daily routines are the regular features of a school's program that occur about the same time every day—snacks, toileting, and group activities—in which language is an associate function. Small and large group times can range from ones with a short announcement to language to literacy-oriented activities the teacher presents or prepares (Figure 6–5).

Gundling (2002) describes preschool practices that support early literacy development.

Good practices that support early literacy development begin with close and dependable relationships with caring adults who are nurturing and responsive to the child's interest and natural curiosity. When adults understand that young children are active learners who delight in engaging in mean-

FIGURE 6–5 A teacher becomes part of the child group while a student teacher leads an activity.

ingful activities, and provide them with multiple opportunities for exploration, they help create a strong early literacy foundation.

Planned activities should have a purpose children can understand and in some way connect to what they already know (Figure 6–6). Most, if not all, learning can be made applicable to the child's life. Early childhood practitioners provide real, hands-on experiences in their classrooms when possible. Secondhand activities are second best.

In an activity planting spring seeds, signs or labels adjacent to planted seeds have a practical

FIGURE 6–6 Teachers consult frequently to determine whether planned activities are relevant to attending children.

purpose. The teacher could read the seed packet instructions to the children to find out about planting particulars. If individual planting pots are used, the children and/or teacher could print their names to label them.

Klein and Starkey (2000), creators of The Berkeley Math Readiness Project, encourage preschool teachers to use number and measurement terms in preschool activities in which counting, comparing, adding, or taking away is encountered in planned or unplanned daily happenings. They believe participation in preschool activities that touch on math knowledge and terminology dramatically reduces the disparities between children from low- and middle-income families.

LANGUAGE ARTS PROGRAMMING

Preplanned language arts programs develop from identified goals: the knowledge, skills, and attitudes that the school intends to teach (Figure 6–7). Early childhood teachers also base teaching techniques on what they believe is best, right, appropriate, and prudent. This, in turn, is connected to views they hold about how, what, when, and where children learn to communicate and use language. The following views about language learning are commonly expressed or implied by staff members involved in planning language arts programs.

◆ Language permeates all planned and unplanned activities.

◆ A dynamic, rich-in-opportunity classroom stimulates communication and exchanges of ideas.

◆ Real experiences are preferred to vicarious ones when practical and possible.

◆ The reciprocal nature of exploring and discovering together should be promoted by teachers.

◆ Play provides many opportunities to learn language.

◆ Teachers' instructional techniques should be skilled and alert to child readiness.

◆ Stressing relationships between objects, events, and experiences is a useful teaching technique.

◆ Individual planning, as well as group planning, is desirable.

◆ Program activities should center on the children's interests.

◆ Literary classics (preschool level) are an important planned-program component.

◆ The entire teaching staff should be committed to and enthusiastic about their planned program and should understand the stated objectives.

FIGURE 6–7 Staff members, consultants, parents, and community representatives may all be involved in language arts program development.

◆ An integrated approach to language arts instruction helps children experience the "connectedness" of language arts areas.

◆ Reading and writing is better conceptualized as a developmental continuum.

Ayres (1998) believes the best type of planned literacy-promoting program is captivating enough to hold the imagination, engaging enough to sustain active involvement for a period of time, and stimulating enough to motivate further literacy exploration.

Okagaki and Diamond (2000) alert early childhood teachers to the idea that teachers' goals for attending children may be much different than parents' goals. Rather than telling parents what they ought to be doing, it is the school's job to support and complement parents' efforts; there is sometimes a need to find community translators to help bridge the gap between home and school.

One can envision an ideal language arts curriculum starting at birth and continuing throughout the child's lifetime. The author sees it as a program of home and life experiences supporting learning and self-discovery in which colorful, interconnected strands of language arts knowledge and skill thread through early childhood and come together in an "'aha' rainbow" when the child successfully decodes her first word, first sentence, or first book. The child then passes through a door equipped to move on into a vast amount of stored human knowledge, discovery, inspiration, creativity, and fantasy. These milestones in development are hopefully accompanied by understanding, rich personal life experiences, natural inquisitiveness, and a belief in the child's own ability and self-worth.

The ideal early childhood curriculum in language arts offers quality child-relevant speaking, listening, early writing, and reading activities in addition to literature opportunities. These activities encourage, sustain, and provide growth, ensuring the necessary foundational knowledge and skill for an easy transition to school and successful kindergarten year and beyond.

Teacher Training

Your classes in early childhood education, self-study, and your life experiences will influence the early childhood literacy program you will attempt to offer young children. Many times, your ideas will be incorporated into a teaching team's effort to design a planned curriculum.

Your training should have encouraged you to continually improve instructional practice and to analyze what is working and what is not. Questioning and researching are parts of the joy of teaching and can lead to what Bruner (1996) termed "new and revolutionary insight." When looking for program ideas, be open-minded and look inside to remember what inspired your own literacy development. Do not discount your ability to really focus on children and discover *their* agenda or your ability as an "innovator" of a language arts program that addresses the needs and interests of each child. The Appendix holds a section of language and literacy specifics that well-prepared candidates (early childhood education majors) should possess. It also cites research-based knowledge and skills.

Recent Research on Teachers' Classroom Skills

Research has identified the following "critical" teacher behaviors.

◆ using new words with children

◆ extending children's comments through questioning

◆ focusing children's attention on an analysis of books read to them

◆ engaging in intellectually challenging conversations

◆ placing an importance on child attentiveness during group times (Dickinson & Tabors, 2001)

◆ obtaining and maintaining children's attention (Dickinson & Tabors, 2001)

◆ believing academic and social goals are both important (Dickinson & Tabors, 2001)

◆ providing literacy-learning opportunities and being *intentional* in instructional efforts to stretch children's thinking (Dickinson, 2001)

◆ supporting children's writing attempts (Dickinson & Tabors, 2001)

Research-based recommendations from others include:

- providing knowledge, phonological sensitivity, and familiarity with the basic purposes and mechanisms of reading to preschoolers with less prior knowledge and skill (at-risk children) (Snow, Burns, & Griffin, 1998).
- giving individual children adequate time to speak (Schickendanz, 2003).
- planning and implementing small group activities (Schickendanz, 2003).
- engaging in extensive conversations (Schickendanz, 2003).
- joining individual children or small groups in the library or writing areas (Schickendanz, 2003).

What constitutes exemplary practice and teacher's modeling skills in language arts first grade instruction?

- varied teaching strategies to motivate literacy learning
- high expectations for student accomplishment
- varied structures for instruction to meet individual needs, such as whole-group, small group, and one-on-one settings with teacher
- literacy-rich classroom environment with accessible materials

- careful organization and management of materials
- opportunities for children to practice skills taught
- guidance in structured lessons for acquisition of skills
- opportunities for children to work independently or in collaborative groups (Morrow, Tracey, Woo, & Pressley, 1999; Pressley, Rankin, & Yokoi, 1996; Ruddell & Ruddell, 1995)

Would these teacher characteristics also suit pre-K teacher educators? That seems highly possible!

Programs for At-Risk Preschoolers

The U.S. Department of Education defines a linguistically and culturally diverse child (an educational term) as a child who either is non-English proficient (NEP) or limited-English proficient (LEP). Educators recognize the difficulties many young children may face when entering child care centers or preschools and children's attempt to learn an unfamiliar language.

High-quality educational programs recognize and promote all aspects of children's development and learning (Figure 6–8). Their

FIGURE 6–8 Observation of children and staff may be undertaken before program planning begins.

goal is to enable all children to become competent, successful, and socially responsible adults.

Preschools and early childhood centers enrolling lower-income families need to consider the following recommendations:

> Failure to develop an adequate vocabulary, understanding of print concepts, or phonological awareness during the preschool years constitutes some risk for reading difficulties. Hence, we recommend interventions designed to promote growth. At the same time, however, we caution that the focus of intervention should not be limited to overcoming these risk factors in isolation but should be more broadly designed to provide a rich language and literacy environment that methodically includes the promotion of vocabulary, the understanding of print concepts, and phonological awareness. (Snow, Burns, & Griffin, 1998)

Culturally Diverse Musical Experience

The songs and music of childhood are a part of our cultural heritage. The folk songs and ballads that have survived to the present day and the regional tunes parents and teachers offer are part of each child's cultural literacy. Early childhood programs attempt to provide the music of various ethnic groups. Most of these musical experiences give young children the opportunity to form beginning ideas concerning the music and language of diverse peoples.

Musical activities have gained new status and are viewed as language-developing activities. Studies conclude that in cultures where musical play is actively encouraged, children acquire heightened competencies in motor and communication skills at early ages (Jaffe, 1992).

Classroom Environment

Yetta Goodman (1990) describes a literacy environment as follows:

> Classrooms need to reflect the rich literate environments in which children are immersed outside of school. There needs to be signs that label materials for children to use; labels for areas where children store their belongings; books and magazines to read; and various sizes, shapes, and colors of paper that children can write on in appropriate ways in their play, their cooking, and their independent time activities.

> All learning experiences need to be organized so that they invite children to participate in literacy events.

> Authentic literacy events need to become the focus of the school day as children:

> - are signed in daily so that the teacher knows who has arrived in school;
> - put away their materials in an appropriate setting, using the signs in the room or their names on their cubbies;
> - read recipes and menus as they cook, eat, and learn about healthy nutritional activities; write prescriptions at the play hospital or take phone messages in the house corner; and
> - read storybooks, write letters, and record observations.

Creating a warm, cozy, friendly environment where children are in a state of relaxed alertness is the goal of educators.

The Importance of Program Quality

University researchers from the University of North Carolina, University of California–Los Angeles, University of Colorado, and Yale University jointly studied early learning and school readiness; they report that children in low-quality care tended to score lower on tests measuring both language and math skills (*The Idaho Statesman*, 1999). The researchers estimate that about 11 percent of the child care centers they studied were judged low quality. Quality child care, researchers concluded, made the most difference to children who were poor or those whose mothers were less educated than other children's mothers (Riley, 1999).

Anderson (2000) points out that using discovery centers, projects, and small group activities provides many child care choices and facilitates high child engagement and opportunities for adult scaffolding of skill development. Many centers use this type of instructional approach.

Determining Program Effectiveness

Goals pinpointed through staff meetings and solicited parent input can be finalized in written form to serve as a basis for planning. For one child or many, goals are achieved when teachers and staff plan interesting and appropriate activities for daily, weekly, monthly, or longer periods. In addition to the actual program, materials, and classroom equipment and arrangement, teacher techniques and interactions and other resources aid in goal realization.

Teacher observation and assessment instruments—teacher-designed and commercial—add extra data that help in planning programs (Figure 6–9).

Assessment may be defined as an ongoing process of gathering evidence of learning in order to make informed judgments about instructional practice (Jones, 2004). The NAEYC's draft position paper on assessment was provided earlier in the chapter. A listing of commercial preschool language assessments is found in the Appendix.

Carefully planned, recorded, and well-conducted teacher observation is an assessment tool that is hard to beat. Standardized tests all too often do not tell observant teachers anything they do not already know about children. Neuman and Roskos (1993) add

> To detect patterns of language and literacy behavior, then, the assessing we do must include multiple sources of information which are gathered over some period of time. And it is our close examination of these diverse indicators of behavior that enhances the credibility of the interpretations we make about children's language and literacy growth.

Some assessments attempt to determine ability and accomplishment in a number of language and communication areas; others may be limited to one language skill.

Literacy Portfolios

Many schools encourage the use of child portfolios to record and visually display a child's accomplishments and progress—in this case, language arts development. With increased focus on prereading skills, portfolios have become increasingly popular for charting children's progress. The teacher collects and dates children's work or photographs. Large album-sized binders are used to accommodate children's artwork. Some schools use page protectors or clear plastic kitchen storage bags to protect inserts. Any related literacy item can be included, and the binder may travel home periodically so that parents can add home-produced work. Items are filed in chronological order and become a personal chronicle of a child's activities. Sharing a child's portfolio—whether teacher-child or child-child sharing—generates considerable interactive conversation.

Teacher Observation

Many child care centers encourage teachers to continually observe the language skills of attending children. Each child and group may have different needs, and the center attempts to fulfill needs and offer a language arts program that will be growth producing and enriching. Many different observation methods and instruments can be used. Some may be school-designed; others may be commercially produced.

A teacher who is a keen observer and listener gathers information, which guides teacher actions and planning. In their efforts to make an activity relevant, teachers observe attending children's needs, desires, and interests and make individual judgments regarding children's already acquired knowledge, attitudes, and language skills. Lunt (1993) believes that assessing beyond children's level of performance by looking at ways children learn and interact provides a much richer portrait of a child than just identifying her level of skill. As teachers observe, some try to answer the following questions.

◆ What individual language characteristics are present?

SAMPLE OF STAFF-DESIGNED LANGUAGE AND LITERACY CHECKLIST

Child _____ Age _____ (Check if present) Date _____

1. can distinguish illustrations, photographs, and so on from print
2. identifies front/back of books   F_____ B_____
3. notices print in the environment
4. is interested in a book's content and illustrations
5. realizes illustrations can tell a story
6. realizes adults are reading printed text in a storybook
7. realizes print contains names and ideas (storylines)
8. realizes books are authored by people
9. realizes a story she creates can be put into print
10. recognizes her name in print
11. can find her printed name in a group of names
12. chooses books regularly in book areas
13. pretend reads
14. makes up stories
15. can act out stories
16. asks or answers questions about books being read
17. listens to a book attentively
18. handles books with care
19. pretend writes
20. uses alphabet letters in art or constructions
21. knows first letter of her name
22. tries to print name or other words
23. can name a few or many alphabet letters
          few _____ many _____ all _____
24. demonstrates she can hear rhyming words
25. creates a rhyme
26. tells a story with a beginning, middle, and end
          beginning _____ middle _____ end _____
27. has a favorite book
28. can identify words with the same beginning sound
29. knows reading starts at the top left on a page
30. knows there are spaces between words
31. wants her name printed on her work
32. can visually discriminate between alphabet letter shapes
                    few _____ many _____
33. can discriminate between two different speech sounds
34. can perform two- or three-part commands
          Two part _____ Three part _____

35. can predict what might happen in a story based on the cover and illustrations
36. can identify and clap how many syllables are in a three-syllable word
37. recognizes that a letter can be written in uppercase and lowercase form
38. recognizes silly orally spoken mistakes are illogical. (The mouse ate an elephant. The cup fell off the table and hit the ceiling.)
39. can predict what would come next in a simple pattern (AooAo?)
40. controls a writing tool with small motor movement
41. has the ability to attend to and understand conversations, stories, poems, and other oral presentations
42. has a vocabulary (three years, more than 2,000 words; four years, more than 4,000 words; five years, more than 5,000 words)
          average_____ complex _____ varied_____
43. asks questions
44. tells feelings, opinions, ideas, needs, desires, and so forth
                    often_____ infrequently _____
45. is a good conversationist
          initiates _____ listens _____ responds _____
46. pronounces words clearly as expected for age
                    clearly _____ average for age _____
47. has increased length of oral sentences
48. uses complex sentences at times
49. discriminates between sounds in words
50. can identify whether a sound in a word is the same or different from another word
51. knows the beginning sound of her name
52. makes an attempt to copy familiar words
53. prints name
54. recognizes common environmental or human symbols
55. is beginning to realize her name is a series of sounds blended together
56. sees visual differences in printed alphabet letters
57. knows the alphabet is a special category of visual graphics
58. can maintain focus of attention in small group instruction (appropriate to age and attention span)

FIGURE 6–9 Sample of a staff-designed language and literacy checklist.

SAMPLE OF STAFF-DESIGNED LANGUAGE AND LITERACY CHECKLIST—cont'd

59. has group social skills such as raising hand, taking turns, asking questions, staying on topic, waiting for answers to her questions, and so on

60. can understand group time rules and participates in formulating them

61. uses language to initiate play with peers

62. makes choices and decisions and verbalizes them

63. can articulate sounds according to developmentally appropriate expectations

64. has developed divergent thinking skills

65. has an adequate grasp of meaningful concepts that are appropriate to age

66. has been exposed to capital alphabet letters used correctly in her name

67. is spacially aware and/or understands up, down, across, top, bottom, right, and left

68. uses visual cues; for example, follows directions on picture cards

69. is aware computer icons have meanings and knows meanings of a few

70. can find commonalities and differences in oral stories and visual representations

71. can create verbal labels for common objects

72. is aware of some punctuation marks in text

73. has been exposed to the use of computers

74. participates in singing

75. knows about a culture other than her own

76. attempts to write words

77. is familiar with graphs and charts and understands their use in visualizing data

78. understands that symbols are used for objects and events

79. can identify sounds in the environment

*Note: This was gathered from a wide collection of individual state standards and goal statements. It is not intended to be a complete or comprehensive list, but rather a sample of one school's efforts to assess its children's readiness for kindergarten. Some duplication of questions is present.

FIGURE 6–9 *(continued)*

◆ How can activities be planned that capture and hold children's interest and enthusiasm?

◆ How do my actions and behaviors affect the children's language arts behaviors?

◆ Which children are interested in which indoor and outdoor areas?

◆ What patterns of language behavior have I noticed?

◆ What do children seem eager to talk about or explore? And with whom?

◆ What can I do to provide experience or exploration just beyond what they already know?

◆ Which children readily express themselves? Which rarely do so?

◆ Which children are socially adept and learn language in play with others?

Assessment is a continual, ongoing process. Observation information is confidential and often useful in program planning. Running accounts of child conversations are difficult to obtain because an adult's presence may affect a child's spontaneity. Also, the child's at-

tention span and mobility make it almost impossible to capture more than a few minutes of speech with preschoolers. Many teachers note a few phrases or speech characteristics on a writing pad they carry with them throughout the day. For many teachers, having time just to observe children is considered a luxury. However, observation is important and can be considered an ongoing teacher responsibility in all areas of instruction.

To ensure a language program's quality, plans are changed, updated, and revised based on both the children's progress and staff members' evaluations and observations. Keeping a planned language arts program vital, dynamic, appealing, and appropriate requires continual revision and overhaul.

GOAL STATEMENTS

A particular center may have many or few goal statements, which can be both general and specific.

If standards exist and affect an early childhood program, goals are often identified and listed. Privately funded early childhood programs in most states may choose to look at standards statements but may or may not incorporate them into their planned program goals.

A good number of program planners use the NAEYC's widely held expectations listing for three- to five-year-olds when identifying goals; this listing is found in the Appendix.

Writing Goals

In the process of literacy development, young children can profit from an understanding of the role of the printed word (Figure 6–10). The uses of writing, including recording and transmitting information, recording self-authored creations, and providing entertainment, are important to the quality of human life. A knowledge of writing uses may lead to a realization of the value of learning to read. Writing and reading open each individual to the thoughts, creations, and discoveries of multitudes of people, living and deceased. This discussion is not intended to promote formal early printing instruction but rather to point out that there are basic ideas about writing that must be considered when planning a language arts curriculum that promotes literacy.

There is a strong connection between the child's familiarity with books (and her book-reading experiences) and literacy. Illustrations of the reasons for writing and how writing can satisfy everyday needs can be incorporated into any center's goals for promoting literacy growth.

Most schools concentrate on exposing children to printed words rather than starting actual writing practice in alphabet letter formation.

Reading Goals

Reading skills are multiple and complex, and they often involve the coordination of other skills and abilities. Some reading goals that will facilitate later reading skills follow:

- reads pictures
- shows an interest in and enjoyment of stories and books
- is able to arrange pictures in a sequence that tells a story
- finds hidden objects in pictures
- guesses at meanings based on contextual cues
- reads own and others' names
- predicts events

FIGURE 6–10 This group is discussing printed signs that they have found in their school environment.

- recognizes letters of own name in other words
- senses left-right direction
- guesses words to complete sentences
- chooses favorite book characters
- treats books with care
- authors own books through dictation
- sees finely detailed differences
- recognizes and names alphabet letters at times
- shows interest in libraries
- shows interest in the sounds of letters
- watches or uses puppets to enact simple stories
- has background in traditional literature appropriate for age and ability
- develops phonemic awareness

Goals That Promote Early Literacy

Preschool teachers planning and conducting programs that promote language development in young children try to provide a "classic" literary experience, featuring appropriate age-level materials collected from many cultures and eras. Such a curriculum would serve as a basis of human cultural understanding and would include a wide range of oral and listening materials and activities: books, poetry, language games, puppetry, and storytelling (Figure 6–11). Most teachers believe that early exposure to and familiarity with literary classics can help the child understand what might be encountered later in literature, media, or schooling.

At present, a widely circulated list of classics for preschool children has not been available, but a list of these works has existed in the minds and hearts of individual teachers. Mother Goose stories are undisputed classics. Two other agreed-upon classic stories are *Goldilocks and the Three Bears* and *Peter Rabbit*. Chapters 9 and 17 present in-depth discussions in this planning area. Whether a story, play, rhyme, or song is considered a "classic," however, is usually a matter of judgment by individual teachers.

FIGURE 6–11 Printed words may accompany new objects in early childhood classrooms.

SOCIOCULTURAL LANGUAGE GOALS

Are there important goals teachers need to consider in a democratic society? Powell (1992) suggests the following:

Goal #1. All students are able to communicate effectively with all persons within a multicultural, diverse society.

Goal #2. All students learn to value linguistic diversity and celebrate the cultural expressions of those who are different from themselves.

Goal #3. All students see the value of language and literacy for their own lives. . . .

Early childhood educators can lay the groundwork and monitor attitudes and feelings that in any way degrade other-than-mainstream-language speakers.

A language arts curriculum should include language activities that celebrate cultural diversity. Family and community literacy activities are important considerations. Family stories and literacy-promoting activities and events can be included in center planning. Collaboration with parents reinforces the unique contributions families and neighborhoods make to child literacy growth.

LANGUAGE ARTS CURRICULUM

Many early childhood **curriculum models** exist. Some are well known; others are little known. Models usually provide well-defined frameworks to guide program implementation. Child development theories are their underlying foundation. Whether a particular model, a combination of models, or an eclectic model is used, early childhood educators are constantly challenged to examine, reflect, and improve children's daily language arts experiences.

Schools and centers differ widely in **curriculum** development; however, two basic approaches can be identified. First a unit or thematic approach emerges from identified child interest and teacher-selected areas, such as families, seasons, animals, and so on. Using this approach, some centers use children's books or classic nursery rhymes as their thematic starting topic. Others introduce a proposed theme (unit) topic to small child discussion groups. This offers input from attending children and lets teachers explore children's past experience, knowledge, and interests. Questions children ask and vocabulary used may aid teachers' thematic unit development. Staff and parent group discussion can also uncover attitudes and resources. Goals are considered, and activities are then outlined and scheduled into time slots. Many teachers believe this type of program approach individualizes instruction by providing many interrelated and, consequently, reinforced learnings while also allowing the child to select activities.

The second common instructional approach is to pinpoint traditional preschool subject areas, such as language arts, science, mathematics, art, cooking, and so forth, and then plan how many and what kind of planned activities will take place. This can be done with or without considering a unifying theme. Some teachers believe that this is a more systematic approach to instruction.

In both approaches, the identification of goals has come before curriculum development. Ages of children, staffing ratios, facility resources, and other particulars all affect planning. After planned curriculum activities take place, teachers evaluate whether goals were reached and modifications and suggestions are noted. Additional or follow-up activities may be planned and scheduled for groups or individual children.

Thematic Inquiry Approach to Language Instruction

Imagine a classroom turned into a pizza parlor or a flower garden. There would be a number of activities occurring simultaneously—some for small groups, others for large groups, and some for individuals. Teachers would be involved in activities, and classroom areas might be set up for continuous, or almost continuous, child exploration. Art, singing, number, movement, science-related, health- and safety-related, and other types of activities would (or could) be preplanned, focusing on the two themes mentioned previously. The sensory activities could be included so that children could experience the smells, sounds, sights, tastes, and so on, associated with each theme. Planning language arts instruction using this approach allows teachers to use creativity and imagination. It also requires planning time to gather and set up material that might not be found in the school storeroom or supply area. It is easy to see that there could be many opportunities for children's use of speech, listening, reading, and writing, and the natural connection among these activities might be more apparent to the children. Most teachers believe that using a thematic approach is an exciting challenge that is well worth teacher time and effort. They see this approach as one that encourages child-teacher conversations and consequently expands children's language usage and knowledge.

Teachers should not limit their program to traditional themes but should explore and discover beyond the familiar. Teachers can follow children's curiosity and their own childhood interests. Many centers believe, as does Moon (1996), that real teaching is found when each

---

curriculum models — refers to a conceptual framework and organizational structure for decision making about educational priorities, administrative policies, instructional methods, and evaluation criteria (Goffin, 2000).
curriculum — an overall plan for the content of instruction to be offered in a program.

staff member gives children what she individually has to offer from the heart as well as the mind.

Develop exciting topics by using a planning strategy with three steps: (1) brainstorming, (2) designing a theme's implementation, and (3) planning specific activities for groups and learning centers.

In constructing a theme, the following steps are usually undertaken.

1. Observe and record a child's interest and/or teacher drawing from past experience.
2. Identify a topic (could be a book, poem, drama, or another category).
3. Try to discover what children know and want to know.
4. Imagine possible activities (in and out of school).
5. Decide on attempted goals of instruction.
6. Pinpoint range, scope, vocabulary, main ideas, and activities.
7. Discuss room environment, staffing, visitors, and helpers. (What will take place in the classroom or yard or in learning centers?)
8. Make specific plans for individual and group activities.
9. List the necessary materials and supplies.
10. Decide on a culminating activity (usually a recap or "grand finale").
11. Set a timetable if necessary. (Daily schedules may be prepared.)
12. Pinpoint evaluation criteria.

Williams (1997) uses a four-step child-teacher interactive process to jointly plan unit (theme) activities for a group of four-year-olds. A description of these steps follows:

1. The teacher asks, "What do you wonder?" or "What do you want to know about— (any particular topic, example: the ocean)?"

   Then the teacher records each child's answer or question in a different color on a wall chart that is posted at children's eye level. Then the teacher adds her own questions.

2. The teacher asks, "What can we do to find out?" Then the teacher records the chil-

dren's ideas on a second piece of chart paper. If no one responded, that is acceptable. The teacher instead develops a list of children's questions or ideas that might come up while the unit is in progress, and these are added to the chart.

3. The teacher asks, "What materials do we need?" on a prepared third chart. Materials suggested by the children that do not seem directly related are gently probed by teacher. A child may have a connection to the topic of study not readily seen by teacher.
4. The teacher asks, "What will you bring (do)?" and "What would you like me to bring (to do)?" The teacher checks with parents about objects and materials suggested by their child. A parent newsletter invites parents to share or bring in additional topic-related items to the classroom.

Burchfield (1996) describes a unit (theme) of study designed by practitioners who consider Gardner's theory of multiple intelligences (1993).

> ... allow children to experience a concept or skill in a variety of ways and demonstrate their learning and understandings by using their strong suits and by being challenged to develop their ability in areas identified (by parents, teachers, and even children) for more emphasis and improvement.

To promote literacy, teachers think about how each theme activity involves listening, speech, reading, and writing and how to logically connect these areas during ongoing activities.

Thematic/Literature-Based Instruction

Literature-based instruction, now mandated or recommended in elementary schools in many states, is very similar to what early childhood educators call thematic instruction. Both levels realize the value of literature and its relationship to literacy. A theme in early childhood could be any topic of interest to children. A literacy-based approach uses a classic book or informational book as its central core (Figure 6–12). A preschool educator would have no

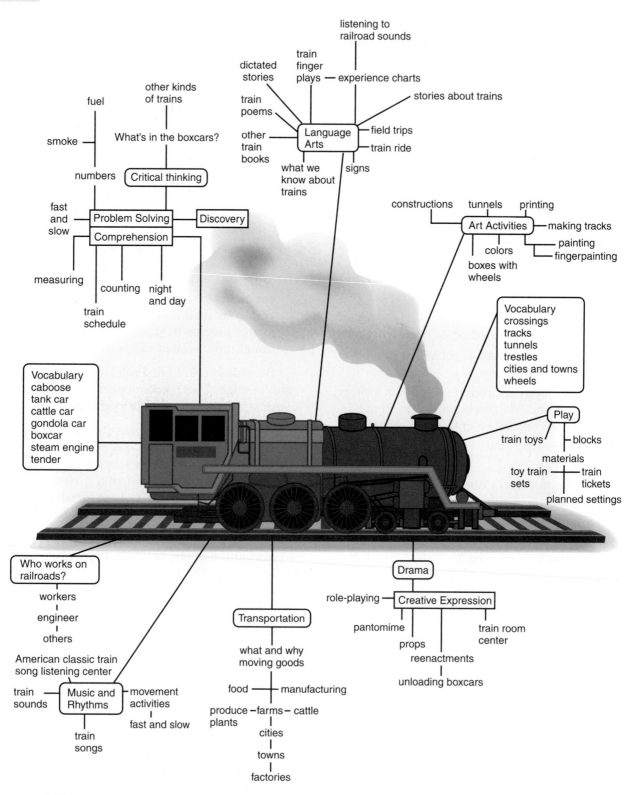

FIGURE 6–12 This webbing example suits a theme based on a picture book about trains, such as Donald Crew's book, *Freight Train*.

problem using a book as a starting place and could plan discussions, drama, art, music, puppetry, and other language arts activities to strengthen various concepts encountered.

Curriculum Webs and Webbing

The use of curriculum webs (or **webbing**) in program planning is popular with some preschool teachers (Figure 6–13). A web can be thought of as a graphic overall picture of what might be included in a theme or unit approach to instruction. Figure 6–14 shows a skeleton web designed for the study of dogs. Under the box "care & needs" one can think of a number of items that could be listed. In fact, the web could become highly detailed as the teacher using it listed concepts associated with the subject—dogs. The object of creating a web is for the teacher to define and refine the web based on the interests and needs of the particular enrolled group. The plan (web) is then translated into planned daily happenings with children's active exploring and participation. The goal is to offer activities to engage the students' interest and imagination and to spark their desire to seek out answers, ponder questions, or create responses. One of the rewards of teaching is to present or set up an activity that children eagerly select, and perhaps ask a million questions about; in other words, one that has "captured" them and engaged their minds.

Webbing is described by one staff member as follows:

> To get a plan, we choose an idea and brainstorm ways that a child could play with hands-on activities we could provide. Putting all the activities on a web gives you a road map full of possible journeys. It's like buying one of those three-month bus or train passes you can use to go anywhere. That's real different from having a nonrefundable, nonstop ticket from Los Angeles to Seattle.
>
> I think webbing has been more important as a process than as a product. (Jones & Nimmo, 1994)

WHY DO WEBBING?

Why do webbing? It gives a staff of adults the chance to explore the possibilities of any material or idea in order to make decisions about use: Is it worth doing? Is it likely to generate developmentally appropriate activities? What are the ways we might want to enrich the activity by being prepared with other materials or questions? How long might children's interest continue?

A web is a *tentative* plan. It does not tell you exactly what will happen or in what order. That depends in large part on the children's response. So, first you plan and then you start trying your ideas, *paying attention to what happens,* evaluating, and moving on with further activities.

FIGURE 6–13 Why do webbing? (From E. Jones & J. Nimmo. *Emergent curriculum* [Washington, DC: NAEYC, 1994], 111. Reprinted with permission from the National Association for the Education of Young Children.)

Reggio Emilia

Early childhood educators studying the Reggio Emilia approach to program planning are reexamining their curriculum. Gandini (1997) describes the teacher's role in the Reggio Emilia approach.

> To know how to plan or proceed with their work, teachers observe and listen to the children closely. Teachers use the understanding they gain in this way to act as a resource for them. They ask questions and discover the children's ideas, hypotheses, and theories. Then the adults discuss together what they have recorded through their own notes, or audio or visual recordings, and make flexible plans and preparations. Then they are ready to enter again into dialogues with the children and offer them occasions for discovering and also revisiting experiences since they consider learning not as a linear process but as spiral progression.

Gardner (1999) identifies how Reggio Emilia curriculum develops.

---

webbing — a visual or graphic method of mapping a possible course of study.

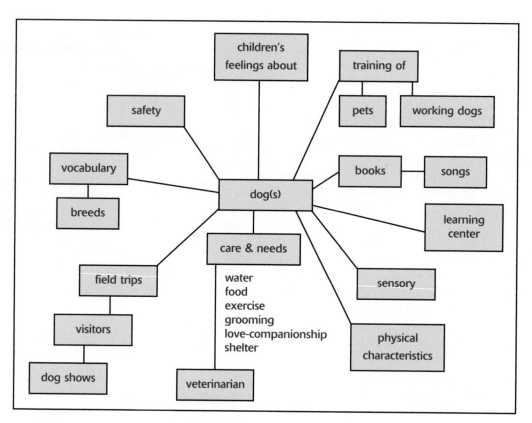

FIGURE 6–14 Topic web—dog(s).

The educators of Reggio Emilia have developed and continuously improved a set of techniques for taking the ideas and actions of young children seriously. Much thought is devoted to the opening exposure to experiences that might constitute themes to be developed in the coming weeks. But it is not possible to plan such a curriculum in advance. Rather, the particular reactions of particular children to particular experiences become the bedrock, the driving force of the "curriculum." The activities of next week (sometimes even the next day) grow out of the results, problems, and puzzles of this week, the cycle is repeated so long as it proves fruitful. Children and teachers are continually reflecting on the meaning of an activity, which issues it raises, how its depths and range can be productively probed.

For Hendrick's comparisons of American and Reggian schools (1997), see Figure 6–15.

A reading list for those exploring the Reggio Emilia approach is found in the Appendix.

The Project Approach

Based on the writings of Katz and Chard (1989), the project approach involves integrated teaching and learning. It encourages meaningful, firsthand, relevant study of child-teacher–developed and child-teacher–chosen activities. This program approach is valued by teachers for its flexible and creative aspects, which fit diverse child groups and geographical communities. Children are involved in decision making, program planning, implementation, and evaluation through active teacher-child shared discussion, brainstorming, and project outlining. Teachers also plan activities and experiences. Children are urged to explore and investigate and become testers of ideas as individuals and in study groups. Teachers using thematic unit instruction may feel the project approach best suits kindergarten and elementary-

AMERICAN	REGGIAN
"Projects" or themes are short lived, extending a day or a week.	"Projects" may be brief but often continue for weeks or months.
"Topics" are used to provide information and (possibly) practice in midlevel thinking skills.	"Topics" are used to pose problems and provoke thought.
Children acquire a shallow smattering of information on many subjects.	Children acquire in-depth knowledge about fewer subjects (i.e., "know more about less").
Inquiry learning focuses on science tables; some problem solving encouraged.	Pronounced emphasis on "provoking" children to propose reasons why things happen and possible ways to solve problems.
Children may show what they know by talking to the teacher about it.	Children show what they know by talking about it but also by using many different media: models, graphics, bent wire, dance, and so forth, to explain their ideas: "You don't know it until you can explain it to someone else."
The individual is emphasized; autonomy, self-responsibility, independence are valued.	Existence within the group is emphasized; sense of community and interdependence are valued.
Children select whatever they wish to participate in each day.	Children select what they want to do but are also encouraged to work in consistent small groups based on their continuing interests.
Time is highly regulated and scheduled.	Time flows easily in an unhurried way.
Record keeping is typically limited to results rather than work in progress—shows what children have learned (checklists, portfolios, observations) or do not know.	Record keeping—Documentation boards record what children "know" at beginning of and during, as well as end of, project; boards used for everyone to *revisit* and *recognize* their work as it progresses.
Teacher changes at least once a year.	Teachers remain with children for 3 years.
Staffing is teacher, or teacher plus aide.	Staffing is two teachers of equal rank plus services of a *pedagogista* and *aterlierista*.
There is a hierarchy of staff positions (i.e., director, teacher, aide).	There are no directors; everyone accepts various responsibilities.
Confrontation is avoided.	Debate and "confrontation" with different points of view between adults and with children are favored methods of learning for everyone.
Teachers tend to be isolated; policy about and regularity of staff meetings varies.	Close collaboration between *all* teachers occurs regularly and frequently.

FIGURE 6–15 A sampling of some additional comparisons of American and Reggian schools. (From Hendrick, J. [Ed.]. [1997]. *First steps toward teaching the Reggio way.* Upper Saddle River, NJ: Prentice Hall, Inc. © 1998. Reprinted by permission of Prentice Hall, Inc.)

aged children. Others have incorporated projects into preschool curriculum.

COMMITMENT TO GOALS AND OBJECTIVES

A number of factors determine whether program goals are met.

◆ enthusiasm and commitment of staff
◆ staffing ratios
◆ staff ingenuity and resourcefulness
◆ methods and techniques used
◆ resources available
◆ general feeling or tone of center
◆ examination of sequence (easy to complex)
◆ parental and community support

Effort and staff creativity translate goals into daily activities.

Daily Activity Plans

Recognizing children's interests stimulates activity-planning ideas based on what captures and holds the children's attention. Part of the challenge and excitement of teaching is finding ways to be creative in daily activity planning.

Although two staff members work toward the same goal, they may approach the task in different ways. Lesson plans are more frequently used in schools using approaches other than the thematic (unit) approach described earlier but can also be used for individual teacher-conducted activities within theme planning.

Lesson plans (or **activity plans**) enable teachers to foresee needs—settings, materials, and staffing. The time that children spend waiting can be minimized. Some teachers pinpoint exactly what words and concepts will be emphasized or what questions asked; other teachers prefer a more spontaneous approach.

Jacobs and Eskridge (1999) describe a teacher's change of feeling concerning the preparation and use of lesson plans.

> Take the new, well-trained teacher who expressed resentment over the school's expectation that teachers prepare lesson plans. Because she fondly remembered the spontaneous classroom of a favorite elementary schoolteacher, she believed that such planning interferes with spontaneity. After discussing her memories of the teacher and the classroom activities that seemed so "spontaneous," she realized that many creative opportunities in the classroom are based on foresight and only look and feel spontaneous because of detailed planning. By clarifying her memory, this young teacher was able to understand the purpose and importance of lesson planning.

Some activities in language arts may require teacher practice beforehand. Others may require visual aids or materials that must be gathered in advance. Planning time is time well spent. Preparation reduces teacher tension and results in child activities that run smoothly.

Teachers must strive to be always aware of child safety and comfort. They must also try to maintain a reasonable level of stimulation somewhere between not very interesting and overly exciting activities so that children are encouraged to process information in a manner that is both pleasurable and efficient. Experienced teachers know when children are interested and are actively participating. Many teachers say this is one of the greatest joys of teaching.

Group size is an important factor in planning. It is easier for teachers to plan for an entire class group, and sometimes staffing demands it. However, many teachers have explored ways to keep children occupied and supervised while working with small groups. Small groups allow greater intimacy, conversational depth, and opportunity for feedback. Research substantiates the idea that both children and adults feel more comfortable sharing their thoughts when in small groups. "Instant replays" with small groups can be planned and coordinated. Beginning preschool teachers may not have seen many small group activities modeled by other teachers, but this text recommends them.

Teachers strive to maintain children's attention during activities. Perry (2000) reminds teachers that attention is mediated by specific parts of the brain and that neural systems fatigue quickly. After 3 to 5 minutes of sustained activity, children need to rest, but they can recover within minutes too. In a familiar and safe classroom, if a child hears factual information for only 4 to 8 minutes and a teacher is not providing novelty, the brain seeks other stimuli. Perry recommends adding "emotional seasoning" like humor and empathy to teacher presentations and linking facts to related child concepts during activities, in addition to taking advantage of the novelty-seeking property of the human brain. He believes this is a challenging task for teachers of all-aged students.

Figure 6–16 describes how a teacher works toward a variety of goals in a planned two-part activity. Note the preplanned materials the teacher has secured or prepared beforehand.

Detailed written lesson plans help early childhood students feel prepared and relaxed (Figure 6–17). After a period of time, most beginning teachers internalize lesson-planning

activity plans — written, detailed, step-by-step teaching plans often including an evaluation section.

NOTE: This is a portion of a longer description. The words in italics show how the teacher works toward a variety of goals.

This episode is an account of a sequence of planned activities culminating in a cooking experience for four four-year-old children. Part 1 of the episode details the preparation in the classroom for the purchase of the food and the group's trip to a local store. Part 2 describes the cooking.

The fresh pears at lunch evoked the excited comment "Apples!" from Spanish-speaking Fernando.

"Well, this is a fruit," said Miss Gordon, encouragingly, "but it has another name. Do you remember the apples we had last week?"

"They were hard to bite," said Joey.

"And we made applesauce," said Rosina.

"This fruit is called a pear, Fernando; let's taste this pear now. We'll have apples again."

The teacher responds to what is correct in the child's response, valuing his category association. First, she wants to support communication and willingness to experiment with language; later she gives the correct name. The children strengthen the experience by relating it to previous experience in which they were active.

"Mine's soft," said Joey.

"Can we make applesauce again?" begged Rosina.

The teacher replied, "Perhaps we could do what Janice wanted to do. Remember? To take some home to her family?"

"To my mommy, and my grandma, and Danny."

"Not to my baby," said Rosina. "He's too little. Him only drink milk."

"Tomorrow we'll buy lots of apples," said Miss Gordon.

The teacher is building a sense of continuity by recalling earlier intentions that had been expressed by the children.

She rarely corrects use of pronouns for four-year-olds. She knows the child will learn through greater social maturity and hearing language.

After rest, Miss Gordon asked the children how they could take home their applesauce. "What can we put it in?"

Rosina ran to the house corner and returned with two baby food jars. "I bringed lots," she said. Miss Gordon remembered that Rosina had come to school lugging a bag full of baby food jars, many of which she had put away. "A good idea! And your mommy said she would keep more for us. Let's write a note to tell her we need them tomorrow."

Rosina dictated a note: "I got to bring bunches of jars to school. We are going to make applesauce. I love you, Mommy." Rosina painted her name with a red marker.

The teacher helps children to think ahead to steps in a process.

The use of a tense form, although incorrect, represents learning for the child. The teacher does not correct at this moment, when she is responding to the child's pleasure in solving the practical problem that had been posed. She is strengthening the connection between home and school.

The teacher helps the children learn that writing is a recording of meaning and a way of communicating.

The next day was jar washing and arranging time. Each of the four children put his or her jars on a tray on which there was a large card with the child's name.

Janice put on one jar for her mother, one for her grandmother, one for her brother, and after a pause, one for herself.

Rosina changed her mind. "My baby can have a little tiny bit," she said. So she needed a jar for her father, her mother, her baby, and herself.

Joey and the teacher figured out that he needed six, and that Fernando needed nine!

The children are actively involved in the steps preparatory to the planned activity—an experience in organization that has personal meaning.

The teacher's plan calls for recognition of one's own name and one-to-one counting of family members.

The teacher turned their attention to a chart near the cooking corner. She had made a recipe chart, pasting colored (magazine) pictures next to the names of the items they would need to make the applesauce and had taped a stick of cinnamon to the chart.

Miss Gordon said, "Let's look at the recipe chart. I have a list so we can remember to buy everything."

The children said, "Apples."

Miss Gordon checked her list.

Then, "Sugar."

The children were silent as they looked at the stick of cinnamon taped to the chart.

Miss Gordon suggested, "Smell it. Have we had it before?"

Joey remembered: "Toast! What we put on toast!"

"Yes," said Miss Gordon, and then gave the word, "cinnamon."

The children are having a dual experience—pictorial representation and formal symbol usage.

The teacher supplies the word after the children have revived their direct experience with the phenomenon (Biber, Shapiro, & Wickens, 1977).

FIGURE 6–16 Multiple-goal approach.

LANGUAGE ACTIVITY PLAN GUIDE

1. Language activity title _____
   _____

2. Materials needed _____
   _____
   _____

3. Location of activity (to be used when plan is developed for a particular classroom or area) _____
   _____

4. Number of children _____

5. Language goal or objective _____
   _____

6. Preparation (necessary teacher preparation, including getting materials or objects, visual aids, etc., ready) _____
   _____
   _____

7. Getting started (introductory and/or motivational statement) _____
   _____
   _____
   _____

8. Show and explore (include possible teacher questions or statements that promote language ability) _____
   _____
   _____
   _____
   _____

9. Discussion of key points, discoveries, conclusions, subjects for further study (what vocabulary and/or concepts might be included?) _____
   _____
   _____
   _____
   _____

10. Apply (include child practice or application of newly learned knowledge or skill when appropriate) _____
    _____
    _____
    _____

11. Transition statement (needed if activity plan is to terminate or if a second activity immediately follows) _____
    _____
    _____
    _____

12. Evaluation: (1) activity; (2) teacher; (3) child participation; (4) other aspects such as setting, materials, outcomes, etc.
    _____
    _____
    _____
    _____
    _____

FIGURE 6–17 Sample activity plan form.

components and discontinue detailed written plans, although they continue to use lists and outlines.

Watching the class carefully, keeping a notebook in a handy pocket, and writing down small observations can help a teacher remember the interests of a young group. A good guide to unearthing new subjects of interest for a particular class is to notice what has already captured the children's attention. What do the children talk about most often? What do they crowd around? Does the activity promote children's interested questions? What has the longest waiting list? Are children eager to explore a particular object with their hands? Who wants to share something discovered or created? For example, if butterflies interest a group, planned butterfly experiences can add depth to the curriculum.

Activities based on teacher enthusiasm for life and growth, skills, talents, hobbies, and pursuits can fit beautifully into language arts goals. Parent and community resources, including borrowed items and field trips, increase the vitality of programs.

Evaluation

Thinking back over planned activities helps teachers analyze the benefits and possibly leads to additional planning along the same line or with the same theme. Oversights in planning frequently occur, and activities may develop in unexpected ways. Hindsight is a useful and valuable tool in evaluating activities (Figure 6–18).

Often, centers evaluate their planned programs by asking themselves questions such as the following:

- Do children share personal interests and learning discoveries with teachers and/or other children?
- Can teachers enter conversations without diminishing children's verbal initiative?
- Do children become involved in planned activities and room centers?
- Are there times when children listen with interest?

THINKING BACK

What I planned and how I went about it:

_____
_____
_____

What effect my actions had:

_____
_____
_____

What I could have done:

_____
_____
_____

What effect this action would have had:

_____
_____
_____

What I will do differently next time:

_____
_____
_____
_____

FIGURE 6–18 Thinking back.

- Are language arts areas (speaking, writing, reading, listening) connected in a natural way during daily activities?
- Is child talk abundant?

SUMMARY

Traditionally, language arts instruction and planning have been based on the educational theories educators believed to be the best and effective. Historically, theories have, over time, changed, evolved, and emerged. Theorists' and researchers' ideas have been accepted and then come into vogue. Currently, research-based information has influenced federal legislation and publicly funded schools.

Language is part of every preschool activity. This text recommends an integrated approach to early childhood language arts, that is, a program that involves listening, speaking, writing, reading, and viewing.

Public centers identify language arts goals through a group process and consider standards. Activities are then planned. Approaches to activity planning are reviewed. Daily plans carry out what is intended. Assessment instruments are evaluated, and decisions are made concerning whether these instruments are to be used or not used. Staff observation provides data on children's abilities, interests, and skill levels, as well as additional insights that are useful in activity planning. Every center has a unique set of goals and objectives, so designing child experiences is done in a variety of ways. Program plans consider attending children's needs and interests.

Evaluating a planned activity after it is presented can pinpoint strengths and weaknesses. This also serves as the basis for further activity planning.

ADDITIONAL RESOURCES

Readings

Bunce, B. H. (1995). *Building a language-focused curriculum for the preschool classroom* (Vol. II). Baltimore: Brookes.

Campbell, R. (1998). *Facilitating preschool literacy.* Newark, DE: International Reading Association.

Hart, C., Burts, D., & Charlesworth, R. (1997). *Integrated curriculum and developmentally appropriate practice.* Albany, NY: State University of New York Press.

Heibert, E. H., & Raphael, T. E. (1998). *Early literacy instruction.* Fort Worth, TX: Harcourt Brace.

Ingraham, P. (1997). *Creating and managing learning centers: A thematic approach.* Peterborough, NH: Crystal Springs.

International Reading Association & National Association for the Education of Young Children (IRA & NAEYC). (1998). *Learning to read and write: Developmentally appropriate practices for young children.* Washington, DC: Author.

Jalongo, M. R. (1992). *Early childhood language arts.* Boston: Allyn and Bacon.

Katz, L., & Chard, C. (1989). *Facilitating preschool literacy.* Norwood, NJ: Ablex.

National Institute of Child Health and Human Development. (2000). *Report of the National Reading Panel. Teaching children to read: An evidence-based assessment of scientific research literature and its implications for reading instruction.* Washington, DC: U.S. Government Printing Office.

Neuman, S. B. (2002). *What research reveals: Foundation for reading instruction in preschool and primary education.* Washington, DC: U.S. Department of Education.

HELPFUL WEB SITES

Early Literacy Advisor
http://www.mcrel.org
This site promotes early literacy development. Search for "early literacy advisor" and then follow the links.

ERIC—Early Childhood Research & Practice
http://ecrp.uiuc.edu
This site provides research articles, theme instruction, project approach information, ERIC standards and assessments, and information about how to develop program goals.

National Association for the Education of Young Children
http://www.naeyc.org
This site is a major resource for information on program planning.

National Reading Panel
http://www.nationalreadingpanel.org
This site reports research-based instructional practices for young children. Select *Publications and Materials* to obtain a full copy of *Teaching Children to Read,* the year 2000 report of the National Reading Panel.

Texas Education Network
http://www.tenet.edu
Provides guidelines (curriculum goals) developed in Texas.

Language and literacy standards for prekindergarten group programs have been developed by Head Start, many states, professional associations, and others. Each set of standards has attempted to identify instructional goals for programs working with young children. The author has put together a combined list of often-mentioned desired outcomes (goals) in language arts by consulting a number of well-regarded sources. An update of the No Child Left Behind Act's progress is also provided, along with Web sites, which provide resources for teachers working with at-risk or language-diverse learners.

STUDENT ACTIVITIES

1. Define literacy in your own words or discuss changes in what skills and knowledge are now required to function in the present "computer age." Share with the class.

2. List 10 reasons for illiteracy in the United States. Then, list 10 ways preschool centers can help a preschooler's early literacy. Ask for a volunteer to make a chart on a large surface that everyone in the classroom can see, listing the reasons for illiteracy that are given by students. Put tallies after ideas so that the class can see what was the most frequently thought of reason. Make a second large listing of the group's ideas concerning how preschools can promote early literacy.

3. Form a discussion group with a few fellow students. Take out one item from your pocket or purse. Describe an activity you could use with children to promote the following skills:

   a. Memory (naming or recalling)

   b. Discrimination

   c. Problem solving

   d. Perceptual-motor skill

   Be aware that each activity planned should

   ◆ be interesting and enjoyable.

   ◆ help children feel competent and successful.

   ◆ stimulate children to discover.

   ◆ promote sensory exploration.

   ◆ include learning by doing.

   ◆ promote language by promoting expression of what the child experienced or discovered.

   Go on to discuss what activities could be planned that would promote the same four skills (a through d) using a box of paper clips or a doll.

4. Form two groups of five students. Each group takes 10 to 15 minutes preparing to react to the following issue.

   Over the last six years or so, kindergarten teachers across the country have been feeling the pressure of a rising tide of academic expectations. When I attend regional conferences and teacher workshops and talk to colleagues and friends, I hear the same concern: Kindergartners are now expected to learn what had once been in the domain of a first grade curriculum.

   Excerpt from DeVault, L. (2003, November). The tide is high, but we can hold on. *Young Children, 58*(6), 90–93.

   Students in the audience are to identify key statements made by either group.

5. Using any activity plan form, make a written plan for a language development activity. Share your plan with others at the next class meeting. Rate the quality of your participation in the discussion using the following scale, or write a beginning outline for a theme of your own choosing or one you believe is of interest to a group of four-year-old children. Share your theme ideas at the next class meeting.

No Input	Very Little	Contributed about as Much as Classmates	A Fair Amount	Offered Lots of Ideas

6. Ask a practicing early childhood teacher to speak about the use of assessment instruments in the language program where the person is employed.

7. Look back into your own childhood before age six. What classics, songs, rhymes, and language activities were part of your childhood? If you do not remember, answer this alternative question: Which literacy-promoting language activities should not be missed by any child? Be specific, and name poems, books, rhymes, stories, or other literary experiences.

8. After reading the following passage, discuss the ability of musical activities to promote cultural understanding.

Music has often been termed "the universal language." It offers one of the most direct and accessible ways of experiencing the aesthetic style and feeling of a particular culture. Incorporating the music of a child's own culture into an early childhood setting creates a more homelike environment in which a child will feel more secure and validated. (Jaffe, 1992)

CHAPTER REVIEW

A. Name the four interrelated language arts areas, arranging them in what you believe is their order of appearance in young children. Include the visual literacy area in your discussion.

B. Write three language arts goal statements (what you would want children to have the opportunity to experience and learn). These should be statements that would be included in a program where you are (or will be) employed.

C. Select the correct answer. Each item may have more than one correct answer.

1. Assessment instruments can be
   a. a checklist.
   b. a child interest inventory.
   c. counted on to be valid.
   d. teacher made.

2. Compiling and identifying a center's goal statements ideally involves
   a. children's input.
   b. staff.
   c. parents.
   d. interested community members.

3. Early childhood language arts should be offered to children using
   a. an approach that helps children see relationships between areas.
   b. techniques that promote the child's realization that spoken words can be written.
   c. separate times of day to explore reading and writing without combining these skills.
   d. identified goal statements as a basis for activity planning.

4. When goals are identified, a school (or center) could
   a. retain its flexibility in activity planning.
   b. lose its ability to fulfill children's individual needs if the same activity plans are used from year to year.
   c. keep its program "personal" by continually evaluating and updating.
   d. periodically take a close look at goals to see whether staff commitment is strong or weak.

5. Using commercial assessment instruments
   a. is questionable because reliability varies.
   b. serves as the basis of professional programming.
   c. can mean using teacher-designed assessments is out of the question.
   d. is a group decision.

6. "There is only one correct way to plan and present activities to children." This statement is
   a. true.
   b. false.
   c. partly true because each individual strives to find the one plan that helps planned activities run smoothly and successfully.
   d. incorrect because the plan itself does not ensure success or goal realization.

7. Although language arts goals may be identified, language
   a. is part of every activity.
   b. can be taught through music activities.
   c. skills may grow whether planned activities are offered or not offered.
   d. activities offered daily cannot ensure that goals attempted will be attained.

INDIVIDUAL ACTIVITY

UNDERSTANDING LOCATIONAL WORDS

Note: This is a self-selected child activity set up during a study of transportation for a class of three- and four-year-olds. A waiting list is available, so children are ensured a turn.

Purpose: Child will be able to place vehicle "under," "over," "behind," and "in front of" when given verbal directions after becoming familiar with the words in the play situation.

Materials: streets and a highway drawn on a large sheet of paper taped to a table; toy vehicles (car, truck, school bus, van, etc.); blocks, a box, or cardboard to make a highway overpass

Procedure:
1. Place box with toy vehicles inside in front of child. "Tell me about what you find in the box." Verbally label each vehicle if child does not.
2. Pause and let child talk about toy vehicles. Introduce overpass and discuss "under" and "over" the bridge.

3. "We're going to take turns. First, I'm going to ask you to put the vehicles in different places. Then, you tell me where you want me to place one of the vehicles."

4. "Can you drive the car *under* the bridge?" Encourage child if necessary. Pause. "Which vehicle do you want me to drive *under* the bridge? The bus?"

5. "My turn. Drive the truck *over* the bridge." Pause. "Which one do you want me to drive *over* the bridge?"

6. "Put the bus in front of the car." "Which one do you want me to move *in front of* the bus?"

7. Proceed until all four locational words are introduced and demonstrated. Then, "Tell me where you choose to drive or park the toys. I'll watch you."

8. Allow child time to play as she wishes. As the child continues with the activity, add comments when appropriate, such as, "You drove the van *under* the bridge."

GROUP ACTIVITY

VISUAL PERCEPTION

Purpose: matching identical stockings game

Materials: enough matching pairs of stockings for each child in the group (more pairs if possible); use of socks of any size but different in color or pattern; two bags (separate, putting one sock of each pair in bags); plastic zip lunch bags

Procedure:
Additional activity ideas include:

1. discussing stockings by examining the differences in socks children are wearing. Talking about how socks are kept together at home, whether a stocking has been lost, and if one visited their home, where stockings are found.

2. introducing intact pairs in a basket. "To play our game, we need to select one pair from the basket, and then put one sock in one of the provided bags and the second in the other bag. We'll take turns. Mary, choose a pair of socks and tell us something about the pair you choose." Give each child a turn.

3. "Now we can start our game. I'm going to mix them all together and make a big pile of stockings, and then we'll try to find two stockings that are the same and put them in a plastic lunch bag so that we can keep each pair together. When you find two that match raise your hand. Here is the plastic lunch bag. Keep the socks you've found and put each pair in a plastic sack in front of you." Continue taking turns until all socks are paired. Count or discuss sock pairs, color, size, pattern, and so on.

Reinforcement Activities:

1. Turn this group activity into an individual activity in which one child can pair all the socks. A standing clothes rack or a clothesline can be used.

2. Mittens or shoes can also be matched in a similar group activity. The closer the distinctions, the more difficult the match.

CHAPTER 7

Promoting Language and Literacy

OBJECTIVES

After reading this chapter, you should be able to:

- List three roles of a teacher in early childhood language education.
- Discuss the balances needed in teacher behavior.
- Describe ways a teacher can promote language growth.

KEY TERMS

closure	explanatory talk
expansion	extension

CHILDREN'S LITERACY PORTFOLIOS

Miss Powell, a kindergarten teacher, planned a home visit to each entering child in her fall kindergarten class. At one home, a mother proudly shared the child's preschool literacy portfolio. Miss Powell was able to sit with both her soon-to-be student and the child's mother as they both commented on items in the binder. She found the child was reading a few words and had a huge interest in cats. Although she knew her district would test each child after school started, she was delighted with this home visit.

QUESTIONS TO PONDER

1. How can Miss Powell put to good use the information she now has about this child?

2. Would you suggest that a child literacy portfolio be part of this child's kindergarten experience also?

A good description of a skilled early childhood educator is a "responsive opportunist" who is enthusiastic, who enjoys discovery, and who is able to establish and maintain a warm, supportive environment. When a reciprocal relationship between a child and an adult or between children is based on equality, respect, trust, and authentic dialogue (real communication), child language learning is promoted. Calkins (1997) points out that talk is at the foundation of a child's learning life. Teachers need to create a classroom atmosphere where children can expect success, see the teacher as a significant person, are allowed choice, and are able to make mistakes. Ideally, children should join in planned activities eagerly. These activities should end before the child's capacity to focus is exhausted. The child should be able to expect the teacher to listen and respond to the child's communication in a way that respects the child's sense of the importance of the communication.

Studies examining the quality of language environments in American preschools found that many preschools serving *poor* children scored in the inadequate range (Snow, Burns, & Griffin, 1998). The quality of group book experiences, cognitively challenging conversation, and teacher use of a wide vocabulary were associated with quality environments and young children's subsequent language and literacy development. Kontos and Wilcox-Herzog (1997) emphasize the importance of adult-child interaction. They are disturbed that some children may rarely interact with a preschool teacher and receive little or no individualized attention. Some preschools may be failing the very children who need a quality literacy environment to prepare them for later schooling.

Barnett (1995) concludes that preschool programs can produce large effects on intellectual growth during early childhood years, but some of those effects may decline over time. This is not always the case. Children enrolled in the Abecedarian Project, an experimental preschool program that emphasizes language and cognitive development, attained significantly higher reading achievement that lasted through grade eight in elementary school (Campbell & Ramey, 1994). The project took place in rural North Carolina with a study sample of poor African-American children. The intervention program included a preliteracy and prephonics curricula emphasizing phoneme identification (Campbell & Ramey, 1995). A school-age follow-up component provided parents with activities to reinforce basic reading concepts being taught at school. Goldenberg (2002) states:

> The preschool intervention alone had a substantial effect, although not as great as that of the combined preschool and school-age intervention.

Barnett (2003) found that the project affected children's reading and literacy scores in a positive way into early adulthood.

TEACHING STRATEGIES AND BEHAVIORS

Three specific teaching functions that encourage the development of language arts and literacy are discussed in this chapter.

1. The teacher serves as a *model* of everyday language use. What is communicated and how it is communicated are important.

2. The teacher is a *provider* of experiences. Many of these events are planned; others happen in the normal course of activities.

3. The teacher is an *interactor*, sharing experiences with the children and encouraging conversation (Figure 7–1).

These three functions should be balanced, relative to each child's level and individual needs. The teaching role requires constant decision making: knowing when to supply or withhold information to help self-discovery and when to talk or listen (Figure 7–2). Basically, sensitivity can make the teacher the child's best ally in the growth of language skills. Calkins (1997) emphasizes the importance of teachers' attitudes toward children's talk and teachers' recognition of children's thinking. Kontos and Wilcox-Herzog (1997) studied teacher-child interactions and

FIGURE 7–1 Sharing books with individual children encourages children to talk about personal interests.

believe teachers with more education are more responsive and sensitive. Newer, stricter licensing regulations regarding the training of child care staff members in Florida's preschool classrooms improved the quality of teacher-child interactions (Howes, Smith, & Galinsky, 1995). Research consistently shows that training is an important predictor of involved, sensitive teacher-child conversations (Kontos & Wilcox-Herzog, 1997).

Observing all elements of a program, as well as children's behavior and progress, involves watching, listening, and recording. This can be the most difficult part of teaching because of time constraints and supervisory requirements. With so much to supervise and provide, teachers can view observation time as a luxury. In-depth observation is best accomplished when a teacher is relieved of other responsibilities and can focus without distractions. Many teachers

Nondirective					Mediating			Directive
Acknowledge	Model	Facilitate	Support	Scaffold	Co-construct	Demonstrate		Direct
Give attention and positive encouragement to keep a child engaged in an activity.	Display for children a skill or desirable way of behaving in the classroom, through actions only or with cues, prompts, or other forms of coaching.	Offer short-term assistance to help a child achieve the next level of functioning (as an adult does in holding the back of a bicycle while a child pedals).	Provide a fixed form of assistance, such as a bicycle's training wheels, to help a child achieve the next level of functioning.	Set up challenges or assist children to work "on the edge" of their current competence.	Learn or work collaboratively with children on a problem or task, such as building a model or block structure.	Actively display a behavior or engage in an activity while children observe the outcome.		Provide specific directions for children's behavior within narrowly defined dimensions of error.

FIGURE 7–2 *Continuum of teaching behaviors.* (From S. Bredekamp & T. Rosegrant, "Reaching Potentials through Transforming Curriculum, Assessment, and Teaching," in *Reaching potentials: Transforming Early Childhood Curriculum and Assessment,* Vol. 2, eds. S. Bredekamp & T. Rosegrant [Washington, DC: NAEYC, 1995], 21. Reprinted with permission from the National Association for the Education of Young Children.)

who do not have duty-free observation time must observe while on duty. Observation often unearths questions regarding children's difficulties, talents, and a wide range of special needs that can then be incorporated into plans and daily exchanges.

The teacher's role as an observer is an ongoing responsibility that influences all daily teacher-child exchanges and allows the teacher to decide on courses of action with individual children. Knowing children's interests, present behaviors, and emerging skills helps the teacher perform the three aforementioned functions, based on group and individual needs. As Ayers (1993) points out, teachers must be part detective and part researcher, sifting through the clues children leave, collecting data, testing hypotheses, and "looking unblinkingly at the way children really are . . ." in order to fill out and make credible the story of their growth and development.

Listening intimately is highly advisable. Providing growth depends partially on being on a child's or group's wavelength. Conversations are more valuable when teachers try to converse and question based on the child's line of thought. Activities provided should increase children's ability to think and rethink and therefore make sense from what they encounter.

Unplanned teacher talk can be viewed as less important than talk in teacher-guided activities. If a teacher thinks this way, it can limit his ability to support problem solving, child discovery, and child expression of events important to the child. The listening and observing behavior of teachers increases the quality and pertinence of teachers' communicative interactions.

THE TEACHER AS A MODEL

Teachers model not only speech but also attitudes and behaviors in listening, writing, and reading. Children watch and listen to adults' use of grammar, intonation, and sentence patterns and imitate and use adults as examples.

Consider the different and similar ways teachers verbally interact with young children (Figure 7–3). After studying British families, Bernstein (1962) theorized that a recognizable

Example A

Child: "It's chickun soup."
Teacher: "That's right."

Example B

Child: "It's chickun soup."
Teacher: "Yes. I see chicken pieces and something else."
Child: "It's noodles."
Teacher: "Yes, those are long, skinny noodles. It's different from yesterday's red tomato soup."
Child: "Tastes good. It's 'ellow."
Teacher: "Yellow like the daffodils in the vase." (Pointing.)

Example C

Child: "Baby cry."
Adult: "Yes, the baby is crying."

Example D

Child: "Baby cry."
Adult: "You hear the baby crying?"
Child: "Uh-huh."
Adult: "Maybe she's hungry and wants some milk."
Child: "Wants bottle."
Adult: "Let's see. I'll put the bottle in her mouth."
Child: "Her hungry."
Adult: "Yes, she's sucking. The milk is going into her mouth. Look, it's almost gone."

FIGURE 7–3 Adult verbal styles.

style of verbal interaction based on social class exists. Working-class speakers, Bernstein believed, used a restricted code type of speech, whereas middle-class speakers used both elaborated code and restricted code speech in some verbal exchanges. Restricted code speech characteristics are described as follows:

- specific to a current physical context
- limited
- stereotyped
- condensed
- inexact
- nonspecific

- short in sentence length
- vague and indefinite

Elaborate code speech, in Bernstein's view, is

- more differentiated.
- more precise.
- not specific to a particular situation or context and affords opportunities for more complex thought.

Speakers' styles of communication were seen by Bernstein as powerful determining factors in the young child's development of cognitive structures and modes of communication. He believed that young children exposed exclusively to restricted code speakers are at an educational disadvantage in school settings where elaborated code speech predominates. The major assumption behind this view is that middle-class ways of talking with children support literacy development, whereas working-class ways inhibit it.

Many other researchers have investigated verbal exchanges between parents and children to pinpoint connections between adult talk and its relationship to child speech, thinking ability, and literacy. Sigel (1982) described parental high-level and low-level distancing strategies in verbal exchanges. High-level distancing strategies include:

- drawing conclusions.
- inferring cause-and-effect relationships.
- planning.
- evaluating consequences.
- evaluating effect.

Low-level distancing strategies include labeling, producing information, and observing. Sigel hypothesized that social class alone does not predict children's cognitive and linguistic outcomes. Early childhood educators observing young children would agree.

Beals (1993) suggested that preschool teachers focus on studying their ability to use **explanatory talk** in child-teacher verbal ex-

changes. Explanatory talk consists of conversation concerning some connection between objects, events, concepts, and/or conclusions that one speaker is pointing out to another (Figure 7–4). Preschool teachers commonly and typically explain their intent and actions to children and provide explanations in response to child comments and questions. This is a preferred behavior in early childhood teachers' verbal interactive exchanges.

> "The blocks go on the shelf. We will know where to find them when we want to use them, and no one will trip on them."

> "The window was open, and the wind blew and knocked over the small cups where our seeds were planted."

> "I'm putting my snack dish in the tub on the table when I'm finished. Mrs. Gregorio will come and get the tub after snack time. She'll wash our snack plates."

FIGURE 7–4 Explanatory talk also occurs when a child explains her connection to a book's illustration.

---

explanatory talk — a type of conversation characterized by a speaker's attempt to create connections between objects, events, concepts, or conclusions to promote understanding in the listener.

This explanatory style sometimes carries over into teachers' personal lives. Teachers report family members often say to them, "Yes, I know why you're doing that!"

Adults should use clear, descriptive speech at a speed and pitch easily understood. Articulation should be as precise as possible. Weiss and Lillywhite (1981) describe appropriate models during infancy and toddlerhood. These teacher characteristics are also desirable in teachers of preschoolers.

> . . . being a good model involves more than merely speaking clearly, slowly, and appropriately. A good model uses a variety of facial expressions and other forms of nonverbal communication; associates talking with love, understanding, affection; provides happy, pleasant experiences associated with talking; demonstrates the importance of clearly spoken words. A good model takes advantage of various timely situations. . . .

Speaking further about infancy, Weiss and Lillywhite note

> A good model imitates what the child says or echoes the sounds the child makes and provides many opportunities for the child to experiment with the vocal mechanism and rewards these early efforts.

Preschool teachers also need to be sure that reward in the form of attention is present in their teaching behavior as they deal with young children's attitudes, skills, and behaviors in language arts activities (Figure 7–5). Teachers should use language patterns with which they feel comfortable and natural and should analyze their speech, working toward providing the best English model possible. Familiar language patterns reflect each teacher's personality and ethnic culture. Knowing what kind of model one presents is important, because knowing that there is room for improvement can help a teacher become more professional. Hutinger (1978) suggests

> Record your own language . . . Listen to your questions, to your sentence structure, your pronunciation.

Modeling the correct word or sentence is done by simply supplying it in a relaxed, natural way rather than in a corrective tone. The teacher's example is a strong influence; when a teacher adds courtesy words ("please" and "thank you," for instance), these words appear in children's speech. Finishing an incomplete word

FIGURE 7–5 Giving attention can be a form of reward for some children.

by adding an ending or beginning may be appropriate with very young speakers. (The child may say, "na na"; the teacher would provide, "banana.") Completing a phrase or offering complete sentences in Standard English suits older speakers. Although adult modeling has its limits in facilitating spontaneous language, it is an essential first step in learning language.

After hearing corrections modeled, the child will probably not shift to correct grammar or usage immediately. It may take many repetitions by teachers and adults over time. What is important is the teacher's acceptance and recognition of the child's idea within the verbalization and the addition of pertinent comments along the same line.

When adults focus on the way something was said (grammar) rather than the meaning, they miss opportunities to increase awareness and extend child interest. Overt correction often ends teacher-child conversation. Affirmation is appropriate; the teacher should emphasize the child's intended message.

Adults can sometimes develop the habit of talking and listening to themselves rather than to the children; it is hypnotic and can be a deterrent to really hearing the child. If one's mind wanders or if one listens only for the purpose of refuting, agreeing, or jumping to value judgments, it interferes with receiving communication from others. Teachers need not be afraid of silences and pauses before answering. The following listening suggestions are recommended.

◆ Work as hard to listen as you do to talk.
◆ Try to hear the message behind the words.
◆ Consciously practice good listening.

One teaching technique that promotes language skill is simple modeling of grammar or filling in missing words and completing simple sentences. This is called **expansion**. It almost becomes second nature and automatic after a short period of intentional practice. When using an expansion, the adult responds to the child by expanding the syntactic composition of the child's utterance. For example, the child's, "It's cold," might be followed by, "The window pane felt cold when you pressed your nose against it." Teacher's expansion is contingent and responsive, focusing on what the child was experiencing. While using expansion, the teacher can also promote wider depth of meaning or spark interest by contributing or suggesting an idea for further exploration. Additional conversation usually occurs.

The teacher is a model for listening as well as speaking. Words, expressions, pronunciations, and gestures are copied, as is listening behavior. A quiet teacher may have a quiet classroom; an enthusiastic, talkative teacher (who also listens) may have a classroom where children talk, listen, and share experiences. The way children feel about themselves is reflected in their behavior. When teachers listen closely, children come to feel that what they say is worthwhile.

Modeling good printscript form (classroom or center manuscript print) should result after studying upcoming chapters in this text. Children seem to absorb everything in their environment, so it is necessary to provide correctly formed alphabet letters and numerals on children's work, charts, bulletin boards, and any displayed classroom print.

Teachers' use and care of books are modeled, as are their attitudes toward story and nonfictional book experiences. Through their observations of teachers' actions, children begin to develop ideas about how books should be handled and stored.

One teacher who wanted to model storytelling of personal stories divided a large paper into eight sections; in each section she drew a picture of different stages in her life. She showed this to her class and asked them to pick a picture, which she then related in storytelling (Mallan, 1994). Teachers also model poetry reading and its use, dramatization, puppet play, and many other language arts activities.

Covey's statement (1989) "What *we are* communicates far more eloquently than any-

expansion — a teaching technique that includes the adult's (teacher's) modeling of words or grammar, filling in missing words in children's utterances, or suggesting ideas for child exploration.

thing we say or do" was not written expressly for teachers of young children; nonetheless it is a good finale to this discussion.

THE TEACHER AS PROVIDER

As providers, preschool teachers strive to provide experiences that promote literacy. Fortunately, the number of interesting language arts activities one can offer children is almost limitless. Teachers rely on both their own creativity and the many resources available to plan experiences based on identified goals. Early childhood resource books, other teachers, teacher magazines, workshops, and conferences all contribute ideas.

Gathering activity ideas and storing them in a personal resource file is suggested, because it is almost impossible to remember all the activity ideas one comes upon. An activity file can include new or tried-and-true activity ideas. Developing a usable file starts with identifying initial categories (file headings) and adding more heads as the file grows. Some teachers use large file cards; others use binders or file folders. Whatever the file size, teachers find that files are very worthwhile when it comes to daily, weekly, and monthly planning. Often, files are helpful when ideas on a certain subject or theme are needed or when a child exhibits a special interest. A file collection is not used as the basis for activity planning but rather as a collection of ideas.

A large number of activity ideas are presented in following chapters. Your creativity can produce other ideas. Suggestions for separate file headings (categories) follow:

- ◆ Audiovisual Activities
- ◆ Bulletin Board Ideas
- ◆ Child Drama Ideas
- ◆ Children's Books
- ◆ Circle Time Ideas
- ◆ Classroom Environment Ideas
  - ◆ Listening Centers
  - ◆ Reading Centers
  - ◆ Writing Centers
- ◆ Dramatic Play Stimulators

- ◆ Dramatic Play Theme Ideas
- ◆ Experience Stories
- ◆ Field Trip Ideas
- ◆ Finger Plays
- ◆ Flannel Board Ideas
- ◆ Free and Inexpensive Material Resources
- ◆ Language Game Ideas
- ◆ Listening Activities
- ◆ Listening Center Ideas
- ◆ Magazine (Child's) Activities
- ◆ Patterns
- ◆ Perceptual-Motor Activities
- ◆ Poetry
- ◆ Printscript Ideas
- ◆ Puppets
- ◆ Reading Readiness Ideas
- ◆ Rebus Stories
- ◆ Seasonal Ideas
- ◆ Speaking Activities Ideas
- ◆ Stories for Storytelling
- ◆ Visitor Resources

Greenberg (1998, November) paints a colorful picture of what early childhood educators might provide as they strive to offer age-appropriate language activities. Her activity ideas follow:

. . . sing lively jingles and soothing lullabies; enjoy laughing lap games and forever intriguing Mother Goose rhymes; recite delightful poems and golden oldie childhood chants; join in choral chanting (or choral reading) of rhymes and fun poems; listen to audio and video cassettes containing songs (including the alphabet song) and rhythmic activities done by real pros—and sing, swing, clap, tap and dance along with them; play traditional preschool and kindergarten games such as London Bridge, Los Pollitos Dicer, and Who Stole the Cookies from the Cookie Jar?; read high-quality books—which have lovely language with pleasing, interesting rhythms, rich vocabulary, and predictable repetitions picking up on a particularly catchy word or phrase and playing with it; act silly with four-, five-, six-, seven- and eight-year-old children, latching onto a word a child says and fooling around with it; or engage in entertaining word games with a few children or the group.

As a provider of materials, a teacher must realize that every classroom object can become a useful program tool to stimulate language. From the clock on the wall to the doorknob, every safe item can be discussed, compared, and explored in some way (Figure 7–6). Because most school budgets are limited, early childhood teachers find ways to use available equipment and materials to their fullest.

Each teacher is a unique resource who can plan activities based on personal interests and abilities. Most teachers are pleasantly surprised to see how avidly their classes respond to their personal interests.

When the teacher shares enthusiasm for out-of-school interests, hobbies, projects, trips, and individual talents, he can help introduce children to important knowledge. Almost anything appropriate can be presented at the child's level. Whether the teacher is an opera buff, scuba diver, gourmet cook, stamp collector, or violin player, the activity should be shared in any safe form that communicates special interest and love of the activity, and the specific vocabulary and materials relating to the activity should be presented. Enthusiasm is the key to inspired teaching.

Providing for Abundant Play

Abundant opportunities for play are important to the child's language acquisition. Considerable research shows that child's play is in fact more complex than it is commonly believed to be. It provides a rich variety of experiences: communication with other children, verbal rituals, topic development and maintenance, turn taking, intimate speech in friendships, follower-leader conversations, and many other kinds of language exchanges. Peer play helps develop a wide range of communicative skills. Except when the children's safety is in question, children's natural ability to pretend should be en-

FIGURE 7–6 The classroom schedule can be an object of discussion.

couraged, and the flow of this kind of play should proceed without the teacher's interference. Children will want to talk to teachers about their play, and the teacher's proper involvement is to show interest and be playful themselves at times.

If a child has chosen to engage a teacher in conversation instead of play, or during play, the teacher should be both a willing listener and a competent, skillful conversationalist. Opportunities for play and opportunities to engage both children and adults in extended, warm, and personal conversations should be readily and equally available to the child.

Young children explore constantly. They want to do what they see others doing. Play opportunities usually involve manipulating something. When deeply involved in play, children may seem to be momentarily awestruck in their search for meanings, but soon they will approach adults with questions or comments.

When one observes preschoolers at play, it is obvious that they learn a great deal of language from each other. They gain skills in approaching other children and asking if they can play, or just nonverbally joining a play group in progress. They begin to understand what attracts others to them, how to imitate another child's actions or words, how to express affection or hostility, how to assume a leadership role, how to negotiate, and how to follow or refuse playmates' requests. These and other play skills help them stay engaged in a play group for a longer period of time.

Preschoolers at play may even argue over correct language use. Some observers believe that the majority of language teaching that takes place in the four-year-olds' classroom is child-to-child teaching.

A resourceful teacher will strive to provide a variety of play by regarding all of a center's area (and furnishings) as a possible place (or object) for safe and appropriate play. Creative use can be made of each foot of floor space.

Children need large blocks of uninterrupted time to construct knowledge and actively explore their problem-solving options in an environment thoughtfully and carefully prepared by the teacher (McMullen, 1998).

Providing Accurate and Specific Speech in All Content Areas

Although this text concentrates on teacher-child interactions in the subject field, language arts, other content areas, such as mathematics (numbers), social studies, health and safety, art, music, movement, and so on, will be subjects of teacher-child conversations and discussions. The same teacher techniques that are useful in building children's language competence and vocabulary in language arts are equally useful for other content areas. Every subject area has its own vocabulary and common terms that can overlap other fields of study. For example, the teacher may discuss "applying" paints during an art activity and "applying" an antibacterial on a wound or scratch. If children are focused on the number of muffins on a tray, or whether

there are enough scissors to go around, then teacher comments include number words.

Teacher comments should be as accurate and specific as possible in light of what the teacher believes the children might already know or have experienced (Figure 7–7). Purposeful teacher conversation adds a little more information than the children know and reinforces and adds depth to words already in the children's vocabulary. When working with numbers or other subjects, the teacher should use terminology that is appropriate to the subject area but at a level the children will understand. For example, the teacher might say, "Let's count the muffins" or "The tool in your hand is a wire whip" or "The metal cylinder attached to the wall is a fire extinguisher. Fire extinguishers have something inside that can be sprayed out to put out fires." In movement or music activities, many descriptive terms can be added to teacher demonstrations and conversations. Terms like *hop, jump,* and *stretch* or *soft, loud, high,* and *low* are easily understood when the child is in the process of experiencing them.

The teacher prompts children's use of the words that the teacher provides. Sometimes a teacher is careful to define new words immediately after using the new terms. In number activities, number words are used in the presence of a corresponding number of objects. In movement activities, types of movement are discussed with quick demonstrations.

It is important to introduce new terms in a natural conversational tone rather than within

FIGURE 7–7 Teachers' comments are based on their knowledge of individual children.

the framework of an obvious lesson. Leading a child or groups of children to new discoveries offers the teacher an opportunity to use specific and accurate terms and also makes children feel like partners in the discoveries.

In the theme (unit) approach to instruction, there is often identifiable terminology attached to the theme. Teachers sometimes outline the terms that might be encountered in a particular unit and try to include these specific terms in conversations. A unit on birds could include many terms and specific names that a teacher might need to research.

THE TEACHER AS INTERACTOR

An interactor can be defined as a person who is always interested in what a child is saying or doing. This person encourages conversation on any subject the child selects. An interactor is never too busy to talk and share interests and concerns and listens with the intent to understand. Understanding will make the interactor's responses more educationally valuable. Time is purposely planned for daily conversations with each child. When teachers talk about what they are doing, explain why particular results occur, and let children ask questions about procedures and results, children will have more exposure to and experience with extended forms of discourse (Snow & Tabors, 1993). These private, personal, one-on-one encounters build the child's feelings of self-worth and open communications. Conversations can be initiated with morning greetings such as the following:

> "Alphonse, I've been waiting to talk to you. Tell me about your visit to Chicago."
>
> "How is your puppy feeling today, Andrea?"
>
> "Those new blue tennis shoes will be good for running in the yard and for tiptoeing, too."

Educators are aware of the "reciprocal opportunity" that is always present in work with young children. A teacher tries to really hear verbal communications and sense nonverbal messages. They give undivided attention (if possible), which lends importance to and shows interest in children's ideas and also rewards children's efforts to use language and initiate social contact. A teacher can respond skillfully, first clarifying what the teacher thought he heard and then adding to the conversation and attempting to stimulate more verbalness, child discovery, some new feature or detail, or a different way of viewing something. The correctness of children's verbal expression of their thoughts, feelings, requests, or other intent is accepted and corrected only when it is socially unacceptable speech.

Tough's study of teacher-child interaction (1977) discovered that some teachers were warm and accepting but offered children little invitation to talk. "Teachers found it quicker and easier to anticipate students' needs and thus failed to seize opportunities that would make children want and need to talk."

Teachers, McMullen (1998) believes, can emphasize the mental or symbolic component of an activity and help children identify problems or dilemas by promoting children to put their ideas into words.

Tough (1977) suggests that teachers may need to raise their own awareness of their interactions with children, in other words, rate themselves on their ability to expand children's verbalness (Figure 7–8). Clay (1991a) alerts

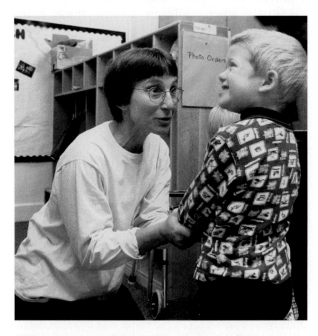

FIGURE 7–8 Notice this teacher's effort to make eye contact with the child as she speaks.

preschool educators to the importance of adult-child language interactions.

> For the first five years the child's language growth is entirely dependent on what people say to him—on how much they speak to him, about what things, in what dialect or language, and in what manner, whether gentle and explaining or peremptory and imperative.

Clay believes

> Through the things a preschool teacher attends to she reveals to children what she values.

> Such valuing of preschoolers' efforts and involvements is continuous, individual, personal, and powerful.

Hendrick (1998) reminds us that it is wise to be aware and up to date on topics of special interest to preschoolers. Current popular toys, cartoon figures, community happenings, sports, and individual family events may often be the focus of young children's conversations. When a teacher has background knowledge, such as what current Disney characters are popular or familiar to her students or which children have a new infant sibling at home, his responses when children discuss these items can be more pertinent and connected to the reality of enrolled children's lives.

Early childhood educators use a technique called **extension**. Building on a child's statement, the teacher adds information, factual data, or additional meaning. This can both add vocabulary and clarify some aspect or concept encountered in the conversational interchange. The child's, "It spilled," might be answered with, "Yes, Quan's hand knocked the cup over."

Many teachers have used a conversational interaction technique called **closure**. It involves pausing, specifically, hesitating in midsentence or at sentence endings. It is a technique that prompts child guessing, and the teacher is willing to accept any guess. Most often, child guesses are logical but may not be what the teacher expected. Those children with a sense of the ridiculous may offer off-the-wall guesses equally acceptable to the teacher. It often promotes further dialogue. The teacher's saying, "The sun disappeared behind a . . . ," might illicit "hill," "mountain," "building," "tree," "cloud," or other possibilities from the child. The teacher's saying, "Coats are hung in the . . . by the front door" is an example of a midsentence closure or fill-in statement.

In looking at individual children, Covey (1989) reminds us of what we know in our hearts to be true, fair, and compassionate. Each child is to be valued for his identity as a person and for his unique individuality, separateness, and worth. Comparisons between children cloud our view. Traits teachers may see as negative can be fostered by the environment we offer and our own perceptions of correct student behavior. An educator's job, according to Covey, is to recognize potential, then coddle and inspire that potential to emerge at its own pace. Weitzman (1992) urges teacher waiting behavior.

> When you wait, you give the child time to initiate or to get involved in an activity. You are, in effect, giving her this message: "You're in control—I know you can communicate, so you decide what you want to do or say. I'll give you all the time you need."

> Studies of adult-child interactions have shown that adults give children approximately one second in which to respond to a question. After one second, the adult repeats and rephrases the question or provides the answer. One second! Most children need much longer than one second to process the question and figure out their response.

---

extension — a teaching strategy in which an adult expands the child's information by adding new, additional, related information or meaning.
closure — a conversation technique that prompts children to verbally guess and complete or fill in a teacher's sentence. The teacher pauses or hesitates, which prompts the child to finish a teacher verbalization.

Adult speech containing a relatively high proportion of statements or declaratives has been associated with accelerated language development in young children (Harris, 1990). Adult-child conversations tend to last longer if adults add new relevant information. If adults verbally accept and react to children's statements with "oh, really?" or "I see," additional conversation seems to be promoted.

When a teacher answers a child by showing interest, this rewards the child for speaking. Positive feelings are read internally as an automatic signal to continue to do what we are doing (Ornstein & Sobel, 1987). Vygotsky's work (1980) suggests that teachers should guide and collaborate to promote children's independent problem solving in any given situation. Most often, teachers show their attention by listening to, looking at, smiling at, patting, or answering a child, or by acting favorably to what a child has said or done.

In Figure 6–16, in the previous chapter, the teacher and children were planning and participating in an activity. Children displayed interest and enthusiasm. This figure illustrates the teacher's thinking. She is guiding, providing, and interacting in a way that promotes children's verbalness and use of writing. It is easy to see that children exposed to this type of interaction with an adult are learning far more than language. In the example, language and thought are paired. There are obvious growth opportunities in both. How many similar situations in joint planning and joint problem solving are possible in the average classroom? The opportunities are limitless!

Note also that in Figure 6–16 not once did the teacher interact in a testlike manner by asking, "What color are apples?" or "What is this called on the recipe chart?" Rather, her verbal comments provoked children's discovery. When she prompted and it was obvious children were unfamiliar with a word (for example, *cinnamon*), the teacher offered it.

For those who want to ask thought-provoking questions, the work of Sanders (1966) provides another guide. As discussed earlier, teachers can get into the habit of asking recall questions that call for a "right" answer. Sanders calls this type of question a *memory question*. These questions do not promote critical thinking. Sanders' other question types are *transition, interpretation, application, analysis, synthesis,* and *evaluation*. Critical thinking, judgment, and problem solving are required to answer these questions. Try to identify to which of Sanders' categories the following belong.

1. What might happen if Emma takes Maria's paint without first asking for it?
2. In our story, Josh carried all the eggs in a basket. Could we use something to carry our small blocks outside? We don't have a basket.
3. Saucedo said he was sorry when he knocked down Kai's block tower. What else might he have done to show Kai he was sorry?
4. What happened to make Ching so angry in our story? Would you do what Ching did?
5. Our pet, Missy, gets so frightened when people gather around her cage. What rules should we make?
6. Noah said, "The ant ate an elephant," and you all laughed. Why?
7. When Latanya said, "It won't work if you do that," what did she mean? Why wouldn't the scissors work?

Although some may seem to fit in more than one category, you should agree that all of these examples required much more thinking than a memory-checking question.

Teachers trying to determine their questioning skills can test themselves using Figure 7–9. In addition, Tough (1977) offers teachers the following interactional techniques to extend conversations.

◆ Invite children to speak by developing a relationship that encourages talking through being a good listener—smiling; nodding; and saying, "mm," "yes," and "really" tell the child to go ahead and you are listening.

◆ Reflecting back on what the child has said, show your understanding.

◆ Use questions that are indirect and give the child the choice of answering or not.

TEST YOUR QUESTIONING AND RESPONDING ABILITIES

Answer the following using A = always, S = sometimes, N = need to work on this, or U = unable to determine.

1. Do I respond to child-initiated comments 100 percent of the time? _____
2. Do I keep to the child's topic and include it in my response? _____
3. Do I ask questions that prompt children to see or discover an aspect that they might not have perceived or discovered? _____
4. Am I aware of the favorite subjects and interests of individual children and ask questions along these lines? _____

   Are my questions appropriate in light of the children's development levels? _____
5. Do I often answer a child's comments using teacher echolalia?

   Child: "I went to the zoo."

   Teacher: "Oh, you went to the zoo."

   Or would my answer more likely be, "What animals did you see?" _____
6. Are my questions usually open ended? _____
7. Are my questions thought-inducing, or are they merely seeking correct answers? _____
8. Do I provide a specific response to children's questions? _____
9. Do my questions take place in the context of mutual trust and respect, based on my genuine friendliness, unconditional acceptance, warmth, empathy, and interest? _____
10. Do many of my questions seem to put a child "on-the-spot" or fluster a child? _____

FIGURE 7–9 Assess your questioning and responding abilities.

◆ Let the child know it is okay not to answer your question by using phrases such as, "Do you want to tell me about . . . ?" or "If you'd like, I'd like to know how . . ."

◆ When the child is eager to talk, use more direct open-ended questions—"What do you see?"

Teachers often act as interpreters, especially with younger preschoolers. The child who says "Gimme dat" is answered with "You want the red paint." Do not worry about faulty teacher interpretations! Most children will let teachers know when they have interpreted incorrectly by trying again. Then the teacher has the opportunity to say, "You wanted the blue paint, Taylor."

Harris (1990) has identified a number of language-developing, teacher speech interactions that may be used in conversations with young children.

1. Use language slightly more complex than the child's.
   Child: "Those are cookies."

Teacher: "Yes, they're called gumdrop mountains because they come to a point on the top."

2. Speak with young or limited-language children by referring to an action, object, person, and/or event that is currently happening.
   Teacher: "You're climbing up the stairs."

3. Base your reactive conversation on the meaning the child intended. There are three ways to do this: (1) *repetition* ("Pet the dog" to child's "Pet dog"); (2) *expansion* (the child says, "play bath," and the teacher expands with, "You want to play with your toys in the bath tub"); and (3) *recasting* (The child says, "You can't get in," and the teacher responds, "No, I can't get in, can I?")

4. Use "I see," "Yes," or a similar expression to indicate you are listening.

Harris (1990) also suggests that conversations be adultlike, allowing children to make comments, tell about happenings and how they feel, and exchange information. This is possible throughout the preschool day (Figure 7–10).

A teacher may find it harder to interact verbally with quiet children than with those children who frequently start conversations with the teacher. The teacher should be aware of this tendency and make a daily effort to converse with all attending children. Morrow (1989) reminds teachers that their role is to associate language with pleasure and enjoyment.

Teachers shift to more mature or less mature speech as they converse with children of differing ages and abilities. They try to speak to each according to his understanding. They use shorter, less complex utterances and use more gestures and nonverbal signals with infants, toddlers, and speakers of foreign languages. Generally, the ability to understand longer and more complex sentences increases with the child's age.

At times, it will be prudent for the teacher to pause or refrain from speaking. Young children who are talking to themselves, directing their actions with self-talk, will appear to be in their own little world. Intrusion by an adult is not expected by the child, nor is it necessary. Children usually think out loud while they are deeply absorbed in self-pursued activities. Adult talk at these times can be interruptive.

The teacher who interacts in daily experiences can help improve the child's ability to see relationships. Although there is current disagreement as to the teacher's ability to promote cognitive growth (the act or process of knowing), attention can be focused and help provided by answering and asking questions. Often, a teacher can help children see clear links between material already learned and new material. Words teachers provide are paired with the child's mental images that have come through the senses. Language aids memory because words attached to mental images help the child retrieve stored information.

Intellectually valuable experiences involve the teacher and parent as active participants in tasks with the child. Adults can label, describe, compare, classify, and question, supporting

FIGURE 7–10 Bending or kneeling puts adults at an appropriate level to engage in intimate conversation.

children's intellectual development. An example of this type of interaction follows:

> Sonja (24 months old) says something about a circus. Mother: "No, you didn't go to the circus—you went to the parade." Sonja: "I went to the parade." Mother: "What did you see?" Sonja: "Big girls." Mother smiles. "Big girls and what else?" Sonja: "Trumpets." Mother: "Yes, and fire engines. Do you remember the fire engines?" Sonja: "You hold my ears a little bit." Mother smiles. "Yes, I did, just like this," and puts her hands on Sonja's ears. Sonja laughs. (Carew, 1980)

As the teacher interacts by supplying words to fit situations, it should be remembered that a new word often needs to be repeated in a subtle way. It has been said that at least three repetitions of a new word are needed for adults to master the word; young children need more.

Teachers often hear the child repeating a new word, trying to become familiar with it. Teacher speech should be purposefully repetitive when a new word is encountered.

There are times when a teacher chooses to supply information in answer to direct child questions. There is no easy way for the child to discover answers to questions like, "What's the name of today?" or "Why is that man using that funny stick with a cup on the end?" A precise, age-level answer is necessary, such as "Today is Monday, May 9" and (while demonstrating) "It's a stick, called a plunger. It pushes air and water down the drain and helps open the pipes so that the water in the sink will run out." As a provider of information, the teacher acts as a reference and resource person, providing the information a child desires. If the teacher does not wish to answer a question directly, he may encourage the child to ask the same question of someone else or help the child find out where the answer is available.

Child: "What's lunch?"

Adult: "Come on, we'll go ask the cook."

or

"I'll have to go and read our posted menu. Come on, let's go see what it says."

A teacher can help the child focus on something of interest. The child's desire to know can be encouraged. Repetition of words and many firsthand activities on the same theme will help the child form an idea or concept. The child may even touch and try something new with the teacher's encouragement.

The teacher's reaction supplies children with feedback to their actions. The teacher is responsible for reinforcing the use of a new word and gently ensuring that the children have good attitudes about themselves as speakers.

Every day, the teacher can take advantage of unplanned things that happen to promote language and speech. Landreth (1972) provides an illustration.

> While children were sitting in a story group, John noticed that a mobile, hung from the ceiling above, was spinning. "Look," said John pointing, "it's moving!"

"How come?" said another child. "Someone must have touched it," said Mary. "Stand up, Mary, and see if you can touch it," added the teacher, standing up and reaching, herself, "I can't reach it either." "Maybe it spins itself," contributed Bill. "No, it can't spin itself," said another child. "Let's see," said the teacher. She got a piece of yarn with a bead tied to the end and held it out in front of the children. It was still. Then she held it near the mobile, which was in a draft of a window. The string swayed gently. "The window, the window is open," suggested the children. "Yes, the wind is coming through the window," said John. "And making it move," said all the children, pleased with their discovery. The teacher held the string so the children could blow at it. "Look, I'm the wind" said one of them. That afternoon, outside, the children were given crepe paper streamers to explore wind direction. They were also read *Gilberto and the Wind*, which tells what happens when wind blows the sail of a boat, the arm of a windmill, the smoke from a chimney, and a child's hat and hair.

Being able to make the most of an unexpected event is a valuable skill. Moving into a situation with skill and helping the child discover something and tell about it is part of promoting word growth (Figure 7–11).

Teachable Moments

You have probably run across the phrase "teachable moments" in your training and perhaps have become adept at using this strategy. It involves a four- to five-step process.

1. Observe a child or a child group's self-chosen actions and efforts.

2. Make a hypothesis about exactly what the children are pursuing, exploring, discovering, playing, and so on.

3. Make a teacher decision to intervene, act, provide, extend, or in some way offer an educational opportunity to further growth or knowledge related to the child-chosen agenda. This can be done a number of

COMMON TEACHER STATEMENT	POSSIBLE CONSEQUENCES
"Tell me more."	expands
"Did you mean . . . ?"	clarifies
"Where did you see . . . ?"	specifying
"Who said . . . ?"	
"When did the bike . . . ?"	
"Whose name shall I write on . . . ?"	specifying possession
"This belongs to . . . ?"	
"Please tell Juan . . ."	conversing with others
"Choose one person to help you."	
"Can you show . . . ?"	provides information
"Tell me again . . ."	rephrase or repeat
"What would happen if . . . ?"	guessing or problem solving
"Thang thinks . . ."	valuing others' ideas
"Taylor says . . ."	
"What could we try . . . ?"	problem solving
"Where should we put . . . ?"	creative thinking
"What's a good name for . . . ?"	
"Who had the last turn to talk . . . ?"	turn taking
"Show me with your hands."	clarifies
"What will you need to . . . ?"	specifies
"What will you do first . . . ?"	
"Do you have a question for me?"	clarifies
"Did something happen that I didn't see?"	
"Did anyone hear a sound?"	listening skill
"Show me your hand when you want to tell us something."	turn taking

*This is not meant to be a complete or comprehensive listing. Each language exchange with children is a challenge and opportunity.

FIGURE 7–11 Sample teacher interaction verbalization.

ways, so this step often involves teacher contemplation.

4. Determine exactly what you will do or provide. Take action. Often, this can be as simple as asking a question such as, "You are putting small pieces of torn paper in Andy's cage. What do you think Andy is going to do with them?" or by silently providing wedge-shaped blocks to a group of children racing small cars down a ramp. Or perhaps you decide to let a child who has been watching the kitchen helper hand-whip eggs try the hand-whip himself.

5. As a final step, consider having the children tell, act out, communicate, dictate, or in some way represent what has been experienced, if this is appropriate.

A watchful teacher who is working to promote early literacy skills, may easily connect teachable moments to relevant opportunities involving literacy skills.

Time Constraints

Comments such as, "You finished," "That's yellow," "How colorful," "It's heavy," "I like that too," or "A new shirt," may give attention, show acceptance, provide encouragement, and reinforce behavior. They feel like suitable and natural comments or responses, and they slip out almost unconsciously. In a busy classroom, they often are said in haste when the teacher may have no time for an extended conversation because he is supervising a group of children. In other words, the best a teacher can do time permitting.

Consciously trying to be specific and expanding takes focus, effort, and quick thinking, but with practice, it can become second nature with teacher statements such as, "You pushed your chair in under the table," "In your drawing I see red and blue," "You helped your friend Alejandra by finding her book," "Those are shoes with lights," "Tell me more about your kitten," and "Returning your crayons to the box helps others find them." Teachers' specific and/or descriptive comments promote literacy.

SCAFFOLDING

Curry and Johnson (1990) describe scaffolding as support with challenge. This refers to a teaching technique that includes responsive conversation, open-ended questions, and facilitation of the child's initiatives. The concept of scaffolding identified with the work of Vygotsky (1987) suggests adults can estimate the amount of necessary verbal support and provide challenging questions for child growth in any given situation. The idea is to promote the child's understanding and solutions. As the child ages, the autonomous pursuit of knowledge will need less adult support. The author is reminded of the four-year-old who described the workings of a steam locomotive. His train knowledge and train terminology was way above that of other children his age and even this teacher. Someone in this child's life had supplied the type of "scaffolding" (support with challenge) that allowed the child to follow an interest in trains.

Vygotsky (1978) suggests inner speech develops as children learn to use language, first to think and then to reason inside their own minds. Language scaffolding by teachers helps children use inner speech and may clarify their thinking. Interactive teachers provide verbal assistance and nudge discovery based on the individual child's degree of sophistication.

It is believed that children need experiences and educational opportunities with adults who carefully evaluate, think, and talk daily occurrences through.

What specific teacher verbalizations and behaviors are suggested in scaffolding? Ones that

- offer responsive and authentic conversation.
- offer a facilitation of the child's initiatives.
- use open-ended questions.
- prompt.
- promote language by using modeling of slightly more mature language forms and some language structures that are new to children.
- offer invitations for children to express thoughts and feelings in words.
- promote longer, more precise child comments.
- invite divergent responses.
- offer specific word cues in statements and questions that help children grasp further information, for example, what, who, why, because, so, and, next, but, except, if, when, before, after, etc.
- provoke lively discussions and quests for knowing more about subjects that interest them.
- increase collaborative communication with adults and other children.

Scaffolding is not as easy as it first may appear to teachers. What is opportunity and challenge for one child may not be for the next. In scaffolding, teacher decision making is constant and complex.

An educator using scaffolding believes understanding, discovery, and problem solving can be guided. Rather than always being dependent on adults for help, the child actually is moved toward becoming an independent thinker. Adults who accompany children at home or at school can use a scaffolding approach to talk through and plan activities as simple as setting the table, cleaning the sink, getting an art area ready for fingerpainting, or taking care of the needs of the school pet.

Langer and Applebee (1986) have identified additional instructional scaffolding. Child ownership of ideas is encouraged. What is right or wrong becomes less important than the child's expression of his own conclusions. The child is encouraged to verbalize the "whys" of his thinking. For example, "Royal thinks the rabbit eats paper because he saw Floppy tearing paper into small pieces inside the cage."

Valuable teacher collaboration with children sustains the momentum of the search, actions, or exploration. Small group projects are often a natural part of children's block area play and can also be promoted in other aspects of daily play and program. For example, a lemonade stand can be managed by a small group, or a present or card can be designed for a sick classmate at home and then completed and mailed by a small group of children.

TEACHER INTERACTIVE STYLES

A central task for the educator is to find a balance between helping a child consolidate new understanding and offering challenges that will promote growth.

Barnes (1976) suggests that there are two teaching styles—transmission and interpretation. Transmission teaching is the traditional, believing child knowledge is acquired through the teacher talking, sharing books, and explaining classroom events and experiences. Interpretation teaching is based on the understanding that children reinterpret information for themselves, and consequently, the teacher's role involves dialogues that support the children's efforts to verbalize their ideas and actual experiences.

One can easily see how easy it is to become a transmission teacher. It is overwhelmingly modeled in a teacher's own schooling. An interpretation teacher really listens and does not monopolize conversations by a display of what the teacher knows. Achieving balance between these two styles is the key. Educators both transmit and interpret.

In promoting developing language arts and literacy in early childhood, an interpretation style would not only help children talk about what they know but also help them put ideas and impressions in print through dictation. The teacher's role is to provide the occasions, resources, and enabling climate for the pursuit of individual meaning.

Teachers can be fun-filled and playful interactors at times, exhibiting their love and enthusiasm for life and child company. This side of teachers comes naturally to some adults and less easily to others. Perhaps some of us remember adults from our own childhood years who were able to engage themselves in adult-child interactions that could be described as joyful playing. Early childhood practitioners bent on language development are careful not to dominate conversations at these times but rather to be responsive companions.

Interaction in Symbolic Play Situations

Pretend play (symbolic play) teacher interactions take both understanding and finesse. The teacher may wish to preserve the child's chosen play direction and not encroach upon self-directed imaginative activity but, at the same time, may wish to promote the child activity by giving attention, and therefore status, to the child's pursuit. There will definitely be many times when teacher interaction may be deemed intrusive because of the child's deep involvement. At those times teachers simply monitor at a distance. In other instances, particularly with younger preschoolers, teacher interaction may enrich the child's experience.

Smilansky (1968) pioneered attempts to train children who were less able to engage in appropriate pretend play. Through adult modeling and assuming a play role in reenacted real-life experiences and through outside-of-play intervention by making suggestions, giving directions, asking questions, and clarifying behavior, Smilansky successfully taught some study children to engage in and sustain sociodramatic play.

Stressing Language Connections

The teacher interested in stressing connections between classroom language arts events and activities, as is done in an integrated approach or a whole-language approach, may often purposefully make the following comments.

> "I am writing down your ideas."
>
> "This printing I am reading says 'please knock'."
>
> "Do you want me to read what is printed on the wall?"
>
> "I can print that word."
>
> "What does the sign for your parking garage need to say?"
>
> "You seemed to be listening to the story I was reading."
>
> "Yes, *s* is the first alphabet letter in your name."
>
> "You want me to print your name on your work, right?"
>
> "I can read what this small printing on the box says."

Accepting Approximations

Just as parents accept and celebrate inaccurate and incorrect language and writing attempts because they are seen as signs of growth, teachers also give attention to beginning attempts and provide encouragement. Lively, interesting environments and experiences where children offer their ideas and comments, feeling safe from criticism and insensitive grammatic correction, help children risk and push ahead.

Handling Interruptions

Children often interrupt adults during planned activities. When an idea hits, they want to share it. Their interruptions can indicate genuine involvement and interest, or they can reflect a variety of unrelated thoughts and feelings. Teachers usually acknowledge the interruption, accept it, and may calmly remind the interruptor that when one wants to speak during group activities, one should raise one's hand first. Other teachers believe preschoolers' enthusiasm to speak is natural and characteristic. These teachers believe that teaching children to raise their hands during group discussions is best reserved for a later age. Interruptions give the teacher an opportunity to make a key decision that affects the flow of the activity. Will the interruption break the flow of what is going on, will it add to the discussion, or is it best discussed at a later time? If the teacher decides to defer a comment, one of the following methods may be used. Or, the teacher may accept being sidetracked and briefly digress from the main subject or develop the interruption into a full-blown teacher-group discussion, as was the case in the previous Landreth (1972) example. Additional examples follow:

> *Situation:* The teacher is telling a flannel board story about a squirrel preparing for winter by hiding nuts in a tree.
>
> *Child:* "My cat climbs trees."
> *Teacher:* "Michael, I've seen cats climb trees."
> (short acknowledgment)
>
> or
>
> *Teacher:* "Michael's cat climbs trees, and the squirrel is climbing the tree to hide the nuts he is storing away for winter."
> (acknowledges, but refers listener back to the story line.)
>
> or
>
> *Teacher:* "Michael, you can tell me about your cat that climbs trees as soon as we finish our story."
> (defers discussion until later.)

Because preschoolers are action-packed, they enjoy activities that include an opportunity to perform the action words they encounter in books, discussions, or daily happenings (Figure 7–12). Teachers can promote "acting out" words with their own behaviors. Some descriptive words are easily enacted. *Pounce, stamp, sneak, slither, creep, slide,* and many other appealing action words exist. *Enormous, droopy, sleepy, tired,* and other descriptive words can be connected to visual reproductions.

Incorporating the children's ideas and suggestions into group conversations and giving

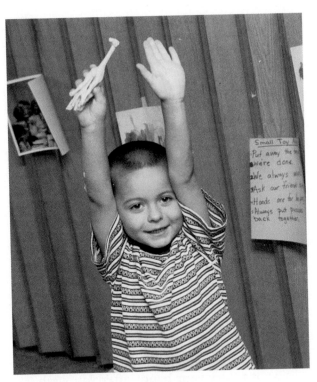

FIGURE 7–12 "I'm this big, teacher."

children credit for their ideas make children aware of the importance of their expressed ideas.

"Kimberly's idea was to . . ."
"Angelo thinks we should . . ."
"Christal suggests that we . . ."
"Here's the way Trevor would . . ."

Using Sequential Approaches to Instruction

Teachers need a clear understanding of how children learn words and concepts. Figure 7–13 includes guidelines for the teacher's words and actions to accompany the child's progress toward new learning.

One approach to teacher interaction during structured, planned, or incidental activities, described by Maria Montessori (1967b), is called three-stage interaction. It shows movement from the child's sensory exploration to showing understanding, and then to verbalizing the understanding. An example follows.

CHILD ACTIVITY	TEACHER ACTIONS
• focuses on an object or activity	• Name the object, or offer a statement describing the actions or situation. (supplies words)
• manipulates and explores the object or situation using touch, taste, smell, sight, and sound organs	• Try to help the child connect this object or action to his past experience through simple conversation. (builds bridge between old and new)
• fits this into what he already knows; develops some understanding	• Help the child see details through simple statements or questions. (focus on identifying characteristics)
	• Use "Show me . . . " or "Give me . . . " prodding statements that call for a nonverbal response. (prompting)
	• Put child's action into words. (Example: "John touched the red ball.") (modeling)
	• Ask the child for a verbal response. "What is this called?" "What happened when . . . ?" (prompting)
• uses a new word or sentence that names, describes, classifies, or generalizes a feature or whole part of the object or action	• Give a response in words indicating the truth factor of the response. "Yes, that's a red ball" or "It has four legs like a horse, but it's called a cow." (corrective or reinforcing response)
	• Extend one-word answers to full simple sentence if needed. (modeling)
	• Suggest an exploration of another feature of the object or situation. (extend interest)
	• Ask a memory or review question. "What did we discover when . . . " (reinforcing and assessing)

FIGURE 7–13 Language learning and teacher interaction.

Step 1: Associating Sense Perception with Words. A cut lemon is introduced, and the child is encouraged to taste it. As the child tastes, the adult says, "The lemon tastes sour," pairing the word *sour* with the sensory experience. Repetition of the verbal pairing strengthens the impression.

Step 2: Probing Understanding. A number of yellow fruits are cut and presented. "Find the one that tastes sour," the teacher suggests. The child shows by his actions his understanding or lack of it.

Step 3: Expressing Understanding. A child is presented with a cut lemon and grapefruit and asked, "How do they taste?" If the child is able to describe the fruit as sour, he has incorporated the word into his vocabulary and has some understanding of the concept.

When using the three-step approach, Montessori (1967b) suggests that if a child is uninterested, the adult should stop at that point. If a mistake is made, the adult remains silent. The mistake indicates only that the child is not ready to learn—not that he is unable to learn.

This verbal approach may seem mechanical and ritualistic to some, yet it clearly illustrates the sequence in a child's progress from not knowing to knowing.

The following example of a variation of the Montessori three-step approach includes additional steps. In this teaching sequence, the child asks the teacher how to open the tailgate of a dump truck in the sandbox.

Teacher Intent	Teacher Statements
1. focus attention	"Look at this little handle."
2. create motivation, defined as creating a desire to want to do or want to know (note that in this situation this is not necessary because the child is interested)	"You want the tailgate to open." Pointing.
3. provide information	"This handle turns and opens the tailgate." Demonstrating.
4. promote child attempt or practice	"Try to turn the handle."
5. give corrective information or feedback or positive reinforcement	"The handle needs to turn. Try to push down as you turn it." (Showing.) or "You did it; the tailgate is open."

Steps 1 through 5 are used in the following situation in which the teacher wants the child to know what is expected in the use of bathroom paper towels.

1. "Here's the towel dispenser. Do you see it?"
2. "You can do this by yourself. You may want to dry your hands after you wash them."
3. Demonstration. "First take one paper towel. Dry your hands. Then the towel goes into this wastebasket."
4. "You try it."
5. "That's it. Pull out one towel. Dry your hands. Put the towel in the wastebasket."
 "Now you know where the dirty paper towels go. No one will have to pick up your used towel from the floor. You can do it without help now like some of your classmates."

Statements of this kind help the child learn both the task and vocabulary. The ability to provide information that the child needs, without talking too much, is one of the skills required of a really excellent teacher. Most theorists believe that the successful completion of a task is a reward in itself. Others believe that an encouraging verbal pat on the back is in order.

The same dump truck scene detailed earlier could be handled using a discovery approach, instead of a teacher-directed sequence, with the following types of questions. "Did you see anyone else playing with this dump truck? Is there a button to push or a handle to turn that opens the tailgate? What happens if you try to open the tailgate with your hand?"

The goal of prompting in a child-adult conversation is to encourage the child to express ideas perhaps more precisely and/or specifically. It is used slightly different with younger preschoolers, as shown in the following examples.

Young preschooler.	*Child:*	"Cookie."
	Adult:	"You want a cookie?"
	Child:	"Dis cookie."
	Adult:	"You want this brown cookie?"
Older preschooler.	*Child:*	"I want that cookie."
	Adult:	"You want one of these cookies. Which kind, chocolate or sugar?"
	Child:	"The chocolate one."
	Adult:	"Help yourself. You can sit here or you can choose to sit in the chair next to Myra."

Can teachers really make a difference in the level and quality of children's language development?

> Very significant correlations were found between both the frequency of informative staff talk, the frequency with which the staff answered the children, and the language comprehension scores of the children. (Tizard, Rankin, Shonic, & Cobb, 1972)

Interaction does require teachers to "wonder out loud." They express their own curiosity while at the same time noticing each child's quest to find out what makes others tick and what the world is all about.

How can teachers interact skillfully?

◆ Expand topics in which the child shows interest.

◆ Add depth to information on topics of interest.

◆ Answer and clarify children's questions.

◆ Help children sort out features of events, problems, and experiences, reducing confusion.

◆ Urge children to put what is newly learned or discovered into words.

◆ Cue children into routinely attending to times when the adult and child are learning and discovering together through discussion of daily events.

Dealing with Children's Past Experiences

As an interactor, a teacher encounters a wide range of children's perceptions as to how the children should communicate with adults. A child's family or past child care arrangements may have taught the child to behave in a certain way. With this in mind, the teacher can almost envision what it means to be a conversationalist in a particular family or societal group. Some families expect children to interrupt; others expect respectful manners. Wild, excited gesturing and weaving body movements are characteristic of some children, whereas motionless, barely audible whispering is typical of others. Teachers working with newly arrived children from other cultures may see sharp contrasts in communication styles. Some children verbally seek help, whereas others find this extremely difficult. Some speak their feelings openly; others rarely express their feelings.

To promote child learning, teachers need to consider both styles and how they interface.

> Because learning means connecting new ideas to what is already known, pupils must have opportunities to verbalize their

unique understandings in order to create the context that encourages further learning. (Healy & Barr, 1992)

Past child care experiences may have left their mark. A four-year-old child named Perry seemed to give one teacher considerable understanding about how speech can be dramatically affected by past undesirable child care arrangements (Busy Bee Children's Center, 1989). The following is that teacher's observation and conclusions.

> Perry sat quietly near the preschool's front door, ignoring all play opportunities, and holding his blanket until his mom's return on his first day at school. He only spoke or looked up when teachers tried repeatedly to engage him in conversation. He sat on adults' laps silently when they tried to comfort him, and ate food quickly and then returned to his waiting place near the door. The real Perry emerged a few weeks later as a talkative, socially vigorous child. Our verbal and behavioral interactions concentrated on rebuilding trust with adults and other children; only later was language developing interaction possible.

It can be difficult for a child to engage an adult in conversation, as was the case with Perry. As Garvey (1977) notes, "Seeking the availability of a teacher and assuring one's right to her attention and reply often calls for persistence and ingenuity." Perry may have long before given up trying.

Children's Inquisitive Honesty

Young children rarely limit their questions or modify their responses to the teacher for the purpose of hiding their ignorance, as older children sometimes do. During conversations, young children intent on answers will probe enthusiastically for what they want to know. Teachers actively promote guesses and appreciate error making in an atmosphere of trust. They interact in conversations by focusing child attention, posing questions, pointing out problems, suggesting alternatives, and provid-

ing information at the teachable moment (Smith-Burke, 1985).

Interacting with Vygotsky's Theory in Mind

A teacher examining Vygotsky's ideas of children's language acquisition might interact in a particular fashion in a preschooler classroom. Believing social interaction builds language learning, the teacher would attempt to stretch above what the child seems to know and say and build on the child's strengths. Vygotsky (1980) suggests

> What the child can do in cooperation today he can do alone tomorrow. Therefore the only good kind of instruction is that which marches ahead of development and leads it.

In Vygotsky's social interaction model, the child engages in meaningful interaction with others, and through this interaction, inner language unfolds (Bartoli, 1995).

THE TEACHER AS A BALANCER

In all roles, the teacher needs to maintain a balance. This means

- giving, but withholding when self-discovery is practical and possible.
- interacting, but not interfering with or dominating the child's train of thought or actions.
- giving support, but not hovering.
- talking, but not overtalking.
- listening, but remaining responsive.
- providing many opportunities for the child to speak.
- being patient and understanding. As Fields and Lee (1987) point out, "When adults already know an answer, we find it hard to be patient as children go through the process of figuring the answer out for themselves."

To maintain such a balance, the teacher is a model, a provider, and an interactor, matching his behavior and speech to the ability of each child. As a model, the teacher's example offers the child a step above—but not too far above—what the child is already able to do. In doing this, the teacher watches and listens while working with individual children, learning as much from the child's misunderstandings or speech mistakes as from correct or appropriate responses and behavior. This does not mean that the motive is always to teach, for the teacher also enjoys just talking with the children. It means the teacher is ready to make the most of every situation, as teacher and child enjoy learning together. The teacher orally reflects and guards against being overly invasive.

There is an old story about two preschool boys who discover a worm in the play yard.

First child: "Boy it tickles! Look at him!" (Holding worm in hand.)

Second child: "Let's show it to teacher."

First child: "No way—she'll want us to draw a picture of it and make us print 'worm'!"

A teacher's attitude toward child growth in language should be one of optimism; provide the best learning environment and realize the child will grow and learn new language skills when he is ready. Early childhood centers plan for as much growth as possible in language abilities with teachers who model, provide, and interact during activities.

Sheldon (1990) urges teachers to thoughtfully use comments and conversation free of sexist, male-oriented attitudes. If a teacher is talking about a stuffed teddy bear or the school's pet guinea pig (whose sex is yet to be discovered), "it," rather than "he" or "she," is recommended.

Giving children the opportunity to re-express what they have discovered, felt, or learned with classroom art materials, building blocks, dramatic play props, and so on, is another way to promote their language growth and further expression of ideas.

SUMMARY

Teachers function as models, providers of opportunities for language growth, collaborators, and interactors. Children copy behaviors and attitudes of both adults and peers. Teacher skills include extending and expanding child conversations. Conversations are a key factor in the child's growing language competence. *Extending* means adding new information, and *expanding* means completing a child's statement so that it is grammatically complete.

Words are symbols for objects, ideas, actions, and situations. The teacher can increase the learning of new words and ideas by helping children recognize links between the past and present.

Teachers observe and listen closely so that teacher comments are pertinent and timely. An atmosphere of adult-child trust and acceptance of child ideas, whether valid or incorrect, is recommended.

The three teacher roles discussed in this chapter are model, provider, and interactor. A delicate balance exists in teaching functions. Decisions are made that affect children's learning opportunities.

ADDITIONAL RESOURCES

Readings

Allison, L., & Weston, M. (1993). *Wordsaroni: Word play for you and your preschooler.* Boston: Little, Brown.

Genishi, C. (1996). Portfolios: Collecting children's work. *Scholastic Early Childhood Today, 11*(1), 60–61.

Grainger, T. (1999). Conversations in the classroom: Poetic voices at play. *Language Arts, 76*(4), 292–297.

Hart, B., & Risley, T. (1995). *Meaningful differences in the everyday experience of young American children.* Baltimore: Brookes.

Isenberg, J., & Jalongo, M. (2001). *Creative expression and play in early childhood.* Upper Saddle River, NJ: Merrill/Prentice Hall.

Routman, R. (2000). *Conversations.* Portsmouth, NH: Heinemann.

West, K. (1998). Noticing and responding to learners. *The Reading Teacher, 51*(7), 550–559.

HELPFUL WEB SITES

Child & Family—Canada
http://www.cfc-efc.ca
Go to Library and then select "literacy" to find library readings.

Iowa State University Extension
http://www.exnet.iastate.edu
Nurturing language skills can be found by searching publications.

National Association for the Education of Young Children
http://www.naeyc.org
Articles, publications, and information are available.

National Parent Information Network
http://npin.org
Family literacy information can be found by searching the library.

 Your rating of teacher verbalizations and actions will be compared with peer ratings. You will be asked to identify additional teacher behaviors that are important and may be missing from the list given. Suggestions for additional readings are also included in the Online Companion™. Some children are more difficult to engage in conversation, and as a teacher, you will need to develop new strategies to reach them. In a suggested exercise, you will first identify these types of children by select descriptors and then devise a possible strategy. Example: the very active child who is always in motion and rarely sits.

STUDENT ACTIVITIES

1. Observe a teacher interacting with a preschool child. Note the type of teacher speech and behavior that makes the child feel that what he says is important.

2. Pretend you are having a conversation about a teacher's car that the children observed being towed away for repair. You are attempting to extend the topic of conversation, wringing as much out of the experience as possible while monitoring child interest and knowledge. Create possible teacher conversational comments in b to g after reading the example in a.

   a. Recap what you noticed and promote children's remembrance.

      Example: "I saw a tow truck driver climb out of the tow truck cab."

   b. *Explain* some aspect of the situation by giving reasons.

   c. Describe a cause-and-effect feature of the situation.

   d. Compare this situation with another.

   e. Talk about what might happen to the teacher's car.

   f. Comment about what the teacher could do in this situation besides calling a tow truck.

   g. Ask how the children would feel if it were their parents' car.

   h. List six other aspects of the situation that could be discussed.

   Compare your answers with those of a group of classmates. Now discuss further teacher-planned activities that could increase and expand children's comments, questions, or understanding. Share with the entire group.

3. Listen intently to three adults. (Take notes.) How would you evaluate them as speech models (good, average, poor)? State the reasons for your decisions.

4. Record a conversation with another classmate. Have the recording analyzed for Standard English speech usage.

5. Tape record or videotape your interaction with a group of young children for a period of 15 minutes. Analyze your listening, questioning, sentence structure, extending ability, and pronunciation.

6. In groups of four or five, develop a listing (on a wall chart or chalkboard) of language-stimulating classroom visitors. Prepare a one-page visitor information sheet to help the visitor understand how to structure the visit to offer a literacy-rich classroom experience. Choose two members of the group to role-play a situation in which the head teacher or director and a guest visitor discuss the visitor information sheet.

7. Consider the following slogans. Explain and elaborate their meanings.
   Intent not correctness.
   Your topic, not mine.
   The wrong answer is right.

Logic not mechanics.
Give them eyes and ears.
Responsive opportunist here!
Shh! Here comes the teacher.

8. Read the following quote. Discuss its relationship to child language growth.

   The small Zulu also didn't have just one daddy. He had the dadoos, his father's brothers and other male adults who talked to him about hunting, showed him how to make a little bow and arrow and all of this kind of stuff. They spent time with him and they "joyed in his presence," as someone once defined love. So on into adult life there was for both the boys and the girls this abundance of love and affection and attention and tenderness. (Lair, 1985)

9. How could the following teachers provide for child awareness and involvement in their special interests: an opera buff, a stamp collector, a gourmet cook, a scuba diver, a cashier, a gardener, a clock collector?

10. Fill out the checklist in Figure 7–14, and compare your ratings with those of your classmates.

	AGREE	CAN'T DECIDE	DISAGREE
1. Every center happening should encourage speech.			
2. It takes considerable time and effort to have personal conversations with each child daily.			
3. Each child is entitled to a personal greeting and goodbye.			
4. "How are you?" is a good opening remark.			
5. A child who bursts out with something to say that has nothing to do with what is presently happening must have something important on his mind.			
6. Pausing silently for a few moments after speaking to a shy child is a good idea.			
7. Most new vocabulary words are learned at group times.			
8. Saying, "John stepped over the green block," is unnecessary, for the child knows what he has done.			
9. All children have home interests that teachers can discuss with them.			
10. At mealtimes, it is best to remain quiet while children enjoy their food.			
11. If the child talks about a bathroom function, ignore it.			
12. When Adam says, "Girls can't drive trucks," tell him he is wrong.			
13. Teachers really need to talk more than they listen.			

FIGURE 7–14 Opinion poll. (continued)

14. Saying, "Tell him you don't like it when he grabs your toy," is poor technique.

15. I don't think it's possible to use a lot of language-building techniques and still speak naturally and comfortably with a child.

16. Teachers should model a playful attitude at times.

FIGURE 7–14 *(continued)*

CHAPTER REVIEW

A. Name three or four basic functions of the early childhood teacher mentioned in this chapter.

B. List five examples of each of the functions you listed for question A.

C. Following is an observation of a teacher and children. After reading it, indicate what you believe was appropriate behavior and inappropriate behavior on the part of the teacher in regard to language development.

Situation: Teacher is conducting a sharing time with Joey, Anna, Maria, and Chris.
Teacher: "It's time for sharing. Please sit down, children."
Joey: "I want to share first!"
Teacher: "You'll have your turn. You must learn to wait."
Anna: "I can't see."
Teacher: "Yes you can. Maria, you're sitting quietly and not talking. You may go first."
Maria: "This is a book about Mickey. Mickey clips."
Joey: "What's clips, teacher?"
Teacher: "You're next, Joey."
Joey: "Mickey on TV, teacher. Tomorrow I went to the fire station. The firefighter let me wear his badge, like this."
Chris: "Firefighter's truck red. Goes whee-whee."
Teacher: "It's Joey's turn, Chris. Would you wait to talk?"
Anna: "I want to go, now!"
Teacher: "Anna, you must have your turn to share before you can go."
Anna: "I see a butterfly on the window."
Teacher: "Later, Anna. You can go outside later."

D. Select the correct answers. All have more than one correct reply.

1. The teacher is a model for
   a. speech.
   b. attitudes.
   c. speech more often than parents may be.
   d. speech only during planned activities.

2. It is more important for young children to
   a. like to speak than to speak correctly.
   b. participate than to sit quietly.
   c. speak than to listen.

d. have the teacher tell them about something than to explore it themselves.

e. feel comfortable with a teacher than to speak clearly.

3. Teachers reinforce learning by
   a. using speech to solve problems.
   b. giving attention to the child's use of a new word.
   c. motivating the child's "wanting to know."
   d. linking the old with the new ideas.

4. When speaking, the teacher should
   a. attempt to use natural language patterns.
   b. speak in full sentences.
   c. make sure each child responds by speaking.
   d. refrain from "overtalking."

5. Preschool children
   a. are also speech models.
   b. rarely teach others new words.
   c. play and use words in play.
   d. have growing vocabularies only when teachers act appropriately.

E. Robert D. Hess and V. C. Shipman believe that different adults have different styles of communicating with young children. The following is a comparison of two mothers trying to teach the same task to their child.

First Mother: "All right, Susan, this board is the place where we put the little toys; first of all, you're supposed to learn how to place them according to color. Can you do that? The things that are all the same color you put in one section; in the other section you put another group of colors, and in the third section you put the last group of colors. Can you do that? Or would you like to see me do it first?"

Child: "I want to do it."

Second Mother (introducing the same task): "Now I'll take them all off the board; now you put them all back on the board. What are these?"

Child: "A truck."

Second Mother: "All right, just put them right here; put the other one right here; all right, put the other one there." (Hess & Shipman, 1966)

Write a brief comparison of the two mothers, but pretend they are two teachers.

F. Choose the one best answer.

1. Briana is staring at the wall clock. The teacher might say
   a. "You're wondering what time it is."
   b. "That's our class clock. It tells us what time it is."
   c. "Tell me about the clock."
   d. "You've noticed our clock. Do you have one at your house?"

2. Scaffolding in teacher-child conversations is
   a. encouragement and laddering.
   b. supportive assistance to help the child express and try out language.
   c. supplying data and information.
   d. telling the child his right and wrong conclusions.
   e. letting the child work things out independently.

234

SECTION 3

Listening:

Literate Beginnings

CHAPTER 8
Developing Listening Skills

OBJECTIVES

After reading this chapter, you should be able to:

◆ List five types of listening.

◆ Discuss teaching techniques that promote good listening habits.

◆ Demonstrate how to plan an activity that promotes a listening skill.

◆ Present a listening activity to a group of preschoolers.

◆ Tell a story that involves purposeful child listening.

KEY TERMS

alliteration	listening	phonemic
continuant	comprehension	awareness
hearing	level	purposeful
listening	onsets	listening
		rimes

STAYING ON TASK

In Karen Crawford's second grade class, Crawford has gathered seven children. The group begins to read a passage on dinosaurs. One student, Glen, starts to look around. Crawford asks him to focus. It works for a moment: Glen offers that "germs" may have killed the dinosaurs. Then he starts pestering the girl next to him. Crawford has him move back to his own desk. As the others reread the dinosaur passage to themselves, Crawford crouches beside Glen, talking about listening and self-control. (Barnes, 2004).

QUESTIONS TO PONDER

1. Have you observed preschoolers who lose focus during read-alouds or discussions? What strategies might hold their attention?

2. Are most teachers as aware of the feedback they are receiving at group times as this teacher?

3. What teacher statements before group instruction promote paying attention?

The world, with its many sounds, bombards children. Although no one formally teaches an infant to listen, certain sounds become familiar and take on meanings from this mass of confusion. The child has begun to listen.

Listening skill is the first language arts skill learned, and it develops before a child speaks. Many children develop the ability to listen carefully to the speech of others during early childhood; others do not. Because language growth has been described as a receiving process followed by a sending process, a child's listening ability is important to speaking and future reading and writing success.

Hearing and listening are quite different. **Hearing** is a process involving nerves and muscles that reach adult efficiency by age four to five. Listening is a learned behavior, a mental process that is concerned with hearing, attending, discriminating, understanding, and remembering. It can be improved with practice. Listening affects social interactions, one's level of functioning, and perhaps one's overall success in life (Weiss & Lillywhite, 1981). Nichols (1984) estimates that we listen to 50 percent of what we hear and comprehend only 25 percent of that.

Listening skill can be described as passive and receptive, but it involves active thinking and interpretation. Lively conversations between adults and young children who feel free to verbalize reactions to life's happenings promote listening and speaking. Children offer more verbal comments in school settings in small, relaxed groups in which comments are accepted and appreciated. Young children sometimes learn that it is best to keep quiet in some classrooms. In other classrooms, every child's opinion counts and classroom discussions are frequent and animated.

There are usually many opportunities to listen in early childhood centers. Teacher-planned or child-created play is a source of many sounds (Figure 8–1). A quality program sharp-

FIGURE 8–1 Children often listen intently to playmates.

ens a child's listening and offers a variety of experiences. Listening is not left to chance; planned programs develop skills.

RESEARCH ON LISTENING

Although limited current research has been done on both listening and whether direct instruction in listening skill is effective, studies conducted in the 1950s and 1960s showed that listening instruction led to measurable gains in listening comprehension. Active involvement following listening activities may help more than passive activities (Pinnell & Jaggar, 1992).

Listening is not a discrete skill or generalized ability, but a cluster of specific abilities closely related to those needed in the reading task. Early childhood professionals should be aware of the early development of a child's **listening comprehension level**.

---

listening — a mental process that includes attending, hearing, discriminating, understanding, and remembering.
hearing — the facility or sense by which sound is perceived.
listening comprehension level — the highest grade level of material that can be comprehended well when it is read aloud to a child.

TYPES OF LISTENING

Listening occurs in many ways. A person does not always listen for knowledge but may listen to a sound because it is pleasing to hear. The first time children discover the sounds made by pots and pans, they are fascinated. Preschoolers often make their own pleasurable or rhythmic sounds with whatever is available.

The human voice can be interesting, threatening, or monotonous to a child, depending on past experience. Silence also has meaning. Sometimes teachers suspect that a child has a hearing problem, only to find that the child was inattentive for other reasons.

Children may listen but not understand. They may miss sound differences or listen without evaluating what they hear. Listening involves a variety of skills and levels. To provide growing opportunities, teachers should be aware of various listening skills, as shown in Figure 8–2. A child may rely on a combination of the skills described.

The goal of a good program in early childhood language arts is to guide the young child toward development of these listening levels. The listening process contains three stages the child moves through in efficient listening (Figure 8–3).

When a sound occurs, it is remembered by thinking about its features: direction, pitch, intensity, newness, and so on.

Appreciative listening. The child finds pleasure and entertainment in hearing music, poems, and stories. It is best to begin with this type of listening because it is passive, but personal, for each child.

Purposeful listening. The child follows directions and gives responses.

Discriminative listening. The child becomes aware of changes in pitch and loudness. Sounds become differentiated in the environment. Eventually, the child is able to discriminate the speech sounds.

Creative listening. The child's imagination and emotions are stimulated by her listening experiences. Thoughts are expressed spontaneously and freely through words or actions, or both.

Critical listening. The child understands, evaluates, makes decisions, and formulates opinions. To encourage this critical listening, the teacher may pose such questions as "What happens when we all talk at once?" or "What if everyone wanted to play in the playhouse at the same time?" The child must think through the responses, decide the most logical solution to the problem, and present a point of view.

FIGURE 8–2 Some of the ways a child listens. (From Scott, L. B. [1968]. *Learning time with language experiences.* New York: McGraw-Hill.)

RESPONDING TO STIMULI	ORGANIZING THE STIMULI	UNDERSTANDING THE MEANING
awareness	sequencing and	(classification;
focus	synthesizing	integration;
figure-ground	scanning	monitoring)
discrimination		

← ——————————————— Memory ——————————————— →

Stage 1—Responding to stimuli. Was there sound? Where was it? Which sound was it? Was there more than one sound? Were the sounds the same?

Stage 2—Organizing the stimuli. What was the sequence of the sounds? What was the length of time between sounds? Have I heard that sound before? Where have I heard it?

Stage 3—Understanding the meaning. What do the sounds and words mean?

FIGURE 8–3 Stages of the listening process.

TODDLER LISTENING EXPERIENCES

Parents and center staff members can engage toddlers in a number of activities to stimulate listening. Body-action play of the old "coo-chee-coo" variety, "This Little Piggy," and simple rhymes and repetitions are recommended. Connecting noises and sounds with toys and objects and encouraging the child to imitate show the child that joy and sound making go hand in hand. Rhythmic clapping, tapping, and pan beating in sequence or patterns can be enjoyable. Musical toys and recordings add variety and listening pleasure. Encouraging children to watch facial expressions as different human sounds are produced and locating environmental sounds together are additional techniques in developing children's listening skills.

Adults exercise care in sound volume and quality; at all age levels, extra loud, shrill, vibrating, or emergency alert sounds can be frightening.

Purposeful Listening Activities

The intent of purposeful listening practice is to increase the child's ability to follow directions and instructions, perform tasks, and respond appropriately in some fashion. Teachers can use a three-step method to help very young preschoolers gain skill in this type of listening.

1. Tell the children what you are going to tell them.
2. Tell the children.
3. Tell the children what you told them.

Example

1. "I'm going to give you an envelope, and tell you where to take it."
2. "Take the envelope to the cook, Mrs. Corelli, and then come back to our classroom."
3. "You took the envelope to Mrs. Corelli and returned. Thank you."

Purposeful, attentive listening takes concentration. Teachers can perfect a "what I'm going to say next is important" tone and consequently create a desire in children to listen. A statement such as, "You might want to know how" or "You can listen closely to find out" or "If you'd like a turn, watch and listen," may also provide the motivation to listen closely.

Planned, purposeful listening activities can include activities that encourage children to listen in order to

- do something for themselves.
- tell another how to do something.
- operate some type of toy or equipment.
- carry a message.
- recall details.
- put objects in a special order or sequence.
- see how many names or facts they can remember.
- learn new skills, such as singing new songs or chanting or doing finger plays.

Appreciative Listening Activities

Appreciative listening deals with light listening when enjoyment or pleasure is paramount. A wide variety of recorded and live appreciative listening experiences is possible. Background music can accompany favorite preschool pursuits. Chanting a remembered selection of words gives the children a double treat of hearing voices in unison and feeling part of a group. Some appreciative listening builds moods, touches emotions, and adds another dimension to experience. The world is full of beautiful and not-so-beautiful sounds.

Possible appreciative listening activities include:

- moving to music.
- discussing music, rhythms, and sounds.
- talking about favorite sounds.
- talking about happy, sad, or funny feelings that sounds produce.
- tapping, clapping, or moving to music or rhythmic speech.

Cole and Cole (1989) list the benefits of introducing a music curriculum to young children.

> Music provides another means of oral expression for children. . . . building vocabulary, establishing a sense of internal rhythm, developing an awareness of pitch and intonation in voice, and creating an understanding of language concepts such as loud, soft, fast, and slow. Providing practice in singing promotes the development of syntax and memorization skills.

There is a predictable pattern in children's learning of any song. Words are learned first, then rhythms and other elements. Traditional nursery songs are plentiful, are appropriately pitched, and contain repetition of melodic and rhythmic patterns. Music is a "language builder."

FAVORITE TRADITIONAL SONGS

"Old MacDonald Had a Farm"
"Dinah"
"Teddy Bear"
"Eensy, Weensy Spider"
"I'm a Little Teapot"
"Hot Cross Buns"
"The Bus"
"Twinkle, Twinkle, Little Star"
"Yankee Doodle"
"Did You Ever See a Lassie?"
"If You're Happy"
"Ring Around a Rosy"
"Oh, Dear, What Can the Matter Be?"
"Skip to My Lou"
"Down by the Station"
"Looby Loo"
"Bingo"
"The Bear Went over the Mountain"

PARTIAL LIST OF LANGUAGE FEATURES FOUND IN SONGS

vocabulary
predictability
story line and sequence
rhyming
repetition
cultural literacy significance
rhythmic beat
concept development

appreciative listening
purposeful listening
discriminative listening
creative listening
coordination of words and physical
    movement

Critical Listening Activities

Critical listening requires the children's evaluation of what is heard and comprehended. It requires contemplation and reflection, and some preschoolers develop considerable skill in this area and use it frequently. These children seem able to weigh the new against what they already know and feel and are eager to discuss differences. Other children seem rarely to hold any opinion or particular viewpoint and are reticent to share thoughts. Activities that involve critical thinking can be ones in which

◆ a problem is discussed and solutions are offered and evaluated.

◆ a probable outcome or guess is prompted.

◆ a real or make-believe feature is pinpointed using some criteria.

◆ personal preferences or dislikes are discussed.

◆ group votes are reviewed and outcomes are anticipated.

◆ errors of some type are discovered or detected.

◆ feelings of others are predicted.

◆ inconsistences are listened for.

Discriminative Listening Activities

Increased attention to discriminative listening has occurred as a result of current research and because of national legislative efforts to improve American children's reading ability. To discern whether a sound or sound pattern is the same or different, one uses discriminative listening skill. This skill is necessary when a child attempts to decode words in early reading.

The preschool teacher who plans a "Listening Detective" activity in which preschoolers catch the teacher in a mistake—such as "he huffed and he puffed and he blew the tree down" after the group is well acquainted with *The Three Little Pigs*—is presenting a discriminative listening exercise. Imitating a clapping pattern is another, as is finding rhyming sounds or matching xylophone notes.

Creative Listening Activities

Many classroom literacy activities create an emotional response or reaction. Audiovisual media can do so also. Discussion after read-alouds and other literacy events may reveal child feelings and imaginative ideas. Children may then be encouraged to create their feelings and ideas in subsequent art, drama, or other form of expression.

Creative listening has been used as a strategy to unleash creative potential. Who among us hasn't had an "aha" experience when listening or had a mental picture form while experiencing a piece of music?

TEACHER SKILLS

Good listening habits are especially important in school situations. Teachers need to assess their own listening habits and abilities in their daily work with children. If they expect undivided attention from children, they must also give undivided attention to them (Jalongo, 1996). Most of us have been told in teacher training to bend or lower ourselves to child eye level when we speak to children, but how often do we do this when we listen to them?

Two factors may decrease teachers' ability to listen and model listening behavior: (1) they may not have experienced teachers in their own schooling (including college professors) who listened with care and valued child inquiry, and (2) they are so busy imparting information that they miss the profound questions and comments of young children. As Grant and Murray (1999) observe, this type of interactive style teaches children to sit passively and withdraw. It teaches most vividly what the teachers least suspect they have transmitted.

Instructions from teachers should be clear and simple, with a sequence of what comes first, next, and last. Usually, instructions need not be repeated when given clearly and simply. Often, when the attention of the group is required, a signal is used. Any distinctive, easy-to-hear, pleasant sound or visual signal can alert children that it is time to listen. The silent pause before beginning an activity can be used effectively to focus attention on listening.

Teachers also use a short song, finger play, or body-movement activity to stimulate interest and draw the group together (Figure 8–4). This helps children focus on what is to follow.

FIGURE 8–4 A body-movement activity helps capture attention.

Encouragement and smiles at any time of the day can reward individual listening. Positive, specific statements, such as, "Ramon, you listened to what Jan had to say before you started talking" or "It's quiet, and now we can all hear the beginning of the story," give children feedback on expected listening behavior.

The following are sample teacher statements that can promote a group's ability to listen.

At the Beginning

◆ "When I see everyone's eyes, I'll know you're ready to hear about . . ."
◆ "We'll begin when we can all hear the clock ticking."
◆ "I'm waiting until everyone can hear before I start. We need to be quiet so that everyone can hear about . . ."
◆ "It seems everyone is listening; it's time to begin."
◆ "We take turns speaking. Skye is first, then . . ."

During Activity

◆ "Wyatt had his hand up. Would you like to tell us about your idea?"
◆ "It's Maria's turn to tell us . . ."
◆ "We can hear best when just one person is talking. Louis, you go first, then Cristalee."
◆ "Ethan, it's hard to wait when you want to talk. Khesia is talking now; you can be next." (Later add, "Ethan, thank you for waiting for Khesia to finish. Now we will hear what you wanted to tell us.")
◆ "Everyone wants to tell us about their own pets. Raise your hand—I'll make a waiting list so that we can hear everyone." (Make the list quickly and hold it up.) "Isaac, your name is first."

At Activity's End

◆ "We listened so quietly. We all heard every word of that story."
◆ "Everyone listened to what their friends said."
◆ "We listened and found out a lot about . . ."

Additional examples of teacher talk that promotes listening are as follows:

◆ "We are going to do two things right now. Listen. Pick up your rug square; that's the first thing to do. Then put your square right here on this pile on the table. You were listening, Polly, thank you."
◆ "Listen and then you'll know who will hold the door open. Today it's Rudy's job. Whose job is it? Right, it is Rudy's job today."
◆ "Eyes open. Lips closed. It's listening time."
◆ "I can't hear when everyone is talking. Mario, tell us what you said. Michelle, you need to wait. We will listen to you next."
◆ "It's Adrian's time to talk now. That means no one else is talking."
◆ "Let's wait until it is quiet, then we are all ready to listen to the story."
◆ "When I see everyone's eyes looking in my eyes, I'll know you are ready to listen."
◆ "That was attentive listening. Everyone was quiet while Joni told us about her painting."
◆ "Josh has something important to say. Let's listen so that we all hear what he is going to tell us."
◆ "I know it's hard to wait, Cleota, but Rick is talking now. Wait. It will be your turn next."
◆ "What are we going to do after we pour the milk in the bowl? Yes, Brenda, we said we had to stir with the spoon. Good listening, Brenda."
◆ "Now let's think of another sound we might hear if we go to the window and listen."
◆ "My turn to talk. Your turn to listen."

Rewarded behavior is usually repeated and becomes a habit. Teachers should consistently notice correct listening behavior and comment favorably about it to the children.

How can one recognize good listening habits? Characteristics of children with listening skills follow. Children

◆ look toward the speaker's face.
◆ filter out distractions.

◆ concentrate on the speaker's message.

◆ can repeat back what the speaker said.

◆ interrupt infrequently (Figure 8–5).

◆ ask clarifying questions that make sense.

◆ seem to think about what has been said.

Examine Figure 8–6; it is an example of a teacher attempting to promote listening skill and other language development strategies.

AUDITORY PERCEPTION

Ears respond to sound waves. These sounds go to the brain and become organized in relation to past experience. The same process is used in early childhood and later when the child learns to read. Language development depends on the auditory process.

Educational activities that give practice and help perfect auditory skills usually deal with the following objectives.

◆ sustaining attention span

◆ following directions or commands

◆ imitating sounds

◆ identifying and associating sounds

◆ using auditory memory

◆ discriminating between sounds (intensity, pitch, tempo)

The intensity of a sound is its degree of force, strength, or energy. Pitch is the highness or lowness of sound. Tempo is the rate of speed of a sound, in other words, the rhythm of the sound that engages the attention.

Auditory Activities

A wide range of auditory activities can be planned. The following goals often serve as the basis for planning. Simple skills come before more difficult ones.

◆ recognizing own name when spoken

◆ repeating two nonsense words, short sayings, chants, poems, finger plays, or any series of words

◆ reporting sounds heard at home

◆ imitating sounds of toys, animals, classrooms, rain, sirens, bells

FIGURE 8–5 These two girls are listening closely to the story and probably will not interrupt the reader.

A GROUP ACTIVITY

At group time, Rachel, a preschool teacher, gathered the children, and silently waited while they settled in before beginning. "Let's see who is with us today. If you hear your name, give me one clap. Gage." Gage claps one time. "Gage heard his name, and I heard one clap. I'll whisper the next name. If you hear your name give me two claps." Two claps are heard. "Good listening, Mara." Rachel continues until all in the group have been recognized by name.

Rachel then reaches for a story book. "In this book there is something Nathan and Nicholas Alexander want, but they can't see it. Let's look at the book's cover and I will read its title. Then I think you can guess." She places her hand under each word and reads *Nathan's Fishing Trip.* Children's hands shoot up, and Skylar guesses fish. Others agree. "Lulu Delacre wrote this story," Rachel continues. She turns to the title page and comments, "Look carefully at the pictures (illustrations), do you see Nicholas Alexander? He has a big two word name, but Nicholas Alexander is a very small mouse." She fans the book closer so that all can see. Rachel starts the story, but interrupts briefly to show a large drawing of a hook and a few colored fishing lures. When the word hook and lure are mentioned on the third page, she traces the hook shape as she talks about its sharpness. The book reading proceeds to its conclusion.

A discussion includes confirming that fish was a good guess. Rachel mentions it was a particular fish, a trout. She asks why Nathan and Nicholas Alexander may have decided to free the trout. Children's ideas are offered and discussed. Rachel then says, "Nathan and Nicholas Alexander have names beginning with the letter 'N' just like Nicole." She makes a quick "N" on a sheet of paper and holds it up.

A fishing game with fish shapes follows. This was prepared by Rachel beforehand. She explains some of the fish in the plastic washtub have the letter "N" printed on them, while other do not. "If you want a turn with the fishing game raise your hand." Rachel says. A waiting list is printed by Rachel, who selects one child and asks, "Do you want to choose a friend to play with you?" The child indicates a friend. Rachel lines out their names on the waiting list, and points to and reads the next child's name who is to have the next turn.

FIGURE 8–6 Rachel's group activity.

- telling whether a sound is near or far, loud or soft, fast or slow, high or low, same or different
- identifying people's voices
- identifying and repeating rhythms heard
- retelling a story, poem, or part of either
- trying to perform first one- and then two-part directions
- recalling sounds in sequence
- coordinating listening skills with body movements in a requested way
- enjoying music, stories, poems, and many other language arts, both individually and in groups

SETTINGS FOR LISTENING

When preparing listening activities, the teacher can plan for success by having activities take place in room areas with a minimum of distracting sounds or objects. Screens, dividers, and bookcases are helpful (Figure 8–7). Heating and lighting are checked, and comfortable seating is provided. Decisions concerning the size of a group are important. In general, the younger the children, the smaller the group and the shorter the length of the activity.

Listening cannot be forced, but experiences can be provided that create a desire to listen. Some schools offer children the choice of joining a group listening activity or playing quietly nearby. Teachers find that an interesting experience will attract children who are playing nearby. When activities are enjoyable and successful, the child who was hesitant may look forward to new experiences. A teacher can turn on or turn off attention by ending, changing, or modifying activities when necessary. The teacher should watch carefully for feedback; this will help the child develop active listening. A skillful teacher will complete the learning activity before the group becomes restless. When an activity is planned for which listening is required, it is important to consider that an active preschooler may have to struggle to remain seated for any length of time.

FIGURE 8–7 Bookcases have been added to make this classroom area a quiet spot.

Evaluating Teacher Behaviors

Teachers planning activities need to consider the following questions. Why will a child listen to this activity? What factors or features could be included? What teacher behaviors, speech, or actions encourage child listening? How do I, as a teacher, develop "a listening habit" in children and promote specific listening skills? Can I judge when I have captured child attention? Can I assess which children listen well and which children listen poorly? These are quite a few questions to be answered, and you may have thought of others. A good place to start is to analyze your own classroom experiences. Hopefully, you experienced a memorable class or teacher whose class you loved to attend. List the factors that made that teacher or class special. Usually mentioned are the teacher's personality, her style of teaching, and techniques that the teacher used to make students feel special, competent, smart, accepted, and so on. Also often mentioned are the classroom's physical space and the activities that took place, which were highly enjoyed, and perhaps other adults or children in the classroom. The author remembers vividly the grammar school teacher who always skillfully read an interesting and exciting book after recess. She read with great enthusiasm, animation, and pleasure. Going back to the questions under discussion we will take a closer look at each. Why do children listen to an activity? A number of reasons are possible.

- The activity relates in some way to past experience.
- The children are curious about something new.
- There is a motivation to listen because of something the children want to know that personally affects them.
- The children enjoy the company of the people present.
- Something has happened to capture their attention.
- They can hear clearly without distractions and/or can easily see what is going on.
- They are physically comfortable.
- They have no physical, emotional, social, or personal distracting life situation upon which they are focused, such as hunger, lack of sleep, emotional pain, and so on.

What teacher behaviors, speech, or actions might influence child listening?

◆ enthusiasm (Figure 8–8)

◆ animation (but not overly so)

◆ acceptance

◆ recognition of children by name

◆ establishment of a you-talk turn, I-talk turn interaction

◆ eye contact

◆ listening skill

◆ patience

◆ clear and appropriately paced and pitched speech

◆ panning of a group with the eyes to gauge children's avid or waning attention and adjusting accordingly

◆ voice variety

◆ appropriate voice volume

FIGURE 8–8 This teacher is enthusiastic about this "listening" activity.

◆ eye-level contact

◆ planning for enough time so that there is not a rushed feeling

◆ elimination of distractions such as two children sitting together who might "act up" or other noises in the classroom that interfere with listening

◆ lowered voice volume to gain attention

◆ stating of rules about turn-taking behavior, hand raising, and interrupting

◆ use of an attention-getting gathering activity at the beginning of the activity

Can I judge when I have captured attention or the activity has captured child attention? Easily. If you watch, you will know when they are with you, all ears so to speak. It is one of the joys of teaching. The feeling of communion never grows old. Ask any practicing teacher.

Can I assess which children listen well and which need help developing listening skill? If you are watchful, yes. However, there are days when even the best listeners will be distracted.

Talk-Listen Group Times

Kindergarten and some early childhood programs are offering older preschoolers "talking-listening" social skill groups. The goal of this activity is to give children who desire to participate the chance to discuss child- and teacher-selected topics in a social setting. This structured activity promotes active listening. In elementary school, this group experience is usually termed "active listening" time or "community circle" (Curran, 1994).

Children are seated in a circle so that they can look at the person speaking and easily hear everyone's comments. In preschools, the circle times are kept short and intimate, with small groups of children.

Teachers structure this type of talking-listening time as follows:

1. The teacher announces a talk-listen circle as a choice of activity.

2. The teacher names the topic or elicits one from the group. It might be *cats* because a

picture book has been shared, or *worms* because one has been found, or it might be an open-ended statement like, "After school I like to go home and . . ."

3. A chart depicting expected talk-listen circle child behavior is introduced or reviewed. "We'll be looking at the person speaking. We'll listen with our ears." The teacher may choose to introduce only looking at others during children's first circle, and listening another time.

4. The teacher states, "Each of us will have a turn to speak. If you don't want a turn to speak, you can say 'pass'."

5. The teacher speaks first, modeling a short sentence—"My cat is gray and likes to sleep in a sunny window." Then she proceeds around the circle.

6. A very short group evaluation can take place when all have had a turn. Was it easy to wait for your turn? Did you see others' eyes while you were talking? (Children's answers are given in turn.)

Teachers may continue if discussion is still of interest with statements such as, "We've all had a turn. Raise your hand if you've something more to tell. Anyone can choose to leave our talking-listening time."

A number of common behaviors occur at preschool discussion times. An egg timer might have to be used with the child who drones on and on. The same children may pass day after day, or the same children may choose to participate in circle discussions. A child may not stick to the announced topic, but all comments are accepted and appreciated by the teacher.

Because listening closely and group discussion may be new to preschoolers and because individual developmental levels vary, children may either quickly or slowly grasp the social and listening skills offered. To encourage listening and speaking in turn, some programs use cardboard cutouts of lips and ears attached to tongue depressors. The speaker holds the stick with the lips while listeners hold ear sticks.

Of course, many unplanned discussions take place in most preschool classrooms. This type of structured group time encourages

young children's social discussion—a skill useful in future classrooms.

Listening Centers

Special listening areas, sometimes called listening posts, can become a part of early childhood classrooms. Enjoying a quiet time by oneself or listening to recorded materials fascinates many children. Headsets plugged in to a jack or terminal help block out room noise. Partitions cut distractions. Clever listening places where children can settle into become favorite spots, such as

- large packing boxes lined with soft fabrics and pillows.
- old, soft armchairs.
- a bunk or loft.

Phonographs, videos, audio cassettes, CDs, photographs, picture sets, and books offer added dimensions to listening centers. Recordings of the teacher reading a new or favorite story can be available at all times for children's use (Figure 8–9). These recordings are sometimes called read-alongs and are also available from commercial sources. Their quality varies widely, so it is recommended that they be reviewed before they are purchased.

When teachers realize how much future educational experience depends on how well language is processed through children's listening, listening activities and listening centers gain importance. As Healy (1990) points out, many of today's children have passively listened to considerable TV but may be particularly lacking in the practice of auditory analysis and logical sequential reasoning.

Children can record, with adult help, their own descriptions of special block constructions together with accompanying drawings or photos. "Why I like this book" talks can be made about a special book. Children can record comments about their own pieces of art. A field-trip scrapbook may have a child's commentary with it. Recorded puppet scripts and flannel-board stories can be enjoyed while the child moves the characters and listens. The child can explore small plastic animals while listening to a recorded story. Possibilities for recorded activities are limited only by preparation time and staff interest.

FIGURE 8–9 Listening with earphones puts this child into deep thought.

Children's ages are always a factor in the use of audiovisual equipment. Listening centers need teacher introduction, explanation, and supervision.

Recordings. Some companies specialize in recordings for children that are designed to improve listening skills. These recordings involve children in listening for a signal, listening to directions, or listening to sounds. Some recordings include body-movement activities along with listening skills.

Not all recordings contain appropriate subject matter for young children. Before purchasing one for children, the teacher should listen to it and judge its quality.

Tape Recorders. Tape recorders can fascinate children. They can be valuable tools for listening activities. Under the teacher's supervision or after being aquainted with instructions for use, children can explore and enjoy listening.

Children's Books with Listening Themes. Books with themes concerned with listening are good springboards to discussions about listening skills. See books listed in Resources at the end of this chapter.

MUSIC AS A LISTENING ACTIVITY

A type of listening Wolf (1992) calls "focused listening" occurs in many music activities. Children may be attending to specific sounds and words that give directions. Singing games often call for child response or child silence (or pause). To remember and sing a song (or parts of songs), staying in tune and rhythm, entails not only focused listening but also auditory discrimination and intellectual processing. Suggestions for music activities in early childhood centers follow:

- songs and recordings that give directions
- songs and recordings that contain certain sounds that serve as a cue for response in speech, movement, or both
- music that highlights particular rhythm instruments, drums, bells, sticks, and so forth
- music with environmental sounds
- music with songs that promote creative child response
- background music accompanying play and exploration

See the Appendix for suggested recordings.

ARE THERE DIFFERENCES IN CHILDREN'S LISTENING ABILITIES?

There are wide differences in children's listening abilities. As teachers become familiar with the children enrolled in their classes, they may notice that some children display abilities that allow them to note fine differences in sounds. Other children, who are progressing normally, will not acquire these skills until they are older.

Some researchers believe that boys have a slight edge in one particular area—listening vocabulary (Brimer, 1969). Theories attempting to explain this difference suggest that boys speak later than girls and consequently depend on discriminative listening for a longer period and gain more skill. It is also believed that mothers respond more frequently to male infant vocalizations, giving males greater vocal input. Chances are that preschool teachers will not notice any significant difference between their male and female students.

PHONOLOGICAL AWARENESS

Phonological awareness skills are believed to be predictive of a child's ease in learning to read. Researchers have begun to investigate how to enhance these skills before children enter kindergarten. Rhyming; segmenting morphemes and syllables in words; using discriminative and critical listening, phonemic contrasting, and phonemic games emphasizing beginning letter sounds in words; commenting on alphabet letter sounds; and engaging in other such sounds-of-language activities could all be categorized as phonological skill-building opportunities. These types of activities might aid all four- and five-year-olds and be particularly valuable for at-risk children. Making these activities relevant and interesting can be a teaching challenge. Activities can become an outgrowth of many daily planned happenings. See the Listening Activities section at the end of this chapter.

Opitz (2000) explains that phonological awareness is developmental—it develops in stages, the first and easiest being the awareness that our language is composed of words. Language learners progress and become aware that words are made up of word parts (that is, syllables), and in the last and most difficult stage, they become aware that syllables are made up of individual sounds (that is, phonemes).

What did the National Reading Panel Report (2000) conclude after reviewing research concerning phonetic awareness?

- Phonetic awareness instruction is effective in teaching children to attend to and manipulate speech sounds in words.
- Phonetic instruction is effective under a variety of teaching conditions and with a variety of learners.
- Teaching sounds in language helps children learn to read.
- It helps children decode novel words as well as remember how to read familiar words.
- It boosts reading comprehension.
- Phonetic awareness helps all types of children, including normally developing readers, readers at risk for future reading problems, disabled readers, preschoolers, kindergartners, and first through sixth grade children learning to read English as well as other languages.
- It helps some children learn to spell in English as well as other languages.
- Instruction is most effective when children are taught to manipulate phonemes with alphabet letters, when instruction is explicitly focused on one or two types of phoneme manipulations rather than multiple types, and when children are in small groups.
- Instruction should be suited to the child's level of development, with easier tasks being used for younger children.
- Teaching alphabet letters is important.
- Teaching children to blend phonemes helps them decode.
- It is important to teach letter shapes, names, and sounds so that children can use letters to acquire phonetic awareness.
- Instruction is more effective when it makes explicit how children are to apply phonetic awareness skills in reading and writing tasks.
- Instruction does not need to consume long periods of time to be effective.
- Computers can be used to teach phonetic awareness effectively.

◆ Phonetic awareness helps learners understand and use the alphabetic system to read and write.

◆ Phonetic instruction is a critical foundation piece.

◆ Instruction should be offered in short periods and be as relevant as possible.

◆ Early phonetic instruction cannot guarantee later literacy success.

Phonological awareness typically begins around age three and improves gradually over many years (Snow, Burns, & Griffin, 1998). Phonological awareness refers to the general ability to attend to (listen to) the sounds of language as distinct from its meaning. A subskill, **phonemic awareness**, can be defined as understanding that spoken language can be analyzed into strings of separate words and that words can be analyzed in sequences of syllables and phonemes within syllables. Young children begin to notice sound similarities in the words they hear. They enjoy rhymes, language play with words, repeated syllables, and **alliteration**. Because children's books contain these features, close listening at story time is certainly one way to develop phonemic awareness.

Eventually, but usually not until kindergarten or early first grade, children can hear all the sounds in a word and can segment a word into each of its sounds, or phonemes (McGee, 2003a). Is there a sequence in the development of phonemic awareness? Most educators agree that simultaneous learning is more characteristic. Activities associated with phonemic awareness are found at the end of this chapter.

Barone (2003) suggests that learning about phonemes is not new. What is new is the importance assigned to phonemes. There is great pressure on teachers to make sure that young children know how to use them to decode words. Barone discusses successful implementation of phoneme instruction in kindergarten:

... teachers built their instruction of phonemes around children's own language and experiences. They moved from what was known by the students to less familiar territory. They expected all of their students to participate and use whole-group sessions for assessment as well. From these activities, they moved to small groups in which individual student needs can be met.

Can an early childhood program include the goal of developing phonemic awareness? Is phonological awareness training helpful in four- to five-year-old preschoolers who are at risk for reading difficulties? Snow, Burns, and Griffin (1998), in *Preventing Reading Difficulties in Young Children,* suggest that available research evidence points to a "yes" answer to both questions. They cite a study by Brady, Fowler, Stone, and Winbury (1994).

Brady and associates (1994) studied 43 inner-city children aged 4 to 5 years. At the outset, fewer than half could generate rhymes, and none could segment simple words into phonemes or read any words. The 21 children who received training were closely matched to 21 who did not on receptive vocabulary, age, and initial phonological abilities.

In the post-tests, 12 of the 21 controls were still unable to generate any rhyme, and only one could segment any words into phonemes. In contrast, all but one of the trained group could generate rhymes, and six succeeded in full phonemic segmentation. (Snow, Burns, & Griffin, 1998)

What exercises were included in this phonemic awareness training?

◆ directing children's attention to rhyme

◆ segmenting morphemes and syllables (e.g., "Say a little bit of butterfly" and "Can you say 'butterfly' without the 'but'?")

◆ categorizing sounds (e.g., "Which word doesn't belong: mop, top, pop, can?")

---

phonemic awareness — the insight that every spoken word can be conceived as a sequence of phonemes.
alliteration — the repetition of the initial sounds in neighboring words or stressed syllables, for example, "The foam flowed free and fizzy."

- identifying syllables ("Do you hear 'doe' in 'window'? In 'candy'?")

- illustrating phonemic contrasts (e.g., /p/ vs. /b/)

- allowing children to experience relevant articulatory gestures

- using segmentation and identification games at the phonemic level (e.g., "Say a bit of 'boat'.")

- segmenting phonemes in two- and three-phoneme words using a "say it and move it" procedure

Educators planning to incorporate phonemic awareness training for at-risk four-year-olds are urged to investigate projects like the Abecedarian Project (Campbell & Ramey, 1994).

PHONEMIC AWARENESS SKILL

A child with phonemic awareness may have *phoneme* segmentation skill, a skill that allows her to hear phoneme segments in a word. A phoneme is the smallest unit of speech distinguishing one utterance from another.

Research in this area is motivated by the accepted conclusion that a good number of children having difficulty learning to read cannot hear sound sequences in words (Clay, 1987).

One clever Danish research team (Lundberg, Frost, & Peterson, 1988) introduced a guessing game in which children listened to phonemic hints by a troll character concerning presents they would receive by guessing the word correctly. In English, this might be done with d-o-ll? c-a-r? and so on. No alphabet letters need to be mentioned in this kind of activity.

Hearing individual phonemes is not an easy task. Hearing the "separate" words in a sentence is also difficult. Weaver (1998b) believes that when researchers and educators talk about developing children's phonemic awareness, they are talking about developing children's ability to hear such sounds, and particularly to analyze words into their separate sounds. Venn and Jahn (2004) point out that children hear and isolate letters with **continuant**, or sustainable, sounds first. The sounds articulated in the letters *a, e, i, o, u, f, l, m, n, r, s, u,* and *z* are easier to sustain than the stop sounds articulated in the letters *b, c, d, g, h, j, k, p, q, t,* and *x.* Therefore, it is easier for children to hear the continuant sounds in the word *mom* than the stop sounds in the word *bat.*

Adams (1990) has identified at least five different levels of phonemic awareness.

1. The most primitive level—that measured by knowledge of nursery rhymes—involves nothing more than an ear for the sounds of words.

2. At the next level, the oddity tasks require the child to methodically compare and contrast the sounds of words for rhyme or alliteration; this requires not just sensitivity to similarities and differences in the overall sounds of words, but also the ability to focus attention on the components of sounds that make them similar or different.

3. The tasks at the third level, blending and syllable splitting, seem to require (1) that the child have a comfortable familiarity with the notion that words can be subdivided into these small, meaningless sounds corresponding to phonemes and (2) that she be comfortably familiar with the way phonemes sound when produced "in isolation" and, better yet, with the act of producing them that way by oneself.

4. The phonemic segmentation tasks require not only that the child have a thorough understanding that words can be completely analyzed into a series of phonemes but further that she be able to so analyze them, completely and on demand.

---

continuant — a consonant or vowel that may be continued or prolonged without alteration during one emission of breath.

5. The phoneme manipulation tasks require still further that the child have sufficient proficiency with the phonemic structure of words that she is able to add, delete, or move any designated phoneme and regenerate a word (or a nonword) from the result.

Phonemic awareness is required to make connections between single alphabet letters and sounds. It is therefore one of the first steps, or first skills, on the road to learning to read. Some preschool children can and do read the printed names of classmates and may have a large number of words memorized by sight, but tackling other words they see and sounding them out is impossible without phonemic awareness.

Weaver (1998c) believes effective teaching would focus on a number of language features, including **rimes** and **onsets**, before single phonemes (other than onsets). In spoken syllables, onsets are any consonants before a vowel in a syllable; rimes are the vowel and any consonants after it in a syllable (Figure 8–10).

Several researchers have shown that young children are competent at analyzing spoken words into onsets and rimes but not into phonemes when onsets or rimes consist of more than one phoneme (Moustafa, 1998). There is usually more than one phoneme in the onset, the rime, or both. Moustafa gives as an example the fact that children can mentally analyze the word smiles into /sm/ and /ilz/, but not into /s/, /m/, /i/, /l/, and /z/. Wylie and Durrell (1970) have identified 500 primary grade words that can be derived from a set of only 37 rimes.

The fact that young children can split spoken words into onsets and rimes more easily than into phonemes (when phonemes are parts of onsets and rimes) raises the possibility that children use onsets and rimes rather than phonemes to pronounce new print words (Moustafa, 1998). Moustafa concludes that research findings suggest that (1) reading instruction predicated on the assumption that young childen learn to pronounce unfamiliar print using phonemes is developmentally inappropriate and (2) young children use their knowledge of onsets and rimes rather than a knowledge of phonemes to pronounce unfamiliar print.

What discussions will early childhood staff members have before providing phonemic awareness activities? (1) Most certainly, "is it developmentally appropriate?" (2) Do children typically develop phonemic knowledge and phonic knowledge without direct teaching? Weaver (1998c) observes that direct teaching does not have to be intensive and systematic to be effective for a majority of children. At least three-fourths of children typically develop phonemic knowledge and phonic knowledge without much direct teaching. (3) Will some children need and benefit from additional help in developing phonemic awareness? Various sources suggest that somewhere between 15 and 20 percent of children show a need for such additional instruction, whether it be provided in the classroom or not (Lyon, 1996). (4) What are recommended instructional techniques to help children gain phonics knowledge and phonemic awareness in the context of meaningful activities and language play? Weaver (1998c), after reviewing the works of many educators and researchers, advocates the following:

1. Read and reread favorite nursery rhymes, and enjoy tongue twisters and other forms of language play together.

ONSET	RIME
b-	-ack
st-	-ale
p-	-ick
s-	-ame
pl-	-ay
cl-	-ick

FIGURE 8–10 Onsets and rimes.

rimes — the vowel and any consonants after it in a syllable.
onsets — any consonants before a vowel in a syllable.

2. Reread favorite poems, songs, and stories; discuss alliteration and rhyme within them; and play with sound elements (e.g., starting with *cake,* remove the *c* and consider what different sounds could be added to make other words, like *take, make, lake*).

3. Read alphabet books to and with children, and make alphabet books together.

4. Discuss words and make lists, word banks, or books of such words that share interesting spelling-sound patterns.

5. Discuss similar sounds and letter-sound patterns in children's names.

6. Emphasize selected letter-sound relationships while writing with, for, or in front of children.

7. Encourage children to play with magnetic letters and to explore letter-sound relationships.

8. Help children write the sounds they hear in words.

9. When reading together, help children use prior knowledge and context plus initial consonants to predict what a word will be, then look at the rest of the word to confirm or correct. This is especially important for helping children orchestrate prior knowledge with context and letter/sound cues in order to not merely identify words but to construct meaning from texts, which, after all, is the primary purpose of reading.

Weaver (1998a) emphatically points out that teaching is embedded within a rich literacy context that also integrates reading, writing, and literature with the use of oral language across the curriculum. It requires children to think, not passively complete worksheets or engage in skill sessions. It focuses on patterns, not rules.

Phonemic Awareness Activities

Teachers of young children should recognize the important role they can play in contributing to young children's phonemic awareness and realize it can become a natural outgrowth of a wide variety of language-related activities and not become relegated to a "one-time-a-day" status.

These activities can take place in the daily context of a developmentally appropriate program. The goal of any phonemic awareness activity is to facilitate children's perception that speech is made up of a series of sounds. Activities that easily fall into the category of phoneme awareness activities are word-play and word-game activities.

It is suggested that the reader study the references found in the Additional Resources section at the end of this chapter and search for other resources to uncover how educators have developed awareness programs for young at-risk children.

Using Book Discussions to Develop Phonemic Awareness

A teacher's comments about a book the teacher is reading aloud can explicitly point out and analyze phonemic features, for example, "Those words start alike. The author did that! Listen: cap, cape, coat" (Yopp, 1995). See Resources at the end of this chapter for a listing of children's books that are helpful in developing phonemic awareness.

LISTENING ACTIVITIES

Listening activities are used to increase enjoyment, vocabulary, and skill. In this chapter, the activities focus on the development of auditory skills through listening and response interactions. Activities that further develop these skills through the use of books and stories are found in later chapters.

Chapter 14 gives a great deal of encouragement and helps you conduct circle or group activities. If you will be trying out activities in this chapter, it is best to skip ahead and read Chapter 14 first.

Every classroom has some signal that alerts children to a change in activities or a new opportunity. This can range from a few notes on a classroom musical instrument to more creative signals. Usually, a short invitational and attention-getting statement will be used to pique children's curiosity, such as

◆ "Gail has a new game for you in the rug area today."

- "Time to finish what you are doing and join Madelyn in the story-time center with a book about Clifford, the big, red dog."
- "Our clapping song begins in two minutes."

In some centers, children are simply requested to finish up what they are doing and join their friends in a particular room area. The enjoyment of already-started finger plays, chants, songs, or movement captures their attention and they are drawn in. This is a great time to recognize all children by name, as in the following (to the tune of "She'll Be Coming Round the Mountain").

"Susie is here with us, yes, yes, yes."
(Clap on yes, yes, yes.)
"Larry's here with us, yes, yes, yes."
(Continue until all children are recognized, and end with the following.)
"We are sitting here together,
We are sitting here together,
We are sitting here together, yes, yes, yes."

AUTHOR'S CHAIR OR CHILD PICTURE-BOOK SHARING

Early childhood programs that promote poetry, child dictation, storytelling, and authorship can institute an author's chair, a listening and discussion activity. Usually, the child-sized chair is specially decorated and used at one time of the day, or a sign is affixed—Author's and/or Reader's Chair. Children are invited to share their own efforts or share a favorite or brought-to-school picture book. Teachers may find a need to establish time limits for ramblers or may allow audiences to choose to leave quietly when they wish.

LISTENING RIDDLES FOR GUESSING

Rhyming Animal Riddles

A tail that's skinny and long,
At night he nibbles and gnaws
With teeth sharp and strong.
Beady eyes and tiny paws,

One called Mickey is very nice.
And when there's more than one
We call them _____. (mice)

He has a head to pat.
But he's not a cat.
Sometimes he has a shiny coat.
It's not a hog, it's not a goat.
It's bigger than a frog.
I guess that it's a _____. (dog)

No arms, no hands, no paws,
But it can fly in the sky.
It sings a song
That you have heard.
So now you know
That it's a _____. (bird)

Sharp claws and soft paws,
Big night eyes, and whiskers, too.
Likes to curl up in your lap,
Or catch a mouse or a rat.
Raise your hand if you know.
Now all together, let's whisper its name
*   very slowly _____. (cat)*

Riddle Game

Children take turns calling on others with raised hands.

I'll ask you some riddles.
Answer if you can.
If you think you know,
Please raise your hand.
Don't say it out loud
Till _____ calls your name.
That's how we'll play
This riddling game.

A beautiful flower we smell with our nose.
Its special name is not pansy but _____.
*   (rose)*

I shine when you're playing and having
*   fun.*
I'm up in the sky and I'm called the _____.
*   (sun)*

If you listen closely you can tell,
I ring and chime because I'm a _____. (bell)

You've got 10 of me, I suppose,
I'm on your feet and I'm your _____. (toes)

I'm down on your feet, both one and two
Brown, black, blue, or red, I'm a _____.
*   (shoe)*

I sit on the stove and cook what I can
They pour stuff in me, I'm a frying _____.
   (pan)

It is helpful to have magazine pictures of a rose, the sun, toes, shoes, and a pan, plus a real bell to ring behind you as you speak. Those appropriate for young children who have little experience with rhyming follow.

Body Parts Riddle

If a bird you want to hear,
You have to listen with your _____. (ear)

If you want to dig in sand,
Hold the shovel in your _____. (hand)

To see an airplane as it flies,
Look up and open up your _____. (eyes)

To smell a pansy or a rose,
You sniff its smell with your _____. (nose)

When you walk across the street
You use two things you call your _____.
   (feet)

If a beautiful song you've sung,
You used your mouth and your _____.
   (tongue)

All these parts you can feel and see
Parts are always with you on your _____.
   (body)

Tracing hands or drawing any body part they choose (on a picture with missing hands, feet, and so forth) is a fun follow-up activity for four-and-a-half-year-olds.

LISTEN AND FOLLOW DIRECTIONS—STORIES AND GAMES

Sit-Down/Stand-Up Story

Say to the children, "Let's see if you can stand *up* and sit *down* when I say the words. Listen: Stand *up!* You all are standing. Sit *down!* Good listening; we're ready to start." Then, tell the children the following story.

When I woke *up* this morning, I reached *down* to the floor for my slippers. Then I stood *up* and slipped them on. Next, I went *down*stairs to the kitchen. I opened the refrigerator, picked *up* the milk and sat *down* to drink. When I finished drinking, I tried to stand *up*, but I was stuck in the chair. I pulled and pulled, but I was still sitting.

"Don't sit on the chairs," my dad called from *up*stairs. "I painted them."

"It's too late! I'm sitting *down*," I answered. "Hurry *down* here and help me."

Dad pulled and pulled, but I didn't come *up*.

"I'll go get our neighbor, Mr. Green. Maybe he can pull you *up*," Dad said. Dad and Mr. Green pulled and pulled. "What'll I do?" I said. "The children will be waiting at school for me." Then I got an idea. "Go get the shovel," I said. Well, that worked. They pushed the shovel handle *down* and I came *up*.

You know, I think I'm stuck in this chair, too. Look, I am. _____ (child's name) and _____ (child's name), please help me. Everyone else please sit.

After my story, let's see if just _____ (child's name) and _____ (child's name) can show us with their hands which way is *up*, and which way is *down*.

A good follow-up is to talk about what can be seen in the room that is up above the children's heads and down below their heads, or say this poem together:

When you're up—you're up,
And when you're down—you're down.
But when you're halfway in between,
You're neither up nor down.

SUMMARY

Listening skill is learned behavior. The ability to listen improves with experience and exposure, although young children vary in their ability to listen. Listening ability can be classified by type—appreciative, purposeful, discriminative, creative, and critical.

Planned activities, teacher interaction, and equipment can provide opportunities for children to develop phonetic and phonemic awareness.

Listening cannot be forced, but experiences can be provided so that a desire to listen is increased. Signals and attentive teacher encouragement can help form habits. Settings that limit stimuli and control the size of groups are desirable. When teachers are watchful and act when children seem restless or uninterested during planned activities, listening remains active. One of the responsibilities of the teacher is to plan carefully so that young children consistently want to hear what is being offered.

ADDITIONAL RESOURCES

Children's Books with Listening Themes

Borten, H. (1960). *Do you hear what I hear?* New York: Abelard-Schuman. (Describes the pleasures to be found in really listening.)

Brown, M. W. (1951). *The summer noisy book.* New York: Harper and Row. (Can be easily made into a "guess what" sound game.)

Fisher, A. (1988). *The house of a mouse.* New York: Harper and Row. (Mouse poems can be read in a tiny teacher voice. Rhyming text.)

Glazer, T. (1982). *On top of spaghetti.* New York: Doubleday. (Teacher sings a silly story.)

Guilfoile, E. (1957). *Nobody listens to Andrew.* Chicago: Follett. (The no-one-ever-listens-to-me idea is humorously handled.)

Johnson, L. (1967). *Night noises.* New York: Parents Magazine Press. (Listening to noises in bed at night.)

Lloyd, D. (1986). *The sneeze.* New York: Lippincott. (The child listens to questions.)

Novak, M. (1986). *Rolling.* Riverside, NJ: Bradbury Press. (The sounds of a storm dominate this story.)

Showers, P. (1961). *The listening walk.* New York: Thomas Y. Crowell. (Good book to share before adventuring on a group of sound walk.)

Spier, P. (1971). *Gobble, growl grunt.* New York: Doubleday. (Lots of variety in animal sounds, with brilliant illustrations.)

Zolotow, C. (1980). *If you listen.* New York: Harper and Row. (A touching tale of a child who, missing her father, turns to listening.)

Children's Books Promoting Phonemic Awareness

Bayer, J. (1992). *A, my name is Alice.* New York: Dutton. (Alliteration.)

Brown, M. W. (1991). *Good night moon.* New York: Harper. (Rhyming.)

Carle, E. (1994). *The very hungry caterpillar.* New York: Scholastic. (Blending and segmenting.)

Christelow, E. (2000). *Five little monkeys jumping on the bed.* New York: Clarion. (Rhyming.)

Guarino, D. (1997). *Is your mama a llama?* New York: Scholastic. (Rhyming.)

Hutchins, P. (1986). *The doorbell rang.* New York: William Morrow. (Blending and segmenting.)

Martin, B., Jr. (1997). *Polar bear, polar bear, what do you hear?* New York: Henry Holt. (Blending and segmenting.)

Peek, M. (1985). *Mary wore her red dress and Henry wore his green sneakers.* New York: Clarion. (Rhyming.)

Trapani, I. (1997). *I'm a little teapot.* Watertown, MA: Charlesbridge. (Rhyming.)

Readings

Adams, M. B., Foorman, B., Lundberg, I., & Beeler, T. (1996). *Phonemic awareness in young children.* Baltimore: Brookes.

Byrne, B., & Fielding-Barnsley, R. (1995). Evaluation of a program to teach phonemic awareness to young children. A two and three year follow up and a new preschool trial. *Journal of Educational Psychology, 87*(3), 488–503.

Elster, C. A. (1994). I guess they do listen: Young children's emergent readings after adult read-alouds. *Young Children, 49*(3), 26–31.

Hennings, D. G. (1990). *Communication in action.* Boston: Houghton Mifflin.

Tough, J. (1976). *Listening to children talking.* London: School Council Publications.

Wolvin, A., & Coakley, C. G. (1996). *Listening.* Madison, WI: Brown & Benchmark.

Readings on Phonological Awareness

Adams, M., Foorman, B., Lundberg, I., & Beeler, T. (1997). *Phonemic awareness in young children: A classroom curriculum.* Baltimore: Paul H. Brookes.

Byrne, B., & Fielding-Barnsley, R. (1993). Evaluation of a program to teach phonemic awareness to young children: A one year follow-up. *Journal of Educational Psychology, 55,* 104–111.

Floyd, S., & Yates, W. (2001). *Curriculum-aligned thematic phonological awareness treatment.* Lake City, SC: Susan Floyd.

Opitz, M. F. (2000). *Rhymes and reasons: Literature & language play for phonological awareness.* Portsmouth, NH: Heinemann.

Paulson, L., Noble, I., Jepson, S., & van den Pol, R. (2001). *Building early literacy and language skills.* Longmont, CO: Sopris West.

Yopp, H. K. (1992). Developing phonemic awareness in young children. *Reading Teacher, 45,* 696–703.

Yopp, H. K., & Yopp, R. H. (2000). *Oo-pples and bo-noo-noos: Songs and activities for phonemic awareness.* Orlando: Harcourt School.

Game Making and Construction

Silberg, J., & Jones, R. (1995). *500 five minute games: Quick and easy activities for 3-6 year olds.* Beltsville, MD: Gryphon House.

Silberg, J., & Noll, C. K. (1997). *300 three minute games: Quick and easy activities for 2-5 year olds.* Beltsville, MD: Gryphon House.

HELPFUL WEB SITES

American Speech-Language-Hearing Association and The Learning Disabilities Association
http://www.ldanatl.org
Find information on central auditory processing problems in children.

KidSource Online
http://www.kidsource.com
Phonemic awareness and reading information is provided.

National Child Care Information Center
http://npin.org
Search for child literacy and early phonetic awareness information.

SIL International LINGUALlinks
http://www.sil.org
Information is provided on developing awareness of sounds.

 Additional listening activities that develop specific skills in six listening comprehension areas are described in the Online Companion™. Listening has been taken for granted for many years and ignored by educators. Now, listening comprehension is a recognized skill that educators believe can be systematically developed starting in the years before kindergarten. More information about phonemes and quotes about phonemes by a number of authors may help you feel comfortable with them.

STUDENT ACTIVITIES

1. Choose one of the listening activities found in this chapter, one from another source, or one you create. Present the activity to a group of preschoolers, modifying the activity to suit the child group if necessary. Then answer the following questions.

    a. Was the activity interesting to the children?

    b. Were they able to perform the auditory perception tasks?

    c. Would you change the activity in any way if you presented it again?

2. Find or create five additional listening activities. Provide information regarding the source, name of activity, materials needed, description of activity, and objective. Cite the source or state the title of the book where you found the activity idea. If the idea is original, indicate this by using the word *self*.

3. Practice the listening story in this chapter entitled "Sit-Down/Stand-Up Story," or find another listening story. At the next class meeting, tell the story to a classmate. Share constructive criticism.

4. Create a recorded activity in which children will in some way analyze what they hear and share responses with the teacher. An activity that requires logical or sequential listening could also be attempted. Share your recording and accompanying objects and/or visuals at the next class session.

5. Watch a listening activity in a preschool center, and then answer the following questions.

    a. How did the teacher prepare the children for listening?

    b. What elements of the activity captured interest?

    c. How was child interest held?

    d. Did the teacher have an opportunity to recognize children's listening skill?

    e. Did children's listening behavior during the activity seem important to the teacher?

    f. Was this the kind of activity that should be repeated? If so, why?

6. Write a one-page paper concerning your feelings about phonological or phonemic awareness instruction for preschoolers. Consider that many other countries, including the United Kingdom, expect preschoolers to know both alphabet letter names and letter sounds before entering kindergarten. Bring your paper to class and pair up with three others to discuss each person's feelings and ideas. Share main points in your discussion with the entire class. Hand in your paper and your four-member discussion-group notes to the instructor.

7. With the new emphasis on phonemic awareness development during preschool years, the commercial development and publication of phonemic awareness activities is bound to happen. What could be the inherent problems preschool teachers might face if they relied heavily on these commercially produced materials? List your main points.

8. Do talk-listen circle times seem overly structured to you, or do you believe they may be appropriate for today's generation of "television-saturated" children? Elaborate.

9. Discuss with two classmates the teacher techniques used in Figure 8–6. List your ideas and share with your training class.

CHAPTER REVIEW

A. Five types of listening have been discussed. After each of the following statements, identify the listening type that best fits the situation.

1. After hearing an Indian drum on a recording, Brett slaps out a rhythm of his own on his thighs while dancing around the room.

2. During a story of *The Three Little Pigs,* Mickey blurts out, "Go get 'em wolfie!" in reference to the wolf's behavior in the story.

3. Kimmie is following Chris around. Chris is repeating, "Swishy, fishy co-co-pop," over and over again; both giggle periodically.

4. Debbie tells you about the little voice of small Billy Goat Gruff and the big voice of Big Billy Goat Gruff in the story of the *Three Billy Goats Gruff.*

5. Peter has asked whether he can leave his block tower standing during snacktime instead of putting the blocks away as you requested. He wishes to return and build the tower higher. He then listens for your answer.

B. Select the correct answers. All have more than one correct reply.

1. Most parents unconsciously teach preschoolers
   a. to develop auditory perception.
   b. attitudes toward listening.
   c. to listen to their teachers.
   d. many words.

2. A teacher can promote listening by
   a. demanding a listening attitude.
   b. using a signal that alerts children and focuses attention.
   c. encouraging a child.
   d. telling a child she is not listening.

3. Critical listening happens when the
   a. child relates what is new to past experience.
   b. child disagrees with another's statement.
   c. child makes a comment about a word being good or bad.
   d. teacher plans thought-provoking questions and the child has the maturity needed to answer them.

4. Children come to early childhood centers with
   a. individual variation in abilities to listen.
   b. habits of listening.
   c. all the abilities and experiences needed to be successful in planned activities.
   d. a desire to listen.

5. Children's ability to follow a series of commands depends on
   a. their auditory memory.
   b. how clearly the commands are stated.

c. how well their ears transmit the sounds to their brains and how well their brains sort the information.

d. how well they can imitate the words of the commands.

C. Assume the children are involved in an activity when they are suddenly distracted by a dog barking outside the window. List four things you could say to the children to draw their attention back to the activity.

If you wished to use their focus on the barking for a spontaneous listening activity, how would you proceed?

D. What elements of music might promote listening skills?

E. Describe three listening activities, stating the objective of each activity and giving a description of the activity.

F. Define phonemic awareness, onset, and rime.

G. What factors have contributed to a new interest in phonological awareness?

LISTENING ACTIVITIES

Note: The following activities will have to be evaluated for age-level appropriateness and use with a particular group of children. They are provided here as examples of listening activities but may or may not be appropriate for your teaching situation.

ACTIVITIES ASSOCIATED WITH PHONOLOGICAL AWARENESS

- read-alouds, especially ones with repetition in words, phrases, and alliteration
- singing songs, especially those with repetitions or word play
- reading nursery rhymes and poetry
- engaging in language play—using silly words
- seeing words as separate entities
- noticing spaces between words
- labeling objects in the classroom; using word lists and charts
- counting words in a sentence or on a picture-book page
- raising one's hand on hearing a designated word

- clapping syllables
- counting syllables
- hearing different sounds in words and identifying them
- recognizing rhyming words
- using name tags; playing name activities and name games
- hearing sounds in their name by "stretching it out"
- playing with fun-to-say words—ratta-ta-ta, bibbity bobbity boo, licky sticky, and so on
- rhyming a word with teacher's word
- allowing children to create their own rhyme
- thinking of words that start the same as teacher's word
- identifying beginning sounds in words
- associating sounds with written words
- matching sounds
- rhyming with children's names
- playing games with children's names
- making an "'A' stands for . . ." list and so on
- finding one's name on a helper's chart

Note: These suggested activities are not presented in a particular order.

261

PHONEMIC AWARENESS ACTIVITIES

- using alphabet books, songs, rhymes, charts, toys, and games
- providing rhyming experiences—recognizing, identifying, and creating
- matching rhyming pictures
- clapping on rhyming words
- recognizing words beginning with the same letter—alliteration
- recognizing words beginning with the same sound
- hearing initial, middle, and ending sounds
- knowing the sounds alphabet letters make
- putting sounds together
- manipulating sounds
- naming words that start with the same letter
- counting sounds in words
- taking away sounds in words
- substituting sounds in words
- writing alphabet letters
- knowing the shapes of alphabet letters
- naming letter shapes
- trying to write words
- trying to read words
- making words with magnetic letters
- typing words or using alphabet stamp sets to form words
- grouping picture cards according to beginning, middle, and ending sounds
- making a list of same-sound beginnings
- matching sounds with alphabet letters
- comparing the number of syllables in words
- finding words with the same beginning and ending sounds
- playing with alphabet letter puzzles
- hunting for alphabet letters in the room
- making personal alphabet books

Note: These are not listed in sequential order, nor is the listing meant to be comprehensive.

RECOGNIZING VOICES GUESSING GAME

Objective

To practice discriminative listening and auditory memory skills

Materials

Individual snapshots of school personnel; a recording of different school staff members' voices reading sequential paragraphs in a story or describing the work they perform

Introduction and Activity

Line up snapshots in view of the children after each is identified. "Here are some snapshots of people we know. Now we're going to listen and try to guess who's talking. Raise your hand if you think you know."

At the conclusion of the activity, show the photos one by one and name each. A great follow-up is guessing children's voices using the same game format.

This can be set up as an individually chosen activity after being introduced at a group time or can be used with a group.

BUILD A BURGER

Objective

To practice purposeful listening

Materials

Cutouts of foods that are added to hamburger buns—onion slices, lettuce, tomato slices, cheese slices, pickles, salsa, meat patties, bacon, mayonnaise, mustard, and catsup; cutout paper buns or clay bun halves; paper plates; chart paper (optional)

262

Introduction and Activity

Ask the children what kinds of food they like on their hamburgers. After the group discusses the things they like, say, "I'm going to show you pictures of some of the things you've said you liked on your hamburger and some things I like. Here are onion slices; Marion said she liked them." Go on to show and name all the cutouts. "You can build a hamburger for a friend in this game. You'll have to listen closely to find out what she chooses to have you put between the buns." Teacher can print each child's selection on chart paper. (Of course, the real thing would be more fun—provide plastic gloves or use plastic sandwich bags for real food handling.)

SOUND CANS

Objective

To match similar sounds by using discriminative listening skills

Materials

Cans with press-on or screw-off lids; cards large enough to hold two cans; outline of circles of can bottoms (made with dark pen); two circles for each card, large different color index cards work well; best to use cans that are impossible for children to open or to securely tape cans shut; pairs of cans filled with same materials, such as sand, paper clips, rocks, rice, beans, nuts, and bolts

Introduction and Activity

This is a solitary activity or one that children can choose to play with others. It can be used in a learning center. An introduction like the following is necessary. "Here are some cans and cards. The way you play this game is to shake one can and then shake all the rest to find the one that sounds the same as the first can. Let's listen to this can." Shake it. "Now I'm going to try to find the can that sounds just like this one when I shake it." Pick up another and ask, "Does this sound the same?"

Shake the first and second cans. "No, this sounds different, so I'm going to shake another can." Go on until the mate is found and placed beside the first can on the card.

This activity is a classic one, and many sound sets are found in preschool programs. (Sets are also commercially manufactured.)

"CAN YOU SAY IT AS I DO?" ACTIVITY

Objective

To imitate sounds

Materials

None

Introduction and Activity

The teacher says, "Can you change your voice the way I can?"

"My name is (teacher softly whispers her name)." With changes of voice, speed, and pitch, the teacher illustrates with a loud, low, or high voice, speaking fast or slow, with mouth nearly closed or wide open, when holding nose, and so on.

The teacher then asks for a volunteer who would like to speak in a new or funny way. "Now, let's see if we can change our voices the way Billy does. Do it any way you want, Billy. We'll try to copy you."

The teacher then gives others a turn. This activity may be followed up with a finger play with voice changes, like the "Five Little Astronauts" activity in Chapter 14.

"LISTEN, OOPS A MISTAKE!—INTERRUPT ME PLEASE."

Objective

To associate and discriminate among word sounds and objects; to listen for inconsistencies

Materials

Four or five common school objects (such as a pencil, crayon, block, toy, cup, and doll) and a low table, or photographs or drawings of objects

Introduction and Activity

Talk about calling things by the wrong name, being sure to discuss how everyone makes mistakes at times. Begin with something like, "Have you ever called your friend by the wrong name?"

> *Teacher:* When you call your friend by the wrong name, you've made a mistake. Look at the things on the table. I am going to name each of them. (Teacher names them correctly.) All right, now see if you can hear my mistakes. This time I'm going to point to them, too. If you hear a mistake, raise your hand and say, "Oops, a mistake!" Let's say that together once: "Oops, a mistake!" Are you ready? Listen: crayon, ball, doll, cup.

Change objects, and give the children a chance to make mistakes while others listen. This activity can later be followed with the story *Moptop* (by Don Freeman, Children's Press), about a long-haired red-headed boy who is mistaken for a mop.

ERRAND GAME

Objective

To follow verbal commands

Materials

None

Introduction and Activity

Start a discussion about doing things for parents. Include getting objects from other rooms, from neighbors, and so on. Tell the children you are going to play a game in which each person looks for something another has asked for.

> *Teacher:* "Get a book for me, please."
> "Can you find a leaf?"

Items to ask for include a rock, a blade of grass, a piece of paper, a block, a doll, a crayon, a toy car, a sweater, a hat, clothes, a hanger, a blanket, and so forth. Send children off one at a time. As they return, talk to each about where the item was found. While the group waits for all members to return, the group can name the returned items. Put them in a row, ask children to cover their eyes while one is hidden, and then ask the children to guess which item was removed.

If interest is still high, the teacher can make a request that the items be returned and repeat the game by sending the children for new items.

BLIND WALK

Objective

To depend on listening to another child's verbal directions

Materials

Scarfs, bandanas, or cloth strips

Introduction and Activity

Discuss blindness and guide dogs. Pair children and blindfold one child. Ask the guide to hold the blindfolded child's hand and take a classroom walk. Ask the guide to talk about where children are going, and urge the blindfolded child to use hands to feel objects, and so forth. Change blindfolds, giving the guide a chance to also go on a guided walk. (Some children may object to blindfolds or act fearful. Respect their wishes.) Conduct a brief follow-up discussion.

Courtesy of WICAP Headstart, Donnelly, Idaho.

JACK-IN-THE-BOX

Objective

To discriminate sounds by listening for a signal and responding to it

264

Materials

None

Introduction and Activity

Recite the following rhyme in a whispered voice until the word *pop* is reached. Using hand motions, hide your thumb in your fist and let it pop up each time the word pop is said.

> *Jack-in-the-box, jack-in-the-box, where can you be?*
> *Hiding inside where I can't see?*
> *If you jump up, you won't scare me.*
> *Pop! Pop! Pop!*

Suggest that children squat and pretend to be jack-in-the-boxes. Ask them to listen and jump up only when they hear the word *pop*. Try a second verse if the group seems willing.

> *Jack-in-the-box, jack-in-the-box, you like to play.*
> *Down in the box you won't stay.*
> *There's only one word I have to say.*
> *Pop! Pop! Pop!*

PIN-ON SOUND CARDS (ANIMALS AND BIRDS)

Objective

To associate and imitate sounds and use auditory memory

Materials

Safety pins or masking tape; file cards (3" × 5") or self-stick memo paper with pictures of birds and animals (gummed stickers of animals and birds are available in stationery stores and from supply houses)

Suggestions: duck, rooster, chick, owl, goose, woodpecker, horse, cow, cat, dog, sheep, lion, mouse, turkey, bee, frog, donkey, seal

Introduction and Activity

Have a card pinned on your blouse or shirt before the children enter the room. This will start questions. Talk about the sound that the animal pictured on your card makes. Practice it with the children. Ask who would like a card. Talk about the animal and the sound it makes. Imitate each sound with the group. Have children imitate animal noises, and ask the child with the right card to raise her hand or stand up. Then prompt the child to finish "That's me; I'm a . . . ?" Children usually like to wear the cards the rest of the day and take them home, if possible.

SOUND STORY

This story contains three sound words. Every time one of the words is mentioned, the children should make the appropriate sound.

Say, "When you hear the word spinach, say 'yum, yum, yum.' When you hear the word dog, bark like a dog. When you hear the word cat, meow like a cat." Then, recite the following story.

> Once upon a time, there was a little boy who would not taste SPINACH. Everyone would say, "Marvin, why won't you taste SPINACH?" Marvin would say, "I think SPINACH is yuk!!!" Marvin's DOG Malcolm loved SPINACH. Marvin's CAT Malvina loved SPINACH. If Marvin didn't eat his SPINACH, Malcolm the DOG and Malvina the CAT would fight over who would get the SPINACH. The DOG and CAT would make so much noise fighting over the SPINACH that everyone in the neighborhood would say, "If you don't stop that noise, you will have to move away." Marvin loved his house and he didn't want to move away from the neighborhood. Malcolm the DOG loved his house and he didn't want to move away from the neighborhood. Malvina the CAT loved her house and she didn't want to move away from the neighborhood. What could they do?

265

Let the children tell you the answer. This game is a great deal of fun, and the children never tire of hearing the story. You can make up your own sound stories. You can also add rhythm instruments to make the sounds instead of voices. Spinach can be changed to any food—enchilada, wonton, bratwurst, grits, sweet potato pie, and so on.

Funny Old Hat Game

Gather a bag of old hats (such as new or discarded paper party hats). Pass the hats out to the children, or let the children choose them.

Say, "We're ready when our hats are on our heads. We're going to put our hats in some funny places and do some funny things. Listen."

Put your hat between your knees.

Put your hat under your arm.

Put your hat over your shoes.

Put your hat under your chin.

Touch the top of your hat.

Sit on your hat.

Stand on your hat.

Encourage the children to choose a place to put the hat, and then say, "Where's the hat? Where's the hat, [child's name]. Can you see the hat, hat, hat?" (This can be chanted.) "Under the chair, under the chair—I can see the hat, hat, hat."

See If You Can Game

Collect objects from around the classroom (for example, scissors, ruler, eraser, cup, chalk). Put them on the floor on a large piece of paper. Say, "I'm not going to say its name. See if you can tell me what object I am talking about. Raise your hand if you know." (Keep giving hints until the children guess.)

"What has two circles for two fingers?" (scissors)

"It's long and thin with numbers printed on one side." (ruler)

"What makes pencil marks disappear?" (eraser)

"You can fill it with milk." (cup)

"What's white and small and writes on the chalkboard?" (chalk)

CAN YOU DO THIS?

Children imitate hand and body movements of teacher or other children. "Can you put your hands on your chin, knees, elbows, and so on?"

WHAT HAS CHANGED? GAME OR CAN YOU KEEP A SECRET? GAME

Materials

A bag with hats, scarves, belts, pins, sock, glove, shoe, and so on.

Introduction and Activity

Teacher can ask a group to examine her closely because something is going to change or look different. The teacher asks the children to close their eyes or look down, or the teacher can turn her back to the children and quickly slip on one item from the bag. "If you know, keep it a secret. We will help your friends by giving them some clues that will help them discover what changed. Is it above my neck? Say yes or no. Is it above my belt?" and so on. Child volunteers can be used to change themselves after game is learned.

SECTION4

Introducing Literature

CHAPTER 9

Children and Books

OBJECTIVES

After reading this chapter, you should be able to:

◆ State three goals for reading books to young children.

◆ Describe criteria for book selection.

◆ Demonstrate suggested techniques for reading a book to a group of children.

◆ Design a classroom library center.

◆ Explain quality book features.

◆ Discuss multicultural and multi-ethnic book use.

KEY TERMS

characterization	genre	realism
fairy tales	narrative	visualization
fiction	nonfiction	

A VOLUNTEER READER

Mr. Mead, LaVon's grandfather, arrives in the four-year-old's classroom shortly after nap time and goes to the rocking chair. There is a small commotion in the book center as a few children dash for the reading shelf. A line of children clutching one book forms. The first in line peeks at Mr. Mead, who is reading a book and already has a child curled up on his lap, the child's face registering the intent of enjoying every minute. There is an air of magic and hopeful anticipation on the waiting children's faces. Mrs. Rex, the teacher, moves a few chairs in a row for the "waiters."

QUESTIONS TO PONDER

1. One can hear Mr. Mead's laughter and a child's giggle. What would you like to know about Mr. Mead's reading technique?

2. What children's attitudes are being formed, and how might these affect their future academic success?

269

Picture books are an important beginning step on the child's path to literacy, as well as an excellent source of listening activities for the young child. Seeing, touching, and interacting with books is part of a good-quality program in early childhood education. Books play an important role in language development. *Becoming a Nation of Readers* asserts that reading aloud is the single most important activity for creating the background necessary for eventual success in reading (Anderson, Hiebert, Scott, & Wilkinson, 1985).

Cox (1981) describes the child's first home being-read-to experience as a curriculum.

> It is a curriculum rich in pleasant associations: a soft lap, a warm bath, a snugly bed ... This initial literature curriculum makes possible the impossible, uses common words in uncommon ways, titillates the senses, nurtures curiosities, stretches the memory and the imagination.

When handled with care, reading experiences at home and at school can create positive attitudes toward literature and help motivate the child to learn to read. A positive attitude toward literacy is most easily established early in life.

Many parents read to their children at home; others do not (Figure 9–1). Children from many low-income families are more dependent on school experiences for their literacy development than middle-class children (Alexander & Entwisle, 1996). In fact, a teacher may offer some children their first contact with stories and books. Teacher and child can share the joy of this very pleasant experience. Trelease (1995) discusses reading to young children and the possible significance to the child and parent.

> Next to hugging your child, reading aloud is probably the longest-lasting experience that you can put into your child's life. Reading aloud is important for all the reasons that talking to children is important—to inspire them, to guide them, to educate them, to bond with them and to communicate your feelings, hopes and fears. You are giving children a piece of your mind and a piece of your time. They're more inter-

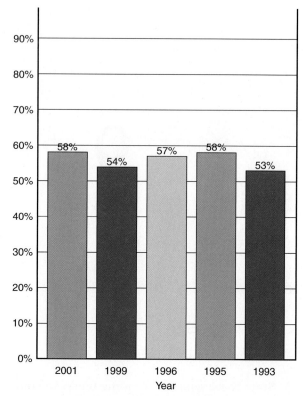

*Based on children who have yet to enter kindergarten.

FIGURE 9–1 Percentage of children ages three to five* who were read to every day by a family member. (From U.S. Department of Education, National Center for Education Statistics, *National Household Education Survey,* 1993, 1999, and 2003.)

ested, really, in you than they are in the story—at least in the beginning.

Snow and Tabors (1993) describe possible literacy happenings during adult book-reading times as follows:

> Book reading is an opportune time for teachers to help children build vocabulary, extend phonological awareness, and develop familiarity with literate forms.

> Reading books aloud to children exposes them to grammatical forms of written language and displays literate discourse rules for them in ways that conversation cannot.

Snow and Tabors (1993) urge teachers to lead discussions that encourage children to analyze the text, and they believe these discussions can have a powerful effect on the development of complex oral language, vocabulary, and story understanding—all critical abilities that young children will need when faced with later literacy tasks.

Early childhood teachers agree that book-sharing sessions are among their favorite times with children. Teachers introduce each new group of children to favorite books that never seem to lose their magic.

There will be times when young children are rapt with enjoyment during picture-book readings, and at such times, the lucky reader will understand the power of literature and realize his responsibility as the sharer of a vast treasure. The value of offering thoughtfully selected books in a skilled way will be readily apparent.

What, exactly, do picture books offer young children? They open the door to literacy and create the opportunity to influence attitudes, broaden understanding, savor diversity, vicariously experience drama, expand the imagination, gain vocabulary and information, hear the rhythm of language and words, and enjoy the visual and aesthetic variety in illustrations.

Clay (1991a) notes another advantage.

> Preschool children learn to respond to the messages in children's stories which are told or read to them and in doing this they use the kind of language and thought processes that they will use in learning to read later on.

As you read through this chapter, other benefits of reading aloud to children will occur to you, and you will clarify your thoughts about the benefits you consider of primary and secondary importance.

Cullinan (1992) suggests that story form is a cultural universal; stories help us remember by providing meaningful frameworks. Stories make events memorable.

A special kind of language is found in books. Oral language differs from written language in important ways. Although many young children communicate well and have ad-equate vocabularies, they do not construct sentences in the same manner found in their picture books. Knowing the way books "talk" makes them better predictors of words they will discover in their early reading attempts.

Each child gets his own meaning from picture-book experiences. Books cannot be used as substitutes for the child's real-life experiences, interactions, and discoveries, because these are what help make books understandable. Books add another dimension and source of information and enjoyment to children's lives.

Although most teachers believe reading books in a preschool classroom is an important classroom literacy activity, Dickinson's research (2001) found that children in about one-third of the preschool classrooms studied listened to books read in a large group for 25 minutes or less each week. In only about 25 percent of the classrooms did children listen to stories in large groups for more than 50 minutes each week. Reading to children individually and in small groups was also rare. Were this study's conclusions an anomaly? Let's hope so.

AGE AND BOOK EXPERIENCES

Careful consideration should be given to selecting books that are appropriate to the child's age. Children younger than three (and many older than this age) enjoy physical closeness, the visual changes of illustrations, and the sound of the human voice reading text. The rhythms and poetry of picture books intrigue them. Beck (1982) points out that very young children's "syntactic dependence" is displayed by their obvious delight in recognized word order. The sounds of language in picture books may be far more important than the meanings conveyed to the very young child. Teachers of two- and three-year-olds may notice this by observing which books children select most often. Four-year-olds are more concerned with content and **characterization**, in addition to what

---

characterization — the way an author presents a character by describing character verbalizations, actions, or thinking, or by what other characters say, think, or do about the character.

they previously enjoyed in picture books. Fantasy, **realism**, human emotions, **nonfiction**, and books with a variety of other features attract and hold them.

BRIEF HISTORY OF CHILDREN'S LITERATURE

The idea that children need or deserve entertainment and amusement is a relatively new development. Until the mid-eighteenth century, books for children instructed and aimed to improve young children, particularly their moral and spiritual natures.

Folk tales were sung and told in primitive times, and stories of human experience were shared. Storytellers often attempted to reduce anxieties, satisfy human needs, fire the imagination, and increase human survival, among other aims. Orally handed down, tales appeared in most of the world's geographical locations and cultures. Much of today's **fiction** reflects elements of these old tales and traditional stories.

Early American children's literature was heavily influenced by English and Puritan beliefs and practices. Books that existed before William Caxton's development of printing in fifteenth-century England were hand-copied adult books that children happened to encounter in private wealthy households. Caxton translated *Aesop's Fables* (1484) from a French version and printed other adult books that literate English children found interesting. *Aesop's Fables* is considered the first printing of talking animal stories. Themes of other books in Victorian England included romances of chivalry and adventure, knights in shining armor, battles with giants, and rescue of lovely princesses and other victims of oppression.

Victorian families read to their children, and minstrels and troubadours were paid to sing narrative verses to the families of rich patrons. The English Puritans were dedicated to a revolution founded on the deep conviction that religious beliefs form the basis for the whole of human life. Writers such as Bunyan, author of *A Book for Boys and Girls* (1686), were intent on saving children's souls.

Chapbooks (paper booklets) appeared in England after 1641. Initially, they were intended for adults, but eventually, they fell into children's hands. They included tiny woodcuts as decoration, and later woodcuts were used to illustrate the text. Salesmen (chapmen) traveled England selling these small, $4'' \times 2\frac{1}{2}''$ editions to the less affluent. Chapbooks written to entertain and instruct children followed, as sales and popularity increased. Titles included *The Tragical Death of an Apple Pie* and *The History of Jack and the Giants.*

John Newbery and Thomas Boreman are recognized as the first publishers of children's books in England. Chapbooks, although predated, are considered booklets. Most of these newly printed books were instructional (Nelson, 1972), but titles like *A Little Pretty Pocket-Book* (Newbery, 1744) were advertised as children's amusement books (Figure 9–2). In 1765, Newbery published *The Renowned History of Little Goody Two Shoes, Otherwise Called Mrs. Margery Two Shoes.* The book chronicles Goody's rise from poverty to wealth. Newbery prospered. Other publishers followed with their own juvenile editions, many with themes designed to help children reason and use moral judgment to select socially correct courses of action.

During the earliest years of our nation, many children had no schooling and could not read. Those few who could read often read works intended for adults, such as Jonathan Swift's *Gulliver's Travels* (1726). Reading was considered unimportant for children in agricultural society. Only the need for a literate workforce in the new industrialized society of the 1800s caused time to be set aside for children's

---

realism — presents experience without embellishment to convey life as it appears in a natural world limited by the senses and reason.
nonfiction — prose that explains, argues, or describes; usually factual.
fiction — imaginative narrative in any form of presentation that is designed to entertain, as distinguished from that which is designed primarily to explain, argue, or merely describe.

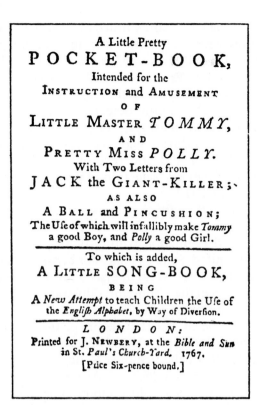

FIGURE 9–2 Excerpts from *A Little Pretty Pocket-Book,* published by John Newbery, 1744.

education and more attention to be paid to books intended for children.

Books used as school readers in early America contained subject matter of both a religious and a moral nature.

By the mid-1800s, adventure stories for older boys gained popularity with Mark Twain's *Adventures of Tom Sawyer,* published in 1876. Louisa May Alcott had created *Little Women* in 1868 as a girl's volume.

Picture Books

Toward the end of the nineteenth century, some picture books became artistic. English and French publishers produced colorful illustrations of charm, quality, and detail. The books of Randolph Caldecott, Maurice Boutet de Monvel, and Kate Greenway had captivating drawings that overshadowed the drab and homely illustrations that were typically found in American picture books.

Although not intended or recommended for children, comic picture sequences, like those of A. B. Frost, appeared in American magazines from 1880 to 1890. Their humor was shared by families. Two American picture books resembling Frost's slapstick humor gained acceptance from American librarians: Gelett Burgess's *New Goops and How to Know Them* (Lippincott, 1928) and Palmer Cox's *Brownies* (1927).

E. Boyd Smith, an American, created illustrations for *The Story of Noah's Ark* (Houghton Mifflin, 1905), which are described as both artistic and humorous. The books Smith created delighted children and adults with colorful panoramic illustrations. Librarians speaking of Smith's illustrative work described it as honest, true, "better than any done by an American artist" (Bader, 1976). The cost of full-color printing escalated, and illustrative color in picture books was not to reappear in the United States and become widely affordable until the later 1920s and 1930s. Little Golden Books became popular, and European books with colorful illustrative art were imported to the United States for those who could afford them.

Lynch-Brown and Tomlinson (1998) believe the establishment of book awards improved American picture books.

> By the 1920s a class of professional writers devoted solely or almost solely to writing literature for children—as opposed to moral reformers, teachers, and clerics as authors—produced a larger quantity and better variety and quality of children's books than had been seen to that point. This development was hastened by the establishment in 1922, under the auspices of the American Library Association, of the first of the great American children's book awards, the Newbery Medal. In 1938, with the establishment by ALA of the Caldecott Medal for illustration, more and better artists were encouraged to enter the field of children's books as well. For the remainder of the 20th century, book award programs were effectively used to create interest in children's books generally and to promote awareness of specific types of books. Competition for the most prestigious awards resulted in better, more original works.

Extraordinary black-and-white illustrations drawn by Wanda Gág in *Farm Sale* (Coward-McCann, 1926) and *Millions of Cats* (Coward-McCann, 1928) and a lithographic technique used in her other books captured both children's fancy and book reviewers' praise. Her drawings complemented and reinforced her text. Together, the effect was polished and eminently suitable for her folk tales. As Bader (1976) notes, the combination of Wanda Gág's text, drawings, and format constitute its lasting distinction.

American picture books for children began to reflect a worldview of children's literature. Colorful illustrations appeared in school readers. Stories for young children set in foreign countries were widely acclaimed during the 1930s. *Madeline* (Simon & Schuster, 1939), by Ludwig Bemelmans, is still found on most suggested early childhood reading lists.

The child-study movement and research at numerous universities and institutions during the late 1920s and 1930s led some well-known researchers to believe small children's interests focused on "the-here-and-now." This was translated as home objects and environments, community settings, airplanes, trains, local workers and professionals, and "everyday matters." Approved and recommended book lists guided parents' selection of preschool books as early as 1913.

It is thought that Russian information and "how-to" books of the 1940s and 1950s increased nonfiction picture-book production in the United States. Books concerning machines and how they worked, insects, and science concepts became abundant. Illustrations included photographs.

Some of the changes in picture-book publishing during the 1960s occurred because several individuals, including Nancy Larrick (1965), spotlighted the lack of African-Americans in story lines and illustrations. The civil rights movement affected the social consciousness of many teachers and parents.

Only a few research surveys conducted in the 1970s and 1980s attempted to pinpoint the numbers of picture-book representations for Mexican-Americans, Asian-Americans, or Native Americans. It is reasonable to say they were minimal in number.

Although published multicultural literature for young children increased and became an important part of language arts education (Bishop, 1990), cultural accuracy that helps young children gain a "true" sense of the culture depicted (a so-called insider's view) is a relatively recent development. This type of picture book is eagerly sought by most early childhood educators.

The current trend toward publishing more multicultural literature to compensate for the almost total absence of it as recently as 35 years ago will continue as schools become more diverse and society becomes more accepting of different voices and viewpoints (Lynch-Brown & Tomlinson, 1998).

Picture books dealing with the reality of young children's daily lives, their families, and living problems (such as stress, fear, moving, and appearance) began appearing in larger numbers in the 1970s and 1980s, broadening subject matter believed appropriate and of interest to children. These books, many classified as "therapeutic," often attempted to build self-esteem or help young children cope in difficult situations. Characters in picture books always had problems to be solved by creative thinking and self-insight, but these new stories dealt more frequently with life situations children could not change themselves.

Literacy concerns and the whole-language movement (1980s to 1990s) have dramatically increased educators' ideas of the importance of quality literature in early childhood curriculum. More and more activities are based on children's reactions to books and language arts activities offered by their teachers.

Creative technology has entered the children's book field with glitz, bang, and flashing color. The computerized picture book has voice, sound effects, and interactive features not previously thought possible. There are an amazing number of book-technology products that capture attention, hold attention, and attempt to teach and entertain preschoolers. Fortunately, many young children treat them as novelties after a short period and seek traditional read-alouds with the special people in their lives. How smart they are! Nothing can replace someone who answers your every question, relates the book to you and your unique life experiences, and treats you special by choosing to spend time with you in an activity they, too, enjoy.

Today's picture books have historical roots. Some have outlived the generation of children for whom they were produced and are classics of quality. It is those that you, as a teacher of young children, will endeavor to find and share along with the "classics of the future."

WHERE TO START

This chapter contains a list of picture books (pages 289 and 310–311) to be considered merely as a starting point. Because the quality of a book is a subjective judgment, your fa-

vorites may not appear on this list. There are many other books of quality; each teacher should develop a personal collection. Librarians and bookstore salespeople can offer valuable suggestions and advice.

QUALITY

Judging quality means reading and viewing a picture book to find out whether it contains something memorable or valuable. For every good book you discover, you may wade through a stack that makes you wonder whether the authors have any experience at all with young children. Remember, appropriate material for a four-year-old may not suit a younger child.

Each book you select may have one or more of the following desirable and valuable features.

- character development (such as *Madeline* by Ludwig Bemelmans, the wolf in *Goldilocks and the Three Bears,* or Beady Bear by Don Freeman)
- color (*Little Blue and Yellow* by Leo Lionni)
- an example of human courage, cleverness, or grit (such as *Peter Rabbit,* created by Beatrix Potter)
- aesthetic appeal (*Rain Rain Rivers* by Uri Shulevitz)
- word play (*Tikki Tikki Tembo* by Arlene Mosel)
- listening pleasure (*Make Way for Ducklings* by Robert McCloskey)
- nonsense (*What Do You Do with a Kangaroo?* by Mercer Mayer)
- onomatopoeia (the naming of a thing or action by a vocal imitation of the sound associated with it, as in *buzz* and *hiss*)
- suspense (*Deep in the Forest* by Brinton Turkle)
- humor or wit (*Nothing Ever Happens on My Block* by Ellen Raskin)
- fantasy (*Where the Wild Things Are* by Maurice Sendak)
- surprise (*Harry the Dirty Dog* by Eugene Zion)

◆ repetition (*The Little Engine That Could* by Mabel Bragg)

◆ hope (*The Carrot Seed* by Ruth Krauss)

◆ charm (*George and Martha* by James Marshall)

◆ sensitivity (*The Tenth Good Thing about Barney* by Judith Viorst)

◆ realistic dialogue (*Can I Keep Him?* by Steven Kellogg)

◆ cultural insight (*On a Hot, Hot Day* by Nicki Weiss)

◆ action (*Caps for Sale* by Esphyr Slobodkina)

◆ predictability (*Brown Bear, Brown Bear, What Do You See?* by William Martin)

The preceding is only a partial listing. A book can excel in many different ways. An outstanding feature of many good stories is that they can cause the reader or listener to smile with recognition and think, "life is like that" or "I've been there myself." This promotes a positive feeling of connectedness.

The theme of respect for individual differences in Bill Peet's *Huge Harold*, the gentleness of Uri Shulevitz's *Dawn*, or the tenderness of Charlotte Zolotow's *My Grandson Lew* may fit your criteria of quality. The runaway fantasy of Frank Asch's *Popcorn* and Tomie de Paola's *Strega Nona* might tickle your fancy.

The panoramic scenes of Mitsumasa Anno's *Anno's Counting Book*, the patterns and contrasts in Ezra Jack Keats' *The Snowy Day*, or the fun of discovery in Janet and Allan Ahlberg's *Each Peach Pear Plum* might help a book become one of your favorites because of visual appeal.

For humor and wit, you might choose Steven Kellogg's *There Was an Old Woman*, Leah Komaiko's *Annie Bananie*, Robert Kraus's *Leo the Late Bloomer*, James Marshall's *Yummers*, Mercer Mayer's *Frog, Where Are You?*, or a selection of others that may make you laugh. You might never forget the way you trip over your tongue while reading about Jack, Kack, Lack, Mack, Nack, Ouack, Pack, and Quack in Robert McCloskey's *Make Way for Ducklings* or Arlene Mosel's *Tikki Tikki Tembo*. If you enjoy surprise or an ending with a twist,

you might be delighted by Brinton Turkle's *Deep in the Forest* or Jimmy Kennedy's *The Teddy Bears' Picnic*. The sound pleasure in Wanda Gág's *Millions of Cats* or the onomatopoeia in Mabel Bragg's *The Little Engine That Could* might make these books memorable.

You might relive your experience of city living in *Tell Me a Mitzi* by Lore Segal. Perhaps discovering the facts through the colorful, precise artwork in Ruth Heller's *Chickens Aren't the Only Ones* will attract you to the world of nonfiction. You may look for books to promote children's phonological awareness, like Bill Martin, Jr., and John Archambault's *Chicka Chicka Boom Boom* or Cheryl Hudson's *Afro-Bets ABC Book*. Unforgettable characters like Leo Lionni's *Frederick*, Don Freeman's *Corduroy* and *Dandelion*, Eugene Zion's *Harry by the Sea*, or Ludwig Bemelman's demure individualist *Madeline* may be counted among your friends as you search for quality. Jewels will stand out, and you will be anxious to share them with children.

You will be looking for fascinating, captivating books. Some captivate by presenting believable characters.

> Character-drawing is like a tremendous, complicated conjuring-trick. Appealing to imagination and goodwill, diverting attention by sheer power of technique, the writer persuades us (for the period of reading and sometimes for long afterwards) to accept the identity of certain people who exist between the covers of his book. (Fisher, 1975)

Some fascinate to the extent that worries are forgotten, and the child lives in the fantasy world of the story during its reading and beyond (Bettelheim & Zelan, 1981).

Speaking about a true literature-based curriculum, Cooper (1993) identifies quality books.

> Teachers need to watch for stories that "catch on," stories that fulfill some deep understanding of human intentions, or express a developmental concern, or arouse our curiosity: these are the stories that should lead a curriculum of hearing stories,

knowing them, and—if they appeal—reliving them through writing, drama, or retelling.

You will want to choose classics so that from the very beginning, the child has a chance to appreciate literature. Not everyone will agree as to what is a modern-day classic. *Where the Wild Things Are*, by Maurice Sendak, continues to cause arguments among adults about whether it is truly a classic. Martinez and Johnson (1987) note that "adults don't like it very much, but nearly all the children really respond to it—Sendak is just on the kids' wavelength."

Knowing about family lifestyles, home language, and community individuality aids book selection and planning. Some schools order 50 percent of their books in the children's home language. The relevance of a farm book is bound to be different for farm children, yet the human universality depicted may make it an attractive choice for inner-city, urban children.

Neuman (1999) notes that early childhood classrooms and child care settings across all geographical boundaries and income levels do not have the resources to build libraries with sufficient numbers of quality books for young children. She adds that far too much reliance is placed on the generosity of parents and community members to supply additional quality literature for classroom libraries. Another problem, she cites, is the lack of adequate guidance (for both parents and teachers) about how to choose quality books that build developmentally appropriate learning skills.

Award-Winning Books

Each year, the Association for Library Services to Children (American Library Association) recognizes the *artist* it believes has produced "the most distinguished American picture book for children" with the Caldecott Medal and Honor awards. Early childhood educators look for these and other award-winning books. Other awards given to books include:

- Newbery Medals
- International Reading Association Children's Book Awards
- The Parent Choice Awards
- Coretta Scott King Awards
- National Jewish Book Awards
- Catholic Book Awards
- newspaper awards
- magazine reviews and recognitions found in *Book Links* (American Library Association) and *Language Arts* (National Council of Teachers of English)
- local public library awards or recognitions

Illustrations

In many quality picture books, the story stands well by itself. The illustrations simply visualize what is written. In others, illustrations play a dominant role and are an integral part of the entire action. Picture books are defined by Glazer (1986) as "those books that rely on a combination of illustrations and **narrative** with both being integral to the complete work." Fortunately, many picture-book illustrations are created by highly talented individuals.

Young children may or may not have grasped the idea that book illustrations are drawn, created, or photographed by real people. The following happened to a student teacher at Evergreen Valley College Child Development Center.

> During a book reading activity the student teacher displayed the cover of the book *The Wide-Mouthed Frog,* and then read the title, the author's name and said "This book's pictures were drawn for us by Jonathan Lambert." One four-year-old girl queried "Was it the frog or a people?" The book's cover has a large colorful green frog illustration.

---

narrative — in general, a story, actual or fictional, expressed orally or in writing.

A wide range of artistic styles exists in picture-book illustration, including line drawings, woodcuts, water colors, collage, crayon, pastels, oil paint, and photography. The style of art can be representational, impressionistic, expressionistic, cartoon, abstract, stylized, surrealistic, or a style that defies categorization. Poltarnees (1972) describes the true artist as one who is able to enter the realm that his work evokes and move as freely there as if it were the kingdom of his birth. As a consequence, the artist can show us things that we would not have seen as mere visitors.

Illustrations help give words reality. For young children, illustrations promote visual literacy. Cox (1981) lists additional benefits.

1. provision of pleasure
2. nourishment of the imagination
3. promotion of creative expression
4. development of imagery
5. presentation and exploration of various styles and forms for the communication of ideas
6. awareness of the functions of languages
7. acquisition of metalinguistic awareness (defined as a sense of what printed language is all about)

Picture-book illustrations are often familiar objects in lifelike settings, and publishers are careful to emphasize figures rather than backgrounds. In addition to the simple, true-to-life depictions preferred by young preschoolers, illustrations of pure fantasy and illustrations that contain more detail appeal to older preschoolers.

Morrow (1990) identifies teacher interactive behaviors that may happen in read-aloud activities.

> Among the interactive behaviors research has identified in read-aloud activities are questioning, scaffolding dialogue and responses, offering praise or positive reinforcement, giving or extending information, clarifying information, restating information, directing discussion, sharing personal reactions, and relating concepts to life experiences.

A teacher reading this description can never again believe that read-aloud book times are the simplest, easiest time of the day, although they will probably remain one of teacher's favorite times (Figure 9–3).

Format

A book's format is defined as its overall and general character, that is, the way it is put together. Decisions concerning format by book publishers and author/illustrators include the size and shape of the cover and interior pages, paper quality, printing colors, typesetting, content of each page, and binding. A book's format can enhance its narrative, appeal, and subsequent enjoyment, or it can confuse, frustrate, and alienate the reader. A book can reflect a thoughtful attempt to create a classic volume of enduring worth and value or represent a sacrifice of quality for the sake of quick profit.

Genre, another way of categorizing books, concentrates on a book's content. Narrative is either poetry or prose. Prose can be further classi-

FIGURE 9–3 Schools provide as many one-on-one readings as staff and time allow.

---

genre — a category used to classify literary works, usually by form, technique, or content.

fied as fiction or nonfiction. The category of fiction includes excursions into sheer fantasy as well as more plausible stories about people or situations that could be, could have been, or might be. The latter group is classified as realistic fiction.

IF ONLY THEY WOULD CHOOSE BOOKS AND BOOK-RELATED ACTIVITIES

Many early childhood teachers are worried that busy parents and money-tight families do not have the time or resources to make books part of children's lives. Consequently, they are expending extra effort and attention to books and book-related activities. Emergent literacy research has alerted educators to the idea that preschoolers who are read to and who are interested in stories and books are more successful students in the beginning years of elementary school and in accomplishing reading. Raines and Isbell (1994) suggest that educators monitor how many children select classroom book-related activities and library areas and also monitor the amount of time each child is so engaged (Figure 9–4).

Teacher planning and thoughtful analysis can increase child interest. Thinking of classroom schedules and book-reading times more critically can initiate change and creative and imaginative presentation of activities. Time spent reading to children can be viewed as only one part of a book's introduction. What precedes and what follows are equally important. Practitioners need to ask themselves the following: How is this book relevant to children's lives? What can I do to increase child involvement and interest? What will make children eager to be part of story times? How can I discover child thoughts about what has been read and then build in further experiences? What can follow this story time, and will children give me clues? In other words, how can this book become part of their lives and at the same time be highly enjoyed? After attempting to answer these and other teacher questions, one can see that simply reading to children may not be enough to reach a teacher's true goals.

READING BOOKS TO YOUNG CHILDREN

Because children can gain so much from books, the teacher's way of presenting them is very important. The primary goal of a read-aloud event is the construction of meaning that develops in the interactive process between adult and child

FIGURE 9–4 This classroom has been able to promote child self-selection of books.

and the development of children's positive attitudes toward the activity.

Becoming this type of teacher requires the teacher to view children as active, individual learners. In previewing Tomie de Paola's picture book *Strega Nona* (Prentice Hall, 1975) for a group reading, a teacher might think as follows:

What past experiences has this group had with pasta?

What follow-up, extending activities could be planned?

What teacher questions would guide a discussion that probes children's feelings and ideas?

How can I make the "overflowing," "too much," concept a real experience?

The teacher's goal should be to lead each child to understand that books can be fun and interesting, can hold new experiences, and can be enjoyed alone or in the company of others (Figure 9–5).

Children who enjoy being read to will seek out books. Fraiberg (1987) urges preschool teachers to think of the preschool years as

... a critical period for becoming addicted, the time when urges are felt as irresistible and objects that gratify the urge are also experienced as irresistible. The educator who wishes to capitalize on the addictability of the child at this age must insure early and repeated gratifications from stories told and stories read.

Books you may review and reject you will recognize as inappropriate or missing their mark with young children. You may judge them as having no redeeming social value; to be dull and uninteresting; or to contain violence, unfortunate representations, unclear messages, or poor models of behavior. A book's construction and format may be undesirable. Of the more than 70,000 children's books currently in print, many will not meet the quality standards you set.

Most educators are eager to learn more about new children's books and are already quite knowledgeable. Picking books for a specific child's interest and then selecting books to

FIGURE 9–5 Creating enjoyment and interest when sharing books involves promoting the child's positive attitude.

suit some unique classroom situation or event are ongoing teacher tasks.

In a diverse society, offering multicultural and ethnically representative literature is a must for young children. Although age-recommended lists are available, most teachers actively pursue additional publications. Librarians, publishers, and children's bookstores are excellent resources. Antibias themes and sex-equity themes are also eagerly sought to ensure book models give young children every chance to value themselves as individuals.

Sales of children's books to affluent parents, who want to give (perhaps literally) their child every educational advantage, are growing. Yet, no one is really sure who—if anyone—is actually reading the books (Healy, 1990).

It is the teacher's responsibility to encourage the children's interest because not every child in preschool is interested in books or sees them as something to enjoy. Although children cannot be forced to like books, they can acquire positive feelings for them. Part of the positive feelings depends on whether children feel successful and competent during reading time. This, in turn, depends on how skillfully the teacher acts and reacts and how well the book sessions are planned. The key is to draw reluctant children into the story by making story times so attractive and vital that children simply cannot bear to stay away.

An important additional goal in reading books to children is the presentation of knowledge. Books can acquaint the child with new words, ideas, facts, feelings, and happenings. These are experienced in a different form than spoken conversation. In books, sentences are complete; in conversation, they may not be. Stories and illustrations follow a logical sequence in books.

Teachers ought to be concerned with whether the child comprehends what is read. To ensure comprehension, the books must offer significant content, something that relates to the child's everyday experience. Humor and fantasy, for example, are common in favorite picture books. Usually, these books are not merely frivolous. A closer reading will often reveal that they deal with universal human emotions or imaginations. Comprehension is aided by open discussion. Children should be free to ask questions that will help them connect the book's happenings to their own past experiences. The more outgoing and talkative children often clear up misunderstandings of the whole group when books are discussed. Those who work with young children often notice children's innate tendency to try to make sense and derive meaning from the happenings in their lives.

Teachers can show that books may also be used as resources. When a child wants to find out about certain things, teachers can refer to dictionaries, encyclopedias, or books on specialized subjects. The teacher can model the use of books to find facts. When a child asks the teacher a question about some subject of special interest and the teacher says, "I don't know, but I know where we can find out," the teacher can demonstrate how books can be used for finding answers. The teacher tells where to look and follows through by showing the child how the information is found. The joy of discovery is shared, and this opens the door to seeking more answers.

Another goal of the teacher should be to encourage the development of listening skills. During listening times, children's attention can become focused. Many different types of listening—discriminative, appreciative, purposeful, creative, and critical—can all be present in one reading experience.

In contrast, "pressure-cooker" programs, which promise to have four-year-olds reading before kindergarten, often feature drill sessions designed to develop technical reading skills (such as decoding words). When these drill sessions, which are usually meaningless and boring to young children, are connected to picture-book readings, they could endanger the young child's budding love affair with books.

Many children pick up reading knowledge and reading skills as they become more familiar with their features. They will see regularities and differences in the book's illustrations and text that will aid them in their eventual desire to break the code of reading. An early type of reading has been witnessed by all experienced preschool teachers. Paul Copperman (1982) calls it "imitative reading." He defines this behavior as "reading the story from pictures, sometimes speaking remembered text that precisely follows the book for a page or more." Certain techniques can be used to encourage imitative reading.

- reading picture books to children daily
- planning repeated reading of new and old favorites
- reliving enjoyed parts in discussions
- being attentive to children's needs to be heard "reading"
- issuing positive encouragement about your enjoyment of what the children have shared
- expecting some creative child deviation from the actual story
- suggesting or providing additional ways children could "read" a book (for example, into a tape recorder)
- viewing the children's activity as emerging literacy and behavior to value as a milestone

Another goal to consider when planning a program is to encourage children to learn how to care for books and where and how they can be used. Attitudes about books as valuable personal possessions should be instilled during early childhood. A number of emerging behaviors and skills will be noticed as children become fond of books. Learning to read is a complex skill that depends on smaller skills, some of which children develop during story times and by browsing through books on their own.

Using Literature to Aid Conflict Resolution Skills

Concerned with rising levels of violence in our society, early childhood teachers are attempting to use picture books and stories to help children identify and define problems, a first step in conflict resolution. Books can be a valuable tool. Illustrations and book text may help child **visualization**, build empathy, provide nonviolent resolution to story-line disputes, portray different types of conflicts, and give examples of peacemaking at work (Schomberg, 1993).

BOOK SELECTION

Teachers are responsible for selecting quality books that meet the school's stated goals; often, teachers are asked to select new books for the school's collection. Book selection is not an easy task for teachers. McCord (1995) points out

> As caregivers or teachers, we have the responsibility to select each book with much thought to its content and relevance to particular children. We must be sensitive to how children might personalize a story we have selected. An awareness of family situations, cultures, religions, and social biases of the "smaller community" in our classrooms must be developed with respect as we choose which stories to tell.

Some books may fill the needs completely; others may only partially meet the goals of instruction. The local library offers the opportunity to borrow books that help keep storytelling time fresh and interesting, and children's librarians can be valuable resources.

Even when careful thought has been put into selecting a book, one child may like a book that another child does not. Some stories appeal more to one group than to another. Stories that are enjoyed most often become old favorites. Children who know the story often look forward to a familiar part or character. MacDonald (1992) points out that selected books should match the children's needs.

> Children need books that reflect their changing interests. They need books that range from simple to more difficult. They need books that are relevant to the social and cultural reality of their daily lives and our multi-cultural, multi-ethnic, multi-racial world.

Children's librarians usually know "kid-appeal" books, that is, books that children return to again and again—books that connect with children's interests, their sense of humor, and their stage of growth.

Professional books and journals abound with ideas concerning the types of books that young children like best. Some writers believe that simple fairy-tale picture books with animal characters who possess lifelike characteristics are preferred. Others mention that certain children want "true" stories. Most writers agree with Self (1987).

> Much of the . . . success of any book for young children depends on its presentation of basic human tasks, needs, and concerns from their perception and at a level at which they can respond. They do not need books which are condescending, which trivialize their concerns and efforts, and which present easy answers to complex problems. Rather, young children need adults and books, and other materials

---

visualization — the process, or result, of mentally picturing objects or events that are normally experienced directly.

which support their right to be children, their efforts to meet both their common and their individual needs, and their efforts to create meaning in the world.

James and Kormanski (1999) provide a list of selection criteria that are sensitive to inter-generational representation in picture books. It follows:

1. Characters should be portrayed realistically, have experiences and emotions with which children can immediately identify, and be believable.

2. The chronological organization of the story should unfold sequentially. There should be tension or conflict to be reduced or resolved. The simple plot necessitated by the length of a picture book should allow young children to become involved immediately in the action, discover the problem, and understand the resolution.

3. Satisfaction and substance are added through the element of theme. The theme should relate to children's needs, understandings, and interests. Even a simple story can develop a significant theme.

4. In addition to establishing time and place, setting can be used to introduce a culture or period in history, develop a mood, and stress symbolic meaning. Older people have been present in all cultures and historical eras, as have children. Illustrations should work hand in hand with the text to convey aspects of the setting.

5. Style involves rhythm, repetition, and a very careful choice of words. Individual elements of style include vivid phrasing, rhyme, understatement, repeated refrains, sound patterns, and exaggeration, all of which give vitality and variety to picture books for children.

Bettelheim (1976) advises that both fairy tales and realism should be offered to young children.

When realistic stories are combined with ample and psychologically correct exposure to fairy tales, then the child receives information which speaks to both parts of a budding personality—the rational and the emotional.

Many parents and educators have concerns about the violent nature of some folk and **fairy tales**. Others believe children already know the world can be a dangerous and sometimes cruel place. Tunnell (1994) explains that many old stories involve justice—good things happening to people with good behavior and bad things happening to people with bad behavior. Tunnell points out

> The old stories have existed for centuries mainly because they speak to us on a deep level concerning the human experience. Because good and evil are the most basic of human traits, children are concerned from an early age with the ramifications of good and bad behavior. In classic fantasy stories, there are few gradations of good and bad—evil characters are truly evil and cannot be swayed toward good. Likewise, the pure in heart remain pure. These stories, then, are a study in justice.

Individual teachers and staff groups may decide that some folk tales are too violent, gory, or inappropriate for the age or living circumstances of attending children. Each book needs examination. It is likely that, at times, staff opinions will differ.

Some beginning teachers worry about book characters such as talking bears and rabbits. Make-believe during preschool years is an ever-increasing play pursuit. Beck (1982) advises

> Children don't mind if bears talk if the message of their speech is something with which they can identify. On the other hand, they will reject stories that seem realistic if the problems the characters face have little to do with their own emotional lives.

---

fairy tales — folk stories about real-life problems, usually with imaginary characters and magical events.

The clear-cut story lines in many folk and fairy tales have stood the test of time and are recommended for a beginning teachers' first attempts at reading to preschoolers. Bettelheim and Zelan (1981) believe that "good literature has something of meaning to offer any reader of any age, although on different levels of comprehension and appreciation." Each child will interpret and react to each book from an individual point of view, based on his unique experience.

Blaska and Lynch (1998) urge early childhood educators to include books depicting people with disabilities so that children can understand and accept people with varying abilities. They believe no other group of individuals has been as overlooked and as inadequately presented in children's books and the popular press. It is prudent to be on the lookout for this type of picture book.

You will want to introduce books with excellent language usage, ones that enchant and create beautiful images using the best grammatical structure, vocabulary, and imaginative style—in other words, memorable quality books.

Kinds of Books

Children's book publishing is a booming business. Many types of books are available, as illustrated in Figure 9–6, which lists various categories in the left column. The figure identifies the major genre classifications and formats of children's books used in preschool classrooms, but it excludes poetry, which is discussed in another chapter. Many books do not fit neatly into a single category; some books may fit into two or more categories.

A vast and surprising variety of novelty books are also in print: floating books for bath time; soft, huggable books for bedtime; pocket-sized books; jumbo board and easel books (Scholastic); lift-the-flap books; movielike flipbooks (Little, Brown & Co.); books that glow in the dark; sing-a-story books (Bantam); potty-training books (Barron's); and even books within books.

Oversized Books (Big Books)

Big, giant, and *jumbo* (24″ × 36″) are descriptors used to identify oversized books. Publishers are mass producing this size book because of their increased popularity with both early

childhood educators and whole-language curriculum advocates.

Because they are easily viewed by groups of children, oversized books have been added to teacher curriculum collections. New and classic titles abound. Because the text is large, it is not overlooked by young children. Found in soft and hard cover versions with brilliant-colored illustrations, some have accompanying audio tapes and small book editions. Teachers use chalkboard gutters or art easels as book holders.

Strickland and Morrow (1990) recommend the use of big books and suggest

> Enlarged texts allow groups of children to see and react to the printed page as it is being read aloud, a factor considered key to the effectiveness of shared reading between parent and child. Many teachers regard Big Book experiences as the closest approximation to family storybook reading one can offer in the classroom.

Active participation and unison participation can be encouraged. Using his hand to underline words while reading, the teacher can focus attention on print and its directionality. Recommended big books are listed in the Additional Resources section at the end of this chapter.

Alphabet Books

Singing and learning the "Alphabet Song" is often a child's first introduction to the alphabet, one that precedes and promotes interest in alphabet books. For a further discussion of alphabet books and print awareness, see Chapter 16.

Nonfiction Books

Teachers may encounter and share nonfiction books that answer child questions, are related to a curriculum theme, or serve another teaching purpose, such as providing pictorial information. Nonfiction books can teach concepts and terms associated with various topics, people, places, and things children may never encounter in real life. A book with a simplified explanation of how water comes out of a faucet serves as an example. Nonfiction (books) may be perceived as more appropriate for older grades, and a real

TYPES	FEATURES TEACHERS LIKE	FEATURES CHILDREN LIKE

Storybooks (picture books)
• family and home
• folktales and fables
• fanciful stories
• fairy tales
• animal stories
• others
	sharing moments
	seeing children enthusiastic and attentive
	making characters' voices
	introducing human truths and
	   imaginative adventures
	sharing favorites
	easy for child to identify with small
	   creatures
		imagination and fantasy
		identification with characters'
		   humanness
		wish and need fulfillment
		adventure
		excitement
		action
		self-realization
		visual variety
		word pleasure

Nonfiction books (informational) also
  referred to as *content books*
	expand individual and group
	   interests
	develop "reading-to-know" attitudes
	encourage finding out together
	provide accurate facts
	contain scientific content
		provide facts; allow for discovery of
		   information and ideas
		discuss reality and how
		   things work and function
		answer "why" and "how"
		supply new words and new
		   meanings

Wordless books	promote child speech, creativity, and
	   imagination
		provide opportunity to supply
		   their own words to tell the story
		promote discovery of meanings
		include color, action, and visual
		   variety

Interaction books (books with active
  child participation built in)
	keep children involved and attentive
	build listening for directions skills
		provide for movement and group
		   feeling
		promote individual creativity and
		   expression
		appeal to senses
		have manipulatable features

Concept books (books with central
  concepts or themes that include
  specific and reinforcing examples)
	promote categorization
	present opportunities to know about
	   and develop concepts
	many examples
		add to knowledge
		visually present abstractions

Predictable books (books with repetitions and reinforcement)	permit successful guessing build child's confidence promote ideas that books make sense	provide opportunity to read along are repetitive build feelings of competence

Reference books (picture
  dictionaries, encyclopedias, special
  subject books)
	provide opportunity to look up questions
	  with the child
	promote individualized learning
		provide answers
		are used with teacher (shared time)
		are resources that answer
		   their questions

Alphabet and word books (word
  books have name of object
  printed near or on top of object)
	supply letters and word models
	pair words and objects
	are useful for child with avid interest in
	   alphabet letters and words
	can include letter and word play
		discover meanings and
		   alphabet letters and words
		see names of what is illustrated

Novelty books (pop-ups, fold-outs,
  electronic books, stamp and pasting
  books, activity books, puzzle books,
  scratch-and-sniff books, hidden
  objects in illustrations, talking books)
	add sense-exploring variety
	stimulate creativity
	come in many different sizes and
	   shapes
	motor involvement for child
	many include humor
		encourage exploring, touching,
		   moving, feeling, smelling,
		   painting, drawing, coloring,
		   cutting, gluing, acting upon,
		   listening to a mechanical voice,
		   and getting instant feedback

FIGURE 9–6 Categories of children's books. *(continued)*

TYPES	FEATURES TEACHERS LIKE	FEATURES CHILDREN LIKE
Paperback books and magazines (Golden Books, *Humpty Dumpty Magazine*)	are inexpensive come in a wide variety many classics available	include activity pages
Teacher- and child-made books	reinforce class learnings build understanding of authorship allow creative expression record individual, group projects, field trips, parties promote child expression of concerns and ideas build child's self-esteem	allow child to see own name in print provide opportunity to share ideas with others are self-rewarding
Therapeutic books (books helping children cope with and understand things such as divorce, death, jealousy)	present life realistically offer positive solutions and insights present diverse family groups deal with life's hard-to-deal-with subjects	help children discuss real feelings
Seasonal and holiday books	accompany child interest may help child understand underlying reasons for celebration	build pleasant expectations add details
Books and audiovisual combinations (read-alongs)	add variety offer group and individual experiencing opportunities stimulate interest in books	project large illustrations can be enjoyed individually
Toddler books and board books (durable pages)	resist wear and tear	are easy to use (ease in page-turning
Multicultural and cross-cultural books (culturally conscious books)	increase positive attitudes concerning diversity and similarity	introduce a variety of people
Oversized books (big books)	emphasize the realities in our society have extra large text and illustrations	are easy-to-see in groups have giant book characters

FIGURE 9–6 *(continued)*

revolution has occurred in recent years in the writing and production of nonfiction books for young children.

Teachers may ignore informational picture books, believing they will not hold children's attention. They may not know that many are related in cumulative story form, some are wordless, and others have rhythmic features or include poetry. Most cover interesting topics, pique curiosity, and offer scientific or precise vocabulary. Figure 9–7 offers tips on selecting quality nonfiction titles. Casbergue and Plauché (2003) suggest that photographs, realistic drawings, paintings, collages, and other images should be accurate because young readers attend most directly to il-lustrations. If informational books sacrifice this, reject them.

Given a choice of reading materials, young children are as likely to state a preference for informational picture books as for fictional picture books (Kletzien & Szabo, 1998). Informational books should be a part of all early childhood classroom libraries. Although as Casbergue and Plauché point out, the effects of immersing young children in nonfiction picture books are not fully documented in research. Most practicing teachers know children readily use and consult them.

Examples of nonfiction books follow:

Arnosky, J. (1985). *Watching foxes.* New York: Lothrop Lee and Shepard Books.

LANGUAGE

Does the material:

- use simple, straightforward vocabulary?
- include some specific scientific or technical terms?
- present special or technical terms or context?
- use short, direct sentences?

IDEAS AND ORGANIZATION

Does the material:

- present one idea at a time?
- provide specific and concrete information?
- show relationships among ideas that are explicit and simple (for example, sequence, cause-effect, descriptions)?
- use short paragraphs that begin with a clear topic sentence followed by details?
- use bold titles and headings?

GRAPHICS AND FORMAT

Does the material use:

- * illustrations and graphics to support and provide content?
- * clear relationship between text and illustrations?
- * illustrations that elaborate and clarify the written text?
- * type size that is 14 point or larger?

FIGURE 9–7 Tips on selecting informational texts.

Coats, L. (1987). *The oak tree.* New York: Macmillan.
Hirschi, R. (1987). *What is a bird?* New York: Walker.
Stein, S. (1985). *Mouse.* New York: Harcourt, Brace, Jovanovich.
Yabuuchi, M. (1985). *Whose footprints?* New York: Philomel Books.

Story Songs

A growing number of favorite books put to music and favorite songs published as books are available. An adult sings as pages are turned. Teachers can introduce this literary experience and encourage children to join in. The added advantage of visual representations helps induce child singing. The novelty of a teacher singing a book also offers a possible incentive for the child to select this type of book because of his familiarity with an already memorized and perhaps enjoyed song. Word recognition is sometimes readily accomplished.

Popular books of this type include:

de Paola, T. (1984). *Mary had a little lamb.* New York: Holiday House.
Kovalski, M. (1987). *The wheels on the bus.* Boston: Little, Brown & Co.
McNalley, D. (1991). *In a cabin in a wood.* New York: Cobblehill/Dutton.

Interactive Technology

Technology and young children's books have been combined by companies like LeapFrog, Fisher-Price (PowerTouch Learning System), and Publications International (ActivePAD). With a touch of the finger or a stylus, a young child can flip pages, hear any particular word pronounced, hear a book read by a clear voice, select the reader's pace, play games, hear word definitions, and take quizzes. Some models have light attachments and a microphone. Some teach phonics; encourage children to pronounce phonemes, words, and sentences; and prompt children to record their names, which are then put into stories. Some models focus on writing skills and enable children to trace alphabet letters, work mazes, or engage in dot-to-dot activities or handwriting exercises. Individual companies have developed as many as 70 children's book titles.

Parents are lured by educative features, and preschools are adding electronic books to their book collections. Prices vary, but they usually are not prohibitive for the average center.

Criteria for Selection

Consider the attention span, maturity, interests, personality, and age of children you are targeting when selecting books. Developing broad literary and artistic tastes is another important idea.

The following is a series of questions a teacher could use when choosing a child's book.

1. Could I read this book enthusiastically, really enjoying the story?

2. Are the contents of the book appropriate for the children with whom I work?
   a. Can the children relate some parts to their lives and past experience?
   b. Can the children identify with one or more of the characters?
      Look at some children's classics such as Mother Goose. Almost all of the stories have a well-defined character with whom children have something in common. Teachers find that different children identify with different characters—the wolf instead of one of the pigs in *The Three Little Pigs,* for example.
   c. Does the book have directly quoted conversation?
      If it does, this can add interest; for example, "Are you my mother?" he said to the cow.
   d. Will the child benefit from attitudes and models found in the book?

   Many books model behaviors that are unsuitable for the young child. Also, consider the following questions when analyzing a book for unfavorable racial stereotypes or sexism.
   a. Who are the "doers" and "inactive observers"?
   b. Are characters' achievements based on their own initiative, insights, or intelligence?
   c. Who performs the brave and important deeds?
   d. Are value and worth connected to skin color and economic resources?
   e. Does language or setting ridicule or demean a specific group of individuals?
   f. Are individuals treated as such rather than as one of a group?
   g. Are ethnic groups or individuals treated as though everyone in that group has the same human talent, ability, food preference, hairstyle, taste in clothing, or human weakness or characteristic?
   h. Do illustrations capture natural-looking ethnic variations?
   i. Does this book broaden the cross-cultural element in the multicultural selection of books offered at my school?

   j. Is the book accurate and authentic in its portrayal of individuals and groups?

3. Was the book written with an understanding of preschool age-level characteristics? See Kathryn Galbraith's *Katie Did!* (Atheneum, 1983).
   a. Is the text too long to sit through? Are there too many words?
   b. Are there enough colorful or action-packed pictures or illustrations to hold attention?
   c. Is the size of the book suitable for easy handling in groups or for individual viewing?
   d. Can the child participate in the story by speaking or making actions?
   e. Is the fairy tale or folktale too complex, symbolic, and confusing to have meaning? See *East of the Sun and West of the Moon* (Norway) or *Beauty and the Beast* (France) (examples of traditional folktales with inappropriate length, vocabulary, and complexity for the young child). Although some educators debate offering "life's realities" to young children, others think folktales may help them face fears.

4. Is the author's style enjoyable?
   a. Is the book written clearly with a vocabulary and sequence the children can understand? See Mercer Mayer's *There's a Nightmare in My Closet* (Dial, 1969). Are memorable words or phrases found in the book?
   b. Are repetitions of words, actions, rhymes, or story parts used? (Anticipated repetition is part of the young child's enjoyment of stories. Molly Bang's *Ten, Nine, Eight* [Greenwillow, 1983] contains this feature.)
   c. Does the story develop and end with a satisfying climax of events?
   d. Are there humorous parts and silly names? The young child's humor is often slapstick in nature (pie-in-the-face, all-fall-down type rather than play on words). The ridiculous and far-fetched often tickle them. See Tomie de Paola's *Pancakes for Breakfast* (Har-

court, Brace, Jovanovich, 1978), a wordless book.

5. Does it have educational value? (Almost all fit this criteria.) (See Figure 9–8.)
   a. Could you use it to expand knowledge in any special way? See Maureen Roffey's *Home, Sweet Home* (Coward, 1983), which depicts animal living quarters in a delightful way.
   b. Does it offer new vocabulary? Does it increase or broaden understanding? See Masayuki Yabuuchi's *Animals Sleeping* (Philomel, 1983), for an example.
6. Do pictures (illustrations) explain and coordinate well with the text? Examine Jane Miller's *Farm Counting Book* (Prentice Hall, 1983) and look for this feature.

Some books meet most criteria of the established standards; others meet only a few. The age of attending children makes some criteria more important than others. Schools often select copies of accepted old classics. These titles are considered part of our cultural heritage, ones that most American preschoolers know and have experienced (Figure 9–9). Many classics have been handed down through the oral tradition of storytelling and can contain archaic words, such as *stile* and *sixpence*. Most teachers try to offer the best in children's literature and a wide variety of book types.

FIGURE 9–8 Color words are easily learned with this book and adjacent real leaves.

A PARTIAL LISTING

"Ba, Ba, Black Sheep"
Chicken Little
"There Was a Crooked Man"
Goldilocks and the Three Bears
"Here We Go Round the Mulberry Bush"
"Hey Diddle, Diddle (the Cat and the Fiddle)"
"Hickory, Dickory, Dock"
"Humpty Dumpty"
"Jack and Jill"
Jack and the Beanstalk
"Jack Be Nimble"
"Jack Sprat"
"Little Bo Peep"
"Little Boy Blue"

"Little Girl with a Curl"
"Little Jack Horner"
"Little Miss Muffet"
The Little Red Hen
"Little Robin Redbreast"
"London Bridge Is Falling Down"
"Mary Had a Little Lamb"
"Mary, Mary, Quite Contrary"
"Old King Cole"
"Old Mother Hubbard"
"The Old Woman Who Lived in a Shoe"
"Peter Piper"
"Pop Goes the Weasel"
"Ride a Cock Horse (Banbury Cross)"
"Rock-a-Bye Baby"

"Row, Row, Row Your Boat"
"Silent Night"
"Simple Simon"
"Sing a Song of Sixpence"
"Take Me Out to the Ball Game"
The Three Bears
The Three Billy Goats Gruff
"The Three Blind Mice"
The Three Little Pigs
"To Market, to Market"
"Twinkle, Twinkle, Little Star"
Ugly Duckling
"You Are My Sunshine"

FIGURE 9–9 Stories, songs, rhymes, and poems considered classics for preschoolers. Many can be found in picture-book form.

CULTURALLY CONSCIOUS AND CULTURALLY DIVERSE BOOKS

Yokota (1993) defines multicultural children's literature as literature that represents *any* distinct cultural group through accurate portrayal and rich detail. She urges teachers to evaluate multicultural children's literature using two criteria: (1) literary quality and (2) cultural consciousness.

Cai and Bishop (1994), searching for a definition of multicultural literature, found that numerous definitions agree that multicultural literature is about some identifiable "other," a person or group, that differs in some way (for example, racially, linguistically, ethnically, culturally) from the Caucasian American cultural group.

The question of authenticity or, more correctly, what constitutes an accurate portrayal of a culture, has plagued children's literature for decades (Harris, 1993). Teachers strive to present an authentic portrayal of cultural reality in the books they select.

The National Council of Teachers of English (NCTE, 1994) points out

> Literature educates not only the head, but the heart as well. It promotes empathy and invites readers to adopt new perspectives. It offers opportunities for children to learn to recognize our similarities, value our differences, and respect our common humanity. In an important sense, then, children need literature that serves as a window onto lives and experiences different from their own, *and* literature that serves as a mirror reflecting themselves and their cultural values, attitudes, and behaviors.

The books listed in the Additional Resources section at the end of this chapter include not only African-Americans, Asian-Americans, Hispanic Americans/Latinos, and Native Americans but also subgroups of different and distinct groups under each heading. Other world groups are also included.

When offering multicultural and multi-ethnic books to young children, no attempt to give these books special status is suggested. Child questions and comments that arise are discussed as all interesting books are discussed. These books are not shared only at certain times of year or for recognized celebrations but are included as regular, standard classroom fare.

Harris (1993) believes the following characteristics are part of authentic multi-ethnic/multicultural literature.

- Books include the range of character types or people found within the culture, although not necessarily in one book. The characters should not be idealized, but neither should stereotypes predominate. There should be doctors, teachers, truck drivers, cooks, and individuals with other occupations.

- Illustrations should not consist of caricatures of a group's physical features. Rather, the illustrations should reflect the variety found among members of any group.

- Speech adopted by characters should have linguistic authenticity.

- Names of characters should reflect cultural traditions of a group.

- Food should not be used as a shorthand signifier of a group; for example, *rice* is not a code word for Asian or Asian-American.

- The beliefs and values of characters as well as their worldviews should reflect the diversity found in the group's communities.

- Writers should understand pivotal family roles and family configurations.

- Members of groups should portray members as intelligent problem solvers.

- Authenticity derives from insider knowledge about a culture acquired as a member or through extensive study, observation, and interaction.

"Hispanic" children's literature does not refer to one culture but rather a conglomerate of Central and South American cultures. Hispanics, although one of the largest and fastest-growing populations in the United States, are poorly represented in children's literature. Books that exist are often folktales or remembrances of an author's childhood. Books always need to be screened thoroughly for classism, sexism, and portrayals of helpless, passive caricatures.

In picture books classified as depicting the Asian culture, one may find Chinese, Japanese, Korean, Taiwanese, Laotian, Vietnamese, Cambodian, and Filipino cultural experiences depicted. Increasingly, published books about Asians deal with Asian assimilation into the American mainstream. One can find numerous books dealing with Asian folktales. Yet to be written are plentiful picture books from the Vietnamese, Cambodian, and Laotian cultures, but they are slowly appearing.

Books concerning Native Americans can be easier to locate. Most are folktales, but some deal with rituals, ceremony, everyday life, family joys, and problems. Books depicting Middle Eastern cultures are scarce. Again, the teacher needs to screen for stereotypical characteristics.

A listing of children's multicultural books is included in the Additional Resources section at the end of this chapter.

MORAL AND NONVIOLENT EDUCATION

A good number of educators are offering picture books whose story lines include moral dilemmas and conflict resolution. These lead to classroom group discussion. Because many stories involve a moral problem or conflict to overcome, it is not difficult to find positive models of character's actions, words, and behaviors. Koc and Buzzelli (2004) recommend selecting books

◆ with well-defined dilemmas.
◆ with characters who model levels of reasoning close or slightly higher than those of the child group audience.
◆ that have a variety of appropriate follow-up activities.
◆ of quality with powerful plots, lively characters, and a satisfying conclusion.

◆ that portray clear and logical consequences.
◆ that promote critical thinking skills.
◆ that have characters who embody a wide mixture of physical, social, and emotional features and show a balanced representation of good and evil.

BIBLIOTHERAPY

Bibliotherapy, literally translated, means book therapy. Teachers, at times, may seek to help children with life problems, questions, fears, and pain. Some professionals believe that books can help children cope with emotional concerns. At some point during childhood, children may deal with rejection by friends, ambivalence toward a new baby, divorce, grief, or death, along with other strong emotions.

Fairy tales can reveal the existence of strife and calamity in a form that permits children to deal with these situations without trauma. These tales can be shared in a reassuring, supportive setting that provides a therapeutic experience. A small sampling of books considered to be therapeutic in nature follows:

Alexander, M. (1971). *Nobody ever asked me if I wanted a baby sister.* New York: Dial. (Jealousy.)
Blegvad, L. (1985). *Banana and me.* New York: Margaret K. McElderry Books. (Fear.)
Brown, M. B. (1960). *The first night away from home.* New York: Franklin Watts, Inc. (Security.)
Dragunwagon, C. (1976). *Wind rose.* New York: Harper and Row. (Birth.)
Gershator, P. (2004). *The babysitter sings.* New York: Henry Holt. (Separation.)
Greenfield, E. (1994). *Sweet baby coming.* New York: HarperCollins. (Birth of a sibling.)
Hazen, B. S. (1987). *Fang.* New York: Atheneum. (Bravery.)
Le Tord, B. (1987). *My Grandma Leonie.* New York: Bradbury Press. (Death.)
Mayer, M. (1968). *There's a nightmare in my closet.* New York: Dial. (Fear.)
Noonan, J. (1971). *The best thing to be.* Garden City, NY: Doubleday. (Feelings about being small.)
Viorst, J. (1973). *The tenth good thing about Barney.* New York: Atheneum. (Death of a pet.)

A much wider selection of such titles is in print. The following resource book is helpful to preschool teachers looking for books dealing with strong feelings.

Griffin, B. K. (1986). *Special needs bibliography: Current books for/about children and young adults regarding social concerns, emotional concerns, the exceptional child.* DeWitt, NY: The Griffin.

READING BOOKS TO YOUNG CHILDREN

Teachers read books in both indoor and outdoor settings, to one child or to many. If a child asks for a story and a teacher is available, the book is shared. Planned reading, called story times, are also part of a quality early childhood program.

Because of the importance of reading to children, teacher techniques need to be carefully planned and evaluated. Adams (1990) suggests

> It is not just reading to children that makes the difference, it is enjoying the books with them and reflecting on their form and content. It is developing and supporting the children's curiosity about text and the relationships of the text's ideas to the world beyond the book. And it is showing the children that we value and enjoy reading and that we hope they will too.

Teachers need to assess their ability to make books and book-reading times exciting and personally relevant and rewarding to each young child. In successful classrooms, observable child behaviors include eager attendance at book-reading times, joyous participation, active dialogue, and self-selected investigation and time spent in the classroom library.

How the teacher achieves this is critical. Most of us have seen well-meaning adults use reading techniques that are questionable and defeat the adult's purpose in reading. Bettelheim and Zelan (1981) emphasize the importance of teaching methods in the following.

> If we wish to induce children to become literate persons, our teaching methods should be in accordance with the richness of the child's spoken vocabulary, his intelligence, his natural curiosity, his eagerness to learn new things, his wish to develop his mind and his comprehension of the world, and his avid desire for the stimulation of his imagination . . . in short, by making reading an activity of intrinsic interest.

The burden of making reading interesting falls on the teacher. A teacher must also strive to make the book's content relevant to each child. This means relating and connecting story elements to children's lives and their past experiences whenever possible. This can be likened to building a bridge to the world of books—a bridge that children will eventually be eager to cross because pleasurable, satisfying emotionally "warm" book readings have been experienced. Building these positive attitudes takes skill. A step-by-step outline is helpful in conducting group story times.

Step 1. Think about the age, interests, and special interests of the child group and consider the selection criteria mentioned in this chapter. Read the book to yourself enough times to develop a feeling for characters and the story line. Practice dialogue so that it will roll smoothly. For example, you might not be able to read *The House That Jack Built* unless you have practiced the incremental refrain (Stewig, 1977). In other words, analyze, select, practice, and prepare.

Step 2. Arrange a setting with the children's and teacher's comfort in mind. The illustrations should be at children's eye level. A setting should provide comfortable seating while the book is being read. Some teachers prefer small chairs for both children and teachers; others prefer rug areas. Avoid traffic paths and noise interruptions by finding a quiet spot in the classroom. Cutting down visual distractions may mean using room dividers, curtains, or furniture arrangements.

Preschoolers, in groups of four children, make greater language gains than when they are read to in larger groups (Whitehurst, Epstein, Angell, Payne, Crone, & Fischel, 1994).

Some classrooms use "instant replays" of story-book readings when adult supervision affects group size.

Step 3. Make a motivational introductory statement. The statement should create a desire to listen or encourage listening: "There's a boy in this book who wants to give his mother a birthday present"; "Monkeys can be funny, and they are funny in this book"; "Have you ever wondered where animals go at night to sleep?"; "On the last page of this book is a picture of a friendly monster." Then briefly introduce the author and illustrator.

Step 4. Hold the book to either your left or right side. With your hand in place, make both sides of the page visible. Keep the book at children's eye level.

Step 5. Begin reading; try to glance at the sentences and turn to meet the children's eyes as often as possible so that your voice goes to the children. Also watch for children's body reactions. Speak clearly with adequate volume, using a rate of speed that enables the children to both look at illustrations and hear what you are reading. Enjoy the story with the children by being enthusiastic. Dramatize and emphasize key parts of the story but not to the degree that the children are watching you and not the book. Change your voice to suit the characters, if you feel comfortable doing so. A good story will hold attention and often stimulate comments or questions. Savor it and deliver each word. Try not to rush unless it adds to the drama in places.

Step 6. Answer and discuss questions approvingly. If you feel that interruptions are decreasing the enjoyment for other children, ask a child to wait until the end when you will be glad to discuss it. Then do it. If, on the other hand, most of the group is interested, take the time to discuss an idea, but be careful to resist the temptation of making a lengthy comment that will disrupt the story. Sometimes, children suck their thumbs or act sleepy during reading

times. They seem to connect books with bed-time; many parents read to their children at this time. By watching closely while reading, you will be able to tell whether you still have the children's attention. You can sometimes draw a child back to the book with a direct question like, "Debbie, can you see the cat's tail?" or by increasing your animation or varying voice volume. Wondering out loud about what might happen next may help.

Step 7. You may want to ask a few open-ended discussion questions at the end of the book. Keep them spontaneous and natural—avoid testlike questions. Questions can clear up ideas, encourage use of vocabulary words, and pin-point parts that were especially enjoyed. "Does anyone have a question about the fire truck?" You will have to decide whether to read more than one book at one time. It helps to remember how long the group of children can sit before getting restless. Story times should end on an enthusiastic note, with the children looking forward to another story. Some books may end on such a satisfying or thoughtful note that discussion clearly is not appropriate; a short pause of silence seems more in order. Other times, there may be a barrage of child comments and lively discussion.

Many children's comments incorporate the story into their own personal vision of things and indicate that the text has meaning for them (Miller, 1990). Personal meanings are confirmed, extended, and refined as children share their interpretations with others. The focus in after-book discussions is on meaning, and the goal is to "make sense of the text."

Judging oneself on the ability to capture and hold children's attention during group reading times is critical. Many factors can account for children's attention wandering, so analyze what can or did interfere with classroom focus. Factors to consider include group size, seating comfort, temperature, the way the light shines on the book, the child who cannot sit next to a friend without talking or touching, and so on, and, of course, the teacher's presentation skills. One teacher who hated distractions created a sign that read, "Storytime;

please wait to enter our room." The book itself may also need closer scrutiny.

Independent Reading

Teachers should examine daily programs to ensure children time to pursue favorite books and new selections (Figure 9–10). It is ridiculous to motivate then not allow self-selection or time for children to spend looking at and examining introduced books page by page at their own pace. Most rooms have book areas or libraries.

Additional Book-Reading Tips

◆ Check to make sure all of the children have a clear view of the book before beginning.

◆ Watch for combinations of children sitting side-by-side that may cause either child to be distracted. Rearrange seating before starting.

FIGURE 9–10 There should be plenty of time to enjoy books with a friend.

◆ Pause a short while to allow children to focus at the start.

◆ If one child seems to be unable to concentrate, a teacher can quietly suggest an alternative activity to the child. Clear understanding of alternatives or lack of them needs to be established with the entire staff.

◆ Moving a distracted child closer to the book, or onto a teacher's lap, sometimes works.

◆ When an outside distraction occurs, recapture attention and make a transitional statement leading back to the story: "We all heard that loud noise. There's a different noise made by the steam shovel in our story. Listen and you'll hear the steam shovel's noise."

◆ Personalize books when appropriate: "Have you lost something and not been able to find it?"

◆ Skip ahead in books, when the book can obviously not maintain interest, by quickly reading pictures and concluding the experience. It is a good idea to have a backup selection close by.

◆ Children often want to handle a book just read. Plan for this as often as possible. Make a quick waiting list for all who wish to go over the book by themselves.

◆ Plan reading sessions at relaxed rather than rushed or hectic times of day.

◆ Handle books gently and carefully.

◆ When a new, multisyllabled word appears, repeat it, emphasizing syllables. Clap word syllables such as festival (fes-ti-val) and interpreter (in-ter-pret-er). This can be done periodically, not every time a new word is encountered, to ensure the story flow is maintained. This technique is primarily used with children nearing kindergarten age.

◆ Remember it is not so much what you are reading but how you read it.

◆ Choose material to suit yourself as well as the group. Select a story type that you like.

◆ Lower or raise your voice and quicken or slow your pace as appropriate to the text.

Lengthen your dramatic pauses, and let your listeners savor the words and ideas (Dopyera & Lay-Dopyera, 1992).

◆ Read a book a child has brought to school before you read it aloud to children. (Share suitable "parts" only if necessary.)

◆ Handle a child comment such as, "I've heard it before," with a recognizing comment such as, "Don't tell how it ends," or "See if you see something different this time."

Teachers who want to enhance children's understanding of a book's story line can elicit children's ideas about what might happen in a new book. Focusing on the book's cover and showing a few select interior illustrations aid children's predictions. The teacher prints these child suggestions on chart paper, labeling each comment with the child's name. An after-book discussion can return to children's predictions. Each suggestion is given merit as another possible story happening. How close the child's prediction comes to the storybook's plot is not the point.

Teale (1995) notes that a key instructional practice in early literacy classrooms is *response-to-literature* activities that include discussions, art, music, dramatic reenactments, written (child-dictated) ideas, or any other child symbolizing attempts encouraged by the content in a book the teacher reads aloud.

Child Interruptions during Story Time

A slight debate exists as to the degree that child questions and comments during story time mar or enhance the experience for all group members. One position holds that a book should be enjoyed without any loss of flow that diminishes the book's intent and effect. The other position is expressed by Bos (1988): "It's important that we keep conversation going even if we never get to the end of the story." Teachers and schools have arrived at a number of techniques, which follow. It is a good idea to discuss courses of action at a school where you are employed, volunteering, or student teaching.

Teachers can decide to

◆ save all comments until the end.

◆ answer and accept comments up to the point that they feel the story is being sacrificed.

◆ deem certain books "taboo" for discussion: "This book is one we won't talk about until the end."

Studies of young children's questions during storybook review show, in general, that questions about the book's pictures predominate and questions about the meaning of the story rank second (Schickedanz, 1993).

Paraphrasing Stories

Paraphrasing means putting an author's text into one's own words. By tampering with the text, the teacher may interfere with a book's intent, message, and style. Many professionals find this objectionable and urge teachers to read stories exactly as they are written, taking no liberties, respecting the author's original text. When a book does not hold the interest of its audience, it should be saved for another time and place, perhaps another group. Some teachers believe that maintaining child interest and preserving the child's positive attitude about books supersedes objections to occasional paraphrasing.

Building Participation

Children love to be part of the telling of a story. Good teachers plan for child participation when choosing stories to read. Often, books are read for the first time, and then immediately reread, with the teacher promoting as much participation as possible. Some books hold children spellbound and usually take many readings before the teacher feels that it is the right time for active involvement other than listening. Listening skills are encouraged when children contribute to read-aloud sessions and become active, participating listeners.

Miller (1990) believes group readings have five distinct benefits.

1. They encourage discussion of the text.
2. Discussions help generate meaning and serve as checks on the meaning constructed by individuals.

3. They cause a social experience to develop around the sharing of literature.

4. Children share knowledge with one another.

5. Classmates answer questions as well as the teacher.

Miller (1990) points out that three-year-olds take a while to settle into appropriate and expected story-time behaviors. A young group may, as Miller observes, "reach out physically in territorial battles over pillows, places for feet, or stuffed toys."

Nonfiction books may not provide as much material for child involvement.

Examining story lines closely can give the teacher ideas for children's active participation. Many of the benefits young children derive from adult-child readings come through active child participation and adult reading strategies:

> Several strategies have proven particularly helpful to children: prompting their responses, scaffolding or modeling responses for them, getting them to relate responses to real experiences, asking them questions, and offering positive reinforcement for their comments and questions. (Strickland & Morrow, 1989)

Following is a list of additional ways to promote child participation and active listening.

1. Invite children to speak a familiar character's dialogue or book sounds. This is easily done in repeated sequences: "I don't care," said Pierre.

2. Pantomime actions: "Let's knock on the door."

3. Use closure: "The cup fell on the . . ." (floor). When using closure, if children end the statement differently, try saying "It could have fallen on the rug, but the cup in the story fell on the floor."

4. Predict outcomes: "Do you think Hector will open the box?"

5. Ask opinions: "What's your favorite pie?"

6. Recall previous story parts: "What did Mr. Bear say to Petra?"

7. Probe related experiences: "Emil, isn't your dog's name Clifford?"

8. Dramatize enjoyed parts or wholes.

Younger preschoolers, as a rule, find sitting without active motor and/or verbal involvement more demanding than older children.

Reading to Individual Children

Teachers without aides and/or volunteers in their classroom may never have undivided time to share books with individual children. One-on-one readings can be the most beneficial and literacy-developing times of all. The dialogue possible and the personalized interaction exceeds group readings. In large groups, some children are reluctant to speak and consequently receive less appreciation and feedback. (Small groups are recommended.)

Busy parents can tend to rely on schools to offer books. Many centers have been clever in promoting home reading. Bulletin boards, lending arrangements, and mandating parent classroom participation are among the most common tactics.

It is not the simple "I-read-you-listen" type of adult-child interaction with books that really counts. It is the wide-ranging verbal dialogue the adult permits and encourages that gives children their best opportunity to construct a full knowledge of how people use books. Schools consequently include and share reading techniques in their communications with parents.

Teachers should plan times to be in the classroom's book center, book corner, library, or book-reading area (whatever it is called). A teacher's presence models interest and allows for individual child readings, questions, and interactions other than at planned group book times.

Rereading Stories

It never ceases to amaze teachers and parents when preschoolers beg to hear a book read over and over. Beginning teachers take this statement to mean they have done a good job, and even veteran teachers confess it still feels good. Ornstein and Sobel (1987) note that young children enjoy repetition more than older children or adults. A teacher who can read the same book over and over again with believable enthusiasm, as if it were his first delighted reading, has admirable technique and dedication. Children often ask to have stories reread because, by knowing what comes next, they feel competent, or they simply want to stretch out what is enjoyable. The decisions that teachers make about fulfilling the request depend on many factors, including class schedules and children's desire but lack of capacity to sit through a second reading. It is suggested that books be reread often and that teacher statements such as, "I'd like to read it again, but . . ." are followed by statements such as, "After lunch, I'll be under the tree in the yard, if you want to hear the story again."

Holdaway (1991) believes the request to "read it again" arises as a natural developmental demand of high significance and an integral part of book exposure. The child's behavior alerts adults to which books hold and preoccupy them. Teachers can think of the behavior as children selecting their own course of study. Multiple copies of favorite books may be deemed necessary and advantageous.

A curious response occurred when the same storybooks were read and reread to four-year-olds in Martinez and Roser's study (1985). The researchers attempted to identify the consequences of rereading familiar and enjoyed stories. Children in the study made more detailed comments centering on characters, events, titles, story themes, settings, and the book's language with rereadings. Other results suggest that as children understand particular aspects of stories (gained through numerous rereadings), they shift focus and attend to additional story dimensions overlooked in initial readings.

Spencer (1987) suggests additional possible benefits in adult's rereading of child favorites. Children experience

- story schema.
- the structure of plots.
- anticipation of events.
- memory of what happened from a previous reading.
- the way in which language is used to create the effects of surprise, climax, and humor.

In a related study, Morrow (1988) found that participation in one-to-one, read-aloud events increased the quantity and complexity of the children's responses.

Following this line of research, early childhood educators intent on literacy development would plan to reread familiar, favorite story books to both groups and individual children.

"I Can Read, Teacher!"

Early childhood practitioners with any experience have encountered children who want to "read" to their teacher or peers. Teachers often smile, hypothesizing that the child is using rote memory, but often the child tells the story in his own words. Holdaway (1991) points out that detailed study of this child behavior suggests some of these children displayed a deep understanding of and response to central story meanings. Comparing older and younger children displaying "I-can-read" behavior, both older and younger children told stories using their own level of spoken language, not by memorizing the book's vocabulary or word-for-word grammar but rather by memorizing the book's meaning.

Using Visuals during Story Times

Teachers decide to introduce books with objects or other visuals for a number of reasons. A chef's hat worn by a teacher certainly gets attention and may motivate a group to hear more about the chef in the picture book. A head of lettuce or horseshoe may clarify some feature of a story. The possibilities are almost limitless. Currently, with the popularity of theme or unit approaches to instruction, a picture book may expand or elaborate a field of study or topic that has already been introduced. If so, some new feature mentioned in a book may be emphasized by using a visual.

When the teacher wears an article of clothing, such as the hat mentioned previously, it may help him get into character. Because children like to act out story lines or scenes, items that help promote this activity can be introduced at the end of the story. Previewing a picture book may make it easier to find an object or person who could add to the storytelling experience.

A teacher at one center wanted to enlarge illustrations in a book that was a classroom favorite. She first used an overhead projector and outlined the enlarged figures on chart paper. She displayed these as she read the book. The experience was enjoyed, and she found posting the enlarged characters around the room drew child interest. Another favorite book was photographed and made into slides. Reading the book in a darkened area with a flashlight while projecting the slides held the children spellbound. One child asked if they could "go to the movies" again.

AFTER-READING DISCUSSIONS

How soon after a story is read should discussion, which promotes comprehension of stories, take place? It is obvious that a discussion might ruin the afterglow that occurs after certain books are shared. Teachers are understandably reluctant to mar the magic of the moment.

Cochran-Smith (1984) sees the teacher's role during storybook readings as acting as a "mediator" who assists children in two ways: (1) by helping them learn to take knowledge they had gained outside of book-reading experiences and use this knowledge to understand the text and (2) by helping them apply the meanings and messages gained from books to their own lives. Teachers often wonder what type of questions to ask to stimulate book discussions. Open-ended questions work well: "What do you think Asam should do?" "How would you try to find the lost shoe?" "In what ways are your toys different from Ling's toys?" Questions concerning how children feel about book features are helpful. Inviting child responses, and reacting with close accepting listening, is suggested. The teacher who conjectures, connects, appreciates, muses, challenges, and questions shows the child how the mature responder interacts with text.

Looking closely at picture books, teachers will find they have a

- beginning, which introduces a setting, characters, and a place.
- desired goal or outcome or problem.
- series of happenings working toward an accomplishment or satisfactory solution often discovered by the main character.
- resolution or attainment of a goal.

Understanding this sequence gives hints to pertinent features teachers can probe in after-book discussions that have much more educational value than "What was the dog's name?" or "Did you like the story?" Teachers build on what children say rather than trying to impart or transmit information. What can early childhood teachers expect when children make comments or have questions after book reading?

- Questions about illustrations or photographs predominate.
- Questions about meaning will be less common.
- Questions about alphabet letters, words, or letter sounds are rare.
- Questions about the author, illustrator, titles, or book's format are asked infrequently.

When a book becomes very familiar through rereadings and text correlates to illustrations, children increasingly comment about print.

The teacher's focus in asking questions in an after-book discussion is not to check children's knowledge but rather to learn from the child. Cochran-Smith (1984) describes preschool teacher's story-reading discussions as negotiated, nonfocused interactions in which teachers become aware of the "sense making" children express.

The process depends on what children say about their confusions and interpretations and what they understand, together with the teacher's response to the meaning the group seemed to make of the story. Teachers who believe children "construct" their own knowledge will be more apt to try this type of after-book discussion.

After children listen and participate at story time, the teacher can assume children have both understandings and questions. Schulz (1999) reminds us what happens to adults when we find an impressive book—we want to talk about it! We share it and experience others' reactions. Responding to literature involves the raising of questions. Discussion after a book reading, if the teacher deems it appropriate, can focus on student responses and questions. Langer (1992) suggests the following teacher questions: "How did you feel at the end of the story (book)?" "Is there anything you want to talk about?" or "Are there any questions about the pictures you saw in the book?"

Anderson (1988), referring mainly to elementary school reading, states that "there needs to be a strong emphasis on teaching comprehension," and early childhood teachers could at times consider asking what Anderson calls "artful questions" that draw attention to major elements of characterization and plot and the moral or deeper implications of a story, if appropriate. The solution that many teachers favor is to wait until children seem eager to comment, discuss, and perhaps disagree, and only then act as a guide to further comprehension. The opportunity may present itself after repeated readings of favorites or after a first reading. Teachers hope children will think out loud, sharing their ideas with the discussion group. All present are given the opportunity to respond or add comments and cite personal experiences. Those children more interested in other pursuits can be allowed to drift away. Discussion is akin to a small community (with teacher included) sharing ideas. Teachers using after-book discussions believe book content, word meanings, and ideas are best remembered if talked about.

Teachers should take special care to avoid asking testlike questions at the conclusion of book readings because it discourages open and natural discussion. Unfortunately, many adults have had this kind of questioning in their own elementary schooling, so they automatically and unconsciously copy it.

Some centers designate a time after a story is read as "story time talk." It is described as a time when children's ideas are recorded by the teacher on a "language chart" made of chart paper or butcher paper. This activity gives importance to children's ideas. Writing the children's names by their contributions affords additional status. Children's art related to the book can be appended. Other schools make basket collections of inexpensive small plastic (or other material) figures of story characters, animals, houses, story objects, and so on, to go along with a book. These are so popular one teacher made home-sewn story dolls for the school basket collection.

Discussions can promote print knowledge. McGee (2003a) points out:

> Children's concepts about print include book orientation, the understanding that books are held in a certain way, and pages are turned from front to back. They learn about beginnings and endings of stories, about title pages, authors, and illustrators. They discover that teachers and other adults read print rather than pictures. Children also acquire concepts about print directionality—in English print is read from left to right and top to bottom—as well as concepts about letters and words—words are made up of letters and are marked by spaces on either side.

STORY OR BOOK DRAMATIZATION

Some early childhood educators encourage child dramatization of favorite picture books and stories. Young children's recollection of literal story details and their comprehension of story features are enhanced if enactment takes place.

Planning for book enactment means teachers start with simple short stories and display various props, objects, costumes, and so forth, to serve as motivator and "get-into-character" aids. In previewing picture books or oral stories for story times, teachers become accustomed to looking for material with repeated words, sentences, or actions (Figure 9–11). These are the

FIGURE 9–11 Reenacting "and Grandma caught Annabella before she could run away" was experienced by this story-time group.

books or story parts that are easy to learn. In the telling of *The Three Little Pigs*, most children will join in with "then I'll huff, and I'll puff, and I'll blow your house down!" after just a few tellings.

PICTURE BOOKS AS THE BASIS FOR THEME INSTRUCTION

Early childhood centers are experimenting with using picture books as the basis for theme programming. Under this approach to program planning, instruction branches out from the concepts and vocabulary present in the book. Usually, the meaning of the story is emphasized, and a number of different directions of study and activities that are in some way connected to the book are conducted. Eric Carle's *The Very Hungry Caterpillar* is a favorite theme opener.

The classroom setting can be transformed into the cabbage patch that Peter Rabbit was so fond of exploring. Activities such as counting buttons on jackets, singing songs about rabbits or gardens, taking field trips to vegetable gardens, and engaging in science experiences in vegetable growing are a few examples of associated activities. A theme webbing exercise included in Chapter 6 was based on a child's picture book. A "Stuffed Toy Animal Day" invites children to bring their own favorites to class for story time. Memorable experiences connected to classic books can aid literacy development, and an increasing number of preschools are using this approach in language arts programming.

LITERATURE-BASED CURRICULUM

Literature-based reading instruction swept the nation in the 1980s. Many states at the time either recommended or mandated this elementary school approach. Advocates, such as Huck (1992), have described a comprehensive literature program as permeating the curriculum. It includes reading aloud to children, making use of informational books, and encouraging children's response to books using drama, art, and child-dictated writing.

Can an early childhood teacher implement a "literature-based" language arts program? Most early childhood teachers would answer, "Yes, if activities are developmentally appropriate, literature can permeate program planning, but many educators are also choosing to add new research-based instructional techniques."

FROM BOOKS TO FLANNEL (FELT) BOARDS AND BEYOND

Teachers find that a number of books can be made into flannel board stories relatively easily; Chapter 12 is devoted to these activities. Five books that are particular favorites have been adapted.

◆ *The Very Hungry Caterpillar* by Eric Carle
◆ *The Carrot Seed* by Ruth Krauss
◆ *Johnny and His Drum* by Maggie Duff
◆ *My Five Senses* by Aliki

◆ *Brown Bear, Brown Bear, What Do You See?* by William Martin

Books often open the door to additional instruction through activities or games on the same subject or theme. Whole units of instruction on bears, airplanes, families, and many other topics are possible.

Teachers have attempted to advertise particular books in creative ways. Enlarged book characters might be displayed, or displays of the book of the week or book of the day may be placed in a special spot in a classroom. An attending child's mother or father may be a special story-time book reader. Bos (1988), in discussing morning greetings to children, states, "Many times I may have a new book in my lap and then share the cover to set the excitement about story time."

LIBRARY SKILLS AND RESOURCES

A visit to the local library is often planned for preschoolers. Librarian-presented story hours often result in the children's awareness of the library as a resource. Selecting and checking out one's choice can be an exciting and important milestone. Most preschools also do their best to encourage this parent-child activity.

Many libraries have well-developed collections and enthusiastic and creative children's librarians who plan a number of activities to promote literacy. Along with books, you may find computers, language-development computer programs, audio and video tape cassettes, records, book and tape combinations, slides, films, children's encyclopedias, foreign language editions, pamphlet collections, puzzles, and other language-related materials and machines.

Finding out more about the authors of children's books can help provide teachers with added insights and background data. One goal of language arts instruction should be to alert children to the idea that books are created by real people. Most children find a photograph of an author or illustrator interesting, and discussions about authors and authorship can help

encourage children to try their hand at writing books.

Becoming more familiar with authors such as Margaret Wise Brown, often called the "Laureate of the Nursery," helps a reader appreciate the simplicity, directness, humor, and the sense of the importance of life that are found in her writings. The following books give helpful background data on authors.

Doyle, B. (1971). *Who's who in children's literature.* New York: Schocken.

Hopkins, L. B. (1969). *Books are by people.* New York: Scholastic Magazine.

Web sites that give information about children's book authors and illustrators are found in the Helpful Web Sites section at the end of this chapter.

The following resources include autobiographical and biographical sketches.

de Montreville, D., & Crawford, E. D. (Eds.). (1978). *Fourth book of junior authors and illustrators.* New York: Wilson.

Hoffman, M., & Samuels, E. (1972). *Authors and illustrators of children's books.* New York: R. R. Bowker Co.

Kirkpatrick, D. L. (1978). *Twentieth-century children's writers.* New York: St. Martin's Press.

Some early childhood centers set up author displays, celebrate author/illustrator birthdays, and encourage visiting authors and illustrators. Letters to authors might be written with child input.

A teacher who has done some reading and wants to mention or quote the children's favorite authors might use items like the following that were found in the preceding resources.

◆ from Steven Kellogg, author/illustrator of *Can I Keep Him?* "I particularly loved [as a child] drawing animals and birds."

or

"I made up stories for my younger sisters." (*Fourth Book of Junior Authors and Illustrators*)

◆ from Mitsumasa Anno, author/illustrator of *Anno's Alphabet,* "The imaginative eye is the source of all the books I have made for children." (*Fourth Book of Junior Authors and Illustrators*)

◆ from Eric Carle, author/illustrator of *The Very Hungry Caterpillar*, "I remember large sheets of paper, colorful paints and big brushes" (speaking of childhood). (*Authors and Illustrators of Children's Books*)

◆ from Leo Lionni, author/illustrator of *Little Blue and Little Yellow*, "I like to write about birds because I have birds at home: parrots, pigeons, chickens and finches." (*Authors and Illustrators of Children's Books*)

CHILD- AND TEACHER-AUTHORED BOOKS

Books authored by children or their teachers have many values. They

◆ promote interest in the classroom book collection.

◆ help children see connections between spoken and written words.

◆ contain material based on child and teacher interests.

◆ personalize book reading.

◆ prompt self-expression.

◆ stimulate creativity.

◆ build feelings of competence and self-worth.

Hostetler (2000) describes child-authored books in her classroom.

The children in my class who are four and five years old love to dictate text and illustrate the pictures for our handmade books. These books become treasures.

The first book the children usually write is about our field trip to the farm. Upon our return from this outing, we encourage the children to each describe something they saw at the farm. Then we add photographs to their transcribed words.

She suggests creating a group-produced classroom book in which each child has his own page. The teacher suggests a focal point subject such as something the children would like to have in their pocket or mom's or dad's work. Another idea is to ask older four-year-olds who will be going to kindergarten soon to help make a book for children coming into their four-year-olds' classroom. The book will give the new children advice about the good things that might happen at preschool, how to play with others, and so on.

If a child-authored book is one of the school's books, the book corner becomes a place where the child's accomplishment is exhibited. Teachers can alert the entire group to new book titles as the books arrive and make a point to describe them before they are put on the shelves.

Child-made books require teacher preparation and help. A variety of shapes and sizes (Figure 9–12) add interest and motivation. Covers made of wallpaper or contact paper over cardboard are durable. The pages of the books combine child art and child-dictated words, usually on lined printscript paper, or print is enlarged with computer help. Staples, rings, yarn (string), or brads can bind pages together (Figure 9–13). Child dictation is taken word for word with no teacher editing.

The following book, dictated by a four-year-old, illustrates one child's authorship.

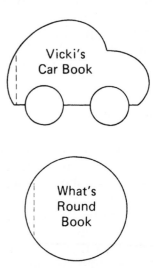

FIGURE 9–12 Book shapes.

BOOKBINDING

1.
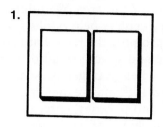

2.
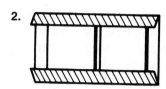

3.
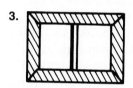

4.
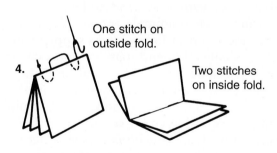

One stitch on outside fold.

Two stitches on inside fold.

5.

Masking tape with adhesive facing cover boards.

FIGURE 9–13 One way to bind pages.

THE WINDOW

Page 1: Once upon a time the little girl was looking out the window.

Page 2: Child's art

Page 3: And the flowers were showing.

Page 4: Child's art

Page 5: And the water was flushing down and she did not know it.

Page 6: Child's art

Teacher-authored books can share a teacher's creativity and individuality. Favorite themes and enjoyed experiences can be repeatedly relived. Books containing the children's, teachers', staff's, parents', or school pets' names are popular. Photographs of familiar school, neighborhood, or family settings are great conversation stimulators. Field trips and special occasions can be captured in book form.

Resources for motivating early childhood teachers to write children's books follow. Some provide insights written by commercially successful children's picture-book authors.

Dahl, K. L. (Ed.). (1990). *Teacher as writer.* Urbana, IL: National Council of Teachers of English.

Holm, K. C. (Ed.). (2001). *Writer's market.* Cincinnati: Writer's Digest Books. (Chapters 5, 17, 21, 32, 36, 85.)

Kovacs, D., & Preller, J. (1993). *Meet the authors and illustrators: 60 creators of favorite children's books talk about their work.* New York: Scholastic Professional Books.

Lentz and Burris (1985) suggest using what they call caption books with young children. Their caption books carefully place the print at the top left of the page; include photographs that give clues to the print message on the same page; and use short, meaningful sentences that repeat on succeeding pages. These writers also suggest teacher-made books that record nature walks, seasonal events, and holiday celebrations. An additional suggestion from Lentz and Burris (1985) involves urging children to illustrate their favorite stories with their own art.

Group authorship is another idea. Books in which every child has contributed one or more pages are enjoyable projects and discoveries.

BOOK AREAS AND CENTERS

Classrooms with inviting book storage areas beckon curious browsers. Teachers have become exceptionally clever at devising eye-catching, comfortable, well-lighted, inviting, visually stimulating book-browsing classroom areas.

If an educator is trying to attract children to the book collection or book display area, thought and effort may be necessary to sell the "look-at-books" activity. Heath (1987) suggests

Make the most of what is at hand, whether it be a sunny interior wall, a tabletop, an old bookcase, or an unused corner.

Thematic and seasonal displays, potted plants, spotlights, and lamps have been used to lure children. Heath (1987) observes that displays in or near the book center can shout, reach out, and grab the eyes and ears of passersby, forcing them to stop and pay attention. She also encourages teachers to tape a story, or fragment of a book, making it available at times so that child listeners can move on from the tape to the exploration of adjoining books.

Books should be at the child's eye level with book front covers in sight. Book-jacket wall displays and life-size book characters (drawings made by using overhead projectors to increase size then tracing on large sheets of paper) have their own appeal. Comfort and color attract. Softly textured rugs and pillows, comfortable seating, and sprawling spaces prolong time spent in book areas. Low round tables and plump pillows used as seating can also be inviting. Quiet, private spaces that are shielded from outside distractions and sounds and that have good lighting increase the child's ability to stay focused. Hideaways where friends can escape together and experience a book that has captured their attention are ideal.

Guidelines that outline the rules and responsibilities of book handling should be developed by the school. Rules should be designed to encourage children to return books to shelves, turn pages carefully, and respect the quietness of the area. Well-defined boundaries of library centers help books stay put. Teachers should promote the idea that using the area is a privilege and should monitor book centers frequently when younger preschoolers, who may have had little past experience with book collections and libraries, enter the area.

What kind of collection should a well-stocked classroom library center have? Collections often reflect a school's budget and priorities. The purchase of classroom favorites and classics should be the first priority; after that, a well-rounded collection that includes a lot of different topics and categories is recommended. Some centers prize nonfiction books, and consequently, these comprise a large percentage of their class library collection. Their goal is to offer more reality and informational resources as well as fiction.

Rotating books by removing and storing some books from time to time and providing a different, previously stored set of books will make the area more interesting. Some centers categorize and store related books together and label them with a sign, identified picture, or drawing (such as animals, trains, things that are blue, and so on). Library books supplement the school's collection and may have special classroom-handling rules. Seasonal and holiday books are provided when possible. Paperbacks round out some collections, and multiple copies are considered for younger preschoolers' classrooms. Constant book repair is necessary in most classrooms because of heavy use. A classroom "Book Hospital" box reflects teachers' concern and esteem for books.

Teachers should browse in book centers, modeling both interest and enthusiasm when time and supervision duties permit. It is sad to think of curious children wandering into the book area, selecting a book, trying to grasp meaning from illustrations, wondering how teachers find a story within, and giving up after studying the book closely. Many teachers set up a system so that the story (or nonfiction) can be heard by using an "I-want-to-know-about-this-book" box. Children's name cards are adjacent. The child can select his book, slip his card inside, and place the card in the box. Younger children can find a name card with their picture and do the same. This system works well only if the staff follow through and find the time to share the child-chosen book.

Group Settings

Most classrooms have areas suitable for picture-book reading in groups, besides areas for individual, self-selected browsing and places where children can be in the company of a few others. If these areas are not available, staff members can create them. The reading area should be comfortable and well lit and as far removed from interruptions and distractions as possible. Generally, lighting that comes from behind the children is preferred. Intense, bright light coming from behind the book can make it hard to see. During group readings, one center put a floor lamp in the reading area and dimmed the overhead lights. This setup worked well to cut distractions and focus the group on the reading. Another teacher brought a large packing case into the classroom, hooked up a light, added comfortable pillows, made a door, and called it the "Reading Box." A large, horseshoe-shaped floor pillow can increase child comfort. Many centers use small carpet sample squares for comfort and to outline individual space. A shady spot in the play yard may be a good site for teachers to read on a warm day.

The number of children in groups is an important consideration; as the size of the group increases, intimacy, the child's ease of viewing, and the teacher's ability to be physically close and respond to each child decrease. The ideal group size for story time ranges from 5 to 10 children. Unfortunately, staffing ratios may mandate a much larger group size. Some preschools do "instant replays"—they have many small reading groups in succession, rather than large group reading sessions.

Most centers have developed rules about what behavior is expected from the child, whether the child chooses either to come or not come to a book-reading time, and whether a child can leave before the book's end. If the center decides to give children a choice, usually the rule is stated thusly, "You need to find a quiet activity inside our classroom until story time is over."

Care and Storage of Books

By setting an example and making clear statements about handling books, the teacher can help children form good book-care habits. However, with time and use, even the sturdiest books will show wear.

Teachers are quick to show their sadness when a favorite book is torn, crayoned, or used as a building block. Some classrooms have signs reading "Books Are Friends—Handle with Care" or "Books are for looking, talking about, and sharing." Teachers are careful to verbally reward children who turn pages gently and return books to shelves or storage areas.

RESOURCES FOR FINDING READING MATERIALS

Public Libraries

Many libraries have book lists of suggested early childhood editions. Often, seasonal books are together in special displays. Ask the librarian about new books, special services, or resources that include films or slides.

Children's Book Stores and Toy Stores

Many stores carry popular new and older titles. Some stock as many as 15,000 titles.

Teacher Supply Houses and School Supply Stores

Often, a wide selection is stocked, sometimes at school discount prices.

Children's Book Publishers

Catalogs listing new titles, with summaries of contents, are available for the asking.

Book Clubs

Book clubs offer monthly selections of a wide variety of titles. These clubs usually reward schools with free books and teacher gifts that include posters and teaching visuals. Enough order forms for each child's parents are sent on a monthly basis. This offers parents an easy way to order books for their children by having school personnel send and receive orders.

Children's Periodicals

A helpful reference book that describes and evaluates nearly 90 children's magazines is *Magazines for Children: A Guide for Parents, Teachers and Librarians* by Selma Richardson, published by the American Library Association.

Book Week

The Children's Book Council has sponsored National Children's Book Week since 1945 to promote reading and encourage children's enjoyment of books. Mobiles, materials, posters, bookmarks, and book-week kits can be ordered from

> The Children's Book Council, Inc.
> 12 West 37th Street, 2nd Floor
> New York, NY 10018

Book Services to Parents—School Lending Libraries

Preschools that have overnight and weekend book-borrowing privileges promote book use and home enjoyment of books. Manila folders or envelopes, preprinted with the center's name, protect books in transit. Book pockets and cards are available at stationery or school-supply stores. This service can operate with minimal teacher supervision. Parents can help their children pull cards on selected titles if they thoroughly understand the school's system and rules for book borrowing.

FAVORITE CHILDREN'S BOOKS

Generally, children's favorites become your favorites. There is really only one way to develop your own list. Preview books and then try them with children. The Additional Resources section at the chapter's end provides a list of books that are young children's favorites. Dopyera

and Lay-Dopyera (1992) urge beginning teachers to consider the following.

> You can help children learn the value of reading first by getting "hooked" on books yourself and then by developing your repertoire for sharing that enjoyment with children.

PARENTAL INFLUENCES ON CHILDREN'S READING-LIKE BEHAVIORS

Parental influences on the attitudes young children hold about books and book-reading times must be considered. When a first book-reading time is announced, a newly enrolled child's behavior can reflect past experience.

Book reading by parents usually starts in infancy, with parents setting up a social book-reading routine. Physical closeness, comfortable seating, and lighting in which the parent acts as if the child is taking part of a two-part dialogue is presently recommended. The parent acknowledges the child's earliest responses, such as looking, pointing, producing vocal imitations of adult speech, turning pages, and so on. The parent may speak for the child, "What's this? A ball, right, that's a ball." As the child responds for himself, the parent subtly asks for more and accepts all attempts. More and more interaction and responsibility for the child's role as a partner in the "reading to" routine is experienced as the child develops. Some parents encourage verbalization and adjust their speech to their child's increasing evolvement and ability. The child experiencing many parent-to-child readings learns what is expected, when to talk, when to listen, when to turn pages, how to answer adult questions, whether to join in with actions or words, whether to ask questions, and so on. Bus (2002) attempted to research key factors of high-quality parent storybook reading. She believes the way in which the adult mediates the reading experience in response to children's interests, personal experiences, conceptions, and knowledge is of prime importance.

Under the right circumstances, young children who have developed a liking for books may be similar to the children Doake (1985) describes in the following.

> By being read to regularly from very early in their lives, children soon begin to demonstrate their growing enjoyment of the experience. Their attention span increases, their repertoire of favorite stories expands, and they begin demanding that these be read over and over. Their avid listening to stories in the secure and close proximity of a loved parent becomes a deeply rewarding, warm, human experience for the children and their parents. . . . The children soon begin to develop very high expectations for books and reading.
>
> Children begin to see books as sources of personal pleasure and derive from them a type of personal satisfaction they can secure in no other way.

Doake (1985) gives insight into parental reading techniques and book-selection criteria that facilitate both development and positive child attitude.

> When a powerful inner drive to want to learn and a natural aptitude for learning are coupled with parents who not only select highly predicable stories (Rhodes, 1981) to read to their children, but who read in a way that invites children to participate, then learning to reproduce stories through reading-like behavior becomes a relatively simple process. This learning becomes even easier when it is permitted to operate in a non-corrective no-fail environment where children are encouraged to experiment and approximate in their attempts to "read." When these conditions prevail, children have the opportunity to take the initiative and direct their own learning.

Parental techniques in the previous quote are also used effectively by teachers, especially when reading with very small groups or in one-to-one classroom reading situations. What exactly are the techniques pinpointed by Doake (1985)?

1. a noncorrective, no-fail environment
2. invited child participation
3. encouragement of the child to experiment and approximate in his attempts to "read"

And the types of books selected? Predictive.

Reading-like child behavior can include "reading" the book to self or others; mumbling words while paging through a book; joining in with the parent on select pages, passages, and/or book character's verbalizations; offering rhyming and repetitive guesses during an adult reading; and echoing by "reading" slightly behind the adult. Children may also embellish or deviate from a known familiar story, and then return to the original text.

Doake (1985) mentions another reading-like behavior termed *completion reading*, which occurs when a reader pauses and the child completes the sentence or story. Parents seem to know intuitively where to pause in order to invite their children to complete a sentence or phrase.

Reading-like behavior may include early child knowledge of print. Parents may have pointed to print in picture books explaining "it says that here" or "this word is . . ." Early elementary school teachers and some parents may move their hands under words as they read, consequently drawing attention to print. This also gives clues to the direction words are read. A parent may point and ask, "What does this say?" Children also may point to words in books asking readers the same question. Many young children come to realize the print in books is significant and connected to what the reader is saying. At this point, children may struggle to understand, and some children actually accomplish the unbelievable feat of the real reading of many words. A few children can read simple books and primers before kindergarten, leaving their teachers in awe of the tremendous capacity of some young minds.

SUMMARY

The teacher has certain goals when reading books to young children.

◆ promoting child enjoyment and attitude development

◆ acquainting children with quality literature

- presenting knowledge

- developing children's listening skills

- encouraging early literacy (Figure 9–14)

A careful selection of books makes it easier to reach these goals and gives reading activities a greater chance for success. Books vary widely in content and format. Teachers who are prepared can interact with enthusiasm by showing their own enjoyment of language; this helps promote the children's language growth.

Good book-reading technique requires study and practice. Professional interaction is crucial to achieving goals and instilling a love of books.

Settings for group times need to be free of distraction, with optimal comfort and lighting. Book care is expected and modeled by teachers.

ADDITIONAL RESOURCES

Children's Big Books

Crowley, J. (1986). *Mrs. Wishy Washy*. Bothell, WA: Wright Group. Humorous.

Hoberman, M. A. (1986). *A house is a house for me*. Ontario: Scholastic-TAB Rhythm and Rhyme.

O'Donnell, E. L. (1995). *I can't get my turtle to move*. New York: Harcourt Brace School Publishers. (Predictive, colorful, and a drama enactment opportunity.)

Trumbauer, L. (1998). *Sink or float?* Delran, NJ: Newbridge Educational Publishing. (Nonfiction, color photo illustrations.)

YOUNGER PRESCHOOLER (AGES TWO TO THREE)

- is able to sit and maintain interest while a quality picture book is skillfully read
- is able to browse through a book from cover to cover
- has a favorite book
- points to and talks about objects, people, or features of illustrations when in individual reading sessions
- can name one book character
- brings a book to adults to read

- wants to be present at most book-reading times
- brings a book to school to share
- discusses or acts out story parts at times
- handles book gently
- enjoys library trips
- may point to words or letters
- wants name on his work

OLDER PRESCHOOLER (AGES FOUR TO FIVE)

- obviously enjoys story times
- asks about words
- picks out own name tag
- knows beginning letters of a few words
- wants his ideas and comments written down
- has favorite books and book characters
- can put book events in sequence
- realizes books have beginnings, middles, and endings
- understands authoring
- explains a number of functions of printed words and signs
- asks about the names of letters of his own name
- can tell a book story from memory
- handles and cares for books properly

- discusses and shares books with others
- finds similar letters in different words
- knows spaces exist between words
- recognizes a few words
- tries to decipher words in books
- knows stories in books do not change with rereadings
- is interested in alphabet games, toys, and activities
- tries to copy words or letters from books
- knows alphabet letters represent sounds
- is interested in machines or toys that print words or letters
- wants to make his own book
- knows books have titles and authors
- creates own stories

FIGURE 9–14 Early literacy indicators.

Multi-ethnic and Multicultural Children's Books

Ashley, B. (1991). *Cleversticks.* New York: Crown. (Multiracial class with Chinese-American child who questions his capabilities.)

Bruchac, J., & Ross, G. (1995). *The story of the Milky Way.* New York: Dial Books. (Presents a Cherokee legend with colorful illustrations.)

Buchanan, K. (1994). *This house is made of mud/Esta casa está hecha de lodo.* Flagstaff, AZ: Northland. (In both Spanish and English, poetic language about a home made of mud.)

Caines, J. (1998). *I need a lunch box.* New York: Harper and Row. (Young child in African-American family wishes for a lunch box like his older sister has.)

Carlstrom, N. (1992). *Northern lullaby.* New York: Philomel. (A poetic lullaby set in Alaska featuring native people. For older preschoolers.)

Cave, K. (2003). *One child. One seed: A South African counting book.* New York: Henry Holt.

Child, L. (2000). *I am not sleepy and I will not go to bed.* London: Orchard Books. (A full-of-excuses child and her patient brother.)

Chocolate, D. M. (1992). *My first Kwanzaa book.* New York: Scholastic. (For older four- and five-year-olds.)

Cummings, P. (1991). *Clean your room, Harvey Moon.* New York: Bradbury Press. (African-American family life.)

Dale, P. (1987). *Bet you can't.* Philadelphia: Lippincott. (African-American brother and sister clean room at bedtime.)

Falwell, C. (1992). *Shape space.* New York: Clarion Books. (An African-American dancer encounters geometric shapes.)

Giovanni, N. (1996). *The genie in the jar.* New York: Holt. (Rhythmic read-aloud with a message of self-esteem and self-discovery.)

Gomi, T. (2001). *I lost my dad.* Brooklyn, NY: Kane/Miller Book Publishers. (A detective story with ethnic characters.)

Greenfield, E. (1991). *I make music.* Inglewood, CA: Black Butterfly Children's Books. (Rhythmic and rhyming, this book encourages young children to join in.)

Greenspun, A. A. (1991). *Daddies.* New York: Philomel. (Photographs of dads and children of diverse cultures.)

Hale, I. (1992). *How I found a friend.* New York: Viking. (Interracial friendship.)

Hamanka, S. (1994). *All the colors of the earth.* New York: Morrow Junior Books. (An exuberant, lovingly illustrated book celebrating the beauty of diverse people.)

Hill, E. S. (1990). *Evan's corner.* New York: Viking Penguin. (African-American family life.)

Hoffman, M. (1987). *Nancy no-size.* New York: Oxford University Press. (A middle child's self-concept in an urban African-American family is examined.)

Hutchins, P. (1993). *My best friend.* New York: Greenwillow. (Friendship between African-American children.)

Keats, E. J. (1964). *Whistle for Willie.* New York: Viking Press. (A well-known classic featuring an African-American child.)

Keller, H. (1995). *Horace.* New York: Mulberry. (About a spotted leopard who feels out of place in his adopted family of striped tigers.)

Kleven, E. (1996). *Hooray, a pinata.* New York: Dutton. (A diverse way to celebrate birthdays and other special days.)

Lee, C. (2001). *The very kind rich lady and her one hundred dogs.* Cambridge, MA: Candlewick Press. (Especially for dog fanciers.)

Machado, A. M. (1996). *Nina Bonita.* New York: Kane/Miller. (A fanciful story about a rabbit and a dark-skinned Brazilian girl.)

Marcellino, F. (1996). *The story of little Baboji.* New York: Harper Collins/Michael di Capua. (An authentic tale set in India.)

Mora, P. (1992). *A birthday basket for Tia.* New York: Macmillan. (A Mexican-American family celebrates a special aunt's birthday.)

Morris, A. (1992). *Tools.* New York: Lothrop, Lee and Shepard Books. (Around the world encountering tool use.)

Pinkwater, D. M. (1997). *The big orange splot.* New York: Hastings House. (Showcases diversity and pressures to conform.)

Rattigan, J. K. (1993). *Dumpling soup.* Boston: Little, Brown & Co. (Different ethnic traditions can be comfortably blended.)

Roe, E. (1991). *Con mi hermano/With my brother.* New York: Bradbury Press. (A loving relationship between Mexican-American brothers.)

Rosen, M. (1996). *This is our house.* Cambridge, MA: Candlewick Press. (Opens discussion concerning exclusion.)

Russo, M. (1992). *Alex is my friend.* New York: Greenwillow. (Child's disability handled with feeling.)

Sage, J. (1991). *The little band.* New York: Margaret K. McElderry Books. (A multi-ethnic band in a multicultural town depicts racial harmony.)

Samton, S. W. (1991). *Jenny's journey.* New York: Viking Penguin. (Interracial friendship.)

Schaefer, C. L. (1996). *The squiggle.* New York: Crown. (Asian child delights in imaginative play.)

Sierra, J. (1996). *Nursery tales around the world.* New York: Clarion. (An international collection of folktales.)

Spinelli, E., & Iwai, M. (2000). *Night shift daddy.* New York: Hyperion Books. (Ethnic family relationships.)

Waters, K., & Slovenz-Low, M. (1990). *Lion dancer: Ernie Wan's Chinese New Year.* New York: Scholastic. (Color photographs capture a Chinese New Year celebration in New York.)

Weiss, N. (1992). *On a hot, hot day.* New York: P. Putnam's Sons. (Multicultural setting deals with ways to cool off in extra heat.)

Williams, V. B. (1990) *"More more more," said the baby.* New York: Greenwillow. (Love and life with multi-ethnic families with babies. Caldecott Honor winner.)

Yolen, J. (Ed.). (1992). *Street rhymes around the world.* Honesdale, PA: Boyds Mill Press/Wordsong. (Children's rhymes and counting songs from a wide range of countries.)

Young, R. (1992). *Golden bear.* New York: Penguin. (A golden bear is this African-American child's friend. Text rhymes.)

Zalben, J. (1988). *Beni's first Chanukah.* New York: Henry Holt. (Family traditions are experienced by a small child.)

VOLUMES LISTING MULTI-ETHNIC AND MULTICULTURAL CHILDREN'S BOOKS

Gilliland, H. (1980). *Indian children's books.* Billings, MT: Montana Council for Indian Education.

Jenkins, E. C., & Austin, M. C. (1987). *Literature for children about Asians and Asian Americans.* New York: Greenwood Press.

Manna, A., & Brodie, C. S. (Eds.). (1992). *Many faces, many voices: Multicultural literacy experiences for youth.* Fort Atkinson, WI: Highsmith Press.

Marantz, K., & Marantz, S. (1993). *Multicultural picture books: Art for understanding others.* Worthington, OH: Linworth Publishing, Inc.

Miller-Lachmann, L. (Ed.). (1992). *Our family, our friends, our world: An annotated guide to significant multicultural books for children and teenagers.* New Providence, NJ: R. R. Bowker.

Multicultural Big Books. New York: Macmillian Publishers.

National Black Child Development Institute. (1995). *Young children and African American literature.* Washington, DC: National Association for the Education of Young Children.

Rand, D., Parker, T., & Foster, S. (1998). *Black books galore! Guide to great African American children's books.* New York: John Wiley and Sons.

Schon, I. (1978). *Books in Spanish for children and adults: An annotated guide.* Metuchen, NJ: Scarecrow Press.

Slapin, B., & Seale, D. (1988). *Books without bias: Through Indian eyes.* Berkley, CA: Oyate Press.

FAVORITE CHILDREN'S BOOKS

Aylesworth, J. (2003). *Goldilocks and the three bears.* New York: Scholastic. (An inquisitive child encounters problems; repetitive dialogue; a classic tale.)

Brown, M. W. (1938, 1965). *The dead bird.* New York: Young Scott Books. (Deals tenderly with the death of a bird.)

Carle, E. (1984). *The very hungry caterpillar.* New York: Penguin-Putnam. (The hungry caterpillar eats through the pictures and emerges as a butterfly on the last page.)

Chorao, K. (1977). *Lester's overnight.* New York: E. P. Dutton. (Family humor about a child's overnight plans and his teddy bear.)

Ets, M. H. (1955). *Play with me.* New York: Viking Press. (A lesson to learn on the nature of animals.)

Flack, M. (1932). *Ask Mr. Bear.* New York: Macmillan. (The search for just the right birthday present for a loved one.)

Freeman, D. (1954). *Beady bear.* New York: Viking Press. (Meet Beady and his courage, independence, and frailty.)

Freeman, D. (1968). *Corduroy.* New York: Viking Press. (The department store teddy who longs for love.)

Gag, W. (1928). *Millions of cats.* New York: Coward-McCann. (Word pleasure and magic—a favorite with both teachers and children.)

Greene, R. G. (2003). *At grandma's.* New York: Henry Holt. (Grandma's house can be a special place.)

Guilfoile, E. (1957). *Nobody listens to Andrew.* New York: Scholastic Book Services. (An "adults-often-ignore-what-children-say" theme.)

Hazen, B. S. (1974). *The gorilla did it.* New York: Atheneum Press. (A mother's patience with a fantasizing child. Humorous.)

Hoban, R. (1964). *A baby sister for Frances.* New York: Harper and Row. (Frances, "so human," deals with the new arrival.)

Hutchins, P. (1968). *Rosie's walk.* New York: Macmillan. (A fox is outsmarted.)

Hutchins, P. (1971). *Changes, changes.* New York: Macmillan. (Illustrations of block constructions tell a wordless story of the infinite changes in forms.)

Hutchins, P. (1976). *Good-night owl!* New York: Macmillan. (Riddled with repetitive dialogue; a delightful tale of bedtime.)

Keats, E. J. (1967). *Peter's chair.* New York: Harper and Row. (A delightful tale of family life.)

Kennedy, J. (1987). *The teddy bears' picnic.* New York: Peter Bedrick Books. (A delight for the child who has his own teddy bear.)

Kraus, R. (1973). *Leo the late bloomer.* New York: Dutton. (Wonderful color illustrations and a theme that emphasizes individual development.)

Krauss, R. (1945). *The carrot seed.* New York: Harper and Row. (The stick-to-it-tiveness of a child's faith makes this story charming.)

Leonni, L. (1949). *Little blue and little yellow.* New York: Astor-Honor. (A classic. Collages of torn paper introduce children to surprising color transformations, blended with a story of friendship.)

McCloskey, R. (1948). *Blueberries for Sal.* New York: Viking Press. (The young of the two species meet.)

McMillan, B. (1988). *Growing colors.* Fairfield, NJ: Lothrop, Lee, and Shepard Books. (Color photographs of bountiful nature.)

Mosel, A. (1968). *Tiki tiki tembo.* New York: Holt, Rinehart and Winston. (A folktale that tickles the tongue in its telling. Repetitive.)

Potter, B. (1987). *Peter Rabbit's ABC.* Bergenfield, NJ: Frederick Warne. (Clever alphabet letter presentation.)

Provensen, A. (2003). *A day in the life of Murphy.* New York: Holiday House. (A memorable animal story for children who own pets.)

Raskin, E. (1975). *Nothing ever happens on my block.* New York: Atheneum Press. (The child discovers a multitude of happenings in illustrations.)

Scott, A. H. (1972). *On mother's lap.* New York: McGraw-Hill. (There's no place like mother's lap!)

Segal, L. (1970). *Tell me a Mitzi.* New York: Farrar. (New York City life.)

Shulevitz, U. (1969). *Rain rain rivers.* New York: Farrar, Straus and Giroux. (Illustrative fine art.)

Slobodkina, E. (1947). *Caps for sale.* New York: William R. Scott. (A tale of a peddler, some monkeys, and their monkey business. Word play and gentle humor.)

Stevens, J. (1987). *The town mouse and the country mouse.* New York: Holiday House. (One's own house is best.)

Viorst, J. (1971). *The tenth good thing about Barney.* New York: Atheneum. (Loss of family pet and positive remembrances.)

Viorst, J. (1976). *Alexander and the terrible, horrible, no good, very bad day.* New York: Atheneum Press. (Everyone relates to the "everything-can-go-wrong" theme.)

Zion, G. (1956). *Harry the dirty dog.* New York: Harper and Row. (Poor lost Harry gets so dirty his family does not recognize him.)

Finding Recommended and Award-Winning Books

American Library Association. (2003). *The Newbery and Caldecott awards: A guide to medal and honor books.* Chicago: Author.

Deeds, S. (2001). *The new books kids like.* Chicago: American Library Association.

Gillespie, J. T. (2002). *Best books for children: Preschool through grade 6.* New Providence, NJ: R. R. Bowker.

Temple, C., Martinez, M., Yokata, J., & Naylor, A. (1998). *Children's books in children's hands: An introduction to their literature.* Boston: Allyn and Bacon.

CHILDREN'S BOOKS CITED IN THIS CHAPTER

Ahlberg, J., & Ahlberg, A. (1979). *Each peach pear plum: An "I spy" story.* New York: Viking Press.

Aliki. (1962). *My five senses.* New York: Crowell.

Anno, M. (1975). *Anno's counting book.* New York: Crowell.

Asch, F. (1979). *Popcorn: A Frank Asch bear story.* New York: Parent's Magazine Press.

Bragg, M. C. (1930). *The little engine that could.* New York: Platt & Munk.

de Paola, T. (1978). *Pancakes for breakfast.* New York: Harcourt Brace Jovanovich.

Duff, M. K. (1972). *Johnny and his drum.* New York: H. Z. Walck.

Gág, W. (1928). *Millions of cats.* New York: Coward-McCann.

Heller, R. (1981). *Chickens aren't the only ones.* New York: Grosset & Dunlap.

Hudson, C. W. (1987). *Afro-Bets ABC book.* Orange, NJ: Just Us Books.

Keats, E. J. (1962). *The snowy day.* New York: Viking Press.

Kellogg, S. (1971). *Can I keep him?* New York: Dial Press.

Kennedy, J. (1987). *The teddy bears' picnic.* New York: Bedrick Books.

Komaiko, L. (1987). *Annie Bananie.* New York: Harper and Row.

Marshall, J. (1972). *George and Martha.* Boston: Houghton Mifflin.

Martin, B., & Carle, E. (1970). *Brown bear, brown bear, what do you see?* New York: Holt, Rinehart and Winston.

Martin, B., Jr., & Archambault, J. (1989). *Chicka chicka boom boom.* New York: Simon & Schuster.

Mayer, M. (1974). *What do you do with a kangaroo?* New York: Four Winds Press.

McCloskey, R. (1941). *Make way for ducklings.* New York: Viking Press.

Miller, J. (1983). *Farm counting book.* Englewood Cliffs, NJ: Prentice Hall.

Peet, B. (1961). *Huge Harold.* Boston: Houghton Mifflin.

Roffey, M. (1983). *Home sweet home.* New York: Coward-McCann.

Sendak, M. (1963). *Where the wild things are.* New York: Harper and Row.

Turkle, B. (1976). *Deep in the forest.* New York: Dutton.

Yabuuchi, M. (1983). *Animals sleeping.* New York: Philomel Books.

Zolotow, C. (1974). *My Grandson Lew.* New York: Harper and Row.

READINGS

Chambers, A. (1996). *The reading environment. How adults help children enjoy books.* York, ME: Stenhouse.

Dickinson, D. K., & Smith, M. W. (1994). Long-term effects of preschool teachers' book readings on low-income children's vocabulary and story comprehension. *Reading Research Quarterly, 29*(2), 104–122.

Gemma, M. (2001, January). Picture books and preschooler's perceptions of school. *Young Children 56*(1), 71–75.

Kupetz, B. N., & Green, E. J. (1997). Sharing books with infants and toddlers: Facing the challenge. *Young Children, 52*(2), 22–27.

Opitz, M. F. (Ed.). (1998). *Literacy instruction for culturally and linguistically diverse students.* Newark, DE: International Reading Association.

Schon, I. (2001, March). Los ninos y los libros: Noteworthy books in Spanish for the very young. *Young Children, 56*(2), 94–95.

Snow, C., Burns, M. S., & Griffin, P. (Eds.). (1998). *Preventing reading difficulties in young children.* Washington, DC: National Academy Press.

Trelease, J. (1995). *The read-aloud handbook.* New York: Viking-Penguin.

Whitehurst, G., Arnold, D., Epstein, J., Angell, A., Smith, M., & Fischel, J. (1994). A picture book reading intervention in day care and home for children from low-income families. *Developmental Psychology, 30,* 679–689.

HELPFUL WEB SITES

American Library Association
http://www.ala.org
Newbery Medal information is presented.

Black Books Galore
http://www.blackbooksgalore.com
The site describes themes in books depicting children and families.

Cal State University
http://www.csusm.edu
Search "Barahona" to find books centered around Latino peoples and culture.

Internet School Library Media Center—James Madison University
http://falcon.jmu.edu
Use to find links to author and illustrator Web sites.

National Parent Information Network
http://npin.org
Select "Web pages" from the site and then a library Web address. Then use "children's literature" as a search term.

The Official Eric Carle Web Site
http://www.eric-carle.com
Children's book author's Web page is available here.

Whispering Coyote Press
http://www.bookcloseout.com
Search for children's book bargains.

 Web resources that include picture-book databases, articles, educational games, and curriculum planning ideas are listed. Public library Web sites that post book reviews, offer readers advisory services, recommend and provide abstracts, and describe book awards are included. Association Web sites that contain news, conference information, journal and article access, and links to additional online resources are also mentioned. Suggested readings will broaden your investigation of children's literature. Top picture-book authors are named, and their individual biographies will enable you to make these authors "real" to young children. Critical thinking questions probe your views about the value of some book-related preschool activities and can be shared in a discussion forum. A "new arrivals" book list, citing picture books published by or after 2000, may include new soon-to-be favorites.

STUDENT ACTIVITIES

1. Select, prepare, and present three books to children. Evaluate your strong points and needed areas of growth.

2. Read a children's book to two classmates or to a video camera; take turns evaluating the presentations.

3. Visit a preschool classroom new to you. After observing, develop a book list (10 books) for the class, indicating why each was selected.

4. Interview a local librarian concerning the children's book collection and library services.

5. Pretend you are to make a presentation about the desirable elements and formats of picture books to sixth, seventh, or eighth grade classes interested in creating and then sharing their picture-book creations with a small group of preschoolers. What would be your key points? What guidelines or tips concerning reading to preschoolers would you present? List your answers.

6. Create a self-authored picture book. Share it with a small group of young children. Share results, outcomes, and your feelings with fellow students.

7. Visit the local library. Using the form for analyzing a children's book (Figure 9–15), review five books.

Name _____ Date _____

Name of Book _____

Author _____

Illustrator _____

Story Line

1. What is the book's message? _____

_____

_____

2. Does the theme build the child's self-image or self-esteem? How? _____

_____

_____

3. Are male and female or ethnic groups stereotyped? _____

4. Why do you consider this book quality literature? _____

_____

Illustrations

1. Fantasy? True to life? _____

2. Do they add to the book's enjoyment? _____

_____

General Considerations

Could you read this book enthusiastically? Why?

How could you involve children in the book (besides looking and listening)?

How could you "categorize" this book? (for example, firefighter, alphabet book, concept development, emotions, and so on)

On a scale of 1–10 (1—little value to 10—of great value to the young child) rate this book. _____

FIGURE 9–15 Form for analyzing a children's book.

8. Do you believe as does Harris (1993) that to author authentic multicultural or multi-ethnic literature the author either has to have "lived" the experience or studied it deeply? Participate in a class discussion after first listing your main points.

9. Make a list of five nonfiction books that could be used with preschoolers.

10. Read the following quotation from Barbara Elleman.

My subject today, however, is stereotypes less noticeable and less noticed that have surfaced over my many years of reading and writing about children's books. Or, perhaps they are noticed after all. In my March editorial, "Intergenerational Relationships," I mentioned that children today most likely have grandparents who are younger and more active than those depicted in most stories, who seem to be closer in age and physical condition to the grandparents of those writing and illustrating the books. The resulting chorus of agreement has made me realize that I am not alone in being bothered by these skewed portrayals of the elderly.

This, in turn, triggered thoughts about another stereotype of the elderly that is perpetrated without much comment. An older character who is scruffily dressed, eccentric, and has a sinkful of unwashed dishes, dust an inch high, and a menagerie of dogs or cats in tow is almost always depicted as warm, caring, thoughtful, and sympathetic. But let a character be neatly dressed and coifed, keep a tidy house and yard, and be meticulous in lifestyle, and the resulting image is nearly always that of, at the least, a disagreeable person.

For some reason, the orderliness-equals-nastiness equation is often associated in children's books with affluence. In addition to being very meticulous, the wealthy are nearly always depicted as mercenary, arrogant, and unscrupulous schemers. And as for offspring of affluent parents, they are too-often portrayed as conceited, haughty, and vain. What books do you know that find the wealthy kid on the block the nice one?

Books containing these or any stereotypes shouldn't necessarily be dismissed because of their failings; instead, portrayals should be talked about with children. They should know that one can be neat and still be nice, that affluence isn't always corrupt, that someone from a monied family isn't necessarily a snob. Stereotypes won't disappear by sweeping them under the rug; they are best met head-on through discussion and sharing. It's another reason to read with and to children. (Elleman, 1995)

Discuss with a group of peers. Report the group's comments.

11. Obtain two copies of an inexpensive paperback picture book. Make stick puppets out of characters, objects, and buildings by cutting them out of one copy. Read the book to a small group of preschoolers, and introduce the stick puppets. Put the book and puppets together in a box or basket. Ask which children would like a turn. Have paper and pencil available for a waiting list. Report your experiences to the class.

12. Janine, a student teacher, made the following observation of her cooperating teacher's story time.

Every child was seated on a carpet square cross legged with hands in laps. Mrs. Cordell asked all to "zip their lips and open their ears." Mrs. Cordell started reading the first page with enthusiasm and expression. She used theatrical talent, changing her voice to fit character dialogue. Josh asked a question and Mrs. Cordell simply put her finger to her lips shushing him and then went ahead with her dramatic presentation that included a loud voice which mesmerized the children. She stopped once to ask Ryan to sit still on his carpet square and a few times to praise individual children for their attention. Children focused on Mrs. Cordell spellbound but seemed later to start wiggling toward the book's end. They bolted from the reading circle after Mrs. Cordell excused them. I was surprised none of them wanted to talk about the book. I felt I'd seen a teacher performance I couldn't match and dreaded the future when I'd read a picture book and she'd watch me.

React with written notes to be used for a class discussion. Write questions about the student teacher's observation that you would like answered in the class discussion.

13. Design a preschool classroom library center. Include materials and furnishings and show room features such as windows and doors and adjacent activity areas.

14. Observe a classmate reading to a small group of preschool children. Complete Figure 9–16.

15. Split the class into two groups. Select someone to read *The Teddy Bears' Picnic* (by Jimmy Kennedy. [1949]. New York: Peter Bedrick Books) in each group. Both groups are to create child activities that could be used as a follow-up after reading the book to a group of four-year-olds.

    Example: Making a dictated list with children about what teddy bears might like to eat. Both groups then share their lists with the rest of the class. Vote on the one activity students would most like to use with young children.

16. Critique one children's magazine using the following terms: literary quality, values found, developmental appropriateness, strengths, and weaknesses. Would you recommend this publication to parents? Why or why not? Identify the publication date, issue, name of publication, and publisher.

		Yes	Can't Determine	No
1. Reader's name: _____				
2. Brief description of group (age, number, etc.): _____				
3. Location: _____				
Setting: _____				
4. How was group gathered? _____				
5. Seating comfort considered? _____				
All saw and heard? If not, explain. _____				
6. Interesting introduction? _____				
7. Title and author mentioned? _____				
8. Reader's voice appropriate? _____				
If not, describe problem. _____				

FIGURE 9–16 Picture-book reading rate sheet. *(continued)*

	Yes	Can't Determine	No
9. Read with expression? Appropriate? If not, explain. _____ _____			
10. Book suitable for group? If not, explain. _____ _____			
11. Book familiar enough for reader to read with ease? _____			
12. Did reader give attention and expression to "special" or "unique" words, phrases, sentences, or dialogue? _____			
13. How did reader initiate group discussion of story? _____ _____			
14. Were child comments respected and accepted? _____ If not, explain. _____			
15. Any unusual child reactions to book? If yes, explain. _____ _____			
16. What reader skills impressed you? _____ _____			
17. What reader skills need attention? _____ _____			
18. How would you rate this book's holding power on a scale of 1 (low) to 10 (high)? _____			

FIGURE 9–16 *(continued)*

CHAPTER REVIEW

A. Read the following comments by a teacher who is reading to children. Select those comments that you believe would help the child accomplish a goal mentioned in this chapter.

1. "Sit down now and stop talking. It's story time."
2. "Kathy, can you remember how the mouse got out of the trap?"
3. "What part of this story made you laugh?"
4. "John, I can't read any more because you've made Lonnie cry by stepping on her hand. Children, story time is over."
5. "Children, don't look out the window. Look at the book. Children, the book is more interesting than that storm."

6. "Donald, big boys don't tear book pages."
7. "Was the dog striped or spotted? If you can't answer, then you weren't listening."
8. "Mary, of course you liked the story. Everyone did."
9. "Tell me, Mario, what was the boy's name in our story? I'm going to sit here until you tell me."
10. "No, the truck wasn't green, Luci. Children, tell Luci what color the truck was."
11. "Take your thumb out of your mouth, Debbie; it's story time."
12. "You all looked at the book and told me what was in each picture."
13. "One book is enough. We can't sit here all day, you know."
14. "Children, we have to finish this book before we can go outside. Sit down."
15. "That book had lots of colorful pictures."
16. "Well, now we found out who can help us if we ever lose mama in a store."

B. Answer the following questions:

1. Why is it important for the teacher to read a child's book before reading it to the children?
2. How can a teacher help children learn how books are used to find answers?
3. Why should a teacher watch for the young child's reactions to the story while reading it?

C. Select the best phrases in Column II that apply to items in Column I.

COLUMN I	COLUMN II
1. fairy tales	a. before teacher starts reading to the group
2. first step in planned reading	b. when children show interest in a subject
3. arrange setting with comfort in mind	c. a book with violence
4. stop storytelling to discuss it	d. book may not be appropriate for this age level
5. not appropriate for early childhood level	e. may be too frightening
6. children become restless	f. "Tick-tock," said the clock
7. directly quoted conversation	g. teacher reads the book beforehand
8. "And I'll huff and I'll puff and I'll blow your house down."	h. repetition in *The Three Little Pigs*
9. "So they all had a party with cookies and milk." The end.	i. identification
10. "The rabbit is just like me, I can run real fast."	j. a satisfying climax to a story
11. a book should be read and held	k. in an upright position with the front cover showing
12. books are more inviting when stored this way	l. at children's eye level

317

D. Describe in step-by-step fashion how you would plan and conduct a group story time.

E. Choose the true statements. Each question may have none or more than one true statement.

1. A book's format
   a. is defined by its content.
   b. includes paper weight.
   c. includes size and shape.
   d. can frustrate children.

2. A teacher's goals when sharing books with children can include to
   a. give information.
   b. promote literacy.
   c. build attitudes.
   d. make them aware of print.
   e. teach listening behavior.

3. Bibliotherapy refers to books that are
   a. nonfiction.
   b. focused on life's happy moments.
   c. helpful in promoting reading skills.
   d. colorful and well illustrated.
   e. written by people with problems.

4. When it comes to different types of books for young children,
   a. most are suitable.
   b. many contain exceptional art.
   c. the fewer words, the greater the enjoyment.
   d. a wide variety exists.
   e. there are more factual than fantasy books published.

5. When preparing to read a picture book to a group of young children, the following was recommended.
   a. Be prepared to dramatize so that children watch you closely.
   b. Skip over old-fashioned words.
   c. Practice until it easily rolls over your tongue.
   d. The larger the audience, the more vivid the experience.
   e. Speak in character dialogue, if it is comfortable for you.

6. Multicultural picture books are
   a. offered to children only at special times and during celebrations.
   b. treated the same as other classroom books.
   c. difficult to find if one is looking for a wide variety of ethnic representation.
   d. widely available and account for about 30 percent of children's picture books published after 1990.

CHAPTER 10
Storytelling

OBJECTIVES

After reading this chapter, you should be able to:

◆ Describe how storytelling can help language growth.

◆ List teacher techniques in storytelling.

◆ Demonstrate the ability to create a story that meets suggested criteria.

◆ Describe promotion of child-created stories.

KEY TERMS

dialogue	participation	semiotics
fable	stories	story
monologue	plot	story map

HEY! GODZILLA!

A tree in our yard was perfect for climbing, with a smooth trunk and a thick layer of tan bark underneath. I watched as Fenton climbed up and out on a limb. He was hanging on the limb with both hands, feet dangling a foot or so above the ground. He seemed unable to let go and unable to swing his legs back up on the limb. As I walked closer to help him, he yelled, "Godzilla help me." Other boys, closer than I, grabbed his legs. He let go, knocking them down with him. They rolled on the ground unhurt. Then Pierre jumped up and said, "My turn," and he headed up the tree.

QUESTIONS TO PONDER

1. Could you create a short story with a beginning, middle, and end about a boy stuck in a tree? Write this story.

2. How would you describe this tree to give listeners a vivid mental image?

Storytelling is a medium that an early childhood teacher can develop and use to increase a child's enjoyment of language. When good stories are told by a skilled storyteller, the child listens intently; mental images may be formed. Fountas (1999) believes told stories become linguistic child resources.

> As they encounter a piece of text like a nursery rhyme or a folktale again and again, children notice more about the **plot**, the characters, the text structure, and the words. In a way, they make it theirs—a linguistic resource that can be tapped again and again in many ways.

Storytelling enables teachers to share their life experiences and create and tell stories in an individual way. It is a teacher's gift of time and imagination.

Rivers (1996) describes the individuality and improvisations possible in storytelling.

> You know you have to hit certain key points in the story, but how you get there is up to you.

Beginning teachers need not worry that their version of a favorite or any story differs from others.

Breneman and Breneman (1983) offer the following definition of storytelling.

> . . . the seemingly easy, spontaneous, intimate sharing of a narrative with one or many persons: the storyteller relates, pictures, imagines, builds what happens, and suggests characters, involving him- or herself and listeners in the total story—all manifested through voice and body.

Storytelling is the act that essentially makes humans human. It defines us as a species. We are shaped by the stories we hear. In storytelling, children leave the "here and now" and go beyond what is seen and at hand. They experience the symbolic potential of language with words themselves, the main source of meaning independent of the time and place

they are spoken. Calkins (1997) emphasizes the "foundational aspect" in children's imaginative scenarios created on the spot in everyday play situations.

> . . . the story those girls [preschoolers] created around their three blobs of clay was foundational to their later writing, reading, and learning.

Early childhood teachers recognize the importance of storytelling in a full language arts curriculum. Good stories that are well told have fascinated young listeners since ancient times. Chambers (1970) believes that storytelling is a form of expressive art.

> The art of storytelling remains one of the oldest and most effective art forms. The oral story, be it aesthetic or pedagogical, has great value. It seems to be a part of the human personality to use it and want it. The art of the storyteller is an important, valuable ingredient in the lives of children.

The art of storytelling is enjoying a renaissance. The National Storytelling Festival's 3-day celebration held in Jonesborough, Tennessee, draws more than 8,000 people each year. Storytelling festivals are held in 40 states. America is rediscovering the magic of storytelling. Regional, intergenerational, multicultural, and multi-ethnic story themes delight audiences.

In many cultures, oral stories have passed on the customs, accumulated wisdom, traditions, songs, and legends. Storytelling is as old as language itself.

The teacher's face, gestures, words, and voice tell the story when books or pictures are not used. Eye contact is held throughout the storytelling period. The child pictures the story in her mind as the plot unfolds.

How could one describe skilled storytellers? Sawyer (1969) describes them as gloriously alive, those who live close to the heart of things and have known solitude and silence and have felt deeply. They have come to know the power of the spoken word. They can remember in-

---

plot — the structure of the action of a story.

credible details about a good story that interests them. Preschool teachers may know silence only at nap times, but they indeed live close to the heart of young children's forming character and personality and growing intellect.

STORYTELLING AND LITERACY

The promotion of oral literacy is an important consideration for preschool program planners. Oral literacy involves a shared background and knowledge of orally told stories plus a level of competence. Being able to tell a story well depends on a number of factors, including observation of techniques. Natural storytellers, if they exist, are overshadowed by storytellers who have practiced the art. Some adult job hunters find telling a story is a requested part of their job interview and is used to assess intelligence, communication ability, and literacy.

Preschools are sure to offer picture-book readings, but storytelling may be neglected. Some teachers shy away from the activity for a variety of reasons, including not being able to hold their child audience's attention. Young children may be so used to illustration and pictures (books and television) that initial storytelling experiences are foreign to them.

Teachers can increase their skills by observing practiced storytellers, taking classes, or engaging in self-study (Figure 10–1). The best suggestion for skill development is starting by relating short, significant happenings in their daily lives—keeping it lively and working with four-year-olds rather than younger children.

As children observe and listen to the teacher's storytelling, they notice common elements, including beginnings, middles, and story endings. They discover stories vary little between tellers. They imitate techniques using hand and body gesturing, facial expression, and vocal variation; they speak in character **dialogue**, and they may even copy dramatic pause. They also may attempt to make their audience laugh or add suspense to their stories.

Acredolo and Goodwyn (2000) suggest how young children begin to get "the idea of story" in the following.

FIGURE 10–1 Watching a skilled storyteller may increase teacher skill.

dialogue — a conversation between two or more persons or between a person and something else.

. . . They hear important people in their lives talking about the past: "Remember what we did today? We went to the zoo! And do you remember what animals we saw?" What's more it's clear that these people are especially pleased when the children themselves also remember. The implication is clear.

Adults literally teach their children about beginnings, middles, and endings by structuring their own narratives in an organized way: "Remember we saw the flamingos when we first went though the gate? And then we went into the snake house and we got scared."

Sharing oral stories and verbally putting daily happenings into words can be cherished for what they are—the building blocks of thinking and imagining, describing, creating, expressing ideas, and later achieving writing and reading skill. Gallas (2003) points out that not only is the storyteller absorbed in thought during the storytelling experience but the audience is as well.

Over the years as I have watched successive classes create stories for sharing time, I have seen that the storytelling child does one kind of imaginative, synthesizing work that takes skill and thought. The listening children, however, do another kind of imaginative, synthesizing work in order to become part of the story. That work is personal, social, and intellectual.

Educators try daily to really engage children in talk and to celebrate its occurrence. Forget quiet classrooms; strive for talk-filled rooms balanced with quiet times!

Wells (1986), author of *The Meaning Makers*, studied 32 children in a longitudinal study that lasted 15 years. In six case studies, which concentrated on the children's later educational achievement, she found stories are the way that children make sense of their lives. Stories, she observed, gave meaning to events by making connections between them and the real world. The number of stories

children heard before schooling had a lasting effect.

Trousdale (1990) sees an additional benefit that is fostered by adult storytelling—child story making.

Storytelling offers ways to bring children into the act of storymaking, ways of creating stories *with* children not just *for* or *to* children.

Other possible child competencies and understandings promoted by storytelling experiences include developing a sense of

- ◆ personal story.
- ◆ curiosity about others stories.
- ◆ drama.
- ◆ a story's power.
- ◆ phonemic awareness.
- ◆ cultural similarities and differences.
- ◆ social and group enjoyment during storytelling.
- ◆ gestures and acting actions effective in communicating ideas, feelings, and moods.

Much current research is encouraging teachers to promote child dictation of child-created stories and subsequent dramatization. The teacher then reads the child's work to child groups. Besides the obvious benefits of the speaking and writing involvement in this activity, it is based on child-relevant material. It is believed to open children's inner feelings and thinking processes to change and growth and to increase child self-awareness and awareness of self in relation to others. All in all, it is a powerful language arts approach.

Gainsley (2003) describes a teacher dictation activity that took place a firehouse field trip. Children were asked what they might see. The teacher made a list that was checked off during the trip. It was discussed later, along with other things children observed and recalled. Other teacher dictation ideas cited by Gainsley were creating grocery lists, creating new verses for songs, and writing letters and cards.

TELLING STORIES WITHOUT BOOKS

Chapter 9 described the merits and uses of picture books with young children. Storytelling without books has its own unique set of enjoyed language pleasures. Storytelling is direct, intimate conversation. Arbuthnot (1953) points out the well-told story's power to hold children spellbound (Figure 10–2).

> It is the intimate, personal quality of story-telling as well as the power of the story itself that accomplishes these minor miracles. Yet in order to work this spell, a story must be learned, remembered, and so delightfully told that it catches and holds the attention of the most inveterate wrigglers.

Teachers observe children's reactions. A quizzical look on a child's face can help the teacher know when to clarify or rephrase for understanding. A teacher's voice can increase the story's drama in parts when children are deeply absorbed.

Many people have noted how quickly and easily ideas and new words are grasped through storytelling. This is an additional benefit. Stories are told to acquaint young children with this enjoyable oral language art. Obvious moralizing or attempts to teach facts by using stories usually turn children away.

Storytelling may occur at almost any time during the course of the day, inside or outside. No books or props are necessary. Teachers are free to relate stories in their own words and manner. Children show by their actions what parts of the story are of high interest. The storyteller can increase children's enjoyment by emphasizing these features.

GOALS

A teacher's goal is to become a skilled storyteller so that she can model storytelling skill while providing another avenue to the development of oral competence. Another goal is to acquire a repertoire of stories that offer children a variety of experiences.

FIGURE 10–2 Storytelling usually takes place with small groups of preschool children, but this teacher is skilled and has enough staff to tell a story to the whole class.

The teacher's goals include:

◆ increasing children's enjoyment of oral language.

◆ making young children familiar with oral storytelling.

◆ encouraging children's storytelling and authorship.

◆ increasing children's vocabulary.

◆ increasing children's confidence as speakers.

◆ increasing children's awareness of story sequence and structure.

An additional goal by Cooper (1993) follows.

> . . . through stories young children can confront their personal and imaginative worlds so that they may come to understand them.

Storytelling is a wonderful way to promote understanding of audience behaviors and performer behaviors. Teachers experience rewarding feelings when their technique and story combine to produce audience enjoyment and pleasure. Child storytellers gain tremendous insights into the performing arts, their own abilities, and the power of orally related stories. Most reading experts agree that oral competence enhances ease in learning to read and promotes understanding of what is read.

Thoughtful writers have questioned the wisdom of always exposing children to illustrations at story time. By not allowing children to develop mental images, they believe we have possibly distracted children from attaining personal meaning (Bettelheim, 1976). On the other hand, discussing what children see in a photograph or drawing and conjecturing with them about what is happening, the details they notice, the feelings that they or the person pictured might be having, and what might happen next can be both a visual literacy experience and a motivational strategy to encourage child storytelling. There are benefits children can accrue from both "with visuals" and "without visuals" literacy experiences.

USING PICTURE BOOKS FOR STORYTELLING

At times, a picture book is the source for storytelling. The teacher later introduces the book and makes it available in the classroom's book center for individual follow-up. Used this way, storytelling motivates interest in books.

Many picture books, however, do not lend themselves to storytelling form because illustrations are such an integral part of the experience (Figure 10–3). Books that have been successfully used as the basis for storytelling can be handled in unique ways. Schimmel (1978) relates her storytelling experiences with *Caps for Sale* by Slobodkina:

> I like to make it an audience participation story. I shake my fist at the monkeys, and the audience, with only the slightest encouragement, shakes its fists at the peddler.

She recommends the following for use with young children:

Asbjornsen, P. C. (1972). *The three billy goats gruff.* New York: Harcourt, Brace, Jovanovich.

Galdone, P. (1961). *The old woman and her pig.* New York: McGraw-Hill.

FIGURE 10–3 *Some picture books are not good sources for oral storytelling.*

Kent, J. (1971). *The fat cat*. New York: Parents Magazine Press.

An increasing number of multicultural picture books are in print as publishers strive to react to America's changing and diverse school populations. The following are suggested as storytelling sources.

Hudson, C. (1999). *Glo goes shopping*. East Orange, NJ: Just Us Books, Inc.

Ketteman, H. (1992). *Not yet, Yvette*. Morton Grove, IL: Albert Whitman & Co.

Tsubakiyama, M. (1999). *Mei-Mei loves the morning*. Morton Grove, IL: Albert Whitman & Co.

An increasing number of classrooms promote acting out stories after they are read. Immediately following this acting experience, children are urged to create their own stories. These can be taped and later written by adults. These child stories can also be enacted with the story's author or teacher selecting her actors or with actor volunteers.

SOURCES FOR STORIES

Story ideas can be found in collections, anthologies, resource books, children's magazines, films, or story records, or they may come from another storyteller. A story idea can also be self-created.

A teacher-created story can fill a void. In any group of young children there are special interests and problems. Stories can expand interest and give children more information on a subject. Problems can possibly be solved by the stories and conversations that take place.

New teachers may not yet have confidence in their storytelling abilities, so learning some basic techniques for selecting, creating, and telling stories can help build confidence. This, together with the experience gained by presenting the stories to children, should convince the teacher that storytelling is enjoyable for preschoolers and rewarding to the teacher.

Teachers telling children personal stories about their lives actually "model" storytelling. They also let children know that their actions and words are the stuff of stories too. Gestures, facial expressions, body language, and variety in tone of voice are observed. This type of storytelling is a natural part of social interaction. With young children, short anecdotes and humorous life incidents work well. "News of the Day times" are often included in daily schedules.

STORY SONGS

Many stories can be introduced through song. Some of us remember the delightful folk story song that begins "A fox went out on a chilly night" and tells of the animal's adventures. These types of songs may include opportunities for children's oral, physical, and creative expression or for child involvement in the storytelling. A creative teacher can use story songs to complement, extend, and reinforce a multitude of classroom learnings. Vocabulary meanings are often more apparent to children when learned in the context of a story song.

Simple, quick definitions by teachers are offered in a conversational tone. Imagine the fun involved in a story song about the saga of a lump of dough becoming a loaf of bread: "... and they pushed and pulled me. Oh, how they pushed and pulled," or "It's warm in here. I'm getting hot. Look at me I'm growing and turning golden brown."

SELECTION

The selection of a story is as important as the selection of a book, because stories seem to have individual personalities. Searching for a story that appeals to the teller and that can be eagerly shared is well worth the time. A few well-chosen and well-prepared stories suiting the individual teacher almost always ensure a successful experience for all. The following selection criteria are commonly used.

Age-Level Appropriateness

Is the story told in simple, easily understood words? Is it familiar in light of the child's life experiences? Is it frightening? Can the child profit from traits of the characters?

Plot

Does the setting create a stage for what is to come? Is there action? Is there something of interest to resolve? Does the story begin with some action or event? Does it build to a climax with some suspense? Does it have a timely, satisfying conclusion? Are characters introduced as they appear?

The stories you will be searching for will have one central plot; a secondary plot may confuse children. Action-packed stories in which one event successfully builds to another holds audience attention.

Style

Does the story use repetition, rhyme, or silly words? Does it have a surprise ending? Does it include directly quoted conversations or child involvement with speaking or movements? Does the mood help the plot develop?

Values

Are the values and models presented appropriate for today's children? Screen for ethnic, cultural, and gender stereotypes that would lead you to exclude the story or discuss the issue with children.

Memorable Characters

Look for a small number of colorful characters who are distinct entities in contrast to the main character and each other. One should be able to identify and recognize character traits.

Sensory and Visual Images

The visual and sensory images evoked by stories add interest. For example, phrases like "gingerbread cookies, warm and golden" rather than "cookie" and the "velvet soft fur" rather than "fur" create different mental images. Taste, smell, sight, sound, and tactile descriptions create richness and depth.

Additional Selection Criteria

Elements that make stories strong candidates include:

- an economy of words—a polished quality
- a universal truth
- suspense and surprise

Themes and Story Structure

Many well-known and loved stories concern a problem that is insightfully solved by the main character. They begin by introducing a setting and characters and have a body of events that moves the story forward to a quick, satisfying conclusion. The story line is strong, clear, and logical. One category of stories described as cautionary seems to have been designed to keep children safe by teaching a truth or moral, consequently helping children make wise decisions.

Storyteller Enthusiasm

Is the story well liked by the teller? Does the teller feel comfortable with it? Is it a story the teller will be eager to share?

Finding a story you love may make it easier for the child to enjoy the story you tell.

> The easiest door to open for a child is one that leads to something you love yourself. All good teachers know this. And all good teachers know the ultimate reward: the marvelous moment when the spark you are breathing bursts into a flame that henceforth will burn brightly on its own. (Gordon, 1984)

MacDonald (1996) advises

> Just jump in. Storytelling is like swimming. You can't do it by sitting on the bank. You have to jump in and start dog paddling. You take a story that you love and think would be fun to tell, and you just start telling it. You keep on doing it until you get good at it. It's that simple, but you've got to start. You'll never do it sitting on the bank (Figure 10–4).

FIGURE 10–4 Dressing up may help a teacher tell her story.

TYPES OF STORIES

Some stories, particularly folktales and fairy tales, have been polished to near perfection through generations of use. Classic tales and folktales may contain dated words and phrases, but these might be important story parts that add to the story's charm. In retelling the story to young children, a brief explanation of these types of terms may be necessary.

A **fable** is a simple story in which animals frequently point out lessons (morals), which are contained in the fable's last line.

Many great stories, called **participation stories**, have opportunities for active child involvement and the use of props. Props, such as pictures, costumes, and other objects, may spark and hold interest. A cowboy hat worn by the teacher during the telling of a Western tale may add to the mood and can later be worn by children in play or during a child's attempt at storytelling.

Repetitive phrases or word rhythms are used in all types of stories, and chanting or singing may be necessary in the telling. Most stories have problems to be solved through the ingenuity of the main character. This sequence can be explored in teacher's self-created stories.

Huck, Hepler, and Hickman (1993) point out that some tales, such as the adventures of Anansi, a spider of African origin, have a rhythm and cadence found in no other stories. Anansi stories, they believe, exist today because of an African oral storytelling tradition.

Stories of children of color should be a planned part of the curriculum. Mooney and Holt (1996) urge teachers to look for stories in their own cultural and ethnic background and believe the right story will fit emotionally, intellectually, and physically.

---

fable — a short tale in prose or verse that teaches a moral, usually with talking animals or inanimate objects as main characters.
participation stories — stories with some feature children can enact through physical movements, verbal expression, or both.

Story Ideas

Teachers often begin by telling stories from classic printed sources.

Classic Tales

Goldilocks and the Three Bears
Little Red Riding Hood
The Three Little Pigs
The Billy Goats Gruff
The Little Red Hen
The Gingerbread Boy

From Aesop's Fables

The Lion and the Mouse
The Hare and the Tortoise
The Ant and the Grasshopper

Traditional Stories

Hans Christian Andersen, *Ugly Duckling*
Arlene Mosel, *Tikki Tikki Tembo*
Florence Heide, *Sebastian*
Beatrix Potter, *Tale of Peter Rabbit*

MacDonald (1993) urges teachers not to waste their time on material that does not inspire them to feel, "I can't wait to tell this!"

PRACTICE AND PREPARATION

When a teacher has selected a story, a few careful readings are in order. Try to determine the story's main message and meaning. Next, look closely at the introduction that describes the setting and characters. Study Figure 10–5 and analyze how the selected story fits this pattern. The initial setting often sets up a problem or dilemma. The story can be outlined on a 4″ × 6″ (or larger) cue card to jog your memory during practice sessions (Figure 10–6). Memorizing beginning and ending lines and interior chants or songs is suggested.

Once the story rolls out effortlessly, practice dialogue, pauses, gesturing, and facial expressions. Particular attention should be given to the rising action in the story's body so that

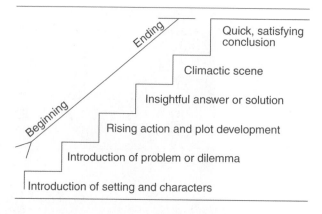

FIGURE 10–5 Common and classic story pattern form.

Intro. "Once upon a time, there were four little rabbits, Flopsy, Mopsy, Cottontail, and Peter. They lived with their mother in a sand-bank, underneath the root of a very big fir tree."

Theme. Mind your mother.

Problem. Peter disobeys and goes into McGregor's garden.

Rising action.

Peter squeezes under garden gate and eats a lot.
McGregor sees him.
McGregor chases him, and he loses a shoe.
Peter gets caught in a gooseberry net and loses his jacket.
Peter hides in the tool shed in a can full of water.
Peter sneezes, almost gets caught, but jumps out a window.
Peter cries and sees cat (another danger).
Peter makes a dash for the gate and gets free.
Peter gets home without clothes and shoes, goes to sleep, and misses dinner. Mother serves him tea.

Ending lines.

"But Flopsy, Mopsy, and Cottontail had bread and milk and blackberries for supper. And that's the end of the Tale of Peter Rabbit!"

FIGURE 10–6 Cue and file card example.

one event builds on another until a quick, satisfying conclusion is reached.

In many cultural rituals, an air of magic, soft flickering embers, were part of the storytelling experience. African storytellers would begin, "A story, a story, let it come, let it go"

(Sivulich, 1977). Ritual can mean entering a particular "distraction-free" classroom area, lighting a candle, wearing a special teacher hat, dimming the lights, saying a chant, or engaging in a special finger play that settles and brings anticipation. One clever teacher created a story sack and reached inside and slowly raised her hand to her mouth before beginning. Another teacher found only short, action-packed stories containing many move-the-body features appealed to his group of three-year-olds.

Sivulich (1977) has advice for early childhood storytellers.

> Having learned a story that you like and that is suited to your group, the next step is to "live" it. The most important part of the process is the desire or urgency to tell the story . . . in a sense, you can think of storytelling as "literary gossip!"

Stewig (1977) suggests the following steps in preparing a story.

> The first is to divide the story into *units of action*. As you read the story, you will notice that most divide into an easily definable series of actions or episodes; these can be summarized in brief form, and then the sequence can be learned. The second task is to identify

those sections which do need to be memorized verbatim. This may include some words, some repeated phrases, or perhaps some larger sections. A discerning storyteller learns verbatim these repeated sections, because the repetition encourages children to join in as the teller recites the lines.

Participation tales hold child attention. MacDonald (1993) points out

> The preschooler demands your attention. Your eyes must be constantly roaming the group, touching *every* face and drawing each listener back into the story over and over again.

See *Just Like Metoo!*, *To Grandmother's House*, *What Was behind the Door?*, and *I'm Going to Catch a Lion for the Zoo* in the Activities section of this chapter.

Select a setting with few distractions where all can hear, and make child seating comfortable. Do not begin until listeners are ready. Be at a level to maintain eye contact and prepare an introduction that piques child interest. Norton (1993) recommends using a prop, telling something about the story's source or author, discussing a related event, or asking a question (Figure 10–7). MacDonald (1993) suggests

FIGURE 10–7 Using pictures or photographs to introduce the setting in your story is sometimes successful.

that your opening phrase is your bridge between the world of ordinary conversation and the world of the story and says this crossing is best when both magical and deliberate.

Additional Techniques

The following techniques and tips should be kept in mind.

- Guard against sounding mechanical. Tell the story in your own personal way.
- Become familiar with the key ideas. Know the key happenings and their order of appearance in the story.
- Develop story sequence pictures.
- Practice before a mirror or with another staff member.
- Enjoy and live the story as you tell it in your own words. Use gestures.
- Maintain eye contact by scanning the group during the telling; watch for children's interest or restlessness.
- Pace the storytelling by going faster during exciting or fast-action parts and slower in serious parts. Adventure stories may feature the unknown or unexpected and include elements of excitement and surprise.
- Use a clear, firm voice. Try changing voice volume and tone to fit the story; in some parts of the story a whisper may be most effective. Change your voice to fit the characters when they speak if you feel comfortable doing so.
- Make gestures natural complements of the story (large and descriptive for younger children).
- Involve the children often, especially with repetitions, rhymes or actions, silly words, or appropriate questions, if the story lends itself to this.
- Sit close to the group; make sure all are comfortable before beginning.
- Include teacher's and children's names and familiar places in the community to clarify meanings or add interest in teacher-created stories.

- Start by telling little personal stories about your family, pets, and daily happenings, if you are a novice; move on to simple stories with lots of repetition.
- Investigate the cultural backgrounds of children in your care and see if you can find stories that reflect these backgrounds.
- Seek out talented storytellers in your community to observe your storytelling or to appear as guest storytellers in your classroom.
- Become very familiar with any pronunciations, including proper names and foreign or unfamiliar terms in stories.
- Use dramatic pauses to build suspense, after an exclamation, or to facilitate transitions between story events.
- Try to communicate characters' attitudes and motivations.
- Consider the flavor and language of the particular tradition from which the story comes.
- Storytelling comes from the imagination. Let it unfold as you picture scenes in your mind.
- Slow down. Tales are best shared when spoken at half of normal conversation speed.
- No two tellers present their tales in exactly the same way, for each person brings another perspective (MacDonald, 1993).
- Move your body with your story.
- End with confidence.

Sierra and Kaminski (1989) believe a storyteller who sees that children are losing interest in a story is free to make changes in it, based on intuition and knowledge of the group. Others would disagree with changing well-known, classic tales, but they do advise changing one's style, pace, or voice volume to draw them back to the story.

It is important to remember that even the best storytellers have an occasional flop. If the storyteller is not able to draw the children back to the story, the story may be ended very quickly and tried at a later time, using a revised version.

Teacher-Created Stories

Many teachers find that they have a talent for creating stories and find that a popular character in one story can have further adventures in the next. Remember that "bad guys" in stories are enjoyed as much as "good guys." Having a problem that needs to be resolved serves as the basis for many well-known classics.

Whenever a teacher cannot find a story that seems tailor-made for a particular group of children, she can create a story. As teachers use their own stories, they tend to cut and add to them based on the reactions of the children. Take care that themes do not always revolve around "mother knows best" episodes, and watch for sexism and stereotypes when creating a story.

Telling Stories for an Educational Purpose

There are five key elements of a good teacher story: audience, content, motivation, timing, and **semiotics** (O'Leary, Newton, Lundz, Hall, O'Connell, Raby, & Czarnecka, 2002). Teachers can consider these elements if storytelling for an educative purpose.

Considering *audience* without one is not storytelling! *Content,* whether the story includes preschool sharing behavior or some other preschool-important concept, needs to be creatively conceived and made interesting. It can be made interesting by relating it to children's lives. *Motivation* is enhanced when children identify with some story element. O'Leary et al. point out that interactive storytelling, where children have some part in the telling, engages unmotivated learners.

Timing involves telling a story in a progression from beginning, to middle, to end. Pacing, at the right speed, holds attention. *Semiotics* considers cultural and cognitive differences. A story set in an imaginary preschool classroom similar to the children's own classroom, and the inclusion of familiar words like *block area* or *bicycle path* will help children connect.

The writings of Vivian Paley (1990, 1994) are full of examples of purposeful educative storytelling.

Child-Created Stories

Storytelling is probably the first situation in which the child must sustain a **monologue** without the support of a conversational partner. It is a complex cognitive endeavor that involves a kind of "story sense" and "story grammar." To be coherent, a child's story needs to be more than an unrelated series of events, as is often the case with beginning child storytellers. Miller and Mehler (1994) alert teachers to the fact that for some preschoolers, including those from low-income and minority backgrounds, personal storytelling is their area of strength.

As children are exposed to stories told and stories read, they construct their own ideas about the linguistic features of narrative storytelling. They use their stories as a way of expressing certain emotionally important themes that preoccupy them and of symbolically managing or resolving these underlying themes (Nicolopoulou, Scales, & Weintraub, 1994).

Cooper (1993) believes that despite our best efforts, we just do not reach young children on the inside, where they hide their stories. She states

> The real tragedy in failing to reach even the youngest children in our care does not stem from the children, or their much publicized "lack of preparation" for school, or their "unreadiness to learn" but from our lack of response to their personal and developmental histories—in other words, to who they are and how they think.

Watching children's dramatic play, teachers will see stories "acted out" rather than told. They will be spontaneous, creative, natural, and seemingly much easier and enjoyable than the act of child storytelling. Teachers can appreciate child actors in dramatic play situations, for they create their own script, impro-

---

semiotics — observant of signs or symbols. The study of how groups come to share meaning.
monologue — literally "speaking alone."

vise, and develop characters in the roles they have chosen or been assigned. At times, dramatic play may seem a series of unrelated events, but surprisingly, the teacher will witness many logically flowing scenarios, such as stories in action or preschool "soaps."

Encouraging child authorship and child storytelling goes hand-in-hand with teacher storytelling. It is an excellent way to develop fluency and elaborated language usage. Calkins (1997) emphasizes the importance of the children's sense of "I am an author" being incorporated into the child's self-concept. She believes this will help children form the habits and knowledge an author needs. One suggestion is to offer activities in which pictures or props are used as motivators (Figure 10–8). Children's attempts are not edited or criticized but simply accepted. Logic should not be questioned, nor should the sequence of events be corrected. Each story is special. Teachers can think of child-dictated stories as print-awareness activities. Young children may have had limited experiences with adults printing their ideas. Child story dictation presents an-

other use of print—a personal important use. Cooper (1993) gives teachers added insights into the possible benefits.

> The fact is that beginning writers don't write because they have something they want to say, they write in order to discover what they have to say, just as they play with blocks, and on the playground, letting ideas flow. This is why I see dictation as so valuable to the young storyteller. Subtly and over time, dictation helps teach the child-author that a written story is merely an oral one put into print.

If recorded or dictated, the story should be taken verbatim. Some teachers initiate discussions that allow the children to tell what they liked best about a story to alert children to desirable story features. Egg timers may be useful if rambling, long-winded children leave little time for others. Asking for child volunteers to retell stories to other children works in some programs; an announcement may be made that Mark or Susie will be sitting in the storyteller's chair after snack. Teachers tactfully remind children before the volunteer starts her story

FIGURE 10–8 Children may be motivated to tell a story about a visiting classroom animal.

that questions or comments will be saved until the story is over. An adjacent box of storytelling props may help a child get into character. If teacher has told *Goldilocks and the Three Bears* using three stuffed bears, a yellow-haired doll, three doll beds, and three dollhouse chairs, chances are children will want to use the same props for their own telling of the story.

Clipboards can be used to list the stories that are created throughout the day. The creation of stories is given status, and sharing these stories is a daily occurrence. Sharing takes place with the child's permission, and the child chooses whether she or the teacher will present the story to the group.

Children's first storytelling attempts often lack sequence, have unclear plots, ramble, and involve long, disconnected events; as children mature and are exposed to stories and books, authorship improves. The goal is not to produce child storytellers but to encourage a love for and positive attitudes toward oral storytelling.

Strickland and Feeney (1992) trace the development of child storytelling.

> ... the first evidence of the developing sense of story in children is their use of language to create a special or private world. This is thought to be the forerunner to the child's use of language to create a world of make-believe, involving dramatic play ... and leading to the gradual acquisition of the specific conventions that constitute a sense of story. As children mature, their stories increase in length and complexity. ... Children gradually gain greater control over the events in their stories, moving from a loose collection of related events to tightly-structured narratives which link a set of events to each other and to a common theme.

Working on Comprehension

One important goal in formal reading instruction is promoting children's comprehension of reading material. Early experiences in **story** comprehension take place in preschools when discussions follow oral stories as well as picture-book stories. The goal is to help children organize and understand the ideas, events, and feelings the story produced. Logic is used when children think about story sequence, cause and effect, emotions felt, fantasy versus reality, incongruities, and other story elements. An after-story discussion led by the teacher might focus on

- making a visual graph of some story element (whether the monkeys ate grapes, bananas, melons, etc.).
- asking if anyone has a question about the story.
- listing on a chart what information about alligators was present.
- asking if someone heard a new word or name.
- asking about story noises or actions.
- discussing how children might change something a character did.
- having the children create a different way to end the story.
- discussing how the children might have solved a problem in the story.
- asking the children if they could show the story in pictures and what would come first and last.
- making a **story map** showing the travels of a story character.
- asking the children's opinion of a story character's behavior as being good or bad—and why.
- asking about a character's possible emotions during story events.

Picture Files Use in Storytelling. Encouraging young children to tell stories while using visuals, pictures, or photographs involves viewing (visual literacy skills) and stimulates creative thinking. What is so interesting to teachers is the diverseness of stories a group of children may relate from the same visual images. Picture files are useful in many language arts activities

---

story — an imaginative tale with a plot, characters, and setting.
story map — a timeline showing an ordered sequence of events.

and are well worth the time spent collecting, mounting, and protecting them with clear contact paper.

Story Sequence Cards

Story sequence cards are popular teaching aids. They have a number of purposes. They can be used as a teacher's cue cards when storytelling. They are also a visual aid for children, who are learning that stories progress from a beginning to an end, with events, actions, and happenings occurring in a sequence between. If sequence cards are made available for child use, children will use them for storytelling and retelling. They often line or prop them up and "picture read."

Cards can be made from two picture books torn apart and pasted on cardboard, with or without adjoining print. They can also be made from teacher drawings, photographs, or other pictorial representations. Examine Figure 10–9, which displays a picture sequence cards for a story found at the chapter's end *(It Was My Idea)*.

SUCCESSFUL DICTATION

Weitzman (1992) suggests the following teacher techniques when taking dictation.

◆ Do encourage storytelling in unstructured situations, for example, during free play, sensory-creative activities, outdoor play, and mealtime and snack time.

◆ Do listen carefully to stories.

◆ Do invite all children to tell stories.

◆ Do make leading statements that invite children to tell a story.

◆ Do make comments that relate to the child's story. You can encourage children to continue their story with comments such as, "That must have been so scary, getting lost in the supermarket!"

◆ Do ask a sincere question to help the child continue with her story.

◆ Do ask questions to make the child aware of information that is unclear or missing.

◆ Do not make children's storytelling a large group activity.

Two snow geese flying

Geese by lake

Turtle

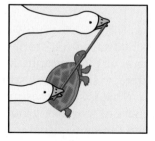

Geese with turtle
flying together

Farmer

Turtle falling
into haystack

FIGURE 10–9 Story sequence cards.

◆ Do not interrupt or change the topic.

◆ Do not turn the story into a "lesson" or "test."

Cooper (1993) suggests that teachers act in the dual role of scribe and facilitator, a role she describes as complicated. Asking questions to clarify and help the child express ideas is deemed appropriate. Younger children seem to run out of steam after 10 minutes or more of storytelling, and some are done in less than 2 minutes.

Statements that help children start dictating stories follow:

◆ "Tell me the words you want me to write down on the paper. I'll write them down."

◆ "Do you have a story to tell?"

◆ "I'll write down your words."

◆ "Let's write down what you said about your new puppy."

◆ "What is the story you would like to tell me?"

◆ "What are the words to your story?"

Kirk (1998) suggests that during dictation a teacher may guide a child toward developing the sequence of a story or help the child find the story's beginning and end. When working with a child who is more advanced, she advises the teacher to encourage the child's use of dialogue or the child's development of descriptive language.

The decisions children make mentally during dictation are complex. The child may pause, start, and stop, all of which reflect the child's attention to the task at hand.

Preschool classrooms that announce that the teacher or volunteers are available and start a waiting list for a child-dictated storytelling time find that children accept and look forward to the opportunity. The success of the dictation activity may rely on the promise of dramatization, Cooper (1993) believes. Linking dictation to children's opportunity to jointly act out before peers what the children have written is believed to be the key (Paley, 1981) (Figure 10–10). Young children's interest in a concrete representation of their stories (the drama or action) coincides with young children's emotional need to

Teacher:	Alexandra's story goes like this: (Paraphrasing) "The lady knocked on the door. Her dog was big and fluffly. The lady said, "Do you want to buy my cookies?" The girl in the house told the lady "yes" if the lady could sing a song that would make her dog bark. She did. They had cookies and lemonade under the tree in the yard."
Teacher:	(to Alexandra) Who do you choose to be the lady with the dog and the cookies? (Alexandra chooses Dana.)
Teacher:	Dana will you be the lady? (Dana nods "yes.")
Teacher:	Alexandra choose your dog. (Alexandra chooses Patrick.)
Teacher:	Patrick can you be a dog that barks? (Patrick says, "Okay.")
Teacher:	Now we need a girl in the house. Who do you choose Alexandra? ("Maria," she answers.)
Teacher:	Maria would you play the girl in Alexandra's story? (Maria nods "yes.")
Teacher:	Dana, Patrick, and Maria, please come up here in front. Everyone else can move to where they can see and sit down. Alexandra's play is going to start. (Children move and sit.)
Teacher:	Dana and Patrick, let's start with you moving to the door of Maria's house. "The lady knocked on the door." "Do you want to buy my cookies?"
Teacher:	"I will if you sing a song and your dog barks."
Teacher:	Dana if you don't know a song to sing you can just sing *la, la, la.* "The dog barks." The teacher and the children finish the play sequence. Maria improvises giving Dana coins.
Teacher:	Good acting. Dana really sang a song. Patrick, what a good job of pretending to be a dog. You walked like a dog. Maria that was a good idea—giving money for cookies. A class discussion follows. Children decide to ask Alexandra if the story can be "acted" again.

FIGURE 10–10 Example of a child's story dramatization. (Courtesy of Busy Bee Preschool, Santa Clara, California.)

establish their individual identity within the group (Cooper, 1993).

Nicolopoulou, Scales, and Weintraub (1994) studied the content of four-year-olds' dictated stories and found differences in boys' and girls' tales. Boys' stories were far less likely than girls' to have either a stable cast of characters or a well-articulated plot; in addition, boys did not develop their themes in the steady and methodical manner as did many girls. Whereas girls' stories focused on creating, maintaining, and elaborating structure, the boys' stories focused on generating action and excitement. Boys' main characters were often big, powerful, and frightening, whereas girls depicted realistic stable family life. Girls' stories created animals that were soft, cute creatures, whereas boys' animals typically were violent, wild, and scary.

Bathroom-type stories appeared at times in child dictation and should be censored if necessary.

Reaching Reluctant Storytellers

Educators may be faced with some young children who seem unable to initiate stories or who are reluctant interactive audience members. Reaching these children can be a challenge. Telling one's own story involves an element of risk. Becoming comfortable speaking before a group may be difficult in light of their innate nature, home culture, or past experience. A classroom alive with "story," dramatization, and performance may slowly reach these children, as the fun, excitement, and "social connectedness" of storytelling become part of their classroom lives. Most child groups have a number of enthusiastic story presenters, who are learning which of their presenter skills or created story parts are enjoyed by their audience. These are willing and eager models.

Some children feel comfortable preforming with physically active body movements and dance, and it has become integral to their storytelling style. The early childhood educator who introduces storytelling discovers that wild fantasy and vivid imagination are alive and well in most young children.

Gallas (2003) describes the shift in some children's storytelling behavior in her kindergarten class.

> By May, many children who had been silent and self-conscious during more spontaneous performances were improvising songs and orchestrating dances and musical events. That signaled to one that the children had made movement toward understanding their roles as co-performers as well as realizing the social benefits of the authoring process and, further that they were comfortable taking the risks that those kinds of performances required.

Storytelling with Young Limited-English Children

Pantomimes of eating dinner, going to bed, dressing, washing face and brushing teeth, opening a door with a key, rocking a baby to sleep, and other pantomime activities intrigue limited-English speakers. Pantomimes can include words in English and other languages enacted by children and adults. Props are sometimes useful. Guessing is half the fun. Using pantomimes can introduce and enhance the world of storytelling.

A Cut-and-Tell Story

Clever teachers have created cut-and-tell stories that readily capture children's attention. While telling these stories, the teacher cuts a paper shape relating to the story line. *The Boy in the Boat,* an example, follows.

Preparation

Step 1. Fold a piece of 9″ × 12″ (or larger) paper in half.

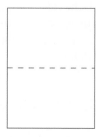

Step 2. Fold top corners down toward the middle.

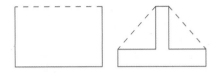

Step 3. Fold single sheet up over triangles.

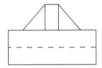

Step 4. Turn over and fold single sheet up.

Those who know how to fold a sailor's hat will recognize the pattern. Tell the story with scissors handy.

Once there was a boy (or girl) who wanted to be a sailor. He had a sailor's hat. (Show hat shape.) *And he had a boat.* (Turn the hat so it becomes a boat.) *One day he climbed in his boat and floated to the middle of a big lake. It was very hot, for the sun was bright. He took off his shirt and pants and threw them into the water. He had a swimming suit on under his clothes, and he felt much cooler. His boat hit a large rock and the front of his boat fell off.* (Cut off front of boat.)

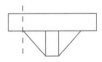

Then a giant fish took a bite out of the bottom of the boat. (Cut off the bottom.)

The back of the boat came off when a big bird flew down and sat on it. (Cut off the back of the boat.)

The boy didn't have but a little boat left and water was reaching his toes, so he jumped overboard and swam to the shore. He watched his boat sink. Then he saw something white floating toward him. What do you think it could be? (Unfold what's left of the boat.)

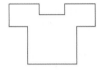

His shirt!

Finding Additional Help

Many metropolitan areas have storytelling clubs and associations. Increasingly apparent are individuals and groups bent on preserving cultural and ethnic stories and techniques. One well-known resource for storytelling is The National Association for the Preservation and Perpetuation of Storytelling, P.O. Box 309, Jonesborough, TN 37659.

PARENTS, VOLUNTEERS, AND COMMUNITY STORYTELLERS

It is surprising how many parents, volunteers, and community elementary school-aged children, teenagers, and adults will rise to the occasion when asked to tell fictional stories or stories concerning significant life experiences. Guidelines of suitability will need to be discussed.

Intergeneration storytelling and its benefits have been given attention and need mentioning here. After briefing possible volunteers and older storytellers on appropriate time length, settings, story features, and so forth, grandparents and other seniors might relate stories from their own unique backgrounds. Stories about contemporary happenings are also valuable. Many of these stories might involve a rich array of multicultural and multigenerational themes and offer wisdom accumulated through many years of living. Stories might also be told in the authentic language of the storyteller.

SUMMARY

Teachers offer orally told stories to promote literacy and encourage children's language enjoyment and development of oral abilities.

One goal of storytelling is achieving a feeling of togetherness and enjoyment through the words of a story. Building listening skills, developing vocabulary, and expanding interest are other important goals.

Stories for storytelling can be found in printed sources or borrowed from other teachers. A story can also be created by the teacher. By following suggested techniques and criteria, a successful activity for both children and teachers is possible.

Stories are told in the teacher's own words, with key events clearly in mind. Watching the children's interest and reactions keeps the teacher aware of how well the experience is accepted. Any skill takes practice; storytelling skills improve with use.

Teachers promote child storytelling by encouraging children and recognizing their efforts.

ADDITIONAL RESOURCES

Readings

Barclay, K. D., & Walwer, L. (1992, March). Linking lyrics and literacy through song picture books. *Young Children, 47*(4), 76–85.

Brett, D. (1998). *Annie stories: A special kind of storytelling.* New York: Workman.

Dyson, A., & Genishi, C. (1994). *The need for story: Cultural diversity in classroom and community.* Urbana, IL: National Council of Teachers of English.

Fujita, H. (1998). *Stories to play with: Kids' tales told with puppets, paper, toys and imagination.* Little Rock, AR: August House Publishers, Inc.

Gillard, M. (1996). *Storyteller storyteacher.* New York: Stenhouse Publishers.

Hamilton, M., & Weiss, M. (1996). *Stories in my pocket: Tales kids can tell.* Golden, CO: Fulcrum Publishing.

McCord, S. (1995). *The storybook journey: Pathways to literacy through story and play.* Englewood Cliffs, NJ: Prentice Hall.

Meyer, R. J. (1995, April). Stories to teach and teaching story: The use of narrative in learning to teach. *Language Arts, 72,* 276–286.

Mooney, B., & Holt, D. (1996) *The storyteller's guide.* Little Rock, AR: August House Publishers, Inc.

Nelson, O., & Linek, W. (1999). *Practical classroom applications of language experience.* Boston: Allyn and Bacon.

Paley, V. (1990). *The boy who would be a helicopter.* Cambridge, MA: Harvard University Press.

Rowe, D. W. (1994). *Preschoolers as authors.* Cresskill, NJ: Hampton.

Trousdale, A. (1990). Interactive storytelling: Scaffolding children's early narratives. *Language Arts, 67*(2), 164–173.

HELPFUL WEB SITES

Brown Bag Bedtime Books
http://www.brownbagbooks.com
Search the stories presented at this site.

The Internet Public Library
http://www.ipl.org
Some story text can be found. Select KidSpace and then click Story Hour.

Reading Is Fundamental
http://www.rifnet.org
Storytelling history and benefits are reviewed.

Read, analyze, and react to elements in classic stories that create drama. Describe why memorable main characters in your favorite stories are well remembered and may guide your actions. What makes Beatrix Potter's Peter Rabbit as real today as he was when you were a child? Answer this during an online discussion forum.

STUDENT ACTIVITIES

1. Create a story. In outline form, write the beginning, middle, and ending. Practice telling it to a fellow student. Use your own title or select one of the following:

   The Giant Ice Cream Cone   *The Mouse Who Chased Cats*
   Magic Shoes   *The Police Officer and Mike*
   The Dog Who Wouldn't Bark   *The Fastest Bike*
   Billy Found a Dollar   *I've Got a Bug in My Pocket*
   The Big Birthday Present

2. Tell a story to a group of children. Write an evaluation of both the story and your skill.

   a. What parts interested the children the most?
   b. What would you change if you told it again?
   c. What techniques were used to hold interest?

3. Create a story song. Share it with your classmates.

4. Find an ethnic or cultural story that could be told to young children. Cite your source and be ready to share the story with fellow classmates.

5. Design an evaluation (rating form) to assess a storyteller's skill.

6. Interview and invite a librarian or experienced adult who tells stories during story hours to share favorite stories with the class.

7. Tell a story and have it recorded on videotape. Play it back. Look for strong points and areas for growth in skill.

8. Read the following kindergarten teacher's description of an oral storytelling situation.

   Once they were drawn in, they became intensely focused during the story. I couldn't help but notice the deep interest in their faces, and they begged for more. They especially liked stories with jokes about themselves, and with issues that weren't too close to home. For example, they wouldn't have enjoyed a vivid description of an angry mother, but they adored the story in which the janitor had mistakenly replaced their table chairs with those from the toddler room. (Cooper, 1993)

   Knowing preschoolers enjoy a slapstick type of humor, create a story for teacher storytelling. What vivid descriptions would you avoid including in tales to preschoolers—ones you feel are "too close to home"?

9. Have a child under the age of five dictate a story to you. Try an "I'll tell you my story, and you tell me your story" technique. Share the results with the class.

10. Listen to a commercial storytelling record. List the techniques used to hold children's interest.

11. List important reasons for teacher storytelling.
12. Using the cue card example (Figure 10–6), tell a fellow student the *Tale of Peter Rabbit*.
13. Read the following storytelling promotion idea.

Create a home-visiting stuffed animal who reports back to school his adventures during his home visit. The class stuffed animal comes in a convenient carrying case with written instructions to parents to help their child record what the stuffed animal experienced. This written and pictorial record (if parents take photos) is presented to the class and becomes part of a book entitled *Geraldo's Adventures*. Often, this book is the most cherished book in the classroom collection.

What would you include in the instructions to parents? Put your instructions in written form.

14. Create a story that can be told while each child in the audience moves props that have been distributed beforehand, such as (1) felt pieces on a square of felt, (2) plastic animals, (3) blocks, (4) paper figures, or (5) other props you create. Test the story and props with a small group of children. Report results to classmates, and write a brief summary for your instructor.

CHAPTER REVIEW

A. Column I lists common preschool characteristics. Select the appropriate storytelling technique or criterion from Column II that matches each item in Column I.

COLUMN I

1. likes to move frequently
2. has had experiences at home, at school, and in community
3. has fear of large animals and bodily harm
4. likes play with words
5. likes to be part of the group
6. likes to talk

COLUMN II

a. selects stories without cruel monsters or vivid descriptions of accidents
b. "Ducky-Ducky and Be-Bop-Boo went to the park to meet Moo-moo the cow"
c. stories contain familiar objects and animals
d. "What did big bird say to baby bird?"
e. "Help Tipper blow out the candle. Pretend my finger is a candle and try to blow it out!"
f. "Stand up and reach for the moon like Johnny did. Now close your eyes; is it dark like night? You couldn't reach the moon, but can you find your nose with your eyes closed?"

B. Briefly answer the following questions.

1. Why should storytelling take place often in early childhood centers?
2. What are three resources for stories?
3. What are stereotypes?

C. Select the correct answers. Each item has more than one correct answer.

1. In storytelling, the storyteller not only uses words but also uses
   a. the hands.
   b. the face.
   c. the eyes.
   d. gestures.

2. Recommended techniques used by storytellers are
   a. changing the voice to fit the character.
   b. changing the personality of a character during the story.
   c. stopping without ending a story so that children will listen quietly the next time.
   d. watching children closely and emphasizing the parts they enjoy.

3. Criteria for story selection include
   a. believable characters.
   b. a plot with lots of action.
   c. a possible problem to be resolved.
   d. making sure the story is one that can be memorized.

4. Teachers should not
   a. let children be inattentive during their story.
   b. feel defeated if a story occasionally flops.
   c. put bad guys in stories.
   d. tell the story word for word.

5. During storytelling time, the
   a. child can form her own mental pictures.
   b. teacher can share interesting personal life experiences.
   c. teacher models correct speech.
   d. teacher models creative use of words.

D. Write a paragraph or two describing appropriate teacher reactions to child-created stories.

E. Give two examples of words, phrases, or sentences that must be memorized when storytelling a particular story. Include story title.

SUGGESTED STORIES

THE LITTLE ELF WHO LISTENS

Author Unknown

Do you know what an elf is? No one ever saw an elf, but we can pretend it is a little boy about the size of a squirrel. This elf I'm going to tell you about lived at the edge of a big woods.

He played with chattering chipmunks, with bushy-tailed squirrels, and with hopping rabbits. They were his best friends.

Now, this little elf had something very special. His fairy godmother had given him *three pairs* of listening ears! That would be *six* ears, wouldn't it?

There was a *big* pair of ears, a *middle-sized* pair of ears, and a *tiny* pair of ears.

When the little elf wore his *big* ears, he could hear the faintest (smallest) sounds in the woods—leaves falling from the trees, the wind whispering to the flowers, the water rippling over stones in the little stream. He could hear the dogs barking far, far away. The little elf always told his friends, the squirrels, the chipmunks, and the rabbits, about the dogs, so they could run and hide. They were very thankful.

The little elf wore his *tiny* ears when the storms came and the wind blew loud and fierce, and when the thunder roared and crashed. The little animals, who had only one pair of ears apiece, were frightened by the loud noises, but their friend, the elf, told them that the wind and the thunder were important. After them would come the rain, and the rain was needed to help the food to grow.

Most of the time the little elf wore his *middle-sized* ears. He liked them best of all. He listened to all the middle-sized sounds with them, not the very loud and not the very soft sounds.

One morning some children came to the woods to pick flowers. "What shall we do with our pretty flowers?" a little girl asked.

A boy called Billy said, "Let's take them to school." "Let's!" the little girl agreed. "We can show them to the other children." The little elf listened, and he wished that he could go to school. He wanted to see and hear what the children did at school.

He told his friends, the squirrels, the chipmunks, and the rabbits, about it, but they said, "No, an elf can't go to school. School is just for children."

The little elf decided he would go to school anyway. So the next morning he crept out of his warm bed of leaves under the toadstool and skippety-skipped down the road toward the school.

Soon he came to a big building. Girls and boys were playing out on the playground. There was a red, white, and blue flag flying high on a pole, so the little elf knew this was really the school.

Just then a bell rang, and the children all went inside. The little elf quietly slipped inside too.

You were the girls and boys playing outside. You are the children that the little elf followed.

Which pair of ears do you think he will have to use?

—His *big* ears because you talk too low, as if you were afraid of your own voice?

—His *tiny* ears because you talk so loud that you sound like a thunderstorm?

—Or his *middle-sized* ears because you are talking just right—loud enough so everyone in the room can hear, but not so loud that you seem to be shouting? Remember, the little elf likes his *middle-sized* ears best!

Suggestion: It is a good idea to show tiny, middle-sized, and big ears drawn on the chalkboard or on paper or on the flannel board.

(A follow-up to this story could be sorting objects into three groups by size.)

LITTLE DUCK

(A good group-participation story. Children imitate the actions with teacher.)

Run = Slap thighs quickly

Walk = Slap thighs slowly

Big steps = Thump fists on chest

Swim = Rub palms of hands together rapidly

Bang = Clap hands once

Little Duck was scolded for eating too many bugs, so he said to his mother, "I am going to run away. Then I can eat anything I like."

So Little Duck left the barnyard and his own dear mother who loved him. He walked down the road on his little flat feet. (Action)

Little Duck met a cow who was munching hay.

"Have some," offered the cow.

Hay was much too rough for Little Duck to eat because he had no teeth to chew it. He thanked the cow for her thoughtfulness and walked on. (Action) Suddenly, he heard a big BANG. (Clap) Little Duck trembled with fright.

"Oh, oh, that must be a hunter with a gun," he cried.

Little Duck ran away from there fast. (Action) Then Little Duck heard some BIG LOUD steps coming toward him. (Action) He hid in some bushes until the big steps went by.

"Why, that was only a HORSE," said Little Duck happily.

Little Duck met a dog with a bone.

"Have some," said the dog.

"No, thank you," said Little Duck as he walked on. (Action)

Little Duck came to a pond. He jumped into the water and swam across the pond. (Action) He climbed out of the water and walked on. (Action)

Suddenly Little Duck heard a fierce sound, "Grrrrrrowl, Rrrrrrruff."

Right in front of Little Duck sat a fox!

"Yum, yum," said the fox, smacking his lips. "Duck for dinner!"

"Oh, oh!" cried Little Duck as he began to run. (Action)

He ran and ran faster and faster. (Action) He came to the pond and swam across. (Action) The fox was right behind him.

Suddenly there was a loud BANG. (Action) When the fox heard the big noise, he turned and ran away. (Action)

Little Duck felt safer now, but he kept right on running. (Action)

He passed the horse—and the cow—and the dog with a bone. Soon he was back in the barnyard with his own dear mother who loved him.

He said:

"I'm a little duck as you can see,

And this barnyard is the best place for me."

Little Duck knew that being scolded was for his own good, and he never ate too many bugs again. He never ran away again, either.

Peck, P. C. (1968). Special permission granted by Weekly Reader Corporation.

I'M GOING TO CATCH A LION FOR THE ZOO

Author Unknown, Traditional

I'll get up in the morning (yawn and stretch)

I'll put on my clothes (go through motions)

I'll take a long piece of rope down from the wall (reach up)

I'll carry it over my shoulder (push up arm to shoulder)

Open the door (pretend to turn door handle)

And close the door (clasp hands)

I'm going on a lion hunt, and I'm not afraid (slap hands on knees)

Whoops—comin' to a hill (climbing with hands)

Now I'm crossing a bridge (pound closed fists on chest)
And I'm crossing a river (motion as though swimming)
Now I'm going through tall grass (rub hands together)
Whoops—I'm walking in mud (poke air-filled cheeks)
I'm going on a lion hunt, and I'm not afraid (slap hands on knees)
Comin' to a lion territory—want to catch a lion
With green stripes and pink polka dots
Have to go tippy-toe (fingertips on knees)
I'm climbing up a tree (climb up and look all around)
No lion!
Going in a dark cave (cup hands around eyes and look around)
Oh, a lion!

> (The trip back home is exactly the same, only in reverse and faster. The cave is first and slam the door is last.)

Home at last. I'm not going on any more lion hunts. I've found a lion, and I'm afraid.

> (This story is full of child participation and action. It takes teacher practice but is well worth the effort.)

Note: This is a variation of "Bear Hunt."

THE LITTLE RED HEN

See the Appendix for story text. Trousdale (1990) relates her experiences with this story as follows:

> To encourage interactive telling . . . I have taken with me stuffed animals for each character. After the story has become thoroughly familiar to the children, the stuffed hen, dog, cat, and rat are given to individual children. I continue to "tell" or narrate the story, but when each character speaks, the child who is holding the hen, or dog, or cat, or rat, speaks that character's words. Holding the animals seems to give the children a sense of security and authority.

In early childhood, many repetitions of the story may be necessary before children remember individual character's lines.

THE LITTLE HOUSE WITH NO DOORS AND NO WINDOWS AND A STAR INSIDE

Author Unknown

(Plan to have an apple, cutting board, and a knife ready for the ending. A plate full of apple slices is sometimes enjoyed after this story.)

Once there was a little boy who had played almost all day. He had played with all his toys and all the games he knew, and he could not think of anything else to do. So he went to his mother and asked, "Mother, what shall I do now?"

His mother said, "I know about a little red house with no doors and no windows and a star inside. You can find it, if you go look for it."

So the little boy went outside and there he met a little girl. He said, "Do you know where there is a little red house with no doors and no windows and a star inside?"

The little girl said, "No, I don't know where there is a little red house with no doors and no windows and a star inside, but you can ask my daddy. He is a farmer and he knows lots of things. He's down by the barn and maybe he can help you."

So the little boy went to the farmer down by the barn and said, "Do you know where there is a little red house with no doors and no windows and a star inside?"

"No," said the farmer, "I don't know, but why don't you ask Grandmother. She is in her house up on the hill. She is very wise and knows many things. Maybe she can help you."

So the little boy went up the hill to Grandmother's and asked, "Do you know where there is a little red house with no doors and no windows and a star inside?" "No," said Grandmother, "I don't know, but you ask the wind, for the wind goes everywhere, and I am sure he can help you."

So the little boy went outside and asked the wind, "Do you know where I can find a little red house with no doors and no windows and a star inside?" And the wind said, "OHHHH! OOOOOOOOOOOO!" And it sounded to the little boy as if the wind said, "Come with me." So the little boy ran after the wind. He ran through the grass and into the orchard and there on the ground he found the little house—the little red house with no doors and no windows and a star inside! He picked it up, and it filled both his hands. He ran home to his mother and said, "Look, Mother! I found the little red house with no doors and no windows, but I cannot see the star!"

So this is what his mother did (teacher cuts apple). "Now I see the star!" said the little boy. (Teacher says to children) "Do you?"

THE PANCAKE WHO RAN AWAY

(a folktale)

Once upon a time there was a mother who had seven hungry children. She made a delicious light and fluffy golden pancake.

"I'm hungry," said one child. "I want some pancake."

Then all the other children said the same thing, and the mother had to cover her ears because they were so loud.

"Hush, shush!" said the mother. "You can all have some as soon as the pancake is golden brown on both sides."

Now the pancake was listening and did not want to be eaten, so it hopped from the pan and rolled out the door and down the hill.

"Stop, pancake!" called the mother. She and all her children ran after the pancake as fast as they could. The pancake rolled on and on.

When it rolled a long way, it met a man.

"Good morning, pancake," said the man.

"Good morning Mandy-Pandy-Man!" said the pancake.

"Don't roll so fast. Stop and let me eat you," said the man.

"I've run away from the mother and seven hungry children and I'll run away from you Mandy-Pandy-Man." It rolled and rolled down the road until it met a hen clucking and hurrying along.

"Good morning, pancake," said the hen.

"The same to you, Henny-Fenny-Hen."

"Pancake don't roll so fast, stop and let me eat you," said the hen.

"No, no," said the pancake. "I've run away from the mother and the seven hungry children, Mandy-Pandy-Man, and I'll run away from you." And it rolled on and on.

It met a rooster.

"Good morning, pancake," said the rooster.

"The same to you, Rooster-Zooster," said the pancake.

"Stop so I can eat you," said the rooster.

"I've run away from the mother and the seven hungry children, Mandy-Pandy-Man, Henny-Fenny-Hen, and I'll run away from you," said the pancake. And it rolled on and on until it met a duck.

"Good morning, pancake," said the duck.

"The same to you, Quacky Duck," said the pancake.

"Stop so I can eat you," said the duck.

"I've run away from the mother and the seven hungry children, Mandy-Pandy-Man, Henny-Fenny-Hen, Rooster-Zooster, and I'll run away from you," said the pancake. And on and on it rolled until it met a goose.

"Good morning, pancake," said the goose.

"The same to you, Goosey-Loosey," said the pancake.

"Stop so I can eat you," said the goose.

"I've run away from the mother and the seven hungry children, Mandy-Pandy-Man, Henny-Fenny-Hen, Rooster-Zooster, Quacky Duck, and I'll run away from you."

And on and on it rolled until it met a pig at the edge of a dark wood.

"Good morning, pancake," said the pig.

"The same to you Piggy-Wiggy," said the pancake.

"That wood is dark, don't be in such a hurry! We can go through the wood together. It's not safe in there," said the pig.

The pancake thought that was a good idea, so they went along together until they came to a river. The pig was so fat he could float across, but the pancake had no way of crossing.

"Jump on my snout," said the pig, "and I'll carry you across." So the pancake did that. "Oink!" said the pig as he opened his mouth wide and swallowed the pancake in one gulp. And that's how it was . . . pancakes are for eating, and the pig had his breakfast.

IT WAS MY IDEA

One winter two snow geese were on their way south flying high in the sky. They looked down and saw a beautiful lake. They were tired and hungry, so they landed together, splashing across the sparkling water. There were seeds and bugs everywhere, and they ate their fill. A talkative turtle poked his head up from the water, and talked, and talked, and talked. "We'll get no rest here," said one goose to the other. The turtle overheard, and said, "I want to see the world. Take me with you. Will you? Will you? Will you?" The geese laughed. "Now, how can we take you with us?" they said. "I'll get a stick. If you both hold it in you beaks, I can clamp down on in the middle with my strong snapping mouth," explained the turtle. "It won't work turtle, you couldn't stop talking that long," laughed a goose. The turtle talked, and talked, and talked. Finally, the geese said, "Yes," just to shut him up. The three took off together with turtle biting the stick and hanging between them. Soon they flew over a farm. A farmer in the field looked up. He had never seen such a sight. He called to his wife, "Look at those clever birds, aren't they smart?" Turtle called back as he fell from the sky, "It was my idea." Turtle was very lucky to fall into a giant haystack. He was happy and ready to start a new adventure on the farm.

(This is a "bare bones" version of this tale. The author suggests you embellish it by adding descriptive words and developing further characterization. Invoke color and use sounds. Add details suiting your own personal style.)

A LUMP THE SHAPE OF A HUMP

Maxwell woke up one bright morning and saw a brown bird walking on his window sill, and that's not ALL he saw! There was a lump the shape of a hump under the covers at the foot of his bed. Maxwell squeezed against the headboard, folded up his knees, and stared at the lump the shape of a hump. It's Bellflower the Beagle, my dog, Maxwell thought, but Bellflower bounded into the bedroom and barked at the lump the shape of a hump at the foot of the bed. It's Tootie, my brother, he thought, but Tootie came into the bedroom and blew his horn, toot-toot at the lump the shape of a hump at the foot of the bed. "Must be Bubbles, my baby sister," Maxwell said to himself, but just then Bubbles crawled into his room. Maybe it's Toady, my best friend, Maxwell thought, but then he remembered Toady (who was called Toady because he loved to play leapfrog) had gone to visit his grandmother. "What's that lump the shape of a hump?" Maxwell's dad said as he walked into the bedroom. "I think it's my pillow," Maxwell said, but they both saw Maxwell's pillow on the floor. "My teddy?" Maxwell said. "Nope," said Maxwell's dad, "Teddy's sitting over there in the chair."

Just then the lump wiggled. It shook from side to side. Tootie blew his horn. Bellflower barked. Maxwell squeezed against the headboard afraid to move. "There is something strange going on here!" Maxwell's dad said.

Then the lump made a sound like a croak. Maxwell grabbed the covers and pulled and pulled. There was Toady all doubled up ready to play leapfrog, and he was laughing and croaking. "Grandma was sick, so I sneaked into your bed," Toady said. "Let's play leapfrog!" So they did. Maxwell, Tootie, Bellflower, and Toady played leapfrog while Dad and Bubbles watched.

PARTICIPATION STORIES

Just Like Metoo!

(Children imitate what Metoo does. Metoo does things a little faster each day. Metoo was always late for school. Speedee was always on time.)

Once upon a time, Metoo came to live at Speedee's house. He thought, "I'd like to do what Speedee does, but I can't learn everything at one time. Each day I'll do one new thing."

On Monday, when the alarm went off, Metoo jumped out of bed just like Speedee and washed his hands and face at 7:30 in the morning. (Jump up, wash hands and face, sit down.)

On Tuesday, when the alarm went off, Metoo jumped out of bed and washed his hands and face and brushed his teeth at 7:30 in the morning. (Jump up, wash hands and face, brush teeth, sit down.)

On Wednesday, when the alarm went off, Metoo jumped out of bed just like Speedee and washed his hands and face, brushed his teeth, and dressed himself at 7:30 in the morning. (Jump up, wash hands and face, brush teeth, dress self, sit down.)

On Thursday, when the alarm went off, Metoo jumped out of bed just like Speedee, washed his hands and face, brushed his teeth, dressed himself, and ate his breakfast at 7:30 in the morning. (Jump up, wash hands and face, brush teeth, dress self, eat breakfast, sit down.)

On Friday, when the alarm went off, Metoo jumped out of bed, just like Speedee, washed his hands and face, brushed his teeth, dressed himself, ate his breakfast, and waved goodbye to Speedee's mother who was on her way to work at 7:30 in the morning. (Very rapidly, jump up, wash hands and face, brush teeth, dress self, eat breakfast, wave goodbye, sit down.) Speedee and Metoo walked to school together. Metoo wasn't late for school!

On Saturday, when the alarm went off, Metoo turned over and shut it off. (Move right arm across body slowly, as if shutting off alarm.) He had heard Speedee say, "This is Saturday. Nobody goes to school on Saturday."

To Grandmother's House

(Before beginning this story, draw the picture in Figure 10–11 on the chalkboard or on a large sheet of paper. During the telling let your finger show Clementine's travels.)

One day Clementine's mother said, "I'm making cookies. I need some sugar. Please go to Grandma's house and borrow

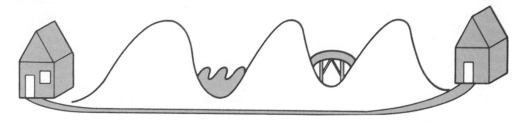

FIGURE 10–11 Clementine's travels.

a cup of sugar." "Yes, Mother, I'll go right away," said Clementine.

Clementine climbed up the first mountain. Climb, climb, climb. (Make climbing motions with arms.) Climb, climb, climb.

When she got to the top of the mountain she slid down. (Make sliding motion with hands.)

At the bottom of the mountain was a wide, wide lake. Clementine jumped in and swam across. Swim, swim, swim. (Make swimming arm motions.)

Clementine climbed the next mountain. Climb, climb, climb. (Make climbing hand motions.) Then she slid down the other side. (Make sliding motions.)

Next, Clementine crossed the bridge. Tromp, tromp, tromp. (Make feet move up and down.) Tromp, tromp, tromp.

Clementine climbed the third mountain. Climb, climb, climb (motions). Then she slid down the other side (motions).

Clementine's grandmother was standing next to her house. "Hello, Grandmother, may I have a cup of sugar? My mother's making cookies." "Yes, dear," said Grandmother, and she came out of the house with a little bag.

"Goodbye, Grandmother," Clementine said. Climb, climb, climb. She slid down the other side and crossed the bridge. Tromp, tromp, tromp. She climbed the middle mountain. Climb, climb, climb (motions). Then she slid down the other side (motions). She swam the lake with the bag in her teeth and her head held high. Swim, swim, swim (motions). Next, she climbed the mountain. Climb, climb, climb (motions). Then she slid down the mountain (motions) to her house.

When she went into the house, she gave her mother the sugar. Her mother said, "This is brown sugar. I wanted white sugar." "I'll go to Grandmother's," said Clementine.

Clementine climbed the first mountain. Climb, climb, climb (motions). She

slid down the other side (motions). Then she swam the lake. Swim, swim, swim (motions).

She climbed the second mountain. Climb, climb, climb (motions). She slid down the other side (motions) and crossed the bridge. Tromp, tromp, tromp (motions).

She climbed the third mountain. Climb, climb, climb (motions). Then she slid down the other side (motions).

Grandmother was working in her garden. "Hello, Grandmother," said Clementine. "Two visits in one day. How nice," said Grandmother.

"But I can't stay this time either. Mother needs white sugar instead of brown," said Clementine.

Grandmother went into her house and came out with a little bag.

"You look so tired, Clementine!" said Grandmother.

"I am," said Clementine.

"Take the shortcut home," said Grandmother.

So Clementine did. She walked straight home on the path at the foot of the mountains.

This story can be lengthened by having the mother request additional ingredients and by Clementine taking cookies to Grandmother after they are baked. White or wheat flour is another possibility, as is raisins or nuts.

WHAT WAS BEHIND THE DOOR?

Dog—"Bow Wow"   Bird—"Peep Peep"
Cat—"Meow"   Lion—"Grrrr"

(Teacher says the following to children: "I need you to help me tell this story! Do you suppose that you can remember all of the sounds that we have talked about? In this story, you can make the animal noises that Granny hears. When the story says, Granny heard a dog, say, 'Bow Wow!' (and so on). Listen carefully."

Granny sat in a big armchair knitting Tommy a sweater. All of a sudden she heard a dog say "..." (Bow Wow).

"Gracious!" said Granny. "I do believe there's a dog behind the door. Should I have a dog in the house?"

"Oh yes," answered the dog behind the door. "I'm a good dog. I don't jump on people."

"Very well," said Granny, and she went on knitting the sweater for Tommy. All of a sudden Granny heard a cat say "..." (Meow).

"Gracious!" said Granny. "I do believe that there is a cat behind the door. Should I have a cat in the house?"

"Oh yes," answered the cat. "I am a good cat. I do not scratch the furniture."

"Very well," said Granny, and she went on knitting Tommy's sweater. All of a sudden Granny heard a bird say "..." (Peep Peep).

"Gracious!" said Granny. "I do believe that I heard a bird behind the door. Should I have a bird in the house?"

"Oh yes," answered the bird. "I am a good bird. I sing very sweetly."

"Very well," said Granny, and she went right on knitting a sweater for Tommy.

All of a sudden, Granny heard a lion say "..." (Grrrr).

"Gracious!" said Granny. "I do believe that there is a lion behind the door. This is too much!" Carefully, Granny opened the door, because she wasn't sure she liked having a lion in the house.

And what do you think she found hiding behind her door? There was Tommy. He had been making those noises after all!

Suggest: "Can you all make the noises Tommy made?"

    Dog   = Bow Wow
    Cat   = Meow
    Bird = Peep Peep
    Lion = Grrrr

"What other animal sounds do you know?"

LITTLE DUCK LOST

(full of sounds and action)

Cow—"Moo Moo"
Cat—"Meow Meow"
Duck—"Quack Quack"
Horse—"Neigh Neigh"
Pig—"Oink Oink"
Mouse—"Squeak Squeak"
Dog—"Bow Wow"
Rooster—"Cock-a-doodle-do"

The animals on the farm were noisy one morning. The rooster (Cock-a-doodle-do) was crowing. The cow (Moo Moo) was mooing. The dog (Bow Wow) was barking, and the cat (Meow Meow) was meowing. Everybody was looking for Little Duck (Quack Quack). Little Duck (Quack Quack) was gone. The cow (Moo Moo) looked all through the sweet clover in the pasture but no Little Duck (Quack Quack). The horse (Neigh Neigh) galloped into the next field, but no Little Duck (Quack Quack). The fat, fat pig (Oink Oink) pushed all the mud out of his puddle. He could not find Little Duck (Quack Quack).

Then the animals hurried down to the pond once more to look for Little Duck (Quack Quack). They all called him. (Everybody calls "Little Duck.") There was no Little Duck (Quack Quack). The animals were quiet as they walked back to the barn. They had looked everywhere, but could not find Little Duck (Quack Quack).

Suddenly, a little mouse (Squeak Squeak) came scurrying out of the barn. How he squeaked! He led the animals back into the barn and over to his nest in a quiet corner and there was Little Duck (Quack Quack) asleep on the mouse's (Squeak Squeak) nest. What a shout the animals gave! (Everybody calls "Wake up!") They had found Little Duck (Quack Quack). They woke him with their shouting. Little Duck (Quack Quack) was rushed back to the duck pond, where, after all, little ducks (Quack Quack) belong.

CHAPTER 11

Poetry

OBJECTIVES

After reading this chapter, you should be able to:

◆ Discuss poetry elements.

◆ Demonstrate the ability to present a poem.

◆ Create a poem with features that appeal to young children.

KEY TERMS

alliteration	figurative	personification
assonance	language	poems
couplets	metaphors	similes
diction	nursery rhymes	verses

FRECKLES

I notice Yolanda staring at my arm one day. She was new and had moved here from Arizona. She asked, "What are those?" It was summer, and my freckles really stood out. "They are called freckles," I said. She answered, "Have you tried to get them off?" I replied, "I tried buttermilk one time because someone told me buttermilk would make them go away. But it didn't work." She thought about that for a moment and said, "Have you tried soap and water?" I laughed, and told her that soap and water didn't work either. Later that day, Yolanda walked by saying, "Sprinkles, speckles, freckles," while smiling up at me. "That's a rhyme, Yolanda," I answered.

QUESTIONS TO PONDER

1. What do you think about Yolanda's logic?

2. Would freckles or Yolanda's created rhyme be something to talk about with children at a sharing time?

3. Were the teacher's verbal responses appropriate?

350

Children's poetry is an enjoyable vehicle for developing listening skills. Activities that involve poetry hold many opportunities to promote language and literacy by associating pleasure with words. Poetry has a condensed quality that makes every word important. It prompts imagery through its sensory descriptions and can introduce enchanting tales. Nonsense verse appeals to the preschoolers' appreciation for slapstick.

Glazer and Burke (1994) believe

> The repetitive format of rhymes makes them "rote-able." Repetition is a strategy for learning with pleasure. Expectancies are set up and gloriously materialize. The desire to hear more is intensified.

> The language of rhyme becomes easily fixed in memory; it can become part of a child's linguistic and intellectual resources for life.

Poetry is a perfect test for what language can do; it is full of word play. Poets have always used language in special ways, and in poetry, we have a vehicle for looking at the use of words, that is, the choosing of the one special word that fits perfectly (Booth, 1999).

We need to share with children words "that taste good"—that tickle the tongue, tease the ear, create images in the minds's eye, delight us with their trickery, and amuse us with their puzzles and complexities (Moore, 1985).

Appropriate children's poetry is plentiful and varied. In addition to fast action and mood building, there is the joy of the rhythm of the words in many **poems**. Some rhythms in classic rhymes are so strong that they can motivate children to move their bodies or clap. The nursery rhymes "Jack and Jill," "Twinkle, Twinkle, Little Star," and "The Little Turtle" are good examples. Norton (1983) notes that "Rhythm encourages children to join in orally, experiment with language, and move to the rhythmical sounds." Some poems appeal to the emotions; others, to the intellect (Figure 11–1).

FIGURE 11–1 Poetry can hold a child's attention.

A preschool child with beginning literacy might be described as a child familiar with Mother Goose rhymes and other contemporary and classic poems, and one who knows rhyming words sound alike. Three-year-olds delight in silly and playful poetry (Miller, 2001).

LEARNING OPPORTUNITIES

Poetry provides an opportunity for a child to learn new words, ideas, and attitudes and to experience life through the eyes of the poet. To remember how many days there are in a month, many people still recite a simple poem learned as a child. If you are asked to say the alphabet, the classic ABC song of childhood may come to mind.

Poetry has form and order. It is dependable and also easy to learn. Simple rhymes are picked up quickly, as most parents have seen

---

poems — metrical forms of composition in which word images are selected and expressed to create powerful, often beautiful impressions in the listener and/or enjoyable rhymic responses in young children.

from their children's ability to remember television commercials. Children in early childhood centers enjoy the accomplishment of memorizing short **verses**. They may ask to share the poems they have learned with the teacher, just as they ask to sing songs they know (which are often poems set to music).

The teacher should provide encouragement, attention, and positive comments to the child who responds to poetry. As with picture-book reading, storytelling, and other language activities, the goal of the teacher in regard to poetry is to offer children pleasure and enjoyment of the language arts while expanding their knowledge and interest.

Poetry, then, is used for a variety of reasons, including the following.

- familiarizing and exposing children to classic and contemporary poetry that is considered part of our literary heritage
- training children to experience the pleasure of hearing sounds
- providing enjoyment through the use of poems with silly words and humor
- stimulating children's imaginations
- increasing vocabulary and knowledge
- building self-worth and self-confidence
- encouraging an understanding of rhyming

POETRY AND EARLY READING ABILITY

Poems, rhymes, and chants acquaint young children with language in repeated pleasant patterns and with catchy rhythms, such as "The Grand Old Duke of York." Drop the words in this rhyming chant (found in Chapter 14). Use *da-Da, da-Da, da-Da*, etc., and see how easy it is to isolate and sense the accented words and syllables. Acredolo and Goodwyn (2000) point out that rhyming words teach a child that different words can share some of the same sounds.

Experts believe children's ability to discriminate, create rhyming words, and sense the rhythm of words is closely related to early reading ability (Healy, 1990).

Goswani (2002) informs educators that a great deal of general evidence indicates that both early awareness of rhyme and nursery rhyme knowledge facilitate literacy acquisition. It is a significant predictor of later progress in reading and spelling. Chaney (1992) reports a relationship between early rhyme awareness and later phonological skills. Other researchers, including Baker, Fernandez-Fein, Scher, and Williams (1998), believe nursery rhyme knowledge is a strong predictor of word attack and word identification skills when children begin early reading. The connection between rhyme awareness and the child's subsequent acquisition of literacy-related skill demonstrates that a developmental pathway to reading involves rhyme (Goswani, 2002). Repetition of consonant sounds in the lyrics of **nursery rhymes** like "cock-a-doodle-doo, dee-doodle-dee doodle-dee doodle-dee-doo" certainly demonstrates rhyme and **alliteration**.

Children develop skill in identifying rhyme at an early age. The relationship between rime units and words that rhyme is obvious: words that rhyme share the same rime unit (Peterson & Haines, 1998). Refer back to the discussion of phonemic awareness and rimes in Chapter 8. Bryant, Bradley, MacLean, and Crossland (1989) note that children's knowledge of nursery rhymes predicted their success in spelling 2 to 3 years later.

SELECTION

Poetry introduces children to characters with fun-to-say names such as

Jonathan Bing by Beatrice Curtis Brown
Mrs. Peck Pigeon by Eleanor Farjeon
Godfrey Gordon Gustavos Gore by William Rands

verses — lines of a poem or poetry without imaginative or conceptual power.
nursery rhymes — folk sayings with rhyming words for very young children.
alliteration — repetition of beginning consonant sounds.

The characters can live in familiar and far-fetched settings.

> under the toadstool, from *The Elf and the Dormouse* by Oliver Herford
>
> straight to the animal store, from *The Animal Store* by Rachel Field
>
> in a little crooked house, from Mother Goose

And they have various adventures and difficulties.

> "The kids are ten feet tall," from *Grown-Up-Down Town* by Bobbi Katz
>
> "Christopher Robin had wheezles and sneezles," from *Sneezles* by A. A. Milne
>
> "Listen, my children, this must be stopped," from *The Grasshoppers* by Dorothy Aldis

Teachers select poetry that they can present eagerly and that they believe children will like. Delight in words is a natural outcome when the poem suits the audience. Teachers look for poems of quality and merit. Three elements exist in good poetry: *distinguished* **diction**, *carefully chosen words and phrases* with rich sensory and associated meanings, and *significant content*. Much of classic poetry has a song quality and a melody of its own. Poetry can say something to children, titillate them, recall happy occasions or events, or encourage them to explore.

Geller (1985), working with three-year-olds, found traditional eighteenth-century nursery rhymes still popular with today's children. Favorite rhymes with strong four-beat **couplets** ("Humpty Dumpty" and others) were repeated with the teacher exaggerating the beat (as children do). This technique held group interest.

Categories of verse popular with most preschoolers have one or more of the following characteristics (Geller, 1985).

1. simple story line ("Jack Be Nimble")
2. simple story line with finger play ("This Little Piggy")
3. story in song with repeated chorus ("London Bridge")
4. verse/story with nonsense words ("Hey, Diddle, Diddle")
5. descriptions of daily actions ("Little Jack Horner")
6. choral reading in which youngsters could join in with rhymed words ("To Market, to Market")

No child should miss the fun, wit, and wisdom of Mother Goose. Literacy, in part, depends on a child's exposure to cultural tradition. Mother Goose is an American tradition. Make a list of Mother Goose characters. You will be surprised at how many you remember.

Galda (1989) shares poetry selection criteria in the following.

> . . . begin with poems which are sure to please: poems which have strong rhythm and rhyme, poems which play with sound, poems which are humorous, tell stories, and are about children and the things that make up their lives. . . . Once children have been bitten by the poetry bug, . . . focus on rhythm and rhyme, and explore how various poets use sound devices such as alliteration or onomatopoeia.

Types of Poetry

Types of poetry are described as follows:

lyric	melodic, descriptive poetry that often has a song quality
narrative	poetry that tells a story or describes an event or happening
limerick	a poem with five lines of verse set in a specific rhyming pattern that is usually humorous
free verse	poetry that does not rhyme
nonsense	poetry that is often ridiculous and whimsical (Figure 11–2)

diction — clarity of speech; enunciation.
couplets — stanzas of two rhyming lines.

"What's did you do?" said the shoe.

"I sat on the hog," answered the dog.

"Is he dead?" asked the bread.

"That is not funny!" said the bunny.

"Is that a hat?" said the cat

"No, it is not," replied the clock.

"Well, what is it then?" asked the hen.

"Stop. This poem is too silly!" said Uncle Willy.

FIGURE 11–2 A whimsical poem.

POETRY ELEMENTS

A particular poem's rhythm is influenced by sounds, stress, pitch, and accented and unaccented syllables. Manipulation of one or all of these features creates a particular idea, feeling, or message. Some rhythms are regular; others are not. The enjoyable quality of the Mother Goose rhymes stems from their strong rhythm and cadence. In poetry, authors use rhythm to emphasize words or phrases, consequently capturing children's immediate attention. Exciting, dramatic rhythms and relaxed, soothing rhythms can be included in the same poem. Poetry's rhythm is capable of making children feel that they are actively participating rather than merely listening.

Children's literature is full of rhyming words and rhyming names. Poetic rhyme can occur within sentences or at line endings. Children often rhyme on their own, spontaneously, during play (Figure 11–3). Nonsense rhymes have given joy to generations of children; sayings like stomper-chomper, icky-sticky, and Dan, Dan, elephant man, can spread immediately among children.

Alliteration (defined as the occurrence of two or more words having the same initial sounds, **assonance**, or vowel sounds) is often used in poetry. All types of repetition are characteristic of children's poetry.

Visual images are stimulated by the poet's use of sensory words and **figurative language** (nonliteral meanings). A poet may provide a new way of looking at things by comparing previously unconnected objects or events. **Similes** (direct comparisons between two things that have something in common but are essentially different) or **metaphors** (implied comparisons between two things that have something in common but are essentially different) are often found in poetry. Giving human characteristics and emotions to inanimate objects and animals

assonance — the repetition of words of identical or similar vowel sounds followed by different consonant sounds.
figurative language — language enriched by word images and figures of speech.
similes — comparisons of two things that are unlike, usually using the words *like* or *as*. Example: "Love is like a red, red rose."
metaphors — figures of speech in which a comparison is implied by analogy but is not stated.

FIGURE 11–3 Darren created the rhyme "High in the sky" during this activity.

(**personification**) is also commonplace, and talking dishes, trains, birds, bears, and pancakes are plentiful in children's poems.

The format of printed poetry (type size and style, page layout, punctuation, and capitalization) has been used to heighten enjoyment and highlight the subject matter. One can find poems printed in the shape of a tree or in one-word, long, narrow columns.

TEACHER TECHNIQUES

If a poem is read or recited in a conversational manner, rather than in a sing-song fashion, the rhyme is subtle and enjoyable. Sing-song reading and recitation may become tiresome and difficult to understand.

Most teachers know that reciting from memory requires practice, so the poems they memorize are a few favorites. However, memorization can create a mechanical quality, as the teacher focuses on remembering rather than enjoyment.

Often, poetry is shared through teacher readings from lap cards. A poem should be read smoothly without uncalled-for hesitation. This means the teacher has to prepare by reading the poem enough times for it to roll off the tongue with ease, savoring the words in the telling.

The enjoyment of poetry, like other types of literature, can be increased by an enthusiastic adult. Glazer (1986) suggests a careful reading of poetry because of poetry's compactness, making every word count.

When encouraging children to join in and speak favorite poetry lines, sensitive handling is in order. A teacher can suggest, "Let's say it together" or "Join me in saying this poem if you like." A child should not be singled out or asked to recite without volunteering. Some gregarious children will want to share poems they have learned. A number of repetitions of a favorite verse may be needed before it is totally remembered. Children usually start with a few words or phrases.

Stewig (1977) offers the following preparatory tips.

> . . . give careful attention not only to pitch and stress, but most importantly to juncture. That is, where we make the breaks in poetry will make or break our presentation. The natural tendency is to break at the end of the printed line. In poetry, this may lead to artificial segmenting, not intended by the poet.

Look at Figure 11–4. Read the first two lines as one sentence without pausing at the word *tree*. Now, read the poem stopping at each line's end and you'll see what Stewig means.

A technique that works well for "a change of pace" is suggested by the work of John Kinderman Taylor (1993). Background music without lyrics but with a strong repeated beat is used as a backdrop for poems or teacher-created rhymed lines. The result is chantlike or raplike and promotes children's joining in and at times also clapping.

---

personification — a metaphorical figure of speech in which animals, ideas, things, etc., are represented as having human qualities.

I am a pine tree
growing on a hill.
I can stand so very,
very still. All at
once the wind
begins to blow.
I bend to and fro,
to and fro, to and fro.

FIGURE 11–4 A rhyming chart.

A POETRY CHART

Be gentle Turn pages slow I don't want to Rip you know! 　　　　by Ashad	Sticky hands Make a mess When I'm clean I look my best. 　　　　by Carla
I fall apart In the rain Pages crinkle It's a pain! 　　　　by Ling	My printed words Will make you laugh This book's about A funny giraffe. 　　　　by Hensie
If after you hold me You put me back Others will find me On the book rack. 　　　　by Rena	Don't walk away I'm lonely today Look at me Before you play. 　　　　by Lori
Inside my cover A story hides Pick me up And look inside. 　　　　by Juan	When you hold me In your hands And turn my pages I feel grand. 　　　　by Omar
If you've never Been to the zoo Animals inside Might frighten you. 　　　　by Sierra	I'm not safe On the floor Where feet kick And make me sore. 　　　　by Bradford

FIGURE 11–5 If books could talk, what would they say?

Poetry charts hanging on a chart stand next to the teacher are a helpful device for capturing attention and freeing a teacher's eyes to meet those of the children. When reading from a chart, quickly glance at a line and then turn so that the words are transmitted to the children. The elementary school poetry chart in Figure 11–5 was posted near the storage of classroom books. Children were encouraged to think of other things a book might say about book care and handling. The teacher wrote these child thoughts and posted them at the chart's bottom and identified them with the child's name.

Young children sometimes create their own rhymes. The teacher can jot them down for display or to be taken home by the children. "Amber, pamber, big fat bamber," created by a child, may interest other children, and the teacher who has recorded it might share it at group time as a rhyme created by a playmate.

Poems dictated by children should be recorded verbatim, with no editing or teacher suggestions. Each creation is regarded as special. Lionni's *Frederick*, a wonderful picture book, helps children understand rhyming. This book's last two lines read

"But Frederick," they said, "you are a poet!"

Frederick blushed, took a bow, and said shyly, "I know it."

Ways to Introduce Children to Poetry

Posting poems in conspicuous places may help create interest, particularly if pictures or illustrations are placed adjacent to the poems. A poetry tree, made by placing a smooth tree limb in plaster of Paris, can have paper leaves with poems on the back that can be selected at group times. A poem of the day (or week) bulletin board has worked well in some classrooms.

Pictures and flannel boards can be used in poetry presentation to interest and help children focus on words. Other props or costumes that relate to the poem (such as a teddy bear or police officer's hat) will gain attention. Some of the best collections of poems have no pictures; others have an illustration for each poem.

A poem can be enjoyed indoors or outdoors, or between activities as a "fill-in" when the teacher or children are waiting.

Mounting cut magazine pictures and trying to think up words that rhyme with what is pictured is a rhyming activity many teachers favor. For example, "Here's a cake, let's give it to . . ."

Nursery songs emphasize rhyme, rhythm, alliteration, and playful enjoyment. Their predictability delights, and children acquire an immediate sense of accomplishment when they join in with words or movement. Classic rhyming nursery songs are listed in Figure 11–6.

OLD CLASSICS

"Here We Go 'Round The Mulberry Bush"
"London Bridge Is Falling Down"
"Rock-a-Bye Baby"
"Row, Row, Row Your Boat"
"Sing a Song of Sixpence"
"Three Blind Mice"
"Twinkle, Twinkle Little Star"
"I'm a Little Teapot"
"Pop Goes the Weasel"

NEW CLASSICS

"You Are My Sunshine"
"Take Me out to the Ball Game"
"Blue-Tailed Fly"

FIGURE 11–6 Nursery songs—old and new classics.

SOURCES

A fine line divides finger plays, body and movement games, chants, songs, and poems. All can involve rhyme and rhythm. Poetry given later in this chapter is primarily the type that children would merely listen to as it is being recited, although some do contain opportunities for child participation.

Many fine picture books contain rhymed verse and can enhance a center's poetry program. Collections, anthologies, and books of children's poetry are available at the public library, bookstores, and school supply stores, as well as in children's and teachers' magazines.

Teachers also can create poetry from their own experiences. The following suggestions for creating poems for young children help the teacher-poet by pointing out the special features found in older classics and quality contemporary poetry.

◆ Include mental images in every line.
◆ Use strong rhythms that bring out an urge to chant, move, or sing.
◆ Use frequent rhyming.
◆ Use action verbs often.
◆ Make each line an independent thought.
◆ Change the rhythm.
◆ Use words that are within the children's level of understanding.
◆ Use themes and subjects that are familiar to the young child.

Teacher-created poems promote child-created poems.

Many teachers search for ethnic poems that allow them to offer multicultural variety. Jenkins (1973) points out

No one cultural group has a corner on imagination, creativity, poetic quality, or philosophic outlook. Each has made important contributions to the total culture of the country and the world.

Recalling the poems and verses of one's own childhood may lead a teacher to research poems by a particular poet. Remembering appealing poetry elements may also help a teacher find poetry that may delight today's young child. Volumes and poetry collections are cited in the Additional Resources section at the end of this chapter.

SUGGESTED POEMS

The poems that follow are examples of the type that appeal to young children.

IF I WERE AN APPLE

If I were an apple
  And grew on a tree,
I think I'd drop down
  On a nice boy like me.
I wouldn't stay there
  Giving nobody joy;
I'd fall down at once
  And say, "Eat me, my boy!"

Old Rhyme

BUTTONS

Buttons on a sweater,
Buttons on a skirt,
Buttons on a dress,
Buttons on a shirt,
Buttons on pajamas,
Buttons on a gown,
Buttons that I button up,
Or I button down,
Buttons that are hidden,
Buttons right in sight,
Buttons that are red and blue,
Yellow, green, or white,
Buttons made of leather,
Buttons made of glass,
Buttons made of bits of wood,
Buttons made of brass,
Buttons, lots of buttons,
Buttons big and small,
Buttons with two eyes or more,
Or no eyes at all.
"You're cuter than a button,"
My Aunt Sue said to me.
Just what button does she mean?
Which one could it be?

Anita E. Posey

ANIMAL CRACKERS

Animal crackers, and cocoa to drink,
That is the finest of suppers, I think;
When I'm grown up and can have what I
  please
I think I shall always insist upon these.

What do you choose when you're offered a
  treat?
When Mother says, "What would you like
  best to eat?"

Is it waffles and syrup, or cinnamon toast?
It's cocoa and animals that I love the most!

The kitchen's the coziest place that I know:
The kettle is singing, the stove is aglow,
And there in the twilight, how jolly to see
The cocoa and animals waiting for me.

Daddy and Mother dine later in state,
With Mary to cook for them, Susan to wait;
But they don't have nearly as much fun as I
Who eat in the kitchen with Nurse standing
  by:
Having cocoa and animals once more for
  tea!

"Animal Crackers," © 1917, 1945 by Christopher Morley. From *Chimneysmoke* by Christopher Morley. Reprinted by permission of Harper and Row Publishers, Inc.

ONE STORMY NIGHT

Two little kittens,
  One stormy night
Began to quarrel,
  And then to fight.

One had a mouse,
  The other had none;
And that's the way
  The quarrel begun.

"I'll have that mouse,"
  Said the bigger cat.
"You'll have that mouse?
  We'll see about that!"

"I will have that mouse,"
  Said the eldest son.
"You shan't have the mouse,"
  Said the little one.

The old woman seized
  Her sweeping broom,
And swept both kittens
  Right out of the room.

The ground was covered
With frost and snow,
And the two little kittens
Had nowhere to go.

They lay and shivered
On a mat at the door,
While the old woman
Was sweeping the floor.

And then they crept in
As quiet as mice,
All wet with the snow,
And as cold as ice.

And found it much better
That stormy night,
To lie by the fire,
Than to quarrel and fight.

Traditional

WHISKY FRISKY

Whisky frisky,
Hipperty hop,
Up he goes
To the tree top!

Whirly, twirly,
Round and round,
Down he scampers
To the ground.

Furly, curly,
What a tail,
Tall as a feather,
Broad as a sail.

Where's his supper?
In the shell.
Snappy, cracky,
Out it fell.

Anonymous

TO MARKET

To market, to market,
To buy a fat pig,
Home again, home again,
Jiggety jig.
To market, to market,
To buy a fat hog,
Home again, home again,
Jiggety jog.
To market, to market,

To buy a plum bun,
Home again, home again,
Market is done.

Mother Goose

SECRETS

Can you keep a secret?
I don't suppose you can,
You mustn't laugh or giggle
While I tickle your hand.

Anonymous

OLIVER TWIST

Oliver-Oliver-Oliver Twist
Bet you a penny you can't do this:
Number one—touch your tongue
Number two—touch your shoe
Number three—touch your knee
Number four—touch the floor
Number five—take a dive
Number six—wiggle your hips
Number seven—say number eleven
Number eight—bang the gate
Number nine—walk the line
Number ten—start again.

Traditional

RAINDROPS

"Splash," said a raindrop
As it fell upon my hat;

"Splash," said another
As it trickled down my back.

"You are very rude," I said
As I looked up to the sky;

Then another raindrop splashed
Right into my eye!

Anonymous

PRETENDING

I'd like to be a jumping jack
And jump out from a box!
I'd like to be a rocking horse
And rock and rock and rock.
I'd like to be a spinning top

And twirl around and round.
I'd like to be a rubber ball
And bounce way up and down.

I'd like to be a big fast train
Whose wheels fly round and round.
I'd like to be a pony small
And trot along the ground.
I'd like to be so many things
A growly scowly bear.
But really I'm a little child
Who sits upon a chair.

Anonymous

SLOW TURTLE, FAST RABBIT

Turtle and Rabbit went walking each day.
They moved along in the funniest way.
Turtle talked s-l-o-w-l-y but he listened
    well.
Rabbit hopped fast and had much to tell.
He hopped in circles around turtle slow.
He talked and talked about all he did
    know.
Rabbit, of course, knew of every disaster
And he spoke out in spurts like a TV
    forecaster.
"Molefellinahole." "Roosterflewintoapole."
Words shot out of his mouth like an arrow
    in flight.
Turtle, a good listener, understood them all
    right.
Turtle answered, "T-o-o b-a-d t-h-a-t i-s s-o
    s-a-d."
Rabbit went on to relate,
    "Snakeateawholecake-
    gottastomachache."
"Bearlosthercub."
    "Antwasswallowedbyabigyellowbug."
Turtle said, "N-o h-a-p-p-y n-e-w-s t-o-d-a-y?"
"OhsureIknowsomething," he did say.
"Skunkfellinthewellandhelosthissmell!"

J.M.M.

THE ISLAND OF A MILLION TREES

I took my ship and put out to sea
Sailing to the Island of a Million Trees.
Lucky Duck flew on the deck
There was Happy Me, and Lucky Duck
    sailing free.

To Million Tree Island we sailed our ship.
Neal the Seal asked to join our trip.
The ship was big so we said, "yes."
Happy Me, Lucky Duck, Neal the Seal, our
    new guest.

The wind did blow and along we flew
Sailing, playing, eating lunch, too.
We heard a meow from a floating raft
And rescued a kitty named Sweet Little Taff.
There was Happy Me, Lucky Duck, Neal the
    Seal, and Sweet Little Taff.
Sailing free to the Island of a Million Trees.

We drifted east and drifted west.
A storm stirred the waves, we could not
    rest.
A voice cried out from the gray fog
And over the side climbed Sailor Bob.

There was Happy Me, Lucky Duck, Neal the
    Seal,
Sweet Little Taff and Sailor Bob.
Off to the Island of a Million Trees.

Off in the distance we spotted land
With a million trees and mile of sand.
Closer and closer our boat did go.
Hands on the oars we started to row.
There was Happy Me, Lucky Duck, Neal the
    Seal,
Sweet Little Taff, and Sailor Bob.
Stepping onto the Island of a Million Trees.

Danielle Tracy

MAYTIME MAGIC

A little seed
For me to sow . . .
A little earth
To make it grow . . .

A little hole,
A little pat . . .
A little wish,
And that is that

A little sun,
A little shower . . .
A little while,
And then—a flower!

Mabel Watts

HARRY T. BEAR LEARNS TO RHYME

Harry T. Bear says he can rhyme.
"Harry," I say. "Rhyme the word game."
He says, "Game rhymes with door."
I say, "Game rhymes with name."
"Give me a better word," says he.
"Well then try to rhyme the word bug."
Harry T. says, "Bug rhymes with bear."
"They start with the 'B' sound that's true
But Harry T. no rhyme is there."
He smiles and says, "Rhymes I can do!
Bug rhymes with rug, jug and mug, too."
"Harry T. you've got it hurray!"
That was the start of a very bad day
He could only talk in rhyme you see
His awful rhymes were bothering me.
When I said, "It's time to eat."
He said, "Meat, feet, sweet, tweet and seat."
I said, "I am going to bed."
He said, "Dead, lead and read."
"Stop please." I said "This is hurting my
*   head!"*
"But I can say rhymes anytime"
"Enough all ready," I then cried.
"Please take your rhymes and go outside."
Away he went out the door
My head ached I wanted no more.
As Harry T. Bear walked out of sight
I heard him say light, kite and bite.
Then his voice disappeared into the night.
He'll be back on my bed when I awake
I hope he has no other rhymes to make.

Danielle Tracy

Permission granted by Danielle Tracy, 2000.

HARRY T. BEAR SAYS HE CAN READ

At night Harry says "Is it time?"
He puts on pajamas when I put on mine
Harry T. Bear hides books in my bed
Under the pillow where I lay my head.

"See," Harry T. says, "Black marks
In a straight row
Are alphabet letters
Making words that I know!"

Harry says, "I CAN read books
But you read them best"
He sits and looks
While I read his requests.

Harry picks books 'bout caves and honey,
Or silver fish swimming in streams.
I like books that are funny,
Or have birthday parties with chocolate ice
*   cream.*

Together we sit all snuggled tight.
I read the pictures by the lamp's golden
*   light.*
Harry T. Bear says, "Please read it again."
But I fall asleep before the book's end.
That's when Harry T. Bear says he reads to
*   me.*

Danielle Tracy

Permission granted by Danielle Tracy, 2005.

I BOUGHT ME A ROOSTER

I bought me a rooster and the rooster
*   pleased me.*
I fed my rooster on the bayberry tree,
My little rooster goes cock-a-doodle-doo,
*   dee-doodle-dee doodle dee doodle dee*
*   doo!*

I bought me a cat and the cat pleased me.
I fed my cat on the bayberry tree,
My little cat goes meow, meow, meow.
My little rooster goes cock-a-doodle-doo,
*   dee-doodle-dee doodle dee doodle dee*
*   doo!*

I bought me a dog and the dog pleased me.
I fed my dog on the bayberry tree,
My little dog goes bark, bark, bark.
My little cat goes meow, meow, meow.
My little rooster goes cock-a-doodle-doo, dee-
*   doodle-dee doodle dee doodle dee doo!*

Traditional

Note: This is a cumulative poem that takes teacher practice; additional verses include as many animals as you wish.

THE CHICKENS

Said the first little chicken,
*   With a queer little squirm,*
"I wish I could find
*   A fat little worm!"*

Said the next little chicken,
*   With an odd little shrug:*

"I wish I could find
    A fat little bug!"

Said the third little chicken
    With a small sign of grief:
"I wish I could find
    A green little leaf!"

Said the fourth little chicken,
    With a faint little moan:
"I wish I could find
A wee gravel stone!"

"Now see here!" said the mother,
    From the green garden patch,
"If you want any breakfast,
    Just come here and scratch!"

                        Anonymous

TALKING ANIMALS

"Meow," says cat.
"Bow-wow," says dog.
"Oink," says pig.
"Croak," says frog.

Hen says, "Cluck."
Lamb says, "Ba."
Cow says, "Moo."
and babies "Wah."

Lion says, "Roar."
Mouse says, "Squeak."
Snake says, "Ssssis."
Chick says, "Peep."

Crow says, "Ca."
Bears growl.
Sheep bleat.
Wolves howl.

Pig says, "Squeal."
Owl says, "Hoot who."
Toad says, "Ree deep."
Cuckoo says, "Cuckoo."

Donkey says, "Hee Haw."
Horse says, "Neigh Neigh."
Turkey says, "Gobble."
And we all say, "HOORAY!"

Note: Last line can also read, "And we say 'Happy Birthday!'"

HERE COMES THE BUS

Lights flashing, gravel crunching, the big
    yellow door swings open shooshing the
    air.

Big kids make faces in the windows and
    the driver smiles down the stairs

When I climb in that bus I'm a big kid
    too.
With my snack in my backpack and my
    new shiny shoes.

I'll wave to mom and kiss the glass
Today I'll be a kindergartner—at last.

I'll make new friends and run and play
There'll be things to do like blocks and
    clay.

I'm going to learn to draw and write
And spell and make my numbers
    right.

Mom says to share, be kind and good
For the teacher has rules to tell.
I'll sit or stand like teacher says
And listen for the bell.

Since I'm five I know a lot
Like alphabet letters, left, right and
    stop.
I can print my name and say colors, too
But being a kindergartner—that is new.

                        J. M. M.

OVER IN THE MEADOW

Over in the meadow, in the sand in the
    sun,
Lived an old mother frog and her little
    froggie one.
"Croak!" said the mother; "I croak," said
    the one,
So they croaked and were glad in the sand
    in the sun.

Over in the meadow in a pond so blue
Lived an old mother duck and her little
    ducks two.
"Quack!" said the mother; "We quack," said
    the two,
So they quacked and were glad in the pond
    so blue.

Over in the meadow, in a hole in a tree,
Lived an old mother robin and her little
    birdies three.
"Chirp!" said the mother; "We chirp," said
    the three,
So they chirped and were glad in the hole
    in a tree.

*Over in the meadow, on a rock by the
      shore,*
*Lived an old mother snake and her little
      snakes four.*
*"Hiss!" said the mother; "We hiss," said the
      four,*
*So they hissed and were glad on a rock by
      the shore.*

Over in the meadow, in a big beehive,
*Lived an old mother bee and her little bees
      five.*
*"Buzz!" said the mother; "We buzz," said the
      five,*
*So they buzzed and were glad in the big
      beehive.*

Traditional

LITTLE BOY BLUE

Little Boy Blue,
Come, blow your horn!
The sheep's in the meadow,
The cow's in the corn.
Where's the little boy
That looks after the sheep?
Under the haystack, fast asleep!

Mother Goose

THE CAT AND THE FIDDLE

Hey, diddle, diddle!
The cat and the fiddle,
The cow jumped over the moon;
The little dog laughed
To see such sport,
And the dish ran away
With the spoon.

Mother Goose

THE LITTLE GIRL WITH A CURL

There was a little girl
Who had a little curl
Right in the middle of her forehead;
When she was good
She was very, very good,
*And when she was bad she was
      horrid.*

Mother Goose

SUMMARY

Poems and verses provide an important literary experience, and exposure to classics is something no child should miss. Poems and verses can be a source of enjoyment and learning for young children. Rhythm, word images, fast action, and rhyme are used to promote listening skill.

Short verses, easily remembered, give children self-confidence with words. Encouragement and attention are offered by the teacher when the child shows interest.

Poems are selected and practiced for enthusiastic, smooth presentations. They can be selected from various sources or can be created by the teacher. Props help children focus on words. Poems are created or selected keeping in mind the features that attract and interest young children.

ADDITIONAL RESOURCES
Readings
Bryant, P. E., MacLean, M., Bradley, L., & Crossland, J. (1990). Rhyme and alliteration, phoneme detection, and learning to read. *Developmental Psychology, 26*(3), 429–438.
Carlstrom, N. W. (1986). *Jesse Bear, what will you wear?* New York: Macmillan.
Cole, B. (1990). *The silly book.* New York: Doubleday.
Cole, J. (1989). *Anna Banana.* New York: William Morrow.
Gable, S. (1999, September). Promoting children's literacy with poetry. *Young Children, 54*(4), 12–15.
Keats, E. J. (1991). *Over in the meadow.* New York: Scholastic.
MacLean, M., Bryant, P., & Bradley, L. (1987). Rhymes, nursery rhymes, and reading in early childhood. *Merrill-Palmer Quarterly, 33*(3), 255–281.
Stevenson, R. L. (1990). *My shadow.* New York: Putnam.

Read-Aloud Rhyming Picture Books
Christelow, E. (1998). *Five little monkeys jumping on the bed.* Boston: Houghton Mifflin.
Collins, H. (2003). *Little Miss Muffet.* Toronto: Kids Can Press.

Guarino, D. (1997). *Is your mama a llama?* New York: Scholastic.

Kalan, R. (1989). *Jump, frog, jump.* New York: Mulberry.

Lansky, B. (2004). *Mary had a little jam.* New York: Meadowbrook Press.

Miranda, A. (1997). *To market, to market.* San Diego: Harcourt.

Mosel, A. (1988). *Tikki tikki tembo.* New York: Henry Holt.

Raffi (1990). *The wheels on the bus.* New York: Crown.

Seuss, Dr. (1960). *One fish, two fish, red fish, blue fish.* New York: Random House.

Poetry Collections

Brady, L., Meirelles, R., & Nikoghosian, A. (1987). *The best of Mother Goose.* Hanford: RozaLinda Publications.

Brown, M. (1985). *Hand rhymes.* New York: E. P. Dutton.

Brown, M. (1998). *Party rhymes.* New York: Dutton.

Carle, E. (1989). *Animals, animals.* New York: Philomel.

Carlstron, N. W. (1989). *Graham cracker animals 1–2–3.* New York: Macmillan.

Cousins, L. (1989). *The little dog laughed and other nursery rhymes.* New York: E. P. Dutton.

Delacre, L. (1989). *Arroz con leche: Popular rhymes from Latin America.* New York: Scholastic.

Gander, F. (1985). *Nursery rhymes.* Santa Barbara: Advocacy Press.

Ghigna, C. (1995). *Riddle rhymes.* New York: Hyperion.

Jones, C. (1992). *Hickory dickory dock and other nursery rhymes.* Boston: Houghton Mifflin.

Lobel, A. (1985). *Whiskers & rhymes.* New York: Greenwillow.

Lobel, A. (1986). *The Random House book of Mother Goose.* New York: Random House.

McClosky, P. (1991). *Find the real Mother Goose.* New York: Checkerboard Press.

Moore, H. H. (1997). *A poem a day.* New York: Scholastic.

Prelusky, J. (1983). *The Random House book of poetry for children.* New York: Random House.

Prelusky, J. (1986). *Read-aloud rhymes for the very young.* New York: Knopf.

Roemer, H. (2004). *Come to my party and other shape poems.* New York: Henry Holt.

Rosen, M. (1993). *Poems for the very young.* New York: Kingfisher.

Schlein, M. (1997). *Sleep safe, little whale.* New York: Greenwillow.

Silverman, J. (1988). *Some time to grow.* Menlo Park, CA: Addison-Wesley.

Sutherland, Z. (1990). *The Orchard book of nursery rhymes.* New York: Orchard Books.

Trapani, I. (1997). *I'm a little teapot.* Watertown, MA: Charlesbridge Publishing.

HELPFUL WEB SITES

The Academy of American Poets
http://www.poets.org
Search poetry benefits.

Famous Poetry Online
http://www.poetry-online.org
Click on *Poetry for Children*, then *Funny poetry*. A listing of humorous poetry selections is also available.

Meadowbrook Press
http://www.gigglepoetry.com
Select *Poetry Class* and learn to write humorous poems.

Poets House
http://poetshouse.org
Click on *Collection* and then *Children's Room* for information about admission-free poetry activities in New York; or click *Collection* and then *Libraries* to find out how the Poets House model can be replicated. Visit *News* to see how poetry has been introduced in community environments.

Story-It
http://www.storyit.com
Select *Rhymes to Print* to print nursery rhymes; then investigate *Top Sites for Teachers*.

 The Online Companion™ holds an additional flannel board poem and additional Mother Goose rhymes. Rhyming picture books are given attention.

STUDENT ACTIVITIES

1. Share with the class a poem you learned as a child.
2. Select five poems from any source. Be ready to state the reasons you selected them when you bring them to the next class meeting.
3. Make a list of 10 picture books that include children's poetry. Cite author, title, publisher, and copyright date for each.
4. Create a poem for young children. Go back and review the features most often found in classic rhymes.
5. Present a poem to a group of preschoolers. Evaluate its success in a few sentences.
6. Find poetry written in free verse that you think might be successful with preschool children.
7. Form groups of three to six students. Using a large sheet of newsprint tacked (or taped) to the wall and a felt pen, list clever ways to introduce poetry to young children; for example, Poem of the Day. Discuss each group's similar and diverse suggestions.
8. Find a source of ethnic children's poetry and share it with class members.
9. Earlier in this chapter it was suggested that you list remembered Mother Goose characters. In a group of four or five classmates, compare your list with others, then with other groups. The group with the longest list then asks other groups with shorter lists to recite a Mother Goose rhyme in unison.

CHAPTER REVIEW

A. List a few reasons why poetry is used with young children.

B. Match each term in Column I to one item in Column II.

COLUMN I	COLUMN II
1. poetry	a. an action verb
2. rhyme	b. self-confidence
3. beat	c. a rhythmic measure
4. order and form	d. mental pictures
5. images	e. words with like sounds
6. remembered	f. consistent and dependable
7. interest	g. teacher attention
8. goal	h. after practice
9. presentation	i. enjoyment
10. reciting	j. promotes listening skill
11. classics	k. never forced
12. song	l. library
13. props	m. Mother Goose rhymes
14. run	n. musical poem
15. source	o. focus attention

C. List the numbers of the statements that you believe agree with the suggestions mentioned in this chapter.

1. Young children must learn to recite.
2. Emphasizing the beat of poetry as you read it always increases the enjoyment.
3. Repeat the poem over and over until a child learns it.
4. Describe to children the mental pictures created by the poem before reading the poem to the children.
5. It really is not too important for young children to memorize the poems they hear.
6. Memorizing a poem can help a child feel competent.
7. Most poems are not shared because teachers want children to gain the factual information the poem contains.
8. Poetry's rhythm comes from its form and order.
9. Memorizing a poem always causes awkward teacher presentation.
10. Teachers may try to author some of their own children's poetry.

D. List elements of poetry that can be manipulated to evoke emotion in listeners.

E. Write an example using a line of poetry or free verse for the following: alliteration, personification, simile, and figurative language.

F. Comment on a poetry reader's tendency to pause at the end of each line when reading poetry aloud.

CHAPTER 12

Flannel (Felt) Boards and Activity Sets

OBJECTIVES

After reading this chapter, you should be able to:

◆ Describe flannel boards and types of flannel board activities.

◆ Make and present three flannel board activities.

◆ Describe teacher techniques in flannel board story presentation.

Flannel (or felt) board activities are a rewarding experience for both the child and teacher. Because the attention of young children is easily captured, the teacher finds the use of flannel board activities very popular and effective. Children are highly attentive during this type of activity—straining to see and hear—looking forward to the next piece to be put on the flannel board.

Stories to be used with flannel board activities are selected by the same criteria used for storytelling (see Chapter 10). In addition to stories poetry, and songs, other listening and learning activities can be presented with flannel boards.

FLANNEL BOARD CONSTRUCTION

Boards of different sizes, shapes, and designs are used, depending on the needs of the center. They may be freestanding or propped up in the chalkboard tray, on a chair, or on an easel. Boards can be covered on both sides in different colors. Many are made by covering a sheet of heavy cardboard, display board, prestretched artist's canvas (Figure 12–1), Styrofoam™, or wood with a piece of solid-colored flannel or felt yardage (Figure 12–2). The material is pulled smooth and held by tacks, tape, glue, or wood staples, depending on the board material. Sometimes an under padding is added. Putting wire mesh or a sheet of metal between the under padding and the covering material makes pieces with magnets adhere. Because all metal does not attract magnets, the mesh or metal needs testing before purchase.

Decisions on which materials to use in flannel board construction are often based on the intended use of the flannel board, material cost, and tools or skills needed in construction. Styrofoam™ is a good choice if having a lightweight board is important; however, wood-based boards are more durable.

Making a board that tilts backward at a slight angle is an important consideration for a freestanding flannel board because pieces applied to a slanted board stick more securely. Stores and companies that sell school supplies have premade boards in various price ranges. See the Additional Resources section at the end

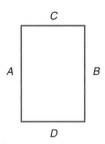

A prestretched *artist canvas* can be obtained at an art and craft store or through artist's supply catalogs. Flannel or felt is available in navy blue or black in 45" widths.

Purchase ¾ yard of 45" yardage to cover a 24" × 36" canvas. Place the flannel or felt on a flat surface, and place the artist canvas face down on the material. Fold over and staple material onto the wood frame in this manner: First, staple side A. Pull the material snugly, and staple side B, then sides C and D making four hospital corners. Trim.

FIGURE 12–1 Directions for artists' canvas flannel board.

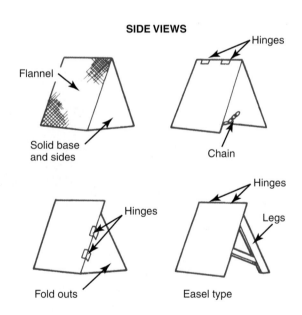

FIGURE 12–2 Freestanding boards.

of this chapter for a listing of commercial board and set manufacturers.

Although flannel and felt are popular coverings for boards, other materials also work well. Almost all fuzzy textured material is usable. The nap can be raised on flannel or felt by brushing it with a stiff brush. It is a good idea to press a small piece of felt or pellon (fabric interfacing) to a fabric to see how well it sticks before buying the fabric.

Some boards have pockets in the back so that flannel pieces can be lined up and ready for use (Figure 12–3). Some early childhood centers have parts of walls, dividers, and backs of pieces of furniture covered with flannel or felt. A simple homemade freestanding board holder is shown in Figure 12–4.

A tabletop flannel board can be made from a cardboard box (see instructions and necessary materials in Figure 12–5). One clever idea is using a secondhand attaché case. Using a case that opens to a 90-degree angle, glue a large piece of flannel to the inside of the top lid. When the lid is open, the flannel will be in view. The case is used for storing sets, and the handle makes it easy to carry.

Display fabrics to which three-dimensional objects will adhere are also available. Special adhesives and tapes are needed for this type of flannel board.

The size of the flannel board's front surface is important. Consider making or purchasing a board no smaller than 24″ × 30″. The attaché case could be used for individual child's play or for small groups, but it may be too small for larger groups. Most centers obtain or construct both a child's flannel board and a staff flannel board.

Activity Sets

Pieces for flannel activity sets can be made in a number of ways and from a number of fabrics and papers. Pellon and felt, because of their low cost and durability, are probably the most popular. Heavy-paper figures with flannel backing or felt tape also stick well. Commercial tape, sandpaper, fuzzy velour-flocked wallpaper, Velcro™, and used foamlike laundry softener sheets are other possibilities for backing pieces. Premade flannel or felt board sets are available at school-supply stores and at most teacher conferences. Most communities have at least one teacher who is a small business entrepreneur specializing in making flannel sets for other teachers.

Shapes and figures can be traced from books, magazines, or coloring books; self-drawn and created; or borrowed from other sources. Tracing paper is helpful for this pur-

Construction:

Obtain a piece of cardboard, of the size you desire for the back of your flannel board, and a large sheet of flannel or heavy wrapping paper. The flannel (or paper) should be several inches wider than the cardboard and about twice as long as the finished chart size. One-inch deep with a back 3 inches high is a good pocket size.

Measure and mark both sides of flannel (paper) at intervals of 3 inches and 1 inch, alternating. Using accordion folds, the first 1-inch section is creased and folded forward over the second 3-inch section, and so on. Pull tight and secure ends.

A pocket chart conveniently holds set pieces in sequence for flannel-board stories and can be useful in other child activities with flannel set pieces.

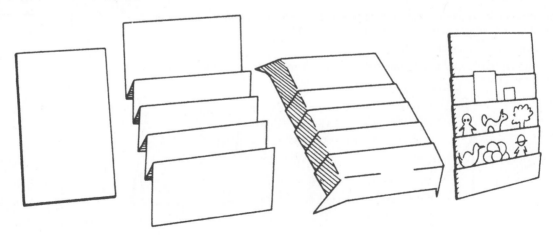

FIGURE 12–3 Pocket chart.

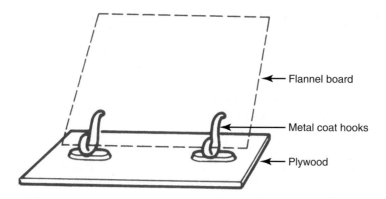

FIGURE 12–4 Two metal coat hooks screwed to a piece of heavy plywood make a good flannel board holder.

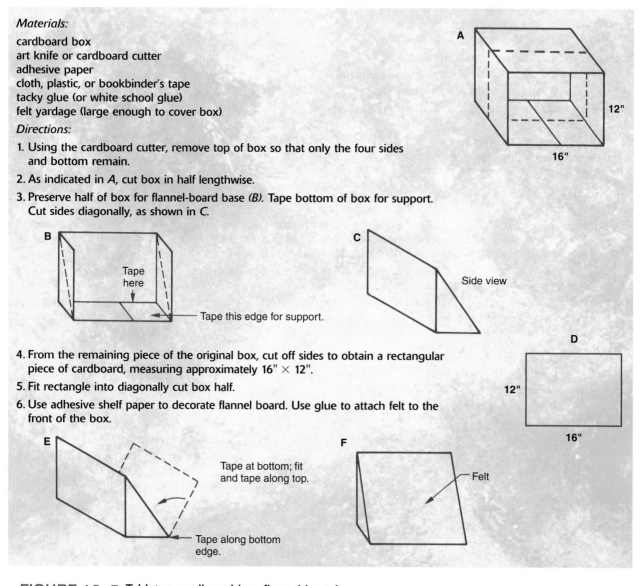

Materials:

cardboard box
art knife or cardboard cutter
adhesive paper
cloth, plastic, or bookbinder's tape
tacky glue (or white school glue)
felt yardage (large enough to cover box)

Directions:

1. Using the cardboard cutter, remove top of box so that only the four sides and bottom remain.
2. As indicated in *A*, cut box in half lengthwise.
3. Preserve half of box for flannel-board base *(B)*. Tape bottom of box for support. Cut sides diagonally, as shown in *C*.
4. From the remaining piece of the original box, cut off sides to obtain a rectangular piece of cardboard, measuring approximately 16" × 12".
5. Fit rectangle into diagonally cut box half.
6. Use adhesive shelf paper to decorate flannel board. Use glue to attach felt to the front of the box.

FIGURE 12–5 Tabletop cardboard box flannel board.

pose. Tracing can be done simply by covering the back of a paper pattern with a heavy layer of pencil lead. Soft art pencils work best. The pattern is then turned over and traced. Another method is cutting the object out, tracing its outline, and then drawing details freehand. Tracing pencils and pens are commercially available and come with directions for use; they can be found at craft stores.

Color can be added to set pieces with felt markers, oil pastels, acrylic or poster paint, embroidery pens, crayons, paints, and colored pencils. Sets take time to make but are well worth the effort. Favorites will be presented over and over again. Pieces can be covered with clear contact paper or can be laminated (fronts only) for durability.

Teachers can be creative with flannel board sets by decorating pieces with

◆ layered felt.
◆ wiggly eyes (commercially available at variety stores).
◆ hand-stitched character clothing.
◆ imitation fur fabric.
◆ liquid glitter.
◆ commercial fluorescent paint or crayons.

Most copy machines have the ability to enlarge figures or shrink them. Set pieces that are too small are difficult to handle and see. Narrow parts on set pieces should be avoided because they tend to tear with use. Also, try to preserve the size relationship between characters (such as between a mouse and a human figure) as well as the cultural and ethnic diversity of characters.

Pattern transfer books are plentiful and available from craft and sewing stores. Patterns can be ironed on cloth quickly, and it is possible to obtain multiple copies. Publishers of transfer books include Dover Publications, New York, and Craftways, Richmond, CA.

Some schools buy inexpensive picture books and use the illustrations as flannel board set pieces. After the pieces are cut, they are glued to oak tag and backed with some of the materials mentioned earlier.

Proper storage and care will preserve pieces and prolong their usefulness. A flat stocking box or large mailing envelope or manila folder is practical for storage. If pieces become bent, a warm iron can often be used to flatten the pieces. Sets can be stored in plastic page protectors used in three-ring binders (available in stationery stores). Large resealable plastic household bags, as well as plastic envelopes available at teacher-supply stores, can also be used to protect pieces.

Nonfiction Sets

You will find that young children are just as interested in nonfiction topics as they are in narrative stories. Educators, in attempting to build on recognized child interest, construct their own nonfiction set pieces or find ones commercially manufactured. True representations of detailed subjects is best. Library or computer research can secure accurate images. Textbooks for elementary schools are another good resource. A robin set piece should look like a robin, not just a bird in general. The same goes for other set figures. Distinguishing features should be depicted.

Nonfiction set pieces can also be easily woven into other designed activities, such as categorizing animals by color or number of legs. Referring back to the discussion in Chapter 9 on nonfiction book selection will be helpful.

Child Flannel Board Activity Sets

Many schools make or purchase flannel set pieces to accompany children's favorite books. Before making set pieces, teachers can discuss children's ideas concerning what pieces are central to the story. In retelling the story with a flannel board, children will decide how set pieces are to be placed on the board to increase audience understanding; they also select what visual pieces are essential in each scene. Children choose the words that coordinate with the visuals. In stories involving "running away" set pieces, children often move a piece in a running movement across the board. The children may also try to manipulate two pieces in an action sequence, such as a monkey riding on a donkey's back. As a child relates a tale, considerable visual literacy thinking is taking place.

PRESENTATION

Like most other listening activities, a semisecluded, comfortable setting should be chosen for presentation. The activity begins with the teacher starting to place pieces on the board in proper sequence as the story or activity unfolds, always focusing on the children's reactions. In this activity, as in many others described in this text, the teacher may be presenting but also watching for reaction. Because pieces are usually added one at a time, they should be kept in an open flat box or manila folder in the teacher's lap, or, better yet, behind the board, stacked in the order they will appear. This is hard to do if the story or activity is not well in mind.

The teacher should periodically check to see whether the set has all its pieces, particularly in large centers where many staff members use the same sets. If pieces are missing or damaged, the teacher or volunteers can make new pieces. New sets are always appreciated by the entire staff and can be developed to meet the needs and interests of a particular group of children.

To present activities with ease, the beginner should

◆ read the story (or activity sequence) and check the pieces to be used.

◆ practice until there is a smooth coordination of words and placement of pieces on the board.

◆ set up the flannel board.

◆ check and prepare pieces in order of their appearance.

◆ place pieces out of view, behind the board within easy reach, or in a lap folder.

◆ gather children. Make seating adjustments if necessary. Respond to children's needs. Group size should be considered carefully; the smaller the group, the more intimate and conversational the experience. As with other language arts presentations, consider two tellings to reduce group size.

◆ introduce the activity with a statement that builds a desire to listen.

◆ tell the story (or present the activity), watching for reactions from the children. Create drama and suspense with pauses, speaking in characters' voices and moving pieces across the board's surface, if the story calls for this. Let your personality guide you (Figure 12–6).

◆ discuss language development or comprehension (optional). Teachers ask questions

FIGURE 12–6 During this flannel board presentation, children are imitating the teacher's gestures.

or discuss story particulars to elicit children's ideas and comments.

◆ keep pieces flat and store them properly, returning sets to where other staff members expect them to be.

◆ allow children to do their retelling with a flannel board and their own activity sets. Most centers construct one set for teachers and another set for child exploration and activity.

In addition to storytelling activities, sets may be used for songs, poetry, numbers, language development, and other activities.

SUGGESTED STORIES AND ACTIVITIES

There are many resources for story ideas. Stories created by teachers can be enjoyed as much as commercial sets and classic stories. Sets can improve listening skills and enhance vocabulary and concept development, often within one activity. The visual shapes or pieces are linked to words and ideas. Occasionally, a child's picture book can be presented as a flannel board activity before the book becomes part of the school's book collection.

An available flannel board placed at children's eye level with an adjacent open box of figures or shapes quickly encourages use and creativity. Remembered words, lines, and whole stories are relived in children's play. They often go beyond the familiar, devising their own events. Even sturdy felt pieces will need to be ironed flat occasionally and replaced because of frequent and vigorous use by children. As suggested previously, children's play with the flannel board often follows a teacher presentation but can also be a free choice activity at other times of the day.

Many centers include flannel boards and sets in their language centers along with alphabet letter cutouts. Teachers can use alphabet letter cutouts in daily activities, and many centers routinely have set pieces, such as a flower shape, labeled with the cut out alphabet letters underneath the shape on the flannel board for viewing. A flannel board with the word *closed* on it may be used to block entrance to a play area or other section of the room.

Suggested picture books that lend themselves to flannel board presentations include:

Brett, J. (1989). *The mitten.* New York: Putnam.

Flack, M. (1971). *Ask Mr. Bear.* New York: Macmillan.

French, V. (1995). *Red hen and sly fox.* New York: Simon & Schuster.

Hobson, S. (1994). *Chicken Little.* New York: Simon & Schuster.

Martin, B. (1972). *Brown bear, brown bear, what do you see?* New York: Holt, Rinehart, and Winston.

Neitzel, S. (1989). *The jacket I wear in the snow.* New York: Greenwillow.

Slobodkina, E. (1947). *Caps for sale.* Glenview, IL: Addison Wesley Publishing Company.

Stevens, J. (1995). *Tops and bottoms.* New York: Harcourt.

Young, E. (1992). *Seven blind mice.* New York: Philomel Books.

Zemach, M. (1977). *It could always be worse.* New York: Farrar.

Zuromskis, D. (1978). *The farmer in the dell.* Boston: Little, Brown & Co.

Commercially made sets and activity ideas can be obtained from sources listed in the Additional Resources section.

Many urban school districts allow private preschool teachers in their community to use their central office curriculum centers, which may also hold flannel board resources. Flannel board stories and patterns are found in the Activities section at the end of this chapter.

SUMMARY

A flannel board presentation is one of the most popular and successful listening activities for the young child. Stories are told while figures and shapes are moved on the board. The children can learn new ideas and words by seeing the visual model while listening to the story.

Beginning teachers practice presentations with words and pieces until the activity flows smoothly. The children's feedback is noted. Flannel board activities in many other learning areas besides language development take place in early childhood centers.

A wide variety of fabrics is available for both boards and pieces; felt and flannel are the most commonly used materials for boards.

ADDITIONAL RESOURCES

Commercial Flannel Board and Flannel Board Set Manufacturers

Childwood, 8040 NE Day Road West, Bainbridge Island, WA 98110; 800-362-9825; http://www.childwoodmagnets.com. (Magnet boards, brightly painted cut-wood pieces, and teaching suggestions.)

G. W. School Supply Inc.; 800-234-1065; http://www.gwschool.com. (Boards and sets in a variety of price ranges.)

Learning Wonders; 866-933-PLAY; http://www.learningwonders.com. (Felt sets and boards, multicultural figures, nursery rhymes, community helpers, fairy tales.)

Little Folk Visuals; 800-537-7227; http://www.littlefolkvisuals.com. (Flannel sets and scenes.)

Books with Flannel Board Stories and Set Patterns

Anderson, P. (1972). *Storytelling with the flannel board* (Books 1 & 2). Minneapolis: T. S. Denison & Co.

Briggs, D. (1992). *Flannel board fun: A collection of stories.* New York: Scarecrow Press.

Kreplin, E., & Smith, B. M. (1995). *Ready-to-use flannel board stories, figures and activities for ESL children.* Denver: Center for Applied Research.

Peralta, C. (1981). *Flannel board activities for the bilingual classroom.* Culver City, CA: La Arana Publishers.

Scott, L. B., & Thompson, J. J. (1984). *Rhymes for fingers and flannel boards.* Minneapolis: T. S. Denison & Co.

Taylor, F., & Vaugh, G. (1980). *The flannel board storybook.* Atlanta: Humanics Learning.

Wilmes, L., & Wilmes, D. (1987). *Felt board fun.* Elgin, IL: Building Books.

Readings

Flood, J., & Lapp, D. (1998). Conceptualizations of literacy: The visual and communicative arts. *The Reading Teacher, 51*(4), 342–344.

Roe, B., Alred, S., & Smith, S. (1998). *Teaching through stories: Yours, mine and theirs.* Norwood, MA: Christopher-Gordon.

HELPFUL WEB SITES

Fabulous Flannel Fun
http://www.lessontutor.com
Search the site for "flannel boards." An author provides flannel board ideas for making boards and creating cutouts.

Homespun Kids
http://www.homespunkids.com
Click on *Educational Themes* or *Science* to view commerical boards and ideas for sets.

Lakeshore Learning Materials
http://www.lakeshorelearning.com
This is a commercial source for boards and sets.

Make Me a Story
http://www.makemeastory.com
This site was created by flannel set specialists.

Preschool Printables
http://www.preschoolprintables.com
Select *Felt Board Stories;* then click on *5 Red Apples.*

A simple method of assessing young children's story comprehension is provided in the Online Companion™. Think of this exercise as a miniresearch study that may tell you if young children can remember more about a story told with the flannel board than a story read aloud from a picture book. A suggested reading list is also included.

STUDENT ACTIVITIES

1. Visit a center to watch a flannel board presentation, or invite a teacher to present an activity to the class.
2. Give a presentation to a small group of classmates. The classmates should make helpful suggestions in written form while watching the presentation, trying to look at the presentations through the eyes of a child.
3. Write an original story for the flannel board. Include patterns for your pieces. Share with your total training group.
4. If videotape equipment is available in your classroom, give a flannel board presentation and evaluate yourself.
5. Make three flannel board sets, using any materials desired.
6. Visit a school supply store and price commercial flannel boards. Compare costs for constructing a flannel board, and report at the next class meeting.
7. Make a personal flannel board.
8. Research stories and sets with multicultural variety.
9. With a group of classmates discuss turning "Roll Over" into a flannel board set. How many set pieces would be needed? How could this set fit into a theme unit? Would you use numeral set pieces? Why? Could set pieces be multicultural? What materials would you need to construct this set? List.

ROLL OVER

Ten in the bed, and the little one said,
"Roll over! Roll over!"
So they rolled over and one fell out.

Nine in the bed, and the little one said:
"Roll over! Roll over!"
They all rolled over and one fell out.

Eight in the bed, and the little one said:
"Roll over! Roll over!"
They all rolled over and one fell out.

Seven in the bed, and the little one said:
"Roll over! Roll over!"
They all rolled over and one fell out.

Six in the bed, and the little one said:
"Roll over! Roll over!"
They all rolled over and one fell out.

Five in the bed, and the little one said:
"Roll over! Roll over!"

They all rolled over and one fell out.

Four in the bed, and the little one said:
"Roll over! Roll over!"
They all rolled over and one fell out.

Three in the bed, and the little one said:
"Roll over! Roll over!"
They all rolled over and one fell out.

Two in the bed, and the little one said:
"Roll over! Roll over!"
They all rolled over and one fell out.

One in the bed, and the little one said,
"Alone at last!"

CHAPTER REVIEW

A. List the types of materials used in board construction.

B. Name the kinds of materials used to make flannel board pieces.

C. In your opinion, what is the best way to color pieces for flannel boards?

D. Why is the use of visual aids valuable?

E. Place the following in correct order.

1. Give a flannel board presentation.
2. Set up area with board.
3. Check pieces.
4. Practice.
5. Place pieces in order of appearance.
6. Gather children.
7. Place pieces out of sight.
8. Discuss what happened during the activity with children (optional).
9. Store set by keeping pieces flat.
10. Introduce the set with a motivational statement if you wish.

F. What color flannel (or felt) would you use to cover your own board? Why?

G. Finish the following statements.

1. A board is set up slanting back slightly because _____.
2. A folding flannel board with handles is a good idea because _____.
3. If children touch the pieces during a teacher presentation, the teacher should say _____.
4. The main reason teachers like to store set pieces in a flat position is _____.

5. One advantage of a flannel board made from a large Styrofoam™ sheet is
_____.

6. One disadvantage of a flannel board made from a large Styrofoam™ sheet is
_____.

BEGINNING TEACHER ACTIVITIES

The following activities and stories are suggested as a start for the beginning teacher. The set piece patterns that follow are shown at a reduced size. Full-size versions are available on the Online Companion™ Web site at http://www.earlychilded.delmar.com.

THE LION AND THE MOUSE

Author Unknown (a classic story)

Pieces   lion, sleeping   rope
lion, awake   mouse
tree   two hunters

(On the board, place the sleeping lion next to the tree. Place the mouse near the lion's back, moving it slowly toward the lion while speaking in a soft voice.)

There once was a little mouse who saw a big lion sleeping by a tree. "Oh, it would be fun to climb on top of the lion and slide down his tail," thought the mouse. So—quietly, he tiptoed close to the lion. When he climbed on the lion's back, the fur felt so soft and warm between his toes that he began running up and down the lion's back.

The lion awoke. He felt a tickle upon his back. He opened one eye and saw the little mouse, which he then caught in his paw.

(Move mouse under lion's paw.)

"Let me go—please!" said the mouse. "I'm sorry I woke you from your nap. Let me go, and I'll never bother you again. Maybe you and I could be friends—friends help each other, you know."

This made the lion laugh. "A little mouse like you, help me? I'm big, I'm strong, and I'm brave!" Then the lion laughed again, and he let the mouse go.

(Take the mouse off the board.)

The mouse ran away, and he didn't see the lion for a long time. But, one day when the mouse was out looking for seeds for dinner, he saw the lion tied to a tree with a rope, and two hunters near him.

(Remove sleeping lion. Add awake lion, placing it next to tree, with rope on top. Put the two hunters on the other side of the tree.)

One hunter said, "Well, this rope will hold the lion until we can go get our truck and take him to the zoo." So the hunters walked away.

(Remove the hunters.)

The mouse ran up to the lion as soon as the hunters were out of sight. He said, "Hello, lion."

(Add mouse.)

The lion answered, "Well, I guess it's your turn to laugh at me tied to this tree."

"I'm not going to laugh," said the mouse, as he quickly started to chew on the rope.

(Move mouse close to rope.)

The mouse chewed, and chewed, and chewed. The rope fell apart, and the lion was free.

(Remove rope.)

"You are a good friend," said the lion. "Hop on my back and hold on. Let's get away from here before those two hunters come back."

(Place lion in running position with mouse on lion's back.)

"OK," said the mouse. "I'd like that."

So you see, sometimes little friends can help big friends. The size of a friend isn't really too important.

← Cut line

Full-size version of this art can be found on the Online Companion™ at http://www.earlychilded.delmar.com

THE SEED

Margie Cowsert (While an ECE student)

Pieces
small roots	leaves
green shoot	beaver
deer	bird
Mr. Man	large trunk
apples (five or more)	large leaves
seed	large roots
small trunk	

Once upon a time, there was a seed named Abraham. He didn't know what kind of plant he would be, so he asked Mr. Bird. Mr. Bird didn't know but wanted to eat Abraham. Abraham asked him to wait until after he found out what he would be, and the bird agreed to wait.

Abraham grew small roots and green shoots. He asked Mr. Deer if he knew what he would grow up to be. "Do you know what I'll be when I grow up?" Mr. Deer said, "No," but wanted to eat the tender green shoot. Abraham said, "Please wait." So Mr. Deer decided to wait.

Abraham grew a small trunk and leaves. He was glad he was a tree but still didn't know what kind. He asked Mr. Beaver, "Do you know what I'll be when I grow up?" Mr. Beaver didn't know but wanted to eat Abraham's tender bark. He decided to wait also.

Abraham grew big roots, a big trunk, and more leaves, but still didn't know what kind of tree he was. He asked Mr. Man,

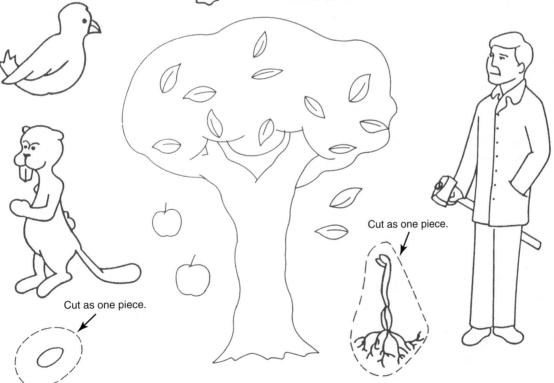

Cut as one piece.

Cut as one piece.

Full-size version of this art can be found on the Online Companion™ at http://www.earlychilded.delmar.com

"Do you know what I'll be when I grow up?" Mr. Man didn't know, but he wanted to chop down Abraham to make a house. He decided to wait.

Abraham grew apples. Hooray! He knew that he was an apple tree. He told Mr. Bird he could eat him now. Mr. Bird said Abraham was too big, but that he would like one of the apples. Mr. Deer thought the tree was too big, too, but he did want an apple. Mr. Beaver took any apples that fell to the ground home to his family. Mr. Man loved apples, so he told Abraham Tree that he wouldn't chop him down.

Abraham Apple Tree was so happy to know what he was and that no one was going to eat him or chop him down that he grew lots of apples.

When I got up this morning, I yawned a big yawn . . .
> *Just like daddy.*
I washed my face, got dressed, and had a big breakfast . . .
> *Just like daddy.*
And then I put on my yellow coat and blue vest and my red boots . . .
> *Just like daddy.*
And we went fishing—Daddy, Mommy, and me.
On the way, I picked a flower and gave it to my mother . . .
> *Just like daddy.*
When we got to the lake, I put a worm on my hook . . .
> *Just like daddy.*
All day we fished, and I caught a big fish . . .
> *Just like mommy!!!*

JUST LIKE DADDY

Pieces

little brown bear	green fish (large)
little brown bear's blue vest	green fish (small)
flower	brown mother bear
brown father bear	red boots for little bear
red boots for father bear	blue vest for father bear
yellow coat for father bear	yellow coat for little bear
purple vest for mother bear	

Flower (cut 1)

Small green fish (cut 1)

Green fish (cut 2)

Yellow coat for father bear (cut 1)

Little bear's blue vest (cut 1)

Little brown bear (cut 1)

Purple vest for mother bear (cut 1)

Full-size version of this art can be found on the Online Companion™ at http://www.earlychilded.delmar.com

380

Brown mother bear (cut 1)

Brown father bear (cut 1)

Yellow coat
for little bear
(cut 1)

Blue vest
for father
bear (cut 1)

Red boots
for father bear
(cut 2)

Red boots
for little bear
(cut 2)

Full-size version of this art can be found on the Online Companion™ at http://www.earlychilded.delmar.com

THE TREE IN THE WOODS

Pieces   grass   bird's nest
          treetop   bird's egg
          tree trunk   bird
          tree limb   wing
          tree branch   feather

(The flannel board can be used to build the song by placing first the grass and then the treetop, trunk, limb, branch, nest, egg, bird, wing, and feather, as each verse calls for them.)

> *Now in the woods there was a tree,*
> *The finest tree that you ever did see,*

And the green grass grew all around,
    around, around,
And the green grass grew all around.

And on that grass there was a trunk,
The finest trunk that you ever did see,
And the trunk was on the tree,
And the tree was in the woods,
And the green grass grew all around,
    around, around,
And the green grass grew all around.

And on that trunk there was a limb,
The finest limb that you ever did see,
And the limb was on the trunk,

And the trunk was on the tree,
And the tree was in the woods,
And the green grass grew all around,
    around, around,
And the green grass grew all around.

And on that limb there was a branch,
The finest branch that you ever did
    see,
And the branch was on the limb,
And the limb was on the trunk,
And the trunk was on the tree,
And the tree was in the woods,
And the green grass grew all around,
    around, around,
And the green grass grew all around.

And on that branch there was a nest,
The finest nest that you ever did see,
And the nest was on the branch,
And the branch was on the limb,
And the limb was on the trunk,
And the trunk was on the tree,
And the tree was in the woods,
And the green grass grew all around,
    around, around,
And the green grass grew all around.

And in that nest there was an egg,
The finest egg that you ever did see,
And the egg was in the nest,
And the nest was on the branch,
And the branch was on the limb,
And the limb was on the trunk,
And the trunk was on the tree,
And the tree was in the woods,
And the green grass grew all around,
    around, around,
And the green grass grew all around.

And on that egg there was a bird,
The finest bird that you ever did see,
And the bird was on the egg,
And the egg was in the nest,
And the nest was on the branch,
And the branch was on the limb,
And the limb was on the trunk,
And the trunk was on the tree,
And the tree was in the woods,
And the green grass grew all around,
    around, around,
And the green grass grew all around.

And on that bird there was a wing,
The finest wing that you ever did see,

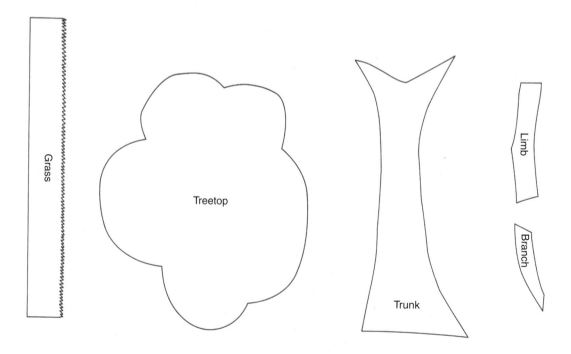

Full-size version of this art can be found on the Online Companion™ at http://www.earlychilded.delmar.com

382

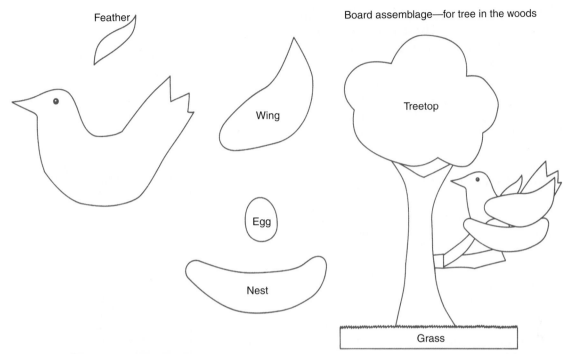

Feather

Board assemblage—for tree in the woods

Wing

Treetop

Egg

Nest

Grass

Full-size version of this art can be found on the Online Companion™ at http://www.earlychilded.delmar.com

And the wing was on the bird,
And the bird was on the egg,
And the egg was in the nest,
And the nest was on the branch,
And the branch was on the limb,
And the limb was on the trunk,
And the trunk was on the tree,
And the tree was in the woods,
And the green grass grew all around,
    around, around,
And the green grass grew all around.

And on that wing there was a feather,
The finest feather that you ever did
    see,
And the feather was on the wing,
And the wing was on the bird,
And the bird was on the egg,
And the egg was in the nest,
And the nest was on the branch,
And the branch was on the limb,
And the limb was on the trunk,
And the trunk was on the tree,
And the tree was in the woods,
And the green grass grew all around,
    around, around,
And the green grass grew all around.

RIDDLE

Pieces Triangles of felt in red, blue, yellow, green, purple, orange, brown, black, and white

Teacher: Riddle, riddle, ree.

What color do I see?

_____ (child's name) has it on his or her

_____ (shirt, pants, and so forth).

What color can this be?

(When the color is identified, the following is said.)

Group: It's _____, _____, _____. (Example: red, red, red)

Mary (instead of Mary substitute name of child who named the color) did say.

Let's see what colors we can find today.

383

(Teacher puts triangle of same color on flannel board. Child whose name was mentioned is asked whether he or she, or a friend of the child's choice, is going to guess the name of the color. Each child is asked whether he or she wants to guess the color. Activity ends with line of triangles that group names as each triangle is removed.)

ONE, TWO, BUCKLE MY SHOE

Pieces

Numerals 1 through 10   crossed sticks
shoe   straight sticks
door   hen

One, two,
Buckle my shoe;
Three, four,
Knock at the door;
Five, six,
Pick up sticks;
Seven, eight,
Lay them straight;
Nine, ten,
Big fat hen.

Cut line →

THIS OLD MAN

Pieces
old man	tree
shoe★	two clouds (heaven)
door★	thumb
sticks★	hive
gate	vine
10 bones	hen★
dog	numerals 1 through 10★

1. This old man, he played one, he played knick-knack on my thumb. With a knick-knack paddy-whack, give a dog a bone.

   This old man came rolling home.

2. This old man, he played two, he played knick-knack on my shoe. With a knick-knack paddy-whack, give a dog a bone.

Full-size version of this art can be found on the Online Companion™ at http://www.earlychilded.delmar.com

This old man came rolling home.

3. This old man, he played three, he played knick-knack on my tree.
   With a knick-knack paddy-whack, give a dog a bone.

   This old man came rolling home.

4. This old man, he played four, he played knick-knack on my door.
   With a knick-knack paddy-whack, give a dog a bone.

   This old man came rolling home.

5. This old man, he played five, he played knick-knack on my hive.
   With a knick-knack paddy-whack, give a dog a bone.

   This old man came rolling home.

6. This old man, he played six, he played knick-knack on my sticks.
   With a knick-knack paddy-whack, give a dog a bone.

   This old man came rolling home.

7. This old man, he played seven, he played knick-knack up in heaven.
   With a knick-knack paddy-whack, give a dog a bone.

   This old man came rolling home.

8. This old man, he played eight, he played knick-knack on my gate.
   With a knick-knack paddy-whack, give a dog a bone.

   This old man came rolling home.

9. This old man, he played nine, he played knick-knack on my vine.
   With a knick-knack paddy-whack, give a dog a bone.

   This old man came rolling home.

10. This old man, he played ten, he played knick-knack on my hen.
    With a knick-knack paddy-whack, give a dog a bone.

    This old man came rolling home.

AFRAID-OF STORY

Pieces   mouse   cat
         dog   bear
         hunter   lion

(Note: Patterns, except cat, can be found in stories in this chapter.)

(Place mouse on board.)

Here is a mouse. Mouse says, "I am the fastest, squeakiest mouse in the forest but I am afraid of cats."

(Add cat. Remove squeaky mouse.)

"I am the cleverest, meowingest cat in the forest but I am afraid of dogs."

(Add dog.)

Cat sneaks away.

(Remove cat.)

"I am the barkingest, bravest dog in the forest but I am afraid of bears."

(Add bear. Remove barking dog.)

"I am the biggest, most ferocious bear in the forest but I am afraid of the hunter."

(Add hunter and remove growling bear.)

"I am the smartest, most fearless hunter in the forest but I am afraid of lions."

(Add lion and remove hunter.)

"I am the fiercest, roaringest lion in the forest but I am afraid of a mouse who runs and squeaks at my feet!"

(Add mouse and remove lion.)

Mouse says "I told you I was the fastest, squeakiest mouse in the forest. Everyone is afraid of something sometimes!"

One can stop at this point or go through the characters again stopping at the "but I am afraid of" part in each animal's dialogue for the children to guess. This is also a good story to dramatize.

SECTION 5

Speech Growth:

Conversation, Expression,

and Dramatization

CHAPTER 13

Realizing Speaking Goals

OBJECTIVES

After reading this chapter, you should be able to:

◆ State five goals of planned speech activities.

◆ Describe appropriate teacher behavior in daily conversations with children.

◆ Give three examples of questioning technique.

◆ Explain the role of the teacher in dramatic play.

◆ Describe activities that promote children's speaking abilities.

KEY TERMS

| convergent thinking | divergent thinking | expressive jargon |
| discourse skills | dramatic play | recasting |

SWORD PLAY

Two four-year-old boys were pretending to fence with paper swords. One kept saying "mustard" as he wielded his. After saying it a few more times, the other boy said, "hot dog" in response. They thought this was hysterical. I didn't get it until later, when I realized the first child must have observed someone saying "en garde" while fencing.

QUESTIONS TO PONDER

1. Is this a type of dramatic play?

2. Do you have any other examples of young children copying words they have heard but not understood ?

In a well-planned classroom, a child has many opportunities to speak. Oral language is the foundation of literacy learning (Pinnell, 1999). While some activities are planned, others just happen. Classroom discussion is paramount; throw away most or all of your ideas about quiet classrooms and instead aim for a dynamic room where discussion reigns. In this type of atmosphere, true literacy emerges. Help children see the uses of speaking in social interactions in their daily lives and tie speech to print and reading activities when possible. Preschool children do a wonderful job of learning to communicate, and the more they talk, the more their talking improves.

Activities can be divided into three groups: structured, unstructured, and child-initiated. Structured activities are those that the teacher plans and prepares. The teacher may be, for a while, at the center of all action—motivating, presenting ideas, giving demonstrations, eliciting child ideas and comments, and promoting conversation. Unstructured activities, on the other hand, may still be prepared by the teacher, but the children decide the action through self-directed play, and the teacher is cast primarily in the role of cohort, confidant, and interested party (Figure 13–1). The teacher remains conversational and supportive. For optimal child learning, teachers need to appreciate and offer authentic dialogue and real human communication in a reciprocal relationship between learner and teacher rooted in equality, respect, and trust (Bartoli, 1995). Educators who are skilled in responsive involvement and responsive conversation make a difference in children's lives. Warm, sensitive, observant, interested listeners who encourage, make suggestions, promote child verbal expression, and are, at times, playful companions of the language arts events are definitely contributing to the quality of children's experiences.

Child-initiated activities are those that follow children's interests and exploration. The teacher may provide materials or activities to further child opportunities. He may act as a resource, someone to share ideas with, someone to discuss discovery, and may also provide help in recording the child's research (Figure 13–2). Teachers take every possible avenue to increase and promote child expression of ideas.

FIGURE 13–1 Teachers often become "coexplorers" who offer pertinent and language-expanding comments.

FIGURE 13-2 When teachers are close, they can share ideas, discuss happenings, or serve as a resource.

PROGRAM GOALS

Each center contains a unique group of children and adults. A center has its own geography and its children come from different segments of society, so the goals and priorities of one program may differ from others. There are, however, some common factors among centers. The following goals are acceptable to most programs. They give the teacher a basis for planning speaking activities and daily conversational exchanges. Each child should be helped to attain

◆ confidence in the ability to use speech with others.

◆ enjoyment in speaking experiences in play, conversations, and groups.

◆ acceptance of the idea that another's speech may be different.

◆ a higher level of interest in the meaning of new words.

In addition, each child should be helped to increase his skill in

◆ using speech for ideas, feelings, and needs.

◆ using speech to solve problems.

◆ using speech creatively in play situations.

◆ coordinating speech and body actions.

◆ waiting for a turn to speak.

Tabors (2002) reminds teachers of the importance of child **discourse skills** that go beyond basic conversation. Discourse skills involve children's use of language in structured ways, like telling a story about a past event, explaining how something works, building a fantasy world with words, explaining classroom rules to a peer, and dictating a "made up" poem. Tabors believes thought-provoking and open-ended adult-child conversations support children's discourse efforts.

---

discourse skills — refers to using language in structured ways to go beyond basic conversation, for example, telling a story, explaining a procedure, creating a fantasy, dictating ideas, and elaborating to provide greater understanding.

The overall goal in the development of speech communication in language arts is to increase each child's ability to use the speech he already possesses and to help the child move, when ready, toward the use of Standard English. Program goals can be realized mainly through the planning of daily activities, daily staff-child and child-child interaction, and the use of equipment and materials.

Skarpness and Carson (1987) note that appropriate child behavior in kindergarten is aided if certain speaking and listening skills have been acquired.

Children who are encouraged to express themselves, practice their speaking skills, and listen carefully to others are likely to adjust more readily to changing situations within the classroom.

A wide variety of different experiences can provide many learning opportunities. An activity can follow, review, and add depth to a previous one. One has to consider how much practice time is available.

The special interests or needs of each child are considered when planning daily programs. Programs then become more valuable and meaningful.

DAILY CONVERSATIONS

Daily teacher-child conversations become amazingly easy when teachers focus on "children's agenda." When classrooms seem always to be too hectic to get eye to eye with the child and listen to and pursue the child's interests, the program, environment, and teaching situation need to be evaluated and overhauled, for intimate conversations are severely limited and infrequent. At the other extreme, teachers defeat their purpose when the objective is always to teach or add a new word to the child's vocabulary. The key is to identify the child's interests; words then become meaningful. When the child is engrossed, he will connect the teacher's words with what has fascinated him (Nelson, 1985).

Excellent teachers make their students feel valuable, competent, and worthwhile. The follow-

ing are the attitudes and behaviors every would-be teacher should cultivate in conversation.

◆ concern for each child's well-being
◆ an unwillingness to interrupt a child's conversation to respond to an adult
◆ a willingness to share the small moments of child accomplishment, sometimes even recognizing a child's achievement in a nonverbal way across a busy classroom
◆ consideration of children's verbal comments as worthy contributions and respect for individual opinions
◆ respect of each child's potential
◆ special regard for children as future leaders and discoverers

Teacher actions, questions, or statements that indicate the listener's genuine interest elicit a wealth of oral language (Figure 13–3).

Some of the best activities happen when the teacher notices what the child or group is focusing on and uses the opportunity to expand interest, knowledge, and enjoyment. A rainbow, a delivery truck, or any chance happening can become the central topic of active speaking by the children.

Whether limited or advanced, a child's speech is immediately accepted and welcomed. Teachers carefully guard and protect each child's self-confidence. By waiting patiently and reading nonverbal clues, teachers become understanding listeners.

Every effort should be made to give a logical response, showing the child that the teacher finds value in the communication. Touching, offering a reassuring arm or hand, and giving one's whole attention to the child often seem to relax the child and increase speech production.

Children are more willing to speak when the proper classroom atmosphere is maintained.

◆ The tone of the room is warm and relaxed, and children have choices.
◆ Speaking is voluntary, not mandatory.
◆ The speaking group is small.
◆ The group listens attentively.

FIGURE 13-3 "You want to fill four buckets with sand using the funnel?"

◆ Any speaking attempt is welcomed.

◆ Effort and accomplishments are recognized.

A teacher's willingness to engage in light-hearted dialogue may make the child more open to talking for the fun of it. When the mood is set for discovery, the teacher becomes active in the quest for answers, carefully guiding children through their exploration and expression.

Adults who emphasize the reasons for events and who take a questioning, thoughtful, and systematic approach to problems become model explorers. Thinking out loud while sharing activities is a useful device. "I wonder what would happen if you put the block there?" a teacher might ask. In their speech, young children often deal with the reality of what is happening around them; teachers' speech should also be based on this concept.

In reacting to young children's sometimes awkward, fractured, or incorrect speech, adults intuitively provide useful corrective feedback. The child's "posta put in" would automatically be accepted and corrected with, "Yes, the blocks go on the shelf." Seasoned teachers listen for content and the ideas behind words and

matter-of-factly model correct usage so smoothly that the child is not made to feel that his speech usage was in any way deficient. The teacher must know how to make alert, sensitive comments that ensure that the children will continue to see the teacher as a responsive, accepting adult.

Halliday (1973) has researched human speech development and classified differing "functions" of human speech. His classifications follow. Teachers observing children will notice the young child's increasing use of speech in social situations.

◆ *Instrumental* speech satisfies wants and needs.

"I want to be next."

◆ *Regulatory* speech helps children control others.

"Don't drop the cup because it will break into a zillion pieces."

◆ *Interactional* speech establishes and maintains contact with others.

"M," that's my letter. I'm Monroe." (Pointing to an alphabet chart with a friend.)

◆ *Personal function* speech expresses and asserts individuality.

"Let's push it under, and make it stay down." (Water play).

◆ *Heuristic function* speech helps children learn and describe.

"You're the baby, who goes wah, wah, wah."

◆ *Imaginative function* speech creates images and aids pretending.

"Look, I'm flying."

◆ *Representational* speech informs.

"I don't like bananas."

Teachers trying to facilitate children's use of Halliday's speech classifications will want to study Figure 13–4. All of these speech functions are present in the average preschool classroom.

What are young children fond of talking about? Themselves and what they are doing! They have their own views and opinions about the world around them. As their social contact increases, they exchange their ideas with other children. When they become older preschoolers, they typically engage in criticism, commands, requests, threats, and questions and answers. As a teacher listens to child-to-child conversations, he can make out both self-interest speech and speech that indicates social-intellectual involvement. Quite a lot of child conversation reflects the child's active, exploring, questioning mind and attempts to try, test, manipulate, control, and discover what speech can do for him. Flights of fantasy and make-believe play are also evident.

Certain teacher behaviors and planned programs enhance children's speaking abilities. Are there factors that work counter to the realization of goals? Hough, Nurss, and Goodson (1984) compared everyday interactions in two child care centers and found one center they describe as lacking language stimulation. They reported that the children spent most of their time in teacher-directed large-group activities and that most of the children's language behavior was receptive, such as listening to and following teachers' directions. Although teachers provided adequate oral language models, they were not active listeners, did not encourage curiosity, and did not spontaneously expand on children's vocabulary or concepts.

During interactions, children need their conversational partners to provide them with information that relates to the topic of the conversation and is relevant and appropriate to their language level so that they can use it to build upon what they already know. Teachers should try to avoid the following behaviors because they discourage healthy speech development.

◆ making inappropriate or irrelevant teacher comments

◆ talking at rather than with children

◆ using a controlling and commanding mode of interaction

◆ repeating oneself often

◆ criticizing child speech

◆ speaking primarily to other classroom adults

These are characteristics of unprofessional practice.

A New York study paired a proficient "talker" with a less proficient preschooler. At a special table, the "talk table," the study authors provided sets of categorized miniature figures and furnishings (Woodward, Haskins, Schaefer, & Smolen, 2004). Rules limited the table to one pair of children for 15 minutes of uninterrupted talk-time play per day. The miniature toys were not to be moved away. Each new set of toys was introduced with vocabulary. Children were urged to "use your words" at the talk table. During the 10-week study, teachers expended efforts to stimulate oral language through interactions and additional literacy activities. Test scores showed statistically significant oral improvement. The authors of the study believe the project clearly indicates that when an assessment suggests that a child has an expressive speech problem, concerned and innovative teachers can do something about it (Woodward et al., 2004).

Personal Speech Expressing Individual Ideas, Feelings, Concerns

Teacher actions include:
1. providing time and opportunity for adult-child and child-adult sharing of personal thoughts and feelings.
2. eye-level listening and impromptu conversations throughout the school day.
3. accepting individual child ideas and feelings and expressing your own.
4. encouraging family visitation, participation, and interaction in classroom activities and affairs.
5. sharing literature that elicits children's personal speech responses.

Speech Helping Children Obtain and Satisfy Wants and Needs

Teacher actions include:
1. listening and responding to children's requests.
2. encouraging children's ability to ask for wants and needs.
3. increasing children's opportunities to help other children by giving verbal directions.
4. explaining in step-by-step fashion the sequence needed to obtain desired results (e.g., how to get a turn with a favorite bike).

Speech That Promotes and Maintains Interaction

Teacher actions include:
1. planning for shared use of materials, areas, or adult help.
2. planning for small group discussion and problem solving.
3. including a mix of child ages and genders in planned activities.
4. celebrating and socializing between children and adults in classrooms.
5. devising activities in which self-worth and diversity are valued.
6. devising activities in which negotiating and compromise are possible.

Speech That Expresses Imaginative Ideas

Teacher actions include:
1. planning for creative individual child and group response.
2. designing activities to promote pretending.
3. prompting child description of creative ideas, actions, and solutions.
4. offering dramatizing, play acting, and role-playing classroom opportunities and providing areas and furnishings.

5. being playful with language and appreciating children's playful language.
6. encouraging children's creative play by providing props and giving teacher attention.
7. using audio or visual taping or group enactment of child creativity to preserve, give status, and promote discussion and provoke additional creativity.

Speech That Enhances Children's Verbal Descriptions and Learning

Teacher actions include:
1. providing child activities to capture child interest and spark curiosity.
2. creating child and group verbal problem-solving opportunities.
3. putting phrases such as the following in daily teacher speech:

    "I wonder what . . ."

    "What would happen if . . ."

    "Let's see if . . ."

    "That's one way, can anyone think of another?"

    "What do we know about . . ."

    "Can we try a new way?"

    "What did we see when . . ."
4. suggesting real rather than contrived problems to solve.
5. listening closely to child discoveries and prompting children to put ideas into words.
6. noticing child interests. Building interest by following up with further activities.

Speech That Is Representational or Informative

Teacher actions include:
1. keeping record charts with children.
2. planning activities that involve observing carefully and analyzing or drawing conclusions.
3. eliciting additional or more precise information from children.
4. recording memorable classroom events, celebrations, and other happenings.
5. posting child birthdays, individual attributes, milestones, or other facts and data enhancing child self-worth or dignity.
6. graphing class composition factors (e.g., height and weight, food preference). Or presenting simple mapping activities involving school or neighborhood.
7. comparing time-related classroom factors.
8. providing activities that report individual child experiences to the group.

FIGURE 13–4 Suggested teacher strategies to promote child speech in differing classifications of human speech.

Children's Conversational Styles

Weitzman (1992) urges early childhood practitioners to observe and notice children's conversational styles. She points out that young children vary in their ability to spontaneously approach others, initiate communicative interactions, and respond. She believes conversational styles evolve from children's past life experiences and interactions with others as they form their own views of themselves as communicators (Figure 13–5). From your own experience with young children, what types of communication styles have you noticed? Eager, shy, self-conscious, self-confident, articulate, silent, questioning, repetitive, loud, advanced, and others? One child may need multiple descriptors, being social yet unclear, or shy but verbal when approached, for example. As one works daily with young children, one makes mental notes (or written ones) to help one decide what possible activities and adult interactions will provide opportunities for speech growth. Beginning teachers need to be aware of teacher tendencies to converse and spend time with children with whom they feel comfortable, perhaps because of that child's particular conversational style, cultural background, ethnic origin, or personality.

Sign Systems

Early childhood educators are aware that young children express themselves in a number of ways. Teachers realize that words are but one of the multiple systems young children use to construct and express meaning. Sign systems, like music, drama, and mathematics, are uniquely different from language yet related. Words often accompany sign systems in both adults' and children's activities. Nonverbal signs, such as gestures, encountered in children's personal experience become associated with particular meanings that may differ widely for individual children.

Teachers meet young children who are more able to express themselves in movement, art, or drama than with words. Actions can sometimes convey more than a child's language ability allows.

Activities that encourage singing, dramatic expression, or use of art media to express what children know and feel expand the "confines" of language, promoting what Newkirk (1989) calls "symbol weaving."

Almost all activities involve communication and expression. It is the teacher's job to see that words are prompted or supplied as a natural part of adult-child interaction so that consequent vocabulary growth is possible. Discussion between teachers and children in all curriculum areas can add and expand meaning to what is jointly experienced. For example, the statement, "You found two cars can fit on the flat bed truck," puts into words the child's discovery. "Joy-lyn is showing us with her body how she feels about the doll she brought to sharing time" is another example.

FIGURE 13–5 Anna uses specific terms and mentions small details as she converses with others.

THE AUTHENTIC TEACHER

"Authentic" teachers are quick to issue appreciative comments about a child's persistence at tasks, creative or new elements in child activities, solutions to problems encountered, or other features of children's actions or behaviors. They are good at spotting every child's advances and accomplishments. They also provide honest comments when necessary, and this can be done with specific, detailed words that expand children's understanding. They promote children's ability to put their own feelings into words daily in conflict situations, empowering children in the process.

Of prime importance to most educators is the goal of enhancing each child's growth of self-esteem and feelings of worth and value. Teachers work daily toward this. They attempt to stretch language skills and realize a confident child will converse freely and risk new experiences.

In social conflict situations, teachers channel child problems back to the conflicting parties so that verbal solutions between children are possible (Figure 13–6). They quietly stand near, hoping confrontations can come to satisfactory solutions, and intercede only when child communication breaks down.

It is obvious to teachers that many young children seek validation of their abilities. Children's "Look at me" or "Look what I did" requests can be answered in ways that are both language expanding and self-worth building. "Oh, that's nice" or "Yes, I see" are weak adult statements. A specific comment is more effective. "Your long blocks are standing on their small ends. You built your bridge very carefully," or "To make your cat's tail you had to cut a long thin piece of paper. It looks like a cat's tail because it comes to a small point on the end." These are valuable teacher comments.

FIGURE 13–6 After listening, the teacher will encourage putting the child's distress into words and will suggest that the child return and negotiate a solution.

INTEGRATING CHILDREN INTO SOCIAL GROUPS

Because adults know children are teachers of other children, they want all children to obtain skills in social interaction. Teachers promote child friendships. The fragile friendships of two- and three-year-olds blossom and stabilize around age four. The conversation of children in group play is a joy to overhear. A reluctant child is encouraged. Books, puppets, and other language arts media can offer friendship themes and empathy-building models. The story *The Lion and the Mouse* is a good example and usually increases child comments concerning what it means to be a friend. The story ends with ". . . little friends can help big friends. The size of a friend isn't really too important."

SUGGESTED INTERACTION GUIDES

A teacher is a speech model for children. Because preschoolers range in abilities, the following guides for teachers in daily verbal conversations are based on understanding the level of each child. These guidelines help develop speaking ability when dealing with young nonverbal, or slightly verbal, children.

- ◆ Let the child see your face and mouth clearly, bend your knees, and talk at the child's eye level.
- ◆ Use simple hand gestures that show meanings.
- ◆ Watch for nonverbal reactions.

◆ Talk to the nonverbal child slowly, stressing key words such as nouns and verbs.

◆ If you cannot understand a word, repeat it back to the child in a relaxed way.

◆ If a child says "lellow," say, "Yes, the paint is yellow." Articulation will improve with age and good speech modeling.

◆ Answer **expressive jargon** (groups of sounds without recognizable words) or jabbering with suitable statements such as "You're telling me."

◆ Play games in which the child copies sounds or words.

◆ Watch for the child's lead. If he is interested in some activity or object, talk about it in simple sentences.

◆ Make directions simple. Indicate actions as you say the words.

◆ Encourage the child's imitations, whether verbal or nonverbal. Show that the effort is appreciated.

◆ Pause and wait patiently for the child's response.

The following guidelines help children who speak in one-word phrases or simple sentences develop speaking ability.

◆ Enlarge a child's one-word sentences into meaningful simple sentences, for example, "ball" to "The ball bounces."

◆ Use naming words to describe objects and actions: "The red ball is round."

◆ Use conjunctions (and, but, so, also, or), possessives (mine, theirs, ours, Billy's, yours, his, hers), and negatives (is not, will not, do not, isn't, don't, won't, am not).

◆ Help the child talk about his feelings.

◆ Use previously learned words with new words: "The black candy is called licorice." "Your dog is a poodle; this dog is a beagle." "It's a kind of hat called a baseball cap."

◆ Ask simple questions that help the child find out and discover while his interest is high: "Where did you find that round rock?"

◆ Play labeling games with pictures and objects.

◆ Correct speech errors such as "wented" or "goed" by matter-of-factly saying the correct word in a sentence: "Yesterday you went to the store." (Omit any corrective tone of voice.) The child may answer by saying it the same as before, but you have modeled correct usage, and in time it will be copied.

◆ Accept hesitant speech and stuttering in a patient, interested way. When a child is excited or under stress, ideas may not develop into words properly.

◆ Wait patiently while a child tries to speak; silently hold eye contact. The thought may get lost, but if you are a good listener, and if you respond with interest to what is said, the child will try again.

When the child speaks in sentences and comes close to mature speech, the teacher should

◆ include appropriate classifications or categories in sentences to help children form concepts: "Dogs and cats are animals."

◆ ask questions that help the child pinpoint identifying characteristics (Figure 13–7): "Does it have a tail?"

◆ ask questions that help the child see what is alike and what is different.

◆ after modeling a sentence pattern in conversation, ask a simple question so that the child can imitate the proper form while it is still fresh in his mind: "I think this lemon tastes sour. How does the lemon taste to you?"

◆ help the child keep ideas in order. What happened first? What happened next? What came last?

◆ state instructions clearly, building from one- to two- or three-part directions: "First wash your hands; then you can choose a cracker."

◆ use prepositions in speech. Say them with gestures: "Put the toy on the shelf. Thank

---

expressive jargon — a term describing a child's first attempts at combining words into narration that results in a mimic of adult speech.

FIGURE 13–7 "Will this brown triangle become the jack-o-lantern's other eye?"

you. The blocks go inside the box." (Use your hand to show position as you speak.)

◆ use adjectives (big, little, bright, red, soft, and so forth) and comparatives (more, less, lighter, heavier, shorter, tallest): "Tell me about the rubber doll." "Yes, this pink doll is bigger."

◆ ask the child to take simple verbal messages to another staff member: "Tell Mrs. Brown it's time to fix the snack." Alert other staff members to the fact that you are trying to promote verbal memory and self-confidence.

◆ help the child discover cause and effect: "Teacher, I'm afraid of bugs." "Why do bugs make you afraid, Billy?"

◆ remember that what is said in response to the child helps the child in many ways. Really listen. Answer every child if possible. When children talk at the same time, say, "I

want to hear each one." "Mary, please say it again." "John, you can tell us next."

◆ give ownership to the ideas children contribute: "Yesterday Nancy told us . . ." "Kate's idea is . . ."

Dumtschin (1988) mentions a technique in adult-child conversation from the work of Fujiki and Brinton (1984) that is termed **recasting**. This is very similar to expansion and feedback, previously mentioned. Recasting fills in what is missing or gently changes the child's incorrect usage in the adult's answering comment and extends the child's idea. If a child says, "I like apples," for example, the teacher could respond, "Apples taste good, don't they?" or "I like green ones, don't you?"

When teachers actively listen and observe, questions and teacher responses can better suit individual children. Teachers can grow to understand speech and conceptual errors, miscues, misconceptions, and the ways certain children express themselves with greater depth. With close observation, teachers begin to build a personal and cultural history of attending children. Some preschool children may have traveled extensively, whereas others have never left their neighborhoods. Both can have rich, full vocabularies but completely different fields of reference. In a conversation about tree blossoms brought into the classroom, the teacher might ask, "Where have you seen trees blossom in your neighborhood?" or "Tell me how the blossoms feel when you rub them gently on your cheek like this," or "What do you see if you look very closely at the blossom in your hand?"

Goodman (1985) suggests the following regarding teachers' verbal interactions with children.

1. When a child achieves success in some communicative setting, the teacher may find ways to extend this to a new and different setting.

2. When children are involved in exploratory activities, the teacher might raise questions

---

recasting — a teaching technique that involves a teacher who supplies children's missing words or gently models correct usage of words or extends the child's idea following the child's verbal statement.

such as, "I wonder why this is so?" or "What do you think is happening here?"

3. When children are observed to be troubled with an experience, the teacher can move in and talk about the situation with them and lead them to what they cannot yet do by themselves.

4. Teachers need to trust in children's learning and in their own ability to learn along with their children.

A number of additional teacher options for extending child conversations can be found in Figure 13–8.

When a child's attention or focus is upon an object, action, event, animal, person, and so on, try the following:

• *Probe* with comments using your five senses. Discuss visual attributes (color, shiny, round, etc.). Comment on tactile qualities (soft, smooth, etc.). Make sound observations (loud, clang, thud, etc.). Describe smell or taste, if present.
• *Suggest* that the child "describe" using his senses.
• *Provide* data or information that is pertinent.
• *Comment* on significant facts and features, such as function, usefulness, category or class, novelty, origin, timeliness, parts, details, construction, mobility, weight, height, bulk, dimension, movement, and so forth.
• *Compare* it with something similar.
• *Relate* it to present, past, or future.
• *Probe* its relationship to other things.
• *Make guesses* in reference to what has captured the child's attention.
• *Discuss* opinions, impressions, conclusions, and problems that are possible or apparent.
• *Mention* likes and dislikes.
• *Fantasize,* imagine, pretend, or dream out loud.
• *Talk* about humorous, ridiculous, or incongruent features.

To assess your skill:

The child is observing a large ice cube melt in the outside yard. Return to the above and generate extending teacher comments.

FIGURE 13–8 Teacher options and ways to extend child conversations.

AWARENESS OF INTELLIGENT BEHAVIOR

Over time, a number of researchers have tried to identify effective thinking and intelligent behavior indicators. Would-be teachers observe children and conjecture how young children "come to know" rather than remember or state what they already know. Most classrooms enroll children whom teachers would call "successful students." By closely observing children, teachers can note behaviors that indicate children's reasoning abilities, insightfulness, strategies, perseverance, creativity, and craftsmanship.

Many indicators are best observed in children's speech behavior. Costa (1991) outlines intelligent behavior characteristics but also notes that the listing may be incomplete.

1. *Persistence:* Persevering when a solution to a problem is not immediately apparent. In preschool some children ask abundant questions, others try various and different approaches to reach goals. A child might ask all other teachers in a room if one teacher admits he/she doesn't know the answer to the question. Many children probe the reasons behind happenings and are persistent in getting more and more data to explain happenings.

2. *Decreasing impulsivity:* A thoughtful pause rather than a quick answer or action may be observed in some preschoolers.

3. *Listening to others with understanding and empathy:* Some young children hear others' points-of-view and can paraphrase another's ideas. Others may not be able to "overcome ego-centrism" at this age as Piaget observes. Both groups are displaying developmentally appropriate behavior. The first group has achieved a maturity in thinking processes, and are usually slow to ridicule, laugh at, or put down other children's ideas.

4. *Flexibility in thinking:* No matter what a teacher or parent tells a child on a certain subject, the child may not believe or accept the information. This isn't flexibility in thinking. As children age, however,

many will at least consider new possibilities and doubt their previous ideas. Some check out new ideas with others with questions like "Do daddies cook?"

5. *Metacognition: Awareness of one's own thinking:* Preschoolers may be able to describe the steps they took to achieve some desired outcome, but rarely can they put into words what went on inside their heads or describe their strategies. More often when asked "How did you do that?" they will be silent or say "I just did it." This is a developmentally appropriate answer.

6. *Checking for accuracy and precision:* The child who shows a printed form to teacher saying "I made an A" may be simply stating a truth as he sees it. With another child who says "That's not an A. Is it, teacher?" The child is checking for accuracy. In discussions a child may seek a correction. Many teachers have learned this lesson with the child who's a dinosaur buff for the child has learned the distinguishing characteristics of each dinosaur well, and may be better informed than the teacher.

7. *Questioning and problem posing:* This is a characteristic of many preschoolers who inquire about the "whys" of things and are alert to discrepancies and uncommon phenomena.

8. *Drawing on past knowledge and applying it to new situations:* At times, teachers have difficulty trying to understand what common element in a present situation the child is connecting to the past. Other connections are readily apparent as when a child reacts negatively to a worker dressed in white.

9. *Precision of language and thought:* Young children use an increasing number of descriptive words and analogous comments when exposed to adult language that is not vague or imprecise.

10. *Using all the senses:* Young children readily probe, manipulate, and savor the sensory opportunities presented to them.

11. *Ingenuity, originality, insightfulness, creativity:* Early childhood professionals treasure child attempts and behaviors in this area, and most teachers can immediately cite examples they've observed.

12. *Wonderment, inquisitiveness, curiosity, and enjoyment of problem solving—a sense of efficacy as a thinker:* Child attitudes toward problems, thinking games, guessing and obstacles can enhance or impede their quest for knowledge and solutions. Adults may model attitudes of "giving up" or "it's too hard" or "I'll never get it right" rather than the preferred "let's find out," "let's see what we can do." Adults can also model enjoyment when in the pursuit of solving some task or dilemma.

In considering Costa's number 6 in preceding list, the teacher may consider a child saying, "Sudeh didn't drink her juice," as checking to see if a rule about juice-finishing exists, rather than tattling. The teacher might reply, "At school we can choose to drink as much juice as we want, but everyone should drink all that he pours in his cup."

How can early childhood teachers support children's emerging intellectual abilities? From Costa's list, there are many clues. A teacher begins by having faith in the ability and intelligence of all children and acknowledges that not all children's homes (or all teachers) value intelligent behavior. Intelligent child behavior can be recognized and appreciated.

Children can absorb the idea that often there is more than one solution or answer or way of doing something and that pausing, gathering more data, and "thinking things over" are good strategies. Children can be asked to share their plans and outcomes on chosen activities. Day-to-day happenings and real dilemmas can be talked about and problems solved through actions and discussions where every child's ideas are valued.

The teacher can rig classroom activities to promote children's thinking, problem solving, creative ideas, and imagination. Children can develop the attitude that what they contribute is worthwhile. When teachers listen, paraphrase children's comments, clarify, and try out student ideas, children feel what they say is meaningful. "Maybe the school's pet bird does eat paper, or maybe it just tears it up. If we watch carefully we can find out, can't we?"

Providing a continually interesting classroom full of exploring opportunities is a must. Classrooms rich in firsthand manipulative experiences and responsive adults is a widely accepted goal in preschool practice.

One of the chief causes for failure in formal education is that we begin with language rather than with real and material action (Costa, 1991). At preschool level this means some teachers have a tendency to tell children about reality rather than "providing" reality—real exploring experiences encountered together. Teachers also need to model their own intelligent behaviors and enthusiasm for learning. Nothing works as well as an example.

SETTINGS FOR PREPLANNED SPEAKING ACTIVITIES

Speaking activities occur when children are inside or outside the classroom or when they are on the move. Preplanned activities are more successful when both children and teachers are comfortable and unhurried and when there are no distractions. Peers will be a valuable source of words and meanings.

Close attention should be given to group size and the seating space between children at group times. It is easier to create an atmosphere of inclusion and intimacy in a small discussion group than in a large group, thereby promoting children's willingness to share thoughts. Lighting and heating in the room must also be considered. Soft textures and rugs add warmth and comfort. A half-circle seating arrangement, with the teacher in the center, provides a good view of both the teacher and what is to be seen.

Ease of viewing depends on eye level and seating arrangement. When possible, the objects children are to look at should be at their eye level. Teachers often sit in child-sized chairs while conducting language arts experiences. Screens, dividers, and bookcases can help lessen distractions.

One inventive teacher thought of a way to promote child speech during a parent-child "Back to School" night. Children were asked to draw a picture of themselves. A large mirror was set up beside various drawing supplies and paper. Children were asked not to write their names on their self-portraits. Before the meeting, child drawings were posted under signs reading "Can you find me?" Signs were done in the home languages of attending children. The activity promoted the children's verbal identification of themelves and classmates and highlighted the children's role as a verbal classroom guide for parents.

QUESTIONING SKILLS

A teacher's questions often prompt children to ponder and wonder. Questions checking whether the teacher has understood the child's comment are common. They provide the child feedback concerning the teacher's attention and interest and clarify whether the child's intended message was understood. This gives the child the opportunity to correct the teacher and send further data or explanation or clear up miscommunication. Questions can also help keep conversations afloat and show that the teacher is interested in child pursuits.

Questions can help children see details they would otherwise have missed. Sometimes questions help a child form relationships between objects and ideas; they may prompt the child to speak about both feelings and thoughts; they can lead the child to a new interest. Skill in questioning is an important teaching ability. Questions asked by a teacher can often lead children to discovery.

Many experts suggest that teachers need help and specific training in questioning strategies so that they can aid children's ability to see contradictions, move them toward rethinking, and assist concept development. Teachers need to ask questions that are readily understood and require easy responses from the very young child and more challenging, thoughtful responses from language-capable preschoolers. This means modifying questions depending on language levels.

Asking questions may be "the most fragile" of all conversation starters. Teachers can make questions less threatening by asking about a child's activities or interests and by using familiar expressions.

In a situation in a classroom when a window has blown shut and one of the children says, "Someone hit that window, teacher!" a skillful question such as "Is anyone standing near the window?" or "Could anyone reach that window from down on the ground?" or "Can you think of something else that might slam a window shut, something that could push it? Let's look out the window and see if other things are being pushed around," could lead the child to a new conclusion.

The following example illustrates the teacher's role in stimulating the thought process that emerges from play. The teacher, who has created the climate for learning by supplying and arranging the equipment, sees a child playing with cars on ramps that he has constructed with blocks. The teacher knows that if a car is placed on a slope made with blocks, the speed with which it descends and the distance it goes are affected by the slope and length of the ramp. The teacher asks, "Johnny, did this blue car go farther than the red one?" The teacher also introduces new words to the child's vocabulary—slant, ramp, slow, faster, above, below, under, tall, smaller than—and uses and elicits this vocabulary in conversation (Danoff, Breitbart, & Barr, 1977).

Teachers need to be sensitive to the anxiety that some children may have. In past experiences, if a child's answers have been overcorrected, or if adults' questions are associated with punishment, teachers' questions can cause children to be silent and tense.

Teachers use "choice" questions at times. It allows them to slip specific, descriptive words into their speech while the child is focused: "Do you want the red paint (pointing) or the blue paint (pointing)?"

Also important in asking questions is the teacher's acceptance of the child's answers. Because each child answers a question based on his own experience, children may give very different answers. The following conversation (observed at the San Jose City College Child Development Center) shows how a teacher handled an unexpected answer.

(Conversation has centered around television sets.)

Teacher: "Where could we go to buy a television set?"

Chase: "Macy's."

Chloe: "At a pear store."

Vanda: "The TV store."

Teacher: "Chase says Macy's sells television sets. Chloe thinks we could buy one at a 'pear' store. Vanda thought at a TV store. Maybe we could go to three places to buy one. Chloe, have you seen television sets at the 'pear' store?"

Chloe: "The pear store has lots of 'em."

Teacher: "You've been to a 'pear' store?"

Chloe: "Our TV broke, and we took it to the 'pear' store."

Teacher: "The repair shop fixed my broken television set, too. Yes, sets can be for sale at a repair shop."

The teacher's task is to keep the speech and answers coming, encouraging each child's expression of ideas. Sometimes a question can be answered with a question. When a child says, "What does a rabbit eat?" the teacher might say, "How could we find out?" The teacher knows that a real experience is better than a quick answer.

When using questions, the level of difficulty should be recognized. Early childhood teachers can use carefully asked questions to find the child's level of understanding. Teachers try to help each child succeed in activities while offering a challenge at the same time. Even snack time can be a time to learn new language skills.

Open-ended questions are very useful, and teachers try to increase their ability to ask them. *Open-ended questions* are defined as questions with many possible answers. Almy (1975) points out

Some teachers are so intent on imparting information to children that they forget to assess the ways it may be assimilated. Thus answers to open-ended questions—"Can you tell me about . . . ?" "What do you think about . . . ?"—are often more revealing than answers to questions with a more specific focus. They can be followed by "Tell me more." "Some people think that . . ." "What do you think?"

Teachers' questions can be classified into eight main types.

1. *Recall:* Asks child to remember information, names, words, and so forth. Recall questions are the type most often asked. Gall (1984) reports that about 60 percent of teachers' questions require students to recall facts, about 20 percent require students to think, and the remaining 20 percent are procedural. Teachers emphasize fact questions, whereas research indicates an emphasis on higher, cognitive questions would be more effective. The Student Activities section of this chapter asks you to conduct an observational study concerning this point. Could it be this type of question was modeled constantly in most teachers' own elementary schooling? Example: What color is this ball?

2. **Convergent thinking:** Asks child to compare or contrast similarities or differences and seek relationships. Example: How are these two toy cars alike?

3. **Divergent thinking:** Asks child to predict or theorize. Example: If the boy steps on the marble, what might happen?

4. *Evaluation:* Asks child for a personal opinion or judgment or asks child to explore feelings. Example: What would be on your plate if you could have your favorite food?

5. *Observation:* Asks child to watch or describe what he senses. Example: What is happening to the ant on the window sill?

6. *Explanation:* Asks child to state cause and effect, reasons, and/or descriptions. Example: The clay feels different today. What do you think happened to it?

7. *Action:* Asks child to move body or perform a physical task. Example: Can you show us how to walk like a duck?

8. *Open-ended:* Many answers are possible. Example: How do children get from their homes to their school in the morning?

Hendrick (1998) also suggests that certain types of teacher questions promote children's thinking processes. These include questions seeking child *opinion,* questions calling for a verbalized child *choice,* questions promoting a child hypothesis, questions asking for *cause-and-effect explanations,* and questions seeking child *solutions.* She urges teachers to question children's past happenings in light of present happenings to help children form relationships.

Teachers should limit "low-quality" questions that center on isolated bits of knowledge and are designed to test what is learned or remembered. Unfortunately, teachers and teacher test question behavior have been paired in the minds of some adults. They doggedly ask continual questions of children, believing this is age-old and appropriate behavior for all "good" teachers. When an adult approaches a young child playing in the sandbox with questions like "What are you doing?" or "What are you making?" the child may wonder why the adult cannot see for himself or whether he is supposed to be making something. It may be hard for this adult to really focus on the child's activity and

---

convergent thinking — the process of analyzing and integrating ideas to infer reasonable conclusions or specific solutions from given information.

divergent thinking — the process of elaborating on ideas to generate new ideas or alternative interpretations of given information.

make pertinent comments, such as "That's a big mountain of sand you've just made," or to pick up a sand toy cup and say, "Please pour some sand in my cup."

Preschool teachers have many opportunities through questioning to explore children's imaginative responses to books, events, and classroom happenings. Their questions can be child-centered, promoting creative and interpretive child responses. Teachers can improve their ability to stop, listen, and learn from what their charges are saying.

The way questions are phrased may produce short or longer answers. Questions using "what" or "where" usually receive one-word or word-phrase answers. Many questions, such as Do you? Did you? Can you? Will you? Have you? Would you? can be answered by yes or no. This type of question fits the level of the very young.

Questions that help a child compare or connect ideas may begin as follows:

What would happen if . . . ?

Which one is longer?

How are these two alike?

Why did you say these were different?

What happened next?

If it fell off the table, what would happen to it?

Can you guess which one will be first?

Could this ball fit inside this can?

I wonder why that is like that?

What do you think is happening?

The following are examples of questions that encourage problem solving or stimulate creative thought.

If you had a handful of pennies, what would you buy?

Could you tell me what you are going to do when you're as big as your dad?

Can you think of a way to open this coconut?

How could we find out where this ant lives?

These questions can be answered by the more mature speakers. Through close listening and observation, the teacher can form questions that the child will want to answer.

USING A VYGOTSKIAN OR CONSTRUCTIVIST APPROACH

According to Bodrova and Leong (1996), a teacher using a Vygotskian approach with younger and older children should

◆ make his actions and the children's actions verbally explicit. Label his own actions as he carries them out. Label the child's actions for him as they occur. "Hand me the blue blocks."

◆ model thinking and strategies aloud. As he solves a problem, talk about what he is thinking about. "I could put them together."

◆ when introducing a new concept, be sure to tie it to actions. "When we want to measure something to see how long it is, we put the ruler at the end of the object and read the numbers here."

◆ use thinking while talking to check children's understanding of concepts and strategies. Get children used to talking about what they think and how they solve problems.

◆ encourage the use of private speech. This type of self-talk has meaning for the child and should not be discouraged. Coach the child on what he might say to himself as he does something, "The knob turns, and then press the button."

SPEECH IN PLAY AND ROUTINES

Children's play opportunities in early childhood centers are planned for, promoted, and wide ranging. An examination of whether an early childhood center has built conversation and discussion times into its daily schedule can reflect a staff's efforts to encourage child talk and oral expression. Calkins (1997) terms this establishing "rituals for conversation." A conversational lunch period is an example of a routinely planned "small talk time." Benefits described here relate primarily to language arts growth.

In play, children can symbolize ideas and feelings through gestures and speech and can collaborate with friends. Children reexamine life experiences, adding their imagination and at times manipulating happenings, settings, and people (Figure 13–9).

Play

Play stimulates much child-to-child conversation, and some kinds of play promote talking more than others. Quiet activities such as painting or working puzzles may tend to limit speech while the child is deeply absorbed.

If teachers observe children's play sequences, they will note many child-initiated play situations that involve print, acting, drawing, "reading," and "writing." Props are improvised as dramas unfold. With writing, art, or construction materials handy, children will incorporate these into child-created and child-directed situations.

Teachers plan opportunities for children to play by themselves and with others in small and large groups. Play with another child or a small group almost always requires children to speak. Toddlers may play near each other in a nonverbal, imitative manner using sounds, squeals, and sometimes screams. Interaction with other children promotes the growth of speaking ability.

Bergen (2001) notes that a smooth transition from simple play to complex social pretend play does not occur for all children. Rubin and Coplan's review (1998) of studies of children with nonsocial or withdrawn play behavior during preschool found this behavior was a strong predictor of peer rejection, social anxiety, loneliness, depression, and negative self-esteem in later childhood. Extra teacher help and encouragement may be necessary, and a case study by staff, conferencing, and referral to diagnostic experts may be needed if the school is unsuccessful.

Early in life, children act out and repeat the words and actions of others. During preschool years, this is called **dramatic play**, and the staff

FIGURE 13–9 Look how intent and careful this child is while she is play ironing.

dramatic play — acting out experiences or creating drama episodes during play.

in early childhood centers plan and prepare for it. Dramatic play is believed to have important benefits for children and holds many learning opportunities. It helps children

♦ develop conversational skills and the ability to express ideas in words (Figure 13–10).

♦ understand the feelings, roles, or work of others.

♦ connect actions with words—actions and words go hand-in-hand in dramatic play.

♦ develop vocabulary.

♦ develop creativity—children imagine, act, and make things up as play progresses.

♦ engage in social interaction with other children.

♦ cope with life, sometimes through acting out troubling situations, thus giving an outlet for emotion (for example, almost every doll in an early childhood center gets a spanking periodically when children play house).

♦ assume leadership and group-participant roles.

Griffing (1983) describes dramatic play after observing it closely.

> The play was rich in symbolic activity—the transformations of self, objects, and situations into characters, objects, and events that existed in imagination only. The play was cognitively complex in its organization, consisting of sequences of related ideas and events rather than isolated pretend behaviors. There was extensive social interaction and verbal communication with children taking roles and carrying them out cooperatively.

Pretend play is no easy task even though it may look to be to the uninitiated observer. It is actually a milestone in development. It requires the ability to transform events and objects symbolically. Bergen (2001) describes pretend play as interactive social dialogue and negotiation involving role taking, script knowledge, and improvisation. Considerable vocabulary growth occurs during its duration. For example, when

FIGURE 13–10 Tea parties are all-time favorites.

playing house, the child can start out as the grandfather and end up as the baby or the family dog. In each role, the child mixes real and pretend factors simultaneously; acts out thoughts, speech, and actions; and may portray emotions appropriate to the play scenario. Joint planning and problem solving using linguistic skill also have taken place. Much time and effort are devoted to this type of play in childhood. The child engages in this type of activity often and has the ability to slide easily from the real world into the make-believe world.

Teachers watch dramatic play develop from the simple imitative actions of toddlers and younger preschoolers to the elaborate dramatic play of four-year-olds, in whom language use blossoms. Teachers support each step along the way by providing the necessary objects and materials that enhance dramatic episodes and by offering assistance (Figure 13–11). To be effective, teachers must observe and be aware of the adult actions and situations that capture child interest enough to prompt reenactment. One surprised student teacher who dreamed up a shaving activity, complete with mirrors, shaving cream, and bladeless razors, found that the boys rolled up their pants legs and shaved their legs. This points out two interesting items: first the wisdom of letting razors, even bladeless

FIGURE 13–11 Pretending to be an animal after a read-aloud about animals is a dramatic play activity.

ones, become play items, and second, how dramatic play often enlightens teachers. Child safety is always the first criterion used to evaluate whether an activity is appropriate.

Four-year-olds engage vigorously in superhero play. As cowboys and Indians, good guys and bad guys, or monster or ghost enactments captured the imaginations of past generations of American children, new heroes have appeared in television cartoons and movies. Robots and space creatures are common dramatic play themes for four-year-olds. The children become the chosen power figures in actions and words. Segal (1987) probes the possible reasons for the popularity of this type of play.

> ... Superhero play is the child's way of restructuring his world according to his own rules. By dubbing himself a superman, a four-year-old can instantaneously acquire major powers and awesome strength. This strength represents access to a powerful force that is missing in their adult-controlled everyday lives.

Many teachers feel ambivalent when they witness the violence enacted in some of these play episodes, which can require special handling and supervisory decisions to keep children safe. Most teachers set up times for group dialogue about superheroes so that reality and fantasy come under group discussion. Discussions can also be seen and handled as possible learning opportunities for the entire class or group. Other teachers worry about the perceived lack of child creativity in this type of play because the same theme and action are generally repeated over and over.

Rich home and school experiences (going places and doing things) serve as building blocks for dramatic play. One would have a difficult time playing "restaurant" or "wedding" if there had been no previous experience with either. Early childhood centers can provide activities and objects that promote dramatic play, such as

◆ field trips.
◆ discussions and readings by visitors and guest speakers.
◆ books.
◆ discussions based on pictures.
◆ films, videos, filmstrips, and slides.
◆ kits (boxed sets), equipment, and settings for dramatic play.
◆ parent career presentations.

In dramatic play, children often use symbols and language to represent objects that are not actually present. An oblong block may become a baby bottle; a pie plate, the kitchen clock; and so on. The enactment of role-appropriate behavior in a make-believe situation is a major step toward literacy. A significant relationship exists between kindergartners' symbolic play and reading achievement. Children with symbolic dramatic play skills have increased ability to comprehend words and understand a variety of syntactic structures.

Smilansky and Shefatya (1990) list growth areas promoted and possible in dramatic play. They include verbalization, vocabulary, language comprehension, attention span, imaginativeness, concentration, impulse control, curiosity, problem-solving strategies, cooperation, empathy, and group participation. Vygotsky's work (1986) has given greater emphasis to the intellectual component of child's play.

> In play the child is always behaving beyond his age, above his usual everyday behavior: in play he is, as it were, a head above himself. Play contains in a concentrated form, as in the focus of a magnifying glass, all the development tendencies: it is as if the child tries to jump above his usual level.

DRAMATIC PLAY SETTINGS

A playhouse area with a child-size stove, refrigerator, table, and chairs encourages dramatic play. An old boat, a service station pump, and a telephone booth are examples of other pieces of equipment that children enjoy using in their play.

Furniture found at early childhood centers can be moved into room arrangements that suggest a bus, a house, a tunnel, or a store. Large cardboard boxes may become a variety of different props with, or without, word labels. Large paper bags, ropes, blankets, and discarded work clothes or dress-up clothing also stimulate the child to pretend. Items for dramatic play can be obtained from commercial school-supply companies, secondhand stores, flea market sales, garage sales, and other sources.

Dramatic Play Kits

Items that go together and suggest the same type of play can be boxed together, ready for use. A shoe-shine kit, complete with cans of natural shoe polish, a soft cloth, a shoe brush, play money, and a newspaper or a magazine, is very popular. Children catch on to the activity quickly. Unfortunately, not many have seen a shoe-shine stand, so a teacher demonstration of this kit may be necessary.

Community theme prop boxes such as bakery, flower shop, bank, car repair shop, and so forth, are suggested. Children using them make decisions about what community people think and do. Incorporating writing materials natural to the play theme promotes an additional language arts dimension.

Ideas for kits to be used in dramatic play follow.

Post Office. Large index cards, used postcards and letters, stamp pads, stampers, stationery, envelopes, greeting cards, crayons or pencils, stamps (Christmas or wildlife seals), mail boxes (shoe box with slot cut in front and name clearly printed), old shoulder bag purses for mailbags, and men's and women's shirts.

Cleaning Set. Several brooms, mops, sponge mops, dust cloths, dustpans, sponges, shirts with logos, aprons, plastic bottles and spray bottles with water, and paper toweling for windows.

Tea Party. Set of cups and saucers, plastic pitchers, napkins, vase, tablecloth, plastic spoons, placemats, place cards, teapot, invitations, small empty food packages such as cereal boxes, and clay or plastic cookies or biscuits.

Doctor. Stethoscope, bandages, masking tape, red stickers for play wounds, tongue depressors, play thermometer, medical exam checklist, paper pad and pencil for prescriptions, billing forms for bill, adhesive tape, cotton balls, armband with a red cross on it, bag to carry, paper hospital gowns, white shirt, and photographs of culturally diverse doctors of both sexes.

Teacher. Notebooks, pencils, plastic glasses, chalk, bell, chalkboard, attendance book, photographs of a variety of teachers' desks, chairs, rulers, books, flannel board with sets, book about the first day at school.

Washing the Car. Towels, spray bottles with soapy water, sponges, buckets, cut hose lengths, window squeegees, old plastic rain coats, feather dusters, window cleaner spray bottles with blue-colored water, wax cans, drying line with clothes pins for wet towels, an old car. (A warm, sunny day in an outside area.)

Supermarket. Cash register, play money, newspaper ads, paper pads and pencils or crayons, hole punch, store name tags, shopping list, paper sacks, empty food cartons, wax fruit, play grocery cart or rolling laundry cart, purse, and wallet.

Hair Salon. Plastic brushes, combs, cotton balls, powder, scarves, colored water in nail polish bottles, old hair dryer (no cord or plug), curlers, water spray bottle, hairpins, book of male and female hairstyles, and mirror.

Service Station. Tire pump, pliers, cans, sponges and bucket, short length of hose and cylinder (for gas pump), hat, plastic charge cards, squirt bottle, paper towels, paper and pencil, and a "Gas for Sale" sign.

Fishing. Hats, bamboo lengths (about 3 feet) with string and magnet at the end, fishing box, a basin, and small metal objects such as paper clips for the fish or cutouts for fish shapes with a paper clip attached to each (to attract the magnet), and bucket.

Gift Wrap. Old wallpaper books, assorted empty boxes or blocks to wrap, used bows, tape, scissors, gift cards, ribbon, crayons, and calendar.

Camping. Old pots and pans, plastic dishes, backpacks, blankets, sleeping bags, foam pads, flashlight, short lengths of logs, red cellophane, large box or tent, food boxes, card table and chairs, old camp stove, canteen, portable radio, pretend child-safe sunlotion, and sunglasses.

Airplane. Chairs in rows, trays, plastic utensils, play food, headphones, little pillows, blankets, tickets, magazines, rolling cart, cups, plastic bottles, napkins, airline attendant clothing, backpack, and snack packages.

More kits can be made for the following:

TV repair person	mail carrier
baker	firefighter
painter	pilot
picnic	circus
restaurant	birthday party
wedding	astronaut
police officer	airport
construction worker	plumber
computer repair person	

The ideas for play kits that have been suggested are based on a few of the many possible themes. Parents are good sources of kit items.

Collecting props for favorite stories and putting them in a storage bag or container that has a picture or illustration of the story on its front is another idea. An example for *Stone Soup* (Brown, 1947) follows:

Materials Needed: large pot, large stone, long-handled spoon, assorted vegetables, aprons for cooks, hats for travelers, three-cornered hats for soldiers.

Costumes

Costumes and clothing props let a child step into a character quickly. Strong, sturdy, child-manageable ties and snaps increase self-help. Elastic waistbands slip on and off with ease. Clothing that is cut down to size (so that it does not drag) can be worn for a longer time. Items that children enjoy are

◆ hats of all types. (*Note:* The use of hats, wigs, and headgear may not be possible in some programs where head lice has occurred.)

◆ shoes, boots, and slippers.

◆ uniforms.

- accessories, such as ties, scarves, purses, wallets, old jewelry, aprons, badges, and key rings.
- discarded fur jackets, soft fabrics, and fancy fabric clothing.
- wigs.
- work clothes.

A clever idea for a child-made costume is using a large-handled shopping bag. Once the bottom of the bag is cut out, the child can step into it, using the bag handles as shoulder straps. The child can decorate the bag and use it as a play prop.

THE TEACHER'S ROLE IN DRAMATIC PLAY

Dramatic play is child-directed instead of teacher-directed. Play ideas come from the child's imagination and experience.

Teachers can motivate dramatic play before they withdraw to remain in the background. They are watchful but do not hover. Sometimes a new play direction is suggested by a teacher to divert the children away from unsafe or violent play. The flow of play preferably is decided by the children. Teachers' close presence and words can stop or change behavior when the situation becomes unsafe or gets out of hand. If things go smoothly, the ideas, words, and dramatic play actions are those of the children.

Periodic suggestions by the teacher and introduction of material may extend and enrich play. Care is taken not to dominate but rather to be available as a friendly resource.

Play is where reading and writing begin. In dramatic play, children understand its pretend or make-believe nature (although, in certain play situations, an occasional child may confuse play with reality).

Older preschoolers' dramatic play becomes increasingly mature, involved, complex, and riddled with abstract symbolic representations.

Smilansky (1968) pioneered attempts to train children who were less able to engage in appropriate pretend play. Teacher modeling, teacher assuming a play role in reenactments of real-life experiences, and teacher interventions

such as suggestions, giving directions, asking questions, and clarifying behavior took place. Study children were encouraged to engage in and sustain sociodramatic play. Teachers let children decide play direction and content. Teachers' actions aided child elaboration of child-chosen play themes.

Traditionally, teachers have been advised to limit or omit adult interaction and domination of young children's dramatic play. Yet research (Schrader, 1989) suggests that teacher behavior involving modeling, making statements of child options (for example, writing a note, selecting menu items, looking at signs, and so on), and teacher play suggestions can increase children's literacy behavior. Teacher behavior of zooming in and out is believed appropriate. This involves adding to child ideas and giving choices for the child to consider without directing or dominating the flow of child ideas and play except where child safety is concerned.

Dramatic Play as an Intellectual Reaction to Book Events

Children's dramatic play and role-playing are ways to synthesize and connect what has been presented in picture books and in their own lives. Any observant teacher knows children's dramatic play mirrors their significant life experiences. The child who first says, "Did you bring home any money?" in a play scenario in which the child playing father enters the play situation has observed or experienced a background event.

What then could be the benefit of dramatic play acting a book? Besides the recreating (retelling) of book parts or themes, the experience offers a number of intellectual and literary benefits. Deeper or clearer meaning might be achieved. Early childhood practitioners can conclude that this activity helps children construct knowledge on a number of levels.

Children often retell more detailed and complex stories when they are supplied with simple props, such as small objects or pictures (McGee, 2003a). McGee also suggests using a story clothesline tied between two pieces of furniture with 6 to 10 pictures (created or selected) to depict major story or book events.

"Story collars," which represent the clothing story characters might wear, such as a farmer's work shirt collar or a faux fur collar for an animal character, were also suggested.

Props like hats, clothes, and objects and settings connected to the picture book can be created using teacher ingenuity. A teacher can examine a book before presenting it for features that lead to easy enactment, such as *The Three Billy Goats Gruff*. It is easy to set up a bridge with the materials and equipment found in most preschools.

Most observant teachers find children reliving favorite or captivating picture books with or without their help in groups or as individuals. It is as if in the reliving, the reenactment, the picture book's message becomes "fitted" into what they already know.

Reenacting a picture book with a teacher's help may surprise the teacher, for as children reenact they will usually insert objects and events from their own lives into the story context (Ferguson & Young, 1996).

Books that lend themselves to child reenactment follow:

Eastman, P. (1960/1993). *Are you my mother?* New York: HarperCollins.
Flack, M. (1971). *Ask Mr. Bear.* New York: Young Readers Press.
Mora, P. (1992). *A birthday basket for Tia.* New York: Macmillan.
Williams, S. (1989). *I went walking.* San Diego: Harcourt, Brace, Jovanovich.

McGee (2003a) believes an intense pressure exists for teachers to justify instructional activities unless they are described as research-based. She notes that research supports "book acting" and cites the following research:

Preschoolers and kindergartners who frequently engage in thematic fantasy play (in which children act out stories that have been read aloud to them) have better vocabularies, use more complex language, and have better story comprehension than children who only draw or talk about stories (Pellegrini & Galda, 1982; Saltz & Johnson, 1974).

McGee also notes that children are more likely to enact stories when teachers repeatedly read them. Other techniques mentioned by McGee include:

◆ providing adult supportive assistance and suggestions during enactments to enhance language learning and story comprehension.

◆ promoting interactive sharing of storybooks, where children take on the role of the storyteller, to improve preschoolers' expressive language.

◆ creating activities for kindergartners, to listen to and then retell information contained in stories. Encouraging kindergarteners to recall information and use the particular language structures found in written information.

◆ maintaining small group size when retelling to improve children's comprehension.

◆ providing playful replays and dramatization of both stories and informational books.

According to McGee, these techniques help children

◆ make inferences.

◆ integrate information across the entire text.

◆ use unique literary and content-specific vocabulary.

◆ speak in sentences with more complex grammatical structures.

◆ in group enactments, negotiate, hear others' perspectives, combine perspectives, and integrate more complex dialogue into their own conception of the story.

Daily Routines

Periods designed especially for conversation are included in the program of an early childhood center. A gathering or group time at the start of the day is used to encourage individual recognition and speaking. Snack and lunch periods are set up to promote pleasant conversation while eating. Activities are planned and structured to provide for as much child talk as possible.

Show-and-Tell. One of the most common daily routines is show-and-tell time. It must be noted here that some early childhood educators believe that this routine is outdated and overused and prefer to eliminate it from their daily schedules. In contrast, show-and-tell advocates believe that this activity encourages children to talk about their special interests in front of others. The child can bring something from home or share something made or accomplished at school. Following are some helpful hints for conducting show-and-tell.

- Encourage, do not force, children to speak. If they do not want to talk, they can just show what they brought.
- Let the child who is showing something to the group stand or sit near the teacher. A friendly arm around the child's shoulders may help.
- Stimulate the other children to ask the child questions: "Mark, you seem to want to ask Gustavo about his blue marble."
- Limit the time for overly talkative children by using an egg timer.
- Limit the time for the activity so that the children do not become bored.
- Thank each child for his participation.
- Try something new such as the following.
  a. Display all articles and have the group guess who brought them.
  b. Have children swap (if possible) what they have brought so that they can talk about each other's items.
  c. Bring in a surprise item to share with the children.
  d. Make a caption for each item and display it on a table (for example, Betty's Green Rock).
  e. Have the child hide the object behind his back while describing it to the others. Then the other children can guess what the object is.
  f. Be sensitive to ethnic and cultural communication styles.

Oken-Wright (1988) points out show-and-tell times can be tedious and stressful, but when well-conducted, they can also be

- an activity for closure (ending activities on a satisfying note) and evaluation and for clarification of feelings.
- a forum for expressive and receptive language development.
- a session for brainstorming, idea catching, and idea expanding.
- an opportunity to reflect and engage in group problem solving.
- a source for curriculum ideas and materials.
- a window into children's thoughts and feelings.

Show-and-tell items are usually kept out of children's reach to prevent the loss of a valued or favorite toy. The teacher can divide the class into groups and name the days on which each group can bring in items, or the teacher may prefer to allow the children to share whenever they wish. Show-and-tell helps children develop vocabulary, responsibility, and the ability to speak in front of others. When making these goals known to parents, teachers explain that the children have choices in these sharing times and that items do not have to be brought to school on a daily or regular basis.

One kindergarten teacher (Edwards, 1996) initiated sharing-time topics related to her classroom theme instruction and alerted parents beforehand. Sharing time consequently became focused, less rambling. Children who brought in objects unrelated to the topic could be given time after topic-centered sharing.

The Daily News or Recap Times. Many centers engage in a daily news or recap group time that focuses on important or interesting events of the day. Teachers and children share news, anecdotes, and happenings in both their home and school life. The teacher can initiate this activity with statements such as the following.

"Keith told me about something new at his house. Would you like to share your news, Keith?"

"Aliki and Todd built something today that I've never seen before! Tell us about it, Todd, or would you like me to tell your classmates?"

As with all other group times, the teacher must be aware of group reaction and response. On some days, there may be excited response and conversation; on others, there may be little response, and the activity should be kept brief. To give children an opportunity to talk about problems and their solutions, recap times can be partially devoted to children's verbalizing success or lack of it in proposed courses of action and projects.

> "Mosaad was going to try to make a spaceship today. Mosaad, do you want to tell us about it?"
>
> "Megan finished making her book today. Would you like to tell us what happened, Megan?"

Promoting Speech Daily. The following are suggestions that can promote more child speech in daily programs.

◆ Have children give verbal messages or directions to other children often: "Petey, please show Flynn our dustpan and hand broom. Tell him how we empty it." (Then follow through by thanking him.)

◆ Let children describe daily projects: "Danielle, tell us about your rocket ship. I know you worked hard making it. What did you do first?"

◆ Relate present ideas and happenings to the children's past when possible: "Shane had a new puppy at his house too. Did your puppy cry at night? What did you do to help it stop? Kathy has a new puppy who cries at night."

◆ Promote child explanations: "Who can tell us what happens after we finish our lunch?"

◆ Promote teacher-child conversations in which the teacher records children's words on artwork, constructions, or any happenings or projects.

◆ Periodically make pin-on badges (for teachers and interested children) like the ones shown in Figure 13–12.

◆ Play "explaining games" by setting up a group of related items on a table and having the children explain how the items can be used. For example, three groups of items might be (1) a mirror, comb, brush, washcloth, soap, and basin of water; (2) shoes, white shoe polish, and new shoelaces; and

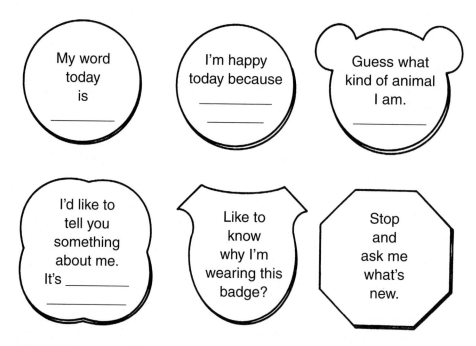

FIGURE 13–12 Pin-on badges.

(3) nuts, a nutcracker, and two bowls. Encourage child volunteers to explain and demonstrate the use of the items by facing the group from the other side of the table. Other possibilities include items to demonstrate peeling an orange, making a sandwich with two spreads, or making a telephone call.

◆ Design and create games that encourage children to speak.

LEADING ACTIVITIES

A child can be chosen to lead others in activities if he is familiar with the routines and activities. The child can alert the others by saying the right words or calling out the names of the children who need items or who are next for a turn at something. One or more children can be at the front of the group, leading songs or finger plays. (Finger plays are discussed in the next chapter.) Often, children can be chosen as speakers to direct routines with words. Also, teachers can promote speaking by asking one child to tell another child something: "Tell Billy when you want him to pass the wastebasket," or "If you're through, ask Georgette whether she wants a turn."

A watchful teacher uses many ways of encouraging the children to speak. The children tend to speak more if their speech is given attention and if speech helps them achieve their ends. It is helpful during group times to point out that the teacher and the other children want to hear what everyone says, and because of this, children should take turns speaking.

SUMMARY

Each early childhood educational program is based on goals. Goals state the attitudes and abilities that a center wishes to develop in children. Planned activities and daily teacher-child conversations help the school reach its goals.

Teachers plan for both group and individual needs. They converse skillfully with children

of varying degrees of fluency. There are specific teacher techniques that promote children's expression of ideas.

Questions are asked by both children and teachers. By observing, listening, and interacting, teachers are better able to encourage speaking abilities.

When there is a relaxed atmosphere with interested teachers and many activities, more talking takes place. Playing with others helps vocabulary development and language acquisition in settings where children interact in real and make-believe situations.

The teacher's role in dramatic play is to set the stage but remain in the background so that the children can create their own activities. Dramatic play settings and kits are made available, and some are boxed and collected by the teacher.

Part of a teacher's work is to encourage children to share their ideas and give children opportunities to lead speaking activities. Teachers ensure that children are talked with rather than talked at. Teachers plan for conversational group times and conduct games and activities that promote verbal comments.

ADDITIONAL RESOURCES

Bloom, P. (2000). *How children learn the meanings of words.* Cambridge, MA: MIT Press.

Boutte, G. S., Van Scoy, I., & Hendley, S. (1996, November). Multicultural and nonsexist prop boxes. *Young Children, 52*(1), 34–39.

Davidson, J. (1996). *Emerging literacy and dramatic play in early education.* Clifton Park, NY: Thomson Delmar Learning.

Katz, L., & Chard, C. (1998). *Engaging children's minds.* Norwood, NJ: Ablex.

Kieff, J. E., & Casbergue, R. M. (1999). *Playful learning and teaching: Integrating play into preschool and primary programs.* Boston: Allyn and Bacon.

Owacki, G. (1999). *Literacy through play.* Westport, CT: Heinemann.

Paley, V. (1981). *Wally's stories.* Cambridge, MA: Harvard University Press.

Paley, V. (1984). *Boys and girls: Superheroes in the doll corner.* Chicago: University of Chicago Press.

Vukelich, C., Christie, J., & Enz, B. (2000). *Helping young children learn language and literacy.* Boston: Allyn and Bacon.

HELPFUL WEB SITES

KidSource Online
http://www.kidsource.com
Areas of intelligence are discussed.

National Academy Press
http://www.nap.edu
Readings in literacy development are provided.

National Association for the Education of Young Children
http://www.naeyc.org
Articles and publications can be found.

Quotes concerning children's vocabulary development and the age when some young children's rate of word acquisition speeds ahead of others are offered. Both focus on the importance of children's opportunity to interact with adults and peers who promote word growth. A question and answer section provides information about speaking goals and vocabulary development.

STUDENT ACTIVITIES

1. List five speaking area goals in your own order of priority.

2. Interview a preschool teacher (or teachers). Ask the question, "If you could do only one thing to help young children's speaking ability, what would that be?"

3. Observe a preschool group. What differences do you notice in the children's ability to solve problems with words? Cite specific examples.

4. Observe a preschool classroom. Write down the teacher's questions (word for word). Using the eight question types from this chapter, tell which recorded questions fit which category. Report your findings to the class. Were more recall questions asked?

5. Pair off with another student. Try to find some object (from your pocket or book bag, for example) that might interest a preschool child. Alternate asking each other two recall, two convergent, two divergent, and two evaluation questions about the objects. Then try asking observation, explanation-seeking, or prediction questions. Which questions were easy to formulate? Which were difficult?

6. List what you believe to be two additional characteristics of intellectual behavior not found on Costa's outline of intelligent behavior characteristics on pages 400–401. How could these behaviors be supported and encouraged as they emerge in a preschool child?

7. With a classmate, describe a dramatic play-kit idea on a theme that was not included in this chapter. List the items for this theme that you believe would be safe and would promote dramatic play. Share with the class. Vote on one play kit created by classmates in this exercise that you believe would be popular with children. Give the reasons for your vote.

8. Review dramatic play items commercially produced by looking in school-supply catalogs. Report on the cost of three items.

9. Discuss your position concerning show-and-tell time.

10. Pretend you have acquired a very large cardboard packing case, big enough for children to crawl into and stand. In what way would this case enhance dramatic play? In what play situations could the case be used?

11. Read the following observed child behavior. Using Costa's characteristics of intelligent behavior, identify child behaviors that match Costa's listing. With a small group of classmates, write teacher statements that might support and appreciate the child's quest. Do not include possible teacher control or behavior-change-attempt statements.

Damian watched intently as Ariela pushed a wheeled popper toy across the floor. Brightly colored wooden balls danced and flew within the toy's transparent dome. Searching for a stuffed animal, Damian selected a green rabbit. With rabbit in hand, he stood in front of Ariela saying "What's up, Doc!" while moving the rabbit in jumping motions. Slyly he grabbed the handle of the popper toy. Ariela tried to scoot around Damian. Damian held on and Ariela howled. As the teacher approached, Damian said, "She won't give me a turn!" Teacher gently removed Damian's hand and said "Let's go find another toy." Damian instead flees to the painting easel. He paints but concentrates on Ariela and the toy by peering over the top of the easel. Ariela, aware of Damian, sees her friend Bettina, and they proceed to push the popper toy back and forth in front of Damian's easel. Damian makes loud zooming noises with his paintbrush as he strokes vigorously up and down.

Bettina becomes interested and walks around to see Damian's artwork. Ariela follows. Damian quickly drops the brush and picks up the popper toy. The girls then paint together at a second easel. The teacher notices Damian has forgotten to take his wet artwork to the drying area, so asks him to do so. With popper toy under his arm, he complies and holds the popper between his knees as he pins the wet painting on the drying line. Damian spends about ten minutes pushing the toy and watching colored balls pop upward. His fingers try to pull off the plastic cover to no avail. He slips outside to the yard to an out-of-sight corner. Teacher notices he is seated bent over the toy. She sees Damian pick up a stick and try to wedge off the plastic top using considerable pressure. She approaches and says "Damian, that's an inside toy." Damian shrugs, picks up the toy, and heads for the classroom.

12. Read and analyze the following from "What's Wrong with This Show-and-Tell?" by Oken-Wright (1988):

Fifteen four-year-olds are seated in a sprawling group. "Today it's Todd's, Teddy's, Joyce's and Karen's turn," says the teacher. "Todd, did you bring anything for us? You always forget, don't you? You need to start remembering when it's Tuesday, that's your day." When it's her turn, Karen drones on in a monotone for five minutes about a plastic bracelet her mother bought her at the mall. Stevie interrupts many times trying to get the teacher's attention to tell about the frog he caught in the morning. After several warnings, the teacher tells Stevie that he has lost his turn to tell on Wednesday because of his discourteous behavior during Karen's turn today. The teacher says, "This way you don't have too many on any one day and they can talk as long as they like."

13. Make a dramatic play prop box collection for a child's picture book. On the outside of the storage container put a book illustration or character illustration. Introduce it to a group of preschoolers. Share the results with your classmates.

CHAPTER REVIEW

A. Explain each of the following terms.
   1. structured activities
   2. possessives
   3. negatives
   4. prepositions
   5. comparatives

B. Answer the following questions related to speaking goals.

1. How can the goals of a program be met?
2. When children are interested in an object or event, what should the teacher do to help the children learn while they are motivated?
3. Where should visual material be placed for viewing with a group of children?

C. Define *dramatic play.*

D. Answer the following questions.

1. What is a dramatic play kit?
2. Name some of the things a teacher does not want to happen during show-and-tell time (for example, one child talking too long).

E. Select the correct answers. Each item may have more than one correct answer.

1. In daily conversations, the teacher should
   a. answer or respond to nonverbal messages.
   b. pair new word meanings with words the children already know.
   c. listen to children who yell in anger.
   d. patiently accept stuttering and hesitant speech.

2. If a child says "richlotti-gongo" to you,
   a. repeat it back if you can, hoping the child will show you what he wants to say.
   b. ignore it and wait until you understand the message.
   c. go along with the statement, saying something like, "Really, you don't say."
   d. ask the child to speak more clearly.

3. In using questions with young children,
   a. suit the question to the children.
   b. always give them the answer.
   c. insist that they answer correctly.
   d. answer some of the children's questions with your own questions, when appropriate.

4. Planned activities are based on
   a. goals only.
   b. children's current interests only.
   c. goals and children's interests.
   d. knowledge instead of attitudes.

F. Name three ways a teacher can give children confidence in their speaking abilities.

G. From the four question types listed, choose the type that matches questions 1 through 8.

    recall   divergent   convergent   evaluative

1. What would happen if we left this glass full of ice on the table?
2. If your shoes and socks are the same color, would you please stand up?
3. Who can tell me this puppet's name?
4. If you had a dollar, how would you like to spend it?
5. What do we need to make a birthday cake?
6. Why did the basket fall over?
7. Did the door open by itself?
8. Who has the smallest cup?

H. Write down teacher questions that could lead a child to a discovery and promote the child's verbal expression of the discovery in the following situations.

1. A bird's nest is found in the yard.
2. The wheel on a bike squeaks.
3. A flashlight is taken apart.

I. SITUATION. Formulate appropriate teacher comments in the following situations (1–3). What might a teacher say in response?

1. Child is complaining that easel paint drips and does not stay where he wants it.
2. It is cleanup time, and Sharie (child) says, "Scott and Keith never put anything away!"
3. Carter is talking about the way water is disappearing in the sun.

NOW WORK ON CONVERGENT-TYPE QUESTIONS. Formulate a possible teacher question.

4. Megan noticed a bug on the floor.
5. Christa says, "Dana has new shoes!"
6. Ryan brings a toy truck to share at group time.

PLAN EVALUATION QUESTIONS. In 7, 8, and 9, plan evaluation questions that a teacher might use.

7. "I don't like peanut butter," Romana says.
8. "This is my favorite book," Linsay declares.
9. Teacher is introducing a new toy with plastic boats.

J. List Costa's characteristics of intelligent behavior.

K. Write a short paragraph that finishes the following:

The reasons some teachers do not actively plan programs with children leading activities in front of the child group . . .

GAMES PROMOTING SPEECH

Suitcase Game

Teacher: I'm going on a vacation trip. I'm putting suntan oil in my suitcase. What will you put in your suitcase?

Child: A swimming suit.

Child: Candy.

Teacher: (After the group has had an opportunity to contribute.) Let's see how many items we can remember that people wanted to bring on vacation.

Grocery Store Game

Have a bag handy with lots of grocery items. Pull one out yourself and describe it. Have the children take turns pulling out an item and describing it. The teacher can make a shopping list of items named and explain a shopping list's use.

Letter Game

Provide a large bag of letters. Pull one letter out. Talk about a letter you are going to send to a child in the group. "I'm going to give this pretend letter to Frankie and tell him about my new car," or "I want to send this thank-you card to Janelle because she always helps me when I ask for cleanup helpers. Who would like to pull out a letter from this bag and tell us the person they would like to send it to?"

Guess What Is in the Box

Collect small boxes with lids. Put small items inside, such as paper clips, erasers, bottle tops, plastic toys, leaves, flowers, and so forth. Have a child choose a box, guess its contents, open it, and talk about what is in the box.

Describe a Classmate

Choose a child out of the group to stand beside you. Describe or list three of the child's characteristics, for example, red shoes, big smile, one hand in pocket. Ask who would like to choose another classmate and tell three things about that person.

Guessing Photograph Happenings

Use photographs showing a sequence of actions. Help children express their ideas of what is depicted. Examples: digging in the garden, planting bulbs, a flowering tulip; mixing pancake batter, frying pancakes, eating pancakes.

The Mystery Bag

An activity children enjoy in small groups is called the mystery bag. The teacher collects a series of common objects. Turning away from the group, the teacher puts one of the objects in another bag. The game starts when a child reaches (without looking inside) into the second bag and describes the object. It is then pulled out of the bag and discussed: "What can we do with it? Has it a name? It's the same color as what else in the room?" The group should be small, because it is hard for a young child to wait for a turn. Examples of objects that could be used include a rock, comb, orange, pancake turner, feather, plastic cup, sponge, hole punch, flower, toy animal, and whistle.

Parts-of-the-Body Guessing Game

I can see you with my _____ (eyes).
I can smell you with my _____ (nose).
I can chew with my _____ (teeth).
I can hear with my _____ (ears).
I can clap with my _____ (hands).
I walk on my _____ (feet).
I put food in my _____ (mouth).
This is not my nose, it's my _____ (point to ears).
This is not my eye, it's my _____ (point to nose).
This is not my mouth, it's my _____ (point to eye).

CHAPTER 14
Group Times

OBJECTIVES

After reading this chapter, you should be able to:

◆ Describe circle and group-time speaking activities.

◆ Perform a finger play with children.

◆ Discuss ways to promote child involvement in simple plays, chants, and circle times.

◆ Plan and lead a group time.

KEY TERMS

chants

circle time

transitory

statements

MR. FUZZ

At a group time, Billy Jay was sharing what had happened to the classroom's visiting teddy over the weekend. Each child in the class has a turn to take Mr. Fuzz home, and Billy Jay had just done so. It was expected that the child taking Mr. Fuzz would then relate some important weekend happenings at Monday morning's circle time. So far, Mr. Fuzz had been hidden by the family dog, accidentally washed in the washing machine, taken up in an airplane, and thrown out of a window on his previous excursions to the children's homes. Billy Jay was excited when he told the group that Mr. Fuzz went to "Three and one." This puzzling statement was soon cleared up when Billy Jay said, "And he likes Jamocca Almond Fudge just like my mom."

QUESTIONS TO PONDER

1. Would it be a good idea to make a book of Mr. Fuzz's adventures for the library corner?

2. Can you think of other literacy activities that also could grow out of the use of Mr. Fuzz?

3. Billy Jay is obviously aware of numbers on signs. Could this lead to an activity for the whole class? If yes, identify one.

The activities in this chapter give children many speaking opportunities. Children involved in the activities have the opportunity to imitate speech, to use creative speech, and to express their own ideas and feelings. However, you should realize that it is difficult to classify activities as listening or speaking activities because they often overlap.

GROUPS

Group time and **circle time** are chances for children to develop understanding about themselves as group members. They enjoy language together by using familiar songs, favorite finger plays, chants, and a wide variety of activities. Children gain self-confidence, feelings of personal worth, and group spirit (Figure 14–1). Group times are often conducted as "sharing times" within programs that are designed for an abundance of child-selected and child-initiated activities.

School administrators and teachers need to clarify their priorities concerning group times. Because it is difficult to conduct intimate conversations and discussions with large groups, many schools prefer working with small groups of children so that conversations can flourish. However, decisions regarding group size may hinge on staffing considerations. Sometimes large groups can be temporarily divided so that there can be "instant replays" of activities for smaller groups.

Many educators are debating the value of larger group activities, especially ones that attempt to teach the school's curriculum through large group instruction. Although many programs use large group instruction, educators doubt its developmental appropriateness. Large group times used for news, announcements, morning welcome, a quick class discussion, or

FIGURE 14–1 Group time—together time.

circle time — an early childhood term describing a planned gathering of children, usually seated in a half-circle configuration, led by a teacher.

closing wrap-up may be part of the established school routine and are common.

When presenting new material during small group sessions, teachers should allow time to receive and react to children's comments and questions. One pitfall in conducting group activities is the tendency for teachers to remain the center of attention, assuming the role of the great dispenser of knowledge. When this occurs, child feedback is ignored.

Calkins (1997) believes that some teachers may be unskilled in drawing conversation from children in group discussions.

> Unfortunately, not enough teachers support small group discussion. In too many instances, what is called discussion is the teacher asking questions and calling on children for answers. Then the teacher rephrases, corrects, or evaluates what a child says before asking a new question. In these so-called discussions, children learn very little about what it means to "talk things over" with a group of people, and this can become a real disadvantage.

Other questionable teacher skills and behaviors are discussed under the heading "Circle-Time Pitfalls" later in this chapter.

In group settings with four-year-olds, early childhood teachers become acutely aware of children who are having difficulty paying attention, following directions, getting along, and controlling negative emotions of anger or distress. McClelland, Morrison, and Holmes (2000) predict these children will do less well in school. Research on early schooling suggests that the relationships children build with peers and teachers are based on their ability to react in social versus anti-social ways; behaviors can help or hurt academic performance (Raver, 2003). At group times, teachers make every effort to keep children focused and involved in language arts activities.

Language activities add sparkle and liveliness to circle times. The following is a list of words that can be used to describe a successful group experience.

active—Children's participation includes motor and speech involvement.

enthusiastic—The teacher's commitment in making a presentation is communicated by the teacher's facial expressions and manner.

prepared—All necessary materials are at the teacher's fingertips and are used with smooth verbal presentations.

accepting—The teacher is open to children's ideas and feelings and is appreciative of children's contributions.

appropriate—The activity suits the particular group.

clear—The teacher provides purposeful clarification of new concepts.

comfortable—The seating and light source are appropriate.

familiar—The activity includes previously learned and enjoyed material.

novel—New ideas and material are presented.

relaxed—The activity does not pressure or threaten children.

sharing—All children are invited to take turns participating in the activity.

IMPORTANT SKILLS FOR ENTERING KINDERGARTEN

Gamel-McCormick (2000) surveyed 240 kindergarten teachers in Delaware, asking them to rate the importance of a set of 20 skills desirable in entering kindergartners. Two communication-related skills appeared in their top 10 choices: (1) communicates needs and preferences and (2) attends to peer or adult talking. The number one teacher selection was exhibits self-control. Kindergarten teachers were also asked for a hand-written definition of readiness. A summary of their answers follows (Gamel-McCormick, 2000):

◆ Except for physical skills, most teachers included components of all domains in their definitions.

◆ Almost all definitions assessed social and behavioral skills and skills that would allow students to be independent.

◆ A significant minority of teachers included preacademic and academic skills in their definitions.

◆ For most teachers, the definitions focused on children's abilities to interact with peers and adults.

Blair (2003) reports similar results in a nationally represented sample of kindergarten teachers who cited child self-regulation as being essential to school readiness. This included a child's being able to

◆ communicate needs, wants, and thoughts verbally.

◆ sustain attention and be enthusiastic and curious in new activities.

◆ inhibit impulses and follow directions.

◆ take turns and be sensitive to other children's feelings.

What can early childhood educators surmise from this study? The work undertaken at the preschool level to promote child self-help, social interaction, and cooperation and to promote both child independence and group participation skills is highly valued by kindergarten teachers. The child's ability to recognize alphabet letters and write her name was also cited by kindergarten teachers, but these choices followed skills concerned with child self-control and self-help.

The time four-year-olds spend in small group or circle-time activities during preschool promotes learning group expectations (rules for group behavior), skills in talking, turn taking, listening with focus, and the communication of individual ideas.

GROUPS OF YOUNGER PRESCHOOLERS

Two- and three-year-olds participating in group times are learning social interaction. Their group participation may depend on their feelings of trust and security. After adjustments to seating comfort are made, the teacher welcomes each child by stating or singing their names, or the teacher starts a simple song or finger play, the teacher watches for child focus and involvement. Often, active participation grows slowly as watchers become doers. In well-conducted circle times, children can choose their own level of participation. Teacher flexibility and preplanning, together with the teacher's obvious enthusiasm and delight in each child's presence, breed social acceptance and success. Time will determine whether a teacher decides to expand highly enjoyed circles or cut others short because of children's feedback signals.

Because younger children's classrooms usually are staffed with more adults and volunteers, nonleading adults can sit near or beside children to encourage child participation. An inviting group time may draw in all attending children after it is in progress.

Group time for very young preschoolers can be described as "loose and light" formations or groupings. Children choose to be present and choose their level of involvement. Teachers count on child curiosity and desire to be part of the action. Think of yourself in a new social situation: Wouldn't you watch briefly before entering conversations with strangers and approach those who seem most open and welcoming? And wouldn't you move on if conversations were boring, irrelevant, or obtuse?

PLANNING SMALL GROUP TIME

After considering child capacity to remain involved, a group can be planned to occupy a specific time period. What happens and when it happens is roughly outlined. A gathering-together activity can be a song, a finger play, or a recording followed by any number and type of activities. A planned closing and transition ends the experience and moves the group in an orderly fashion onto other classroom pursuits. If group time is of considerable length, then standing and moving activities are interspersed with seated ones.

The seating arrangement needs consideration because it may cause attention to wander. If a large rug is used for circle time and children are asked to sit on the periphery or edge at a distance from the teacher, then intimacy and the ability to see visuals and hear well may be lost. Teachers may need to break up child combinations in seating when children are seated in a "pack." The teacher's physical closeness is part of the "circle-time" experience. In other words, circle time does not necessarily mean children must sit in a circle. A half-circle or arc is a more common seating arrangement.

GROUPS

A group activity is begun by capturing group attention. A signal or daily routine can be used. To make sure all children are focused, a short silence (pause) adds a feeling of anticipation and expectation.

Occasionally varying the signals keeps one signal from becoming old hat. A visual signal, a xylophone ripple, a tap on a musical triangle, an attention-getting record, a puppet announcing a group activity, or reminder stickers placed on children's hands related to the theme of the activity are a few alternatives.

A musical recording can set the mood as children form a group. Singing can serve as a magnet that pulls the group together, and a quiet song is a great means of relaxing and bonding a group.

Opening activities that recognize each child help build group spirit. Such recognition is a way of communicating to each child that "You're an important person; we're happy to have you with us." The children can then begin group activities on the right note.

No One Said Leading Groups Would Be Easy

Harker and Green (1985) describe one teacher's decision making and internal dialogue while leading a group of children.

Are they going to understand this? Should I rephrase this question? How can I get Tony or Sue to participate?

To the outside observer, a skilled teacher leading and interacting with a group may look like a relaxed, interested individual. Under the surface of the teacher's enthusiastic manner, many decisions are being made. Reciprocal interchange is happening; there's internal dialogue going on. The teacher may be watching the clock for time length, watching for both interested and restless behavior, or listening intently for child comments and framing appropriate verbal interaction. With all this going on, many beginning teachers are not able to truly relax.

Circle time often starts with a few children, and others join as they finish chosen pursuits and/or become attracted to circle activities. Centers differ in philosophy concerning required participation. Staffing may permit other choices.

CIRCLE STARTERS

MacDonald (1995) suggests the following for group openings.

I like to open and close with special "hello" and "goodbye" songs. I recommend using the same songs from week to week, as the children love these familiar opening and closing times. During the opening songs I take time to sing to each child by name, welcoming them to the storytime ("Jenny, Jenny, are you here?"). This singing time quiets the children, allows latecomers to enter the group unobtrusively, acknowledges the importance of each child as he or she is named, and melds the children into a unit ready to listen.

Harris and Fuqua (2000) also describe an initial group time "stop" where each member of the group is acknowledged as an individual. Children may be individually touched, and eye contact is maintained.

The following activities are circle-time starters, attention getters, socializers, and wiggle reducers.

CIRCLE TIME

I've just come in from outside.
I'm tired as can be.
I'll cross my legs

And fold my hands,
I WILL NOT MOVE.
My head won't move.
My toes are still.
I'll put my hands on my chin,
And when it's quiet, we'll begin!

WHO'S THAT?

(Chant or sing to tune of "Ten Little Indians.")

Who's that _____ in the _____
        (boy, girl, lady, man)   (red, blue, etc.)

_____?
(shirt, pants, shoes, etc.)

(Repeat twice.)

Oh, _____ is _____ name, oh.
   (child or adult gives name)   (his/her)

(Teacher supplies name when child is hesitant.)

FRIENDSHIP SONG

(Sing or chant the song "The More We Get Together," using hand movements.)

The more we get together, together, together, (Hug yourself.)

The more we get together, the happier we'll be. (Pull up cheeks in a smile.)

'Cause your friends are my friends, (Point around the circle.)

And my friends are your friends.

The more we get together, the happier we'll be. (Pull up cheeks in a smile.)

A PHONEMIC AWARENESS VERSION

We can find a "t," a "t," a "t" (Hold up a print "t.")

We can find a "t," if we just look around. (Hand by side of eye panning room.)

There's your "t," and my "t," (Pointing.)

And my "t," and your "t," (Pointing.)

We can find a "t," if we just look around.

There is tongue (Touch.)

And t-shirt, (Point; substitute attending children's names when possible.)

And table, (Point.)

And teacher, (Point.)

We can find a "t" word, if we just look around.

WIGGLES

I'll wiggle my fingers
And wiggle my toes.
I'll wiggle my arms
And wiggle my nose.
And now that all the wiggle's out,
We'll listen to what circle's about.

CLAPPING START

Turn around and face the wall. Clap, Clap, Clap.

Down upon your knees now fall. Clap, Clap, Clap.

Up again and turn around. Clap, Clap, Clap.

Turn around and then sit down. Clap, Clap, Clap.

Not a sound.

WHERE ARE YOUR _____?

Where are your eyes? Show me eyes that see.

Where are your eyes? Shut them quietly.

Where is your nose? A nose that blows.

Where is your nose? Show me your nose and wiggle it so.

Where is your mouth? Open it wide.

Where is your mouth? With teeth inside.

Smile—Smile—Smile.

CIRCLE ACTIVITIES

A circle group keeps its lively enthusiasm and social enjoyment when well planned. The activities that follow involve both language and coordinated physical movement.

Passing Games

Have children arranged in a circle. Pass a small object around the circle. Start by passing it in front of the children, then behind, then overhead, and then under the legs. Directions can be changed on command of the teacher, such as "pass it to your left, pass it to your right," and so on. Ask children for suggestions for other ways to pass the object. Passing a toy microphone can also promote a child's verbal contribution. When a child is done, the microphone is passed to the next child.

TEDDY BEAR CIRCLE PASS

(Have bear in bag behind leader.)

Love somebody, yes, I do.

Love somebody, yes, I do.

Love somebody, yes, I do.

Love somebody, but I won't tell who.

(Shake head sideways.)

Love somebody, yes, I do.

Love somebody, yes, I do.

Love somebody, yes, I do.

Now I'll show (him or her) to you!

Here's a hug—Pass it on.

(Group continues to chant as each child hugs and hands teddy to next child. When teddy returns to leader, last verse is repeated, ending with the following line.)

Now back in the bag; our hugs are through!

(Substituted for last line.)

Taking Turns and Directing Attention

During circle times, conversations, and other group activities, the following teacher statements are helpful in emphasizing to children the importance of taking turns.

◆ "It's Monica's turn now."

◆ "Barry's turn to talk, and everyone's turn to listen."

◆ "Listen to Bonnie. Bonnie's lips are moving, and ours are resting."

◆ "Just one person talks at a time."

◆ "I am guessing that you really want to say something, Jason, but that you are waiting for your turn."

◆ "Sierra was telling us a story, so it's her turn. What happened next, Sierra?"

◆ "Time to give Angel a turn to talk, Aki. Angel, do you live in an apartment house?"

◆ "Heiko is answering my question now. Wait and you can answer next, Bradford."

◆ "Raise your hand if you're waiting to tell us about your pet. I see four hands up—September, Ariel, Alexander, and Alwin. You will all have a turn. Alwin, it's your turn now."

◆ "Wait, Collette, Rio hasn't finished his turn."

◆ "My turn to talk, Elias. Your turn to listen."

Being a member of a group provides children with two conditions essential for learning: a sense of security and opportunities for social interaction.

Closing Group Activities

Exciting circles and other group activities sometimes need a quiet, settling close. The following can be used to wind down group activities and prepare excited children for the change to another activity or play.

UP AND DOWN

Up and down,

Up and down,

Clap your hands and turn around.

Up and down,

Up and down,

Clap your hands and sit down.

RAG DOLL

I'm just a limp rag doll.

My arms are limp.

My legs are limp.

My head is limp.

I'm just a limp rag doll.

UP, DOWN, AND REST

Up and down,

Up and down,

Round, round, round,

Up and down.

I stretch, I stretch, I yawn.

I rest and then I start again.

Up and down

(Second time—"I rest, I rest, I rest" is the fifth and ending line.)

GOING TO GRANDMA'S HOUSE

Wash the face.
Wash the hands.
Put on a jacket.
Shoes to lace.
Down the stairs.
Open the door.
Shut the door.
Jump in the car.
It's not far.
Goodbye

Transitions

Disbanding a circle or group at an activity's ending calls for a planned approach. If the group is of any size, you will need to excuse a few at a time. When carpet squares are to be picked up and stacked or small chairs returned to tables, a reminder is in order: "When you hear your name, pick up your carpet square and carry it to the stack."

Transitional statements that relate to the just-completed activity work well: "Crawl like Victor the Boa Constrictor to the block center," or "Let the wind blow you slowly to the water table like it blew in the little tree."

TRANSITION POEM

Wiggle both ears.
Touch your nose.
Wiggle your fingers.
Stamp your toes.
Point to your eyes.
Your mouth open wide.
Stick out your tongue.
Put it inside.
Trace your lips.
Go "shh!" Don't speak.
Hands on your neck.
Touch both cheeks.
Shake your hands.
Now let them sleep.
Bend your knees.
Sit on your feet.

Now we finished with this play,
Take your feet and walk away!

GOING TO LINE UP

(To the tune of "The Bear Went Over the Mountain.")

_____ *is going over to line up.*
1st child's name

_____ *is going over to line up.*
1st child's name

_____ *is going over to line up.*
1st child's name

And _____ *is going next.*
2nd child's name

_____ *went over to line up*
1st child's name

_____ *went over to line up*
2nd child's name

_____ *is going over to line up*
3rd child's name

And _____ *is going next.*
4th child's name

Last line when all have gone.

And all are standing tall.

Additional Transitions. A fun way to move children one by one is to recite the rhyme "Jack Be Nimble," substituting the child's name for "Jack": "(Child's name) be nimble, (child's name) be quick, (child's name) jump over the candlestick." (Children clap for the child who jumps over a plastic candleholder and unlit candle.)

Another way to disband a group is to make a "tickler" from a 3-foot-long dowel and some yarn. Say to the children, "Close your eyes. When you feel a tickle on your head, it's time to stand and walk carefully through your classmates to the . . ."

Some statements that are helpful in moving a group of children in an orderly fashion are listed here. Many identify language concepts and serve a dual purpose.

- "Everyone with brown shoes stand up. Now it's time to . . ."
- "If your favorite sandwich is peanut butter and jelly (ham, cheese, tuna, and so forth) raise your hand. If your hand is up, please tiptoe to the . . ."

transitional statements — teacher statements made to disperse students in small groups or in an orderly fashion.

◆ "Richie is the engine on a slow, slow train. Richie, chug chug slowly to the . . ." "Darlene is the coal car on a slow, slow train." (The last child is, naturally, the caboose.)

Multicultural Considerations and Activities. If second-language learners are present, circle times need to include special considerations. Routines that include recognition of children by their names aid acceptance and inclusion. Activities within circle times that are repeated each day add predictability and promote children's successful participation. Tabors (1997) suggests the words to songs be introduced without music before singing them. This gives children a better opportunity to catch on and join in. Second-language learners frequently "find their voice" or "go public" for the first time in their new language as they sing, chant, or try physical motions or actions.

The inclusion of multicultural and multiethnic aspects to group activities is not a new idea. Songs and finger plays in the native languages of attending children promote acceptance of diversity. Teachers may need parental help in discovering literary material or for translation. Children usually eagerly learn motions and translated words presented with catchy rhythms. Introduce the name of the language when presenting. "This is a song with Russian words. Gregor's mom taught me how to sing it." As with multicultural and multiethnic picture books, stories, and poetry, these activities are not given extra or special status but are everyday, standard activities—ones that many teachers do not wish to neglect. The problem, at times, is finding them when teacher resources abound with "Anglo-intense" examples.

Circle-Time Pitfalls. Circle times can fall apart for a number of reasons. An examination of the teacher's goals and planning decisions prior to conducting a circle time may clarify what caused child disinterest or lack of enthusiasm. When circles go poorly, child behavior may be focused away from the circle's theme and action.

Before examining teacher behaviors, other factors should be reviewed, such as the setting, length, and age-level appropriateness of the activity. Then examine whether the children enjoyed and participated enthusiastically in the activity and how teacher behavior contributed to this. If the activity was not a success, the activity failed the children rather than vice versa.

A teacher whose goals include child conversation and involvement will not monopolize the activity with a constant up-front presentation. Unfortunately, some beginning teachers seem to possess an overwhelming desire to dispense information, eliminating children's conversation and reactions. When this happens, circle times become passive listening times (Figure 14–2).

The size of the circle has also been discussed in this chapter. Dodge (1988) describes the possible reasons teachers attempt large circle times.

> **Possible Causes:** Teachers are more comfortable with their ability to maintain control when the whole group is involved in the same activity. They want to be sure everyone in the group learns the same concepts and skills. Several teachers said that they do most of their teaching at circle time.

Teachers need to understand that large group instruction at preschool level may cause group disinterest and restlessness by becoming impersonal.

There seems to be a type of adult who is unable to talk to the child, no matter how important or pertinent the child's comments. It is as if a planned step-by-step circle time must be followed. The teacher has become inflexible, a slave to a plan. One-sided conversations turn everyone off but the speaker.

Waiting a long time for a turn during circle time leads to frustration, which may cause children to tune out. A simple fact that all experienced teachers know is that active, involved children stay focused.

A teacher who constantly asks questions to maintain child attention may defeat her purpose. Some teachers do not understand the difference between asking a question with one right answer (to test a child) and asking ques-

FIGURE 14–2 In successful group times, children offer their comments, ideas, and questions.

tions that encourage thinking. Most adults remember from past school experiences how it felt when they missed a question. Unskilled teachers may make children afraid to answer or share their ideas.

Hints for Successful Circle Times. Before you conduct your circle

◆ review your goals for circle times periodically.

◆ plan for active child participation and involvement.

◆ make proposed circle-time duration appropriate to the group's age.

◆ practice language games and activities so that you can focus on the children.

◆ think about group size and settings.

◆ remember that it is better to stop before enthusiasm wanes.

◆ consider child comfort.

◆ identify possible room distractions.

◆ keep rules simple, clear, and at a minimum.

Note that some centers also institute the word *pass* as a circle-time signal that the child does not want to contribute during a discussion. This releases pressure to talk when a child cannot think of a response or chooses not to share her ideas.

During a circle time

◆ focus children at the beginning (Figure 14–3).

◆ state what you expect early, if necessary: "Sit where you can see." "My turn to talk; your turn to listen."

◆ proceed with enthusiasm.

◆ try to enjoy and be unhurried.

◆ think about including activities that promote child decisions, guessing, voting, creativity, expression of personal preferences, problem solving, prediction making, and child questioning.

◆ give children credit for their comments, ideas, and participation. "Jason's moving his arms and head." "Shawnita told us what she saw in the mirror." "Maron thinks our plants need water."

FIGURE 14–3 A finger play is used to focus three-year-olds at small group time.

◆ stop the rambling child speaker with "It's time for your friends' turn now, Clyde."

◆ make eye contact with all children.

◆ watch for feedback and act accordingly.

◆ use wind-down activities if the group gets too excited.

◆ use wiggle reducers.

◆ draw quiet children into participation.

◆ reduce waiting times.

◆ watch the length of time allowed for the activity.

◆ think of an orderly transition to the next activity, which may include the children's taking carpet squares to a storage area.

◆ remember that your skill increases with experience.

◆ be aware that sitting still may be a problem for some children.

Children aren't being rebellious by moving around. They are just moving and they're moving because they need to do it. (Hunter, 2000)

Educators will always have children, particularly very young preschoolers or culturally diverse preschoolers, who do not readily choose to participate with speech or actions at group times. French (1996) points out that teacher insistence, although well intended, is inappropriate.

The preschool years are a time of rapid language development, and many preschool teachers are appropriately concerned with supporting and fostering this language development. Unfortunately, many teachers translate this concern into an insistence that a child speak up individually in group situations—for example, participating in show-and-tell or responding to questions about a story the teacher has read.

Aides or volunteers attending a circle time need to be alert to child distractions. Moving closer to or between two children may be helpful, or quietly suggesting an alternative activity to a disinterested child can aid the teacher leader.

Occasionally one child's silliness or mimicking behavior can lead to circle-time disruption as the attention-getting child's behavior challenges the teacher's hold on group focus. Teacher restatement of a circle-time rule may be necessary.

Watching Children's Participation Level. As teachers scan faces and observe child vocalization and movement during circle times, obvious differences in children's ability to focus, stay focused, and participate as fully functioning group members are apparent. Many conditions influence each child's ability to concentrate, actively contribute, and follow group activities—age, health, language deficiencies, weather, distractions, home problems, disabilities, and a multitude of other factors may change child behavior at circle on any given day. After a teacher has become familiar with her group and leads a few circle times, she mentally categorizes child behaviors. Often, at circle time teachers can tell who is having a bad day. Possible child-attending behavior will vary from not focused to completely focused and participating, with other behaviors between these two end points. A child may tune in and out, attend but not participate verbally or with body involvement, or attend and participate sporadically.

As teachers monitor children's group behavior, they become increasingly aware of how teacher behaviors and verbalizations affect children's attendance and participation. Ask any practicing teacher about the teacher satisfaction felt at the conclusion of a well-planned and conducted group time where child interest was held and maintained and something of educational quality or value was accomplished. When teachers feel their child group was eager, responsive, and enjoying the group experience and feel that as the teacher they interacted skillfully, it is a memorable teaching moment.

Chants and Choruses

Throughout history, rhythmic **chants** and choruses have been used in group rituals and ceremonies. The individuals in the group gain a group identity as a result of their participation.

Natural enjoyment of rhythmic word patterns can be seen in a child's involvement in group chants. The child and teacher can also playfully take part in call and response during the preschool day. "I made it, I made it," the child says. "I see it, I see it," the teacher answers, picking up the child's rhythm.

This verbal play is common. Sounds in the community and school yard can be brought to the children's attention by teachers who notice them and make comments. Weir and Eggleston (1975) point out that

> Urban sounds are sometimes syncopated and rhythmical, such as the fire siren, people walking on side walks, jack hammers or nailing in nails. These are rhythms that children imitate verbally and that adults can point out to children.

Chants and choruses are mimicked, and sound and word patterns that have regularity and predictability are imitated. Choruses usually involve a back-and-forth conversation (one individual alternating with another) and involve the rise and fall of accented sounds or syllables.

Children need the teacher's examples and directions, such as, "When it's your turn, I'll point to you" or "Let's say it together," before they can perform the patterns on their own. Chants printed on charts with simple illustrations can enhance chanting and chorus times and tie the oral words to written ones.

Chanting promotes successful language experiences regardless of children's background or talent and helps children learn the importance of clear and expressive pronunciation. Teacher charts developed for chanting can be used over and over and are another way for children to discover the relationship of spoken words and print. Many strong-rhythm chants invite clapping, foot stomping, or a wide variety of other physical movements. The chants that follow are some tried-and-true favorites.

CHANTS

THE GRAND OLD DUKE OF YORK

The grand old Duke of York
He had forty thousand men.
He marched them up the hill.
He marched them down again.
And when you're up, you're up!
And when you're down, you're down.
And when you're half-way-in-between,
You're neither up nor down.

---

chants — rhythmic monotonous utterances.

And It Was Me!

I looked in my soup, and who did I see?
Something wonderful . . . and it was me.

Additional verses:
I looked in the mirror, and who did I see?
I looked in the puddle . . .
I looked in a window . . .
I looked in the river . . .
I looked in the pond . . .
I looked at a snapshot . . .
I turned off the television . . .

Ending:
When I'm grown up, I'll still be there.
Right in reflections everywhere.
When I'm grown up, how will it be?
A wonderful world with you and me.

It's Raining It's Pouring

It's raining, it's pouring.
The old man is snoring.
He went to bed and he bumped his head
And he couldn't get up in the morning.
Rain, rain go away—come again some other day.

Miss Mary Mack

Miss Mary Mack, Mack, Mack
All dressed in black, black, black
With silver buttons, buttons, buttons
All down her back, back, back.

She asked her mother, mother, mother
For fifteen cents, cents, cents
To see the elephants, elephants, elephants
Jump the fence, fence, fence.

They jumped so high, high, high
They touched the sky, sky, sky
And never came back, back, back
Till the fourth of July, ly, ly.

July can't walk, walk, walk
July can't talk, talk, talk
July can't eat, eat, eat
With a knife and fork, fork, fork.

She went upstairs, stairs, stairs
To say her prayers, prayers, prayers
She made her bed, bed, bed
She hit her head, head, head
On a piece of corn bread, bread, bread.

Now she's asleep, sleep, sleep
She's snoring deep, deep, deep
No more to play, play, play
Until Friday, day, day
What can I say, say, say
Except hooray, ray, ray!

Fill in the Blank Poem

If I had a <u>dollar</u>,
I'll tell you what I'd do.
I'd <u>spend it all</u> on <u>ice cream,</u>
And I'd give <u>it all</u> to you.
'Cause that's how much I like you! <u>Child's name!</u>

(Child's name is said with a deep voice in vaudeville style.)

'Cause that's how much I like you, <u>Child's name.</u>

Substitute other words for ice cream that children suggest, such as hamburgers, toys, and so on. Those not wishing to promote sugar can substitute vegetables or other items.

Example:
a. *If I had a bike*
   I'll tell you what I'd do
   I'd <u>pedal</u> on the pedals
   And I'd give a ride to you
   'Cause that's how much I like you <u>Tracy</u>
   'Cause that's how much I like you <u>Tracy.</u>

b. *If I had an elephant*
   I'll tell you what I'd do
   I'd put it on a truck
   And take it to the zoo.

Using Accessories

Teachers often use accessories or props at circle time. The following example, "Little Things," is an accessory that is highly enjoyable and provokes giggles and "do-it-again" requests.

LITTLE THINGS

(to the tune of "Oh My Darling" or chanted)

Little black things, little black things
Crawling up and down my arm.
I am not afraid of them
For they will do no harm.
(Substitute any color for black.)

Materials. The following colors of yarn are needed.

red	green	black	pink
orange	blue	brown	gray
yellow	purple	white	

Instructions. You will need to make a set of 11 colored things for each child. These can be stored easily in resealable sandwich bags.

Step 1: For each colored thing, cut five yarn pieces, each measuring 8 inches long.

Step 2: Put one yarn piece aside and, keeping the other four together, fold them in half.

Step 3: Using the fifth piece of yarn, tie it around the other four, 1 inch from the folded ends and knotting it well, to form a "head" and "legs." Fold the knotted ends down to form more legs.

Give each child a bag of "things." Let the children tell you what color to use. While chanting or singing, have the colored thing crawl up and down arms.

FINGER PLAY

Finger play is a classic preschool group (or individual) activity that parents have probably already introduced to children with "Peek-a-Boo" or "This Little Piggy." Finger plays use words and actions (usually finger motions) together. Early childhood play frequently goes beyond finger movements and often includes whole body actions.

When learning a finger play, the child usually practices and joins in the finger movements before learning the words. Words can be learned and retained by doing the play over and over again.

Finger plays are often done with rhymes. Easy-to-remember rhymes give the children pleasure in listening and a chance to feel good about themselves because (1) they quickly become part of a group having fun and doing the same thing, and (2) they experience a feeling of accomplishment when a rhyme has been learned.

Teachers use finger plays to encourage enjoyment of language, to prepare children for sitting, to keep children active and interested while waiting, and as transitions between activities. Finger plays are also used for special purposes, such as quieting a group or getting toys back on the shelves. They can build vocabulary as well as teach facts and can help a child release pent-up energy.

Teachers should practice a finger play and memorize it beforehand to be sure of a clear and smooth presentation. It should be offered enthusiastically, focusing on enjoyment. As with other activities, the teacher can say, "Try it with me." The child who just watches will join in when ready. Watching comes first, one or two hand movements next, and then repetitions, using words and actions together. Each child learns at her own rate of speed.

Suggested Finger Plays

Finger plays can be found in many books for early childhood staff members or can be created by the teacher. The following are recommended because of their popularity with both children and teachers.

HICKORY, DICKORY, DOCK

Hickory, dickory, dock! (Rest elbow in the palm of your other hand and swing upraised arm back and forth.)

The mouse ran up the clock; (Creep fingers up the arm to the palm of the other hand.)

The clock struck one. (Clap hands.)

The mouse ran down. (Creep fingers down to elbow.)

Hickory, dickory, dock! (Swing arm as before.)

OMITTING SOUNDS POEM (PHONEMIC AWARENESS)

This is the "at" I like best. (Make pointed hat with hands on head.)

I mean my hat. (Make an "oh no" face.)

This is an "op," here on my chest. (Hands on chest.)

No, no, it's my top! (Make face.)

This is my "ants." (Touch pants.)

Oops, I meant pants. (Make face.)

This is my "hoe." (Push out shoe.)

No, its my shoe. (Make face.)

What's wrong with me today? (Hands on head.)

Letters left off words that I say. (Point to mouth.)

I think I better walk out and "lay." (Walk fingers up arm.)

I did it again, I meant play! (Make face.)

CHOO! CHOO!

Choo-o! Choo-o! Choo! Choo! (Run fingers along arm to shoulder slowly.)

This little train goes up the track.

Choo! Choo! Choo! Choo! (At shoulder, turn "train" and head down arm.)

But this little train comes quickly back.

Choo-choo-choo-choo! Choo-choo-choo-choo! (Repeat last line.) (Run fingers down arm quickly.)

Whoo-o! Whoo-o! Whoo-o! (Imitate train whistle.)

WHERE IS THUMBKIN?

Where is thumbkin, where is thumbkin? (Hands behind back.)

Here I am, here I am. (One hand out, thumb up. Other hand out, thumb up.)

How are you today, sir? (First thumb bends up and down.)

Very well, I thank you. (Second thumb bends up and down.)

Run away, run away. (First thumb behind back; second thumb behind back.)

Repeat with:

Where is pointer? (Use first finger.)

Where is tall man? (Use middle finger.)

Where is ring man? (Use ring finger.)

Where is pinkie? (Use little finger.)

Where are all the men? (Use whole hand.)

Newer, less well-known but still popular and enjoyable finger plays appear in the Activities section at the end of this chapter.

BODY-ACTION PLAYS

Encourage children to jump in rhythm to this chant while doing what the rhyme says. Use this for working out pent-up energy.

HEAD, SHOULDERS

Head, shoulders, knees, and toes (Stand; touch both hands to each part in order.)

Head, shoulders, knees, and toes.

Head, shoulders, knees, and toes.

That's the way the story goes. (Clap this line.)

This is my head, this is not. (Hands on head, then feet.)

These are my shoulders, these are not. (Hands on shoulders, then knees.)

Here are my knees; watch them wiggle, (Wiggle knees.)

Touch my armpits and I giggle. (Hands under armpits with laugh.)

Head shoulders, knees, and toes. (Touch in order.)

That's the way the story goes. (Clap.)

BEAT ONE HAMMER

My mother told me to tell you

To beat one hammer (Pound one fist.)

Like you see me do.

My mother told me to tell you

To beat two hammers (Pound two fists.)

Like you see me do.

My mother told me to tell you

To beat three hammers (Pound two fists; stamp one foot.)

Like you see me do.

My mother told me to tell you

To beat four hammers (Pound two fists;
 stamp two feet.)
Like you see me do.
My mother told me to tell you
To beat five hammers (Add nodding head.)
Like you see me do.
My mother told me to tell you
To beat no hammers (Stop!)
Like you see me do.

SUMMARY

Speaking activities are planned for the young child. Some require simple imitation of words, whereas others call for the child's creative or expressive response.

Finger plays use words and actions together. They are actively enjoyed by children and build feelings of self-worth. Teachers can memorize finger plays and use them daily.

Circle times instill group spirit and social enjoyment of language. Opening activities capture attention. Chants and choruses add rhythmic word play and often involve physical movement. A smooth transition to other activities takes place when teachers are well prepared.

Teachers evaluate circle times comparing outcomes with goals. They monitor child reaction to their behaviors, strategies, and presentation skills. They critique their ability to plan lively, enjoyable, relevant, and language-abundant circle times.

ADDITIONAL RESOURCES

Finger Play Collections

Beckman, C., Simmons, R. G., & Thomas, N. (1982). *Channels to children*, P.O. Box 25834, Colorado Springs, CO 80936. (A wonderful collection of activities based on a theme approach to teaching. Many cross-cultural activities described in last chapter.)

Crowell, L., & Hibner, D. (1976). *Finger frolics*. First Teacher Inc., Box 29, Bridgeport, CT 06602.

Dowell, R. L. (1987). *Move over Mother Goose*. Pollyanna Productions, Mt. Ranier, MD: Gryphon House Inc.

Ellis, M. J. (1978). *Fingerplay approach to dramatization*. Minneapolis: T. S. Denison.

Finger plays for young children. Scholastic, 2931 East McCarty St., P.O. Box 7502, Jefferson City, MO 65102. (An easel book.)

Glazer, T. (1973). *Eye Winker, Tom Tinker, Chin Chopper: Fifty musical finger plays*. New York: Doubleday.

Kable, G. (1979). *Favorite finger plays*. Minneapolis: T. S. Denison.

Redleaf, R. (1993). *Busy fingers, growing minds: Finger plays, verses and activities for whole language learning*. St. Paul, MN: Redleaf Press.

Rockwell, R., Hoge, D. R., & Searcy, B. (1999). *Linking language and literacy activities throughout the curriculum*. Beltsville, MD: Gryphon House Inc. (Circle-time ideas.)

Wilmes, L., & Wilmes, D. (1981). *Everyday circle times*. Mt. Ranier, MD: Gryphon House Inc. (A collection of ideas for exciting group times.)

Phonemic Awareness Circle-Time Ideas

Jordano, K., & Callella, T. (1998). *Phonemic awareness: Song and rhymes*. Cypress, CA: Creative Teaching Press.

Readings

Carner, K. (Ed.). (1996). *The giant encyclopedia of circle time and group activities for children 3 to 6*. Beltsville, MD: Gryphon House Inc.

Claycomb, P. (1998). *The learning circle: A preschool teacher's guide to circle time*. Beltsville, MD: Gryphon House Inc.

Colgin, M. L. (1982). *One potato, two potato, three potato, four! 165 chants for children*. Beltsville, MD: Gryphon House Inc.

Dowel, R. I. (1995). *Mother Ruth's rhymes: Lyrical finger plays and action verse*. New York: Pollyanna Productions.

Orozco, J. L. (1997). *Diez deditos/ten little fingers and other play rhymes and action songs from Latin America*. New York: Dutton Childrens Books.

HELPFUL WEB SITES

Ask the Preschool Teacher
http://www.askthepreschoolteacher.com
Select *Search the Site*. Enter "circle time" in Find box and view questions and answers about circle times. A free newsletter is offered.

Child Care Resources, Training and Consultation
http://www.childcarelounge.com
Select *Resources for Caregivers;* then choose
fingerplays for a collection of finger plays.

Early Head Start National Resource Center
http://www.ehsnrc.org
This site provides tips concerning group
instruction.

Gayle's Preschool Rainbow—Activity Central
http://www.preschoolrainbow.org
Click *The Preschool Rhyme Theme Collection.* Next
select *Transition Activity Theme* for nursery
rhymes, finger plays, and action poems.

 A new finger play to an old rhyme can be used at group time. Resource books promoting additional circle-time teacher skills are listed, along with a book review on a newly published book whose content focuses on clever transitions.

STUDENT ACTIVITIES

1. With a small group of classmates, practice and present a finger play, chant, chorus, or body-action play. Have each student present the activity until it is learned by the others.

2. Make a list of at least five books that are resources for finger plays.

3. Present a finger play, chant, or chorus to a group of young children.

4. List possible reasons that children become disinterested at circle times.

5. Find a finger play that is seasonal (generally used at only one time a year). Bring a copy to class.

6. Create a finger play, chant, or chorus for young children.

7. Observe a circle time and evaluate it. Share it with the class.

8. Tape record or videotape a few of your teacher-led discussions at group time. Analyze your listening skills and whether you dominate conversations. Look at your ability to keep group time lively with child participation. If a child-teacher discussion did not hold children's interest, determine the reasons.

9. If you know a song, rhyme, finger play, or movement activity in another language, share it with the class.

10. Create a finger play about making tortillas or using chopsticks. Share with the class.

11. Create finger play motions for one of the following. Share with a small group of peers.

PIZZA

Let's make a pizza big and round
Take tomato sauce and spread it around.
Onions, olives, peppers, and cheese
Add mushrooms, sausage if you please.
Put it in the oven. Careful it's hot!
Bake 'til a warm brown crust you've got.
It's bubbly, spicy, and tastes so nice.
Raise your hand if you'd like a slice.

TAKING OFF

The airplane taxis down the field
And heads into the breeze.
It lifts its wheels above the ground.
It skims above the trees
It rises high and higher
Away up toward the sun.
It's just a speck against the sky
and now—
and now—it's gone.

CHAPTER REVIEW

A. Finish the following:

1. A transitional statement at the end of group time is necessary because

   _____.

2. History shows that chants and choruses were used for

   _____.

3. A successful circle time for young children can be described by the following terms:

   _____.

B. Why are finger plays so popular with young children?

C. Rearrange and place in the best order or sequence.

1. Child knows words and actions of a finger play.
2. Teacher knows words and actions of a finger play.
3. Teacher practices finger play.
4. Child participates with actions only.
5. Child watches.
6. Teacher presents finger play to children.
7. Teacher evaluates the results of the finger play.
8. Teacher encourages children to join in actions and words.

D. List five signals or attention getters that a teacher could use at the beginning of a circle time.

E. In what ways should an assistant teacher be helpful when another teacher is leading group language activities?

F. Rate the following teacher statements during planned circles.

   G = Good Technique   P = Poor Technique

1. "It's my turn to talk."
2. "Stop wiggling, Jimmy."
3. "Everyone's listening; it's time to begin."
4. "When Kate, Tran, and Nancy join us, we'll all be together."
5. "The first one standing can be the first one to leave the circle."
6. "We're finished. Let's go."
7. "Speak up, Gisela. It's time to answer."
8. "Thuy is doing our new finger play the 'right' way."
9. "Watch closely, and make your fingers move just like mine."
10. "Everyone listened to what their friends said and took turns talking today."

ADDITIONAL GROUP STARTERS

I LIKE YOU

(Chant or sing.)

I like you.
There's no doubt about it.
I like you.
There's no doubt about it.
I am your good friend.
You like me.
There's no doubt about it.
You like me.
There's no doubt about it.
You are my good friend.
There's my friend (child's name), *and my friend*
(child's name).
(Continue around circle.)

OH HERE WE ARE TOGETHER

(Chant or sing.)

Oh here we are together, together, together,
Oh here we are together
At (insert school name) *Preschool*
There's (child's name) *and* (child's name), *and* (names of all children).
Oh here we are together to have a good day.

WE'RE WAITING

(Circle starter.)

We're waiting, we're waiting, we're waiting for (child's name).
(Repeat until group is formed.)
We're here, because we're here, because we're here, because we're here.
And my name is _____, and my name is _____. (Around the circle.)

HELLO

Hello (child's name). *Hello, hello, hello.*
Shake my hand and around we'll go.
Hello (child's name). *Hello, hello, hello.*

Shake my hand and around we'll go.

(Teacher starts; children continue around the circle chanting until all are recognized.)

SECRET

I've got something in my pocket
That belongs across my face.
I keep it very close at hand
In a most convenient place.
I know you couldn't guess it
If you guessed a long, long while.
So I'll take it out and put it on
It's a great big friendly SMILE!

TEN FINGERS

I have ten little fingers
And they all belong to me.
I can make them do things.
Would you like to see?
I can shut them up tight
Or open them wide.
I can put them together
Or make them all hide.
I can make them jump high.
I can make them jump low,
I can fold them quietly
And hold them just so.

EVERYBODY DO THIS

Refrain:
Everybody do this, do this, do this.
Everybody do this just like me.

Actions:
Open and close fists
Roll fists around
Touch elbows
Spider fingers
Pat head, rub tummy
Wink
Wave hand good-bye

(Ask children to create others.)

ADDITIONAL CIRCLE ACTIVITIES

ONE AND ONLY

I have two eyes to see all around.
I have two feet to stand on ground.
I have two ears to listen and to hear
Every sound, both far and near.
I have two arms to reach and to fold.
I have two hands to work and to hold.
So many twos it takes to be
The one and only single me.

Reprinted with permission of the publisher Early Years, Inc. From the January 1997 issue of *Teaching K-8 Magazine*, Norwalk, CT 06854.

IF YOU'RE HAPPY AND YOU KNOW IT

If you're happy and you know it, clap your hands.
If you're happy and you know it, clap your hands.
If you're happy and you know it, then your face will surely show it.
If you're happy and you know it, clap your hands.

(Additional verses.)

If you're sad and you know it, wipe your eyes.
If you're mad and you know it, pound your fist.
If you're hungry and you know it, rub your stomach.
If you're silly and you know it, go tee-hee.
If you're cold and you know it, rub your arms.
If you're hot and you know it, wipe your brow.
If you're sleepy and you know it, go to sleep . . . snore, snore.

HANDS ON SHOULDERS

Hands on shoulders, hands on knees.
Hands behind you, if you please.
Touch your shoulders, now your nose.
Now your ear and now your toes.
Hands up high into the air.
Down at your sides then touch your hair.
Hands up high as before.
Now clap your hands,
One, two, three, four.

BALL ROLLING CIRCLE

The ball will roll across our circle.
Touch toes with your neighbors.
Here comes the ball, Susie. "I roll the ball to Susie."

(Teacher says: "Susie roll the ball across the circle and say your friend's name.")

"I roll the ball to _____."

THE CARROT SEED WILL GROW

Carrots grow from carrot seeds,
I'll plant this seed and grow one.
I won't be disappointed if my seed doesn't grow.
What makes seeds grow? I don't know!
So I won't be disappointed if my seed doesn't grow.
My brother said "Na, na. It won't come up. Na, na. It won't come up.
Na, na. It won't come up. Your carrot won't come up."

(Repeat above, ending with the following.)

Oh, carrots grow from carrot seeds.
I planted one, it grew. I watered it. I pulled the weeds.
No matter what he said.
Carrots grow from carrot seeds.

ADDITIONAL CHANTS

PANCAKE

Mix a pancake.
Stir a pancake.
Pop it in the pan.
Fry a pancake.
Toss a pancake.
Catch it if you can.

THE BIG CLOCK

Slowly ticks the big clock
Chorus: *Tick-tock, tick-tock*
(Repeat twice.)
But the cuckoo clock ticks double quick
Chorus: *Tick-a-tock-a, tick-a-tock-a*
Tick-a-tock-a, tick!

LITTLE BROWN RABBIT

Little brown rabbit went hoppity-hop,

All: *Hoppity-hop, hoppity-hop!*
Into a garden without any stop,

All: *Hoppity-hop, hoppity-hop!*
He ate for his supper a fresh carrot top,

All: *Hoppity-hop, hoppity-hop!*
Then home went the rabbit without
any stop,

All: *Hoppity-hop, hoppity-hop!*

WHO ATE THE COOKIES IN THE COOKIE JAR

All: *Who ate the cookies in the cookie*
jar?
All: (Child's or teacher's name) *ate*
the cookies in the cookie jar.
(Teacher points to different child for
each verse.)
Named person: *Who me?*
All: *Yes you.*
Named person: *Couldn't be.*
All: *Then who?*
Named person: (Child or teacher) *ate*
the cookies in the cookie jar.
Newly named person: *Who me? (and*
so forth).

LOCK AND KEY

(A back-and-forth chorus.)

I am a gold lock;   *I am a gold key.*
I am a silver lock;   *I am a silver key.*
I am a house lock;   *I am a house key.*
I am a car lock;   *I am a car key.*
I am a monk lock;   *I am a monk-key*
(whoo, whoo, whoo).

ADDITIONAL FINGER PLAYS

THE CAR WASH

The car wash machine, the car wash
machine
The strangest thing I've ever seen
We drive the car in dirty and drive
it out clean (Pretend to drive
car.)
A little light flashes and a door opens
wide (Move arms as if opening
door wide.)
We go very slowly and drive inside
(Driving car motions.)
Water squirts out all over the
place (Pretend to squirt
water.)

And the brushes seem to be running
into my face (Roll hands and move
up to face.)
They slide over the car to wash off the
dirt (Rub hands.)
I wonder if it's going to hurt. (Cover face.)
It feels like the car is moving away
But the moving brushes make it feel
that way!
The car wash machine, the car wash
machine
The strangest thing I've ever seen
The car went in dirty and came out clean.

Reproduced by permission. Rhoda Redleaf, Busy
Fingers, Growing Minds.

443

FRIENDS AT PLAY

One little child with nothing to do (Hold up one finger.)

Found a friend to play with

And then there were two (Hold up two fingers.)

Two little children, playing happily

Along came another and then there were three (Hold up three fingers.)

Three little children playing grocery store

Along came a customer and then there were four (Hold up four fingers.)

Four little children with cars and trikes to drive

Along came a friend in a wagon, and then there were five. (Hold up all five fingers.)

Reproduced by permission. Rhoda Redleaf, Busy Fingers, Growing Minds.

FAMILY OF RABBITS

A family of rabbits lived under a tree, (Close right hand and hide it under left arm.)

A father, a mother, and babies three. (Hold up thumb, then fingers in succession.)

Sometimes the bunnies would sleep all day, (Make fist.)

But when night came, they liked to play. (Wiggle fingers.)

Out of the hole they'd go creep, creep, creep, (Move fingers in creeping motion.)

While the birds in the trees were all asleep. (Rest face on hands, place palms together.)

Then the bunnies would scamper about and run (Wiggle fingers.)

Uphill, downhill! Oh, what fun! (Wiggle fingers vigorously.)

But when the mother said, "It's time to rest," (Hold up index finger.)

Pop! They would hurry (Clap hands after "Pop.")

Right back to their nest! (Hide hand under arm.)

FIREFIGHTERS

Ten little firefighters, sleeping in a row,

Ding, dong goes the bell, down the pole they go.

Jumping on the engine, oh, oh, oh,

Putting out the fire, shhhhhhhhhhhhhhhhhhhh.

And home again they go

Back to sleep again,

All in a row.

LITTLE HOUSE

I'm going to build a little house (Fingers form a roof.)

With windows big and bright. (Make square with hands.)

With chimney tall and curling smoke (Arm up in the air—waving in spiral.)

Drifting out of sight

In winter, when the snowflakes fall (Hands flutter down.)

Or when I hear a storm (Cup hand to ear.)

I'll go sit in my little house (Stand, then sit down.)

Where I'll be nice and warm. (Hug chest.)

THIS IS THE MOUNTAIN

This is the mountain up so high, (Form a triangle.)

And this is the moon that sails through the sky. (Make a circle with thumbs and index fingers.)

These are the stars that twinkle so bright. (Make a small circle with thumb and index, other three fingers moving.)

These are the clouds that pass through the night. (Make fists.)

This is the window through which I peep, (Make a square with thumb and index.)

And here am I, fast asleep. (Close eyes.)

CLAP YOUR HANDS

Clap your hands high,

Clap your hands low,

Pat your head lightly,

444

And down you go.
I'll touch my hair, my lips, my eyes,
I'll sit up straight, and then I'll rise.
I'll touch my ears, my nose, my chin,
Then quietly, sit down again.

BUTTERFLY

Roly-poly caterpillar
Into a corner crept.
Spun around himself a blanket
Then for a long time slept.
A long time passed (Whisper.)
Roly-poly caterpillar wakened by and by.
Found himself with beautiful wings
Changed to a butterfly.

HAMBURGER

A big hamburger for you. (Cup hands together.)
Open it too. (Hands side by side, palms up.)
What do you see? (Point to palm with one hand.)
A meat patty? Yes. (Nod head yes.)
Yellow mustard we spread. (Spreading motion.)
Squeeze catsup that's red. (Pretend to squeeze bottle.)
Pickle in the middle. (Pretend to place a pickle.)
Close it tight. (Hands cupped together.)
Yum. Take a bite. (Pretend to bite and rub tummy.)

Note: Teacher can provide mustard, catsup, and pickles to taste and lead a discussion of who prefers what and where they like (or do not like) to eat hamburgers. Some classes have expanded this finger play into a theme day with many related activities planned such as a fast food dramatic play center, hamburger patty–forming center, bun-baking area, sign making, order counter, chart-preference activity, visit to a fast food restaurant, money-counting activity, and so on.

SLEEPY TIME

Open wide your little hands,
Now squeeze them very tight.
Shake them, shake them very loose,
With all your might.
Climb them slowly to the sky.
Drop down like gentle rain.
Go to sleep my little hands,
I'll wake you once again.

A FUNNY ONE

'Round the house
'Round the house (Put fingers around the face.)
Peep in the window (Open eyes wide.)
Listen at the door (Cup hand behind ear.)
Knock at the door (Knock on head.)
Lift up the latch (Push up nose.)
And walk in (Stick out tongue and walk fingers in mouth.)
—I caught you! (Bite gently down on fingers.)

TWO LITTLE APPLES

Two little apples hanging on a tree, (Put hand by eyes.)
Two little apples smiling at me. (Smile.)
I shook that tree as hard as I could. (Shake tree.)
Down came the apples. (Make falling motions.)
Mmmm—they were good. (Rub stomach.)

PEANUT BUTTER AND JELLY

First you take the peanuts and you crunch them and you crunch them. (Repeat.)
Peanut butter—jelly! Peanut butter—jelly!
Then you take the grapes and you squish them and you squish them. (Repeat.)
Peanut butter—jelly! Peanut butter—jelly!
Then you take the bread and you spread it and you spread it. (Repeat.)
Peanut butter—jelly! Peanut butter—jelly!

Then you take the sandwich and you eat it and you eat it. (Repeat. Then with your mouth closed hum the refrain as if you had a mouth full of sandwich.)

Peanut butter—jelly! Peanut butter—jelly! ("Peanut butter" is said in the following fashion: "Pea" [medium pitch] "nut" [low pitch] "but" [medium] "ter" [high pitch with hands above head, fingers shaking to side in Vaudeville-type motion]. "Jelly" is said in a low, throaty voice, accompanied by hands to opposite side shaking at knee level.)

FIVE LITTLE ASTRONAUTS

Five little astronauts (Hold up fingers on one hand.)

Ready for outer space.

The first one said, "Let's have a race."

The second one said, "The weather's too rough."

The third one said, "Oh, don't be gruff."

The fourth one said, "I'm ready enough."

The fifth one said, "Let's Blast Off!"

10, 9, 8, 7, 6, 5, 4, 3, 2, 1, (Start with 10 fingers and pull one down with each number.)

BLAST OFF!!! (Clap loudly with "Blast Off!")

ADDITIONAL BODY-ACTION PLAYS

MY LITTLE THUMBS

My little thumbs keep moving.

My little thumbs keep moving.

My little thumbs keep moving. Tra-la tra-la tra-la.

My thumbs and fingers keep moving.

My thumbs and fingers keep moving.

My thumbs and fingers keep moving. Tra-la tra-la tra-la.

My thumbs and fingers and hands keep moving.

My thumbs and fingers and hands keep moving.

My thumbs and fingers and hands keep moving. Tra-la tra-la tra-la.

My thumbs and fingers and hands and arms keep moving.

My thumbs and fingers and hands and arms keep moving.

My thumbs and fingers and hands and arms keep moving. And then I stand right up.

My thumbs and fingers and hands and arms and feet keep moving.

My thumbs and fingers and hands and arms and feet keep moving.

My thumbs and fingers and hands and arms and feet keep moving. Tra-la tra-la tra-la.

My thumbs and fingers and hands and arms and feet and head keep moving.

My thumbs and fingers and hands and arms and feet and head keep moving.

My thumbs and fingers and hands and arms and feet and head keep moving. Tra-la tra-la tra-la.

THE MUSIC'S BEAT

I jump

I hop

I march in place

I twirl around

With style and grace

I wiggle

I squirm

I spin and shake

I move back and forth

Like a human earthquake

I twist

I turn

I kick my feet

I love to move

To the music's beat.

Charley Hoce

Reprinted with permission of the publisher, Early Years, Inc. From the March 2004 issue of *Teaching K-8 Magazine*, Norwalk, CT 06854.

446

CHAPTER 15

Puppetry and Beginning Drama Experiences

OBJECTIVES

After reading this chapter, you should be able to:

◆ Use puppetry in language arts programming.

◆ Describe young children's puppet play.

◆ List five teaching techniques that offer young children opportunities for simple dramatization.

KEY TERMS

audience

characters

dramas

pantomime

SANTA PUPPET

Blaine, a student teacher, was pleased to be invited to a classroom Christmas party. Blaine's cupcake had a small, inch-and-a-half-high, Santa Claus decoration. Other cupcakes had trees, bells, wreathes, and snowmen, but he was served the only one with a Santa. He slipped the small decoration on his little finger and playfully uttered, "Ho, ho, ho, Santa's here." Every child near was interested and wanted to talk to Santa. Blaine could not believe such a tiny finger puppet could hold their attention. The activity went on until all who wanted to talk to Santa did so. Blaine was amazed at the young children's ability to so quickly accept the fantasy. He then remembered that children don't seem to put together the differences in the Santas they see: the red coat, hat, and beard seem to be enough.

QUESTIONS TO PONDER

1. Was Blaine's activity appropriate? Why or why not?

2. Could you make up a quick, simple poem Santa might say or a simple song Santa might sing that emphasizes the alphabet letter "H"?

3. Are you aware of a way children can create a Santa puppet?

Puppets provide countless opportunities for children's speech growth. They match and fulfill many of the preschooler's developmental needs, besides being of high interest. Koons (1986) describes the power of puppet play.

> Imagine a lifeless puppet lying on a table. Suddenly, a child slips his hand into the puppet and it awakens to a life and personality of its own. Magic happens and the world of make-believe begins. Children love to pretend and puppetry allows them to create their own magic.

When used by a child, puppets can be

◆ moved and controlled by the child (Figure 15–1).

◆ a challenge involving coordination of speech and movement.

◆ talked to as an accepting companion.

◆ used individually and in group play.

◆ used to create and fantasize.

◆ used to explore another's personality.

◆ used as a way to release pent-up emotions.

◆ used to relive and imitate experiences.

◆ seen as an adultlike activity.

◆ used to entertain others.

◆ constructed by children.

Many of these uses build and develop children's confidence in their own speaking ability.

There are many ways the *teacher* can use puppetry in language development activities. When used by a teacher, puppets can

◆ motivate.

◆ gain and hold attention.

◆ provide variety in the presentation of ideas and words.

◆ provide a model to imitate.

◆ present stories.

◆ promote child creativity and pretending.

◆ provide a play opportunity that encourages speech and motor-skill coordination.

◆ introduce new information.

◆ promote positive attitudes toward speaking and dramatic activities.

◆ build audience skills.

◆ provide construction activities.

◆ help children express themselves.

◆ build vocabularies.

◆ offer entertaining and enjoyable activities.

◆ provide a wide range of individual personalities through puppets.

FIGURE 15–1 Controlling puppet actions can be great fun.

What can puppets offer both children and their teachers? Hunt and Renfro (1982) believe

> For the child, the introduction of puppets can create a fresh and creative learning environment. Young children can generally accept the puppet as a non-threatening, sympathetic friend to whom they can entrust their thoughts and feelings without fear of ridicule or reprimand. This friend is privy to the child's inner world and is able also to communicate with the outer world as an intermediary. It is perhaps here that the teacher finds in puppetry its most valuable asset for contributing to the process of education. A skillful teacher can take advantage of special moments of puppet-inspired communication to tune into the child's thinking and to open up new avenues for learning.

AUDIENCE SKILLS

Audience skills are quickly learned, and teachers encourage them through discussion and modeling. Clapping after performances is recommended. Listening and being a quiet audience is verbally appreciated. Teachers and staff need to decide whether a child in the audience can leave during a performance. Most schools adopt this plan of action, and the child is expected to choose a quiet play activity that does not disturb others.

STIMULATING CHILDREN'S USE OF PUPPETS

Teachers can expand children's experiences with puppets in the following ways.

- Present puppet plays and skits.
- Find community resources for puppet presentations: puppeteer groups, children's theater groups, high school and elementary classes, and skilled individuals.
- Introduce each puppet periodically and provide new ones when possible.
- Store puppets invitingly.
- Provide props and puppet theaters.
- Keep puppets in good repair.

A puppet carried in a teacher's pocket can be useful in a variety of teaching situations, as mentioned previously. Children imitate the teacher's use of puppets, and this leads to creative play.

TEACHER PUPPETRY

Children sit, excited and enthralled, at simple skits and dialogues performed by the teacher. Continually amazed by young children's rapt attention and obvious pleasure, most teachers find puppetry a valuable teaching skill (Figure 15–2).

Prerecording puppet dialogue (or attaching puppet speeches inside the puppet stage) helps beginning teacher puppeteers. With practice, performance skills increase and puppet coordination can then become the main teacher task.

Hunt and Renfro's *Puppetry in Early Childhood Education* (1982) includes many valuable suggestions for increasing teacher puppetry skill, among them developing a puppet voice and personality.

> Discover a voice contrasting to your own. Look at the puppet and see what characteristics its physical features suggest. A deep commanding voice, for example, may be appropriate for a large mouth while sleepy eyes may connote a slow, tired voice. Become fully involved with the character and experiment freely.

They go on to state

> A puppet's personality does not develop immediately; rather it evolves over a span of days, weeks, sometimes months.

> ... it is sometimes easier to pattern a character after a real person than to try to create one that is entirely imaginary. ... Give the puppet a name.

---

audience — the respondents to drama presentation; a group of listeners or spectators.

FIGURE 15–2 A teacher delights this child with impromptu puppet interaction.

Naturally, puppet **characters** in plays or from printed sources already have built-in personalities, but a teacher's daily puppets have no such script and challenge teacher creativity.

Planning and performing simple puppet plays requires time and effort. The plays are selected for suitability and then practiced until the scene-by-scene sequence is firmly in mind. Good preparation helps ensure a smooth performance and adds to children's enjoyment.

Several helpful tips on puppetry follow.

◆ A dark net peep-hole enables performers to watch audience reactions and helps dialogue pacing.

◆ Puppets with strong, identifiable personality traits who stay in character are well received. Another way to enhance a puppet's personality is to give it an idiosyncrasy that sets it apart (Hunt & Renfro, 1982).

◆ Plan your puppet's personality in advance and stick to it. For example, Happy Mabel has the following characteristics: she is always laughing; says "Hot Potatoes!" often;

likes to talk about her cat, Christobel; lives on a farm; is an optimist; speaks in a high-pitched voice; lives alone; and likes young visitors.

◆ Use your favorite puppet in at least one activity weekly.

PUPPET ACTIVITIES

Child participation with puppets can be increased when planned puppet activities are performed. The following are a few of the many puppet play activities.

◆ Invite children to use puppets (with arms) and act out that a puppet is sleepy, hungry, dancing, crying, laughing, whispering, saying "hello" to a friend, climbing a ladder, waving good-bye, and shaking hands. (A large mirror helps children build skill.)

◆ Ask two volunteers to use puppets and act out a situation in which a mother and child are waking up in the morning. The teacher creates both speaking parts, then prompts

---

characters — persons (or puppets) represented in or acting in a story or drama.

two children to continue on their own. Other situations include a telephone conversation, a child requesting money from a parent to buy an ice cream cone, and a puppet inviting another to a party.

◆ Urge children to answer the teacher's puppet. For example:

Teacher: "Hi! My name is Mr. Singing Sam. I can sing any song you ask me to sing. Just ask me!"

or

Teacher: "I'm the cook. What shall we have for dinner?"

or

Teacher: "My name is Randy Rabbit. Who are you? Where am I?"

◆ Record simple puppet directions (such as the following) and have a large mirror available so that the children can see their actions.

1. Make your puppet touch his nose.
2. Have your puppet clap.
3. Kiss your hand, puppet.
4. Rub your eyes, puppet.
5. Reach for the stars, puppet.
6. Hold your stomach.
7. Scratch your ear.
8. Bow low.
9. Hop.

◆ Set up this activity in an individual, room-divided space.

◆ Record simple puppet **dramas**. After a teacher demonstration, make them available to children on a free-choice basis. Provide a mirror, if possible.

◆ Let children speak for a puppet who has not learned to talk.

◆ Give one special puppet the role of the teacher's helper. This puppet gives directions, rings the clean-up or snack-time bell, and introduces new children.

◆ Invent a singing puppet who sings new songs or sings to pieces of music karaoke style.

◆ Have puppets say character lines in a simple drama.

◆ Have a puppet read a picture book.

◆ Make a set of alphabet letter stick puppets that sing the alphabet song. (It is best to line these up beforehand in an upright position on a foam block.)

Storage and Theaters

Store puppets in an inviting way, face up, begging for handling; shoe racks, wall pockets, or upright pegs within the child's reach are suggested. An adjacent puppet theater tempts children's use. Old television cabinets (with insides removed and open backs) make durable theaters that the children can climb into. Other theaters can be constructed by the teacher using large packing crates that can be painted and decorated by the children.

Hunt and Renfro (1982) describe what might happen in a puppet corner.

> As soon as a child physically picks up a puppet, he wants to make it talk. By giving it a voice, he also gives it life. In the puppet corner children will experiment without inhibition using different vocal sounds and character voices. No other form of expression, except creative dramatics, offers such a broad range of opportunities for verbal experimentation.

In most centers, rules are set for using puppets. The puppets should stay in certain designated areas and should be handled with care.

Visiting Puppet Idea

Rowley (1999) created a "visiting puppet." This puppet was sent to children's homes in a bag containing a pen and pad for a parent to record the child's diary account of what the puppet did during its visit. During group time, on the

---

dramas — plays; stories in dramatic form, typically emphasizing conflict in and among key characters.

day the puppet returned to school, the teacher read the parent's recorded comments and invited the visited children and/or other children to elaborate on the puppet's adventures.

Puppet Plays

Familiar and favorite stories make good puppet dramas. Many contain simple, repetitive lines that most of the children know from memory. Children will often stray from familiar dialogues in stories, however, adding their own lines, actions, or settings. Older preschoolers speak through puppets easily; younger children may be more interested in manipulating alone or simple imitating (Figure 15–3). McGee (2003a) uses wooden spoons with cut-out felt details for use in *The Three Billy Goats Gruff* reenactments.

When children enlarge or change dialogue or a character's personality, their own individuality directs and creates. Schools can wind up with many versions and interpretations of familiar favorites.

Other Puppetry Tips

◆ Some children are fearful of puppets. They may even think that a puppet has died when they see the puppet limp on the shelf. With reassurance and additional exposure to teacher puppet use, fear subsides.

◆ The act of becoming the puppet's persona (such as an alligator or wolf, for example) may be frightening to three-year-olds (Figure 15–4).

FIGURE 15–4 Children can feel comfortable or uncomfortable with puppet play at any age.

FIGURE 15–3 These puppeteers have a rapt audience.

◆ Aggressive puppet play of the "Punch and Judy" type should be avoided. Having puppets punch and hit is common behavior in traditional Punch and Judy shows, and consequently is not presented to young children in school settings. Any modeling of aggressive and violent behavior in puppetry is inappropriate, for it is quickly imitated by some children.

◆ Most public libraries offer puppet shows periodically.

◆ Parents and volunteers can help construct sturdy classroom puppets.

◆ Commercial school-supply companies offer well-made, durable puppets and theaters for group use.

◆ Elementary or high school drama classes may provide puppet shows.

PUPPET CONSTRUCTION

Puppets can be divided into two general categories—those worked with the hands and fingers and those that dangle on strings. Hand puppets are popular in the preschool because they are so versatile and practical. Teacher-made, child-made, and commercially manufactured hand puppets are an essential part of most centers.

Moving arms and pliable faces on puppets increase the possibilities for characterization and action. Rubber, plastic, and papier-mâché puppet heads are durable. Cloth faces permit a wider variety of facial expressions.

Teacher Puppet Presentations

Many simple stories can be shared with children through teacher puppetry. The following story is an example of a tale that lends itself to a puppet presentation. Teachers can create their own stories that appeal to the interests of the children with whom they work.

THE PANCAKE

Narrator: Once upon a time, an old woman made a pancake. When it was nice and golden brown, it hopped out of the frying pan and began rolling down the road, saying:

Pancake: Whee! I'm free! Nobody will ever eat me! What a nice day! I'll just roll along till—hey! I wonder what that funny looking round thing is by the river!

Narrator: He didn't know it, but it was a bridge.

Pancake: I'll bet I can roll over that thing. Watch this! I'll just get a head start back here—(backs up) one . . . two . . . three! (As the pancake starts over the bridge, frog comes up and grabs it.)

Pancake: Let me go! Let me go!

Frog: I want to eat you! I love pancakes! (Pancake pulls away and rolls out of sight.)

Frog: Oh, dear . . . it got away . . . (Frog down. Bridge down. Pancake rolls in.)

Pancake: That was a close one! I hope I do not meet any other—(Off stage is heard the sound of barking . . .)

Pancake: What's that sound? I do not think I like it . . . (Dog in, tries to grab pancake.)

Dog: I want a bite! I love pancakes! (Pancake cries "No! No!" and rolls off.)

Dog: It got away. Well, better luck next time . . . (Dog out, pancake rolls in.)

Pancake: Goodness! Everybody seems to love pancakes, but I do not want to be loved that way! (Off stage is heard the sound of "meow!")

Pancake: Meow? What kind of animal makes that sound? (Cat in, tries to grab pancake, pancake escapes as before.)

Cat: Meow? Meow, no breakfast now! (Cat out, pancake rolls in panting.)

Pancake: This is dreadful! Everybody I meet wants to eat me! (Bird flies in.)

Bird: A pancake! Delicious! I'll just peck a few pieces out of it! (Bird starts to peck at pancake, which rolls away crying, "No! No!" Bird follows, then returns alone.)

Bird: It's too hot to chase it. Besides, it can roll faster than I can fly. (Bird out. Put bridge up again.)

Narrator: And all day long the pancake rolled until it finally found itself back at the same bridge. (Pancake rolls in.)

Pancake: (Wearily) Oh, dear . . . here I am again, back at the same bridge . . . I must have been rolling around in circles. And I'm too tired to roll another inch. I must rest. I'll just lie down here next to this round thing over the river . . . (Pancake lies down flat, or leans against the bridge, if possible. Now puppeteer has two free hands to put on frog and dog. But before they come in, we hear their voices.)

Frog's Voice: (half-whisper) It's mine!

Dog's Voice: (half-whisper) No, it's mine. I saw it first!

Frog's Voice: (same) You did not! I saw it first!

Dog's Voice: (same) Who cares—I'm going to eat it! (Dog and Frog enter and grab the pancake between them.)

Pancake: Let me go! Let me go! (Frog and dog tussle, drop pancake out of sight, look after it.)

Frog: Oh no! You dropped it in the water!

Dog: Not me! You're the one who dropped it!

Narrator: And as the pancake disappeared beneath the water, they heard it say, (far away voice) "Nobody will ever catch me . . ." and nobody ever did. (Sloane, 1942)

Teachers find that play situations containing a puppet, animal, or other character that is less knowledgeable and mature than the children themselves promote a feeling of bigness in children. The children are then in the position of taking care of and educating another, which often produces considerable child speech and self-esteem. A well-known commercial language development kit (program) cleverly contains a puppet that has no eyes. Children are urged to help this puppet by describing objects and events.

SIMPLE DRAMA

Children often playact familiar events and home situations. This allows them to both try out and work out elements of past experiences that they remember for one reason or another. Their playacting can be an exact imitation or something created by their active imaginations.

Much of children's imaginative play (pretend play) reenacts life situations and leads to creative embellishment (Figure 15–5). It happens all the time in preschool. Children often need only a jumping-off place provided by a room setting, story, or teacher suggestion. Picture what might happen if a teacher says

"Here comes the parade, let's join it and march."

"A kitten is lost in the play yard, what can we do? Where can we look?"

"The bus just stopped at the gate. Let's go places. Where will we go first? First we need to step up inside and pay our money."

FIGURE 15–5 In today's world, almost everyone has a telephone.

"The astronauts' rocket ship crashed on the moon. Our rocket ship is here. Let's get on and rescue them."

"Let's pretend we're hummingbirds searching for sweet nectar in all the brightly colored flowers."

"My goodness, teddy bear has fallen out of the bed. His leg is hurt. What can we do?"

The teacher's watchfulness and skillfulness will be necessary. Unfortunately, exposure to television violence may seep into play or play may lead to unwise, unsafe actions depending on one's particular play group. The teacher may need to redirect or stop children's actions. More commonly, however, the astronauts will be rescued and returned to earth, the kitten will be found, and the bus ride will lead to adventures without difficulties.

In creative drama, the teacher wishes to be a coparticipant with children and follow their creative lead. The benefits of creative drama experiences are multiple—social, intellectual, lin-

guistic, and sometimes therapeutic. Creative language use and increased self-esteem are natural outcomes.

Four-year-olds, because of their ability to conceptualize and fantasize, are prime candidates for beginning exposure to this literary form. They pick up both acting skill and audience skill quickly. Three-year-olds enjoy drama presentations and are good audiences. They profit from exposure but can have a difficult time with the acting role. Imitative, pretend play, and **pantomime** suit their developmental level. Pantomime becomes the foundation on which four-year-olds build their acting skills for created and scripted parts.

Young preschoolers will need teacher prompting and suggestions for acting out. Teachers can ask children how someone might feel or act under certain circumstances. They can also ask children to think about what takes place in their homes, at school, at various times of the day, or in other life settings and situations to determine possible acting scenarios. Positive, appreciative teacher and peer comments concerning convincing or appropriate acting behavior provide additional pointers.

In both drama and pantomime, children can act out all the joy, anger, fear, and surprise of their favorite characters. This gives children the opportunity to become someone else for a few minutes and to release their frustration and energy in an acceptable way.

After young children become familiar with stories, they thoroughly enjoy reenacting or dramatizing the stories. By using both physical motions and verbal comments, children bring the words and actions of the stories to life. Because most stories deal with a character with a problem, decision, or challenge, part of the draw of drama for young children is their interest in figuring out how the characters are going to resolve their dilemmas.

---

pantomime — creative communication done with nonverbal physical actions.

Playacting Tips

Children will act out parts from favorite stories as well as scenes from real life. The teacher sets the stage, keeping some points in mind.

- The children must be familiar with the story to know what happens first, next, and last.

- Activities in which the children pretend to perform certain actions, to be certain animals, or to copy the actions of another help prepare them for simple drama.

- Videotaped plays and films are good motivators.

- A first step is to act without words or while listening to a good story or record.

- The teacher can be the narrator, while the children are the actors.

- Children should be encouraged to volunteer for parts.

- Props and settings can be simple. Ask, "What can be used for a bridge?" or a similar question so that children can use their creativity.

- Any of the children's imaginative acts should be accepted, whether or not they are a part of the original story, unless they endanger others.

- Individual and group dramatizations should be appreciated and encouraged. Every child who wishes a turn playing the parts should be accommodated.

- No-touching guidelines are necessary when vigorous acts are part of dramas.

- With large groups, the teacher can limit acting roles to a manageable number to prevent chaos.

- In child-authored dramas, the teacher may need to clarify the child's intent in story sequences.

- Reenacting stories with different children playing parts is usually done with popular stories.

- Include multicultural stories when possible.

Some classic stories that can be used for playacting (drama) include:

- *Goldilocks and the Three Bears*
- *The Three Little Pigs*
- *The Little Red Hen*
- *The Gingerbread Boy*
- *Little Red Ridinghood*
- *Little Miss Muffet*

Fast-action and simple story lines are best for the young child. Playacting presents many opportunities for children to develop

- self-expression.
- use of correct speech.
- coordination of actions and words.
- creative thinking.
- self-confidence.
- listening skills.
- social interaction.

As mentioned in Chapter 10, children's own dictated stories are excellent vehicles for dramatization. In child-authored stories, the most popular procedure is for the child-author to choose the role he would like to play, and then which classmates will play the rest. Teachers read previously dictated stories before and as children act the roles.

Problem-Solving Drama

Early childhood practitioners may want to try problem-solving dramas with older preschoolers. Imaginary problem-solving situations are suggested by the teacher and are then enacted creatively by children working toward a solution. Children are not given words to say, but character parts are assigned.

Sample problems follow:

- A child's shoes are missing, and it is time to go to a party. Characters include the mother, grandmother, dog, cat, brother, and sister.

- While at the zoo on a preschool field trip, the class learns that a giraffe is loose. The teacher asks a group of children to guess where a giraffe might hide. Characters include a zookeeper, police officer, four children, and their preschool teacher.

Teachers trying this type of creative drama may need to slip in and out of the dramatization serving as a confidant, collaborator, and helpful but not dominating coach.

Drama from Picture Books

Bos (1983), a well-known California workshop leader, tells a funny story about children's love of dramatization. Because picture books are often enacted at Bev's center, a child who readily identifies with a particular book character often speaks up, saying, "I want to be the rabbit," long before the reading session is finished.

In enacting stories from books or storytelling sources, the teacher may have to read the book or tell the story many times so that it is digested and becomes familiar to the children. A discussion of the story can promote children's expression of opinions about enjoyed parts, the feelings of characters, and what might be similar in their own lives. The teacher can then ask, "Who's good at crying and can go 'Boo-hoo'?" or "Who can act mad and stomp around the floor?" Most child groups have one or more children ready to volunteer. The teacher can play one of the parts.

The following is a step-by-step teacher guide for child enactment of a book.

◆ *Start* by keeping dramatization simple. Forget props or rehearsing. Props can be added later after subsequent readings or when highly enjoyed enactments are identified.

◆ *Read* the book (or child's dictated book or story).

◆ *Announce* that you will reread the book and that children can pretend to be book characters by acting out what happens in the story.

◆ *Select* roles from volunteers by asking questions such as, "Who can bark like a big red dog?"

◆ Ask the children to stand together in front of the group to the side of teacher or in any classroom space that lends itself to drama production.

◆ *Reread* the story.

◆ *Feel* free to interrupt the text and give clues to actors, such as, "Beady Bear was surprised. How might his face look?"

◆ *Promote* audience skills, such as clapping, and cast skills, such as holding hands and taking bows.

◆ Time permitting, *go through* a second enactment giving all children a chance to act or change characters.

◆ *Think* about asking another group (class) in as an audience occasionally.

Many action- and dialogue-packed picture books, such as the following, lend themselves to child reenactment.

Carle, E. (1996). *The grouchy ladybug.* New York: HarperCollins.
Gág, W. (1999). *The funny thing.* New York: Smithmark.
Galdone, P. (1975). *The gingerbread boy.* New York: Seabury Press.
Hogrogian, N. (1971). *One fine day.* New York: Macmillan.
Hutchins, P. (1972). *Rosie's walk.* New York: Simon & Schuster.
Keats, E. J. (1998). *Peter's chair.* New York: Viking.
Krauss, R. (1974). *The carrot seed.* New York: Scholastic.
Mayer, M. (1983). *Me too!* New York: Golden Press.
Rylant, C. (1987). *Birthday presents.* New York: Orchard Books.

A number of well-known children's songs and popular poems set to music can also be enacted, including:

Aliki. (1996). *Go tell Aunt Rhody.* New York: Aladdin Paperbacks.
Cauley, L. B. (1992). *Clap your hands.* New York: Putnam.
Oxenbury, H. (1999). *Clap hands.* New York: Simon & Schuster.
Oxenbury, H. (1999). *Say goodnight.* New York: Simon & Schuster.

Dramatizing Fairy Tales and Folktales

A number of educators, including Howarth (1989), urge teachers to dramatize classic fairy tales and folktales. She suggests

for two-and-a-half- and three-year-olds:

The Three Little Pigs
The Three Billy Goats Gruff
Goldilocks and the Three Bears

for four-year-olds:

Cinderella
Jack and the Beanstalk
The Wolf and the Seven Little Kids
The Shoemaker and the Elves

Howarth (1989) believes some teachers are reluctant to offer children many of these classic tales because of their inherent violence, and she offers the following to persuade them.

In order to solve life's problems one must not only take risks, one must confront the worst that might happen. Children, like the rest of us, ruminate and worry about these worst things. Fairy tales confront them. This is the chief reason many adults have trouble with fairy tales. They think they can protect children from the hard realities of life. That is the real myth and the children know it.

What a relief it is for a child to find that things she is worried about are taken seriously! Children think a lot about death, separation, and divorce. None of us wants to think about these painful possibilities, yet we must.

Nonfiction books can also be dramatized; as Putnam (1991) observes

... dramatize such things as bears hibernating in their dens, dinosaurs moving through swamps, thunderstorms brewing. ... Invariably, the children appear to be thoroughly absorbed and enjoying themselves, as if at play. They also appear to retain more of the information presented during the reading.

Nonfiction books should not be overlooked by early childhood teachers when looking for dramatization possibilities.

Progressive Skill

Dramatizing a familiar story involves a number of language skills—listening, auditory and visual memory of actions and characters' speech lines, and remembered sequence of events—as well as audience skills. Simple pantomime or imitation requires less maturity. Activities that use actions alone are good as a first step toward building children's playacting skills. Children have imitated others' actions since infancy, and as always, the joy of being able to do what they see others do brings a feeling of self-confidence. The children's individuality is preserved if differences in ways of acting out a familiar story are valued in preschool settings.

Pantomime

Among the all-time favorites for pantomime is the following.

THE BEAR HUNT

We're going on a bear hunt
We're going where?
We're going on a bear hunt.
OK, let's go! I'm not afraid!

Look over there!
What do you see?
A big deep river.
Can't go around it.
Can't go under it.
Have to swim across it.
OK, let's go. I'm not afraid!

What's this tall stuff?
What do you see?
Tall, tall grass.
Can't go around it.
Can't go under it.
Got to go through it.
OK, let's go. I'm not afraid!

Hey, look ahead.
What do you see?
A rickety old bridge.
Can't go around it.

Can't go under it.
Got to go across it.
OK, let's go. I'm not afraid!

Now what's this ahead.
It's a tall, tall tree.
Can't go under it.
Can't go over it.
Have to climb it.
OK, let's go. I'm not afraid!

Do you see what I see?
What a giant mountain!
Can't go around it.
Can't go under it.
Got to climb over it.
OK, let's go. I'm not afraid!

Oh, look at that dark cave.
Let's go inside.
It sure is dark in here.
I think I feel something.
I think it's a nose.
And two furry ears.
HELP! It's a bear!!!!!!!!!!!!!
Let's get out of here . . . I'm afraid.

(Pretend to climb back over the mountain and down the tree, run across the bridge, swish through the tall grass, swim the river, open the door, run in, slam the door, collapse in a heap.)

Whew . . . Home at last . . . I was afraid!

CREATIVE DRAMA PROGRAMS

Starting a language program that includes creative drama requires planning. Props and play materials must be supplied for children to explore. When children see simple plays and pantomimes performed by teachers, other children, and adult groups, they are provided with a model and a stimulus. Some drama activity ideas for the older preschool child include:

- pantomiming action words and phrases: tiptoe, crawl, riding a horse, using a rolling pin.
- pantomiming words that mean a physical state: cold, hot, itchy.
- pantomiming feeling words: happy, sad, hurt, holding a favorite teddy bear lovingly, feeling surprise.

- acting out imaginary life situations: opening a door with a key, climbing in and out of a car, helping to set the table.
- acting familiar character parts in well-known stories: "She covered her mouth so the clown couldn't see her laugh." "The rabbit dug a big hole and buried the carrot." "He tiptoed to the window, raised the shade, and opened it."
- saying familiar lines from known stories: "And he huffed and he puffed, and he blew the house down."
- playing a character in a short story or song that involves both spoken lines and actions.
- pantomiming actions of a character in a short, familiar story that the teacher reads (or from a teacher-recorded story tape). There are a vast number of commercially recorded stories available at school-supply stores.
- making story sequence cards for a favorite book.

Kranyik (1986) suggests the following pantomimes for young children.

- Drink a glass of water. Oh! It turned into hot soup and burned your mouth!
- Eat a bowl of spaghetti.
- Row a boat.
- Pour your milk from the carton to a glass. Drink it.
- Play the piano, trumpet, drums, guitar.
- Try to open a jar that will not open.
- Touch something soft and furry.
- Chew a piece of bubble gum and blow a bubble. It gets bigger, bigger, and bigger. Suddenly it breaks.
- You and your mom are in a supermarket. Suddenly, you cannot find her and you feel scared. You look up and down all the aisles trying to find her. There she is. You see her.

COSTUMES, PROPS, AND STAGE

Imagination and inexpensive, easy-to-make costumes are a great performing incentive. Accessories such as aprons, shirts, canes, and gloves can be used in a variety of play and drama

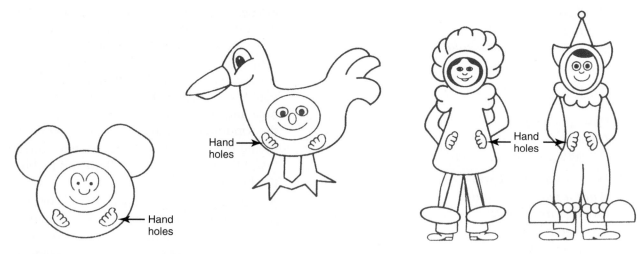

FIGURE 15–6 Story character boards.

situations, and hats are popular when head lice problems do not exist. A "stage" area can be a semipermanent part of the classrooms. Comfortable audience seating and viewing should be considered.

Cutout chartboard or cardboard heads and figures held by the child quickly aid his ability to step into character (Figure 15–6). (Make sure that the chartboard is lightweight and the hand holes are comfortable.) Older children may be able to draw their own patterns, or patterns for figures can be found in children's books and can be enlarged with the use of an opaque projector. These props allow children to put their faces into the spaces cut out of the characters' faces and are useful in child dramatization. Some teachers feel these props are physically awkward and prefer, instead, simple costumes.

SUMMARY

Using puppetry for language development is a widely accepted practice in preschools. Many puppet types are available to choose from. The ability to coordinate puppet actions and words takes practice and maturity. Teachers find that the more children watch puppets being used, the more they will use them. Puppets that are

stored attractively and upright near puppet theaters encourage children's exploration.

There is a wide range of uses for puppets as instructional devices. Puppets are interesting and capture attention as an enjoyable play activity.

Drama is another step on the road to literacy. Simple child dramatizations of favorite stories begin during preschool years. Language programs provide many playacting opportunities. Props, playacting, and pantomime activities motivate this expressive art. Skills are acquired through increased experiences with drama. Plan-ning by the teacher aids children's acquisition of dramatization abilities.

ADDITIONAL RESOURCES

Sources for Puppet and Drama Visuals

Career dress-ups, Dexter Educational Toys, P.O. Box 630861, Aventura, FL 33163.

Door puppet playhouse. Fabric Farms, 3590 Riverside Drive, Columbus, OH 43221.

Dress-ups for dramatic play. DRESS-UPS, 652 Glenbrook Road, Stamford, CT 06906.

Felt puppets. Pat's Puppets, 121 W. Simmons, Anaheim, CA 92802.

Puppet patterns. Plaid Enterprises Inc., P.O. Box 7600, Norcross, GA 30091.

Books for Creative Dramatization

Burton, B. (1973). *Buzz, buzz, buzz.* New York: Macmillan.

DePaola, T. (1975). *Strega Nona.* New York: Scholastic.

Domanska, J. (1969). *The turnip.* New York: Macmillan.

Ets, M. H. (1955). *Play with me.* New York: The Viking Press.

Ets, M. H. (1963). *Gilberto and the wind.* New York: The Viking Press.

Flack, M. (1952). *Ask Mr. Bear.* New York: Macmillan.

Green, N. B. (1975). *The hole in the dike.* New York: Harper and Row.

Hutchins, P. (1969). *The surprise party.* New York: Macmillan.

Hutchins, P. (1972). *Goodnight owl.* New York: Macmillan.

Hutchins, P. (1986). *The doorbell rang.* New York: Greenwillow Books.

Keats, E. J. (1962). *The snowy day.* New York: The Viking Press.

Keats, E. J. (1966). *Jennie's hat.* New York: Harper and Row.

Lionni, L. (1969). *Alexander and the wind-up mouse.* New York: Pantheon.

Mayer, M. (1968). *There's a nightmare in my closet.* New York: The Dial Press.

McGovern, A. (1976). *Too much noise.* New York: Scholastic.

Miller, E. (1964). *Mouskin's golden house.* Englewood Cliffs, NJ: Prentice Hall.

Murphy, J. (1980). *Peace at last.* New York: The Dial Press.

Slobodkina, E. (1947). *Caps for sale.* New York: William R. Scott Inc.

Young, M. (1964). *Miss Susy.* New York: Parent's Magazine Press.

Readings

Breyer, M. A., & Seho, R. (1999). *A guide for using the master puppeteer in the classroom.* Westminister, CA: Teacher Created Materials.

Fox, M. (1987). *Teaching drama to young children.* Portsmouth, NH: Heinemann.

MacLennan, J. (1988). *Simple puppets you can make.* New York: Sterling.

McCaslin, N. (1996). *Creative drama in the classroom.* White Plains, NY: Longman.

Roberts, L. (1985). *Mitt magic: Finger plays for finger puppets.* Beltsville, MD: Gryphon House.

Wagner, B. (Ed.). (1998). *Educational drama and language arts: What research shows.* Portsmouth, NH: Heinemann.

Walker, L., Walker, H., & Christoffer. N. (Eds.). (1991). *Instant puppet resourcebook for teachers.* Portsmouth, NH: Heinemann.

HELPFUL WEB SITES

Axtell Expressions
http://www.axtell.com
Puppet manipulation is discussed.

Drama Kids International
http://www.dramakids.com
Read about an American company that offers worldwide franchises for children's drama programs.

Folkmanis Puppets and Children's Books
http://www.kidsbooksandpuppets.com
This is a commercial site that sells puppets and puppet-book combinations.

National Academy Press
http://www.nap.edu
Publications concerned with early literacy are summarized.

Pioneer Drama Service, Inc.
http://www.pioneerdrama.com
Search catalog for folktales or fairy tales that are appropriate for young children. This site is a resource for inexpensive scripts (800-333-7262).

 Have you attempted to use a puppet to read a picture book? The Online Companion™ suggests you do so and then critique the experience for your training group. Paper-plate puppets are also described. Phoneme puppets have been used in some classrooms; read about them.

STUDENT ACTIVITIES

1. Make a puppet described in this chapter, or make one of your own choosing.
2. Present a simple puppet play with a few classmates.
3. Collect 10 easy-to-make costume ideas that promote creative drama. Share your ideas with the class.
4. Record a puppet drama and enact the drama with the help of classmates.
5. Construct a puppet theater.
6. Invite a local puppeteer group to share ideas with the class.
7. Bring one simple puppet play script or drama script to class.
8. Create a short puppet play.
9. Find commercial resources for ethnic puppets. Share names of companies and the prices for puppets.
10. Create a puppet from a household item such as a cup or a tube. Share with the class.
11. List community resources that might help young children in your community become more familiar with drama.
12. What nonfiction books dealing with the African-American experience or the Vietnamese-American experience might be appropriate for a preschool dramatization activity? List and discuss with a group of three to four classmates. Report your findings to the class.

CHAPTER REVIEW

A. Write a short paragraph describing the reasons puppets are a part of preschool language arts programs.

B. Rate the following teachers using this scale.

+	?	—
definitely promotes puppet interest and use	unable to determine or cannot decide	will probably turn children off

1. Mrs. G. (teacher) pulled a small puppet from her smock pocket. Reaching behind Mark, age three, she talked through the puppet. "Mark Allen Graham? Rupert sees what you're doing, and he doesn't like children who break crayons." Mark returns the crayon to the container.

2. Miss R. (teacher) is introducing a small group of children to an activity involving a poem on a chart. "Well, there's Petey, Sam, Scott, Adam, Renee, and Jonathan," Miss R. begins. The puppet in her hand moves and claps, and the puppet's voice is low pitched and deep. "I came to talk to you about rabbits. Does anyone know what rabbits look like? I live in a pocket, you know. I've heard about rabbits, but I've never seen one."

3. Mr. O. (teacher) has a large packing carton in the middle of the classroom. Two children notice the carton and ask, "What's that for?" Mr. O. tells the two children that he noticed the school puppets do not have a puppet theater. "How could we make one from this box?" he asks the children. "You need a window," one child says. "Yes, that's true. I'll draw one. Stand here, please. I'll need the window the right height." The conversation and the project have drawn a larger group of children.

4. Mr. T. (teacher) has noticed a puppet lying on the ground in the playground. He picks it up, examines it, and puts it in his pocket. During circle time, he says, "Orvil (puppet's name) was on the ground in the yard today. Raise your hand if you know where he should be put after we play with him. Olivia, I see your hand. Would you please put Orvil in the place in the classroom that's just for him? Thank you, Olivia. What could happen to Orvil, our puppet, if we left him on the floor or ground?" "He'd get stepped on," Thad offers. "That could happen, Thad," said Mr. T. "Can anyone else think of what might happen to Orvil on the ground outside?" Mr. T. continues. "The ants would crawl on him," Jessica comments.

5. Ms. Y. (teacher) announces to a group of children, "It's talking time. Everyone is going to talk to Bonzo (the puppet dog) and tell him their names." She reaches behind her and pulls Bonzo from a bag. "Willy, come up and take Bonzo," Ms. Y. directs. "Now, Cleo, you come up here, too. Willy, have Bonzo say, 'Woof, woof, I'm Bonzo.'" Willy fiddles with the puppet and still has not slipped it onto his hand. "We need a barking Bonzo. Who would like to come up, put Bonzo on his hand, and bark?" Ms. Y. asks.

6. Miss W. (assistant teacher) has created an alphabet puppet set. In storytelling and other activities, these puppets brag about how many words start with their letter names.

C. Select the best answer for each statement.

1. Because puppets are so appealing, teachers
   a. motivate, model, and plan child activities to enhance the children's experiences.
   b. rarely use puppets in a conversational way, because it interrupts children's play.
   c. feel the large expense involved in supplying them is well worth it.
   d. find child language develops best without teacher modeling.

2. Puppets in preschool centers are used
   a. only by children.
   b. most often to present teacher-planned lessons.
   c. by both teachers and children.
   d. only when children ask for them.

3. Creative playacting (dramatization) is probably more appropriate
   a. for younger preschoolers, aged two to three years.
   b. for older preschoolers.
   c. when children are chosen for familiar characters' parts rather than selected from those children who volunteer for parts.
   d. when teachers help children stick to story particulars rather than promoting new lines or actions.

4. Identifying with a familiar story character through puppet use or playacting may give the child
   a. skills useful in getting along with others.
   b. greater insight into others' viewpoints.
   c. speaking skill.
   d. a chance to use creative imagination.
   e. all of the above.

5. If one is looking for a puppet with an expressive and active movement ability, one should use a
   a. plastic-headed puppet.
   b. papier-mâché-headed puppet with arms.
   c. cloth-headed puppet with arms.
   d. stick puppet.
   e. all the above are equally active and expressive.

6. Punch and Judy types of child's play with puppets are
   a. to be expected and needs teacher attention.
   b. a rare occurrence.
   c. best when teacher's performance sticks to the script.
   d. expected and should be ignored.
   e. a good puppetry modeling experience.

TEACHER-CONSTRUCTED AND CHILD-MADE PUPPETS

PAPIER-MÂCHÉ PUPPET HEADS

Materials

styrofoam egg or ball (a little smaller than the size you want for the completed head), soft enough to have a holder inserted into it

neck tube (made from cardboard—about 1.5 inches wide and 5 inches long, rolled into a circle and taped closed, or plastic hair roller)

bottle (to put the head on while it is being created and to hold it during drying)

instant papier-mâché (from a craft store)

paints (poster-paint variety)

spray-gloss coat (optional)

white glue

(Use instant papier-mâché in well-ventilated teacher work areas.)

Construction Procedure

1. Mix instant papier-mâché with water (a little at a time) until it is like clay—moist, but not too wet or dry.

2. Place Styrofoam™ egg on neck tube (or roller) securely. Then place egg (or ball) on bottle so that it is steady.

3. Put papier-mâché all over head and half way down neck tube. Coating should be about a half-inch thick.

4. Begin making the facial features, starting with the cheeks, eyebrows, and

464

chin. Then add eyes, nose, mouth, and ears.

5. When you are satisfied with the head, allow it to dry for at least 24 hours in an airy place.

6. When the head is dry, paint the face with poster paint. When that is dry, coat it with spray gloss finish to seal paint (optional).

7. Glue is useful for adding yarn hair, if desired.

SOCK PUPPETS

Materials

old sock
felt
sewing machine

Construction Procedure (Figure 15–7)

1. Use an old wool or other thick sock. Turn it inside out and spread it out with the heel on top.

2. Cut around the edge of the toe (about 3 inches on each side).

3. Fold the mouth material (pink felt) inside the open part of the sock and draw the shape. Cut the mouth piece out and sew into position.

4. Turn the sock right side out and sew on the features.

Easy Puppet

Obtain a stuffed animal. Try yard sales or outgrown shops. Cut a slit in the back of the animal large enough to insert a hand and remove the stuffing from the upper half. Use stiff cardboard or paper folded and cut for the animal's mouth. A sock or soft glove can be sewn to the slit opening to prevent stuffing escape. *Note:* Choose a stuffed animal with a cloth instead of molded face.

PAPER-BAG PUPPETS

Materials

paper bags
scissors
crayons or marking pens
paste
yarn or paper scraps
paint (if desired)

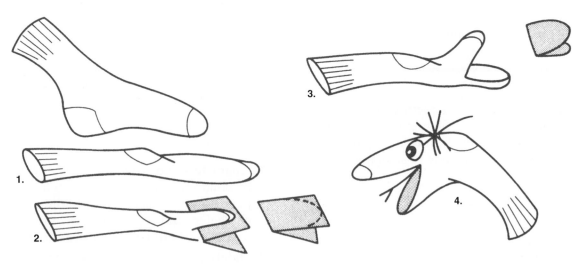

FIGURE 15–7 Sock puppet construction.

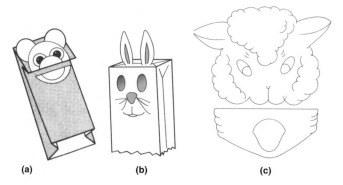

FIGURE 15–8 Paper-bag puppets.

Construction Procedure

1. Making paper-bag puppets is quick and easy. Give each child a small paper sack. (No. 6 works well.)
2. Show the children how the mouth works and let them color or paste features on the sack (Figure 15–8a).
3. You may wish to have the children paste a circle on for the face. Paste it on the flap part of the bag and then cut the circle on the flap portion so the mouth can move again.
4. Children may want to add special features to their paper-bag puppets, for example, eyes, tail, or ears (Figure 15–8b). Another puppet face pattern is found in Figure 15–8c.

STICK PUPPETS

A stick puppet is a picture or object attached to a stick (Figure 15–9). It moves when the puppeteer moves the puppet up and down or from side to side, holding the stick.

Materials

paper
glue
scissors

FIGURE 15–9 Stick puppets.

crayons
craft sticks (or tongue depressors or cardboard strips)

Construction Procedure

1. Characters and scenery can be drawn by children or can be preoutlined. Depending on the age of the children, the characters and scenery can then be colored or both colored and cut out.
2. Older children may want to create their own figures.

Stick puppets with verse pasted or written on their backs can introduce a poem. Stick puppets are easily made by tracing book characters or coloring-book figures, cutting them out, adding a stiff backing, and attaching a tongue depressor.

POP-UPS

Materials

heavy paper
glue
yarn
stick (tongue depressor or thinner sticks)
scissors
plastic
Styrofoam™ or paper cup
felt pens

Construction Procedure

1. Cut circle smaller than cup radius. Decorate face.
2. Slit the cup bottom in the center to allow sticks to move up and down.
3. Glue the face to the stick. Glue on yarn hair.
4. Slip puppet in the cup with stick through cup bottom so that the puppet disappears and can pop up.

SHADOW PUPPETS

Shadow puppets are easy to construct. Simple shapes made of stiff paper allow the audience to see the puppet's mass.

Materials

stiff paper
scissors
doweling sticks (hardware store)
tape
fabric
staple gun or thumb tacks
large picture frame (thrift store)

Construction Procedure

1. Cut puppet.
2. Attach rods using heavy tape (adhesive or electrical).
3. Stretch fabric over frame using a staple gun.

Hints

When purchasing fabric, take a flashlight to make sure light shines through it.

Fabric, such as an old sheet, can be stretched and secured across a doorway.

Make sure a strong light source is available. It should be strong enough to shine on the back of the puppet when it is held up to the screen (Figure 15–10).

BOX PUPPET

Materials

one small (individual size) box with both ends intact
one piece of white construction paper, 6″ × 9″
crayons or poster paints and brush
scissors
sharp knife
glue

Construction Procedure

1. Refer to Figure 15–11. Cut box in half as in view 1, with one wide side uncut. Fold over as in view 2.
2. On construction paper, draw the face of a person or an animal. Color or paint features and cut out the face.
3. Add yarn for hair, broomstraws for whiskers, and so on, if desired.
4. Cut face along the line of the mouth and glue to box, as in view 4, so that lips come together as in view 5.

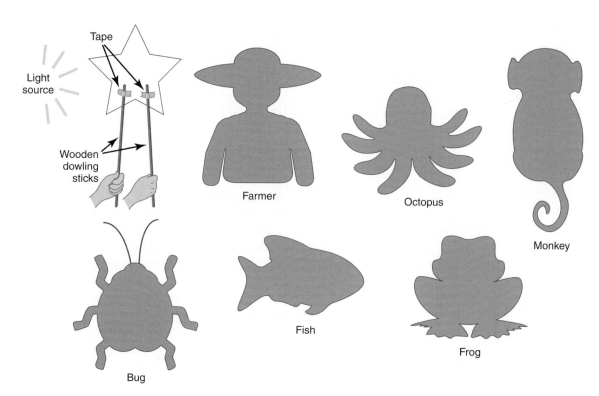

Tape

Light source

Wooden dowling sticks

Farmer

Octopus

Monkey

Bug

Fish

Frog

FIGURE 15–10 Shadow puppets.

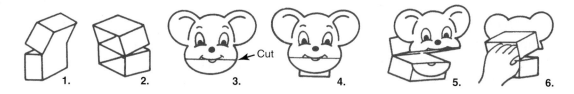

1.　2.　3.　Cut　4.　5.　6.

FIGURE 15–11 Box puppet.

JUMPING JACK

Materials

stiff paper or oak tag
brads
string
hole punch
dowel
glue
curtain pull (optional)

Construction Procedure

1. Design and cut pattern, making arms and legs long enough to secure behind figure. Cut two body pieces (Figure 15–12).

2. Glue figure to dowel by inserting between front and back.

3. Brads act as joints. Hole punch and add arms, legs, and string.

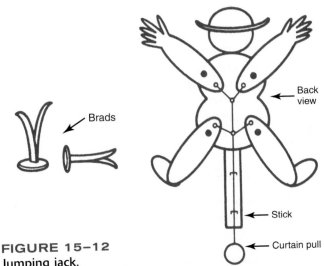

Brads

Back view

Stick

Curtain pull

Front view

Stick

Curtain pull

FIGURE 15–12
Jumping jack.

FINGER PUPPETS

Materials

fabric or cardboard
scissors
sewing machine
pattern
elastic ribbon

Construction Procedure

Cut and sew pieces. Insert stuffing after attaching elastic ring. Stiff paper or cardboard can also be used to make a puppet front.

Additional Puppet Ideas

◆ plastic-bottle-head puppet
◆ dustmop-head puppet
◆ favorite-television-character puppet
◆ garden-glove puppets (different faces can be snapped on or Velcro™ used) (Figure 15–14)
◆ suspended-toy-from-stick puppets (Adding beads to feet give them sound effects.)
◆ basic puppet body and hand pattern (Figure 15–15)

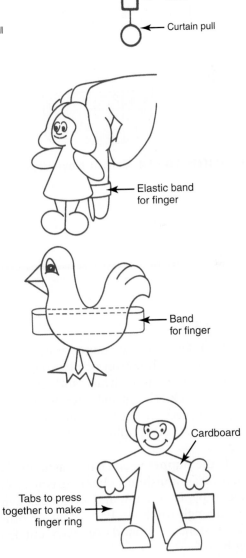

Elastic band for finger

Band for finger

Cardboard

Tabs to press together to make finger ring

FIGURE 15–13 Finger puppets.

469

FIGURE 15–14 Garden-glove puppets.

Materials

 5″ × 8″ paper bag
 string
 crayons or paint
 newspapers or cotton
 paste
 crepe paper or cloth for dress
 scissors

Movement

Place forefinger in neck tube to create movement.

STUFFED CLOTH PUPPET

Construction

Draw head pattern and cut around it on a fold of cloth (white, tan, or pink). Sew around front and back, turn inside out, and stuff with cotton or rags. Insert neck tube and tie. Paint on face. Cut body (Figure 15–15) and sew to neck tube. Add hands and feet.

Materials

 cloth (for head and dress)
 scissors
 needle and thread
 tag board for hands and feet

 material for hair (cotton, yarn, and so forth)

DECORATED PAPER-BAG PUPPETS

Construction

Draw a face on the upper part of bag; color. Stuff with cotton or newspaper. Put neck cylinder into head and tie string around neck. (Neck cylinder is made by rolling a piece of tag board and taping together. The roll should fit around the first finger.)

 If the puppet needs hair, paste on. Add other distinguishing characteristics. Cut hole in paper or cloth and stick neck cylinder through the hole. Paste, sew, or otherwise fasten. Add hands or paws cut from tag board.

STUFFED PAPER PUPPET

Construction

Have the child draw himself or any character the child chooses on a piece of butcher paper. Then trace and cut second figure for the back. Staple edges together and stuff with crumpled tissue paper or other stuffing. Attach stick to up end.

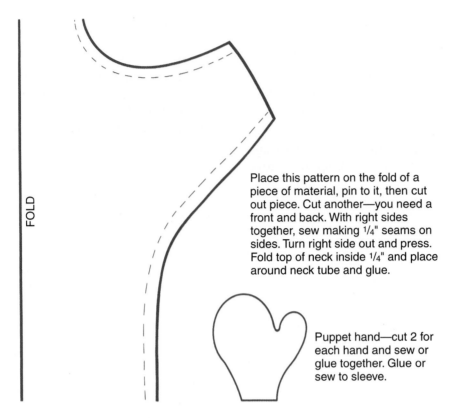

FOLD

Place this pattern on the fold of a piece of material, pin to it, then cut out piece. Cut another—you need a front and back. With right sides together, sew making 1/4" seams on sides. Turn right side out and press. Fold top of neck inside 1/4" and place around neck tube and glue.

Puppet hand—cut 2 for each hand and sew or glue together. Glue or sew to sleeve.

FIGURE 15–15 Basic puppet body.

Full-size version of this art can be found on the Online Companion™ at http://www.earlychilded.delmar.com

DRAMA OUTLINE—ITSY BITSY SPIDER

Materials

black yarn spider with metal washer sewn on back or stomach
rainwater spout
flashlight
yellow cellophane circle big enough to cover flashlight's end
rubber band
watering can

Preparation

1. Make spider from black yarn. Sew on washer.
2. Buy water spout tubing from hardware store or construct from two milk cartons.
3. Cover flashlight front with yellow cellophane using rubber band. (The sun.)
4. Fill water can. Place bucket.

Procedure

1. Present lyrics with hand motions or use sequence cards to refresh children.
2. Ask for child volunteers to act as spider, spout, rain, or sun. Give props.
3. Place volunteers in order of appearance.
4. Sing lyrics, hesitating to demonstrate parts: moving spider up spout to top, making rain in bucket, dropping spider down spout, shining sun, and crawling spider up spout.
5. Go through "Itsy, Bitsy Spider" with total group, cueing volunteers with hand motions.
6. Repeat with other volunteers if group is still interested.

(Use imaginary water.)

SECTION 6

Writing:

Print Awareness

and Use

CHAPTER 16

Print—Early Knowledge and Emerging Interest

OBJECTIVES

After reading this chapter, you should be able to:

◆ Discuss the child's development of small hand-muscle control.

◆ Outline the probable sequence of events occurring before a child prints her first recognizable alphabet letter.

◆ Describe printscript alphabets.

◆ Print both the lowercase and uppercase printscript alphabet.

◆ Describe classroom equipment and settings that promote printscript development.

◆ Plan a print-awareness activity.

KEY TERMS

alphabetic principle

interactive writing

invented spelling

orthographic awareness

print awareness

sight reading

writing

UPS

Cheney and Ong, four-year-olds, are busy stuffing toy animals into boxes provided by their teacher, Mr. Sanchez. They ask for tape, and their teacher supplies strips of masking tape. He watches them struggle to carry the box outside and then pretend to knock on the door. Mr. Sanchez goes to the door. "Well hello. Is this for me?" he says. Cheney pretends to look at his hand and says, "Is this Cherrywood Preschool?" "Yes," the teacher answers. "Are you the deliverymen?" "No, were from U-P-S," Ong says.

QUESTIONS TO PONDER

1. What does this vignette tell you about Ong and Cheney?

2. Could the teacher turn this dramatic play into some kind of additional print-awareness learning?

3. What type of teacher-supplied materials could have added depth to the boys' play and print knowledge?

Two pertinent questions preschool teachers ask themselves concerning print and teaching children to write in printscript are, (1) is it appropriate to offer lessons (activities) that teach print letter recognition and formation at this age? and (2) how is instruction in printscript undertaken? Resolving these questions is made easier by this chapter's discussion.

Currently, ideas about the child's development of **writing** (printing) skill has undergone a major change. Preschool children are seen as writers. Older ideas promoted the idea that teaching children to print and read should not be undertaken until children are in kindergarten or first grade. It was believed that at that stage children are mature enough or possess the readiness skills that would make these tasks much easier. Writing and reading skills were thought to be different from listening and speaking skills. Speech was accomplished without direct or formal teaching over a long period, beginning in infancy. Educators have revised their thoughts.

The concept of early literacy suggests that the foundations of literacy develop from a child's early experiences with print before the onset of formal reading instruction. Calkins (1997) recommends that educators take children's writing seriously, listening to their intended message and supporting writing development.

Dyson (1993) observes "symbol making is the essence of what it means to be human." Young children often talk about what they have done, constructed, and drawn, and they "read" meaning into their creations, a meaning they wish to communicate to others. Through talk with others, children invest their marks with meaning (Dyson, 1993). Giving attention to children's work prompts children to translate their work's meaning to the interested adults. Vygotsky (1978) believes that this type of child speech, "graphic speech" as he named it, paves the way for the eventual use of children's written forms.

At some point, children gain the insight that *print is categorically different from other kinds of visual patterns in their environment*, and eventually, they learn that *print symbolizes language* and *can be produced by anyone* (Adams, 1998). Adams notes children also begin to realize that *print holds information*. Calkins (1997) urges parents and educators to help children see that print holds ideas, observations, stories, and plans.

Snow, Burns, and Griffin (1998) present the following review of current research.

> Research with preschoolers has demonstrated that (a) adult-child shared book reading that stimulates verbal interaction can enhance language (especially vocabulary) development and knowledge about concepts of *print,* and (b) activities that direct young children's attention to the sound structure within spoken words (e.g., play with songs and poems that depend on switching sounds within words), and to the relationships between *print* and speech can facilitate learning to read.

Preschool children already know something about the world of print from their environment. Most children form primitive hypotheses about letters, words, and messages, both printed and handwritten. West, Denton, and Germino-Hausken (2000), studying kindergartners, found 37 percent of children entering kindergarten have a basic familiarity with print. It is a widely held view that learning to read and write will be easier for the child who has had rich preschool literacy experiences than for the child who has had little or limited literacy opportunities.

Much of young children's writing is a kind of exploratory play, common in the developmental beginnings of all symbolic media. **Print awareness** and beginning printing skill and reading awareness and beginning reading skills are now viewed as developing at younger ages, simultaneously with children's growing under-

---

writing — the ability to use print to communicate with others.
print awareness — in early literacy, the child's growing recognition of the conventions and characteristics of a written language. It includes recognition of directionality in reading (left to right and top to bottom), that print forms words corresponding to speech, and that spaces separate words and other features.

standings of a number of other symbol systems. Print awareness describes the child's sensitivity to the presence and use of print in the environment. As Sulzby (1992) points out

> When given a supportive context . . . young children compose connected written discourse using emergent forms long before they hold conventional ideas about writing.

Sulzby goes on to say

> . . . children's scribbling, drawing-used-as-writing, non-phonetic strings of letters, and invented spellings are now accepted and honored as reflecting underlying understandings about writing.

The clues have been there for some time. Early childhood educators have always had children who asked questions and displayed early attempts and interest in printing, reading, number concepts, and representing lifelike objects in drawings. Preschool children can respond to and learn about visual features of print, know some letters, write some words, make up pretend writings such as letters to people, and dictate stories they want written before they have begun to consider how the words they say may be coded into print, and in particular how the sounds of speech are coded in print (Clay, 1993). Through informal daily literacy events and adult-child interactions (such as making useful signs), children learn the many purposes and the power of print in their lives and in those of adults. Adults expect children to talk before they read but may not have noticed that children are interested in writing before they can read.

Alphabet letters appear in four-year-olds' drawings. Young children go through the motions of reading books, and some have a keen interest in numbers and measurement. This supports the idea that children are attempting to make sense out of what they encounter and are expanding their understandings of symbol systems on a number of fronts (Figure 16–1).

Children do not leap from illiteracy to an understanding that our writing system is alphabetic. They may have hypothesized many conclusions, and they may have tried writing with

FIGURE 16–1 Young children pick up early ideas about print when they have experiences with books.

a variety of their own inventions after puzzling over the relationship between print and speech.

Professional practice promotes teachers' supporting, welcoming, and recognizing child efforts and accepting correct and incorrect child conclusions about printing, just as they accepted and supported incorrect or incomplete speech and welcomed it. Earlier practice may have led some teachers to either ignore or defer supportive guidance in printing, the rationale being that this instruction would come later in the child's schooling. Teachers are encouraged to have faith in children's ability to discover and develop their own writing theories and symbol systems, as they did when they taught themselves to speak. This takes place in a print-rich environment with responsive adults. Roskos and Christie (2001) caution educators about providing too many "literacy props" in classrooms, thus displacing other toys and materials. This, they suggest, may turn children's *play* into literacy *work*.

Teachers must be willing to introduce, demonstrate, and discuss print's relationship and use in daily activities to pique child interest. Optimal developmental opportunities can be missed in the very best equipped and print-prolific classroom environments. Adams (1998) describes an environment conducive to a child's development of print awareness as a place where print is important and where interactions with print are a source of social and intellectual pleasure for individual children and the people who surround them. Preschoolers who observe and interact within a print-rich environment with sensitive and responsive teachers may discover

- print is different from other kinds of visual marks and patterns.
- print appears on all kinds of surfaces and objects (Figure 16-2).
- print is almost everywhere.
- adults read picture books aloud but also read silently at times.
- print symbolizes oral language.
- print holds information.
- lots of different people and children know how to print and know what print says.

Through being read to frequently, preschoolers may know

- where one starts reading on a page.
- that reading moves from left to right.
- that at the end of a line, the reader returns to the left margin.

- that pages in a book are in a sequence usually starting with page 1.
- there is a difference between letter, word, and sentence.
- there are spaces between words.
- there are marks, called punctuation marks, that have different names and meanings.
- there are uppercase (big) and lowercase (little) letters.

Preschoolers will also discover a number of other print-related concepts. For example, they also may become aware that written language functions to label, communicate, remind, request, record, and create.

Ohl (2002) points out:

A child will not learn the name of the letter "A", the sound of the letter "A", or how to print it, simply by being with adults who know these things, or by being with an adult who reads a great deal for pleasure. Children learn these critical concepts because adults take the time and effort to teach them in an exciting, engaging, and understanding manner.

Figure 16-3 is an example of a teaching assistant's approach.

FIGURE 16-2 Print is at eye level and saturates this classroom area.

GRADUATE TEACHING ASSISTANT'S APPROACH

Child 1: (3-year-old): I'm writing a letter to my daddy. How do you write "Daddy"?

Teacher: Well, let's think about that. /d/, /d/, /d/. What letter do you think we might use to write /d/?

Child 2*: [5-year-old]: D!

Teacher: Yes. We do use D, but let's let Ana (fictitious) think about it. She's the one who is writing the word. If she needs help, I'll tell you and then you can tell me what your idea is.

Child 2: OK.

Child 1*: I can't make a D.

Child 2: I can. I will show you. (*Gets up from his chair and puts his arm down next to the child's paper, indicating that he is ready to demonstrate.*)

Teacher: Well, actually, wait just a minute. I'll grab the chart. (*Reaches toward an alphabet letter chart that is hanging from a book on the side of the paper display shelf in the writing center.*)

Child 2: But I know how. I can show her.

Teacher: I know that you know how, but Ana might like to know how you learned it, and she might like to know that this chart can show us how, so we'll just take a quick look at it, and, Allen (fictitious), get another piece of paper, honey. Let's not do our demonstration on Ana's paper. She'll write her own *D* after we show her how.

Child 2: (*Draws a straight, vertical line, very deliberately on his paper.*)

Child 1: (*Watches Child 2 with eyes wide and bright.*)

Teacher: Ok, that's just great. Now, Ana, you make that part of the D on your paper. Where was it you thought you wanted to write "Daddy"?

Child 1: (*Points to the middle of her paper.*)

Teacher: Ok, you want it down here in the middle. OK, start a little over here (*gesturing to the left side of the paper, across from where the child had pointed*) so that you will have enough room for all of the letters we'll need to write "Daddy."

Child 1: (*Moves to the spot indicated by the teacher's finger and draws a pretty good straight, vertical line.*) Now what?

Teacher: Well, now, there's a curved line that comes out like this (*uses index finger to trace curved line in the D on the chart*), and then it goes back in to touch the line down here. Allen is going to show you how to do that on the *D* he is making on his paper.

Child 2: (*Draws the curved line very carefully to complete the* D.)

Teacher: OK, now you can add that curved line to finish your *D*. Start right up here at the top of the vertical line you have already drawn, and then move your marker out this way and then gradually down to touch the line down here (*uses finger to trace the path*).

Child 1: (*Draws curved line.*) Now what?

Teacher: Well, let's see. D /ae/, /ae/, Daddy. That's a really hard sound to know how to write.

Child 2: No it isn't. My name starts with that sound.

Teacher: That's right, it does, and you know what's really funny? Ana's name also starts with that sound, and the sound in her name is spelled with the same letter as the sound in your name. What a coincidence! (*Said as if she had just noticed this herself and thought that it was a remarkable discovery.*)

Child 2: A!

Child 1: A?

FIGURE 16–3 A teaching assistant helps a child print the word *daddy.* *Child 1 = Ana; child 2 = Allen. (Reprinted with permission from Barone, D. M., & Morrow, L. M. [Eds.] [2003]. *Literacy and young children* [pp. 136–137]. New York: The Guilford Press.) *(continued)*

GRADUATE TEACHING ASSISTANT'S APPROACH—cont'd

Teacher: Yes, *A*. Just as in (*says both names, one after the other, isolating the first vowel phoneme in each name before saying the rest of it.*)

Child 1: I know how to write *A*! (*Proceeds to do it.*) Now, what is next?

Teacher: Da /d/, /d/ . . .

Child 1: D?

Teacher: Yes, there are two of them.

Child 1: I already did one.

Teacher: Well, I mean there are two more in the middle.

Child 1: (*Writes the two D's.*)

Teacher: (*Offers verbal guidance to support recall of lines needed and their direction.*)

Child 1: OK. Now what?

Teacher: Daddy, Dadd /i/.

Child 1: E! (*Child begins to position her marker to begin making an E.*)

Teacher: Well, the sound is /i/, but we write it with the letter Y. Let me show you one on the chart. (*Same process as was used before is used to instruct Child 1 on making Y and then to help Child 1 to make one of her own.*) OK, that says "Daddy." (*Underlines it with her finger.*) Did you want to write something else?

Child 1: No, I'm finished.

FIGURE 16–3 (*continued*)

Writing awareness and beginning writing attempts make more sense to children who have experienced an integrated language arts instructional approach. The areas of speaking, listening, reading, and writing are interrelated. The child's ability to see how these areas fit together is commonly mentioned in school goals. Adults in classrooms communicate with others daily—both orally and in written form. Written communication offers daily opportunities for teachers to point out print's usefulness. Print's necessity can be discussed and shared.

Increased focus on children's early reading success in the United States has provided additional impetus for researching early writing and reading relationships. An increasing number of experts believe children establish early ideas about printing (writing) that serve as a basis for early printing and reading attempts. Calkins (1979) suggests that children can begin printing the first day they enter kindergarten and that 90 percent of all children come to school believing that they can write. She points out that most children's first drafts concentrate on messages rather than perfec-tion. Generations of children have been asked to learn the letters of the alphabet, sound-symbol correspondences, and a vocabulary of sight words before they learned to write or read. If the same were true of learning to speak, children would be asked to wait until all letter sounds were perfected at age seven or eight before attempting to speak. Throne (1988) suggests that print awareness aids literacy development.

> . . . children . . . begin to understand that reading is getting meaning from print and become aware of the different functions and uses of written language.

Based on the notion that the child constructs from within, piecing together from life experiences the rules of oral language, educators believe that if children are given time and supportive assistance, they can crack the writing and reading code by noticing regularities and incongruencies, thus creating their own unique rules. Children would progress at their own speeds, doing what is important to them and doing what they see others do. Without formal instruction, they experiment with and explore the various facets of the writing process. They decorate letters and invent their own symbols— sometimes reverting to their own inventions even after they are well into distinguishing and reproducing different, recognizable alphabet letters. Some children expect others to know what they have written, regardless of their coding system.

Natural curiosity leads children to form ideas about print and its use in their lives. Schickedanz (1982) suggests that it has often been assumed that children know little or nothing about written language before they receive formal instruction. However, evidence indicates that children have extensive knowledge of some aspects of written language.

A few children may have developed both *phonological awareness* and *phonemic awareness.* Chaney (1992) reports that 14 percent of three- and four-year-old children in their study group could identify words that began with a particular phoneme and 25 percent could reliably identify rhyming words. Tests designed to measure print awareness have been found to predict future reading achievement (Adams, 1998).

Children who live in an alphabetical, literate environment begin to hypothesize that there are relationships between oral and written language. Written language is invented by children in response to their own social and cultural needs as they interact with the objects of literacy in society and with the literate members of society (Goodman, 1990).

The concept of writing readiness began with some important figures from the past who influenced the directions that early childhood education has taken (Charlesworth, 1985). It became popular to talk about writing readiness as being that time when an average group of children acquired the capacity, skills, and knowledge to permit the group to accomplish the task. Figure 16–4 compares traditional, readiness, and "natural" instructional approaches. It would be difficult to find a center that does not use some elements of each of the three approaches in the instructional program.

TRADITIONAL APPROACH

- providing play materials and free time
- supplying art materials, paper, writing tools, alphabet toys and games, chalkboard
- reading picture books
- planning program that excludes instruction in naming or forming alphabet letters
- providing incidental and spontaneous teaching about print

READINESS APPROACH

- providing writing materials and models
- planning program with introduction to tracing, naming alphabet letters, and naming shapes
- reading picture books
- providing a language arts classroom center
- channeling interested children into print and alphabet activities by offering supportive assistance

NATURAL APPROACH

- providing writing and reading materials and models
- planning program that emphasizes print in daily life
- promoting dramatic play themes that involve print, such as grocery store, restaurant, newspaper carrier, print shop, and office
- creating a writing center for the classroom
- supplying alphabet toys and models
- answering questions and supporting children's efforts
- making connections between reading and writing and speaking
- reading picture books

FIGURE 16–4 Comparisons of instructional approaches in printing.

STARTING FROM A DIFFERENT PLACE

At about 16 to 20 months, some toddlers become interested in scribbling. One sees them grasp a drawing or marking tool in their fist and use it in sweeping, whole-arm motions to make marks. Crosser (1998) observes that the experience seems to provide sensory enjoyment. Motions can be vigorous, rhythmic, scrubbing, and repetitive and may include sharp stabs at the paper, which tears because of the pressure applied. Adults can wisely provide sturdy, large pieces of paper taped down onto a surface that can take the punishment. Large flattened brown grocery bags work well.

Scribbling involves decision making. It coincides with young children's emerging sense of autonomy. Crosser points out

> Not only do children make decisions about line, color, and placement, they also exercise their sense of autonomy by using and gaining control over tools of the culture—crayons, markers, pencils, paper—to engage in an activity valued by the culture.

Teachers need to consider all enrolled children ready to learn and progress in language and literacy, with each child possessing a different past experience. Past opportunity may have dramatically molded the individual child's literacy behaviors and language competency. Teachers hope to expand language competencies that exist and introduce children to new activities and opportunities.

Much of young children's writing is exploratory. When children show interest and share in discussions about written marks, they begin to understand print's meaning and functional use.

Through personally motivated and personally directed trial and error—a necessary condition of their literacy development—children try out various aspects of the writing process (Morrow, 1989). They sometimes interact and collaborate with peers who are more literate (Figure 16–5). Competent others provide what Vygotsky (1978) calls "scaffolding," and eventually children function without supportive assistance.

RESEARCH IN WRITING DEVELOPMENT

In *Literacy before Schooling* (1982), Ferreiro and Teberosky revolutionized educators' thinking about young children's development of print knowledge and writing. Subsequent research in children's self-constructed knowledge of alphabet forms and printing has resulted, using anthropological, psychological, and other investigative approaches. Ferreiro and Teberosky identified three developmentally ordered levels.

First Level

Children

◆ search for criteria to distinguish between drawing and writing. Example: "What's this?" referring to their artwork.

FIGURE 16–5 Teachers promote both individual and collaborative printing activities.

- realize straight and curved lines and dots are present but organized differently in print. Example: Rows and rows of curved figures, lines, and/or dots in art.
- reach the conclusion that print forms are arbitrary and ordered in a linear fashion.
- accept the letter shapes in their environment rather than inventing new ones. Example: Rows of one letter appear in linear fashion in art.
- from literacy-rich environments recognize written marks as "substitute objects" during their third year. Example: "What does this say, teacher?" or "This says 'Mary'."

Second Level

Children

- look for objective differences in printed strings.
- do not realize there is a relationship between sound patterns and print.

Third Level

Children

- accept that a given string of letters represents their name and look for a rational explanation of this phenomenon.
- may create a syllabic hypothesis.
- may print letter forms as syllables heard in a word. Example: I C (I see).
- may develop knowledge about particular syllables and what letters might represent such a syllable.
- may look for similar letters to write similar pieces of sound.
- begin to understand printing uses alphabet letters that represent sounds; consequently, to understand print, one must know the sound patterns of words.

What conclusions of Ferreiro's landmark research may affect language arts program planning and early educators' interaction techniques? Certainly, teachers will note attending children's active attempts to understand print. They will realize each child constructs her own ideas and revises these understandings as more print is noticed and experienced.

The seemingly strange questions children ask or off-the-wall answers some children give in classroom discussions about print may now be seen as reflecting their inner thoughts at crucial points in their print knowledge.

As teachers view children's artwork, they will see more readily early print forms. Ferreiro's research will also confirm educators' attempts to provide literacy-rich, print-rich classroom environments.

Some preschoolers demonstrate that they know the names and shapes of alphabet letters. They may also know letters form words and represent sounds. They might have grasped the idea that spoken words can be written and then read. They may be able to express daily uses of written words. Why would a young child write or pretend to write? It is not an easy motor task. Is it simply imitation? done for adult reaction? done because there is an inner drive to know or become competent? Research has yet to answer these questions. Teachers conjecture reasons with each young child they meet who has beginning printing skills. The reasons are not as important as teacher reaction and plan to provide additional opportunities to nourish and expand what already exists.

YOUNG CHILDREN'S PROGRESS

Dyson (1993) believes there is not a linear progression in written language development.

> Rather its development is linked in complex ways to the whole of children's symbolic repertoires; its evolution involves shifts of function and symbolic form, social give-and-take, as children explore and gradually control new ways to organize and represent their world and to interact with other people about that world.

At some point, children learn that written marks have meaning. Just as they sought the names of things, they now seek the names of these marks and, later, the meanings of the marks. Because each child is an individual, this may or may not happen during the preschool years. One child may try to make letters or numbers. Another child may have little interest in or knowledge of written forms. Many children are somewhere between these two examples.

Preschool children may recognize environmental print words before they know the name of any alphabet letters. This is termed **sight reading**, and some preschool children may recognize most of the children's names in their group. Quite a few researchers believe a period of time exists when a young child conceives of a certain alphabet letter as representing a person or object (for example, all "B" words remind the child of her own name). At that point, the child may say, "'B', that's my name." A child may not understand that the alphabet is a complete set of letters representing speech sounds used in writing, but rather, she may have a partial and beginning view of the **alphabetic principle**. Figure 16-6 displays possible child understandings concerning the alphabetic principle.

Writing (printscript) is complex. Many subcomponents of the process need to be understood. Development may occur at different rates, with spurts and lags in different knowledge areas. Besides the visual learning of letter features and forms, the ability to manually form shapes, and knowing that writing involves a message, a writer must listen to the sounds of her inner speech and find matching letters representing those sounds. Because letter follows letter in printing, the child needs to make continuous intellectual choices and decisions.

Atkins (1984) also discusses events between the ages of three and five.

> . . . children begin to vary their patterns and move from imitation to creation. They produce a mixture of real letters, mock letters, and innovative symbols. They write messages which they expect adults to be

THE ALPHABETIC PRINCIPLE

The child may:
- understand that letters have different shapes.
- identify some letters by name.
- notice some words start with the same letter.
- realize letters make sounds.
- match some sounds to letters correctly.
- possess a sight word vocabulary—usually her own and peer's names.
- realize alphabet letters are a special category of print.

FIGURE 16-6 The alphabetic principle.

able to read. These actions signal several new discoveries which the children are making.

- They are attending to the fine features of writing, noting shapes and specific letters.
- They are developing an early concept of sign—the realization that symbols stand for something.
- They are recognizing that there is variation in written language.

Children refine and enlarge these concepts by playing around with writing. They draw, trace, copy, and even invent letter forms of their own.

Print awareness is usually developed in the following sequence.

1. The child notices adults making marks with writing tools.
2. The child notices print in books and on signs. As Chomsky (1971) notes, "When this time comes, a child seems suddenly to notice all the print in the world around him—street signs, food labels, newspaper headlines, printing on cartons, books, billboards, everything. He tries to read everything, already having a good foundation in

---

sight reading — the ability to immediately recognize a word as a whole without sounding it out.
alphabetic principle — the awareness that spoken language can be analyzed as strings of separate words and that words, in turn, as sequences of syllables and phonemes within syllables.

translating from pronunciation to print. If help is provided when he asks for it, he makes out wonderfully well. It is a tremendously exciting time for him."

3. The child realizes that certain distinguishable marks make her name.

4. The child learns the names of some of the marks—usually the first letter of her name. While building a sizable store of words recognized on sight, children will begin to make finer and finer distinctions about print by using more and more visual cues. They begin to pay attention to individual letters, particularly the first ones in words.

The usual sequence in the child's imitation of written forms follows:

1. The child's scribbles are more like print than artwork or pure exploration (Figure 16–7).

2. Linear scribbles are generally horizontal with possible repeated forms. Children's knowledge of linear directionality may have been displayed in play in which they lined up alphabet blocks, cut out letters and pasted them in a row, or put magnetic board letters in left-to-right rows (Figure 16–8).

3. Individual shapes are created, usually closed shapes displaying purposeful lines (Figure 16–9).

4. Letterlike forms are created.

5. Recognizable alphabet letters are printed and may be mirror images or turned on sides, upside down, or in upright position (Figure 16–10).

FIGURE 16–8 Linear scribbles.

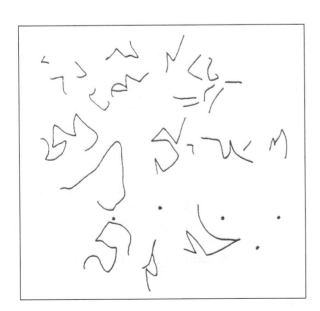

FIGURE 16–7 Scribbles are sometimes printlike.

FIGURE 16–9 This boy has just made a closed-shape letter with purposeful lines.

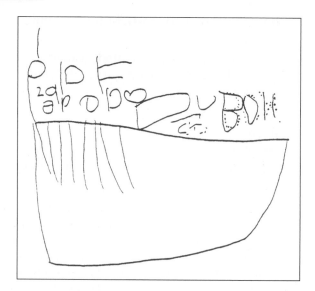

FIGURE 16–10 Recognizable alphabet letters.

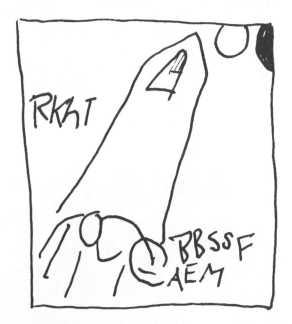

FIGURE 16–11 Child read as "Blast off rocket to the moon."

6. Words or groupings of alphabet letters with spaces between are formed.

7. **Invented spelling** appears; this may include pictured items along with alphabet letters (Figure 16–11).

8. Correctly spelled words with spaces separating words are produced.

INVENTED SPELLING (DEVELOPMENTAL SPELLING)

Invented spelling is something children do naturally. It is a temporary phenomenon that is later replaced with conventional spelling. Teachers, until the mid to late 1980s, gave young children the idea that until they learned to read, they needed to write only those words they had memorized or copied. Research has changed educational philosophy and methods. It suggests children's literacy emerges during a span of several years. As young children slowly begin to understand what letters mean and how to string them together, some children will invent spelling. Often, the beginning consonant sound of a particular word is printed. A whole sequence might shortly appear and consist of single-letter words.

The invented spelling stage casts teachers in the role of detectives trying to ascertain meanings that the child may perceive as obvious. In their early attempts to write, preschool children invent a system of spelling that follows logical and predictable rules before they learn the conventional forms.

According to Sulzby (1996), most kindergartners use drawing, scribbling, and nonphonetic letter strings as they write. She believes only a few children can be expected to use invented and conventional spelling and those who do primarily do so when writing isolated words at this age.

Vowels are commonly omitted in invented spellings. Words appear that may look like a foreign language—*dg* for *dog*, and *jragin* for *dragon*.

Identifiable stages in invented spelling are followed by some children and are given here for teacher reference.

1. Spelling awareness—alphabet letters represent words. Example: C (see), U (you).

---

invented spelling — the result of an attempt to spell a word whose spelling is not already known, based on a writer's knowledge of the spelling system and how it works.

2. Primitive spelling with no relationship between spelling and words—numbers and letters are differentiated. Example: tsOlf..DO.

3. Prephonetic spelling—initial and final consonants may become correct. Example: KT (cat), CD (candy), RT (write), WF (with).

4. Phonetic spelling—almost a perfect match between the symbols and sounds. Some vowels are used. Some sight words may be correctly spelled. Example: SUM (some), LIK (like), MI (my), ME (me).

5. Correct spelling.

Invented spelling serves as an important stage in the process of deciphering the sound-symbol system of written language (Fields & Lee, 1987). It is believed that at this point, phonics becomes important to children. Early on, the child selects letters in her inventive spelling that have some relationship to how the word is pronounced. Large items like "elephants" may be written in huge letters and with more letters than small objects, because the child is operating under the misconception that bigger necessitates more letters (Ferreiro & Teberosky, 1982). A perfectly logical conclusion! The names of letters may represent words (*u* for *you*) or parts of words. Atkins (1984) defines young writers' invented spelling as using personal logic rather than or in conjunction with standard spelling. Atkins points out that the child's strategy of using a name of a letter has a frustrating side.

> There are only 26 letters in the alphabet but almost twice that many phonemes or sound units. What do children do when they encounter a sound for which there is no ready letter-name match? They use a system of spelling logic based primarily on what they hear but also influenced by subconscious knowledge of the general rules of language usage and of how sounds are formed in the mouth when spoken.

What should an early childhood educator do when confronted with invented spelling in a child's work? Faith that children who are given help will evolve toward conventional spelling is needed. As Sowers (1982) writes

> Invented spelling gives young writers early power over words. Professional writers don't worry about correct spelling on their first drafts and neither do inventive spellers.

Many primary teachers write out the standard spelling for words below a child's invented spelling. By doing so, teachers honor the original but give children experiencing the tension between their spelling inventions and regular standard spellings further information. This enables interested children to compare. Inventive spellers who realize their spelling differs from text in books and the world around them may experience frustration and confusion. Teachers at this juncture may introduce phoneme spelling by "sounding out" words that they print.

Calkins (1997) offers another suggested course of action. She describes putting a small translation on papers containing invented spelling.

> During the first year as an independent speller (which may be when a child is four, five, six or seven depending mostly on what instruction the child receives), it can be difficult to decipher what the child's words say. Some teachers will record the child's intended message (or a translation of what the child has written) in tiny adult cursive letters on a remote corner of the page. This is a very satisfying arrangement, I find, because an adult can glance covertly at the translation and then, pointing to the child's letters, join the child in decoding the intended message.

In this way a parent examining "sent home papers" can possibly understand the thought processes the child used to write the message and understand the child's great accomplishment. A parent-teacher discussion is usually necessary for parents to realize that beginning attempts are not immediately corrected.

Teachers need to use these techniques carefully with older preschoolers, being mindful of the child's inventiveness and pride in her work. Many preschoolers object to teachers adding any marks on their papers.

When a child asks the teacher to write a specific word, the teacher has a chance to help the child with letter sounds (rather than letter names), saying d-o-g as she writes it. Time permitting, the teacher can add, "It starts with the alphabet letter *d*, like Dan, *D-a-n*."

GOALS OF INSTRUCTION

Providing experiences that match a child's interests and abilities is the goal of many centers. Most schools plan activities for those children who ask questions or seem ready and then proceed if the child is still interested. Others work with children on an individual basis. Yet others believe in providing a print-rich environment where the child will progress naturally with supportive adults who also model an interest in print and point out uses of print in daily activities. Teachers should plan activities involving authentic writing (printing), that is, writing done for the "real world" rather than for contrived school purposes. An authentic written message often involves a child's need or desire. It is possible to combine these approaches.

As with other language abilities, goals include stimulating further interest and exploration. This should be done in such a way that the child is not confused by instruction that is too advanced or boring.

As stated previously, an important goal concerning print awareness is relating writing to other language arts areas. It is almost impossible to not do so. Teachers are encouraged to consciously mention connections so that children will understand how writing fits in the whole of communicating. Figure 16-12 is a listing of both print- and book-awareness understandings that early childhood educators endeavor to promote before a child begins kindergarten.

PRINT AND BOOK AWARENESS GOALS

The child understands that:
- reading obtains information from books.
- writing communicates thoughts and ideas.
- print can carry messages.
- letters are different from numerals.
- book illustrations carry meaning.
- print can be read.
- books have authors who create books and their titles.
- print is read from left to right and top to bottom.
- alphabet letters in print can form words.
- alphabet letters have names.
- words are separated by spaces.
- spoken words can be written down.
- print has everyday functional uses (for example, shopping lists, messages, recipes, signs).
- one can follow print with one's eyes as it is read aloud.

FIGURE 16-12 Print and book awareness goals.

A teacher's goal would include the ability to print every lowercase and uppercase alphabet letter in excellent form, offering children the best model possible.

WHOLE-LANGUAGE THEORY

The **whole-language approach** suggests that reading is a multifaceted process involving more than just learning to read but also learning to read by writing. Early childhood educators who adopt whole-language theory give attention to children displaying an interest in printing alphabet letters and invented spelling. The role of the teacher in this approach is that of a supportive assistant. Conversations focus on meaning and helping children trying to print something they have in mind. The teacher might pair children with similar interests to encourage

whole-language approach — a philosophy and reading-instruction approach integrating oral and written language. Advocates believe that when children are given literature-abundant and print-rich environments, they will follow their natural curiosity and learn to read as they learned to speak. A thematic focus is used. Teachers seize opportunities to connect and interrelate language arts areas.

child collaboration. Whole-language early childhood classrooms have well-equipped writing centers furnished with abundant child aids.

Teachers encourage children to "reason it out." Approximations of alphabet letters and words are accepted and given recognition. They preserve and encourage the child's attempts. As more exposure to letter forms takes place and when more precise motor control develops, the child will produce closer approximations to recognizable alphabet letter forms.

COORDINATION

Children's muscle control follows a timetable of its own. Control of a particular muscle depends on many factors—diet, exercise, inherited ability, and motivation, to name a few. A baby can control her neck and arms long before her legs. A child's muscle control grows in a head-to-toe fashion. Muscles closer to the center of the body can be controlled long before those of the hands and fingers. Large-muscle control comes before small-muscle control (Figure 16–13). Think of a toddler walking; the

toddler's legs seem to swing from the hips. Just as each child starts walking and develops muscle control at different ages, so too does each child develop fine motor control, which influences her ability to control a writing tool.

Schickedanz (1989) discusses problems preschoolers may encounter if they are *required* by "overeager" teachers to print the letters of the alphabet.

> . . . precise writing is extremely difficult for three- and four-year-olds, who typically grasp writing tools in their fists and guide them with movements started at the shoulder, elbow, or wrist. With the pivot and the writing tool point so far apart, children can't help but write large. . . . Furthermore, because preschoolers' spatial skills are limited, it's difficult for them to construct and combine lines in the ways that writing lessons often demand. Four-year-olds who do have advanced fine motor skills that allow them to hold a pencil in a well-controlled finger and thumb grasp still might conceptualize letters in ways that differ from conventional form (Figure 16–14).

FIGURE 16–13 The small-muscle control Ria is using to trace a leaf will be needed when she begins to print.

FIGURE 16–14 This child displays a well-controlled finger-and-thumb grasp.

COGNITIVE DEVELOPMENT

Realization that written symbols exist is a first step in writing. The discovery that written language is simply spoken language, ideas, or communication is another step. Mental growth, which allows a child to see similarities and differences in written symbols, comes before the ability to write. The child recognizes that a written mark is a shape made by the placement of lines.

Donoghue (1985) lists seven prerequisite skill areas for handwriting.

- small-muscle development and coordination
- eye-hand coordination
- ability to hold writing tools properly
- ability to form basic strokes (circles and straight lines)
- letter perception
- orientation to printed language, which includes a desire to write and communicate, including the child's enjoyment of writing her own name
- left-to-right understanding

The last three skills deal with the child's cognitive development.

PLAY AND WRITING

Print, signs, and writing imaginary messages often become part of a dramatic play sequence. During play, children may pretend to read and write words, poems, stories, and songs, and they may actually make a series of marks on paper. Play encourages children to act as if they are already competent in and able to control the activity under consideration (McLane & McNamee, 1990). Through pretend play, they may feel they are already readers and writers; at least a beginning move toward eventual literacy takes place. Children observe mom, dad, teachers, and older brothers and sisters using reading and writing in their daily lives. These activities are given status. Early childhood teachers can build on children's early attitudes by modeling, demonstrating, and providing dramatic play opportunities involving print, which promote collaborative peer printing.

DRAWING EXPERIENCE

A young child scribbles if given paper and a marking tool. As the child grows, the scribbles are controlled into lines that she places where desired (Figure 16–15). Gradually, the child begins to draw circles, then a face, later a full figure, and so on. Children draw their own symbols representing what they see around

FIGURE 16–15 Children start writing by scribbling and, when older, drawing symbols of the world around them.

them. Clay (1991a) urges teachers to examine one child's drawings over a few weeks time and discover the child is working on a basic plan.

> His ideas are organized and he produces the same pattern or schema again and again. It seems as if the child has learned a plan of action which produces the pattern or schema. This gives the child enough control over pencil and paper to play with variations, which often leads to new discoveries.

The length of time it takes this process to develop differs with each child.

A profound connection exists between experience and ability in drawing and interest in and ability to write (Figure 16–16). Drawings and paintings not only communicate children's thinking (when they reach the level of drawing that is representative of the environment) but also often display early attempts to create symbols. Some of these symbols may be recognized by adults, but others seem to be unique and represent the world in the child's own way. Children often want to talk about their work and create stories to accompany graphics.

FIGURE 16–16 Nontoxic felt-tip pens (markers) are standard preschool materials.

Because alphabet letters are more abstract than representative drawing, some educators suggest that drawing precedes writing. Brittain's research (1973) found that children who were making closed forms and recognizable letters in their drawings made closed forms and recognizable letters if they attempted writing. Durkin (1966) identifies a characteristic that was common to almost all children in her research study who read early and continued to hold their lead in reading achievement: the children were described by their parents as "pencil-and-paper kids," whose starting point of curiosity about written language was an interest in scribbling and drawing.

WRITING AND EXPOSURE TO BOOKS

Probably the most common experience that promotes a child's interest in print is hearing and seeing picture books read over and over. Through repeated exposure, the child comes to expect the text to be near or on the same page as the object depicted. Two- and three-year-olds think that pictures in a book tell the story; as they gain more experience, they notice the reader reads the print, not the pictures (Schickendanz, 1999). Throne (1988) points out that "children begin to understand the conventions of print and how stories work by using familiar and significant texts." Memorized story lines lead to children's questions about print on book pages. Once a word is recognized in print, copying that word onto another piece of paper or manipulating magnetic alphabet letters to form the word is a natural outgrowth. This activity usually leads to parent attention and approval and further attempts. Scribblers, doodlers, drawers, and pencil-and-paper kids are all labels researchers have used to describe children who have an early interest in writing, and much of what they do has been promoted by seeing print in their favorite books.

Clay (1991b) and Ferreiro and Teberosky (1982) have tried to discover what young children think about pictures (illustrations) and text and the relationship between the two. Similar conclusions were drawn by both researchers. Ferreiro and Teberosky (1982) describe a sequential change in child behaviors.

- At first the text and the picture are not differentiated.
- Then the children expect the text to be a label for the picture.
- At the third stage the text is expected to provide cues with which to confirm predictions based on the picture.

Some important concepts that young children gradually understand concerning print are

- the print, not the pictures in a book, tells the story.
- there are alphabet letters.
- words are clusters of letters.
- there are first letters and last letters in words.
- alphabet letters exist in uppercase and lowercase.
- spaces in printing are there for a reason.
- punctuation makes words have meaning.

Children may notice the left-to-right and top-to-bottom direction of printing and also the left-page-first directional feature.

The acquisition of skills in writing and reading and the development of the attitude that books are enjoyable are not simply academic or technical learning. These skills flourish with a warm physical and emotional base with shared enjoyment and intimacy. Most experts believe considerable support exists for the notion that oral language provides a base for learning to write. The importance of emotionally satisfying adult-child interactions in all areas of language arts cannot be overestimated.

Alphabet Books

Children's books in print before the twentieth century were mostly informational and moralistic. Alphabet books suited the then prevailing public view that a good children's book should promote child learning. Presently, school libraries for young children include alphabetic books as valuable volumes in their collection. Although many are in print and some are classic favorites, new titles continually appear. It is said that almost every author of young children's literature yearns to develop a unique alphabet book. Recommended titles follow:

Cleary, B. (1998). *The hullabaloo A-B-C*. Boston: Morrow Junior Books. (Alphabet experiences through farm noises explored by three children.)

Isadora, R. (1999). *ABC pop!* New York: Viking Press. (A clever introduction of alphabet letters.)

Kalman, B. (1998). *Community helpers from A to Z*. New York: Crabtree Publishing Inc. (Community workers are associated with alphabet letters.)

Lester, A. (1998). *Alice and Aldo*. Boston: Houghton Mifflin. (Alphabet letters A to Z introduced through Alice's chronological daily activities [like breakfast in bed].)

Paul, A. (1999). *Everything to spend the night from A to Z*. New York: DK Publishing, Co. (The overnight bag brought for an overnight stay with grandpa yields A to Z objects.)

When children are asking for alphabet letter names and alphabet letters are appearing in their art or writing, alphabet books can become favorites. Teachers notice that a first interest in alphabet letters often appears when the child sees her printed name and then notices similar letters in friend's names.

Ideas for ways to build alphabet books into further classroom activities follow:

- Paint on a giant alphabet letter shape.
- Hide an alphabet letter in a large drawing and have children search for it.
- Make a class alphabet book by outlining large alphabet letters on pages and encouraging interested individual children to decorate a letter.
- Create a "Who looked at this book today?" chart. Add children's names to the chart if they browsed the book.

Additional alphabet books and activities are found in the text's Online Companion™.

PLANNING A PROGRAM FOR PRINT AWARENESS AND PRINTING SKILL

Program planning is often done on an individual basis. If group instruction is planned, it deals with general background information concerning print use during the school day and how it relates to children's lives, including print use in the home and community.

A great deal of spontaneous and incidental teaching takes place. Teachers capitalize on children's questions concerning mail, packages, signs, and labels. In most preschool settings, print is a natural part of living, and it has many interesting features that children can discover and notice when teachers focus attention on print.

Most teachers realize that children will explore graphic symbols on their own, often inventing as they go and constructing and revising understandings as they proceed. Martens (1999) describes the type of supportive classroom environment that allows children to design their own route to further knowledge about print.

> It is critical for children to have a literacy-rich, risk-free environment that includes time to invent, to play, and to experiment with written language for meaningful purposes in an authentic context while interacting with knowledgeable others. Such experiences allow children to work through questions and perplexities, and to build conceptualizations and understandings in ways meaningful to them.
>
> As children compare their inventions with the written language around them, particularly their names, they deepen their understandings of the complexities of our written language system.

A discussion is necessary here concerning the practice of asking the child to form alphabet letters and practice letter forms. The dangers in planning an individual or group experience of this nature are multiple. One has to consider whether a child has the physical and mental capacity to be successful and whether the child has an interest in doing the exercise or is simply trying to please adults.

Adams (1998) believes the logical progression in learning about letters is to first learn letter names and then learn letter shapes. The child then has a solid mnemonic peg to which the percept of the letter can be connected as it is built. Hand and Nourot (1999) suggest that playful activities such as singing the alphabet song, reading alphabet books, and playing with alphabet magnets or puzzles help preschoolers learn letters. Adams (1998) points out that research suggests uppercase letters are more discriminable from one another and thus easier for preschoolers.

Parents often offer only uppercase letters when asked by their child to print. Before learning to read, a child will need to know both forms. Preschools often present "big" and "little" together in the school's visual environment. It is the uppercase letters that most children recognize when they enter kindergarten, and preschool and kindergarten teachers print children's names with an uppercase first letter followed by lowercase letters in printscript.

Teachers encourage children to print ("write") their own names on their artwork when they believe children have an interest in printing. Any child attempt is recognized and given attention. These teachers may also say, "May I write your name on the back? With two names, one on the front and one on the back, we will find your work quickly when it's time to leave school." Teachers print names on the upper left corner of the children's work because that is the spot reading starts on any given page written in English.

Early writing instruction is not a new idea. Maria Montessori (1967b) (a well-known educator and designer of teaching materials) and numerous other teachers have offered instruction in writing (or printing) to preschoolers. Montessori encouraged the child's tracing of letter forms using the first two fingers of the hand as a prewriting exercise. She observed that this type of light touching seemed to help youngsters when writing tools were later given to them. Montessori (1967a) designed special alphabet letter cutouts as one of a number of prewriting aids. These cutouts were thought to help exercise and develop small muscles and create sight-touch sensations, fixing the forms in memory.

In seventeenth- and eighteenth-century England, a gingerbread method of teaching alphabet letters was developed. As a child correctly named a letter-shaped cookie or a word formed by cookies, she was allowed to eat it (or them). This is offered here to point out past educators' practices rather than to recommend.

This text recommends print activity planning that concentrates on awareness of print and its uses in everyday life plus helpful teacher interaction and encouragement given to children who show more than a passing interest. When a child asks for information concerning print or asks to be shown how to print, she is displaying interest and following her own curriculum.

How to Make the ABCs Developmentally Appropriate

When a print-rich classroom environment includes books, charts, labels, printed children's names, and other functional daily use of print in the classroom's daily activities, children are bound to see alphabet letters as a natural part of their world and develop curiosity about them.

Teachers examine activities and take advantage of teachable moments. Educators realize alphabet knowledge prompts phonemic awareness. Teachers promote children's fluency in naming alphabet letters. Fluency can be defined as speed and accuracy. Children fluent in alphabet letter names can recognize and correctly name alphabet letters without hesitation, thereby indicating that letter names have been well learned.

Introduction of alphabet books is probably the most common and professionally acceptable vehicle for teaching letter names, followed only by the alphabet song. Alphabet activities can be enjoyable and gamelike or can be a natural outgrowth of daily schedules and happenings.

Following are samples of alphabet-related activities.

Name of the Day. One child's name is chosen and discussed at circle time. The first alphabet letter in the child's name is named and searched for in room displays.

Alphabet Letter Sorting Game. A teacher-made box with slots under alphabet letters is provided, along with a deck of teacher-made alphabet cards. A child (or children) decide what card is slotted, and then the box is lifted and the cards retrieved for the next child. The box can be a large cardboard box upended with letters on the box and adjacent cut slots. This game needs a simple introduction and demonstration.

Alphabet Chart Game. The teacher posts large alphabet letters on large paper around the room. Child volunteers choose how to get to one letter from the starting place to touch the letter and then how to get to the next. (Every child gets a turn.) The teacher may have to start by saying, "Let's tiptoe to the letter C." "Who can think of a way to get to 'M'"?

Designing Game Activities. When designing games, remember that in developmentally appropriate games

- everyone gets a turn.
- clear directions (rules) are introduced.
- everyone wins.
- competition is inappropriate.
- cooperation is promoted.
- praise or prizes are omitted.
- musical games are enjoyed.
- movement games are wiggle reducers if they end on a cooling down note.
- every child who wants to play is included.
- game parts or visuals are sturdy.
- frustrating game elements should not be included.

Remember also that these games are meant to promote listening skills and problem solving. It is recommended that alphabet letters be introduced. Most early childhood program staffs specifically designate exactly which letter form they will offer first and affirm alphabet letters named by children in either uppercase or lowercase. Teaching the sounds of alphabet letters is an instructional decision based on children's age, interest, and ability. Schools decide if it is developmentally appropriate and whether it is done only on a one-to-one basis.

A phonetic alphabet pronunciation guide is found in the Appendix. Teachers offering letter sounds should know it well.

ENVIRONMENT AND MATERIALS

Children's access to drawing tools—magic markers, chalk, pencils, crayons, brushes—is important so that children can make their own marks (Figure 16–17). It is suggested that teachers create a place where children can comfortably use these tools.

The following early childhood materials help the child use and gain control of small arm and finger muscles in preparation for writing.

◆ puzzles
◆ pegboards
◆ small blocks
◆ construction toys
◆ scissors
◆ eyedroppers

Most schools plan activities in which the child puts together, arranges, or manipulates small pieces. These are sometimes called tabletop

FIGURE 16–17 Some children develop unique ways to hold drawing and writing tools.

activities and are available for play throughout the day. A teacher can encourage the use of table-top activities by having the pieces arranged invitingly on tables or resting on adjacent shelves.

The following are examples of materials common in print-immersion classrooms.

◆ *Labels*—pictures or photographs accompanied by corresponding words
◆ *Charts and lists*—charts that convey directions, serve as learning resources (pictures and names of children in alphabetical order), organize the class (attendance roster or class calendar), show written language as a reminder (children sign-up lists)
◆ *Materials and activities*—various materials, including alphabet toys, puzzles, stamps, magnetic letters, and games, along with clever teacher-made (Figure 16–18) or commercial furnishings, such as blocks, stuffed alphabet-shaped pillows, alphabet rugs, and wall hangings
◆ *Books and other resources*—a variety of books and magazines, poetry, newspapers, computer software, picture dictionaries, riddle and novelty books, and other printed material

Early childhood centers create rooms that are full of symbols, letters, and numbers in clear view of the child. Room print should reflect teacher and child interests. Many toys have circles, squares, triangles, alphabet letters, and other common shapes.

Recommended symbol size for preschool playroom display is at least 2 to 2½ inches in height or larger.

Labeling

Labeling activities revolve around the purpose and function of labels and signs in daily life. In a classroom, many needs usually exist. A "Park bikes here" sign alerts bike riders to the proper storage area and may prevent yard accidents and be useful for a child looking for an available bike.

A labeling activity initiated by a teacher to introduce the need for road signs and environmental signs can lead to an activity in which children decide the appropriate wording.

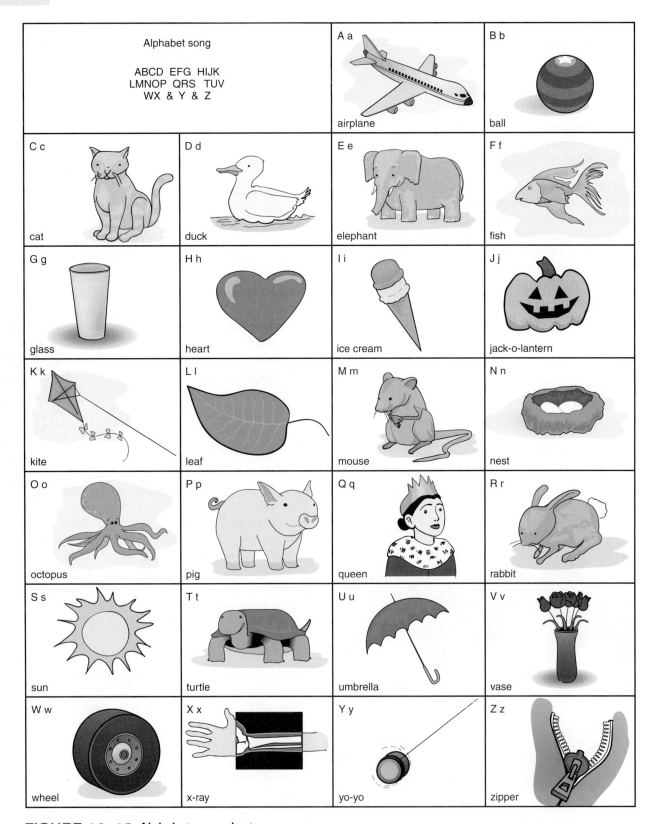

FIGURE 16–18 Alphabet song chart.

Common classroom labeling includes the following.

◆ artwork

◆ name tags

◆ lockers and storage areas (Figure 16–19)

◆ belongings

◆ common objects in the room, such as scissors, paper, crayons, fishbowl, chair, water, door, window, sink

◆ school areas, such as block, library or reading center, playhouse, art center, science center

◆ place cards for snacks

Display Areas

Display areas often include the following.

◆ magazine pictures with captions

◆ current interest displays, for example, "Rocks we found on our walk"

◆ bulletin boards and wall displays with words

◆ wall alphabet guides (Aa Bb . . .)

◆ charts

◆ child's work with explanations, such as "Josh's block tower" or "Penny's clay pancakes"

◆ folding table accordian (Figure 16–20)

◆ signs for child activities, such as "store," "hospital," "wet paint," and "Tickets for Sale Here"

Message-Sending Aids

Classroom mailboxes, suggestion boxes, and message boards are motivational and useful. Writing short notes to children piques an interest about what is said. Large-sized stick-on notes are great for this purpose and can be attached to mirrors, plates, toys, and so on.

Teacher-Made Materials, Games, and Toys

brightly colored alphabet letters from felt, cardboard, sandpaper, leather, plastic

games with letters, numbers, or symbols

alphabet cards

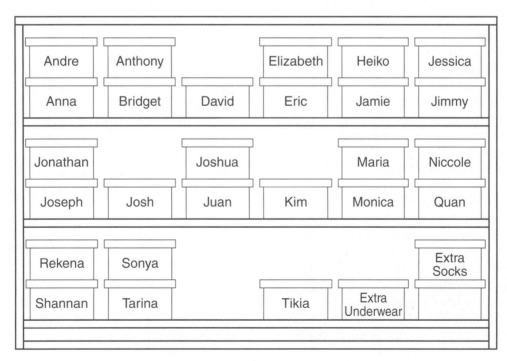

FIGURE 16–19 Large printscript letters are used to label boxes.

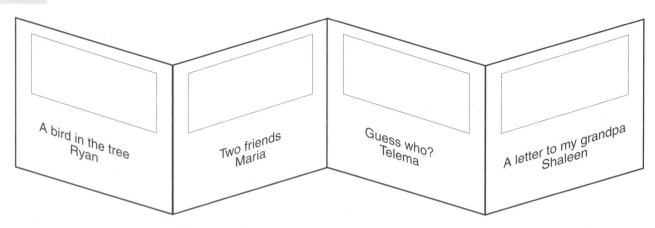

A bird in the tree
Ryan

Two friends
Maria

Guess who?
Telema

A letter to my grandpa
Shaleen

FIGURE 16–20 Folding table accordion.

games with names and words

greeting cards

hats or badges with words

Writing Centers

Writing centers are planned, teacher-stocked areas where printing is promoted. A writing center can be a separate area of a room, or it can exist within a language arts center. Child comfort and proper lighting are essential, along with minimized distractions. Often, dividers or screens are used to reduce outside noise and activity. Supplies and storage areas are provided at children's fingertips so that children can help themselves. Teacher displays or bulletin board areas that motivate printing can be close by. If water-based marking pens are provided, pens with distinct bright colors are preferred.

Through dialogue and exploration at a writing table or center, children are able to construct new ideas concerning print and meaning in a supportive minisocial setting.

There should be a variety of paper and writing tools. Printing stamps and printing ink blocks, a hole punch, and brads are desirable. Old forms, catalogs, calendars, and computer paper may be inviting. Scratch paper (one side already used) or lined paper and crayons placed side-by-side invite use. Most local businesses or offices throw away enough scratch paper to supply a preschool center.

Colored or white chalk has an appeal of its own and can be used on paper, chalkboards, or cement. For variety, use oil pastels, which have bright colors, or soft-lead pencils on paper. Most schools install a child-high chalkboard; table chalkboards are made quickly by using chalkboard paint obtained at hardware or paint stores and scrap wood pieces. Easels, unused wall areas, and backs of furniture can be made into chalkboards.

Primary print typewriters and computers capture interest. Shape books with blank pages and words to copy and trace appeal to some children, as do large rub-on letters or alphabet letter stickers (these can be made by teachers from press-on labels). Magnetic boards and magnetized letter sets are commonly mentioned as the favorite toy of children interested in alphabet letters and forming words.

Letters, words, and displays are placed for viewing on bulletin boards at children's eye level. Displays in writing centers often motivate and promote print.

FIRST SCHOOL ALPHABETS

Parents may have taught their children to print with all capitals. Early childhood centers help introduce the interested child to the letter forms that are used in the first grades of elementary school.

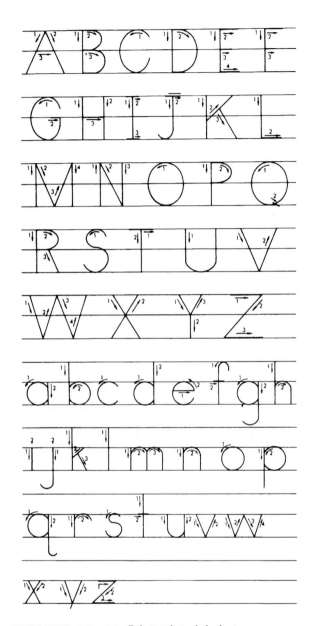

FIGURE 16–21 Printscript alphabet.

ā d k H́ R U
ā d k H́ R U
2 4 7 9 10

FIGURE 16-22 Samples of D'Nealian print and numerals.

child to learn the right way than to be retrained later. All printing seen by young children in a preschool should be either printscript, using both uppercase and lowercase letters, or D'Nealian style. Names, bulletin boards, and labels made by teachers should model correct forms. Printscript letters are formed with straight lines, circles, and parts of circles. In Figure 16–21, the small arrows and numerals show the direction to follow in forming the letters as well as the sequence of the lines.

The D'Nealian form, developed by teacher-principal Donald Neal Thurber and introduced in 1978, has grown in acceptance. Its popularity stems in part from its slant and continuous stroke features, which provide an easy transition to slant and stroke used in cursive writing introduced to children after second grade. Thurber (1988) notes that it takes 58 strokes to print the circle-stick alphabet but only 31 to print D'Nealian. Further information about this alphabet and teaching suggestions can be obtained from Scott, Foresman, Glenview, IL 60025.

Numbers in printed form are called numerals. Children may have used toys with numerals, such as block sets. Young children will probably hold up fingers to indicate their ages or to tell you they can count. They may start making number symbols before showing an interest in alphabet letters. Numeral forms (Figure 16–23) are also available from elementary schools. The numeral forms in one geo-

In kindergarten or first grade, printing is done in printscript, sometimes called manuscript printing (Figure 16–21) or in a form called D'Nealian print (Figure 16–22). Centers should obtain guides from a local elementary school, because letter forms can vary from community to community.

Teachers need to be familiar with printscript (or any other form used locally). It is easier for a

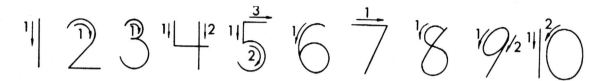

FIGURE 16–23 Printscript numerals.

graphical area may also be slightly different from those of another town, city, or state.

BEGINNING ATTEMPTS

In beginning attempts to write, children commonly grasp writing tools tightly and press down hard enough to tear the paper. With time and the mastery of small muscles, children's tense, unschooled muscles relax and forms and shapes start to resemble alphabet forms and recognizable shapes. Deep concentration and effort are observed. All attempts are recognized and appreciated by early childhood teachers as signs of the children's growing interest and ability.

Figure 16–24 arranges alphabet letters in manuscript print from the easiest for children to manage and form to the most difficult. **Orthographic awareness** is the ability to notice and use critical features of the graphic symbols in written language (Pinnell, 1999). Pinnell points out that children learn what makes a letter unique and that these features are often very finely drawn. The visual difference between the alphabet letters *n* and *m*, or *n* and *h* are subtle, but many preschoolers have no difficulty. Lyons (1999b) believes each child's knowledge is a very personal matter, with children finding their own ways of weaving understanding around a letter to help them remember it and reproduce it.

PLANNED ACTIVITIES—BASIC UNDERSTANDINGS

Most planned activities in this language arts area, and most unplanned child-adult exchanges during the school day, involve basic

1. I	14. V	27. Z	40. Y
2. o	15. c	28. t	41. d
3. L	16. x	29. B	42. R
4. O	17. T	30. Q	43. G
5. H	18. h	31. s	44. a
6. D	19. w	32. n	45. u
7. i	20. J	33. z	46. k
8. v	21. f	34. r	47. m
9. I	22. C	35. e	48. j
10. X	23. N	36. b	49. y
11. E	24. A	37. S	50. p
12. P	25. W	38. M	51. g
13. F	26. K	39. U	52. q

FIGURE 16–24 Listing of letters from easiest to form to most difficult.

understandings. Rules exist in this graphic art as they do in speech. Children form ideas about these rules.

Print concerns the use of graphic symbols that represent sounds and sound combinations. Symbols combine and form words and sentences in a prescribed grammatical order. Alphabet letters are spaced and are in uppercase and lowercase form. They are written and read from left to right across a page. Margins exist at beginnings and ends of lines, and lines go from the top to bottom of pages. Punctuation marks end sentences, and indentations separate paragraphs. It is amazing how many rules of printing interested children discover on their own and with teacher help before they enter kindergarten.

orthographic awareness — the ability to notice and use critical features of graphic symbols in written language.

DAILY INTERACTIONS AND TECHNIQUES

The techniques listed in this section are purposeful actions and verbalizations used by teachers in printscript instruction. The teacher uses a natural conversational style rather than a formal teaching tone.

Putting the children's names on their work is the most common daily use of printscript. The teacher asks the children whether they want their names on their work. Many young children feel their creations are their very own and may not want a name added. When a paper is lost because it has no name on it, children see the advantage of printing a name on belongings.

All names are printed in the upper left corner of the paper, if possible, or on the back if child requests. This is done to train the children to look at this spot as a preparation for reading and writing. Children's comments about their work can be jotted down at the bottom or on the back of their papers.

The teacher can be prepared to do this by having a dark crayon or felt-tip pen in a handy place or pocket. Dictation is written without major teacher editing or suggestions concerning the way it is said. The teacher can tell the child that the teacher will be writing down the child's ideas and then follow the child's word order as closely as possible. Some teachers prefer to print the statement, "Chou dictated these words to Mrs. Brownell on May 2, 2006," before or after the child's message. Most teachers would print the child's "mouses went in hole" as "mice went in the hole," which is minor editing. All teacher printing should be in printscript, using both uppercase and lowercase letters and proper punctuation.

When a child asks a teacher to print, the teacher stands behind the child and works over the child's shoulder (when possible). This allows the child to see the letters being formed in the correct position. If the teacher faces the child while printing, the child sees the letters upside down. Some teachers say the letter names as they print them.

Letters or names written for the child should be large enough for the child to distinguish the different forms—more than 1 inch high. This may seem large to an adult (Figure 16–25).

Some schools encourage teachers to print examples on lined paper if a child says, "Make an *a*" or "Write my name." Others suggest that teachers blend letter sounds as they print words. Many centers expect teachers to respond to the child's request through conversation and by searching for letters on alphabet charts. This encourages the child to make her own copy before the teacher automatically prints it.

Teacher techniques often depend on the circumstances of a particular situation and knowledge of the individual child. One technique common to all centers is supportive assistance and voiced appreciation of children's efforts. Teachers can rejoice with a young child over approximations of intent in writing, just as we do with a toddler who makes an imprecise attempt to say a new word.

Children may show their printing attempts to the teacher or point out the names of letters they know. A positive statement to the child is appropriate: "Yes, that is an *a*" or "I can see the *a, t,* and *p*" (as the teacher points to each), or "Marie, you did print the letters *a* and *t*."

With these comments, the teacher encourages and recognizes the child's efforts. Often, the child may have the wrong name or form for a letter. The teacher can react by saying, "It looks like an alphabet letter. Let's go look at our wall alphabet and see which one" or may simply say, "Look. You made a *w*."

Maryellen
Donald

FIGURE 16–25 Letters should be large enough for the child to see easily.

Atkins (1984) describes supportive assistance in the following way.

> ... children need ... adults to provide the tools needed for writing and the time and opportunity to use those tools. They need adults to ensure an atmosphere conducive to exploration and to good feelings about writing. They need adults to accept what is written as worthwhile, and to appreciate the work and effort that goes into learning to write. And, children especially need adults who understand that the errors they make are an important part of the learning process.

Encourage, welcome, and keep interest in print alive by providing attention. Children have many years ahead to perfect their skill; the most important thing at this early stage is that they are interested in the forms and are supplied with correct models and encouragement.

One technique is to have children who ask for letter forms trace over correct letter models or symbols. This can be done with crayons, felt-tip pens, or other writing tools. To explain the meaning of the word *trace,* the teacher gives the child a demonstration.

When reading charts or books to children, a teacher may move her hand across the page beneath words. This is done to emphasize the left-to-right direction in reading and writing and separations between words. Introducing authors' names periodically helps children realize that they also can create stories, and what they create can be written.

Proponents of Vygotskian theory Bodrova and Leong (1996) suggest the following teacher actions.

- Encourage children to write to communicate even if they scribble. Then write teacher notes about what the child says the writing means or print beneath the work.
- Revisit children's writing and reprocess their ideas. Talk about what they might add.
- Incorporate writing into play. Dramatic play situations might use writing. Acting out stories with peers will also encourage the use of language and writing.

ENVIRONMENTAL PRINT IN DAILY LIFE

A teacher of young children makes connections between print and daily classroom happenings. This is not difficult, but it does require teacher recognition and purposeful action. Print can be noticed starting with children's names and print on clothing, shoes, food, toys, and almost every object in the classroom, including light switches and faucet handles. Print is part of classroom life.

Children need to learn what print can do for them in satisfying personal needs. This makes print real. As Throne (1988) notes, "children become aware of print by using it for real and meaningful purposes when they dictate and write stories, make signs for the block area, read names on a job chart, write messages, look for EXIT signs, follow recipes, have conversations and discussions, or listen to stories." Children may need teacher assistance in recognizing the usefulness of written messages. Many instances of sending or reading print messages are possible during a school day. For example, because print often protects one's safety, there are many opportunities to discuss and point out words that serve this function.

Dramatic play themes that involve print and printing labels for dramatic play props are offered in Figure 16–26. Teachers are advised to not fill play settings with literacy props that "may shove aside" other playthings that children enjoy and prefer (Roskos & Christie, 2001).

Teachers look for functional activities such as

- making necessary lists of children's names with children. Example: Teacher creates a waiting list.
- making holiday or special occasion cards.
- making group murals and labeling parts at a later date. Example: Teacher uses color words or children's ideas (Jane says, "This looks like a cat.").

PLAY THEMES

Classroom Post Office

Suggested play items:

stamps (many come with magazine advertisements), old letters, envelopes, boxes to wrap for mailing, scale, canceling stamp, tape, string, play money, mailbag, mailbox with slots, alphabet strips, writing table, felt-tip pens, counter, postal-employee shirts, posters from post office, stamp-collector sheets, wet sponge, teacher-made chart that lists children by street address and zip codes, box with all children's names on printed individual strips, mailboxes for each child

Taco Stand

Suggested play items:

counter for customers, posted charts with prices and taco choices, play money, order pads, labeled baskets with colored paper taco items (including cheese, meat, lettuce, salsa, sour cream, avocado, shredded chicken, and onions), customer tables, trays, bell to ring for service, folded cards with numbers, receipt book for ordered tacos, plastic glasses and pitchers, cash register, napkins, tablecloth, plastic flowers in plastic vase, cook's jacket, waiter/waitress aprons, busperson suit and cleaning supplies, taped ethnic music, plastic utensils, soft pencils or felt-tip pens, line with clothespins to hang orders, paper plates

A hamburger stand or pizza parlor are other possibilities.

Grocery Shopping

Suggested items:

shopping-list paper, bookcase, pencils or felt-tip pens, chart with cut magazine pictures or labels from canned goods or vegetables labeled in print by teacher for children to copy if they desire, empty food cartons and cans, plastic food, shopping cart, purse and wallet, play money, brown bags, cash register on box, dress-up clothes for customers and store clerks

Letter-Writing Classroom Center
(for writing to relatives and friends)

PRINT-AWARENESS ACTIVITIES

Classroom Newspaper

Make a class newspaper. Print children's dictated news or creative language after sharing a local paper with them. Child drawings on ditto master can be duplicated. Add teacher and parent news, poems, captions, drawings, and so forth. Some children may wish to print their own messages. These may range from scribble to recognizable forms and words.

T-Shirt Autograph Day

Each parent is asked to bring an old T-shirt (any size) to school for T-shirt autograph day. Permanent felt markers are used by children under teacher supervision. (Washable markers can also be used, but teachers must iron or put T-shirts in a clothes dryer for 5 minutes on a hot setting.) T-shirt forms are necessary and can be made of cardboard. Material must be stretched over a form so marks can be added easily. It is a good idea to have children wear plastic paint aprons to protect clothing from permanent markers. Children are free to autograph shirts in any manner they please. A display of T-shirts with writing usually prompts some children to add letters to their own shirts. Most teachers own or can borrow T-shirts with writing.

FIGURE 16–26 Dramatic play themes and activities that promote print awareness and use.

- writing what-we-found-out activities. This can be done with many discovery experiences. Example: What floats, and what does not?

- classifying experiences. Example: "Shoes Are Different"—Teacher elicits from the group the kinds of shoes children see others wearing, then lists the names.

RED SHOES	SHOES WITH LACES	SANDALS
Tony	Becky	Micki
Tonelle	Trent	Nekolla
Star	Tony	Blair
DeShawn	Anna	Tomar

- sharing the lunch or snack menu by discussing printed words on a chart or chalkboard.

- making classroom news announcements on a large sheet of paper posted at children's eye level. Examples follow:

Enrico moved to a new apartment.

Mrs. Quan is on a trip to Chicago.

Lia's cat had three kittens.

Ali is our new friend's name.

Blue flowers are blooming on the patio.

Where is our Elmo doll hiding?

Alonzo is home sick today.

- using children's names. See the Activities section at the end of this chapter.

WRITING TABLE OR AREA

Many classrooms include a writing table or area for children's daily free-choice exploration. Stocked with different paper types, a variety of writing instruments, alphabet letter stencils, letter stamps, and letter model displays, this type of setup makes daily access available and inviting. However, just providing a writing center is not enough. Teachers need to be in it daily, as motivators and resources. Some writing areas have considerable use. In other classrooms, teachers spend little or no time there

(Smith, 2001). Whether a writing center appeals to children, grabs children's attention, and is child-functional depends on the ingenuity of teachers.

Respecting "I'll Do It My Way!"

Recognizing that children need time as well as opportunity, teachers notice individual children involve themselves in classroom literacy events based on their maturity and interest. When a child senses a reason and develops a personal interest in writing or reading, she acts on her own timetable. There seems to exist at this point a desire to proceed her own way, retaining ownership for early literacy behaviors. The child who examines a classroom alphabet chart and then copies letter forms may choose to share her marks with other children and avoid the teacher. Another child the same age may prefer to consult the teacher. Other children may ask, "What's this say?" or "What's this called?" In all situations, teachers aim to preserve and promote each child's idea of her own competency as a writer or reader.

LEFT-HANDED CHILDREN

Left-handedness or right-handedness occurs as the child's nervous system matures. Preschool teachers notice hand preferences when children use writing tools. Some children seem to switch between hands as though hand preference has not been established. Most left-handers uses their right hands more often than right-handers use their left hands. Writing surfaces in preschools should accommodate all children, and both right-handed and left-handed scissors should be available.

Teachers should accept hand preference without attempting to change or even point out a natural choice. Seating left-handed children at the ends of tables (when possible) during activities or making sure left-handers are not crowded against right-handers is a prudent course of action.

TEACHER PRACTICE

Printscript should come automatically to the teacher. Practice is in order if one cannot easily and correctly print the entire alphabet in both uppercase and lowercase.

LINED PAPER

Some children acquire the necessary motor control and can use lined, printed paper (Figure 16–27), so some programs provide it.

Lines can easily be drawn on a chalkboard by the teacher. This provides a large working surface and an opportunity for children to make large-size letters.

CHART IDEAS

Printscript can be added to playrooms by posting charts that have been made by the teacher. Charts can be designed to encourage the child's active involvement. Pockets, parts that move, or pieces that can be added or removed add extra interest. Charts made on heavy chart board or cardboard last longer. Clear contact paper can be used to seal the surface. Some ideas for charts include:

◆ experience charts (Figure 16–28).
◆ color or number charts.

The Picnic
We had lunch
in the park.
We sat
on the grass.

FIGURE 16–28 Experience chart.

◆ large clock with movable hands.
◆ chart showing the four seasons.
◆ picture story sequence charts.
◆ calendars.
◆ room task charts ("helpers chart").
◆ texture charts (for children to feel).
◆ poetry charts (Figure 16–29).
◆ recipe charts using step-by-step illustrations.
◆ classification or matching-concepts charts.
◆ birthday charts.
◆ height and weight charts.
◆ alphabet charts.
◆ rebus charts (Figure 16–30).

Cromwell (1980) suggests making "key word" charts. Key words can be words inspired by a picture-book title, character, and so forth; words solicited from children; or words taken from some classroom event or happening. The chosen word is printed by the teacher at the top of a chart. The teacher then asks a small group, "When I say this word, what do you think of?"

FIGURE 16–27 Example of a five-year-old's printing accompanying art.

FIGURE 16-29 Poetry chart.

Mix a pancake
Stir a pancake
Pop it in a pan,
Fry the pancake,
Toss the pancake,
Catch it
If you can!

FIGURE 16-30 Rebus chart.

or "Salt and pepper go together. We see them in shakers sitting on the kitchen table. What goes with [key word]?" or "Tree is the word at the top of our chart. What can we say about the trees in our play yard?" or some such leading question. Children's offered answers are put below the key word on the chart. This activity suits some older four-year-olds, especially those asking, "What does this say?" while pointing to text.

Charts of songs or rhymes in the native languages of attending children have been used successfully in many classrooms. Parent volunteer translators are often pleased to help put new or favorite classics into their native tongue. *Uno, Dos, Tres Inditos,* a Spanish version of *Ten*

Little Indians, has been frequently enjoyed and learned quickly.

A technique adopted by Williams (1997) involves using a color-code system when recording individual child contributions to a group dictated chart.

I often record each child's question (comment) in a different color or put the child's name beside it so the child can come back and find what he/she contributed.

Think of all the charts that can include a child's choice, vote, or decision! These charts are limitless. A child can indicate her individual selection under the diverse headings by making a mark, printing her name, using a rubber stamp and ink pad, or moving her printed name to a basket or pasting it onto the chart as shown in Figure 16–31.

It is easy to see that placing pictures alongside print makes the task of choosing easier. Simple pictures drawn by the teacher work well. The best charts relate to classroom themes or happenings.

In making a chart, first draw sketches of the way words and pictures could be arranged. With a yardstick, lightly draw on guidelines with a pencil or use a chart liner (see Activities section). Then, add printscript words with a felt-tip pen or dark crayon. Magazines, old elementary school workbooks, old children's books, and photographs are good sources for pictures on charts. Brads or paper fasteners can be used for movable parts. Book pockets or heavy envelopes provide a storage place for items to be added later to the chart.

EXPERIENCE CHARTS AND STORIES

The purpose of these charts is to have children recognize that spoken words can be put in written form.

Materials

large paper sheets (newsprint)

felt-tip pen or black crayon

Activity

After an interesting activity, such as a field trip, visit by a special speaker, party, celebration, or cooking experience, the teacher can suggest that a story be written about the experience. A large sheet of paper or chart sheet is hung within the children's view, and the children dic-

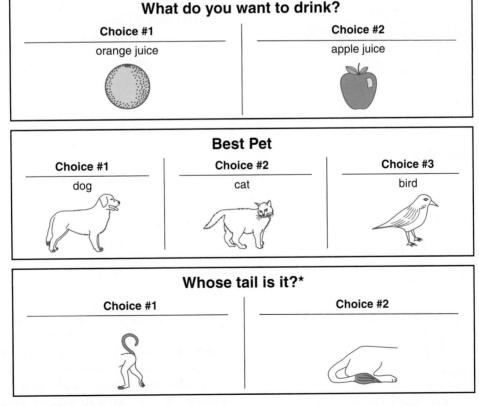

FIGURE 16–31 Examples of charts. *Note: Teacher writes child's answer, reads it aloud, and later displays a complete animal drawing to discuss. Example: "Tia says a dog."

tate what happened. The teacher prints on the sheet, helping children sort out what happened first, next, and last.

Figures 16–32 and 16–33 show examples of other word and picture charts.

Chart Stands

Homemade chart stands can be made by teachers. Commercial chart holders, chart stands, chart rings, and wing clamps are sold at school-supply stores. Teachers using charts daily will attest to preferring commercially manufactured chart stands because of their mobility and stability.

Letter Patterns

Commercially made letter patterns or teacher-made sets are useful devices that can be traced for teacher use in game making or

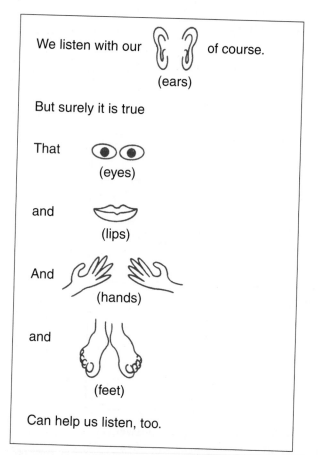

FIGURE 16–32 Rebus listening chart.

1 line is a flagpole

2 lines a mountain make

3 lines form a tiny chair

And 4 a garden rake.

5 lines make a little house

And 6 a ladder tall.

7 lines form a TV antenna

And 8 a puppy small.

9 lines make a playground swing

And with 10 lines you can make most anything!

FIGURE 16–33 A chart using line drawings.

for wall displays. Made of sturdy card stock or oak tag paper, they can be quickly and easily traced. See the Activities section for letter pattern samples.

CHART BOOKS

A number of books called chart books, big books, or easel books are in print. These giant books are poster size and easily capture children's attention. The print stands out and cannot be missed. Creative teachers have produced their own versions with the help of overhead projectors that enlarge smaller artwork. Chart paper or poster board is used. Commercial big books are plentiful and sell at book stores and teacher-supply stores.

Throne (1988), a kindergarten teacher, points out the benefit of using big books and charts.

> . . . these shared experiences bring the benefits of the bedtime story situation into the classroom because the large, clear print allows the whole class to see the text as we read the story together.

Although preschools prefer to use smaller child groups, Throne's comments concerning large, clear print and group sharing appeal to teachers interested in promoting print awareness.

GENERATING STORY SENTENCES

Story sentence activities are similar to chart activities. A child or a small group of children becomes an author. After a classroom activity or experience, the teacher encourages generating a story (a written sentence). The activity is child-centered thereafter, with the teacher printing what the child or group suggests. The teacher can use a hand-wide space between words to emphasize the end of one word and spacing between words, and may talk about letters or letter sounds found at the beginning or end of children's names. It is not unusual for all children in a four-year-old group to recognize all the names of other students in their class. Individual children's ideas and contributions are accepted, appreciated, and recognized by the teacher, and generated sentences are read and reread with the group. Long strips of chart paper or rolled paper can be used. Story sentences are posted at children's eye level.

See the Activities section and the Online Companion™ for additional teacher-created printscript activity ideas.

Interactive and Scaffolded Writing

Interactive, or *shared*, **writing** times take place in many kindergartens and first-grade classrooms. They are described here to ac-

quaint preschool practitioners with what lies ahead and what might be adapted, modified, or individualized for the few individual children who read (not memorize) simple text in picture books and write messages during their preschool years.

This kindergarten strategy is receiving an increased amount of use and attention from educators. McCarrier, Pinnell, and Fountas (2000) define interactive writing as an instructional context in which a teacher shares a pen—literally and figuratively—with a group of children as they collaboratively compose and construct a written message. Children participate in every element of the writing process—deciding on a topic, thinking about the general scope and form of the writing, determining the specific text to write, and writing it word by word, letter by letter. Rereading, revising, and proofreading take place during and after the experience and usually lead to a child's (or children's) reading words, phrases, sentences, and the whole of what has been written.

Using the interactive writing process, a teacher focuses attention on letter sounds, names, forms, left-to-right and top-to-bottom progression, spaces between words, capitalization, punctuation, and spelling. McCarrier, Pinnell, and Fountas (2000) believe interactive writing is an instructional strategy that works well for children of all linguistic backgrounds.

Looking at a skilled kindergarten or first-grade child composing and constructing a message, one finds the child must think about and keep in mind the message, choose a first word, decide where to place it on the paper, consider what alphabet letter she knows makes the wanted sound, remember how the letter is formed, manually form it, decide if there are other sounds and other letters needed, know when the word ends, and know a space is needed before the next word. Immediately, an early childhood educator can see foundational understandings concerning writing must have been well learned.

---

interactive writing — (1) an instructional strategy popular in American kindergartens; (2) a process involving a teacher who verbally stretches each word so that the child (children) can distinguish sounds and letters. Also known as shared writing.

PARENT COMMUNICATION

A conversation with or note to the parents of a child who has asked about or started printing can include the following.

◆ The teacher has noticed the child's interest in printing alphabet letters, numerals, and/or words.

◆ The teacher is including a printscript and numeral guide for parents who wish to show their children the letter forms at home.

◆ The early childhood center encourages printing attempts but does not try to teach printscript to every child. Many children are not interested, and others would find it too difficult at their present developmental level.

◆ A parent can help by having paper and writing tools for the child at home and by noticing and giving attention to the child when she comes to the parent with written letters.

◆ Children who start printing early often write letters and numerals in their paintings. The printing may be backward, upside down, or sideways; this is to be expected. (Many parents worry unnecessarily when this is noticed.)

Parents also may need an explanation concerning child-dictated papers or child printing, which teachers accept rather than edit or correct.

Centers plan parent meetings for joint discussion of the appropriateness of printing instruction during preschool years. If the center's position is clear, staff members will be able to give articulate answers concerning the center's programming. Most parents are responsive when teachers explain to them that early child dictation is written with only minor editing, respecting early attempts. As children become more skilled, more teacher corrective help is offered. The assurance teachers give parents that they will provide both basic experiences and opportunities on an individual basis most often satisfies the parents' need to know that the school cares about each child's progress.

SUMMARY

The alphabet and printed words are part of preschool life. A center's goals rarely include teaching all attending children to print, but instead attempt to offer a print-rich environment. For the great majority of preschool children attending child centers, sit-down practice of letter forms is developmentally inappropriate. Some preschool children, on the other hand, will attempt repeatedly to form alphabet letters and practice writing them on their own or with the teacher's supportive guidance. However, many children will show beginning interest in the uses of print and print in books.

Numerals are also interesting to young children. These symbols appear daily at school, at home, and in the neighborhood.

The ability to print depends on the child's

◆ muscle control.

◆ skill in recognizing symbols.

◆ ability to note the placement of lines in a symbol.

Printscript is used in preschool, kindergarten, and first grade. Letters are formed with lines and circles in uppercase and lowercase symbols.

Children are ready for printing at different ages. They learn alphabet letters at different rates. Printscript is used for display and other activities at early childhood centers.

Equipment and settings for giving children an opportunity to explore printing are available in a childhood center. Materials are arranged within reach. Printing seen on wall displays and charts helps motivate interest.

Printscript is used in a variety of ways. The most common is in planned activities and labeling artwork. A name or sentence should start in the upper left corner and move toward the right.

New teachers practice that so that good print models are supplied. It is also important to encourage children and to recognize their efforts, even if they cannot make correct forms.

Parents should be alerted to children's printing attempts and to the center's policy and practices concerning this language arts skill.

ADDITIONAL RESOURCES

Readings

Bloom, C. A. (1997). *Playing with print: Fostering emergent literacy*. Glenview, IL: Good Year Books.

Collins, J. L. (1998). *Strategies for struggling writers*. New York: Guilford.

Dufflemeyer, F. A. (2002). Alphabet activities on the Internet. *The Reading Teacher, 55*, 631–635.

Johnson, P. (1997). *Pictures and words together: Children illustrating and writing their own books*. Portsmouth, NH: Heinemann.

Jones, E., & Villarino, G. (1994, January). What goes upon classroom walls—and why? *Young Children, 49*(2), 38–40.

Prior, J., & Gerard, M. R. (2004). *Environmental print in the classroom*. Newark, DE: International Reading Association.

Roskos, K., & Christie, J. (2001, May). On not pushing too hard: A few cautionary remarks about linking literacy and play. Young Children, 56(3), 64–66.

Strickland, D. S., & Schickedanz, J. A. (2004). *Learning about print in preschool*. Newark, DE: International Reading Association.

Thurber, D. N., & Jordan, D. R. (1987). *D'Nealian handwriting. Teachers Edition*. Glenview, IL: Scott, Foresman and Company.

U.S. Department of Health and Human Services. (2003). *The Head Start path to positive child outcomes* [The Head Start Outcomes Framework]. Retrieved May 21, 2004, from http://www.hsnrc.org/CDI/outcontent.cfm

Children's Books with Writing Themes

Ahlberg, J., & Ahlberg, A. (1986). *The jolly postman*. Waltham, MA: Little, Brown & Co. (Letter writing.)

de Groat, D. (1996). *Roses are pink, your feet really stink*. New York: HarperCollins. (Writing or dictating Valentine rhymes.)

de Paola, T. (1978). *Pancakes for breakfast*. New York: Harcourt Brace Jovanovich. (Recipes.)

Numeroff, L. (1991). *If you give a moose a muffin*. New York: HarperCollins. (Recipes.)

Alphabet Books

Catalanotto, P. (2002). *Matthew A. B. C.* New York: Atheneum. (A child's adventures.)

Cleary, B. (1998). *The hullabaloo A-B-C*. Boston: Morrow Junior Books. (Alphabet experiences through farm noises explored by three children.)

Isadora, R. (1999). *ABC pop!* New York: Viking Press. (A clever introduction of alphabet letters.)

Lester, A. (1998). *Alice and Aldo*. Boston: Houghton Mifflin. (Alphabet letters A to Z introduced through Alice's chronological daily activities [like breakfast in bed].)

Marzollo, J. (2000). *I spy little letters*. New York: Scholastic. (Finding letter shapes.)

Paul, A. (1999). *Everything to spend the night from A to Z*. New York: DK Publishing, Co. (The overnight bag brought for an overnight stay with grandpa yields A to Z objects.)

Satin, A. S. (2004). *Mrs. McTats and her house full of cats*. New York: Simon & Schuster. (Alphabet cats.)

HELPFUL WEB SITES

America Writes for Kids
http://usawrites4kids.drury.edu
Child writers are encouraged.

KidSource Online
http://www.kidsource.com
Helping your child write.

National Association for the Education of Young Children
http://www.naeyc.org
Select position statements on reading and writing.

SIL International
http://www.sil.org
Search invented spelling topics.

Putting together a "birthday" gift book is an activity idea that combines children's art and children's dictated messages. It is definitely a print-awareness activity. Critical thinking quotes are provided. In a discussion forum, students are asked to brainstorm and create activities that promote children's concepts about the printed text in picture books.

STUDENT ACTIVITIES

1. Observe a morning program for four-year-olds. Cite as many examples as possible of adults' use of written communication.

2. Expand the following statement: Practicing alphabet letter formation when a teacher requests it could result in the child's . . .

3. Without turning back to review the printed alphabet guide given in this chapter, print the alphabet in both uppercase and lowercase letters in printscript. Obtain a printscript alphabet from the nearest public school. With a red crayon or pen, circle letters that differ (even slightly) from your attempted alphabet. Print all letters you circled on the remaining lines using proper form.

4. Observe a preschool program. Notice and list all printscript forms found in the playroom that are within the children's view. Report the findings to classmates.

5. Secure some examples of young children's attempts to make letters and numerals in their drawings. What do you notice about the symbols? Are the lines large, small, slanted, or straight? Are capitals or small letters used? What else do you notice?

6. Take tracing paper to a four-year-old's classroom. Trace examples of child printing (writing) and bring to your next class period. (Talk to your instructor first concerning making school visits and appointments.)

7. Use the following checklist to observe a four- or five-year-old child. Interview the child's teacher for items you were unable to determine. (*Note:* Make sure the teacher knows that this is not a test but an instrument to make you aware of children's emerging abilities.)

Checklist of Print Interest and Understandings

Rate each item as follows. Y = Most of the time
S = Sometimes
H = Has not attempted as yet
U = Unable to determine

The child:

_____ sits through a book reading and enjoys it.

_____ asks for a book's rereading.

_____ "reads" to another parts or lines of a book from memory.

_____ shows an interest in alphabet letters.

_____ shows an interest in books or environmental print.

_____ reads children's name tags or signs.

_____ puts alphabet letters in artwork.

_____ knows when words are skipped in favorite books.

_____ plays with marking tools.

_____ shares written letters or words with others.

_____ points to print in the work of others.

_____ wants name on work.

_____ wants to write own name on work.

_____ knows that print says something.

_____ produces a row of symbols.

_____ attempts to copy symbols, letters, or words.

_____ reads symbols she has written.

_____ invents spellings.

_____ discusses a use of print.

_____ knows print can be read.

_____ wants her talk written down.

_____ recognizes individual alphabet letters.

_____ recognizes words that start with the same letter.

_____ can read some environmental signs.

_____ follows along in chart activities.

_____ looks at books while alone.

_____ has an active interest in something else that then gives a low priority to literary activities.

_____ is best described by which of the following statements?
   a. has yet to develop an interest in print
   b. is developing a possible interest
   c. has about the same degree of interest as others her age
   d. has a fairly strong interest
   e. has a continual interest that has led to experimentation and printing attempts
   f. is very interested in some other area that takes up her time and energy
   g. prints almost daily and has invented spellings or spells many words correctly

8. Watch the children's use of crayons or other writing tools. Take notes. Make observations about the following.
   a. time spent with marking tools
   b. manner used (for example, how do the children hold the crayons?)
   c. whether they have good control of both paper and marking tool

9. Role-play with peers the following scenario.

   Arianna's dad meets her preschool teacher in the hallway and says, "How come you don't correct Arianna's papers? Look at these I'm taking home today. Don't you have time to print *car* right? How is she going to learn?"

10. Make chart paper or tag board patterns for the full uppercase and lowercase alphabet. Teacher-supply stores and practicing teachers are good resources for letter models.

CHAPTER REVIEW

A. Select the correct answer. Most questions have more than one answer.

1. Child care programs
   a. teach all children to print.
   b. try to teach correct printscript form.
   c. all teach the same printscript form.
   d. help children with printing attempts.

2. Small-muscle control
   a. comes after large-muscle control.
   b. depends on many factors.
   c. is difficult for some preschoolers.
   d. is the only thing involved in learning to print.

3. If drawings have upside-down alphabet letters, teachers should
   a. immediately begin printing lessons.
   b. know that the child may be interested in activities with printed forms.
   c. quickly tell the child that the letters are upside down.
   d. worry about the child's ability to form the letters perfectly.

4. A child's readiness to print may depend on her
   a. ability to gather information from her senses.
   b. knowledge that letters are formed by placing lines.
   c. home and family.
   d. feelings for the teacher.

B. Answer the following questions.

1. What are some possible reasons that children ages two to five years may start to print?
2. What should teachers consider about the printscript form they use?
3. Muscle control is only part of learning to write. What other factors affect readiness for written communication?
4. When a child says, "Is this M?" how should one reply?
5. If a child says a *b* is an *f,* what might a teacher say?

C. Describe a print-rich classroom.

D. Answer the following questions.

1. If a child goes to a teacher to show letters she has drawn, how should the teacher react?
2. If two children are arguing over the name of a letter, how should the teacher handle the situation?
3. List three ways a teacher can use printscript during the school day.

E. Referring to Figure 16–34, list all of the things the teacher might have done to encourage the children's attempts.

F. Select the correct answers. All have more than one answer.

1. When a child's first name is to be printed on her work, it should be
   a. in the center on top.
   b. in the upper right corner.

514

FIGURE 16–34

c. in the upper left corner.

d. done with an uppercase first letter and then lowercase letters.

2. The size of the printscript used with young children
   a. does not really matter.
   b. should be large enough to see, at least 1 inch.
   c. can be of any size.
   d. should be at least 2 inches high.

3. The teacher who does not know how to form printscript letters can
   a. practice.
   b. use an individual style.
   c. get a copy from an elementary school.
   d. write instead.

G. A note to the parents of a child who is interested in learning to print should include what kind of information? State four points that should be included.

ANOTHER CHART IDEA

NAME A PART CHART

Enlarge a figure of a face, animal, house, car, bird, bike, or any familiar object that has parts or features children can name. (Draw freehand or use an overhead projector to enlarge a small drawing.) After introducing the chart, discuss and have the children identify what is pictured or a part of what is pictured. Make a printscript label or strip following chil-dren's suggestions. Children can glue strips or labels on the chart. Glue sticks work well, or children can apply glue to back of the label or strip. Children sometimes creatively think up silly names and that is part of the fun. At other times, they may discuss seriously what they believe are the correct labeling words. In a variation of this activity, the teacher draws an outline and parts are drawn as they are named by children.

CHART LINER INSTRUCTIONS

INSTRUCTIONS TO MAKE A CHART LINER

Cut a piece of Masonite® 12" by 36". Make 7 sawcuts 1½" apart, beginning and ending 1½" from either end. Then glue or nail 1½" square pieces of wood 12" long to each end.

Note: A teacher-made chart liner is a useful device that helps teachers make evenly spaced guidelines on charts that use lines of print. By placing the chart liner over chart paper, quick guidelines are accomplished by inserting a sharp pencil in sawcut slots.

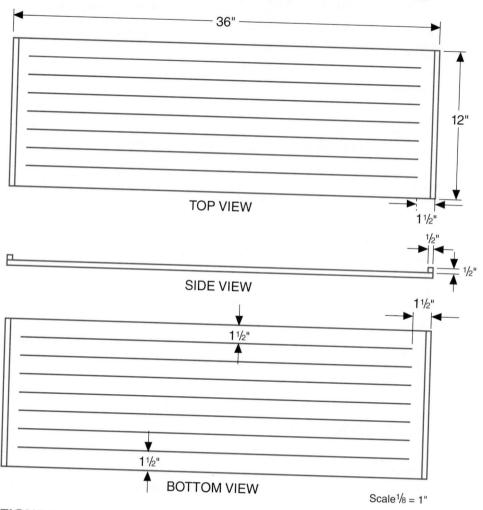

FIGURE 16–35 Making a chart liner.

LETTER PATTERN SAMPLES

ABCDEF
GHIJKL
MNOPQ
RSTUV
WXYZ

FIGURE 16–36 Letter patterns. Note: Letters will need to be enlarged for display in the classroom. *(continued)*

517

abcdef
ghijkl
mnopq
rstuv
wxyz

FIGURE 16–36 *(continued)*

PRINTSCRIPT ACTIVITIES

These were based on (1) a particular group of enrolled children, (2) an individual child's interest, or (3) a classroom's project or theme study. Some suit younger preschoolers; others were enjoyed by older preschoolers who had developed considerable interest in print and print form. Activities suggested represent a variety of skill levels and do not appear in a simple-to-complex order.

Clay-on Patterns

These patterns can be used to enhance small, manipulative-muscle use and tracing skills.

Materials
clay
contact-covered cardboard sheets with patterns (Figure 16–37)

Activity. Child rolls and forms clay over the cardboard patterns.

Commercial Names and Trademarks

Some children delight in reading their favorite brand names. Many trademarks and product logos have appeared on television, in magazines, in fast-food restaurants, or on products seen in the home. It is surprising how familiar children are with this type of print.

Materials
scissors
cardboard
contact paper (optional)

Use commercial print cut from ads or packaging of home products. Mount on stiff paper or cardboard. Get as close to the color and original letter type as possible. Collect pictures of the product, toy, food, drink, cereal, and so on, the print represents. Mount on cardboard or stiff paper. Cover with clear contact paper.

Activity. Child pairs print with picture. Child may want to "read" print labels to adult or another child.

Connecting Dots

The dot patterns for this activity can be made quickly by the teacher on paper or chalkboard and used as a free-play choice. The purpose of this activity is to enhance small-muscle use and children's skills in forming and recognizing symbols.

Materials
paper
writing tools (or chalkboard and chalk)

Activity. Dots are connected to form symbols (Figure 16–38).

Sorting Symbols

This activity enhances small-muscle use and children's skills discriminating symbol differences.

Materials
paper
writing tool
scissors
paste

FIGURE 16–37 Patterns.

FIGURE 16–38 Connecting-dots activity.

519

Activity. After the teacher cuts the symbols in squares from sheets, the children are asked to mix them all together and then find the ones that are the same to paste onto another sheet of paper.

Variation. The teacher can make a cardboard set of symbols that can be sorted by children as a table game (Figure 16–39).

Alphabet Song Slowly

The rhyming song is an easy and fun way for children to recognize letter names. Sing it slowly, exposing each letter as it is named.

Materials
a long printscript alphabet line (Figure 16–40)

Song
ABCDEFG
HIJKLMNOP
QRS and TUV
WX and Y and Z.
Now I've said my ABCs,
Tell me what you think of me.

Activity. Children sing the song while one child or the teacher touches the corresponding letter on the alphabet line. The teacher can ask the group to sing slowly or quickly, in a whisper or a loud voice, or in a high or low voice.

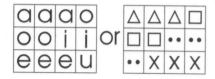

FIGURE 16–39 Symbol card for sorting game.

Gift Wrap

Children are given the opportunity to creatively wrap gifts while learning the usefulness of print.

Materials
empty boxes
wrapping paper
scissors
decorative stickers
thin-line markers
list that includes the names of all in the class (including teachers)
stamps
masking tape
card strips or paper strips preprinted with "To" and "From"
small inexpensive gift items or clay child-made objects

Activity. Children wrap the gifts in boxes with wrapping paper and dictate messages or try to write names on paper or card strips.

Secret Words

This activity promotes visual discrimination and children's recognition of symbols.

Materials
white crayon
white paper
water colors
brush

Activity. The teacher uses white crayon to write a symbol or word on white paper. The crayon should be thickly applied. The teacher demonstrates how the symbol appears when water color is painted over the whole paper. The children can guess the shape names.

Aa	Bb	Cc	Dd	Ee	Ff	Gg	Hh	Ii	Jj

FIGURE 16–40 Printscript alphabet line.

Sticker Pictures

The children are shown the relationship between objects and words.

Materials
stickers
paper strips
felt markers

Activity. The teacher has each child choose a sticker for her paper strip. The child names the sticker, and if the child desires, the teacher writes the name of the sticker on back of the strip. The children can then decorate the sticker strips.

Label Fun

The children recognize the print word forms for classroom objects.

Materials
press-on labels (large size)
felt marker

Activity. Each child is given 5 to 10 labels and told to choose items on the child's body or in the room on which she will stick word labels. Child is told to stick labels on something that has not been labeled by another. Teacher prints child's dictated word(s).

Alphabet Walk

This is another group activity to promote children's recognition of alphabet letters.

Materials
large newsprint art paper
felt marker or dark crayon
masking tape

Activity. The teacher makes giant letters on art paper, one letter per sheet. The children are told that the teacher is going to place giant letters around the room. Have two children choose one friend to walk to the letter A, which teacher points out to them. Teacher selects another child to think of a way, besides walking, that the four children can move to the second letter. The teacher can give suggestions like crawling, hopping, tiptoeing, walking like an elephant, and so forth. Children clap for first four, and another four are selected and directed to walk to another letter.

Find Your Shoe

This group activity shows the usefulness of print.

Materials
press-on labels
marking pen

Activity. The children are asked to take off their shoes and put them in front of them. The teacher asks what will happen to the shoes if everyone puts the shoes in one pile and the teacher mixes up the pile. The teacher introduces the idea that shoes would be easier to find if the children's names were added to each shoe by putting a press-on label on the inner sole. Labels preprinted with the child's name are given to each child. The child puts the labels on her shoes. The shoes go in a pile, which the teacher mixes. Each child describes her shoes to a friend and asks the friend to find the shoes. Two or three friends look in the pile for the shoes at a time.

Alphabet Macaroni Prints

This activity promotes shape discrimination and small-muscle activity.

Materials
alphabet soup macaroni (sand, rice, or salt
    can also be used)
glue and brushes
paper
felt-tip pen

Activity. Each child traces her name or a shape by painting over lines with thinned white glue. The macaroni is then spooned over the glue. When the glue is dry, shake the loose macaroni into a container. The result will be raised, textured letters (Figure 16–41). The teacher should demonstrate this process.

ABC "Paste-on" Group Wall Poster

Small-muscle use and symbol recognition are enhanced.

Materials
alphabet letters or words cut or torn from magazines or newspapers
large-size poster paper or chart paper

FIGURE 16–41 Alphabet macaroni pictures.

Activity. A montage effect is created by having children paste letters where they choose on a piece of paper. During a period of 1 week, the children can return to the work and paste on more letters. At a group time, children are asked to point to three letters or words (or phrases) that they wish the teacher to read.

Alphabet Eaters

Large-muscle use and visual discrimination are enhanced.

Materials
cards with printscript alphabet letters (small enough to be slipped into animal's mouth)
sturdy boxes on which animal heads and alphabet strips are glued (holes are cut in the opposite sides of boxes so that children can reach in for cards)

Activity. A child selects a card and "feeds" it to the animal that has a similar alphabet letter on the strip under its mouth (Figure 16–42).

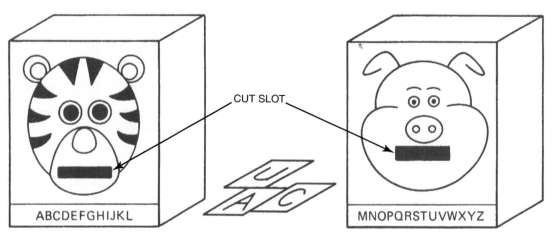

FIGURE 16–42 Alphabet "eaters" and cards.

Footprint Alphabet Walk

This activity promotes large-muscle use and symbol recognition.

Materials

large cardboard (or cloth) on which 26 footprints have been traced

cardboard footprint cutouts each with a printscript alphabet letter (three sets can be made—lowercase, uppercase, and numerals, if desired), covered with clear contact paper or made from plasticlike material.

Activity. Children place cutout footprints over footprint of the correct letter (Figure 16–43).

Tracers

Tracers can be used over and over again. Waxy crayons or felt markers wipe off with a soft cloth. They can be used to help children recognize and discriminate among symbols and enhance small-muscle coordination.

Materials

acetate or clear vinyl sheets
cardboard
scissors
strapping or masking tape
paper
felt-tip pen

Construction. Attach acetate to cardboard, leaving one side open to form a pocket. Make letter or word guide sheets. Simple pictures can also be used (Figure 16–44).

Activity. A child or the teacher selects a sheet and slips it into the tracer pocket. A wax crayon or marker is used by the child to trace the guide sheet. A soft cloth erases the crayon or marker.

DRAWING ACTIVITIES

Words on Drawings

In this labeling activity, children select words that can be added to their drawings.

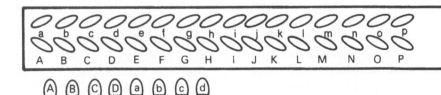

FIGURE 16–43 Footprint alphabet walk.

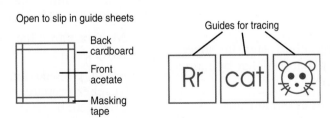

FIGURE 16–44 Tracers.

Materials

felt-tip pen or crayons

Activity. The teacher asks each child individually whether words can be added to her painting, drawing, or illustration. Make sure the child realizes that the teacher is going to write on the drawing. It is a good idea to show the child what has been done to another child's picture beforehand. Most children will want words added, but some will not. It is best to limit this activity to the children who are making symbols of faces, figures, houses, and so forth, in their work. Younger children might not be able to decide what to have written on their work when asked, "Would you like me to put a word name on something you've drawn in your picture?"

Rebus Stories

Teachers can use drawings or photographs to encourage child participation during storytelling time. At a crucial point in the story, the teacher pauses and holds up a picture, and the children guess the next word in the story. Teachers can name the picture and resume the story if the children have not guessed the word. Any guess that is a close approximation is accepted; for example, "It is a truck, Josh, a fire truck." The rebus story in Figure 16–45 is an example of teacher authorship. Many additional teacher-created rebus stories are possible.

Activity Ideas Using Children's Names
Preschool

◆ Use a morning child sign-in sheet. Give choice of placing sticker by name or printing name.

◆ Sing name games at circle time.

> *Mara's name starts with M, starts with M, starts with M, (repeat), and she is sitting next to Elizabeth.*

(To the tune of "Mary had a Little Lamb.")

◆ Make name tags with raised letters. Use white glue.

> Soak thick yarn in glue and place over letters, or pour sand over the glue painted-on letters while it is still wet. "Can you feel the letters in your name? Here's a 'A' ; It comes first," and so on.

◆ Find and circle the children's names on a chart or chalkboard.

◆ Paint oversized cutout letters of the children's names.

◆ Use an ink stamp set of alphabet letters to stamp their names.

◆ Find and match name cards.

◆ Have children find their place at a table that has name place mats.

◆ Play the name bag game. The cutout letters of the children's names are put in a bag. The children decide the order in which to paste them. Preparation includes making cutout letters for each child and putting them in individual brown bags.

◆ Shake materials on letters. Children use a glue stick or liquid white glue to trace letter shapes and then sprinkle on hole-punch confetti circles or another similar fine-grained material.

◆ Have children place colored letter cutouts on waxpaper. Teacher covers with a sheet of waxpaper the same size and irons with a warm iron. They are displayed on windows.

◆ Make name necklaces. Use hole-punched colored discs.

◆ Make a name hat and paste on cutout letters.

◆ Make pancake letters at snack time. Teacher prepares and bakes while children watch.

◆ Create a teacher-made personalized name book. Polarized photos are added. Child dictates captions.

DUCK AND BEAR TAKE A TRIP

This is and this is his friend .

 cried one day and said, "Let's take a vacation!" had not

learned to fly. "I get tired walking," said . "Let's ask

wise old how we can take a trip when a won't walk

and a can't fly." Wise old  said, "That's not a problem.

Both of you can ride your to the airport. Buy a ticket

FIGURE 16–45 This rebus story, created by a teacher, uses computer-generated graphics. *(continued)*

- Line up printed letter cars and let them roll down a block incline. Children choose letters to roll.
- Have children find their names somewhere in the room. Teacher has hidden names beforehand.
- Hang the children's names on a clothesline one letter at a time. Make letter cards with T-shirt shapes.
- Lick and stick names. Use gummed paper cutout alphabet letters.
- Play stick-it note name activities. Print children's names on stick-it notes. Children stick their notes on something they choose to do or play with.
- Make craft stick names. Stick in clay, play dough, thick Styrofoam™, or slits in a box.

and watch the . On an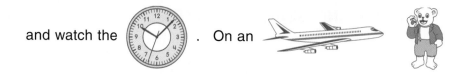

can sit down and  doesn't have to know how to fly.

When the  lands, rent a .

In a   can sit and can sit too."

"Thank you, wise old  ." "You're very welcome, ."

"Now take along a so you can write me a postcard," said .

FIGURE 16–45 *(continued)*

◆ Make generic cookie-cutter figures. Children decorate and name their figures. They are added to a large wall display.

Kindergarten

◆ Count letters in name.
◆ Think of a word that rhymes with a child's name.
◆ Ring a bell for each letter of name.
◆ Draw alphabet letters in the air.

◆ Clap syllables in names.
◆ Cut apart your name and paste it back together.
◆ Find alphabet letters that are a full circle or have a full circle.
◆ Find alphabet letters that are made with straight lines only and both circles and straight lines.
◆ Create a name word wall with names starting with a similar letter in groups.

SECTION 7

Reading:

A Language Art

CHAPTER 17

Reading and Preschoolers

OBJECTIVES

After reading this chapter, you should be able to:

◆ Describe reading skills.

◆ List three methods used to teach reading.

◆ Discuss the early childhood teacher's role in reading.

KEY TERMS

phonetic instruction

reading method

transitional kindergarten

MACKENZIE'S ABILITY

During group time, Mackenzie's teacher makes a discussion chart that reflects what the children in her class of three-year-olds "love to eat" at breakfast. Later, she notices the following poorly formed letters in Mackenzie's painting: BBRY PNKS.

QUESTIONS TO PONDER

1. What does the teacher know about Mackenzie's literacy development?

2. Is this precocious behavior or just precious behavior?

3. What course of action should Mackenzie's teacher pursue?

4. Could it be assumed that Mackenzie may be reading a few words?

At one time, it was thought that there was a magic age when all children became ready for "sit-down" reading instruction. Now it is believed that early childhood teachers at every level must be considered teachers of reading, even if they do not offer formal reading instruction. Research and theory suggest that teachers of young children need to be actively engaged in providing experiences that will build children's language and eventually lead children to become readers. These experiences are deemed appropriate if they match the individual child's level of language development and promote new competence in oral and written language. Stahl (1998) points out that when children learn to read, they use what they know about oral language to comprehend written language.

A wide range of age-appropriate activities involving understanding oral language, awareness of print, intimate experiences with picture books, dramatization, listening, musical activities, and diverse kinds of language arts activities discussed in this text promote early literacy and prepare children for the discovery of reading.

Some children who are in early childhood centers and kindergartens can read. Some have picked up the skill on their own; others have spent time with an older brother or sister, parents, or others. Although reading is considered the fourth language art, this chapter does not intend to suggest reading instruction for groups of young children or even encourage formal instruction for those 1 to 5 percent of children who can read words during preschool years.

It is clear from research that the process of learning to read is a lengthy one that begins very early in life. A lot of teacher effort during preschool years involves setting up young children to learn to read with ease. Adams (1990) discusses "a disposition to read." This disposition can be defined as a desire; a positive attitude toward the act of reading; or a feeling that reading is worthwhile, enjoyable, and fun (Figure 17–1). It includes the knowledge that one can find helpful or important information if one can read.

There is now empirical evidence that differences in preliteracy experiences are associated with varied levels of reading achievement during the early years of elementary school (Bodrova, Leong, Paynter, & Semenov, 2000). Children who begin school with few experiences in and less knowledge about literacy are

FIGURE 17–1 Enjoying their books? Oh yes!

unable to acquire the prerequisites quickly enough to keep up with formal reading instruction in the first grade (Snow, Burns, & Griffin, 1998).

Preschoolers who are given training in phonological awareness evince significant acceleration in their later acquisition of reading (Adams, 1990). Prereaders' letter knowledge was found to be the single best predictor of first-year reading achievement, with the ability to discriminate phonemes auditorily ranking a close second. Strickland (2003) believes a child's ability to write his own name is also a predictive characteristic. Children who will probably need additional support for early language and literacy development should receive it as early as possible (Snow, Burns, & Griffin, 1998). Preschool practitioners should be alert for signs that children are having difficulties.

Children Who May Need Special Help

The National Research Council's publication *Preventing Reading Difficulties in Young Children* (1998) has identified children who are likely to begin school less prepared. Their characteristics include:

1. living in low-income families or poor neighborhoods.
2. having limited English proficiency.
3. being slated to attend an elementary school where reading achievement is chronically low.
4. speaking a dialect of English that differs substantially from one used in schools.
5. having specific cognitive deficiencies, hearing impairments, and early language impairments.
6. having parents who have a history of reading problems.

Preschool educators are increasingly involved in individual state efforts to increase children's present and future ability to learn to read with ease. They have been identified as instrumental and important contributors to their elementary school educators' efforts to increase child success.

Early childhood educators are looking closely at what their individual language arts curricula contain and how to provide supportive assistance for those individual children and individual families they assume to be at risk.

Research-derived indicators for potential problems include:

- in infancy or during the preschool period, significant delays in expressive language, receptive vocabulary, or intellectual capacity (IQ).
- at kindergarten or elementary school entry, delays in a combination of abilities, including the following (Snow, Burns, & Griffin, 1998).
  - –letter identification
  - –understanding of the functions of print
  - –verbal memory for stories and sentences
  - –phonological awareness
  - –lexical skills such as naming vocabulary
  - –receptive language skills in the areas of syntax and morphology
  - –expressive language
  - –overall language development

Preventing Reading Difficulties in Young Children (1998) identifies some of the prior experiences necessary for young children to acquire reading skill. They follow:

- Children have had experiences in early childhood that fostered motivation and provided exposure to literacy in use.
- Children get information about the nature of print through opportunities to learn letters and to recognize the internal structure of spoken words.
- Children get explanations about the contrasting nature of spoken and written language.

Optimal environments in preschool and kindergarten require teachers who are well prepared and highly knowledgeable and who receive ongoing administrative support (Snow, Burns, & Griffin, 1998).

READING

The language arts approach and whole-language approach to reading consider reading as one part of the communication process. The language arts are interrelated—not separate, isolated skills. The teacher is responsible for showing the relationship between the various areas of language arts. In other words, the goal is to help children understand that communication is a whole process in which speaking, listening, using written symbols, and reading those symbols are closely connected (Figure 17–2).

In the past, the logical connection between listening, speaking, using written words, and reading was overlooked. The subjects were often taught as separate skills, and the natural connection between each area was not clear to children. In a language arts, whole-language, or natural approach, the connection (the way these areas fit together) is emphasized.

The preschool teacher realizes that certain skills and abilities appear in children before others, as well as appearing concurrently.

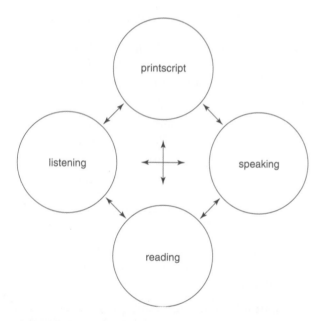

FIGURE 17–2 The four language arts are interrelated and interdependent. Note: Some educators accept a fifth language art—viewing and visual representation.

Barone (1994) studied the literacy development of a group of four- and five-year-old children exposed prenatally to maternal drug use (Figure 17–3). She believes the children's literacy development was appropriate and similar to unexposed four- and five-year-old children.

Early learning in listening and speaking serve as beginnings for further language and communication. Children's beginning ideas about print, writing, and reading form concurrently, and children may display understanding and skill in all of these areas.

Activities with young children can move easily from listening, speaking, seeing, or using printscript to beginning reading attempts: from passive to active participation. It is not uncommon for preschool youngsters to be able to read most of the names of the children in their group after being exposed to the daily use of name tags.

CURRENT THINKING CONCERNING EARLY READING INSTRUCTION

The National Reading Panel Report (2000) and the Elementary Education Act, which includes the No Child Left Behind Act passed in 2002, deal with ways to improve early literacy instruction and prepare young preschool children for school success. Morrow and Asbury (2003) describe what was suggested.

> The report suggests that instruction in early literacy needs to be organized and systematic. It also identifies areas on which to concentrate during instruction. The elements identified are (1) phonemic awareness, (2) phonics, (3) comprehension, (4) vocabulary, and (5) fluency.

> The report also highlights the importance of qualified teachers in developing successful readers.

Early childhood educators are taking these research-based suggestions to heart and are concerned about the approximately 30 to 40

NAME	BOOK CONCEPTS	READING	ORTHOGRAPHIC KNOWLEDGE	CONCEPT/ WORD
Jose	tight scribble	aware of book organization	retells/oral and book connected	not aware of letters	no/focus on illustration
Jamal	beginning letter/ unable to make letters	aware of book organization	only listens to stories when storytelling strategy used	not aware of letters	no/focus on illustration
Anna	yes	aware of book organization	retells/oral and book connected	aware of letters in name	pointing synchronized to rhythm not to words
Mark	yes	aware of book organization	retells/oral and book connected	aware of letters in name	aware of words/not able to track
Billy	yes	aware of book organization	retells/oral and book connected memorizes predictable text	initial consonants semiphonemic	rudimentary
Jennifer	yes	aware of book organization	retells/oral and book connected	initial consonants semiphonemic	rudimentary

"Getting the Idea of Reading and Writing"

NAME	BOOK CONCEPTS	READING	ORTHOGRAPHIC KNOWLEDGE	CONCEPT/ WORD
Mario	yes	aware of book organization	retells/prefers book language	initial consonants semiphonemic	track/not pointing to words
Donette	yes	aware of book organization not aware of word	retells/prefers book language	initial consonants semiphonemic	track/not pointing to words
Melisha	initial letter then circles	beginning/end top/bottom sequence of pages	retells/oral and book language	initial consonants semiphonemic	track/not pointing to words
Melina	yes	aware of book organization	retells/oral and book language predictable	initial consonants semiphonemic	rudimentary

"Beginning Readers and Writers"

NAME	BOOK CONCEPTS	READING	ORTHOGRAPHIC KNOWLEDGE	CONCEPT/ WORD
Ray	yes	aware of book organization	fluent nonpredictable text/word X word	letter-name	full
Curtis	yes	aware of book organization	fluent nonpredictable text/word X word	letter-name	full
Josh	yes	aware of book organization	fluent nonpredictable text/word X word	letter-name	full

FIGURE 17–3 Four-year-olds' literacy summary. "Getting the Idea of Reading and Writing." (From Barone, D. [1994]. The importance of classroom context: Literacy development of children prenatally exposed to crack cocaine. *Research in the Teaching of English, 28*[3], 286–312. Copyright 1994 by the National Council of Teachers of English. Reprinted with permission.)

percent of children who do not have an easy time learning to read in elementary school. They have increased recognition that young children, especially disadvantaged ones, often need concentrated instructional support. These children should learn important skills and strategies that they would have difficulty discovering on their own. Teachers are doing more assessment and documentation to help them identify children's individual needs and progress. Their efforts include attention to guidelines for developmentally appropriate practice and standards. They are planning a full and well-balanced early childhood language arts curriculum.

Professional literature urges preschool teachers to use an integrated approach to language arts. Concerns over national literacy and children's reading success have promoted study and discussion. Twenty state legislatures have passed new child literacy laws reacting to the enactment of the Federal Reading Excellence Act (1998). Most experts recommend a literature-based program for both elementary school and preschool. Ideal classrooms are described as "language rich" or "literacy developing." Key ideas presently stress instruction offered in meaningful contexts with children developing strategies to achieve skills they view as useful to them.

Many researchers agree that early school experiences play a crucial role in the child's future literacy development. They believe teachers should explore effective ways to facilitate language learning by involving children in authentic language uses.

Early childhood professionals want to make sure that their programs of activities offer the best in children's literature, not watered-down versions of classics (Figure 17–4). There is thought to be both older and contemporary literature and language-related activities that have depth, meaning, and linguistic charm that preschoolers should encounter. Meaning and comprehension are aided by discussion and familiarity and can be guided by sensitive teachers who also monitor the appropriateness of what is offered.

FIGURE 17–4 Quality children's literature is offered by professional early childhood educators.

PRESSURE FOR FORMAL READING INSTRUCTION IN PRESCHOOLS

Some parents, for one reason or another, may hold the mistaken idea that their child will have an educational advantage if he receives formal reading instruction in preschool. This idea is often expressed during initial enrollment interviews. Fortunately, early childhood educators can explain that foundational literacy experiences and activities are a standard part of a quality preschool curriculum and that individual growth activities are planned for each child based on his developing capabilities. Durkin's research in the 1960s received considerable publicity, and subsequent studies by many others cite instances of young children reading before kindergarten. Some parents and educators intrigued by this idea have attempted formal, sit-down instruction with three- and four-year-olds. Cullinan (1977) explains the error of this plan of action.

> . . . a major fallacy in basing programs on early reading studies is that children who learned to read early did not do so from exposure to formal reading instruction. Findings show that children who learned to read early were the ones who were read to, who showed interest in paper and pencil activities, and who were interested in visual distinctions in signs and labels. Their families valued reading as an activity. Someone answered their questions. Children learned messages encoded in writing can be decoded, or read, and that letters represented sounds used in speaking.

In other words, typically children who learned to read while quite young did so by discovering decoding in responsive, literacy-enriched family situations. Both Gallagher and Coche (1987) and Piaget and Inhelder (1969) fear that concentrating on early reading-skill instruction may reduce time for play and take away symbolic enrichment time. Play provides the interaction of imagery, imitation, and language, which builds a foundation necessary for learning to read.

The pressure preschool staffs may feel to begin formal reading instruction grates against the belief system of most early childhood educators (Winn, 1981). Many react to the tragedy of finding a number of children in a few preschools with worksheets to complete before they can play. Researchers have yet to find that early reading instruction is advantageous or better than later instruction. In fact, starting formal academics too early may do more harm than good, Elkind (1988) believes. He points out that formal reading instruction in Denmark, where illiteracy rates are very low, is delayed until age seven. Kelly (1985) voices an opinion and observation that many educators feel is valid.

> Studies show that children who are pushed to read early may not be such avid readers when they're older—which is when it matters—while their classmates who started slower may read often and spontaneously.

Gallas (2003) believes to read a text with understanding and insight, children must move inside the text, pulling their life along with them, and that they incorporate the text into their lives, thus forming a new understanding of the world.

Standards, Benchmarks, and Behaviors

A research-based document helping preschool curriculum planners identify their standards for prekindergarten reading and writing curriculum is available. Based on work sponsored wholly, or in part, by the Office of Educational Research and Improvement (OERI), a publication titled *A Framework for Early Literacy Instruction: Aligning Standards to Developmental Accomplishments and Student Behaviors: Pre-K through Kindergarten* (Bodrova et al., 2000) is available. A *standard* is defined in the publication as a general statement that represents information, skills, or both that a child (student) should understand or be able to do by the end of their pre-K school experience. A *benchmark* is defined as a subcomponent of a standard.

The authors state that their publication was not intended as an assessment checklist and that curriculum should not be "dumbed-down" versions of higher-grade benchmarks. Supporting knowledge listings in reading and writing standards will be of particular interest to early childhood educators and provide clarity as to the purposes of their planned activities and daily interactions. Preschool teachers will be more able to recognize emerging preschool behaviors after studying the document in total.

This document is available from McREL (Mid-continent Research for Education and Learning), 2550 S. Parker Rd., Ste 500, Aurora, CO 80014. In examining supporting knowledge sections of the publication, early childhood educators may be able to more effectively examine their language arts curriculum, their teaching behaviors, and their daily interactions.

Most states have developed state reading standards for public school instruction.

Standards for Reading Teacher Preparation

Standards for Reading Professionals (2003), developed by the professional standards and ethics committee of the International Reading Association (IRA), is a reference used by community colleges, college and university faculties, and state departments of education. It is designed to guide the development of elementary school teacher preparation programs and the evaluation of teacher candidates and their training programs through the use of identified candidate performance-based assessment. The standards recognize five categories of professionals: the paraprofessional (2-year degree with specific course work), the classroom teacher, the reading specialist/literacy coach, the teacher educator, and the administrator.

Newly graduated reading professionals must demonstrate they can meet the needs of all students and that they possess the following capabilities or attitudes:

1. Candidates have knowledge of the foundations of reading and writing processes and instruction.

2. Candidates use a wide range of instructional practices, approaches, methods, and curriculum materials to support reading and writing.

3. Candidates use a variety of assessment tools and practices to plan and evaluate effective reading instruction.

4. Candidates create a literate environment that fosters reading and writing by integrating foundational knowledge, use of instructional practice, approaches and methods, curriculum materials, and the appropriate use of assessments.

5. Candidates view professional development as a career-long effort and responsibility.

TEACHER AWARENESS OF CHILD INTEREST AND UNDERSTANDING

Each child will probably hold a totally different view concerning reading (Figure 17–5). Possible understandings a preschooler may have include:

◆ pictures and text have different functions.

◆ print contains the story.

FIGURE 17–5 An interest in books can lead to an interest in printed words.

- the words the reader says come from the pictures.
- stories tend to have some predictable segments and features.
- it is possible to write messages.
- there are words, and written words are made up of letters.
- letters are arranged from left to right.
- letters appear in linear fashion to represent the sequence of sounds in spoken words.
- spaces delineate word boundaries.
- letters come in capitals, in small print, and even in script, but they all have the same significance.
- some marks are used to show beginnings and ends of text.

The ability to read is present if the child understands and acts appropriately when he sees a printed word. In other words, the child must be able to understand the concept that (1) all "things" have a name, (2) the name of the thing can be a written word, (3) the two are interchangeable, and (4) the "word symbols" can be read.

Most teachers have had children "read" to them from a favorite, memorized storybook. Generally, a word from the book will not be recognized out of context and read by the child when seen elsewhere. However, this behavior—imitative reading—can be an indication of early literacy development.

A child may develop the ability to recognize words because of an interest in printing letters. Another child may pick up the sounds of alphabet letters by listening and finding words that start with the same letter. Books and stories can also lead children into early interest and recognition of words. Some children have the ability to distinguish one word from another by sight and can easily remember words. Other children do not develop this ability until a later age.

Early readers are children who have a desire to read. They also have had interactions with others who have answered their questions and stimulated their interest. A few children will read between the ages of four and five, but many will not have the capability or interest to read until a later age. Kelly (1985) estimates that only one to three preschoolers out of a hundred can read simple books. A teacher should be aware of each child's capabilities. Fields (1996) reminds teachers that reading pictures is beginning reading (Figure 17–6). In daily observations and verbal conversations, a child's responses give valuable clues. The wrong answers are as important as the right ones.

A 3-year research study conducted by Strommen and Mates (1997) attempted to identify young children's emerging ideas about the act of reading. Children were asked what they knew about reading at age three and the study continued through ages five or six. The following developmental sequence seemed apparent to the researchers.

Young children:

1. see reading as one aspect of an interpersonal routine. A book was considered a relatively minor part of a situation with a

FIGURE 17–6 Reading pictures (illustrations) is beginning reading.

parent or loved one at a certain time of day (usually bedtime). Children commented upon or demonstrated looking at the book and page turning.

2. notice that readers focus on a book. When asked for reading behavior, children in the study turned pages (front to back), silently looked, labeled objects or actions, carried on a book monologue, asked rhetorical questions, gave general information, and stated their preferences related to book features.

3. develop the idea that readers construct a meaningful sequence when reading that is determined by a series of illustrated pages. Some children point to print but "read" from the pictures. Other children orally mimic and intone in an oral reading style voice.

4. believe readers reconstruct an account that is unique to each particular book. They sense each book has a specific story one can tell in his own words. Some children believe that a book must be memorized word for word, and many associate reading ability as something "big" people do.

5. develop the idea that print provides cues to written language. The sounding out of simple words was displayed. Some children abandon efforts to decode words in books because it hinders getting the books' meaning. They read their own names and attempt to or actually do print their name.

6. use multiple strategies to interpret the language encoded by print. Children began to apply graphophonemic, syntactic, and semantic information, as well as cues provided by illustrations (or by collaborators) to interpret the language encoded by print (Strommen & Mates, 1997).

Kindergarten teachers facing a wide range of enrolled children's language arts abilities often attempt to assess children's progress in letter identification, phonemic awareness (sound-symbol relationships), sight words, concepts of words, and printing skill. In a typical kindergarten class, children's literacy skills and func-

tioning may span a 5-year range; that is, some may possess skills typical of three-year-olds and others, those of eight-year-olds (Riley, 1996). Informal testing is common. Some common informal testing probes and questions follow:

1. Cards with an uppercase and lowercase printscript alphabet are displayed one by one.
   "What alphabet letter do you see?"
   "Can you tell me the sound it makes?"
   "Do you know a word that starts with this letter?"

2. The child is given paper and pencil.
   "Please write alphabet letters you know."
   "Tell me about the letters you've written."

3. The child is asked to write known words.
   "Write all the words you know."
   "Can you write your name?"

4. The child is presented a list of common sight words.
   "Do you know any of these words?"

5. The child is asked to describe/tell about his favorite book.

Individualized activities can become an easier task when assessment data have been gathered.

Cambourne (1988) has identified "reading-like" child behaviors, which follow:

1. recreating text from memory, turning pages randomly

2. recreating a text from pictures only (Each picture represents a complete text—no continuity of story line.)

3. same as 1 and 2, with a continuous story line that may or may not match the text in the book

4. recreating text from memory, running eyes and/or finger over text but not one-to-one matching of print with meaning

5. just turning pages, frontward and backward, but obviously engaging with pictures

6. Sitting next to someone else engaged in behaviors 1 through 5 and sometimes collaborating with or intervening in others' reading-like behavior

Child Knowledge of Alphabet Letters

In comparing two children—one who knows the alphabet and reads a few words and one who crudely writes his own name and makes up barely understandable stories—one may conclude that the first child is bright. However, creativity and logic are important in literacy development, and the second child may be outdistancing the first by progressing at his own speed. Literacy at any age is more than merely naming letters or words. Adams (1998) adds another perspective.

First, it is not simply the accuracy with which children can name letters that gives them an advantage in learning to read; it is the ease or fluency with which they can do so—it is their basic familiarity with the letters. Thus, even in studies with relatively small numbers of children and limited differences in accuracy, the speed with which they can name individual letters is both a strong predictor of success for pre-readers and a strong correlate of reading achievement among beginners.

Adams goes on to state

The speed and accuracy of letter naming is an index of the thoroughness or confidence with which the letters identities have been learned.

Adams (1998) mentions that children's effortlessness may indicate an ability to see letters as "wholes" and then see words as patterns of letters. She also theorizes a comfortable knowledge of the names of letters hastens children's learning of their sounds.

Mason (1980) suggests it is other knowledge that is learned along with the ability to name letters that is crucial. More often than not, alphabet letter names are first encountered in the alphabet song (to the tune of "Twinkle, Twinkle Little Star") or in alphabet books at ages two, three, and four. Children usually memorize the oral names of a few alphabet letters. Children then develop a sense that different letter shapes have different names, and it is

an easy jump to children understanding that their names are different in print than their friends' names. "That's my letter," a child may say when encountering a letter in the environment that is similar to or the same shape as the first letter of his first name.

Adams (1990) urges preschool teachers and parents to understand that young children have 2 to 4 years to master the letter shapes before entering kindergarten. She also urges that instruction in letter recognition be begun long before the child enters primary school.

The goal is to ensure that letter shapes are highly familiar and discriminable to the children before they are faced with the task of learning the letters' sounds or, more generally, of learning to read words.

The sounds that letters make are introduced only after letter names are very well learned. Overlearned letter names protect children from possible confusions. Adams (1990) points out

Children will know that the letter names are in fact names. In short, such separation in time must play a significant role in allowing the children to learn the letter sounds with only the help and not the hindrance that may be had from their names.

Understanding the alphabetic principle involves the knowledge that there is a systematic relationship between letters and sounds. Neuman, Copple, and Bredekamp (1999) note that teachers can involve children in comparing letter shapes and help them visually differentiate a number of letters. They suggest alphabet books and alphabet puzzles as keys to efficient and easy learning.

Adams (1998) believes a child's grasp of the alphabetic principle may be the single most important step toward acquiring the code that eases early reading. She points out that many prereaders figure it out on their own. Letter-to-sound correspondence teaching has currently and historically been the subject of countless arguments and disputes among reading instruction professionals. Adams believes the answer may be that, although knowing the names of letters helps some children remember sounds, it helps others induce them.

Increasingly, early childhood educators are finding or creating new ways to include more focus on alphabet letters by capitalizing on opportunities to point out print and its uses in classroom life, by saturating their classrooms with print, and by reading quality picture books with ABC themes. It is not beneficial to force print instruction on children, rather teachers should draw it into conversations and design an environment where print is hard to miss.

A growing number of early childhood teachers are studying and putting into action the developmental accomplishments cited in *Preventing Reading Difficulties in Young Children* (1998), state standards, the No Child Left Behind Act's goals for preschool learners, and the Head Start Outcomes Framework (U.S. Department of Health and Human Services, 2003). They are working on preschool children's ability to identify at least 10 alphabet letters, their knowledge of sound-letter associations, their ability to pay attention to separate and repeating sounds, their ability to form lines and circles, and their attempts to form alphabet letters. These teachers are also busy relating the uses and functions of print to young children's lives.

Word Recognition

The typical four-year-old relies on idiosyncratic cues to identify words, rather than intuitively making use of letter sounds (Mason, Herman, & Au, 1992). For example, when name tags are used with different types of stickers accompanying different children's names, the sticker is usually read (recognized) rather than the print.

A CLOSER LOOK AT EARLY READERS

Researchers studying both gifted children and early readers notice that parents overwhelmingly report that they have read to their children from birth on or from the time the children learned to sit up. As Strickland (1982) points out, research shows that early readers who learned to read without system-

atic instruction had one common experience, despite their different backgrounds: they were all introduced to books between the ages of three and five. A study (Anbar, 1986) of activities mentioned by the parents of early readers is shown in Figure 17–7. Usually, someone reads aloud to those children on a regular basis. Elkind (1988) notes

> . . . a Gallup survey of people who have attained eminence makes it very clear that parents of gifted children did not impose their learning priorities upon their young offspring. They followed the child's lead, emphasizing play and a rich, stimulating environment rather than formal instruction.

Studies of the early reader indicate that the child was usually exposed to a variety of reading material and enjoyed watching educational television, spending close to equal time in both pursuits (Schnur, Lowrey, & Brazell, 1985). An interest in print characterizes precocious read-

TYPE OF ACTIVITY	FREQUENCY OF REPORT
daily readings with pointing at words	6/6
showing words in magazines	2/6
teaching names of letters	6/6
teaching sight vocabulary	5/6
making rhymes with words	5/6
playing letter games	6/6
helping learn sounds of letters	6/6
helping put words together	6/6
playing spelling games	6/6
playing add-a-letter games	1/6
listening to child read aloud	5/6
having child read after parent	1/6
doing alternate reading	2/6
working on sounding out words	2/6
providing books on an appropriate level	3/6

FIGURE 17–7 Six parents' reading activities with their children. (Reprinted from Anbar, A. [1986, March]. Reading acquisition of preschool children without systematic instruction. *Early Childhood Research Quarterly, 1*[1], 69–83, with permission from Elsevier Science.)

ers, and their parents are described as responsive—noticing child interests and providing help when asked. Many child-centered family activities were part of the early reader's family lifestyle. These children seemed fascinated and obsessed with the alphabet, and parents reported that they answered questions, read to the child, and engaged in play activities with letters and words but had not set out with a systematic plan to teach reading.

Anbar (1986), in completing a study of early readers, has identified possible stages in these children's learning process (Figure 17–8).

If we could examine parent-child storybook readings closely, simply reading aloud does not describe most parent actions accurately. Pointing out book features, relating book happenings to shared family experiences, defining words, engaging in turn-taking dialogue, prompting children's identification and naming of illustra-

Stage I	a preliminary period of gaining awareness and general knowledge of books and print (starting any time during the first year)
Stage II	learning to identify and name the letters and acquiring beginning sight vocabulary (starting around 12–18 months)
Stage III	learning the sounds of the letters (starting around 20–24 months)
Stage IV	putting together words (starting around 24–32 months)
Stage V	active reading from familiar books (starting around 20–30 months)
Stage VI	sounding out short, unfamiliar words (starting around 32–34 months)
Stage VII	reading easy, unfamiliar books (around 36 months)
Stage VIII	reading for enjoyment of content (around 48 months)

FIGURE 17–8 Stages in the learning process of early readers. (Reprinted from Anbar, A. [1986, March]. Reading acquisitions of preschool children without systematic instruction. *Early Childhood Research Quarterly, 1*[1], 9–83, with permission from Elsevier Science.)

tions, listening to children's memorized "readings," and engaging in other parental interactions are all part of the experience (Figure 17–9). Educators use the same techniques.

Calkins (1997), in *Raising Lifelong Learners: A Parent's Guide,* describes how she recognizes and supports the efforts of early readers.

Children who are learning to read will tap into many support systems. They might look over a book before tackling any one line of words, trying to gain a sense for how the book goes, for "the trick of the book," before attempting to do the printwork of reading. Sometimes children essentially memorize the story. The child will read in a word-by-word way as if she is following the print even when she isn't. The child may, for example, look at a page which says, "Where is my father?" and read, "I-can't-find-where-my-father-is."

Calkin's supportive efforts include:

◆ finding good books in which the pictures closely match words.

◆ prompting, "Will you point to the words as you read them?"

◆ letting children ponder the problem that what they are saying does not match the number words they are pointing to in the print and hoping children self-correct themselves.

◆ saying, "Great self-correcting," when it happens.

My goal is for the black marks on the page to give [the child] enough feedback that the child adjusts his/her approximation. This marks a huge step in the process of learning to read. (Calkins, 1997)

◆ watching for confusion and modeling the strategies readers use when they encounter problems. Examples: pausing to see whether the child backs up and rereads on his own or saying, "Try it again, that's what I usually do."

FIGURE 17–9 Teachers, like parents, often point out and discuss features in books.

Calkins lists other effective strategies that early readers use.

- orienting themselves to a book as a whole
- studying the pictures to heighten their sense of what the words say
- guessing at what the print probably says
- checking to confirm or disprove their guesses
- pointing to words

For early readers, Calkins recommends books with repetitive, patterned text and books with a jazzy, rhythmic phrase on every page that may change just a word or two as text moves ahead; however, she notes that some books can consist of meaningless, silly ditties, so select carefully. Looking for logical books that are both interesting and tailored to a child's life and past experience is the prudent course of action.

Suggested books follow:

Barton, B. (1984). *Building a house.* New York: Puffin Books.

Christelow, E. (1989). *Five little monkeys jumping on the bed.* New York: Clarion Books.

de Paola, T. (1980). *The knight and the dragon.* New York: Putnam.

Hutchins, P. (1968). *Rosie's walk.* New York: Macmillan.

Krauss, R. (1974). *The carrot seed.* New York: Scholastic Book Services.

Shaw, C. G. (1947). *It looked like spilt milk.* New York: Harper.

What should happen when a child expects to learn to read the first day of school or kindergarten? Clements and Warncke (1994) suggest

Because of this expectation teachers may want to "make it happen" even on the first day of school. It does not matter to the child that what she read was simple by adult standards—even if the only thing that the child goes home able to read at the conclusion of the first day of school is the simple sentence that states, "My name is _____." On all following days this simple, close-type reading can be used to enhance the child's perceptions that she can read. A big portion of the battle to improve children's self-esteem and allow the child to believe that she can read and write is won if, indeed, the teacher has the child write and read some every day.

HOW SHARED READING IS DONE

Many prekindergartens, kindergartens, and lower elementary school classes conduct group reading activities called shared readings. Often, 14″ by 17″ or larger books, called Big Books, or teacher-made charts are introduced, discussed, and read. On a first reading, the book's cover and illustrations are examined. Predictions about the story or other content take place. Text is large, and colorful illustrations are directly connected to the text. Words are repeated frequently. After a first reading, children may be prompted to share something they noticed in the book. While reading, the teacher puts one hand under each word and moves from top to bottom and left to right. Children may be asked to guess words or predict story outcomes.

Shared reading promotes both letter and sound recognition, especially after repeated readings. In the course of shared reading, children query what a particular word says, notice that some words rhyme, and notice words with the same sound or letter. The teacher encourages discussion and children's touching or pointing to book features. Pleasant attitudes toward the experience are built through accepting and appreciating each child's comments and ideas. It is easy to see, that this exercise will result in children's efforts to point out letters, words, or rhymes that they know. Both fiction and nonfiction titles are used.

Vocabulary and Early Readers

Child vocabulary is strongly related to child comprehension and child ease of learning to read (National Reading Panel, 2000). Reading comprehension involves applying letter-sound correspondence to a printed word and matching it to a known word in the reader's oral vocabulary. Oral vocabulary is a key in making the transition from oral to written forms. Many studies agree that reading ability and vocabulary size are related (National Reading Panel, 2000).

In trying to measure children's vocabulary, one finds different vocabularies exist. *Receptive* vocabulary is seen in toddlers, who follow requests such as "get Grandpa's brown shoes," before they can say the words. *Productive* vocabulary is used when we speak or write to another. *Oral* vocabulary refers to words that are recognized in speaking or listening. For example, the toddler may bring Grandpa's *black* shoes because color words are not part of his oral vocabulary. *Reading* vocabulary refers to words that are used or recognized in print. Many young children can be described as having a reading vocabulary when they correctly recognize street signs and commercial fast-food symbols. *Sight* vocabulary is a subset of reading vocabulary (National Reading Panel, 2000). A sight word is immediately recognized as a whole and does not require word analysis for identification (Harris & Hodges, 1995). Early childhood teachers rarely know the size of preschoolers' sight vocabularies unless they do assessments. When they do, they find some preschoolers have amazingly large ones.

Early childhood educators consciously promote and prompt vocabulary development. They relish and model an interest in words, their definitions, and dictionary use. New words enter children's vocabularies daily in a developmental environment. Teachers explain new words and relate them to children's experience by giving examples. Sight vocabulary words are composed of alphabet letters that can be named and sounded out, so-called teaching moment naturals. Kindergarten classrooms (and some preschools) have word charts, word lists, word walls, words used for labeling, and words in displays. Preschools have abundant alphabet letters and words used in functional ways.

Considerable study suggests a small vocabulary is one major determinant of poor reading comprehension for Latino children and others who lag in readiness in the first grades of elementary school (Carlo et al., 2004). Every effort in early childhood centers is made to aid children's oral vocabulary and work toward depth of understanding through firsthand experience, exposure to books, classroom discussion, play with peers, and the scheduling of frequent daily literacy events.

Some preschools develop a "Words I Know" file box for children who wish to have one. It can be taken home occasionally. Words are dictated by children then printed by the teacher. An oblong box with strips of sturdy paper works well. Printing with a wide-tip black marker is recommended. Strips can be used for tracing and other activities, when appropriate. Some preschoolers have sizable sight word vocabularies, as was mentioned. Sylvia Ashton-Warner (1963) believed, as do many other early childhood educators, that first words have intense meaning for a child. Ashton-Warner's conviction gave rise to her articulation of what she called the *organic reading method,* which used key vocabulary for teaching reading and writing (Gallas, 2003).

OBJECTIVES

Differences exist in the objectives of instruction between (1) educators who believe in readiness activities and (2) educators who advocate natural self-discovery of reading skills. The first group hopes to facilitate learning and enjoyment of reading. The second group foresees the child's experimentation—creating ideas about reading, based on his notions of the use of writing and reading, and attempting to crack the code with supportive assistance. Both groups favor a print-rich classroom, and objectives in many programs are based on a consideration of a blending of the two positions. Both groups also agree that experiences with classic and quality literature and dramatic activity help children's early literacy.

Programs that choose to include reading readiness among their instructional goals (objectives) plan activities that promote the following skills and attitudes.

◆ recognizing incongruities—the ability to see the inappropriateness of a situation or statement, such as "The mouse swallowed the elephant"

◆ recognizing context clues—realizing that pictures on the same page give visual clues to the words

◆ acquiring the ability to listen

◆ building vocabulary through firsthand experiences
   a. recognizing likenesses and differences
   b. identifying through sight and sound
   c. rhyming
   d. increasing memory span
   e. recalling sequence and content
   f. following directions

◆ increasing speech output
   a. developing attitudes of each child's ability and worth
   b. increasing imaginative and creative speech

◆ building critical thinking and problem solving with language
   a. identifying through clues
   b. classifying, sorting, and organizing
   c. developing concepts and recognizing relationships
   d. anticipating outcomes
   e. seeing cause-and-effect relationships

◆ developing self-confidence—attitudes of competence

◆ increasing interest and motivation through enjoyment of and success in language activities

◆ developing left and right awareness

◆ developing positive attitudes toward books and skills in book use
   a. turning pages
   b. storing and handling books with care

Phonemic awareness, the awareness that words are composed of sounds, is important in facilitating learning to read. What can early childhood educators do to encourage phonemic awareness? Griffith and Olson (1992) suggest literature that focuses on some kind of play with the *sounds of language* to help children "naturally" develop awareness. Books including alliteration, rhyme, repetition, and sound substitution fit this category.

Educators seriously consider each child's attitude development concerning reading times and reading in general. In both their actions and words, teachers convey their attitudes. If actions and words value reading and express enthusiasm (and joy) for finding out what enjoyment or information is possible in a book, young children also tend to adopt an "Oh boy, a book" orientation. They may then accept the idea that reading books can be a pleasurable pursuit—a treat, a door to adventure, fantasy, fun!

SEQUENCE OF READING BEHAVIOR

In the absence of adult intervention that emphasizes another sequence, children generally seem to develop reading and writing abilities as follows:

1. The child develops an awareness of the functions and value of the reading and writing processes before becoming interested in acquiring specific knowledge and skills. As Putnam (1994) points out

   We know that children learn to read by reading and by following along with the print as they are read to. Children who sit beside a reader and follow the print from an early age learn to read quite "naturally." We know that the modeling has a lasting effect; children do what they see others do.

2. The child is likely to give greater attention to words and letters that have some personal significance, such as his name or the names of family, pets, and so forth.

3. The child develops both reading and writing skills simultaneously as complementary aspects of the same communication processes, rather than as separate sets of learning. Neugebauer (1981) urges that

   The most important issue is the quantity and quality of experiences the child has with print and with adults who help make print "work." It is through such interactions

with print that the child acquires the information needed to find out what reading is.

4. The child develops an awareness of words as separate entities (as evidenced when he dictates words slowly so that the teacher can keep pace in writing them down) before showing awareness or interest in how specific letters represent sounds.

5. The child becomes familiar with the appearance of many of the letters by visually examining them, playing games with them, and so forth, before trying to master their names, the sounds they represent, or their formation.

6. The child becomes aware of the sound similarities between high-interest words (such as significant names) and makes many comparisons between their component parts before showing any persistence in deciphering unfamiliar words by blending together the sounds of individual letters (Dopyera & Lay-Dopyera, 1992).

As stated earlier, the teacher will probably encounter a few preschool children who have already learned how to read simple words and simple books, but there may be others reading at much higher levels. Some children, usually older four-year-olds, seem quite interested in alphabet letters, words, and writing. Teachers know the center's goals for each child.

It is important for teachers to be able to help the child's existing reading abilities and actively plan for future reading skill.

Any teacher of young children over the age of three can anticipate working with some children who already have interest in and abilities for reading and writing. As a teacher you should be aware of various methods used to teach reading. This is no less true for the teachers of three-, four-, and five-year-olds than for teachers of six- and seven-year-olds. (Dopyera & Lay-Dopyera, 1992)

Figure 17–10 lists accomplishments during kindergarten.

KINDERGARTEN ACCOMPLISHMENTS

- knows the parts of a book and their functions
- begins to track print when listening to familiar text being read or when rereading own writing
- "reads" familiar texts emergently (i.e., not necessarily verbatim from the print alone)
- recognizes and can name all uppercase and lowercase letters
- understands that the sequence of letters in a written word represents the sequence of sounds (phonemes) in a spoken word (alphabetic principle)
- learns many, although not all, one-to-one letter sound correspondences
- recognizes some words by sight, including a few very common ones (a, the, I, my, you, is, are)
- uses new vocabulary and grammatical constructions in own speech
- makes appropriate switches from oral to written language situations
- notices when simple sentences fail to make sense
- connects information and events in texts to life and life to text experiences
- retells, reenacts, or dramatizes stories or parts of stories
- listens attentively to books teacher reads to class
- can name some book titles and authors
- demonstrates familiarity with a number of types or genres of text (e.g., storybooks, expository texts, poems, newspapers, and everyday print such as signs, notices, labels)
- correctly answers questions about stories read aloud
- makes predictions based on illustrations or portions of stories
- demonstrates understanding that spoken words consist of sequences of phonemes
- given spoken sets like "dan, dan, den," can identify the first two as being the same and third as different
- given spoken sets like "dak, pat, zen," can identify the first two as sharing a same sound
- given spoken segments, can merge them into a meaningful target word
- given a spoken word, can produce another word that rhymes with it
- independently writes many uppercase and lowercase letters
- uses phonemic awareness and letter knowledge to spell independently (invented or created spelling)
- writes (unconventionally) to express own meaning
- builds a repertoire of some conventionally spelled words
- shows awareness of distinction between "kid writing" and conventional orthography
- writes own name (first and last) and the first names of some friends or classmates
- can write most letters and some words when they are dictated

FIGURE 17–10 Kindergarten accomplishments in reading. (Reprinted with permission from Snow, C., Burns, S., & Griffin, P. [Eds.]. [1998]. *Preventing reading difficulties in young children.* Washington, DC: National Academy Press. Copyright 1998 by the National Academy of Sciences. Courtesy of the National Academies Press, Washington, DC.)

The Transition to Kindergarten

A relatively new entity, the **transitional kindergarten**, exists in some communities. It may have a curriculum designed to support each child's early skill or at-risk status through special summer intervention classes and/or increased parental and community participation in the child's learning. Its goal is to offer children a transitional period to enhance their effectiveness as prereaders. The goals of most

transitional kindergarten — a relatively new feature of some elementary school districts that offers supportive literacy activities and classroom access (usually during the summer before the child is to enroll in kindergarten).

transitional programs involve both child self-regulation and social interaction. Playing appropriately with others, collaborating, planning play directions, sharing, taking turns, approaching peers to play, and knowing some of the other children's names are social interaction skills. Self-regulation includes watching peers to find out what is expected, imitating behaviors, following classroom routines and rules, changing behavior when necessary, waiting, standing in line, and taking care of personal items. To perform some of these tasks the child needs to accept the teacher as an authority figure.

The communication goals that a transitional program might target are similar to those targeted in preschool, such as responding to teacher questions; offering ideas in group discussions; expressing needs, fears, and feelings; following simple "school-talk" directions; remembering items and actions previously seen or heard; and knowing how to appropriately ask for adult help. In a transitional program, children are expected to listen when it is time to listen, sit when it is time to sit, and finish assigned tasks. The child's ability to make a transition from a parent at arrival and back to parent's authority at departure is another program goal.

READING METHODS

Research studies conducted to try to pinpoint the one best **reading method** for teaching children to read have concluded that there is no proven best method. The important factors seem to be the teacher's (1) enthusiasm for the method or technique used and (2) understanding of the method used. The ideal situation for a child learning to read is a one-to-one child/teacher ratio, with the reading activity suited to the child's individual capacity, learning style, and individual interests. This is difficult to fulfill in an early childhood learning center because of the number of children per group and the many other duties required of a teacher. Other limitations can include the

teacher's amount of training, knowledge of a variety of methods to teach reading, and ability to plan interesting and appropriate activities within a print-rich classroom.

What preschool teachers need to understand is that advocates of many differing methods used to teach reading agree that a rich, strong base in quality children's literature and well-developed oral language and listening skill aid success in whatever reading method is eventually used. Gill (1992) states

> ... since reading research was first formalized, whether or not a child has been read to from a young age has been one of the strongest predictors of first-grade reading success.

Another factor most reading experts will not dispute is that children need experiences that have focused on the meaning of language. Whichever prereading or reading method is used, it is important for children to recognize that "talk" can be written and that "written talk" can be read.

Preventing Reading Difficulties in Young Children (Snow, Burns, & Griffin, 1998) has captured nationwide interest. The publication's core message concerning reading instruction recommends that reading instruction *integrate* attention to the alphabetic principle with attention to the construction of meaning and opportunities to develop fluency. The report's definition of integration follows:

> Integration means precisely that opportunities to learn these two aspects of skilled reading should be going on at the same time, in the context of the same activities, and that the choice of instructional activities should be part of an overall coherent approach to supporting literacy development, not a haphazard selection from unrelated, though varied, activities. (Snow, Burns, & Griffin, 1998)

How best to teach beginning reading may be the most politicized topic in the field of education (Adams, 1990).

reading method — any of several relatively specific procedures or steps for teaching one or more aspects of reading, each procedure embodying explicitly or implicitly some theory of how children learn and of the relationship between written and spoken language.

The Natural Approach

Popular approaches to reading include what has been termed *natural reading*. The basic premise of this method centers on the idea that a child can learn to read as he learned to talk, that is, with adult attention and help with early skills. As Bartoli (1995) explains

> We learn to read in a literate society such as ours the same way we learn to talk, walk, draw, sing: by seeing and hearing reading modeled skillfully for us, by noticing and understanding that this is an interesting and useful thing to do, by being invited to join the process with those who can do it better than we can, by being allowed to try it for ourselves when we desire (occasionally with a little help from our friends), and by being allowed to learn unselfconsciously from our own mistakes.

In the natural approach, an interest in print (words) leads to invented spelling and reading. Huey (1908) anticipated "organic" and natural reading systems by proposing that children learn to read by authoring from their own experiences. He suggested that it was important to expose children to great classic literature as well as child-authored literature (writings) if one wished to promote true literacy.

Educators associated with natural reading include Ashton-Warner (1963), Johnson (1987), and Fields (1987). The well-known work of Allen (1969) has led to a method called the *language-experience approach* and can be thought of as a popular early form of the natural method. Stauffer (1970) points out the specific features of the language-experience approach that he believes make it especially appropriate for young children.

- a base in children's language development and firsthand experiencing
- stress on children's interests, experiences, and cognitive and social development
- respect for children's need for activity and involvement
- requirement for meaningful learning experiences
- integration of school and public library resources with classroom reading materials
- encouragement of children's creative writing as a meaningful approach to using and practicing reading and writing skills

Johnson (1987), influenced by the work of Sylvia Ashton-Warner, recommends starting five-year-olds reading through a procedure that elicits children's images. The images are then connected to printed captions. Individual important images merge as meaningful words to be shared with others through sight reading. Slowly, visual discrimination, capitalization, sentence sense, phonetics, and punctuation are accomplished at each child's particular pace.

Sylvia Ashton-Warner's method of teaching reading inspired a whole generation of teachers during the 1960s. Thompson (2000) believes Ashton-Warner gives today's teachers an early model for teaching multicultural children to read. Thompson describes Ashton-Warner's techniques.

> What she called her "scheme" for working in the New Zealand bicultural context may be, in some very basic ways, universally adaptable to intercultural or transcultural education for the new millennium. Organic teaching requires the teacher to listen to the pupils, to truly hear them and encourage what is important to them, and to use that as the working material for teaching and learning. This concept, Ashton-Warner asserts, embodies the kind of attitude necessary for building transcultural bridges for sharing understanding of cultures, ultimately a possible direction leading to peace in our shrinking global village.

The author recommends, as most teacher-training programs recommend, the early childhood educator's reading of Ashton-Warner's book *Teacher* (1963), for it is as pertinent today as it was more than 40 years ago.

To many people, the terms *natural* and *organic methods* and *language-experience* and *language arts approaches* are synonymous and describe the same or similar methods of reading instruction. Robisson (1983) recommends the *language-experience* approach to young children's teachers because this method is a natural way to build on children's expressive and cognitive activities and because it is flexible and adaptable. She suggests that new teachers collect a large repertoire of activities from the many writers who have contributed to the development of this method. Allen and Allen's *Language Experience Activities* (1982) is a valuable resource. Because no one reading method is superior, teachers should be able to use features of phonic, linguistic, or sight-word recognition that seem useful at any given time (Robisson, 1983). In other words, combine methods.

The language arts approach to reading instruction introduces children to written words through their own interest in play, through their enjoyment of speaking, and by listening to language. Often, children's first experience with written words comes from their own speech and actions. A sign that says "John's Block Tower" or "Free Kittens" may be the child's first exposure to reading. The emphasis is on the fact that words are part of daily living.

Educators' attitudes toward reading instruction have been influenced by various factors: current research, some American children's struggle to read, poor national reading performance (National Assessment of Educational Progress, 1995), and children's lack of school success because of their reading ability. Natural and organic approaches have lost favor. They are thought to be incomplete—good as far as they go, but not as systematic or explicit as they might be.

The Whole-Language Movement

Enthusiasm for a reading philosophy and approach called "whole language" is apparent in some elementary schools.

Whole-language advocates believe in offering children meaningful and functional literature in full literary texts rather than through worksheets or dittoed handouts. The approach emphasizes the interrelated nature of the language arts. It believes that learning in any one area of language arts helps learning in others.

The *whole-language approach* is similar to what is termed the *natural-language approach* in early childhood books, journals, and professional teacher-training literature. Ferguson (1988) describes the whole-language approach as a philosophy that suggests that children learn language skill by following the natural learning behavior that governs the way they learn to talk. She notes that it is important that writing, listening, reading, and speaking activities grow from a child's experiences and interests (Figure 17–11). The teacher directs natural curiosity into activities that develop skills.

All sorts of literature (instead of basal readers) are used in whole-language classrooms, including posters, comics, classic literature, quality books, magazines, and newspapers, to mention a few. Poetry, songs, chants, and simple drama activities are among the language activities offered. The whole-language teacher presents opportunities for learning and development by relating activities to a single theme. Spontaneous conversational exchanges are typical and seen as enhancing and extending learning. Teachers using this approach draw attention to connections between

FIGURE 17–11 Because Evan has displayed an interest in a special topic, the teacher provides a related book.

speaking, writing, and reading by saying things like, "I heard you say *boat*. This is how you write that. Now let's read it." There are usually no ability-grouped reading circles, and classrooms are described as busy, active, and full of talk.

K. Goodman (1986) has listed basic beliefs that most early childhood educators attempting whole-language instruction believe are crucial.

◆ Whole-language learning builds around whole learners learning whole language in whole situations.

◆ Whole-language learning assumes respect for language, for the learner, and for the teacher.

◆ The focus is on meaning, not on language itself, in authentic speech and literacy events.

◆ Learners are encouraged to take risks and invited to use language, in all its varieties, for their own purposes.

◆ In a whole-language classroom, all the varied functions of oral and written language are appropriate and encouraged.

Critics point out that there are no formulas for planning, developing, organizing, and managing whole-language curriculum and that consequently, whole-language teachers with similar philosophies may differ in what curriculum they present. Other criticism usually centers on the teacher's ability to assess each child's reading progress and the lack of instruction in phonics. Walmsley and Adams (1993) speak about the challenge apparent in translating whole-language theory into practice.

Letting go some or all of the traditional teacher's control of the classroom's activities and behaviors does not come easily to teachers, even if they subscribe to a child-centered philosophy. And the consequences of liberating oneself from traditional practice are often not easy to accept. Many of the teachers are finding it hard to adjust to a changed classroom environment, even though few of them have serious doubts about the instructional philosophy they have newly embraced.

Walmsley and Adams (1993) predict the whole-language movement will survive but not dominate American public education. This has proved to be true. Exclusion of phonics instruction by some whole-language teachers and lower reading achievement test scores in some whole-language classrooms have caused additional concern. In 1987 California adopted a reading program focused on teaching children to read simply by exposing them to literature. Reading achievement scores fell, and California fourth graders tied for last place among states in the 1994 National Assessment of Educational Progress' reading report card.

In Weaver's view (1998c), whole language has become a full-fledged, although still evolving, theory of learning and teaching. It exemplifies a constructionist view of learning, believing concepts and complex processes are constructs of the human brain; therefore, research suggests the greater the intellectual and emotional involvement in learning, the more effectively the brain learns, uses, and retains what is learned.

Resources for early childhood teachers wishing to know more about reading instruction are found in the Additional Resources section at the end of this chapter.

Literature-Based Reading Programs

A *literature-based reading* curriculum has been adopted or recommended in many states. Huck (1992) believes that teachers using this approach to reading instruction fall into three groups (or types) depending on how "literature-based" is defined and carried out in their classrooms. The three types Huck identifies may vary somewhat with each teacher.

1. *Literature-based readers.* Basal reading programs that use literature content texts are adopted. In about 80 percent of these texts, the stories are faithful to the original writing. Books are based on selections of stories, not whole books. Teachers' guides and workbooks suggest fragmented kinds of word study and fill-in-the-blank exercises.

2. *Basalization of literature.* A literature-based reading program uses real books to study but treats them as basal readers.

3. *Comprehensive literature program.* Literature permeates the curriculum. Teachers read aloud to children; they give children a choice of real books for their own reading; they make use of the fine informational books that we have today to use literature in every area of the curriculum; and they encourage children's response to books through discussion, drama, art, and writing. Their primary goal is to produce children who not only know how to read but also become readers.

Educators are examining New Zealand's literature-based reading approach because New Zealand is recognized as the most literate country in the world. New Zealand's instructional approach is similar to whole-language theory put into practice. The instructional model was instituted after educational research pointed to the success of literature-based models. An influx of culturally diverse children who were not adequately progressing in reading prompted New Zealand's use of new instructional methodology.

Decoding–Phonetic–Reading Approach

Decoding, using a *phonetic approach* to reading instruction, is based on teaching children the 44 language sounds (*phonemes*), which are 26 alphabet letters and combinations (*graphemes*). This approach assumes that, to read, children first must be able to "decode"; that is, they must be able to pronounce the letter sequences they see on a page based on what they know about the link between spelling and sound. An underlying skill is phonemic awareness, the understanding that words, even simple ones like *cat,* are composed of individual sounds called phonemes, which make a difference in meaning. Only one phoneme makes the difference between *rope* and *soap.*

Although phonetic approaches differ widely, most users believe that when children know which sounds are represented by which letters or letter combinations, they can "attack" an unknown word and decode it. Some schools using this approach begin decoding sessions when all sounds have been learned; others expose children to select sounds and offer easily decoded words early. A few phonetic approach systems require teachers to use letter sounds exclusively and later introduce the individual letter names, such as *a, b, c,* and so forth.

Five "word-attack" (or decoding) skills are helpful in the complicated process of learning to read.

1. *picture clues*—using an adjacent picture (visual) to guess at a word near it (usually on the same page)

2. *configuration clues*—knowing a word because you remember its outline

3. *context clues*—guessing an unknown word by known words that surround it

4. *phonetic clues*—knowing the sound a symbol represents

5. *structural clues*—seeing similar parts of words and knowing what these symbols say and mean

Calkins (1997) believes that phonics is most useful when a reader already has some general notion of what a word should be. A child trying to guess a word he does not know at the end of a sentence read by an adult, such as "the cup fell on the f____" might guess "fire." Such a guess would be phonetically reasonable, but a child relying on meaning would guess "floor."

Cunningham (2003), who attempted to identify the best way to teach phonics, cites the findings of The National Reading Panel:

> The National Reading Panel (2000) reviewed the experimental research on teaching phonics and determined that explicit and systematic phonics is superior to non-systematic or no phonics, but that there is no significant difference in effectiveness among the kinds of systematic phonics instruction. They also found no significant difference in effectiveness among tutoring, small-group, or whole-class phonics instruction.

Advocates of **phonetic instruction** are often critical and vocal about the exclusive use of any one reading approach that neglects phonics. Most teachers recognize that some children can learn to read with little or no phonetic instruction. They also note that many children may have difficulty without it.

See additional readings on phonetic instruction in the Additional Resources section at this chapter's end.

Look-and-Say Method

Many of the children who do read during preschool years have learned words through a "look-and-say" (whole-word) approach. That is, when they see the written letters of their name or a familiar word, they can identify the name or word. They have recognized and memorized that group of symbols. It is believed that children who learn words in this fashion have memorized the shape or configuration of the word. They often confuse words that have similar outlines, such as "Jane" for "June" or "saw" for "sew." They may not know the alphabet names of the letters or the sounds of each letter. This approach was prevalent in public school reading instruction in the twentieth century, but it is rarely used today. Children who are good at noticing slight differences and who have good memories seem to progress and become successful readers.

Other Approaches to Reading Instruction

Many elementary school districts emphasize that their approach to reading instruction is a *combined* or *balanced approach*. This approach offers a rich diet of quality literature and literary experiences plus a sound foundation of phonics.

Morrow and Asbury (2003) recommend and describe a *comprehensive approach* as follows:

> A comprehensive approach that acknowledges the importance of both form (pho-

netic awareness, phonics mechanics, etc.), and function (comprehension, purpose, meaning) of the literacy processes, and recognizes that learning occurs most effectively in a whole-part-whole context. This type of instruction is characterized by meaningful literacy activities that provide children with both the skills and the desire to achieve proficient and lifelong literacy learning (Gambrell & Mazzoni, 1999).

There are multiple experiences with word study activities; guided, shared, silent, collaborative, independent, and content-connected reading and writing; and oral reading to build fluency. The reading and writing take place in whole-class, small-group, one-on-one, teacher directed, and social center settings in which children can practice what they have learned. Materials used include instructional texts, manipulatives, and meaningful children's literature. The instruction is spontaneous, authentic, and not only involves students in problem solving, but it is also direct, explicit, and systematic.

Cassidy and Cassidy (2004) conducted a survey of 25 literacy leaders from the boards of prominent literacy organizations. They found that scientific evidence-based reading research and instructional approaches are the hottest topics in literacy learning.

Other survey topics of very decided interest were reading comprehension, direct/explicit instruction, English as a second language learners, fluency, high-stakes assessment, literacy coaches/reading coaches, phonemic awareness, phonics, and political/policy influences on literacy.

Reading Instruction in Public Elementary Schools

The National Reading Panel (2000) points out that an individual teacher's method of reading instruction is heavily influenced by many factors, including teacher experience regarding

---

phonetic instruction — instruction in phonics is instruction that stresses sound-symbol relationships. Used especially in beginning reading instruction.

what works, politics, economics, and the popular wisdom of the day.

Cunningham and Creamer (2003) have reviewed what has happened since 2000.

> In 2000, the National Institute of Child Health and Human Development (NICHD) published the report of the National Reading Panel. This panel, commissioned by the NICHD and the U. S. Secretary of Education at the request of the U. S. Congress in 1997, was charged to review and assess the research on teaching reading, with implications for both classroom practice and further research. This report has already been used to inform policy on literacy education and has begun to serve as a means of enforcement for these policies.

These authors also note that reading instruction up to the present has experienced a "pendulum swing"—in the middle to late 1990s from whole language and silent reading to intensive phonics and oral reading. Other eras are identified as follows:

◆ phonics era (1956–1964)
◆ language, literature, and discovery-learning era (1965–1974)
◆ individualized specific skills instruction era (1975–1986)
◆ language, literature, and discovery-learning era (1987–1995)
◆ phonics and oral reading era (1996–)

In a review of current reading instruction, one finds the terms *balanced, eclectic, research-based, accountable, phonetic awareness, phonics instruction, fluency, comprehension,* and *alphabetics.* The field of reading instruction seems to lack consensus concerning what constitutes the best practices for the teaching of reading.

Cunningham and Creamer (2003) believe that educators' understanding of different eras and schools of thought can make a real contribution to children's literacy learning. Teachers, they believe, influence most schools and construct their own version of best practices in reading instruction.

Standards, assessment, and accountability are current factors in public school classrooms. The No Child Left Behind Act is driving change. School boards and school districts are promoting reading instruction based on standards. Teachers and teacher groups realize their instructional methods and strategies must match and fit within identified language arts parameters. Testing will take place, and the results will be published. Every effort is being made to make parents and early childhood educators aware of the foundations of literacy, particularly the language skills and abilities necessary for successful participation in kindergarten. These include phonological and phonemic awareness, an understanding of the alphabetic principle, alphabet letter recognition, social and group skills, concepts about print, an adequate vocabulary, oral language, listening ability, early reading, writing and invented spelling development, and visual-perceptual skills.

THE READING RECOVERY PROGRAM

Reading Recovery (RR), a well-known beginning reading intervention program, was designed for first-graders experiencing difficulty learning to read. The program provided one-on-one tutoring by teachers who received extensive training in beginning reading theory and practical application. Marie Clay (1993), a New Zealand educator, is credited as being the "architect" of the program.

Teacher-tutors' daily routine with identified children included the rereading of familiar books, working with alphabet letters, writing a sentence, and learning a new book (Invernizzi, 2003). Tutored lessons lasted 30 minutes and continued for 12 to 20 weeks, or until the child reached the level of the classroom's middle level reading group.

RR evaluation studies conducted by Shanahan and Barr (1995) found

> . . . children who received Reading Recovery instruction make sizable gains in reading achievement during the first grade year [comparing] favorably with those of higher achieving first graders who received only classroom instruction, along with compensatory support.

Other researchers suggest that earlier intervention aimed at preventing problems would yield more powerful benefits than later attempts of remediation (Slavin, Karweit, & Wasik, 1994). In other words, intervention should occur before problems are apparent.

RR, a model used by many other later tutoring programs, has its critics. These criticisms mention RR's use of an incidental, student-centered approach to phonics and vocabulary development and its expense.

A controversy exists concerning the stability of RR student gains. Some evaluators believe gains diminished substantially during the students' third and fourth school years.

THE ROLE OF STORY TIMES AND BOOK-READING EXPERIENCES

Many teachers who are faced with the responsibility of teaching reading believe that the ease in learning to read is directly related to the amount of time a child has been read to by parents, teachers, and others. Think of the difference in exposure hours between a child who has been read to nightly and one who has not.

Books have a language of their own; conversation is quite different. Books are not just written oral conversation but include descriptions, primarily full sentences, rhythm, dialogue, and much more. Listen to adults as they read books to young children; they adopt special voices and mannerisms and communicate much differently from everyday speech. Through repeated experience, children learn that illustrations usually reflect what a book is saying; this knowledge helps them make educated guesses of both meanings and printed words adjacent to pictures.

Storybook sessions are reading sessions and can greatly affect the child's future with books. Yaden, Smolkin, and Conlon (1989) speak about the foundation for later mastery of reading, which children can acquire from storybook reading.

> . . . storybooks provide a variety of information about the way print communicates meaning and represents the sounds of oral language just as environmental print may influence children's acquisition of print knowledge.

If teachers wish to evaluate how well they are doing in making books important to children in their programs, the following set of questions (Cazden, 1981) will help.

- During free-choice periods, how many children go to the library corner and look at books by themselves?
- How many requests to read during the day do adults get from children?
- How many children listen attentively during story time?
- How many books have been borrowed by parents during the week?
- Which books have become special favorites, as shown by signs of extra wear?

PARENTS ROLE IN READING

Parents often want to find ways to help their children succeed in school. Because the ability to read is an important factor in early schooling, parents may seek the advice of the teacher.

Many programs keep parents informed of the school's agenda and goals and the children's progress. An early childhood center's staff realizes that parents and teachers working together can reinforce what children learn at home and at school.

The following are suggestions for parents who want to help their children's language and reading-skill development. Many are similar to suggestions for teachers in early childhood centers.

- Show an interest in what children have to say. Respond to children, giving clear, descriptive, full statements.
- Arrange for children to have playmates and to meet and talk to people of all ages.
- Make children feel secure. Encourage and accept their opinions and feelings.
- Develop a pleasant voice and offer the best model of speech possible.

◆ Encourage children to listen and to explore by feeling, smelling, seeing, and tasting, when possible.

◆ Enjoy new experiences. Talk about them as they happen. Each community has interesting places to visit with young children—parks, stores, museums, zoos, buses, and trains are only a few suggestions.

◆ Read to children and tell them stories; stop when they lose interest. Try to develop children's enjoyment of books and knowledge of how to care for them. Provide a quiet place for children to enjoy books on their own.

◆ Listen to what children are trying to say rather than how they are saying it.

◆ Have confidence in children's abilities. Patience and encouragement help language skills grow.

◆ If parents have questions about their children's language skills, they should consult the children's teachers.

SUMMARY

The fourth area of the language arts is reading. Early childhood centers do not offer formal reading instruction because it is developmentally inappropriate. A few preschoolers do have actual reading skill. Most preschoolers, however, are only beginning to form ideas about reading. Early childhood educators offer systematic and explicit instruction in literacy skills. They work to prepare and promote children's ability to learn to read with ease when formal reading instruction begins.

The goal of the teacher is to blend the language arts skills—listening, speaking, reading, printscript, and viewing—into successful experiences. Because the skills are so closely connected, one activity can flow into another activity in a logical fashion. This gives young children a clearer picture of communication.

Experiences in classic and contemporary, quality literature and other language arts activities provide a background for reading. Abilities, attitudes, skills, and understanding grow at an individual rate. There are many methods of teaching language arts; each center decides which course of action or activities are best suited for attending children. Children exposed to a rich offering of language opportunities that includes paying attention to the understanding of written and oral materials are judged to have the best chance of becoming competent and lifelong readers.

This chapter reviewed a number of reading methods and approaches used to teach reading, and it cited current practice and the factors influencing it. The child's crucial development of positive attitudes concerning reading, books, and their own communicating competencies was emphasized.

Parents and teachers work together to give children the opportunity to gain reading skill and to keep children's interest alive and personally rewarding.

ADDITIONAL RESOURCES

Readings

Adams, M. J. (1998). *Beginning to read.* Cambridge, MA: The MIT Press.

Ashton-Warner, S. (1963). *Teacher.* New York: Simon & Schuster.

Calkins, L. M. (2000). *The art of teaching reading.* New York: Longman.

Clay, M. M. (1997). *The early detection of reading difficulties.* Portsmouth, NH: Heinemann.

Morrow, L. M. (2005). *Literacy development in the early years: Helping children read and write.* Boston: Allyn and Bacon.

Pianta, R., & La Paro, K. (2003). Improving early school success. *Educational Leadership, 60,* 24–29.

Snow, C. E., Burns, M. S., & Griffin, P. (Eds.). (1998). *Preventing reading difficulties in young children.* Washington, DC: National Academy Press.

Venn, C., Jahn, M., & Shreve, R. (2002). *All ready reading and writing preschool guidebook.* Casper, WY: All Ready LLC.

Readings on Phonetic Instruction

Cunningham, P. M. (2000). *Phonics they use: Words for reading and writing.* New York: Addison-Wesley/Longman.

Ehri, L. C., & Nunes, S. R. (2002). The role of phonemic awareness in learning to read. In A. E. Farstrup & S. J. Samuels (Eds.), *What research has to say about reading instruction* (pp. 110–139). Newark, DE: International Reading Association.

National Reading Panel. (2000). *Teaching children to read: An evidence-based assessment of the scientific research literature on reading and its implications for reading instructions.* Washington, DC: National Institute of Child Health and Human Development.

Yopp, H. K., & Yopp, R. H. (2000). Supporting phonemic awareness development in the classroom. *The Reading Teacher, 54,* 130–143.

Children's Books

Barton, B. (1984). *Building a house.* New York: Puffin Books.

Christelow, E. (1989). *Five little monkeys jumping on the bed.* New York: Clarion Books.

de Paola, T. (1980). *The knight and the dragon.* New York: Putnam.

Hutchins, P. (1968). *Rosie's walk.* New York: Macmillan.

Krauss, R. (1974). *The carrot seed.* New York: Scholastic Book Services.

Shaw, C. G. (1947). *It looked like spilt milk.* New York: Harper.

HELPFUL WEB SITES

ERIC Clearinghouse on Disabilities and Gifted Education
http://ericec.org
Search digests for early reading ability articles.

High/Scope Educational Research Foundation
http://www.highscope.org
This site explains how children learn to read in High/Scope programs.

Indiana University
http://www.indiana.edu
Search for "digest readings."

International Reading Association
http://www.reading.org
This site provides additional standards information and readings. Search for IRA's position statement "What Is Evidence-Based Reading?"

KidSource Online
http://www.kidsource.com
Look for phonemic awareness information.

New York Public Library
http://www.nypl.org
Select *Children* for lists of recommended books.

Starfall
http://www.starfall.com
This free educational Web site focuses on learning to read.

On the Online Companion™, you will find a checklist for children's social and developmental behaviors. These behaviors have been associated with school readiness and learning to read. This is not a screening instrument but rather an inventory of the possible behaviors that indicate a successful beginning kindergarten experience. A child could have a few or many of the behaviors listed. Preschool alliteration activities can be fun and challenging. The Online Companion™ gives you a list of activity ideas. A suggested activity involves purposely connecting picture books to children's personal lives.

STUDENT ACTIVITIES

1. Invite a kindergarten teacher and a first-grade teacher to discuss their experiences and knowledge about young children and reading.

2. Observe a kindergarten class. List and describe any activities that increase a child's interest in reading or actual reading instruction.

3. Make a chart of printscript words (common words such as *dog* and *cat* and highly advertised words such as those naming commercial beverages or cereals; include children's names). Test these words with a group of four-year-olds in a gamelike way. Describe the children's response to your game.

4. Observe an older four-year-old. Using Figure 17–12, attempt to rate the child's behavior. Interview the child's teacher, putting his ratings in another color ink. Discuss the outcome of this exercise with others in your training group.

Rating Scale

    1 = often
    2 = frequently
    3 = sometimes
    4 = infrequently
    5 = rarely
    6 = unable to determine

1. requests adult to read a picture book
2. asks about story time
3. shares a book with a friend
4. spends time in classroom library area
5. has a favorite book
6. likes to leaf through picture books
7. joins story times eagerly
8. hurries to story time
9. pretends to read
10. says remembered words while book browsing
11. spends time choosing a book to browse
12. shares pages in books that have captured his attention
13. memorizes repeated words or phrases in books with others
14. looks focused or displays delight in book's happenings
15. wants to take books home
16. displays knowledge of a book taken home
17. talks about his home book collection
18. talks about visits to a community library
19. laughs at humorous portions of picture books
20. asks about illustrations at times
21. treats books with care
22. enjoys books on certain topics of interest to him
23. discusses book characters
24. loses self in a book and blocks out room happenings
25. can describe a book's story line (in part)
26. asks questions about book's happenings at times

Additional Comments:

_____

_____

_____

_____

FIGURE 17–12 Checklist of reading attitudes and behaviors.

5. In a small group, discuss what you would do and what your limitations would be if you were working with a group of young children and found that two of them were reading a few words.

6. Stage a debate. Divide the class into two groups: one presenting the disadvantages of teaching young children to read before first grade and the other presenting the advantages. Do some research at the library. Have each group discuss its position separately. Debaters from each team need to substantiate arguments by citing experts or written sources. Each team gets one point for each substantiation used during the actual debate.

7. Have volunteers role-play the following situation.

   A parent states to a teacher: "I know you believe in teaching Jonathan (her child) the alphabet, and all the other parents are teaching it to their children. Jonathan is just unable to learn it. The other children will seem bright to their kindergarten teacher, while Jonathan will seem slow. What should I do to help him?"

8. Read the following excerpt and write your reaction in preparation for a class discussion.

   Children begin reading signs and other environmental print (Jell-O and cereal boxes, McDonald's milk cartons, soup cans, toothpaste tubes) on their own when they find it useful or interesting to do so. If you can stand the pressure, take any 3-year-old to the grocery store, and you will quickly see what they are capable of reading. (Bartoli, 1995)

9. State your position concerning the need to offer children (who may be at risk for learning to read easily) selected activities and experiences before kindergarten.

CHAPTER REVIEW

A. Discuss the following situations briefly.

   1. A child asks you to listen while he reads a favorite book to you.

   2. You have noticed a young child who is able to read all of the printscript in the playroom.

   3. A parent notices his child is reading a few words and asks advice as to what to do.

B. How can a teacher include the four language arts in activities?

C. Explain what is meant by the following terms.

   reading   phonics
   readiness   configuration
   method   incongruities

D. Select the phrase that best completes each of the following sentences.

1. Between the ages of four and five,
   a. many children learn to read.
   b. a few children learn to read.
   c. children should be given reading instruction.
   d. most children will be ready to read.

2. The language arts are
   a. reading, printscript, and listening.
   b. speaking, reading, and listening.
   c. listening, speaking, writing (print), and reading.
   d. reading readiness, listening, speaking, and alphabet knowledge.

3. Children may begin reading because they
   a. have an interest in alphabet letters.
   b. have an interest in books.
   c. want to see what they say written down.
   d. have an interest in speaking, listening, or writing (printscript).
   e. all the above

4. Reading-like behavior
   a. includes a variety of skills, motives, and attitudes.
   b. can be defined as having an interest in reading.
   c. means at a certain age a child will perfect all the skills needed to read.
   d. means that reading should be taught to most preschoolers.

5. Parents and early childhood teachers work together so that
   a. parents will teach their children to read at home.
   b. teachers can teach reading during preschool years.
   c. what children learn at home and school can be reinforced by both parents and teachers.
   d. children's experiences at home and school will be the same.

E. Describe which of the reading instructional methods reviewed in this chapter seems more logical to you and why. Mention the distinguishing features of the method you choose.

F. What factors tend to predict child ease in learning to read?

SECTION 8

Settings Promoting Literacy:

At School and Home

CHAPTER 18

Developing a Literacy Environment

OBJECTIVES

After reading this chapter, you should be able to:

◆ Explain the need for materials in language-development activities.

◆ Assist teachers in the care, storage, and replacement of materials.

◆ Describe early childhood language games.

KEY TERMS

audiovisual
equipment

language
center

listening center

software

SAM AND THE ALPHABET CHART

When I asked four-year-old Sam, our new child, if he wanted his name put on the corner of his artwork, he nodded and said, "S for shoe, A for ape, M for milk." Later, I noticed our alphabet chart had those same pictorial representations.

QUESTIONS TO PONDER

1. Should this teacher talk to Sam about the alphabet chart? Why or why not?

2. How is a teacher to know if children in the class are using a posted alphabet chart as a reference?

3. What other alphabet materials might one find in a classroom?

This text has emphasized the need to provide children with a variety of interesting classroom materials, objects, and furnishings. Such materials are important in keeping programs alive, fascinating, and challenging.

Classroom materials and objects promote language skills in many ways.

- They provide the reality behind words and ideas.

- They provide the child with opportunities for sensory exploration, which increases children's knowledge of relationships and ability to identify the things around them.

- Materials capture attention, motivate play, and build communication skills.

- Familiar and favorite materials can be enjoyed over and over, with the child deciding how much time to devote to them.

- Many materials isolate one language and perceptual skill, allowing it to be practiced and accomplished.

In language arts centers, related instructional materials are located in one convenient area. Stocking, supervision, and maintenance of materials, furnishings, and equipment are easily accomplished. The classroom can be a place to grow, expand, test ideas, and predict outcomes of questions. A prepared environment provides successful experiences for all children in a climate in which ideas and creative learning flourish.

Neuman and Roskos (1992) state that a limited body of knowledge exists regarding how the physical features of a literacy-based classroom enhance learning. A preliminary study examining the impact of literacy-enriched play areas (ones with meaningful print) found preschool children spontaneously used almost twice as much print in their play (Neuman & Roskos, 1990). Consequently, teachers are urged to experiment and creatively design language arts centers and other play centers and monitor the effect of the room and its furnishings on children's language arts skills.

Suggestions for Print-Rich Environments

The following ideas for print-rich classrooms are from Du and Stoub (2004). Note that labels can be symbols, pictures, photos, or stickers.

- Label all area signs with pictures and words.
- Label all shelving units and containers.
- Label everything in the classroom as you find connections to current curriculum—doors, windows, tables, lights, and so on.
- Post a picture of the children's daily routine.
- Create a message board or daily newsletter where teachers can relate messages to children and vice versa.
- Create a place where children can sign in and out daily.
- Create a question for the day in print and discuss it.
- Use name cards that children select and put in slot pockets, if an area holds only a certain number of children.
- Make classroom games that include print and symbols.
- Have a helper chart.
- Have a pocket attendance chart.
- Design graphs with children's names.
- In housekeeping areas include cookbooks, phone books, recipe books, menus, and newspapers.
- Make lists with children concerning the functional use of print.

LANGUAGE ARTS CENTER

Full of communication-motivating activities, every inch of floor and wall space of a language arts center is used. Small areas are enlarged by building upward with lofts or bunks to solve floor-space problems in crowded centers (Figure 18–1). Adding areas that children can climb into is another useful space-opening device.

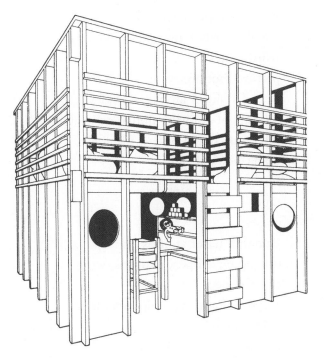

FIGURE 18–1 Solving space problems.

A **language center** has three main functions: (1) it provides looking and listening activities for children, (2) it gives children an area for hands-on experiences with communication-developing materials, and (3) it provides a place to store materials. The ideal area has comfortable, soft furnishings with ample work space, proper lighting, and screening to block out other areas of active classrooms. Miller (1987) urges teachers to make centers cozy and inviting with pillows, a covered crib mattress, or a bean bag chair or two. He believes the area can become a place of refuge for the child who needs to get away from the bustle of the group and a nice place for the teacher to spend some time with children individually.

Language arts centers should be quiet places that are separated from the more vigorous activities of the average playroom. Suggested furnishings are listed by category.

General-Use Materials
    one or more child-size tables and a few chairs

shelving
dividers or screens
soft-cushioned rocker, easy chair, or couch
soft pillows
crawl-into hideaways, lined with carpet or fabric (Figure 18–2)
individual work space or study spots
audiovisuals and electrical outlets
book racks that display book covers
chalkboard
storage cabinets
flannel board
pocket chart
children's file box (Figure 18–3)
bookcase (Figure 18–4)
bulletin board
carpet, rug, or soft floor covering
chart stand or wall-mounted wing clamps
wastebasket

FIGURE 18–2 A crawl-into area for quiet language activities.

language center — a classroom area specifically set aside and equipped for language arts–related activities and child use.

Writing and Prewriting Materials

paper (scratch, lined, newsprint, and typing paper in a variety of sizes)

table

file or index cards

paper storage shelf

writing tools (crayons, nontoxic washable felt markers, and soft pencils in handy contact-covered containers)

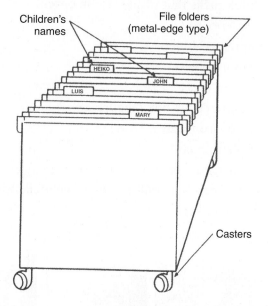

FIGURE 18–3 Children's work file box.

primary typewriter

small, sturdy typewriter table or desk

word boxes

picture dictionary

wall-displayed alphabet guides

cutouts of colorful alphabet letters

tabletop chalkboards with chalk

blank book skeletons

scissors

tape

erasers

alphabet letter stamps and ink pads

tracing envelopes, patterns, wipe-off cloth

chart paper

magnet board with alphabet letters

hole punch

yarn

write-on, wipe-off boards

stick-on notes

notepads

pencil sharpener

envelopes

baskets, desk trays, and flat boxes

stationery

FIGURE 18–4 Children are using a bookcase for puppet play.

brass paper fasteners

set of printscript strips with attending children's and staff's names

stickers

glue sticks

stencils

Reading and Prereading Materials

books (including child-made examples)

book and audiovisual combinations (read-alongs)

cutouts of favorite story characters

rebus story charts

Speech Materials

puppets and puppet theaters

flannel board sets

language games

Audiovisual Equipment

overhead projector

record, tape, or CD/DVD player; headsets; and jacks (Figure 18–5)

story records

language master, recording cards

picture files

television screen and VCR

computer and printer

video camera

digital camera

Adults usually supervise use of **audiovisual equipment** in a language center, and a number of the simpler machines can be operated by children after a brief training period. Tape recorders, CD/DVD players, and headsets require careful introduction by the teacher.

THE TEACHER'S ROLE IN LANGUAGE CENTERS

Teachers are congenial, interested companions for the children: sharing books; helping them with projects; recording their dictation; playing and demonstrating language games; making words, word lists, signs, or charts (Figure 18–6);

FIGURE 18–5 Listening to prerecorded books is possible in some classrooms.

audiovisual equipment — any mechanical or nonmechanical item useful in offering sight or hearing experience.

Hurt no living thing:
Ladybug nor butterfly,
Nor moth with dusty wing,
Nor cricket chirping cheerily
Nor grasshopper
so light of leap,
Nor dancing gnat,
Nor beetle fat,
Nor harmless worms
that creep.

FIGURE 18–6 Language center chart.

and helping children use the center's equipment.

Teachers slip in and out as needed and monitor equipment use. Vigorous or noisy play is diverted to other room areas or outside yard areas. Children who have been given clear introductions to a language center's materials and clear statements concerning expectations in use of the center's furnishings may need little help. It may be necessary, however, to set rules for the number of children who can use a language center at a given time.

The teacher explains new materials that are to become part of the center's collection. The materials are demonstrated before they are made available to the children.

Posting children's work on the center bulletin board and planning chalkboard activities and printing messages that may catch the children's attention motivate interest in and use of the center. Plants and occasional fresh flowers in vases add a pleasant touch. To help children use equipment, materials, and machines on their own, teachers have become inventive, using step-by-step picture charts posted above or near materials. Color-coded dots make buttons or dials stand out. Some centers control machine use by giving training sessions in which children obtain "licenses." Children without licenses need to have adult companions.

Another task the teacher may want to undertake is making read-along recordings to accompany favorite books. The popularity of read-alongs cannot be denied, nor can the educational benefits. Children who use read-alongs are learning word recognition as well as some of the more advanced reading skills. For fun and pleasure, the lure of read-alongs makes them another gateway into the world of books. Teachers should consider the following when making recordings:

> A narrator's pacing is important. It cannot be too fast, or the child trying to follow along will be lost. If it is too slow, the child will become bored. The inflection and tone of the voice are also vital. The narrator cannot be condescending or patronizing; neither should there be an attempt to "act out" the story and run the risk of making the story secondary to the performance. (Ditlow, 1988)

Besides these factors a teacher needs to estimate audience attention span and use a pleasant page-turning signal.

HOUSEKEEPING AND BLOCK AREAS

Educators emphasize the importance of housekeeping and block areas, both of which encourage large amounts of social interaction and the use of more mature, complex language. High levels of dramatic play interaction are also encouraged in theme (unit) centers. Teachers design spacious, well-defined, well-stocked (theme-related) partitioned room areas for block play and dramatic play.

DISPLAYS AND BULLETIN BOARDS

Interesting eye-level wall and bulletin board displays capture the children's attention and promote discussion. Displaying children's work (with children's permission), names, and themes based on their interests increases their feelings of accomplishment and their sense of pride in their classroom. Displays that involve active child participation are suggested. Many can be designed to change daily or weekly.

Printscript is used on bulletin boards with objects, pictures, or patterns. Book pockets, picture hooks, $1/4$-inch elastic attached to clothespins, and sticky bulletin board strips allow pieces to be added and removed.

Figure 18–7 shows one bulletin board idea. The child selects a spot to paste her picture (photo) and name. A colored line is drawn between the photo and name. Later, colored lines can be drawn connecting friends' pictures.

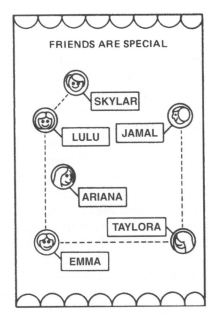

FIGURE 18–7 Bulletin board idea.

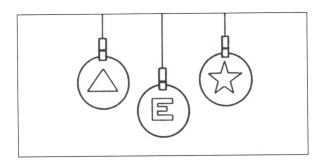

FIGURE 18–8 Plastic lid chalkboard activity.

CHALKBOARD ACTIVITIES

One of the most underutilized instructional items in early childhood centers can be the chalkboard. The following chalkboard activities are suggested to help children's language development.

◆ *Tracing templates and colored chalk*
Using a sharp tool, cut large plastic coffee can lids into a variety of patterns (Figure 18–8). Suspend the patterns on cord (or elastic with clothespins) over the chalkboard.

◆ *Pattern games*
Draw Figure 18–9 on the chalkboard. Ask the children what shape comes next in the pattern. Then draw Figure 18–10 and see whether the children can make a line path from the dog to the doghouse.

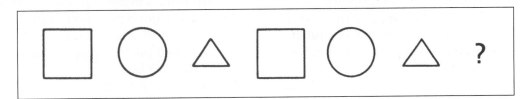

FIGURE 18–9 What comes next in the pattern?

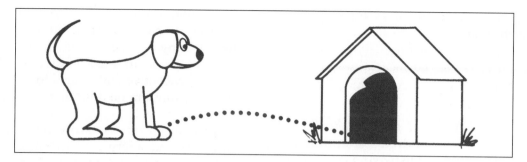

FIGURE 18–10 A left-to-right skill builder.

AUDIOVISUAL EQUIPMENT

Budgets often determine the availability of audiovisual materials in a center. Care of equipment and awareness of operating procedures are important. Special fund-raising projects, rental agreements, borrowing arrangements, or donations have secured audiovisuals for some programs. The machine's instruction manual should be studied for the proper care and maintenance necessary for efficient use.

The following audiovisual equipment enriches a center's language arts program activities.

Camera (Including Polaroid and Video Cameras). A camera can be used to provide images and photos that are useful in speaking activities, displays, and games.

Projector and Screens. Common home, school, field trip, and community scenes can be discussed, written about (experience stories), or used for storytelling.

Lite-bord™. This is a special display board that uses nontoxic erasable crayons for making colorful drawings and words that glow.

Video Cameras. Children enjoy being recorded while displaying and explaining their creations. It has multiple uses.

Overhead Projectors, Screens, and Transparencies. Stories with silhouettes or numerous transparency activities can be designed. Small patterns and alphabet letters can be enlarged and copied by teachers for a variety of uses. McDonald and Simons (1989) suggest drawing or placing images on the screen while storytelling or reading poetry (for example, using a Humpty Dumpty picture sequence while reciting the rhyme). Meier (2004) recommends supplying children with overhead projector sheets, or other kinds of plastic sheets, so that they can project their images and words onto a large screen. Some, but not all, picture books work well with this instructional technique. If text and illustration appear on the same page, this type of sharing is recommended. Teachers may have limited access to equipment used to make transparencies, but if available, the author strongly recommends this type of alternative storybook reading. Illustrations can be enlarged and enjoyed. Text appears giant-sized.

Opaque Projector. Pages of picture books can be projected on wall areas to offer a new way to read books. Guessing games are also possible. Characters from picture books can become life-size companions.

Listening Center *Equipment.* Headsets accommodating up to eight children at one time adapt to cassette, CD, and record players. Volume control is set on the jack box.

CD Players. Most centers have this piece of equipment. Commercial suppliers of story CDs are plentiful.

Digital Camera. Classroom photographs can be displayed on the computer, and prints can be made for display. Photo printers are available from many manufacturers.

Digital Camcorder. Classroom action photography can be displayed on television sets and computers, or prints can be made.

Pocket Wall Charts with Stands. This handy teacher's aid displays alphabet letters, words, sentences, shapes, pictures, colors, names, and so on. It is easy to use. Teachers prefer see-through pocket styles. These can be teacher-made.

Big Book Storage Rack. See-through individual hanging bags can be used for big books and oversized materials; this visual solves the problem of storing large items.

Write and Wipe Boards and Easels. Colored markers glide on and wipe off quickly. They are useful for teacher activities or child use. They are made in freestanding or tabletop styles, and some are magnetic, so plastic alphabet letters and numerals with magnets will stick.

Computer. Besides computer use with software programs and use as a word processor, the computer has become a versatile piece of equipment.

Tape Recorders. This is still a popular audiovisual aid that is used in early childhood centers. The tape recorder opens up many activity ideas. Suggestions for language development activities with tape recorders follow:

- Record children's comments about their artwork or project. "Tell me about . . ." is a good starter. Put the tape and artwork together in the language center so that it is available for the children's use.
- Let the children record their comments about a group of plastic cars, human figures, animals, and so on, after they arrange them as they wish.
- Have children discuss photographs or magazine pictures.
- Record a child's comments about a piece of fruit that she has selected from a basket of mixed fruit.
- Record a "reporter's" account of a recent field trip.
- Gather a group of common items, such as a mirror, comb, brush, and toothbrush. Let the child describe how these items are used.
- Record a child's description of peeling an orange or making a sandwich with common spreads and fillings.
- Record a child's comments about her block structures. Take a Polaroid photo and make both tape and photo available in the listening and looking area.

Television Sets and VCRs. These can be purchased as separate units or as combined machines. Children's classic literature is available. Local video rental stores and public libraries stock a variety of titles. Active discussion of what is viewed is recommended.

Discussion or Study Prints. A collection of large posters, photographs, mounted magazine pictures, and life-size book characters can be used in activities. Visuals can increase child verbalization and serve as creative "jumping off" spots.

The Use of Picture Files

Picture files consisting of collections of drawings and photographs are made available to children in classroom language centers. Teachers find they are invaluable motivators for many language-related child activities. Magazine photos and photos showing classroom scenes or attending children are popular with children. Images can be rotated and used to supplement a present course of study.

It is a good idea to start with enlarged photographs of each child and staff (affix to a firm backing). Resources for pictures include coloring books, shape books, inexpensive children's books, calendars, catalogs, trade journals, travel folders, and toy advertisements.

Suggested activities include:

- writing captions.
- storytelling from a series of pictures.
- giving names to animal pictures.
- finding hidden objects.
- categorizing pictures.
- finding objects that have alphabet letters printed on them.
- putting illustrations in a sequence and telling a story.
- matching pictures with related objects.
- finding alphabet letters in signs.
- identifying logos or outdoor signs from familiar fast-food restaurants or other local businesses.
- singing or creating a song to go with a picture.
- rhyming with pictures.
- finding things of the same shape, color, and category.
- classifying pictures by season.
- making a sound to fit a picture.
- writing a letter to someone shown in a picture.
- finding an object in the classroom that looks like something in a picture.
- choosing a favorite from a picture collection of food or other objects.
- labeling everything in a picture.
- finding things that start with the same alphabet letter sound.

It is easy to see there are many possibilities. Teacher ingenuity creates others. Teachers often protect pictures with clear contact paper or lamination. Classrooms may have a teacher's set and a children's set. Smart teacher substitutes pack them along for "filler" or "spur of the moment" activities.

Technology and Literacy Learning

What do early childhood educators believe concerning the use of technology? Most will agree that machines, whether computers or other audiovisuals, can teach, support, assist, motivate, and be used for the practice and application of literacy skills. Technology cannot "be the teacher of literacy," but it can be a useful tool in assessing and tracking children's literacy skill development.

PLANNING LANGUAGE CENTERS AND COMPUTER CENTERS

Once rooms or areas are designated as language centers, staff members classify materials into "looking and listening" or "working with" categories (Figure 18–11). Display, storage, working space, and looking and listening areas are determined. Activities that require concentration are screened off when possible. Many different arrangements of materials and equipment within a language arts center are possible. Most centers rearrange furnishings until the most functional arrangement is found. For sample arrangements with different functions, refer to Figure 18–12.

Many children like to escape noise with a favorite book or puppet. Most centers provide these quiet retreats within a language arts center. School staffs have found creative ways of providing private space. Old footed bathtubs with soft pillows, packing crates and barrels, pillow-lined closets with doors removed, tepees, tents, and screened-off couches and armchairs have been found workable in some classroom language arts areas.

With the fears mentioned earlier in this text concerning the overuse of television and videos, some educators see computer programs as offering a "cartoon world" rather than the real experiences and human interactions upon which real knowledge and literacy depends. Early childhood educators realize that computer skills and knowledge may be necessary in elementary school grades; however, they may be unsure about the best time to introduce them to young children.

FIGURE 18–11 A puppet theater is often portable and can be moved around classrooms.

Slowly but steadily computer centers are becoming standard in three- and four-year-olds' preschool classrooms. Staffing, expense, and time for teacher preview of programs are important considerations. Many educators agree that computer centers are compatible with developmentally appropriate practice. Computers can offer problem solving, creative experiences, and literacy opportunities. Benefits cited by many early childhood advocates of child computer use include the following.

- Child cooperation and turn taking are promoted.
- The need for adult supervision is minimal once "rule use" is accepted and initial child training on mechanics has taken place.
- Children can work at their own speed.
- Opportunities for child collaboration, mentoring, negotiation, and joint solutions to problems are provided.
- Use builds children's self-confidence and also builds children's feelings of independence.

Benefits related to language arts include children's

- verbal interactions with a peer partner or others (Figure 18–13).

- experiences with alphabet letters, print, and words.
- ability to see uses of print, which include recording, informing, sending, and receiving messages.
- opportunity to create literary works that then can be recorded.
- experience in making greeting cards.
- exposure to rhyme.
- opportunity to match letters, patterns, rhymes, and words with pictorial representations.
- exposure to visual and interactive storybooks.

Teachers with computers in their classrooms will agree that it is appropriate to step in when children are frustrated or lack necessary user skills. They tend to offer minimal help if they believe the child can work out a problem on her own, thereby allowing the child to experience mastery and the resulting feeling of accomplishment. Most teachers periodically join children at the computer to ask questions or make comments that encourage the expansion of skill.

Centers develop simple computer area rules that are appropriate to their classroom, children, and equipment. Rules usually involve clean hands, number of children allowed at one time, how to ask for help, taking turns, time allowed per turn, use of earphones, and what training is required before use.

Haugland (1992) believes research suggests that three- and four-year-old children who use computers that support and reinforce the major objectives of their programs have significantly greater developmental gains when compared with children who have not had computer experiences in similar classrooms. Among the gain areas researched were nonverbal skills, verbal skills, problem solving, and conceptual skills (Figure 18–14).

Interestingly, computer program use has been found to improve the speech skills of children with dyslexia and other language-based learning disabilities (Kotulak, 1996). Researchers noted language comprehension improved to normal,

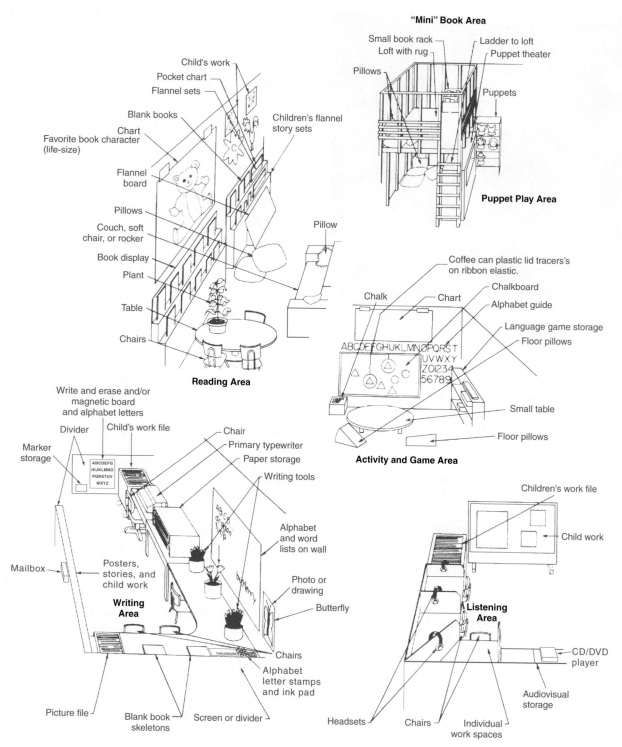

FIGURE 18–12 Language arts center.

near-normal, or above normal in children who had been 2 to 3 years behind peers in speech skills. The findings are especially encouraging for children who have difficulty learning to talk (developmental dysphasia) or who have subsequent reading problems (developmental dyslexia).

For preschool classrooms, Haugland (2000) recommends an initial training period, turn taking, cooperative learning in small groups, peer tutoring, hands-on experience, waiting lists, and a sufficient number of adults who make an "adult time" investment. **Software** variety should also be offered.

Software Selection

Kneas (1999) recommends making a list of program goals and believes developmentally appropriate integration begins with selecting

FIGURE 18–13 One peer can often instruct another.

FIGURE 18–14 Problem-solving programs can be experienced by one child or with a peer.

software — a wide range of commercial programs developed for computer users' convenience, education, entertainment, and so on.

hardware and software that will complement goals. She lists software features to check.

- does not include violence
- provides positive verbal and visual cues and responses (feedback)
- allows the child to control pace and action
- allows option of practicing a skill or moving on
- supports working alone or with others

Haugland and Wright (1997) and Fisher and Gillespie (2003) provide another guide to software selection.

> When teachers provide open-ended software that encourages creativity, rather than drill-and-practice software, this is developmentally appropriate. (Haugland & Wright, 1997)

> Open-ended programs encourage children to explore and to extend their thinking. They spark children's interest as well as social and cognitive development. (Fisher & Gillespie, 2003)

Other software features teachers need to examine include content, age appropriateness, pacing, child choices available, meaningful graphics and sound, clear directions for yet-to-read children, approaches to learning, and appropriate cost. The integrity and craftsmanship in a software program determines its effectiveness and quality.

Haugland (2000) cites the following four critical steps to maximize children learning through computer use.

1. selecting developmental software
2. selecting developmental Web sites
3. integrating these resources into the curriculum
4. selecting computers to support these learning experiences

She estimates only 25 percent of the increasingly available software designed for young children (using the Haugland Developmental Software Scale) was deemed developmentally appropriate.

Web sites, she believes, offer many rich educational opportunities and provide opportunities that appear to enhance problem solving, critical thinking skills, decision making, language skills, knowledge, research skills, the ability to integrate information, social skills, and self-esteem.

A resource magazine for selection of software follows:

> *Children's Technology Revue* (magazine)
> 120 Main Street
> Flemington, NJ 08822
> (Reviews software programs, rating each in six areas using a 1 to 5 rating scale. Lists features and describes a program and what it attempts to teach.)

Computer Software Programs

- Curious George: Reading and Phonics
  Publisher: Knowledge Adventure; ages: 3–6
  Identifying alphabet letters
- Destination Reading
  Publisher: Riverdeep, I; ages: 4–10, level K–3
  Stories with alphabet letter names and sounds
- Kidspiration 2.0
  Publisher: Inspiration Software, Inc.; age: preschool
  Oral language, print rich, letter recognition components
- Photo Kit Junior
  Publisher: APTE Inc; ages: pre-K–2
  Creation of slide shows, books, and so on; aids literacy skills
- Putt-Putt Pep's Birthday Surprise
  Publisher: Atari; ages: 3–6
  Critical thinking, listening, and memory skills

Other resources are included in this chapter's Additional Resources section.

Computer Location

Haugland (1997) states that an ideal classroom location for computers is a visible location where monitors can be seen throughout the classroom, enabling supervision and quick assistance (Figure 18–15). A computer center or

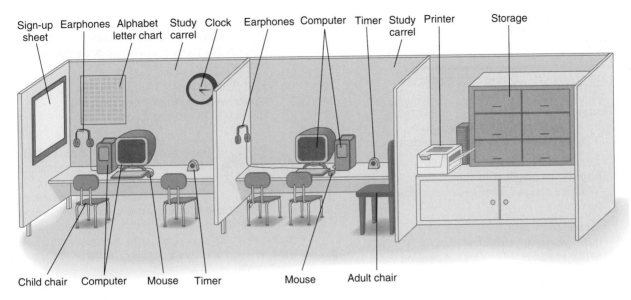

Sign-up sheet · Earphones · Alphabet letter chart · Study carrel · Clock · Earphones · Computer · Timer · Study carrel · Printer · Storage

Child chair · Computer · Mouse · Timer · Mouse · Adult chair

FIGURE 18–15 Computer center.

activity area in a preschool or kindergarten classroom will operate well with two or three computers and one or two printers (Haugland & Wright, 1997).

SUMMARY

When there is a language arts center within an early childhood playroom, language development materials are arranged in one central room location. Children follow their own interests, according to their preferences, which increases the children's interaction with materials and expands language skills.

A language center's material can include a wide range of teacher-made and commercially purchased items. Activities in listening, speaking, writing, and reading (or combinations of these) are side-by-side, promoting the child's ability to see relationships among them.

Audiovisual materials and equipment are useful language center devices. Costs sometimes limit their availability. Training in the use and care of audiovisual machines is necessary for efficient operation. Computer use in young children's classrooms continues to expand, and teacher screening of software programs is important.

ADDITIONAL RESOURCES

Readings

Anderson, G. T. (2000, March). Computers in a developmentally appropriate curriculum. *Young Children, 55*(2), 90–93.

Children's Technology Revue (monthly magazine), Scholastic Active Learning Associates, 120 Main St., Flemington, NJ 08822.

Clements, D. H. (1987, November). Computers and young children: A review of research. *Young Children, 43*(1), 34–44.

Elkind, D. (1996, July). Young children and technology: A cautionary note. *Young Children, 51*(6), 28–34.

Greenman, J. T. (1988). *Caring spaces: Learning places: Children's environments that work.* Redmond, WA: Exchange Press.

Haugland, S., & Wright, J. (1997). *Young children and technology: A world of discovery.* Boston: Allyn and Bacon.

Ingraham, P. (1997). *Caring and managing learning centers: A thematic approach.* Peterborough, NH: Crystal Springs.

Kritchevsky, S., & Prescott, E. (1996). *Planning environments for young children: Physical space.* Washington, DC: National Association for the Education of Young Children.

Papert, S. (1993). *The children's machine: Rethinking school in the age of the computer.* New York: Basic Books.

Shade, D. D., & Watson, J. A. (1990). Computers in early education: Issues put to rest. *Journal of Educational Computing Research, 6*(4), 375–392.

Weinstein, C., & David, T. (Eds.). (1987). *Spaces for children.* New York: Plenum.

HELPFUL WEB SITES

Computing with Kids
http://www.computingwithkids.com
This site offers a free weekly newsletter.

Constructive Playthings
http://www.playdesigns.com
This site reviews commercial equipment and furniture.

Earlychildhood.com
http://www.earlychildhood.com
Select readings or articles concerning early childhood computer use.

Kid Source Online
http://www.kidsource.com
Research articles on computers in the early childhood curriculum.

Lakeshore Learning Materials
http://www.lakeshorelearning.com
This site reviews commercial equipment and furniture.

NAEYC Technology & Young Children
http://www.techandyoungchildren.org
This site is an interest forum.

 The digital camera is a new tool to be added to the teacher's collection. The Online Companion™ describes how some pre-K teachers are using these cameras. A suggested student activity involves the creation of a rebus recipe chart. A reference list will acquaint the reader with readings concerning computers and young children, classroom work spaces, and language arts bulletin boards.

STUDENT ACTIVITIES

1. Observe an early childhood program. Describe the use and storage of language development materials.
2. Listen to three commercial story recordings. Judge and compare the quality of the recordings.
3. Invite an audiovisual company's sales representative to the class to demonstrate the company's product. (Seek instructor approval first.)
4. Develop a price list for five pieces of audiovisual equipment found in this chapter.
5. Interview two early childhood teachers on their use of audiovisuals in their language arts curriculum. Report the findings to the group.
6. Plan and conduct an activity for a group of preschoolers using a tape recorder.
7. Investigate three children's computer (software) programs. Report your findings.
8. Observe preschoolers interacting with a computer in an early childhood classroom. Take written notes during a 15-minute observation period. Share notes with a group of peers. Develop a list of classroom rules for child computer use.
9. Make an "L" chart by cutting out pictures of "L" words (or use another alphabet letter). Introduce it to a group of older four-year-olds. Think about how you will connect the chart to children's interests and lives while creating the chart. Print the items recognized in a list or on the chart and underline the beginning letter. Report your experiences.

CHAPTER REVIEW

A. List the advantages of an early childhood language arts center. What are the disadvantages?
B. List the teacher's duties in a well-functioning classroom language arts center (for example, supervision).
C. Describe or draw a picture of an imaginary language arts center that has a crawl-into bunk or loft area. It should be a place where a child could be alone to enjoy a book.
D. List seven useful machines mentioned in this chapter for classroom language arts centers.
E. Describe a well-designed classroom computer center.

CHAPTER 19

The Parent-Center Partnership

OBJECTIVES

After reading this chapter, you should be able to:

◆ Describe the parent-teacher partnership that affects language arts programs.

◆ List types of parent-school communications.

◆ Identify ways in which parents can strengthen a child's language growth.

KEY TERMS

family literacy   outreach
    programs   socioeconomic

THE POWER OF PERSISTENCE

At pick-up time, when Martin's mother arrived, Mei Lin, Martin's teacher, observed a behavior she had not seen in Martin. Martin immediately started what Mei Lin would describe as vocal badgering. His verbal assault included a steady stream of, "But you promised . . . , I want one . . . , You said so . . . , I didn't have one yesterday . . . , I want it . . . , You told me I could . . . , I'm ready . . . , Let's go." His voice got louder and louder and didn't stop when his mother attempted to talk to Mei Lin. It continued as Martin and his mother exited to the porch. Mei Lin then heard Martin's mother say, "All right. We'll go to McDonalds!"

QUESTIONS TO PONDER

1. What is happening here?

2. Should Mei Lin conference with Martin's mother? Why or why not?

3. Does this have anything to do with language development?

4. Is there anything positive about Martin's way with words?

Although parents and teachers are partners in a child's education, parents are always the child's foremost teachers and models, and the home is the child's first and most influential school (Figure 19–1). A poll conducted by *Newsweek* magazine indicates that parents are eager consumers of information about what is best for their offspring (Raymond, 2000). Six in ten parents read books about parenting or early childhood before their children were born; 32 percent took classes for new parents (Kantrowitz, 2000).

Parents are usually informed of the school's language and literacy curriculum during enrollment interviews. Most parents want to find out how teachers interact with their children on a daily basis to realize their instructional goals. Many educators believe that some parents have a great need to be told what to do in terms of their children's education and are vulnerable as a result. It is suggested that anxious parents need reassurance and can be encouraged to trust their instincts.

Okagaki & Diamond (2000) discuss the impossible task early childhood educators may face and caution against assumptions educators might make.

FIGURE 19–1 The child's foremost teachers and educators—parents.

Given the great diversity in our country it is virtually impossible to know what parents from each cultural group believe about child development and parenting practices. Even if it were possible to learn what each cultural group believes, great variation always exists within each group in terms of what individuals value and practice.

What can early childhood teachers do to enhance their ability to work with all families of children in their classrooms? We should not make assumptions about a family's practices. Within any cultural group— be it ethnic, racial, **socioeconomic**, or religious—individuals and families vary in their beliefs and adherence to the social conventions of their community.

Significant changes in family structure have occurred in the last decade. Twenty-five percent of all children, and fifty-seven percent of African-American children are living with an unmarried parent (Fields, 2001).

Bruns and Corso (2001) recommend that early childhood teachers examine a wide range of strategies to enhance their relationships with families. Researchers urge educators to consider a family-by-family approach. Intragroup differences may be as great as intergroup differences (Lynch & Hanson, 1998). Efforts should include hiring bicultural and bilingual staff to increase a program's ability to create trust.

Child literacy at home and school is influenced by three important factors: (1) setting, (2) models, and (3) planned and unplanned events. The setting involves what the home or school provides or makes available, including furnishings, space, materials and supplies, toys, books, and so forth. Family "connectedness" is crucial. Interactions with parents, siblings, grandparents, and other relatives enrich children's lives. Sharing hobbies, trips, chores, mealtimes, community and neighborhood happenings, conversations, and stories are all language-development opportunities. Access to additional settings outside the home is also

socioeconomic — relating to or involving a combination of social and economic factors.

considered. Time allowed or spent in community settings can increase or decrease literacy.

Preschools planning to influence the continued literacy development of attending children must face the fact that the low socioeconomic status of the home may greatly influence literacy. Differences in literacy achievement among children as a result of socioeconomic status are pronounced (Snow, Burns, & Griffin, 1998). Middle-class families usually offer their children the advantage of more joint book reading, more library visits, and more print-related experiences. Parents with low educational aspirations for their children and low motivation, which sometimes results from poverty, stress, fatigue, and unfortunate living conditions, are the parents who most need sensitive professional **outreach** from their children's teacher and school.

Family economics may determine the opportunities and materials that are available, and family ingenuity may overcome a lack of monetary resources. Most things that parents can do to encourage reading and writing involve time, attention, and sensitivity rather than money. All parents can be instrumental in fostering literacy if they spend time doing so. The usefulness of speaking, writing, and reading can be emphasized in any home. Children's literature may be borrowed from public libraries and other sources in almost all communities.

Although preschools are not as programmed as elementary schools and much of the learning in preschools goes hand-in-hand with firsthand exploration, parents still have a big edge over group programs in offering intimate, individualized adult-child learning situations. Family interactions during activities involve both the quality and quantity of communication (Figure 19–2). The supportive assistance given at home, the atmosphere of the home, parent-child conversations, and joint ventures can greatly affect the child's literacy development.

King (1985) describes parental actions and conversations that successfully promote language.

Successful parents listen to *what* children say and respond to them. They interpret

FIGURE 19–2 Some parents consult their child's teacher for language-developing ideas.

the child's language attempts and reply with related action accompanied by words and sentences. Learning is greater where children are supported by caring adults who share their world with them and enter into the children's worlds of play and talk, tuning in to their feelings and experiences. The essential element is the intimacy between child and adult who share a common environment which fosters the understanding of meanings intended.

McKenzie (1985) notes that children who found their efforts and attempts at language received and valued developed the confidence to continue. Children's learning flourishes when they are allowed some degree of control over their own actions and when they interact with adults who are receptive, less concerned with rightness and wrongness, and more likely to respond in ways that stretch thinking.

Early childhood centers design their own unique parent involvement programs. With increased federal and state emphasis on early childhood educators' working cojointly with parents and families, educators working in publicly funded programs will need to clarify their goals and analyze their efforts. Most educators

---

outreach — an early childhood program's attempt to provide supportive assistance to attending children's families to promote their children's success in school and developmental growth.

would agree any parental involvement must start with the development of a beginning relationship (Figure 19–3).

Developing Trust

Developing trust grows from parental feelings of being respected, accepted, and valued for their individual and cultural diversity, and it also grows when staff are sensitive to family economics. Educators need to be aware of what parents desire for their children. All of this starts the day parents walk through the school's door. What is on the walls and how they are welcomed and treated by staff are important. This calls for a consideration of parents' comfort and requires staff preparation and planning.

Identifying Supportive Assistance

Identifying exactly what a center can offer in supportive assistance is a necessary task. A school's list can be long or short depending on the financial and human resources available. Some schools have generous budgets; others do not. Some have committed and dedicated staff members who realize working with and through parents and families is a priority. Most educators are familiar with data and research showing that a family's socioeconomic status, cultural and linguistic group membership, parenting style, and home literacy experiences correlate with the knowledge and skills that children bring to school. They realize excellent instructional help will be necessary to prepare some children for kindergarten.

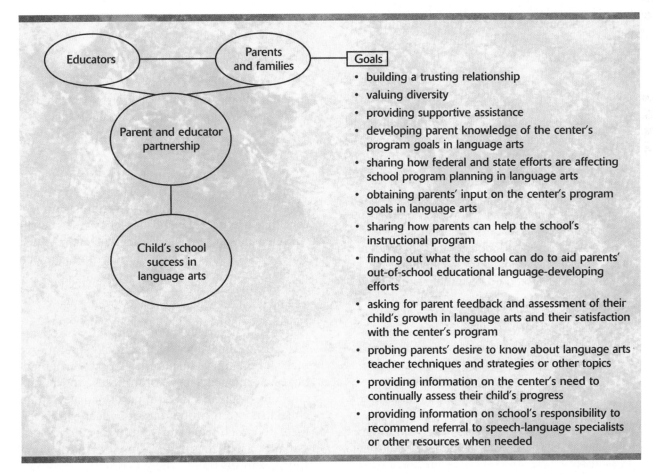

FIGURE 19–3 Parent involvement goals.

Current Early Childhood Language Arts Program Planning

It is a staff's task to explain how a center's program addresses "the whole child" and, in this case, especially language arts instruction. In some states, early childhood programs will need to follow curricular standards and requirements specified in licensing and/or federal or state guidelines or standards. Individual states have established practices to ensure program quality after their state legislators became aware of research concerning young children's brain capacity and growth. President Bush's No Child Left Behind Act (U.S. Department of Education, 2002a) led to an additional focus on early reading and the skills developed during preschool years. Many programs, including Head Start, have updated program standards in language arts. Other groups have developed or are currently developing standards. These groups include the U.S. Department of Education, the International Reading Association, the NAEYC, the National Reading Panel, the Administration for Children and Families, and the National Goals Panel. All are making every effort to develop research-based goals and standards. Goldenberg (2002) lists what he terms the "emerging consensus" of current instructional practices (preschool through third grade) in beginning literacy:

1. Literate environments in which print is used for diverse and interesting purposes, including opportunities for student choice and ample time for looking at books and reading or "pretend reading."

2. Direct, explicit, systematic instruction in specific skills (e.g., phonological awareness, letter names/sounds, decoding, and comprehension strategies), with sufficient practice in successful use of skills in order to promote transfer and automaticity.

3. Discussions and conversations about materials children read or that are read to them.

4. Focus on word-recognition skills and strategies (direct instruction, but also use of techniques such as word walls and making words).

5. Strategically sequenced instruction and curriculum materials to maintain optimal challenge (instructional or independent, as appropriate).

6. Organizational and classroom management strategies to maximize academic engagement and appropriate use of materials.

7. An explicit focus on language (including vocabulary development).

8. Valid and frequent assessments, using multiple measures as needed and appropriate, to allow teachers to gauge developing skills and target instruction appropriately.

9. A home-school connection component that links the school's efforts with children's home experiences and enlists parents in supporting their children's academic development.

Some of this curriculum may be difficult to explain to parents without using specific examples over an extended period. Schools and centers that are privately funded may not use the "consensus" goals listed and instead may use other goals as the basis for their language arts instruction.

Obtaining Parental Input

Schools have developed vehicles to ensure parental input is part of a school's operational plan. These include parent (classroom) mailboxes, parent advisory committees, and parent councils. Parent questionnaires, surveys, and checklists often probe parents' ideas. Other efforts to reach out and communicate include e-mail, parent reading groups, planning workshops, and on-the-fly daily contacts.

PARENT GUIDELINES FOR LITERACY AND LANGUAGE DEVELOPMENT

The techniques or actions recommended to help children's language and literacy development apply to both teachers and parents. Parents have different and more varied opportunities to use these techniques. The following guidelines have been gathered from various sources dealing primarily with parent-child relations, and some have been mentioned previously in this text.

How Parents Can Promote Literacy

◆ Spend some time with your child every day. At school, the teacher has many children to attend to and may not give a child individual attention.

◆ Have your child match buttons, beans, blocks, or toys by colors, shapes, sizes; this kind of categorizing is an important thinking skill.

◆ Sort groceries by categories (canned goods, vegetables, fruits, and so on).

◆ Keep in mind that your child's early experiences with print, writing tools, alphabet letters, and books can be puzzling. When your child asks questions, he should readily be given assistance and answers, while he is focused.

◆ Slip quickly in and out of your child's play, encouraging child discovery. This type of on-the-move teaching is natural and different from sit-down structured teaching to which your child tunes out as interest wanes.

◆ Offer what is just a little beyond what your child already knows in a supportive, enthusiastic, discovery setting. Interactions should be shared and enjoyable.

◆ Turning conversations into commands aimed at teaching language arts turns your child away.

◆ Arrange things so that your child has many opportunities to see operations from beginning to end. For example, make butter from whipping cream or applesauce from picked apples. Your child may not be aware of the origins of the things adults take for granted.

◆ Encourage each success or honest effort with a smile of approval or loving words.

◆ Be available as a resource person. When your child asks questions that you cannot answer, do not hesitate to seek help from others or books.

◆ Help your child feel secure and successful. Your interactions can build feelings of self-worth, if your child's ideas and opinions are valued, or feelings of worthlessness, if his ideas and opinions are negated or ignored.

◆ Realize young children's self-control is developing and is necessary in group activities. In preschool and kindergarten, behavioral expectations create the climate for learning. Parenting means setting behavioral standards. Disciplined work habits promote school success.

Stimulating Speaking Abilities

◆ Talk to children lovingly, taking care to speak naturally and clearly. Listen when children want to tell you something; do not nag or interrupt children when they are speaking (but do make an effort to correct speech errors casually, that is, without drawing attention to the error).

◆ Read stories, poems, jingles, and riddles to children.

◆ Encourage play with puppets, bendable family dolls, dress-up clothes, play stores, doctor kits, and play telephones, letting the children act out various events and practice the language patterns we use in our daily lives.

◆ Encourage children to tell you stories.

◆ Increase your attempts to build vocabulary by including new and descriptive words in your vocabulary.

◆ Give attention; listen for intent rather than correctness. Show children that what they say is important. Communicate with children at their eye level, when possible. Expand and tactfully extend children's comments; talk on the children's chosen subjects.

◆ Use your best speech model—Standard English, if it comes naturally. If you speak a language other than English, provide a good model of that language.

◆ If one is a member of a cultural or ethnic group, examining attitude concerning adult-child verbal interactions is prudent. Meager quantity of home conversations can limit a young child's vocabulary development.

◆ Become a skilled questioner by asking questions that promote thinking, predicting, and a number of possible answers based on the children's viewpoints.

◆ Encourage children to talk about whatever they are making, but do not keep asking them, "What is it?"

◆ Talk frequently, give objects names, describe the things you do, speak distinctly and be specific, use full sentences; encourage children to ask questions, and include children in mealtime conversations.

The following are 11 suggestions from Mavrogenes (1990).

◆ Talk about what children are interested in and patiently answer their questions.

◆ Encourage children to develop their interests and talk about them.

◆ Do things together and talk about them: trips to stores, the zoo, museums, movies, concerts, and worship services; television; library visits; sports; and hobbies.

◆ Allow children to take the lead and direct the talk.

◆ Listen to your children so that you learn about them and show that you are interested in them.

◆ Provide young children with a play telephone and teach them how to use it.

◆ Ask children to describe objects they see.

◆ Talk with children to describe objects they see in a picture. Then hide the picture and see how many objects they can recall.

◆ Sing to and with children.

◆ Make games of spontaneous rhyming.

◆ Make up chants to do chores by.

Building Print Awareness and Skill

◆ Provide literature and a language-rich setting in the home.

◆ Write down the things children tell you about their pictures. Make books of each child's work and photographs, and talk about the books.

◆ Read family letters and mail to children, along with circulars, junk mail, restaurant menus, wrappers and packaging, signs, labels, building identifications, catalogs, brand names, and calendars.

◆ Provide scrap paper and writing tools, and reserve an area in the home as a writing center for children's use (Figure 19–4).

◆ Make or buy alphabet letter toys or word books.

◆ Ask teachers for copies of the alphabet your children will use in kindergarten.

◆ Encourage scribbling and doodling.

FIGURE 19–4 Some homes provide home "writing" areas and parents who show an interest in children's writing attempts.

◆ Write messages to children or make signs for their play, such as "Mark's boat."

◆ Talk about what you are writing and its use to you.

◆ Read signs when driving or walking, especially safety signs.

◆ Point out print on home equipment and products.

◆ Encourage interest in paper-and-crayon activities by showing children their names in print. Give attention to their attempts to copy their names or write them from memory.

The following are seven suggestions from Mavrogenes (1990).

◆ For pretend play, provide bank forms, memo pads, doctors' prescription pads, school forms, store order pads, and ordering pads used in restaurants. This kind of play stretches children's imaginations and broadens their experiences.

◆ Help children in writing letters to grandparents, sick friends, book authors, or famous people.

◆ Put little notes in children's lunch boxes or backpacks. These can be picture notes or simple messages like "Hi, I love you."

◆ Make "books" for children's writing and drawing. Fold several sheets of paper together or staple sheets together.

◆ Model writing for children; write private notes, grocery lists, and recipes with children. These things show how useful writing is.

◆ Praise children's attempts to invent their own spelling; these show that they are learning the relationship between print and speech. "Correct" spelling will follow later.

◆ Do not criticize neatness, spelling, or grammar; it is important that children learn that writing is communication and fun.

Cooper (1993) describes the many ways parents can introduce young children to print in the environment.

... their own names, street signs, stop signs, business signs, price tags, and so on. Young children at home also observe parents actively engaged in meaningful writing activities, such as composing a grocery list, looking up a telephone number, or sending a get-well card.

Putting in print shared experiences or often-told family stories can support early readers by helping them anticipate a sequence of events or by helping them figure out words of personal importance emphasized in the story. "Where does it say zoo?" can be natural outgrowth of reading a joint parent adventure.

Providing Experiences Outside the Home

◆ Take trips to interesting places: bowling alley, shoe-repair shop, bakery, zoo, farm, airport, different kinds of stores. Also consider train and bus trips. When you get back, make drawings related to the trip. Talk about it. Recreate it in creative dramatics. Effective trips can be quite simple but need careful planning. Visit community events such as 4-H fairs, craft shows, antique-auto shows, new-car shows, and farm-equipment displays.

◆ Having children accompany you to the store, bank, post office, zoo, or park can turn the trip into an educational excursion. A home has many advantages that a school cannot duplicate.

Promoting Listening

◆ Try teaching children to listen and identify sounds, such as the whine of car tires, bird calls, insect noises, and sounds of different kinds of doors closing in the house. Recordings, television, and storybooks also stimulate interest in listening.

◆ Be a good listener—pause before answering, and wait patiently for children to formulate answers or speech.

Promoting an Interest in Reading

Calkins (1997) describes how she promoted reading with her own sons.

One way to create an environment that supports reading is to make sure it's impossible to avoid books. Like many families, we always bring a backpack full of books along on car rides, and we kept books in the pockets on the back of our car seats.

It is crucial to understand that young children can make tremendous progress as readers while being in what the uniformed adult might think of as "the nowhere land of 'just pretending'." This happens when a child pretends to read books, reads illustrations, or flips pages as he/she tells his/her own story or imitates the actions or voices of those who've read to him/her.

Parents with positive attitudes about reading will usually find that their children are more motivated, spend more time at reading, and expend more effort in learning to read. Put simply, parents who value reading have children with a greater interest in reading skills.

More advice follows:

◆ Reading is dependent on facility with oral language. Children who talk easily, handle words skillfully, ask questions, and look for answers usually become good readers. Parents have an easy job compared with teachers who have groups of children to help.

◆ Stop reading to a child who has lost concentration. Search for enthralling books. Calkins (1997) urges not going overboard in attempts to educate children.

Reading aloud to our kids will have educational payoffs only if we stop worrying about those payoffs. We must stop pointing at and calling attention to each word as we read it, stop nudging our kids to read parts of the book themselves, stop instructing them on vocabulary words, stop checking that the story means the same to them as it does to us. In short, stop grilling them with little questions.

◆ Children who are more fluent and positive about reading have parents who have fun

reading to their children, keep stories moving with a "semantic" rather than a strict "decoding" orientation, encourage child questions, and add humor (at times) to the reading together experience (Lancy & Bergin, 1992).

◆ Read to children every day. Figure 19–5 displays the amount of time children are reading or being read to compared with time spent engaging in other activities, as reported in a survey by the Kaiser Family Foundation (2003). Ask librarians for help. See Figure 19–6 for a listing of books with an element of predictability. Finding predictable picture books that include repetitive features enhances the child's feelings of being part of the telling. Competency increases when the child knows what comes

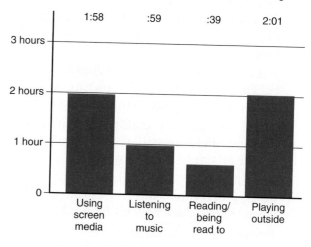

Amount of time children 0–6 spend each day, on average

Note: Average is among all children, across all days of the week, including those who don't do certain activities yet at all.

FIGURE 19–5 *"Zero to Six: Electronic Media in the Lives of Infants, Toddlers, and Preschoolers,"* (#3378), The Henry J. Kaiser Family Foundation, Fall 2003. (This information was reprinted with permission of the Henry J. Kaiser Family Foundation. The Kaiser Family Foundation, based in Menlo Park, California, is a nonprofit, independent national health care philanthropy and is not associated with Kaiser Permanente or Kaiser Industries.)

AUTHOR	TITLE	PUBLISHER
Arno, E.	*The Gingerbread Man*	Crowell
Bang, M.	*Ten, Nine, Eight*	Greenwillow
Baum, A., & Baum, J.	*One Bright Monday Morning*	Random House
Berenstain, S., & Berenstain, J.	*Bears in the Night*	Random House
Bonne, R., & Mill, A.	*I Know an Old Lady Who Swallowed a Fly*	Holiday House
Brown, M. W.	*Goodnight Moon*	Harper Festival
Charlip, R.	*What Good Luck! What Bad Luck!*	Scholastic
Charlip, R., & Supree, B.	*Mother Mother I Feel Sick Send for the Doctor Quick Quick Quick*	Tricycle Press
Flack, M.	*Ask Mr. Bear*	Simon & Schuster
Galdone, P.	*The Three Billy Goats Gruff*	Seabury
Graham, J.	*I Love You, Mouse*	Harcourt Brace
Hoban, T.	*Just Look*	Greenwillow
Hogrogian, N.	*One Fine Day*	Macmillan
Hutchins, P.	*The Surprise Party*	Simon & Schuster
	Rosie's Walk	Simon & Schuster
Isadora, R.	*Max*	Simon & Schuster
Langstaff, J.	*Oh, A-Hunting We Will Go*	Simon & Schuster
Martin, B., Jr.	*Brown Bear, Brown Bear, What Do You See?*	Holt
Mayer, M.	*What Do You Do with a Kangaroo?*	Macmillan
Sendak, M.	*Chicken Soup with Rice*	HarperCollins
Shaw, C. B.	*It Looked Like Spilt Milk*	HarperCollins
Slobodkina, E.	*Caps for Sale*	HarperCollins
Spier, P.	*The Fox Went out on a Chilly Night*	Doubleday
Stevenson, J.	*"Could Be Worse!"*	Morrow, William & Co.
Stover, J.	*If Everybody Did*	McKay
Thomas, P.	*"Stand Back," Said the Elephant, "I'm Going to Sneeze"*	HarperCollins
Viorst, J.	*Alexander and the Terrible, Horrible, No Good, Very Bad Day*	Simon & Schuster
Zolotow, C.	*If It Weren't for You*	HarperCollins

FIGURE 19–6 Predictable books.

next after a few readings. An appealing book selected by a parent can be read with enthusiasm and animation.

◆ Get children actively involved, participating in reading by chanting lines, pointing, speaking in different voices for each character, or doing whatever is natural and logical for the book's text or format.

◆ Give reading status and importance; read recipes and directions (Figure 19–7).

◆ A child's age will determine, in part, what he will find interesting in a book. The preschooler is interested in rhyming words, repetitions, characters the child's own age, bright colors, and fun things to feel. The more a child is exposed to plea-

AUTHOR	TITLE	PUBLISHER
Brown, M.	*Stone Soup*	Simon & Schuster
Carle, E.	*The Very Hungry Caterpillar*	Putnam
de Paola, T.	*Pancakes for Breakfast*	Harcourt Brace Jovanovich
de Regniers, B. S.	*May I Bring a Friend?*	Simon & Schuster
Galdone, P.	*The Gingerbread Boy*	Houghton Mifflin
	The Little Red Hen	Houghton Mifflin
Hoban, R.	*Bread and Jam for Frances*	HarperCollins
Marshall, J.	*Yummers*	Houghton Mifflin
Mayer, M.	*Frog Goes to Dinner*	Dial
McCloskey, R.	*One Morning in Maine*	Viking
	Blueberries for Sal	Penguin Putnam
Patz, N.	*Pumpernickel Tickle and Mean Green Cheese*	Baltimore Sun
Sendak, M.	*Chicken Soup with Rice*	HarperCollins
Seuss, Dr.	*Green Eggs and Ham*	Random House

FIGURE 19–7 Books that encourage reading recipes and home cooking experiences.

surable reading activities, the greater will be his interest in reading. Read aloud and provide books for browsing and a special place to keep the collection. Enjoy reading and encourage children to read a variety of materials. Go to the library. Arrange a time to read with children. You may read your own materials separately or read the same story together. Provide reading-related activities. Encourage children to write stories. Try storytelling without a book.

◆ Children will become readers only if their emotions are engaged and their imaginations are stretched and stirred by what they find on the printed page. The truly literate are not those who know how to read, but those who read fluently, responsively, critically, and because they want to.

◆ It is wise to select from among the best books for even the youngest children. The best are well-designed with uncluttered pages, interesting print, and colorful pictures that stimulate young imaginations.

◆ Parents often think that children learn about reading in school. The truth of the matter is that many children already know a lot about reading when they enter kindergarten, because parents have been teaching their children about reading since they were born. Methods that parents use to teach differ from those used by school teachers. Parents help children every day—when they take them to the grocery store or point out street signs. Experience with print gives a broad and meaningful introduction to reading. Reading really cannot be learned very well if it is first taught only with lessons on isolated letters and sounds. If reading is to make sense to children, they must see how it is used in life.

◆ When children select books, show a genuine interest; do not criticize children's selection.

◆ When children ask for the pronunciation of words, tell them the words; do not analyze the words or sound them out.

◆ Discuss authors and illustrations at times.

◆ Enjoy humor or fun in books. Relate book happenings to the child's real-life experiences.

◆ Subscribe to children's magazines or borrow copies from libraries.

◆ Ask warm-up questions to set the stage and help children anticipate what will happen.

◆ Point as you read. For very young children, point to things in pictures as you talk about them. Pointing helps focus attention, thus lengthening the time children will sit still for a story. It also develops visual literacy— the idea that pictures have meaning.

◆ Try asking what the child expects the book to be about from looking at the cover.

◆ Look for ways to involve the child during readings.

◆ Stop and let the child supply words.

◆ Talk about words (unusual ones) the child may not understand.

Strickland (1990) has pinpointed specific parental reading behaviors that promote positive effects.

> Research on home storybook readings has further identified a number of specific interactive behaviors that support the positive effects of read-aloud activities. Those behaviors include questioning, scaffolding (modeling dialogue and responses), praising, offering information, directing discussion, sharing personal reactions, and relating concepts to life experiences. Although many parents engage their children in such interactive behaviors rather naturally, teachers need to share these facts with parents and encourage them to read to their children daily.

Parents can benefit from knowing they have a greater chance to instill a love of books than teachers do because of their intimate knowledge of their child's life experiences. Parents are able to connect book story features not only to past happenings experienced together but also to the unique characteristics of their child's personality, interests, desires, and abilities. They have an emotional bond that can connect book-reading times to "pleasantness." They can start book reading during infancy and toddlerhood and make parent-child book time a special "together" time. Parents can promote active and verbal child participation when they

are reading aloud, thereby stimulating their child's vocabulary. This is more difficult for teachers reading to groups. Parents can ask questions, do "point-to's," and prompt their child to see details and cause-and-effect relationships, guess, and describe. All will increase the child's literacy and vocabulary. Parents can become active listeners who add information a little above what the child knows. Accepting child comments and ideas, parents can reinforce children's efforts and desire to share their ideas. Storybook illustrations can also be "read" and discussed in detail. Parents can find books along their child's particular line of interest and select ones that challenge by presenting more complex ideas or information.

Encouraging parents to read in their native language is an important consideration. Schools enrolling other-than-English-speaking children include foreign language picture books in their classroom collection and often stock additional copies that parents can borrow. Local library staffers may be able to provide others.

Parents who may wish to rate themselves using Figure 19–8 may discover they are already promoting child language and literacy in a number of ways.

Starting out Right (Burns, Griffin, & Snow, 1999) is a wonderful resource for parents. It is full of practical child-adult activity ideas, and the text is based on research. It explains why activities promote literacy and a child's learning to read with ease.

Parent Storytelling

The magic of parental storytelling not only improves child listening but also broadens child interests and opens new worlds of discovery (Fredericks, 1989). Following are tips from professional storytellers.

1. Select a story that will interest both you and the children. Your enthusiasm for a story is important in helping the children enjoy the story too.

2. Practice the story several times before you share it with the children. Learn all you can about the characters, settings, and events within the story.

Use the following ratings: O = often, S = sometimes, I = infrequently, D = does not apply

Parent attempts to:

_____ 1. initiate family discussions at mealtimes.

_____ 2. give full attention to child's comments.

_____ 3. add descriptive or new words in conversation.

_____ 4. take child to library.

_____ 5. take time at post office to discuss letters and postage.

_____ 6. discuss children's books.

_____ 7. read to child daily.

_____ 8. point out print around the house.

_____ 9. accept child's opinions.

_____ 10. use dictionary with child.

_____ 11. talk on the child's chosen subject.

_____ 12. ask questions that promote child's descriptions or predictions.

_____ 13. listen patiently.

_____ 14. discuss television programs.

_____ 15. plan community outings.

_____ 16. invite interesting people to home and promote interactions with child.

_____ 17. correct child's speech casually with little attention to errors.

_____ 18. encourage child hobbies.

_____ 19. answer questions readily.

_____ 20. discuss care and storage of books.

_____ 21. play word games or rhyme words playfully.

_____ 22. talk about how print is used in daily life.

_____ 23. find books on subjects of interest to child.

_____ 24. consult with child's teacher.

_____ 25. give attention and notice accomplishments.

_____ 26. take dictation from child.

_____ 27. try not to interrupt child's speech frequently.

_____ 28. initiate family reading times and family discussions of classics.

_____ 29. establish a book center in the home.

_____ 30. create child writing or art center in the home.

_____ 31. give books as gifts.

_____ 32. provide different writing tools and scrap paper.

_____ 33. provide alphabet toys in the home.

FIGURE 19–8 Parent self-rating.

3. Decide how to animate the story. Practice some hand gestures, facial expressions, or body movements that will spice up the story for the children.

4. Practice different accents, voice inflections (angry, sad, joyous), and loud and soft speech patterns to help make characters come alive and to add drama to your presentation.

5. Create some simple puppets from common household objects such as wooden picnic spoons, paper plates, or lunch bags. Draw individual character features on each item and use them during your story.

6. Promote your storytelling time. Make an announcement about an upcoming story or design a simple "advertisement" for a story and post it in advance.

7. Design a simple prop for the children to use during the telling of a story: a paper boat for a sea story, a magnifying glass or camera for a mystery story, or a paper flower for a springtime story.

8. Have the children suggest new props, gestures, or voice qualities that would be appropriate for retelling of the story at a later date.

9. After telling a story, talk about it with the children. Ask them to tell you the most enjoyable or memorable parts.

Being a good storyteller takes a little practice, but the time invested can make a world of difference in helping children appreciate good literature.

Games with Rules

A lot of family language interaction takes place in family game playing. Games have rules and encourage child self-regulation, focused attention, and memory. Outdoor games have an added physical component. To play by the rules, children must regulate their behavior and regulate the rule-abiding behavior of others. Acquiring self-regulation, a skill appropriate and desired in further schooling, is a major accomplishment during early childhood. Raver and Knitzer (2002) point out that the emotional, social, and behavior competence of young children (such as higher levels of self-control and lower levels of acting out) predicts children's academic performance in their first grades of school, over and above their cognitive skills and family backgrounds.

Home Reading and Writing Centers

Home reading centers are a lot like school reading areas. A comfortable, warm, private, well-lighted place free of distraction works best. Adjacent shelving and a chair for parent comfort is important to book-sharing times. Window seats and room dividers make cozy corners. Parents can get creative in selecting and furnishing reading centers.

Family book collections build children's attitudes concerning books as personal possessions and give books status. Families model appropriate storage and care in home reading centers. A special area with writing supplies, an alphabet chart, table, and chair should be suggested to parents.

Parents interested in book purchase can be alerted to the opportunity to buy books through school-sponsored book clubs, local library book sales, used-book stores, thrift shops, and yard sales. Pointers should be shared concerning selecting quality.

Library Services

Parents are sometimes unaware of children's library services. Children's librarians are great sources of information and often offer children a wide-ranging program of literary events and activities. They are good at finding books that match a particular child's interest. Teachers who are in touch with a preschool child's emerging interests can alert parents.

Building home book collections can be a real problem for some parents. Economics and library availability may thwart parent desires. Some parents living in the inner city in unsafe neighborhoods may leave their homes only to get food and to take children to school.

Home Visits

In trying to understand attending children, especially "silent ones" or culturally diverse ones, a home visit may help to plan for children's individual needs.

Parents Who Speak Languages Other Than English

Centers have become increasingly sensitive to other-than-English-speaking parents who are often eager to promote their child's literacy. The National Research Council's publication *Preventing Reading Difficulties in Young Children* (1998) points out

> Many Hispanic children with limited English proficiency also have in common that their parents are poorly educated, that their family income is low, that they reside in communities in which many families are similarly struggling, and that they attend schools with student bodies that are predominantly minority and low achieving.

Family literacy programs attempt to break the cycle of intergenerational illiteracy by providing services to both parent and child. Programs vary from community to community as each program tries to meet the needs of participants. Participants are often parents who lack basic literacy skills and may need to acquire positive self-concepts to encourage their children's school success. Family literacy programs and adult literacy programs can be located through County Offices of Education or state agencies.

---

family literacy programs — community programs attempting to provide literacy-building opportunities and experiences for families. Services are available for both adults and children.

Directors and administrators can receive information and a multitude of resources concerning exemplary family literacy programs from

National Center for Family Literacy
325 W. Main St., Suite 300
Louisville, KY 40202-4237

Division of Adult Education and Literacy
    Clearinghouse
U.S. Department of Education
400 Maryland Ave. S.W.
Washington, DC 20202-7240

Early childhood centers can often locate family literacy programs and identify resources by contacting the Director of Adult Education in their state.

A growing number of communities are instituting publicly funded family literacy programs. Many of these programs are designed to provide

- child care.
- transportation.
- introduction to literacy-building home activities.
- access to community services.
- involvement in children's school activities.
- bilingual support and promotion of pride in language and culture.
- increased parental self-esteem.

Many parent education projects working with immigrant parents reject the idea that the best way to help parents is to hold group parenting classes. They instead attempt to increase parents' confidence in their teaching abilities by other means. They encourage parent picture-book readings and after-book discussions in the child's native language. They provide books, book bags with suggested activities, or recorded books or may use other strategies.

African-American School Success

Murphy (2003) conducted case studies on four high-achieving elementary school children of African-American heritage. She states

These children's academic success is no accident. All four benefitted from continuous,

active involvement of their parents in guiding and influencing their school success.

She describes five factors that "maintained and sustained" these African-American families:

- a high-achievement orientation
- strong kinship bonds
- strong work orientation
- adaptability of family roles
- a religious orientation

Murphy also cites additional contributing family characteristics. These include:

- the family's beliefs and values.
- the quality interactive behavior of parents.
- parents' placing an extraordinarily high value on education.
- their maintaining a social environment in which learning flourished.

Early childhood educators working with diverse groups of children will find this study interesting, for it alerts teachers to the strength, resolve, and commitment to education that exists in many American families.

One of the four children studied by Murphy, a 10-year-old, was asked why he has done so well in school. He stated

"great teachers, parents who cared about my school work, friends who helped me with my school work, and a great staff"; and about his parents, he said, "They helped me learn about the world and my environment"; and he added, "I'm special because God made me special. He sent me to this earth to have fun, get an education, and go to college."

What child wouldn't do well with a similar attitude toward school, teachers, parents, and self?

Parent Education Projects—Working Together

Minnesota initiated parent training programs during the late 1970s, and Missouri is credited as the first state in the United States to mandate that all school districts provide parent education and support services (Winter & Rouse, 1990). The Parents as Teachers (PAT) project was initiated in 1981 with 350 families. It has been replicated under different names in more than 50 sites nationwide. Starting at a child's birth, the project helps parents understand their child's individual development and promotes early literacy. Personalized home visits, group meetings, ongoing monitoring, periodic screening, and referral and guidance services have effectively worked toward the project's goal of having children reach age three without undetected developmental delay or handicapping conditions. Among the literacy-building activities considered "particularly powerful" in the PAT methodology is in-home parent storybook reading. Read-aloud activities seemed to influence family social-interactional quality as well as child literacy. Further information about the project is available by contacting Parents as Teachers National Center, 2228 Ball Drive, St. Louis, MO 63146.

The fact that many young parents today may be less prepared to care for children than were their predecessors has not escaped educators. Nor has it escaped our national government. In April 2002, the President announced his *Good Start, Grow Smart* early childhood initiative to help states and local governments strengthen early learning for young children (Ohl, 2002). The initiative focused on young children's literacy, cognitive, social, and emotional development. Ohl points out that 25 percent of the nation's children from families *without* any risk factors, such as poverty, parents with limited education, single-parent homes, or lack of English-language experience, entered kindergarten in 1998 bereft of the necessary oral language or early literacy skills critical for learning.

THE FEDERAL EVEN START FAMILY LITERACY PROGRAM

Even Start, a federally funded program (1989–1997), consisted of a variety of family literacy projects that integrated low-income children's early childhood education classes with parent education and family supportive services. Family participation criteria included

(1) family eligibility for adult basic education (ABE), (2) a child younger than eight years of age, and (3) residence in a geographical area receiving funds for Even Start services.

The Even Start program was modeled after a 1980s Kentucky program that involved parents with low-literacy skills and their three- to four-year-old children. Even Start was based on the following assumptions:

- Intervention is more effective when focused on the family rather than just on the parent or just on the child (St. Pierre & Layzer, 1998).

- A planned, structured classroom time involving parent and child in literacy skill development might also promote parent-child relationships when staff guidance was present.

- Families need supportive services and help in accessing them.

The goals of Even Start were to intervene and offer a developmentally appropriate, meaningful, and useful child curriculum that promoted school readiness and children's language and literacy skills. It also aimed to increase parents' involvement in their child's schooling by decreasing parental barriers, such as fear of school, transportation problems, and low self-esteem. It attempted to provide a stable, capable staff that could integrate all services.

Federal legislation required an evaluation of Even Start at both local and national levels. These evaluations took place from 1989 to 1997. Results showed that adults gained literacy skills similar to those of adults in the control group, but more Even Start adults earned a GED (general education diploma). Even Start children learned school readiness skills significantly faster than children in the control group, but those in the control group caught up after receiving school services. Tao, Gamse, and Tarr (1998) summarize Even Start results in the following:

> At this point we do not have consistent patterns of positive outcomes for children and their families from these evaluations.

Many current educators accept the assumptions espoused by Even Start. Current programs and projects have adopted similar ones, believing they have value and merit.

Television Viewing and Young Children's Language Development

Parents often ask teachers about the value of television and videos and about their children's viewing habits. A national survey of more than 1,000 parents conducted by the Henry J. Kaiser Foundation (Antonucci, 2003) suggests that parents have divided opinions concerning whether television viewing "mostly helps" (43 percent) or "mostly hurts" (27 percent) children's learning. The Foundation's survey also notes that in homes where television is on for the longest periods, children were less likely to be able to read. A review of research generally supports the idea that children's television viewing casts children as "watchers" rather than active participants in language exchanges with others. The effect of viewing on particular children differs. After children become readers, studies show reading development is adversely affected when viewing is excessive.

Children ages three to five spend an average of 13 hours and 28 minutes a week watching television (Hofferth, 1998). Child development experts suggest parents limit the amount and kind of television children watch and seek out educational television or videos from the library that can be discussed with children.

Owens (1999) studied children's sleep and television-viewing habits. He questions whether the sedating effect of television watching for adults is also true for children, because 40 percent of parents reported sleep problems, struggles over going to bed, or a child's difficulty falling asleep. In other words, television watching seems to be a stimulant to some children. Figure 19–9 displays percentages of children of different ages who have television sets in their bedroom.

Television programs that stress educational or informative material do not seem to have harmful potential. Again, the amount of view-

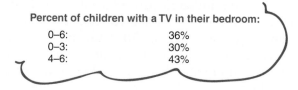

Percent of children with a TV in their bedroom:

0–6:	36%
0–3:	30%
4–6:	43%

FIGURE 19–9 *"Zero to Six: Electronic Media in the Lives of Infants, Toddlers, and Preschoolers,"* (#3378), The Henry J. Kaiser Family Foundation, Fall 2003. (This information was reprinted with permission of the Henry J. Kaiser Family Foundation. The Kaiser Family Foundation, based in Menlo Park, California, is a nonprofit, independent national health care philanthropy and is not associated with Kaiser Permanente or Kaiser Industries.)

ing time is critical. Because research offers so many conflicting views, teachers cannot give definitive answers to parents. Educators can express their concern that heavy television and video viewing rob a child of a literacy-rich home environment, one that is necessary for the child's optimal growth. Real firsthand experiences, exposure to books, and conversations with interested and responsive family members stack the odds in the favor of early literacy and cannot be replaced by television or videos.

What is excessive viewing? Research suggests more than 10 hours of viewing weekly is excessive (U.S. Department of Education, 1991). Young Americans, on average, now spend more hours in front of the set than at any other activity except sleeping (Healy, 1990).

An increasing number of alarmed educators and researchers warn that excessive, unsupervised television and video viewing by young children promotes negative effects, including

- aggressive and violent behavior.

- decreased imagination, cooperation, and success in relationships.

- vulnerability to stimulus addiction, resulting in the child needing overstimulation to feel satisfied.

- immunity to vicarious emotional stresses resulting in inability to produce socially acceptable emotional responses.

◆ poor reading comprehension and inability to persevere to an outcome (DeGaetano, 1993).

◆ listening problems.

◆ pronunciation difficulty.

◆ inability to make mental pictures (visual imagery).

◆ inability to remember or decipher meaning from what is viewed or heard because of the passive aspect of television viewing.

◆ hindered development of metalinguistic awareness (examples: child's understanding that letters make up words, written words are linked together into meaningful sentences, a word is made from printed marks, one reads from left to right in English, and terms such as author, title, illustration, etc.) (Healy, 1990).

◆ decreased verbal interactions with family.

◆ decreased opportunities to experience life and exercise verbal problem solving.

Very few research studies have attempted to reduce preschooler's television watching. Dennison, Russo, Burdick, and Jenkins (2004) were successful in doing so. Their 2-year study with 16 early childhood centers was funded in part by the National Institutes of Health. Intervention sessions emphasized reading and alternatives to television viewing. They also stressed the importance of families eating meals together. Children in the study group were rewarded with stickers for choosing television alternatives. A children's book, *The Berenstain Bears and Too Much TV,* featuring an antitelevision theme, was introduced to children in the study. Results indicated that children in the study session reduced television watching time by 3.1 hours per week. For a full description of the intervention program, consult the February 2004 issue of the *Journal of the Archives of Pediatrics & Adolescent Medicine.*

Barry (1999) notes that children, even those who have been taught critical analysis skills, do not generate critical thinking during television commercials. She explains that children and adults think differently, using differ-

ent parts of their brain. In other words, they tend to believe the images they see!

Educators are beginning to believe that children's excessive television viewing and societal attitudes concerning reading and intellectual pursuits are our nation's greatest threat to literacy and the development of our children's thinking abilities.

Healy's advice (1990) to parents concerning television viewing follows:

◆ Place firm limits on television and video use, and encourage children to plan ahead for favorite shows.

◆ Participate with children when possible.

◆ Talk with children about television content, methods of audience manipulation, point of view, and so forth.

◆ If you want children to become readers, show them how to turn off the tube and pick up a book.

◆ Remember, what is pleasantly relaxing to your brain may not be good for theirs.

◆ Give substitute caregivers strict guidelines regarding television and video use.

Most educators suggest that parents limit and guide children's viewing. Screening programs and videos is wise because of the varying quality and values presented. Conversational follow-up after watching programs together gives parents their best opportunity for promoting language development. Children learn best from educational television shows if adults who watch television with them explain difficult words and ideas and build on the concepts that were introduced. Parents can talk about what has happened, what could have happened, and what may happen.

HOME-SCHOOL COMMUNICATION

Schools differ widely both in the amount of written home-school communication and time spent talking or meeting with parents. Teachers are struggling, particularly in urban, coastal, and border states, to learn about family practices, beliefs, and educational needs and desires. They wish to find common ground and acknowledge parents' cultural values while also sharing their programs' philosophies and teaching techniques. In areas such as California's Silicon Valley, it is common to find children from 10 to 29 different ethnic or culturally diverse groups in one elementary classroom.

Most preschool teachers desire more time and more conversations and additional written communication with parents. This suits some parents who seem to be seeking supportive assistance in child-rearing. Each parent group and center is unique, and consequently, tremendous differences exist in the degree to which preschools and parents work together. Most centers try to provide some type of parent assistance. Parents who receive help and support feel more open to contribute to the school's activities.

Parent-school contacts usually take place in at least four ways.

1. daily conversations
2. written communications
3. planned parent meetings, workshops, and social events
4. individual conferences

At the beginning of the child's school year, a telephone call welcoming the family establishes communication. Weekly newsletters and personal notes from teachers open links thereafter.

On the Fly

Teachers have a good chance to share children's interests and favorite school activities with the parent at the end of the day, when parents arrive to take their children home from the center: books, play objects, and child-created or constructed work can be mentioned. Children spend time with and talk about what excites them; the observant teacher is aware of attending children's at-school play and work. Parents are usually interested in what their children have shared about their homes and out-of-school activities.

Bulletin Boards

Many schools use "parent" bulletin boards as a communicative device. Schools receive more announcements of literary happenings in their communities than do parents. Language-developing local events and activities can be advertised to parents. Short magazine and newspaper articles of interest can be posted at eye-catching levels.

Planned Meetings

Planned meetings include individual and group gatherings (Figure 19–10).

Conferences. Parents need to know how the school plans for their children's individual interests and growth. When children have interests in alphabet letters, dramatizing, or special-topic books, parents and teachers can discuss related school and home activities.

Method-and-Material Review Meetings. A meeting can be planned to take a closer look at the preschool's planned language program, materials, and language arts center. Parents get a firsthand look and an opportunity to explore. Teachers conduct sample activities and demonstrate material and equipment use. Parents may ask questions

FIGURE 19–10 Parents' wishes and concerns are often aired in parent-staff meetings.

about their children's use of or interest in a center's planned opportunities.

Parent-Teacher Study Meetings. Some possible themes of study meetings include (1) the effects of television viewing on children's language development, (2) bilingualism, or (3) free and inexpensive home toys that promote language. The center's staff, parents, outside experts, or films can present ideas to be studied and discussed. This type of meeting helps inform all who are present. Differing views clarify everyone's thinking.

It is a good idea to analyze what is really important to communicate to parents concerning children's language arts development. The following items are the author's high-priority topics.

1. Many parents show concern over their children's articulation and vocabulary. Clay (1991b) discusses how children's speech errors may unnerve and worry parents.

   Parents may be disconcerted to find that a child's language, which at three was apparently error-free and highly grammatical, becomes full of errors a year later. But research has shown that this often indicates progress. At each successive stage the child masters a limited range of simple structures. When he tries more complicated structures to deal with his more complicated thinking, his attempts again become hypotheses which are again tested by whether he is understood or not.

   It is helpful to assure parents that the school's staff monitors fluency and to share typical child speech characteristics. Such discussions often relax parents and dispel their fears. Hints concerning simple modeling of correct forms are well received by most parents.

2. Sharing information on school interaction techniques that the staff uses to increase children's speech by listening, following children's leads, and expanding interest in daily conversation is very important.

3. Parents need to know how influential they are in modeling an interest in and positive attitudes toward reading, writing, and speaking. Their ability to listen closely to ideas rather than judging correctness of grammar or ideas should be discussed. Alexander (2004) notes that research has found that before a child reaches age 14, parents are twice as important as school is for a child's learning. Dickinson and Tabors (2002) urge adults to engage in intellectually challenging conversations, offer new and increasingly descriptive words, and extend conversations with unpressured questioning.

4. Another topic to discuss with parents is the warm, unpressured social environments that promote conversations about pleasurable happenings.

5. Reading picture books and sharing stories with the family at home will stimulate children's desire for more. Discussing quality books and "advertising" books to children can perhaps combat a television dominance in the home. Analyzing books, pictures, text, and their messages is a great idea.

6. The child's home access to creative materials, such as drawing and marking tools, is important.

7. Parents have many questions about early reading and writing of alphabet letters. Both reading and writing acquisition is aided by a widely enriching home and preschool curriculum that preserves children's feelings of competence by offering that which is slightly above their level and related closely to their present interests.

8. The last on this list may be the most important topic teachers can discuss with parents. A lot of language development is possible when parents and other adults share activities they love—the ones they can speak about enthusiastically in detailed specific terms; the ones that are vital to them and for which they have a passionate interest.

   Examples are easy to find and role-play for a parent group: the dad who does carpentry, the grandma who grows garden vegetables, the aunt who dances the flamenco, the mom who makes noodles from scratch, the brother who plays the flute, the sister who collects butterflies, and the uncle who restores motorcycles.

So many times parents do not see themselves as resources and do not understand the power of *shared experiences* with their young child. Parents supply the daily experiences that give words meaning and depth, as do teachers, but parents are more instrumental because of the amount of time spent with the child and their access to the world of children's lives out of school.

Video Games. Video games may be a topic of interest for some parents. Barry (1999) posits

> Because video games are interactive in nature, causing players to imitate violence and not merely to watch it in the process of play, their potential for altering brain structures and function is even more significant than repeated film or television viewing.

It is a good idea to review the video material available to one's child. Cartoon graphics that look like they suit young children are often misleading. More than 2,000 research studies link media violence to children's violent behavior (Barry, 1999).

Fathers and Language Development

More than 25 percent of children do not live with their fathers (Child Care Bureau, 2004). For young children, good fathering contributes to the development of emotional security, curiosity, and math and *verbal* skills (U.S. Department of Health and Human Services, 2001). Many preschools are rethinking their parent involvement and planning to include fathers and children's male relatives to a greater degree. Some schools require "father classroom time,"

and parent meetings are designed to cleverly interest and increase male attendance.

Gadsden and Ray (2002) believe fathers play an important role in their children's school achievement, and the earlier they become involved with their children's learning and socialization, the better. Educational research suggests that a father's ability to support his child's learning can affect the child's engagement with books.

Explaining Phonemic Awareness to Parents

Many parents are well read, but a definition of phonetic awareness and why it has become important is a good idea. Main points to transmit follow:

- Current research suggests that it is an essential skill in learning to read.
- Preschoolers become aware and play with sounds, rhymes, and silly words frequently.
- Speech is composed of small units called phonemes (sounds).
- Each phoneme represents a particular sound. (In *cat*, c - a - t, there are three different phonemes.)

What can parents do to help make their child aware?

- Clap to music.
- Clap to syllables.
- Sing repetitive and rhyming songs.
- Say words slowly and stretch sounds out in a gamelike way at times.
- Play games with rhyming words.
- Blend sounds together in games.
- Say "When I say 'c-a-r' slowly, what word do you hear?"
- Find things that start with "T," and so on.
- Seek computer games that play with word sounds.
- Make up stories with word sounds.
- Have plenty of alphabet books, games, and toys available.

◆ Know that a child's knowing an alphabet letter's name precedes introducing its sound.

◆ Look for teachable moments rather than planned sit-down instruction.

School Lending Libraries

Increasingly, centers are aware of the benefits of school lending libraries. Although extra time and effort are involved in this provision to parents, centers are sensitive to the plight of parents who are economically distressed and pressed for time. Lending libraries should give parents book-reading tips and pointers in parental reading technique as well as calm possible parent fears that a borrowed book might get lost or defaced. Books in the first language of enrolled children should be included in a center's book collection.

Parents may feel inadequate when assessing a book's quality and appreciate both a school's family library selections and its convenience. Some schools interview or question parents concerning their child's favorite reading topics and make every effort to probe family book choices and needs. Multicultural sensitivity is an important interview consideration.

Rules and procedures for checkout and return are prepared in print for parents. Staff time, center budget, and staff availability are key factors in deciding whether a family lending library is a viable activity. A family lending library is one way teachers can collaborate with parents to share specific knowledge about reading, as well as the joys of reading, which may enable children to grow and blossom into lifelong readers.

Working with Hard-to-Reach Parents

Centers incorporate family dinners and provide child care to increase parental attendance at home-school meetings. Every effort is made to make the center staff and facility as nonintimidating as possible and to convince every parent they can contribute to child literacy.

Chang (2001) describes *family literacy night* meetings to engage parents, grandparents, siblings, and family friends as a way to more effectively share ideas and activities. Night sessions helped families apply research-based classroom interventions, strategies, and activities at home. Called "The Scaffold for Family Literacy Development," family literacy night's six major guidelines follow:

1. *Always work with and help your child produce something that conveys what and how much he really knows.* This involves working jointly to produce something that will clarify and reflect the child's learning.

2. *Always help your child develop language used at home and in school by modeling, talking, or working together. Always give your child opportunities to use new words in different ways.* This informs families of the importance of talking and listening to their child while restating, probing, or praising the child's ideas, opinions, or judgments related to specific topics in a calm and encouraging manner. Families were urged to use multiple paths to encourage learning and the discovery of similarities and differences in words or phases.

3. *Always help your child relate what he has learned in school to daily life.* Families were encouraged to use related events to strengthen vocabulary comprehension.

4. *Always help your child think or ask questions using on- and under-the-surface questions. Always help your child see how ideas or concepts are related. Always give positive feedback.*

5. *Always talk with your child about school or lifelong learning. Always listen to your child when discussing how he can think about learning and what he can plan or do for it.*

6. *Always value your child's abilities in multiple ways. Always help your child learn through multiple paths that he would like to try.* This enhances families' abilities to verbalize how their child may develop a healthy and productive sense of self-respect and confidence.

Although Chang's described family literacy evening meetings for parents and families were used at elementary school level, they also suit preschool-level parents.

Washington Elementary School and Preschool (Santa Ana, California) devotes the first 20 minutes of every school day to classroom reading. They call it "Book Choice Time." Family members, volunteers, and older brothers and sisters attending the same elementary school enjoy good literature together, often in their home language. More than 600 family members participate on any given day.

DAILY CONTACTS

Greeting both parents and children as they arrive starts a warm, comfortable atmosphere; encourages talking; and sets the tone for conversation. Short, personal comments build parent-school partnership feelings and help children enter the school discussing the morning's happenings. Children are offered choices of possible activities through certain statements such as, "We've put red play dough on the table by the door for you" or "The matching game you told me you liked yesterday is waiting for you on the shelf near the bird cage."

Parent mailboxes can hold daily teacher messages. Important milestones, such as the child's first interest in or attempt at printing alphabet letters or his name or his first created stories, should be shared. A short note from the teacher about a child's special events is appreciated by most parents. A note about special daily happenings such as, "I think Toni would like to tell you about the worm she found in the garden" or "Saul has been asking many questions about airplanes," keeps parents aware of their children's expanding interests.

WRITTEN COMMUNICATION

Often, centers prepare informal letters or newsletters that describe school happenings or daily themes. Figures 19–11 and 19–12 are two examples of this type of teacher-parent communication.

SMALL, SMALLER, SMALLEST

Dear Parents,

We are studying the size of things and will have many discussions this week comparing two or more objects or people. In similar discussions at home, emphasize the endings of size words (*-er, -est*).

Following are some activities you may wish to try where size can be discussed. Note the words *big, bigger,* and *biggest* or *tall, taller, tallest,* or others could also be appropriately used.

1. Sort bottle caps, canned food cans, spoons, or crackers.

2. Discuss your pet's size in relation to a neighbor's pet.

3. Take a large piece of paper and cut into square pieces. Discuss small, smaller, smallest.

4. Look for round rocks or pebbles and compare sizes. Ask the child to line them up from small to smallest.

5. Play games involving finding objects smaller than your shoe, finger, a coin, and so on, or smaller than a ball but larger than a marble.

You will find many opportunities to compare size in your neighborhood or on walks, or in the course of daily living.

Sincerely,

Your partner in your child's education

Your child's preschool teacher

FIGURE 19–11 Sample of informal letter to parents to strengthen school learning. Note: Adding child drawings might create additional interest.

Dear Parents,

This week we have talked about many means of transportation—of how we use animals and machines to take us from one place to another.

We built things, painted things, and learned songs and heard stories about different vehicles such as bikes, cars, trucks, buses, boats, trains, airplanes, horses and wagons, etc., and we even took a bus ride.

Here are some suggested home activities to reinforce school learning.

• Talk about places you go together in your car.
• Save large cardboard boxes—line them up, and pretend they are railroad cars.
• Save old magazines. Let your child find "vehicles that move things from place to place." The child may want to find, cut, and paste pictures.
• Take a walk, and find all the moving vehicles you can.
• Sing a train song, "I've Been Working on the Railroad," or any other.
• Plan a ride on or in a vehicle that is new to the child.

As you enjoy life together, you may want to point out and talk about transportation.

Sincerely,

P.S. Here's a rebus poem to share.

 Sam wanted to go to the zoo.

The family wanted to go there too.

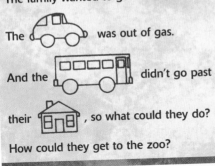

The [car] was out of gas.

And the [bus] didn't go past

their [house], so what could they do?

How could they get to the zoo?

FIGURE 19–12 A partnership letter.

A written communication may concern the following.

◆ local library addresses or a description of services or programs, such as story hours or puppet shows
◆ local children's theater or drama productions
◆ children's book stores
◆ film presentations of interest to the young child
◆ special community events
◆ adult programs, workshops, meetings, and so forth, that include topics concerned with the development of children's language arts
◆ requests for donated materials useful in language arts games or activities

Monthly Newsletters

If a school is trying to help parents expand their children's experiences, newsletters can suggest family outings and excursions to local community events and low-cost and free entertainment. Dates, times, costs, telephone numbers, and simple maps can be included. Wardle (1987) describes newsletter distribution.

> Completed newsletters can be handed out to parents at pick-up or drop-off time. Try to keep the newsletter upbeat and fun with jokes, quotes, and anecdotes scattered throughout the pages.

PARENT RESOURCES

Centers sometimes provide informational articles, magazines, and books that may be borrowed for short periods or available at the school's office. Photocopied magazine articles in manila folders that have been advertised on the school's parent bulletin board are a good resource for busy parents.

Descriptions of home activities that reinforce center topics can aid children's language development. Information on children's books and reading can be obtained from

American Library Association, 50 E. Huron St., Chicago, IL 60611.
Children's Book Council Inc., 12 West 37th St., 2nd Floor, New York, NY 10018-7480.
Cullinan, B. E. (1992). *Read to me: Raising kids who love to read.* New York: Scholastic.

PARENTS AS PROGRAM VOLUNTEERS

The role of parents, relatives, neighbors, and community has changed. Early childhood educators realize home and school literacy learning are intimately intertwined. Parents and community volunteers and resources are seen as vital parts of language arts instruction (Figure 19–13). The teacher's goal is to involve and invite parents, community figures, and resource people to participate in a relationship that urges them to become active participants in children's language learning and literacy. Parents can help teachers plan relevant curriculum topics. Most parent groups include willing volunteers who donate their time, talents, skills, and abilities or share hobby collections with the

FIGURE 19–13 This parent volunteer adds cultural songs with vigorous movements.

children. The following are some of the ways parents can contribute.

- Celebrate "book week."
- Explain occupations. Encourage parents to be guest speakers, discussing their occupations. Ask them to bring in items used in their occupations and to wear the clothing associated with their jobs.
- Demonstrate special skills. From yoga to weaving, parents' simple demonstrations interest children.
- Provide cooking demonstrations. Cooking demonstrations can add words to children's vocabularies.
- Organize field trips. Parents may volunteer their time or provide suggestions.
- Organize fund-raisers.

Many parents often work in businesses where useful language arts materials are discarded, such as scrap paper, cardboard, and so forth. The parent is usually more than willing to obtain these previously discarded materials, especially if they are unable to volunteer their time to the center.

Many parent volunteers enjoy making language-developing games and visuals. Art, photography, sewing, and carpentry talents lend themselves to creating and constructing many classroom materials. Repairing a school's books, flannel board sets, and puppet collections can be an ongoing task. Even the busiest parents seem to find time to share their expertise as visiting guest speakers. Through the joint efforts of home and school, centers are able to provide a wider range of language-developing experiences for attending children.

SUMMARY

Schools differ in both the amount and types of interactions between families and the center. School personnel need to clarify priorities that they wish to communicate to parents concerning children's language development. By teachers and parents working together, children's learning experiences can be reinforced and expanded. A first step involves gaining parents' trust.

Contact with parents takes place in a variety of ways, both planned and unplanned, including daily conversations, written communications, meetings, and scheduled conferences. Centers are interested in promoting the reading of quality books in the home and alerting parents to community opportunities. Parent volunteers can aid goal realization in the language arts by sharing their talents, hobbies, labor, time, and energy. Together, home and school work toward children's language growth and competence.

ADDITIONAL RESOURCES

Readings

Berenstain, S., & Berenstain, J. (1984). *The Berenstain bears and too much TV.* New York: Random House. (A child's book that deals with television issues).

Hydrick, J. (1996). *Parent's guide to literacy for the 21st century.* Urbana, IL: National Council of Teachers of English.

International Reading Association (2002). *Beginning literacy and your child.* Newark, DE: Author.

Lipson, E. R. (2000). *Parent's guide to the best books for children.* New York: Three Rivers Press.

National Association for the Education of Young Children & International Reading Association (IRA). (1998). *Raising a reader, raising a writer: How parents can help.* Washington, DC: NAEYC. (Brochure.)

Schon, I. (2002, July). Pars los ninos . . . Picture books in Spanish for young children. *Young Children, 57*(4) 92-85.

Thernstrom, A., & Thernstrom, S. (2003). *No excuses: Closing the racial gap in learning.* New York: Simon & Schuster.

Williams, D. L., & Chavkin, N. F. (1989). Essential elements of strong parent involvement programs. *Educational Leadership, 47,* 18–20.

International Reading Association Brochures

The following brochures are free with a self-addressed, stamped envelope. Send to requests to 800 Barksdale Rd., P. O. Box 8239, Newark, DE 19714-8139. Brochures are also available in Spanish.

Get Ready to Read! Tips for Parents of Young Children

Explore the Playground of Books: Tips for parents of beginning readers.

Summer Reading Adventure! Tips for Parents of Young Readers.

Making the Most of Television: Tips for Parents of Young Viewers.

See the World on the Internet: Tips for Parents of Young Readers—and "Surfers."

Library Safari: Tips for Parents of Young Readers and Explorers.

HELPFUL WEB SITES

ECRP—Early Childhood Research & Practice
http://www.ecrp.uiuc.edu
Look for readings describing how new teachers develop relationships with parents.

KidSource
http://www.kidsource.com
Find articles about helping children learn to read.

National Academy Press
http://www.nap.edu
Search for report titled "Starting out Right."

National Center for Family Literacy
http://www.famlit.org
Research the final report of the National Early
Literacy Panel.

The National Institute for Literacy
http://www.nifl.gov
This is a federal organization that supports state,
regional, and national literacy services.

Reading Is Fundamental
http://www.rif.org
Locate articles for parents.

University of Calgary
http://www.acs.ucalgary.ca
Find links to sites for parents. Search "dkbrown"
and "index."

U.S. Department of Education
http://www.ed.gov
Look for publications in English and Spanish
concerning children's language development.
Search for "Ready to Learn initiative."

An online discussion forum delves into the issue of parents' and kindergarten teachers' opinions concerning children's school readiness skills. It is based on a U.S. Department of Education survey done in 1998. Additional parent and teacher Web sites are cited in the Online Companion™, as well as a parent's brochure developed by the California Department of Education's Special Education Division. The brochure is helpful to early childhood educators who wish to explain different types of assessments to parents and is especially valuable to teachers affected by the No Child Left Behind legislation.

STUDENT ACTIVITIES

1. Photocopy the following, and cut the sections into cards. Rate each card before joining a group of classmates to discuss ratings.

Rating Scale

1	2	3
teacher used good judgment	uncertain about teacher's behavior	teacher used poor judgment

A field trip is in progress. Mrs. Winkler, a parent, is acting as a volunteer supervisor. A teacher overhears Mrs. Winkler tell her group to be quiet and listen to her explanation of what is happening at the shoe factory. The teacher tactfully suggests to Mrs. Winkler that the children may wish to ask questions.	During a study meeting, two parents are having a heated discussion concerning television's value. A teacher offers her views. Her views happen to support one side of the argument.
Mr. Sousa is a violinist. He is also Tami's father. Tami's teacher sends a special note to Mr. Sousa, inviting him to share his talents with the class. The note mentions that he will be allowed to play the violin for a 5-minute period.	Mr. Thomas, a teacher, knows about a book sale at a local children's book store. He includes the item in the school's newsletter to parents.
Sending written messages to parents is not personal, Ms. Garcia (a teacher) feels. She telephones parents in the evening with news of milestones their children have accomplished in the school's language arts program.	Parent bulletin board posting is part of Miss Alexian's duties. She feels parents rarely read posted materials. At a staff meeting, she asks others for helpful ideas for displays that would grab parents' attention.
Mr. Washington, a teacher, greets the children by waving from across the room or saying, "Hi, Mark. I'm glad you're here."	"Oh, that's not the right way to ask a child about his artwork," Mrs. Yesmin, a teacher, says to Patsy's father.
"You're her teacher. Why ask me what she does at home? It's what goes on at school I'm interested in!" says Mrs. McVey, Pam's mother. "Knowing how Pam spends her time at home helps me plan school activities," explains Mrs. Lerner, Pam's teacher.	"Do you read to your child?" Miss Hernandez asks Mike's mother. "Of course, didn't you think I did?" the child's mother answers.
"There's an article on the parent bulletin board about children's use of slang words that you might want to look over, Mrs. Chung," says Mr. Benjamin (a teacher) to one of the parents.	During a parent-teacher meeting, Mrs. Texciera says, "Jill's work is always so messy." Miss Flint, the teacher, answers, "With time, it will improve. She's working with small puzzles and painting. This will give her more practice and control."
"Oh, don't worry about Jon watching television, Mr. Dunne."	"There isn't one good video for preschoolers, Mr. Perez!"

2. With a group of classmates list ideas for parents to obtain inexpensive quality books for home libraries and book corners.

3. Plan a parent newsletter for a local preschool center with helpful information concerning children's language development.

4. Invite a school's director to discuss parent involvement in a school's language arts goals.

5. Identify three books that might help parents understand children's language development or that might provide home activity ideas. Cite the title, author, and copyright date.

6. If you were to design a literacy packet for parents to use over the summer before their child starts kindergarten, what would it include and why?

7. Interview a few parents of preschoolers. Ask, "What three communication skills do you believe are important for your child's success in elementary school (which he will attend after preschool)?"

8. Visit a public library in a multilingual, culturally and racially diverse community to search for other-than-English picture books. Were other literacy-promoting resources available to parents who do not read English? Report back to your training group.

9. Visit a family literacy program and interview its director. Report findings to the class.

10. Discuss the things you observe concerning the lives of single parents you know that you think might have escaped the notice of their child's teachers. Especially mention factors that may affect children's language arts development.

11. Arreola (2003) believes many Latino parents are intimidated and are reluctant to visit their child's school:

   Our culture believes that it is their territory, you don't get in their territory—if you do, you're not respecting them.

   How could you encourage these parents to visit school?

CHAPTER REVIEW

A. In a short paragraph, describe parent involvement in an early childhood center's language arts program.

B. List the teacher's duties and responsibilities in school-home communications.

C. What is the meaning of the following statement? "Early childhood centers reinforce home learnings just as homes can reinforce center learnings." Be specific.

D. Describe the kinds of problems schools may face when they plan parent-teacher study meetings on enhancing young children's ease in learning to read.

APPENDIX

SUGGESTED MUSIC (CHAPTERS 2 AND 8)

The following are available from Educational Activities, P.O. Box 87, Baldwin, NY 11510, 516-223-4666; and from Kimbo Educational, P.O. Box 477, Long Branch, NJ 07740, 732-229-4949.

Tonja Evetts Weimer

Fingerplays and Action Chants (1986)
Vol. 1—Animals (1994)
Vol. 2—Family and Friends (1995)
Pittsburgh, PA: Pearce-Evetts Productions

Kathy Poelker

Look at My World (1983)

Amazing Musical Moments! (1985)

Wheeling, IL: Look At Me Productions

Raffi

Singable Songs for the Very Young (1976)

More Singable Songs (1979)

Corner Grocery Store (1979)

Baby Beluga (1980)

Rise and Shine (1982)

Raffi's Christmas Album (1983)

One Light, One Sun (1985)

Ontario, Canada: Troubadour Records

Hap Palmer

Sea Gulls (1978)

Walter the Waltzing Worm (1982)

Freeport, NY: Educational Activities

Greg and Steve

We All Live Together, Vols. 1–4 (1975–1980)

On the Move with Greg and Steve (1983)

Holidays and Special Days (1989)

Los Angeles, CA: Youngheart Records

L. Campbell Towel

"Spotlight," Cat Paws: Music for playing (1993)

Milwaukee, WI: Hal Leonard Publishing

Tom Glazer

Tom Glazer's Treasury of Songs for Children (1998)

Garden City, NY: Doubleday

J. Warren

Piggyback Songs for Infants and Toddlers (1985)

Everett, WA: Totline Press

J. Weissman

The I Love Children's Song Book (1996)

Overland Park, KS: Miss Jackie Music Co.

Fred Koch

Did You Feed My Cow? (1989)

Lake Bluff, IL: Red Rover Records

DEVELOPMENTALLY APPROPRIATE PRACTICE (CHAPTER 6)

Language and Communication Development— Widely Held Expectations

For 3-year-olds—

- shows a steady increase in vocabulary, ranging from 2,000 to 4,000 words; tends to overgeneralize meaning and make up words to fit needs
- uses simple sentences of at least three or four words to express needs
- may have difficulty taking turns in conversation; changes topics quickly
- pronounces words with difficulty; often mistakes one word for another
- likes simple finger plays and rhymes and learns words to songs that have much repetition
- adapts speech and style of nonverbal communication to listeners in culturally accepted ways but still needs to be reminded of context
- asks many *who, what, where,* and *why* questions but shows confusion in responding to some questions (especially *why, how,* and *when*)
- uses language to organize thought, linking two ideas by sentence combining; overuses such words as *but, because,* and *when;* rarely makes appropriate use of such temporal words as *before, until,* or *after*
- can tell a simple story but must redo the sequence to put an idea into the order of events; often forgets the point of a story and is more likely to focus on favorite parts

For 4-year-olds—

- expands vocabulary from 4,000 to 6,000 words; shows more attention to abstract uses
- usually speaks in five- to six-word sentences
- likes to sing simple songs; knows many rhymes and finger plays
- will talk in front of the group with some reticence; likes to tell others about family and experiences
- uses verbal commands to claim many things; begins teasing others
- expresses emotions through facial gestures and reads others for body cues; copies behaviors (such as hand gestures) of older children or adults
- can control volume of voice for periods of time if reminded; begins to read context for social cues
- uses more advanced sentence structures, such as relative clauses and tag questions ("She's nice, isn't she?") and experiments with new constructions, creating some comprehension difficulties for the listener
- tries to communicate more than his or her vocabulary allows; borrows and extends words to create meaning
- learns new vocabulary quickly if related to own experience ("We walk our dog on a belt. Oh yeah, it's a leash—we walk our dog on a leash")
- can retell a four- or five-step directive or the sequence in a story

For 5-year-olds—

- employs a vocabulary of 5,000 to 8,000 words, with frequent plays on words; pronounces words with little difficulty, except for particular sounds, such as *l* and *th*
- uses fuller, more complex sentences ("His turn is over, and it's my turn now")
- takes turns in conversation, interrupts others less frequently; listens to another speaker if information is new and of interest; shows vestiges of egocentrism in speech, for instance, in assuming listener

will understand what is meant (saying "He told me to do it" without any referents for the pronouns)

- shares experiences verbally; knows the words to many songs
- likes to act out others' roles, shows off in front of new people or becomes unpredictably very shy
- remembers lines of simple poems and repeats full sentences and expressions from others, including television shows and commercials
- shows skill at using conventional modes of communication complete with pitch and inflection

- uses nonverbal gestures, such as certain facial expressions in teasing peers
- can tell and retell stories with practice; enjoys repeating stories, poems, and songs; enjoys acting out plays or stories
- shows growing speech fluency in expressing ideas

Excerpt from Bredekamp, S., & Copple, C. (Eds.). (1997). *Developmentally appropriate practice in early childhood programs.* Washington, DC: NAEYC.

PROFESSIONAL STANDARDS (CHAPTER 6)

Language and literacy. Early language and literacy form the basis for much later learning, and well-prepared candidates possess extensive, research-based knowledge and skill in the area, regardless of the age group or setting in which they intend to practice.

Listening, speaking, reading, and writing are integrated elements. Verbal and nonverbal communication in its diverse forms, combined with competence as a reader and writer, are essential for children's later development. Even as infants and toddlers, children are building the foundations for literacy through early experiences.

Candidates—including those who are not currently teaching linguistically diverse young children—also demonstrate knowledge of second-language acquistion and of bilingualism. They know the home language environments of the children they teach and the possible effects on children when their classroom environment does not reflect the home language. Candidates know the sociopolitical contexts of major language groups and how those may affect children's motivation to learn English. Candidates understand the benefits of bilingualism and the special needs of young English language learners (ELLs), building on the home language systems that children already have developed and assisting them to add a second language to their repertoire. For young ELLs who are learning to read, candidates use, adapt, and assess research-based literacy activities and teaching methods that build on prior knowledge and support successful transitions for those learners.

Candidates are able to articulate priorities for high-quality, meaningful language and literacy experiences in early childhood, across a developmental continuum. Across the years from infancy through third grade, those experiences should help children to, for example:

- Explore their environments and develop the conceptual, experiential, and language foundations for learning to read and write
- Develop their ability to converse at length and in depth on a topic in various settings (one-on-one with adults and peers, in small groups, etc.)
- Develop vocabulary that reflects their growing knowledge of the world around them
- Use language, reading, and writing to strengthen their own cultural identity, as well as to participate in the shared identity of the school environment
- Associate reading and writing with pleasure and enjoyment, as well as with skill development
- Use a range of strategies to derive meaning from stories and texts
- Use language, reading, and writing for various purposes
- Use a variety of print and non-print resources
- Develop basic concepts of print and understanding of sounds, letters, and letter-sound relationships

From Hyson, M. (Ed.). (2003). *Preparing Early Childhood Professionals NAEYC's Standards for Programs.* Washington, DC. Reprinted with permission from Association for the Education of Young Children.

REGGIO EMILIA READING LIST (CHAPTER 6)

Edwards, C. (1993). Partner, nurturer and guide: The roles of the Reggio teacher in action. In C. Edwards, L. Gandini, & G. Forman (Eds.), *The hundred languages of children: The Reggio Emilia approach to early childhood education.* Norwood, NJ: Ablex.

Gandini, L. (1993). Fundamentals of the Reggio Emilia approach to early childhood education. *Young Children, 49*(1), 4–8.

Hendrick, J. (Ed.). (1997). *First steps toward teaching the Reggio way.* Upper Saddle River, NJ: Prentice Hall.

ASSESSMENT TOOLS (CHAPTER 6)

Clay, M. (1996). *Observational survey of early literacy achievement.*
Portsmouth, NH: Heinemann.

PALS PreK: *Phonological Awareness Literacy Screening for Preschool* (2002).
Publisher: University of Virginia Press (http://pals.virginia.edu/default.asp)

Peabody Picture Vocabulary Test (3rd. Ed.) (1997).
Publisher: American Guidance Service; ages: $2\frac{1}{2}$ and up.

Preschool Language Scale (4th Ed.) (1992).
Publisher: Psychological Corporation; ages: birth to 7.

Preschool Outcomes Checklist
Venn, E. C., & Jahn, M. C. (2004). *Teaching and learning in the preschool: Using individually appropriate practices in early childhood.* Newark, DE: International Reading Association. (May be copied for classroom use.)

Reading Skills Competency Tests—Readiness Level
Publisher: The Writing Company (http://www.writingco.com)

Test of Early Language Development (1999)
Publisher: PRO-ED; ages: 2–7.

Test of Early Reading Ability (2001)
Publisher: PRO-ED; ages: 3–10 years.

Test of Oral Language Development
Publisher: PRO-ED (http://www.proedinc.com)

Test of Phonological Awareness
Publisher: PRO-ED; level: kindergarten

Woodcock-Johnson Educational Battery
Publisher: Riverside Publishing; ages: 2 and up.

Woodcock-Johnson Reading Mastery
Publisher: American Guidance Services; level: K–12

ADDITIONAL STORY (CHAPTER 10)

THE CROOKED-MOUTH FAMILY

There are many versions of this action story. This one, however, appeals to young children and never fails to bring laughter and requests to have it repeated. Before beginning the story, quietly light a candle—preferably a dripless one.

Once there was a family called The Crooked-Mouth Family.

The father had a mouth like this.

(Twist mouth to the right.)

The mother had a mouth like this.

(Twist mouth to the left.)

The Big Brother had a mouth like this.

(Bring lower lip over upper lip.)

The Big Sister had a mouth like this.

(Bring upper lip over lower lip.)

But the Baby Sister had a pretty mouth just like yours.

(Smile naturally.)

(Repeat mouth positions as each character speaks.)

One night they forgot to blow the candle out when they went upstairs to bed.

The father said, "I'd better go downstairs and blow that candle out."

(With mouth still twisted to the right, blow at the flame being careful not to blow it out.)

"What's the matter with this candle? It won't go out."

(Repeat blowing several times.)

"I guess I'd better call Mother. Mother! Please come down and blow the candle out."

Mother said, "Why can't you blow the candle out? Anybody can blow a candle out. You just go like this."

(She blows at the flame, mouth still twisted to the left.)

"I can't blow it out either. We'd better call Big Brother."

(Change to father's mouth.)

"Brother! Please come down and blow the candle out."

Big Brother said, "That's easy. All you have to do is blow hard."

(With lower lip over upper, hold the candle low and blow.)

Father said, "See. You can't blow it out either. We'll have to call Big Sister. Sister! Please come down and blow the candle out!"

Big Sister said, "I can blow it out. Watch me."

(With upper lip over lower, candle held high, blow several times.)

Father said, "That's a funny candle. I told you I couldn't blow it out."

Mother said, "I couldn't blow it out, either."

Big Brother said, "Neither could I."

Big Sister said, "I tried and tried, and I couldn't blow it out."

Father said, "I guess we'll have to call Baby Sister. Baby! Please come down and blow the candle out."

Baby Sister came downstairs, rubbing her eyes because she had been asleep. She asked, "What's the matter?"

Father said, "I can't blow the candle out."

Mother said, "I can't blow it out either."

Big Brother said, "Neither can I."

Big Sister said, "I can't either."

Baby Sister said, "Anybody can blow a candle out. That's easy." And she did.

Author Unknown

FLANNEL BOARD ACTIVITY SETS (CHAPTER 12)

THE HARE AND THE TORTOISE

(Adapted from Aesop)

Pieces: rabbit   dog   rabbit running   finish-line flag
            turtle   hen   rabbit sleeping   tree

One day the rabbit was talking to some of the other animals. "I am the fastest runner in the forest," he said. "I can beat anyone! Do you want to race?"

"Not I," said the dog.

"Not I," said the hen.

"I will race with you," said the turtle.

"That's a good joke," said the rabbit. "I could dance around you all the way and still win."

"Still bragging about how fast you are," answered the turtle. "Come on, let's race. Do you see that flag over there? That will be the finish line. Hen, would you stand by the flag so that you can tell who wins the race?"

"Dog, will you say the starting words—get on your mark, get ready, get set, go!"

"Stand there," said the dog. "Get on your mark, get ready, get set, go!"

The rabbit ran very fast. He looked over his shoulder and saw how slowly the turtle was running on his short little legs. Just then he saw a shady spot under a tree. He thought to himself—that turtle is so slow I have time to rest here under this tree. So he sat down on the cool grass, and before he knew it, he was fast asleep.

While he slept, the turtle was running. (Clump, Clump—Clump, Clump) He was not running very fast, but he kept on running. (Clump, Clump—Clump, Clump) Pretty soon the turtle came to the tree where the rabbit was sleeping. He went past and kept on running. (Clump, Clump—Clump, Clump)

The turtle was almost to the finish line. The hen saw the turtle coming and said, "Turtle, keep on running. You've almost won the race."

When the hen spoke, the rabbit awoke. He looked down by the finish line and saw the turtle was almost there. As fast as he could, the rabbit started running again. Just then he heard the hen say, "The turtle is the winner!"

"But I'm the fastest," said the rabbit.

"Not this time," said the hen. "Sometimes slow and steady wins the race."

Put on turtle, dog, hen, rabbit at left edge of board.

Add finish-line flag on right edge of board. Move hen by flag.

Put on running rabbit. Remove standing rabbit.

Add sleeping rabbit while removing running rabbit.

Change sleeping rabbit to running rabbit.

THE BIG, BIG TURNIP

(Traditional)

Pieces:	farmer	turnip	daughter	cat
	farmer's wife	large piece of ground	dog	mouse

A farmer once planted a turnip seed. And it grew, and it grew, and it grew. The farmer saw it was time to pull the turnip out of the ground. So he took hold of it and began to pull.

He pulled, and he pulled, and he pulled, and he pulled. But the turnip wouldn't come up.

So the farmer called to his wife who was getting dinner.

Fe, fi, fo, fum.

I pulled the turnip,

But it wouldn't come up.

And the wife came running, and she took hold of the farmer, and they pulled, and they pulled, and they pulled, and they pulled. But the turnip wouldn't come up.

So the wife called to the daughter who was feeding the chickens nearby.

Fe, fi, fo, fum.

We pulled the turnip,

But it wouldn't come up.

And the daughter came running. The daughter took hold of the wife. The wife took hold of the farmer. The farmer took hold of the turnip. And they pulled, and they pulled, and they pulled, and they pulled. But the turnip wouldn't come up.

So the daughter called to the dog who was chewing a bone.

Fe, fi, fo, fum.

We pulled the turnip,

But it wouldn't come up.

And the dog came running. The dog took hold of the daughter. The daughter took hold of the wife. The wife took hold of the farmer. And the farmer took hold of the turnip. And they pulled, and they pulled, and they pulled. But the turnip wouldn't come up.

The dog called to the cat who was chasing her tail.

Fe, fi, fo, fum.

We pulled the turnip,

But it wouldn't come up.

Place farmer on board. Cover turnip so that only top is showing with ground piece, and place on board.

Move farmer next to turnip with hands on turnip top. Place wife behind farmer.

Place daughter behind farmer's wife.

Place dog behind daughter.

And the cat came running. The cat took hold of the dog. The dog took hold of the daughter. The daughter took hold of the wife. The wife took hold of the farmer. The farmer took hold of the turnip. And they pulled, and they pulled, and they pulled. But the turnip wouldn't come up.

So the cat called the mouse who was nibbling spinach nearby.

Fe, fi, fo, fum.

We pulled the turnip,

But it wouldn't come up.

And the mouse came running.

"That little mouse can't help," said the dog. "He's too little." "Phooey," squeaked the mouse. "I could pull that turnip up myself, but since you have all been pulling, I'll let you help too."

So the mouse took hold of the cat. The cat took hold of the dog. The dog took hold of the daughter. The daughter took hold of the wife. The wife took hold of the farmer. The farmer took hold of the turnip. And they pulled, and they pulled, and they pulled. And up came the turnip.

And the mouse squeaked, "I told you so!"

Place cat behind dog.

Place mouse behind cat.

Remove ground.

Full-size version of this art can be found on the Online Companion™ at http://www.earlychilded.delmar.com

Full-size version of this art can be found on the Online Companion™ at http://www.earlychilded.delmar.com

THE LITTLE RED HEN

Pieces: cottage   sticks   fox   little red hen
         fire   sack   mouse   pot
         two large rocks rooster   table

It was morning. In the cottage where the little red hen and the rooster and the mouse lived, little red hen was happily setting the table for breakfast.

"Who will get some sticks for the fire?" said little red hen.

"I won't," grumbled the rooster.

"I won't," squeaked the mouse.

"Then I'll do it myself," said the little red hen, and off she went to gather them.

When she returned with the sticks and had started the fire, she asked, "Who will get water from the spring to fill the pot?"

"I won't," grumbled the rooster.

"I won't," squeaked the mouse.

"Then I'll do it myself," she said and ran off to fill the pot.

"Who will cook the breakfast?" said the hen.

"I won't," grumbled the rooster.

"I won't," squeaked the mouse.

"Then I'll do it myself," said the hen, and she did.

When breakfast was ready, the hen, the mouse, and the rooster ate together but the rooster spilled the milk, and the mouse scattered crumbs on the floor.

Place cottage, table, and hen on board.
Add rooster.
Add mouse.

Remove hen.

Replace with hen and sticks. Place fire over sticks.

Place pot over fire.

Remove hen. Return hen.
Move hen, mouse, and rooster near table.

"Who will clear the table?" said the hen.

"I won't," grumbled the rooster.

"I won't," squeaked the mouse.

"Then I'll do it myself," said the hen. So she cleared everything and swept the floor.

The lazy rooster and mouse by this time had moved closer to the fire and had fallen fast asleep.

Move rooster and mouse near the fire.

"Knock, knock, knock," the noise at the door awakened them.

"Who's that?" said the rooster. "Oh it might be the mail carrier with a letter for me," so the mouse went to the door and opened it without looking out the window first to see who was there.

It was a fox. "Help," said the mouse, but the fast old fox, quick as a wink, caught not only the mouse, but also the rooster and the little red hen. Quickly he popped them all into his sack and headed off toward home, thinking about the fine dinner he was bringing to his family.

Place fox and sack on board. Hide rooster, mouse, and hen behind sack.
Remove cottage.

The bag was heavy, and home was a long way, so the fox decided to put it down and rest.

Put fox in horizontal position.

"Snore, Snore, Snore," went the fox.

Little red hen said to the rooster and mouse, "Now we have a chance to escape. I have a pair of scissors and a needle and thread in my apron pocket. I've cut a hole in the bag. Hurry and jump out, find a rock, the biggest one you can carry, and bring it back quickly. "Snore, Snore, Snore," went the fox. Soon the mouse and the rooster returned with large rocks. They pushed them into the sack, and the hen sewed the hole up. Off they ran to their home. They closed the door and locked it, and they bolted the windows. They were safe now.

Remove hen, rooster, and mouse from sack.
Add rocks.
Move rocks behind sack.

The fox didn't know he'd been fooled until he got home and opened his sack.

Remove fox and sack with rocks.

The mouse and the rooster were so happy to be home that they didn't grumble and fight anymore; they even helped to cook the dinner with smiles on their faces.

Place cottage, hen, rooster, and mouse beside it on board.

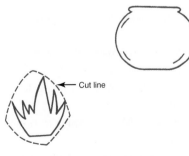

Cut line

Cut line

Full-size version of this art can be found on the Online Companion™ at http://www.earlychilded.delmar.com

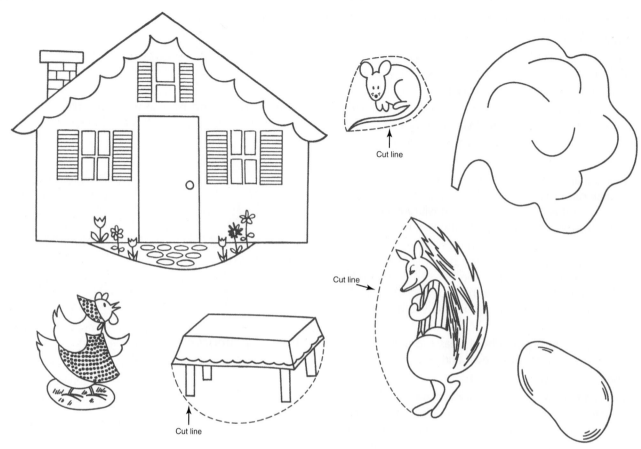

Full-size version of this art can be found on the Online Companion™ at http://www.earlychilded.delmar.com

HUSH, LITTLE BABY

(Flannel-board song)

Pieces:	mother	billy goat	sleeping baby	cart
	crying baby	bull	mocking bird	dog
	ring	horse	looking glass	

Courtesy of *Adventures in Felt* © Copyright 1972.

Hush, little baby, don't say a word, Mama's going to buy you a mockingbird.	Place mother and crying baby on her lap.
If that mockingbird won't sing, Mama's going to buy you a diamond ring.	Add ring.
If that diamond ring turns to brass, Mama's going to buy you a looking glass.	Add looking glass.
If that looking glass gets broke, Mama's going to buy you a billy goat.	Add billy goat.
If that billy goat won't pull, Mama's going to buy you a cart and bull.	Add cart and bull.

If that cart and bull turn over, Mama's going to buy you a dog named Rover.

If that dog named Rover won't bark, Mama's going to buy you a horse and cart.

If that horse and cart break down, YOU'LL be the sweetest little baby in town.

Lullaby, baby sweet of mine, you'll be asleep by half past nine.

Add dog.

Add horse and move cart from bull.

Replace crying baby with sleeping baby.

← Cut line

ALPHABET PRONUNCIATION GUIDE (CHAPTERS 16 AND 17)

Symbols	Sounds as in the Words	Symbols	Sounds as in the Words
a	fat, apple, asks	m	him, me, custom
ā	ate, name	n	sun, not, even
b	rib, big	o	ox, on, not
c	traffic, cat, certain	ō	go, open, home
d	lid, end, feed	p	sip, pat
e	end, wet, pen	r	ran, rip, very
ē	me, Elaine, eat	s	kiss, so, last, sugar
f	if, leaf, full	t	hit, top
g	rag, go, gem	u	up, rug, custom
h	hat, how, high	ū	useful, unite
i	it, individual, pin	v	give, have, very
i	piece, niece	w	we, win, watch
ī	ice, while	x	box
j	jump, jeep	y	yea, you
k	lick, kiss, milk	ȳ	my, cry
l	will, late, little	z	zoo, fuzz

Vowel Digraph Sounds

ai . . . snail
ay . . . say
ea . . . lead
ea . . . tea
ee . . . sheep
ei . . . receive
ie . . . believe

ey . . . key
ey . . . they
oa . . . float
oe . . . hoe
ow . . . grow
ou . . . though

Vowel Diphthongs

oa . . . foal
oi . . . toil
ou . . . though
oy . . . soy

ue . . . sue
ew . . . new

A

accent — prominence or emphasis given to a word or syllable through one or more of the following factors: loudness, change of pitch, and longer duration (Harris & Hodges, 1995).

accommodation — the process by which new experiences or events change existing ideas or thought patterns.

activity plans — written, detailed, step-by-step teaching plans often including an evaluation section.

acuity — how well or clearly one uses senses; the degree of perceptual sharpness.

affective sphere — the affectionate feelings (or lack of them) shaped through experience with others.

alliteration — the repetition of the initial sounds in neighboring words or stressed syllables, for example, "The foam flowed free and fizzy."

alphabetic principle — the awareness that spoken language can be analyzed as strings of separate words and words, in turn, as sequences of syllables and phonemes within syllables.

articulation — the adjustments and movements of the muscles of the mouth and jaw involved in producing clear oral communication.

assessment — a broad repertoire of behaviors involved in noticing, documenting, recording, and interpreting children's behaviors and performances. Testing is a subset of assessment behaviors in which performances are controlled and elicited in standardized conditions (Johnston & Rogers, 2002).

assimilation — the process that allows new experiences to merge with previously stored mental structures.

assonance — the repetition in words of identical or similar vowel sounds followed by different consonant sounds.

attachment — a two-way process formed through mutual gratification of needs and reciprocal communication influenced by the infant's growing cognitive abilities. Sometimes referred to as bonding or a "love affair" relationship.

audience — the respondents to drama presentation; a group of listeners or spectators.

audiovisual equipment — any mechanical or nonmechanical item useful in offering sight or hearing experience.

auditory — relating to or experienced through hearing.

auditory processing — the full range of mental activity involved in reacting to auditory stimuli, especially speech sounds, and in considering their meanings in relation to past experience and to their future use (Harris & Hodges, 1995).

B

babbling — an early language stage in sound production in which an infant engages in vocal play with vowel and consonant sounds, including some sounds not found in his or her language environment.

behaviorism — the theoretical viewpoint, espoused by theorists such as B. F. Skinner, that behavior is shaped by environmental forces, specifically in response to reward and punishment.

bilingual — refers to an individual with a language background other than English who has developed proficiency in the primary language and a degree of proficiency in English.

Black English — a language usually spoken in some economically depressed African-American homes. A dialect of non-Standard English having its own rules and patterns. Also called African-American English.

C

chants — rhythmic, monotonous utterances.

characterization — the way an author presents a character by describing character verbalizations, actions, or thinking, or by indicating what other characters say, think, or do about the character.

characters — persons (or puppets) represented in or acting in a story or drama.

child-initiated curricula — a basic tenet underlying this type of curriculum is the belief that *true* growth occurs when children are free to develop intrinsic interests naturally.

circle time — an early childhood term describing a planned gathering of children usually seated in a half-circle configuration led by a teacher.

classify — the act of systematically grouping things according to identifiable common characteristics, for example, size.

625

closure — a conversation technique that prompts children to verbally guess and complete or fill in a teachers' sentence. The teacher pauses or hesitates, which prompts the child to finish a teacher verbalization.

cluttering — rapid, incomplete speech that is often jerky, slurred, spoken in bursts, and difficult to understand; nervous speech (Harris & Hodges, 1995).

cognition — the process that creates mental images, concepts, and operations.

communication — the giving (sending) and receiving of information, signals, or messages.

concept — a commonly recognized element (or elements) that identifies groups or classes; usually has a given name.

conceptual tempo — a term associated with Jerome Kagan's theory of different individual pacing in the perceptual exploration of objects.

consonant — (1) speech sound made by partial or complete closure of the vocal tract, which obstructs air flow. (2) An alphabet letter used to represent any of these sounds.

constructivist theory — a theory such as that of Jean Piaget, based on the belief that children construct knowledge for themselves rather than having it conveyed to them by some external source.

continuant — a consonant or vowel that may be continued or prolonged without alteration during one emission of breath.

convergent thinking — the process of analyzing and integrating ideas to infer reasonable conclusions or specific solutions from given information.

cooing — an early stage during the prelinguistic period in which vowel sounds are repeated, particularly the *u-u-u* sound.

couplets — stanzas of two rhyming lines.

cues — prompts or hints that aid recognition, such as a parent pointing to and/or saying "teddy bear" when sharing a picture book illustration. This is done because the infant is familiar with his own teddy bear.

cultural literacy — literacy that reflects a culture's knowledge of significant ideas, events, values, and the essence of that culture's identity.

culture — all the activities and achievements of a society that individuals within that society pass from one generation to the next.

curriculum — an overall plan for the content of instruction to be offered in a program.

curriculum models — refers to a conceptual framework and organizational structure for decision making about educational priorities, administrative policies, instructional methods, and evaluation criteria (Goffin, 2000).

D

deafness — hearing is so impaired that the individual is unable to process auditory linguistic information, with or without amplification.

dialect — a variety of spoken language unique to a geographical area or social group. Variations in dialect may include phonological or sound variations, syntactical variations, and lexical or vocabulary variations.

dialogue — a conversation between two or more persons or between a person and something else.

diction — clarity of speech; enunciation.

discourse skills — refers to using language in structured ways to go beyond basic conversation, for example, telling a story, explaining a procedure, creating a fantasy, dictating ideas, and elaborating to provide greater understanding.

divergent thinking — the process of elaborating on ideas to generate new ideas or alternative interpretations of given information.

dramas — plays; stories in dramatic form, typically emphasizing conflict in and among key characters.

dramatic play — acting out experiences or creating drama episodes during play.

dual coding — the belief that infants' experiences and emotions influence cognition.

E

early literacy — speaking, listening, print awareness and writing behaviors, reading of alphabet letters and words, and other skills that evolve and change over time, culminating in conventional literacy.

Ebonics — a nonstandard form of English, a dialect often called Black English that is characterized by not conjugating the verb "to be" and by dropping some final consonants from words.

echolalia — a characteristic of the babbling period. The child repeats (echoes) the same sounds over and over.

equilibrium — a balance attained with consistent care and satisfaction of needs that leads to a sense of security and lessens anxiety.

expansion — a teaching technique that includes the adult's (teacher's) modeling of words or grammar, filling in missing words for children's utterances, or suggesting ideas for child exploration.

explanatory talk — a type of conversation characterized by a speaker's attempt to create connections between objects, events, concepts, or conclusions to promote understanding in the listener.

expressive jargon — a term describing a child's first attempts at combining words into narration that results in a mimic of adult speech.

expressive (productive) vocabulary — the vocabulary a person uses in speaking and writing.

extension — a teaching strategy in which an adult expands the child's information by adding new, additional, related information or meaning.

F

fable — a short tale in prose or verse that teaches a moral, usually with talking animals or inanimate objects as main characters.

fairy tales — folk stories about real-life problems, usually with imaginary characters and magical events.

family literacy programs — community programs attempting to provide literacy-building opportunities and experiences for families. Services are available for both adults and children.

fiction — imaginative narrative in any form of presentation that is designed to entertain, as distinguished from that which is designed primarily to explain, argue, or merely describe.

figurative language — language enriched by word images and figures of speech.

G

gaze coupling — infant-mother extended eye contact.

genre — a category used to classify literary works, usually by form, technique, or content.

grammar — the rules of a specific language that include both written and spoken utterances and describe how that specific language works and the forms of speech that conform to the rules that well-schooled speakers and writers observe in any given language.

H

hearing — the facility or sense by which sound is perceived.

hearing disorders — characterized by an inability to hear sounds clearly. May range from hearing speech sounds faintly or in a distorted way, to profound deafness.

holophrases — the expression of a whole idea in a single word. They are characteristic of the child's language from about 12 to 18 months.

I

impulsive — quick to answer or react to either a simple or complex situation or problem.

inflections — the grammatical "markers" such as plurals. Also, a change in pitch or loudness of the voice.

inner speech — mentioned in Vygotsky's theory as private speech that becomes internalized and is useful for organizing ideas.

interactionists — those who adhere to the theory that language develops through a combination of inborn factors and environmental influences.

interactive writing — (1) an instructional strategy popular in American kindergartens; (2) a process involving a teacher who verbally stretches each word so that the child (children) can distinguish sounds and letters. Also known as shared writing.

invented spelling — the result of an attempt to spell a word whose spelling is not already known, based on a writer's knowledge of the spelling system and how it works.

J

joint attention — child's awareness that he or she must gain and hold another's focus during communicational exchanges to get his or her message understood.

L

language — the systematic, conventional use of sounds, signs, or written symbols in human society for communication and self-expression. It conveys meaning that is mutually understood.

language center — a classroom area specifically set aside and equipped for language arts–related activities and child use.

listening — a mental process that includes attending, hearing, discriminating, understanding, and remembering.

listening center — a classroom area designed to accommodate children's listening experiences.

listening comprehension level — the highest grade level of material that can be comprehended well when it is read aloud to a child.

literacy — involves complex cognitive interactions between readers and their texts and between background knowledge and new information. It involves both skill and knowledge and varies by task and setting. Different types of literacy are described — prose, document, quantitative, academic, workplace, and functional.

M

mental image — a "perceptual representation" or mental picture of a perceptual experience, remembered or imagined.

metalinguistic awareness — a conscious awareness on the part of a language user of language as an object in itself.

metalinguistic skills — the ability to think about language as a separate entity.

metaphors — figures of speech in which a comparison is implied by analogy but is not stated.

moderation level — an individual preferred state of arousal between bored and excited when learning and pleasure peak.

modifiers — words that give a special characteristic to a noun (for example, a *large* ball).

monologue — literally "speaking alone."

morpheme — the smallest unit in a language that by itself has a recognizable meaning.

morphology — the study of the units of meaning in a language.

N

narrative — in general, a story, actual or fictional, expressed orally or in writing.

nativists — those who adhere to the theory that children are born with biological dispositions for learning that unfold or mature in a natural way.

neurolinguistics — a branch of linguistics that studies the structure and function of the brain in relation to language acquisition, learning, and use.

nonfiction — prose that explains, argues, or describes; usually factual.

nursery rhymes — folk sayings with rhyming words for very young children.

nurturist — one who adheres to the theory that the minds of children are blank or unformed and need educational input or direct instruction to develop and "output" knowledge and appropriate behavior.

O

onsets — any consonants before a vowel in a syllable.

orthographic awareness — the ability to notice and use critical features of graphic symbols in written language.

otitis media — inflammation and/or infection of the middle ear.

outreach — an early childhood program's attempt to provide supportive assistance to attending children's families to promote their children's success in school and developmental growth.

overextension — in the early acquisition of words and their meanings, the application of a word to include other objects that share common features, such as "water" being used to describe any liquid.

overregularization — the tendency on the part of children to make their language regular, such as using past tenses like -ed on verb endings.

P

pantomime — creative communication done with non-verbal physical actions.

parentese — a high-pitched, rhythmic, singsong, crooning style of speech. Also known as motherese or baby talk.

participation stories — stories with some feature children can enact through physical movements, verbal expression, or both.

perception — mental awareness of objects and other data gathered through the five senses.

personification — a metaphorical figure of speech in which animals, ideas, things, etc., are represented as having human qualities.

phonation — exhaled air passing through the larynx's vibrating folds and producing "voice."

phoneme — one of the smallest units of speech that distinguishes one utterance from another.

phonemic awareness — the insight that every spoken word can be conceived as a sequence of phonemes.

phonetic instruction — instruction in phonics is instruction that stresses sound-symbol relationships. Used especially in beginning reading instruction.

phonetics — pertaining to representing the sounds of speech with a set of distinct symbols, each denoting a single sound.

phonological awareness — the whole spectrum from primitive awareness of speech sounds and rhythms to rhyme awareness and sound similarities; at the highest level, awareness of syllables or phonemes (Neuman, Copple, & Bredekamp, 1999).

phonology — the sound system of a language and how it is represented with an alphabetic code.

plot — the structure of the action of a story.

poems — metrical forms of composition in which word images are selected and expressed to create powerful, often beautiful impressions in the listener and/or enjoyable rhythmic responses in young children.

pragmatics — the study of how language is used effectively in a social context; varying speech patterns depending on social circumstances and the context of situations.

print awareness — in early literacy, children's growing recognition of the conventions and characteristics of a written language. It includes recognition of directionality (left to right and top to bottom), that print forms words corresponding to speech, and that spaces separate words and other features.

prosodic speech — the child's use of voice modulation and word stress to give special emphasis and meaning.

psychosocial theory — the branch of psychology founded by Erik Erikson; development is described in terms of eight stages that span childhood and adulthood.

R

reading method — any of several relatively specific procedures or steps for teaching one or more aspects of reading, each procedure embodying explicitly or implicitly some theory of how children learn and of the relationship between written and spoken language.

realism — presents experiences without embellishment to convey life as it appears in a natural world limited by the senses and reason.

recasting — a teaching technique that involves a teacher who supplies children's missing words or gently models correct usage of words or extends the child's ideas following the child's verbal statement.

receptive (comprehensive) vocabulary — the comprehension vocabulary used by a person in listening (and silent reading).

reflective — taking time to weigh aspects or alternatives in a given situation.

regularization — a child's speech behavior that indicates the formation and internalization of a language rule (regularity).

resonation — amplification of laryngeal sounds using cavities of the mouth, nose, sinuses, and pharynx.

responsive mothers — mothers who are alert and timely in responding to and giving attention to infants' needs and communications.

rhythm — uniform or patterned recurrence of a beat, accent, or melody in speech.

rimes — the vowel and any consonants after it in a syllable.

S

scaffolding — a teaching technique helpful in promoting languages, understanding, and child solutions. It includes teacher-responsive conversation, open-ended questioning, and facilitation of children's initiatives.

selective (elective) mutism — a behavior that describes child silence or lack of speech in select surroundings and/or with certain individuals.

semantics — the study of meanings associated with words and the acquisition of vocabulary.

semiotics — observant of signs or symbols. The study of how groups come to share meaning.

sensory-motor development — the control and use of sense organs and the body's muscle structure.

sight reading — the ability to immediately recognize a word as whole without sounding it out.

signing — a body positioning, sound, action, or gesture or combination of these undertaken by an infant that represents an effort to communicate a need, desire, or message.

similes — comparisons of two things that are unlike, usually using the words *like* or *as*. Example: "Love is like a red, red rose."

social connectedness — a term associated with the following human characteristics: is stable and secure, develops close relationships with others, has supportive family and friends, and is deemed a worthy individual by others. Often seen by others as able to transcend stress and possess an individual identity.

social constructivist theory — such as Vygotsky's emphasis on the importance of language and socially shared cognition, scaffolded exchanges, and the child's private speech.

socioeconomic — relating to or involving a combination of social and economic factors.

software — a wide range of commercial programs developed for computer users' convenience, education, entertainment, and so on.

spatial-temporal reasoning — the mental arrangement of ideas and/or images in a graphic pattern indicating their relationships over time.

speech and language disorders — communication disorders that affect the way people talk and understand; range from simple sound substitutions to not being able to use speech and language at all.

Standard English — substantially uniform formal and informal speech and writing of educated people that is widely recognized as acceptable wherever English is spoken and understood.

story — an imaginative tale with a plot, characters, and setting.

story map — a timeline showing an ordered sequence of events.

subculture — an ethnic, regional, economic, or social group exhibiting characteristic patterns of behavior sufficient to distinguish it from others within an embracing culture or society.

symbols — things that stand for or suggest (such as pictures, models, word symbols, and so forth).

synapses — gaplike structures over which the axon of one neuron beams a signal to the dendrites of another, forming a connection in the human brain. Concerns memory and learning.

syntax — the arrangement of words as elements in a sentence to show their relationship.

T

telegraphic speech — a characteristic of young children's sentences in which everything but the crucial word(s) is omitted, as if for a telegram.

transitional kindergarten — a relatively new feature of some elementary school districts that offers supportive literacy activities and classroom access (usually during the summer before the child is to enroll in kindergarten).

transitional statements — teacher statements made to disperse students in small groups or in an orderly fashion.

V

verses — lines of a poem or poetry without imaginative or conceptual power.

visual literacy — the ability to interpret and communicate with respect to visual symbols in media other than print.

visualization — the process, or result, of mentally picturing objects or events that are normally experienced directly.

vowel — a voiced speech sound made without stoppage or friction of air flow as it passes through the vocal tract.

W

webbing — a visual or graphic method of mapping or planning a possible course of study.

whole-language approach — a philosophy and reading-instruction approach integrating oral and written language. Advocates believe that when children are given literature-abundant and print-rich environments, they will follow their natural curiosity and learn to read as they learned to speak. A thematic focus is used. Teachers seize opportunities to connect and interrelate language arts areas.

writing — the ability to use print to communicate with others.

Acredolo, L., & Goodwyn, S. (1985). Symbolic gesturing in language development. *Human Development, 28,* 53–58.

Acredolo, L. & Goodwyn, S. (2000). *Baby minds: Brain-building games your baby will love to play.* New York: Bantam Books.

Adams, M. J. (1990). *Beginning to read: Thinking and learning about print.* Cambridge, MA: The MIT Press.

Adams, M. J. (1998). *Beginning to read: Thinking and learning about print* (Rev. ed.). Cambridge, MA: The MIT Press.

Ainsworth, M. D. S., & Bell, S. M. (1972). Mother-infant interaction and development of competence. *ERIC Document,* ED 065 180.

Alexander, K., & Entwisle, D. (1996). Schools and children at risk. In A. Booth & J. Dunn (Eds.), *Family and school links: How do they affect educational outcomes?* (pp. 67–88). Mahwah, NJ: Erlbaum.

Alexander, L. (2004, Summer). Putting parents in charge. *Education next, 4*(3), 39–44.

Allen, R. V. (1969). *Language experiences in early childhood.* Chicago: Encyclopedia Britannica.

Allen, R. V., & Allen, C. (1982). *Language experience activities.* Boston: Houghton Mifflin.

Allen, V. G. (1991). Teaching bilingual and ESL children. In J. Flood, J. M. Jensen, D. Lapp, & J. R. Squire (Eds.), *Handbook of research on teaching the English language arts* (pp. 356–364). New York: Macmillan.

Almy, M. (1975). *The early childhood educator at work.* New York: McGraw-Hill.

American Speech-Language-Hearing Association. (2001). *How does your child hear and talk?* [Brochure]. Rockville, MD: American Speech-Language-Hearing Association.

Anbar, A. (1986, March). Reading acquisition of preschool children without systematic instruction. *Early Childhood Research Quarterly, 1*(1), 69–83.

Anderson, G. T. (2000, March). Computers in a developmentally appropriate curriculum. *Young Children, 55*(2), 90–93.

Anderson, R. (1988, October). Putting reading research into practice. Interview with C. H. Goddard. *Instructor, 98.*2, 31–37.

Anderson, R. C., Hiebert, E. H., Scott, J. A., & Wilkinson, I. A. (Eds.). (1985). *Becoming a nation of readers: The report of the National Commission on Reading.* Washington, DC: National Institute of Education.

Andress, B. (1991, November). From research to practice: Preschool children and their movement responses to music. *Young Children, 47*(1), 22–27.

Angelou, M. (1969). *I know why the caged bird sings.* New York: Random House.

Antonucci, M. (2003, October 29). Gaga over TV. *San Jose Mercury News,* pp. 1A, 5A.

Arbuthnot, M. H. (1953). *The Arbuthnot anthology of children's literature.* Glenview, IL: Scott, Foresman.

Arreola, A. (2003, October 17). Quote in Slonaker, L., Learning a lesson about school visits: Parent-teacher meetings key for kids, experts say. *San Jose Mercury News,* pp. 4A, 12A.

Ashton-Warner, S. (1963). *Teacher.* New York: Simon & Schuster.

Atienza, H. (2004, June 27). Kindergarten: As a parent, you knew the day would come eventually. *The Idaho Statesman,* p. L2.

Atkins, C. (1984, November). Writing: Doing something constructive. *Young Children, 40*(6), 31–36.

Au, K. (1993). *Literacy instruction in multicultural setting.* Orlando, FL: Harcourt Brace.

August, D., & Hakuta, K. (Eds.). (1997). *Improving schooling for language minority children.* Washington, DC: National Academy Press.

Ayers, W. (1993). *To teach: The journey of a teacher.* New York: Teachers College Press.

Ayres, L. R. (1998). Phonological awareness training of kindergarten children. In C. Weaver (Ed.), *Reconsidering a balanced approach to reading.* Urbana, IL: National Council of Teachers of English.

Bader, B. (1976). *American picturebooks from Noah's Ark to the beast within.* New York: Macmillan.

Baker, L., Scher, D., & Mackler, K. (1997). Home and family influences on motivations for reading. *Educational Psychologist, 32*(2), 24–30.

631

Baker, L., Fernandez-Fein, S., Scher, D., & Williams, H. (1998). Home experiences of word recognition. In J. L. Metsala & L. C. Ehri (Eds.), *Word recognition in beginning literacy* (pp. 263–287). Hillsdale, NJ: Erlbaum.

Barnes, D. (1976). *From communication to curriculum.* Harmondsworth, England: Penguin Books.

Barnes, J. E. (2004, March 24). Unequal education. *U.S. News and World Report, 136*(10), 68–75.

Barnett, W. (1995). Long-term effects of early childhood programs on cognitive and school outcomes. *The Future of Children, 5*(3), 18–21.

Barnett, W. S. (2003). Preschool education for economically disadvantaged children: Effects on reading achievement and related outcomes. In S. B. Neuman & D. K. Dickinson (Eds.), *Handbook of early literacy research* (pp. 421–443). New York: The Guilford Press.

Baron, N. (1989, December). Pigeon-birds and rhyming words: The role of parents in language learning. *Digest Monograph,* Language in Education Series. Report EDO-FL-89-08, ERIC/CLL.

Barone, D. (1994, October). Importance of classroom context: Literacy development of children prenatally exposed to crack/cocaine—Year two. *Research in the Teaching of English, 28*(3), 286–312.

Barone, D. M. (2003). Caution apply with care. In D. M. Barone & L. M. Morrow (Eds.), *Literacy and young children: Research-based practice* (pp. 291–308). New York: The Guilford Press.

Barrett, J. (2003, November 10). Tune in or tune out? *Newsweek,* 71.

Barrio-Garcia, C. (1986, December). The silent handicap. *American Baby, 47*(12), 32–41.

Barry, A. M. (1999, June 23–27). Images as thought and persuasive communication: An advertising perspective. Visual Communication Conference. Lake Tahoe, CA.

Bartoli, J. S. (1995). *Unequal opportunity: Learning to read in the U.S.A.* New York: Teachers College Press.

Bateson, M. (1979). The epigenesis of conversational interaction. In M. Bullowa (Ed.), *Before speech.* London: Cambridge University Press.

Beals, D. E. (1993). Explanatory talk in low-income families' mealtime conversations. *Applied Psycholinguistics, 14,* 489–513.

Beck, M. (1982). *Kidspeak.* New York: New American Library.

Begley, S. (2000, Fall/Winter). Wired for thought [Special Edition]. *Newsweek,* pp. 25–29.

Bellugi, U. (1977). Learning the language. In R. Schell (Ed.), *Readings in psychology today.* New York: Random House.

Benard, B. (1993, November). Fostering resiliency in kids. *ASCD Educational Leadership, 51*(3), 44–48.

Bergen, D. (2001, November). Pretend play and young children's development. *ERIC Digest,* EDO-PS-01-10.

Berk, L. (1994). *Child development.* Needham Heights, MA: Allyn and Bacon.

Berk, L., & Winsler, A. (1995). *Scaffolding children's learning: Vygotsky and early childhood education.* Wash-

ington, DC: National Association for the Education of Young Children.

Berko Gleason, J. (1997). *The development of language* (4th ed.). Boston: Allyn and Bacon.

Bernstein, B. (1962). Social class, linguistic codes and grammatical elements. *Language and Speech, 5,* 31–46.

Bettelheim, B. (1976). *The uses of enchantment.* New York: Alfred A. Knopf.

Bettelheim, B., & Zelan, K. (1981). *On learning to read.* New York: Alfred A. Knopf.

Bialystok, E., & Hakuta, K. (1994). *In other words: The science and psychology of second language acquisition.* New York: Basic Books.

Biber, B., Shapiro, E., & Wickens, D. (1977). *Promoting cognitive growth: A developmental-interaction point of view.* Washington, DC: National Association for the Education of Young Children.

Bishop, R. S. (1990). Walk tall in the world: African American literature for today's children. *Journal of Negro Education, 59*(4), 556–565.

Blair, C. (2003, July). Self regulation and school readiness. *ERIC Digest,* EDO-PS-03-7.

Blaska, J., & Lynch, E. (1998, March). Is everyone included? Using children's literature to facilitate the understanding of disabilities. *Young Children, 53*(2), 17–21.

Bloodstein, O. (1975). *A handbook on stuttering.* Chicago: National Easter Seal Society of Crippled Children and Adults.

Blum, I., Koskinen, P. S., Tennant, N., Parker, E. M., Straub, M., & Curry, C. (1995). *Using audiotaped books to extend classroom literacy instruction into the homes of second-language learners* [Reading Research Report No. 29]. Athens, GA: NRRC, Universities of Georgia and Maryland College Park.

Bodrova, E., & Leong, D. (1996). *Tools of the mind.* Englewood Cliffs, NJ: Prentice Hall.

Bodrova, E., Leong, D. J., Paynter, D., & Semenov, D. (2000). *A framework for early literacy instruction: Aligning standards to developmental accomplishments and student behaviors: Pre-K through kindergarten.* Aurora, CO: Mid-continent Research for Education and Learning.

Booth, D. (1999). Language delights and word play. In I. Fountas & G. S. Pinnell (Eds.), *Voices on word matters: Learning about phonics and spelling in the literacy classroom* (pp. 121–137). Portsmouth, NH: Heinemann.

Bornstein, M. (December 1991–January 1992). In S. Goodman (Ed.), Presumed innocents, *Modern Maturity, 34*(6), 24–28.

Bos, B. (1983). *Creativity.* San Jose City College Workshop.

Bos, B. (1988, January). Working the magic. *Pre-K Today, 2.6,* 21–23.

Bowen, C. (1998). *Speech and language development in infants and young children.* Retrieved August 16, 2004, from http://members.tripod.com/Caroline_Bowen/devel1.htm

Brady, S., Fowler, A., Stone, B., & Winbury, S. (1994). Training phonological awareness: A study with inner-city kindergarten children. *Annals of Dyslexia, 44,* 27–59.

Braine, M. D. S. (1973). The ontogeny of English phrase structures: The first phase. In C. A. Ferguson & D. Slobin (Eds.), *Studies of child language development.* New York: Holt, Rinehart, and Winston.

Brazelton, T. B. (1979). Evidence of communication in neonatal behavioral assessment. In M. Bullowa (Ed.), *Before speech.* London: Cambridge University Press.

Bredekamp, S., & Copple, C. (1997). *Developmentally appropriate practice in early childhood programs* (Rev. ed.). Washington, DC: National Association for the Education of Young Children.

Bredekamp, S., & Rosegrant, T. (Eds.). (1995). *Reaching potentials: Transforming early childhood curriculum and assessment* (Vol. 2, p. 21). Washington, DC: National Association for the Education of Young Children.

Bregman, J. (1997, October 27). Quote in Wingert, P., & Kantrowitz, B., Why Andy couldn't read. *Newsweek,* pp. 56–64.

Breneman, L. N., & Breneman, B. (1983). *Once upon a time.* Chicago: Nelson-Hall.

Brimer, M. A. (1969). Sex difference in listening comprehension. *Journal of Research and Development in Education, 9,* 19–25.

Brittain, W. L. (1973, March). Analysis of artistic behavior in young children. Final Report, *ERIC Document,* ED 128 091. Ithaca, NY: Cornell University.

Brophy, J. E. (1977). *Child development and socialization.* Chicago: Science Research Associates.

Brown, R., Cazden, C., & Bellugi-Kilma, U. (1969). The child's grammar from I to III. In J. P. Hill (Ed.), *Minnesota Symposium on Child Psychology* (Vol. 2). Minneapolis: University of Minnesota Press.

Brown, R. W. (1973). *A first language.* Cambridge, MA: Harvard University Press.

Bruner, J. (1996). *The culture of education.* Cambridge, MA: Harvard University Press.

Bruner, J. S. (1966). *Toward a theory of instruction.* Cambridge, MA: Harvard University Press.

Bruno, H. E. (2003, September/October). Hearing parents in every language: An invitation to ECE professionals. *Child Care Information Exchange, 153,* 58–60.

Bruns, D., & Corso, R. M. (2001, August). Working with culturally and linguistically diverse families. *ERIC Digest,* EDO-PS-01-4.

Bryant, P., Bradley, L., MacLean, L., & Crossland, J. (1989). Nursery rhymes, phonological skills and reading. *Journal of Child Language, 16,* 407–428.

Burchfield, D. (1996, November). Teaching all children: Four developmentally appropriate curricular and instructional strategies in primary-grade classrooms. *Young Children, 52*(1), 4–10.

Burmark, L. (2002). *Visual literacy: Learn to see, see to learn.* Alexandria, VA: Association for Supervision and Curriculum Development.

Burns, M. S., Griffin, P., & Snow, C. (Eds.). (1999). *Starting out right: A guide to promoting children's reading success.* Washington, DC: National Academy Press.

Bus, A. G. (2002). Joint caregiver-child storybook reading: A route to literacy development. In S. B. Newman & D. K. Dickinson (Eds.), *Handbook of early literacy research* (pp. 179–191). New York: The Guilford Press.

Cai, M., & Bishop, R. S. (1994). Multicultural literature for children: Towards clarification of the concept. In A. H. Dyson & C. Genishi (Eds.), *The need for story* (pp. 11–27). Urbana, IL: National Council of Teachers of English.

Calkins, L. (1979). Speech given at Columbia University.

Calkins, L. (1997). *Raising lifelong learners: A parent's guide.* Reading, MA: Perseus Books.

Cambourne, B. (1988). *The whole story: Natural learning and the acquisition of literacy in the classroom.* New York: Ashton Scholastic.

Campbell, D. (1997). *The Mozart effect: Tapping the power of music to heal the body, strengthen the mind, and unlock the creative spirit.* New York: William Morrow.

Campbell, F., & Ramey, C. (1995). Cognitive and school outcomes for high-risk African-American students at middle adolescence. Positive effects of early intervention. *American Education Research Journal, 32,* 743–772.

Campbell, F. A., & Ramey, C. T. (1994). Effects of early intervention on intellectual and academic achievement: A follow-up study of children from low-income families. *Child Development, 65,* 684–689.

Carew, J. V. (1980). Experience and the development of intelligence in young children at home and in day care. *Monographs of the Society for Research in Child Development, 45.187,* 56–78.

Carlo, M., August, D., McLaughlin, B., Snow, C., Dressler, C., Lippman, D., Lively, T., & White, C. (2004, April/May). Closing the gap: Addressing the vocabulary needs of English-language learners in bilingual and mainstream classrooms. *Reading Research Quarterly, 39*(2), 188–228.

Casbergue, R. M., & Plauché, M. B. (2003). Immersing children in nonfiction: Fostering emergent research and writing. In D. M. Barone & L. M. Morrow (Eds.), *Literacy and young children: Research-based practices* (pp. 243–260) New York: The Guilford Press.

Casserly, M. (2004, Summer). Driving change. *Education Next, 4*(3), 32–37.

Cassidy, J., & Cassidy, D. (2004, December/2005, January). What's hot, what's not for 2005. *Reading Today, 22*(3), 1, 8.

Cawlfield, M. E. (1992, May). Velcro time: The language connection. *Young Children, 47*(4), 26–30.

Cazden, C. B. (1972). *Child language and education.* New York: Holt, Rinehart, and Winston.

Cazden, C. B. (1981). Language development and the preschool environment. In C. B. Cazden (Ed.), *Language in early childhood education.* Washington, DC: National Association for the Education of Young Children.

Center for Research on Education, Diversity & Excellence. (2001, Summer). Some program alternatives for English language learners. *Practitioners Brief #3.* Santa Cruz, CA: University of California.

Chambers, D. W. (1970). *Story telling and creative drama.* Dubuque, IA: Brown.

Chaney, C. (1992). Language development, metalinguistic skills, and print awareness in 3-year-old children. *Applied Psycholinguistics, 13*(4), 488–514.

Chang, J. (2001, April). Scaffold for school-home collaboration: Enhancing reading and language development. *Research Brief #9.* Santa Cruz, CA: Center for Research on Education, Diversity, & Excellence, University of California.

Charlesworth, R. (1985, Spring). Readiness—Should we make them ready or let them bloom? *Day Care and Early Education, 11.4,* 53–58.

Child Care Bureau. (2004, May). *Promoting responsible fatherhood through child care.* Washington, DC: U.S. Department of Health and Human Services, Administration for Children and Families, Administration on Children, Youth and Families.

Chomsky, C. (1971, August/September). Write now, read later. *Childhood Education, 47.2,* 42–47.

Chomsky, N. (1968). *Language and mind.* New York: Harcourt, Brace, and World.

Chugani, H. T. (1997). Neuroimaging of developmental non-linearity and development pathologies. In A. Thatcher (Ed.), *Developmental neuroimaging: Mapping the development of brain and behavior* (pp. 111–134). San Diego: Academic Press.

Chukovsky, K. (1963). *From two to five.* Berkeley, CA: University of California.

Clark, E. V. (1975). Knowledge, context, and strategy in the acquisition of meaning. In D. P. Dato (Ed.), *Georgetown University Round Table on languages and linguistics, 1975. Developmental psycholinguistics: Theory and applications.* Washington, DC: Georgetown University Press.

Clay, M. (1966). *Emergent reading behaviors.* Unpublished doctoral thesis, University of Auckland Library.

Clay, M. (1987). *The early detection of reading difficulties.* Hong Kong: Heinemann.

Clay, M. (1991a). *Becoming literate: The construction of inner control.* Portsmouth, NH: Heinemann Educational Books.

Clay, M. (1991b). Child development. In J. Flood, J. M. Jensen, D. Lapp, & J. R. Squire (Eds.), *Handbook of research on teaching the English language arts* (pp. 40–45). New York: Macmillan.

Clay, M. (1993). *An observational survey of early literacy achievement.* Auckland, New Zealand: Heinemann.

Clements, N. E., & Warncke, E. W. (1994, March). Helping literacy emerge at school for less-advantaged children. *Young Children, 49*(3), 22–26.

Cochran-Smith, M. (1984). *The making of a reader.* Norwood, NJ: Ablex.

Cohen, N. E., & Pompa, D. (1996). In S. L. Kagan & N. E. Cohen (Eds.), *Reinventing early care and education: A vision for a quality system* (pp. 81–98). San Francisco: Jossey-Bass.

Cole, M. L., & Cole, J. T. (1989). *Effective intervention with the language impaired child* (2nd ed.). Rockville, MD: Aspen.

Coles, G. (2004, January). Danger in the classroom: 'Brain glitch' research and learning to read. *Phi Delta Kappan,* pp. 344–351.

Cooper, P. (1993). *When stories come to school.* New York: Teachers & Writers Collaborative.

Copperman, P. (1982). *Taking books to heart.* Menlo Park, CA: Addison-Wesley.

Costa, A. L. (1990). Personal communication, June 1988. In J. M. Healy, *Endangered minds: Why children don't think and what we can do about it.* New York: Simon & Schuster.

Costa, A. L. (1991). The search for intelligent life. In *Developing minds: A resource book for teaching thinking.* Alexandria, VA: Association for Supervision and Curriculum Development.

Covey, S. R. (1989). *The seven habits of highly effective people.* New York: Simon & Schuster.

Cowley, G. (1997, Spring/Summer). Off to a good start [Special Edition]. *Newsweek,* pp. 27–34.

Cowley, G. (2000, Fall/Winter). For the love of language [Special Edition]. *Newsweek,* pp. 12–15.

Cox, V. E. L. (1981). The literature curriculum. In L. Lamme (Ed.), *Learning to love literature* (pp. 1–12). Urbana, IL: National Council of Teachers of English.

Cromwell, E. (1980). *Early reading through experience.* Washington, DC: Acropolis Books Limited.

Crosser, S. (1998, November/December). When children draw. *Early Childhood News, 10*(6), 6–15.

Cullinan, B. E. (1977). Books in the life of the young child. In B. E. Cullinan & C. W. Carmichael (Eds.), *Literature and young children* (pp. 1–16). Urbana, IL: National Council of Teachers of English.

Cullinan, B. E. (1992, October). Whole language and children's literature. *Language Arts, 69*(6), 426–430.

Cummins, J. (1979). Linguistic interdependence and the educational development of bilingual children. *Review of Educational Research, 49,* 222–251.

Cunningham, J. W., & Creamer, K. H. (2003). Achieving best practices in literacy instruction. In L. M. Morrow, L. B. Gambrell, & M. Pressley (Eds.), *Best practices in literacy instruction* (pp. 333–346). New York: The Guilford Press.

Cunningham, P. M. (2003). What research says about teaching phonics. In L. M. Morrow, L. B. Gambrell, & M. Pressley (Eds.), *Best practices in literacy instruction* (pp. 65–85). New York: The Guilford Press.

Curran, L. (1994). *Language arts & cooperative learning.* San Clemente, CA: Kogan Cooperative.

Curry, N. E., & Johnson, C. N. (1990). *Beyond self-esteem: Developing a genuine sense of human value.* Washington, DC: National Association for the Education of Young Children.

Danoff, J., Breitbart, V., & Barr, E. (1977). *Open for children.* New York: McGraw-Hill.

de Villiers, P. A., & de Villiers, J. G. (1979). *Early language.* Cambridge, MA: Harvard University Press.

Dean, B. (2004, July 15). Quote in Today's debate: Improving public education. Our View. *USA Today,* p. 11A.

DeGaetano, G. (1993). *Television and the lives of our children.* Redmond, WA: Train of Thought Publishing.

DeGraw, B. (1999, March 15). Quote in letters. *U.S. News and World Report,* p. BC-14.

Delacre, L. (1988). *Nathan's fishing trip.* New York: Scholastic.

Delpit, L. (1995). *Other people's children: Cultural conflict in the classroom.* New York: The New Press.

DeMarie, D. (2001, Spring). A trip to the zoo: Children's words and photographs. *Early Childhood Research and Practice, 3*(1), 27–49.

Dennison, B. A., Russo, T. J., Burdick, P. A., & Jenkins, P. L. (2004, February). An intervention to reduce television viewing by preschool children. *The Archives of Pediatrics and Adolescent Medicine, 158,* 170–176.

Descartes, R. (1978). *Descartes: His moral philosophy and psychology.* New York: University Press.

Dewey, J. (1916). *Democracy and education.* New York: Free Press.

Dickinson, D. K. (2001). Putting the pieces together. In D. K. Dickinson & P. Tabors (Eds.), *Beginning literacy with language* (pp. 257–287). Baltimore: Brookes.

Dickinson, D. K., & Tabors, P. O. (Eds.). (2001). *Beginning literacy with language.* Baltimore: Brookes.

Ditlow, T. (1988, May–December). Making a book into a successful cassette. *CBC Features, 41.3,* 4–6.

Doake, D. B. (1985). Reading-like behavior: Its role in learning to read. In A. Jaggar & M. T. Smith-Burke (Eds.), *Observing the language learner* (pp. 82–98). Newark, DE: International Reading Association, and Urbana, IL: National Council of Teachers of English (co-publishers).

Dodge, D. (1988, May). When your program is off track. *Child Care Information Exchange, 61,* 42–48.

Donegan, P. (2002). Normal vowel development. In M. J. Ball & F. E. Gibbon (Eds.), *Vowel disorders* (pp. 1–35). Woburn, MA: Butterworth-Heinemann.

Donoghue, M. R. (1985). *The child and the English language arts.* Dubuque, IA: Brown.

Dopyera, J., & Lay-Dopyera, M. (1992). *Becoming a teacher of young children.* New York: McGraw-Hill.

Douglass, R. (1959, March). Basic feeling and speech defects. *Exceptional Children, 35.4,* 18–23.

Du, L., & Stoub, S. (2004, February 21). *Options pre-K literacy curriculum.* Session guide. California Association for the Education of Young Children, Annual Conference. San Diego, CA.

Dumtschin, J. U. (1988, March). Recognizing language development and delay in early childhood. *Young Children, 43.3,* 16–24.

Dunn, L., Beach, S. A., & Kontos, S. (1994). Quality of the literacy environment in day care and children's development. *Journal of Research in Childhood Education, 9,* 24–34.

Dunn, L., & Kontos, S. (1998, March/April). Developmentally appropriate practice: What does research tell us? *Journal of Early Education and Family Review, 5*(4), 16–25.

Durkin, D. (1966). *Children who read early.* New York: Teachers College Press.

Dyson, A. H. (1993). From prop to mediator: The changing role of written language in children's symbolic repertoires. In B. Spodek & O. Saracho (Eds.), *Yearbook in early childhood education* (Vol. 4, 21–41, pp. 132–146). New York: Teachers College Press.

Edwards, C., Gandini, L., & Forman, G. (Eds.). (1998). *The hundred languages of children: The Reggio Emilia approach—Advanced recollections.* Greenwich, CT: Ablex Publishing.

Edwards, P. (1996). Creating sharing time conversations: Parents and teachers work together. *Language Arts, 73*(5), 344–349.

Elkind, D. (1971). Cognition in infancy and early childhood. In J. Eliot (Ed.), *Human development and cognitive process.* New York: Holt, Rinehart, and Winston.

Elkind, D. (1988, January). Educating the very young: A call for clear thinking. *NEA Today, 6.6,* 37–39.

Elleman, B. (1995). Handling stereotypes. *Book Links, 4*(5), 4.

Epstein, A., Schweinhart, L., & McAdoo, L. (1996). *Models of early childhood education.* Ipsilanti, MI: High/Scope Press.

Erikson, E. (1950). *Childhood and society.* New York: W. W. Norton.

Erickson, E. (1993). *Childhood and society* (Rev. ed.). New York: Norton.

Eveloff, H. H. (1977). Some cognitive and affective aspects of early language development. In S. Cohen & T. Comiskey (Eds.), *Child development contemporary perspectives* (pp. 140–155). Itasca: F. E. Peacock.

Fackelmann, K. (2000, July 10). Infants who learn gestures may later do better on IQ tests. *The Idaho Statesman,* p. 2D.

Falk, D., (2004, July). Quote in Wong, K., Baby talk beginnings: Infant pacification may have led to the origins of language. *Scientific American, 291*(1), 30–32.

Farr, M. (1992). Dialects, culture, and teaching the English language arts. In J. Flood, J. M. Jensen, D. Lapp, & J. R. Squire (Eds.), *Handbook of research on teaching the English language arts* (pp. 365–369). New York: Macmillan.

Ferguson, P. (1988, May). Whole language: A global approach to learning. *Instructor, 97.9,* 23–28.

Ferguson, P., & Young, T. (1996, December). Literature talk: Dialogue improvisation and patterned conversations with second language learners. *Language Arts, 73*(8), 597–600.

Ferreiro, E., & Teberosky, A. (1982). *Literacy before schooling.* Exeter, NH: Heinemann.

Fields, J. (2001). *The living arrangements of children, Fall 1996.* Current population reports. Washington, DC: U.S. Census Bureau.

Fields, M. (1987). *NAEYC developmentally appropriate guidelines and beginning reading instruction.* Presentation made at the annual conference of the National Association for the Education of Young Children, Chicago.

Fields, M. (1996, November). *Authentic reading and writing activities for beginners.* Presentation made at the annual conference of the National Association for the Education of Young Children, Dallas.

Fields, M., & Lee, D. (1987). *Let's begin reading right.* Columbus, OH: Charles E. Merrill.

Fifer, W. P., & Moon, C. M. (1995). The effects of fetal experience with sound. In J. P. Lecanuet, N. A. Fifer, A. Krasnegor, & W. P. Smotherman (Eds.), *Fetal development: A psychobiological perspective.* Hillsdale, NJ: Erlbaum.

Fischer, K. (1986). What do babies know? In O. Friedrich (Ed.), *Human development, Annual editions 85/86.* Guilford, CT: The Dushkin Publishing Group.

Fischer, M. A., & Gillespie, C. W. (2003, July). Computers and young children's development. *Young Children, 58*(4), 85–91.

Fisher, M. (1975). *Who's who in children's books.* New York: Holt, Rinehart, and Winston.

Fountas, I. (1999). Word matters. In I. Fountas & G. S. Pinnell (Eds.), *Voices on word matters: Learning about phonics and spelling in the literacy classroom* (pp. 164–178). Portsmouth, NH: Heinemann.

Fraiberg, S. (1987). *Selected writings of Selma Fraiberg.* Athens, OH: Ohio State University Press.

Fredericks, A. D. (1989, October/November). The magic of storytelling. *Reading Today, 7*(2), 13.

French, L. (1996, January). "I told you all about it, so don't tell me you don't know": Two-year-olds and learning through language. *Young Children, 51*(2), 17–20.

Froebel, F. (1974). *The education of man.* Clifton, NJ: Augustus M. Kelly.

Fujiki, M., & Brinton, B. (1984). Language, speech, and hearing services in schools, *Journal of Learning Disabilities, 15.2,* 98–109.

Gadsden, V., & Ray, A. (2002, November). Engaging fathers: Issues and considerations for early childhood educators. *Young Children, 57*(6), 32–41.

Gainsley, S. (2003, Summer). Write it down. *High/Scope Resource, 22*(2), 26–27.

Galda, L. (1989, October). Children and poetry. *The Reading Teacher, 43*(1), 66–71.

Galda, L., Cullinan, B., & Strickland, D. (1993). *Language, literacy, and the child.* Orlando, FL: Harcourt Brace.

Gall, M. D. (1984). Synthesis of research on teachers' questioning. *Educational Leadership, 42,* 40–47.

Gallagher, J. M., & Coche, J. (1987, September). Hothousing: The clinical and education concerns over pressuring young children. *Early Childhood Research Quarterly, 2.3,* 203–210.

Gallas, K. (2003). *Imagination and literacy: A teacher's search for the heart of learning.* New York: Teachers College Press.

Gambrell, L. B., & Mazzoni, S. A. (1999). Principles of best practice: Finding the common ground. In L. B. Gambrell, L. M. Morrow, S. B. Neuman, & M. Pressley (Eds.), *Best practices in literacy instruction.* New York: The Guilford Press.

Gamel-McCormick, M. (2000, November). *Exploring teachers' expectations for children entering kindergarten and procedures for sharing information between pre-K and K programs.* Conference presentation at the annual conference of the National Association for the Education of Young Children, Atlanta.

Gandini, L. (1997). Examples of practice. In J. Hendrick (Ed.), *First steps toward teaching the Reggio way.* Upper Saddle River, NJ: Prentice Hall.

Garcia, E. (1991). Effective instruction for language minority students: The teacher. *Journal of Education, 173*(2), 130–141.

Garcia, E., & McLaughlin, B. (Eds.). (1995). *Meeting the challenge of linguistic and cultural diversity in early childhood education.* New York: Teachers College Press.

Garcia-Barrio, C. (1986, August). Listen to the music! *American Baby, 48*(8), 46, 67–69.

Gardner, H. (1993). *Multiple intelligences.* New York: Basic Books.

Gardner, H. (1999). *Disciplined mind: What all students should understand.* New York: Simon & Schuster.

Gardner, H. (2000). *Intelligence reframed. Multiple intelligences for the 21st century.* New York: Basic Books.

Garvey, C. (1977). *Play.* Cambridge, MA: Harvard University Press.

Garvey, C. (1984). *Children's talk.* Cambridge, MA: Harvard University Press.

Geller, L. G. (1985). *Word play and language learning for children.* Urbana, IL: National Council of Teachers of English.

Gelman, S. A. (1998, January). Categories in young children's thinking. *Young Children, 53*(1), 32–41.

Genesee, F., & Nicoladis, E. (1995). Language development in bilingual preschool children. In E. Garcia & B. McLaughlin (Eds.), *Meeting the challenge of linguistic and cultural diversity in early childhood education.* New York: Teachers College Press.

Genishi, C. (1985). Observing communicative performance in young children. In A. Jaggar & M. T. Smith-Burke (Eds.), *Observing the language learner* (pp. 131–142). Newark, DE: International Reading Association, and Urbana, IL: National Council of Teachers of English (co-publishers).

Genishi, C. (1993). Assessing young children's language and literacy: Tests and their alternatives. In B. Spodek & O. Saracho (Eds.), *Yearbook in early childhood education* (pp. 121–138). New York: Teachers College Press.

Genishi, C. (2002, July). Young English language learners. *Young Children, 57*(4), 66–72.

Gesell, A. (1940). *The first five years of life.* New York: Harper & Brothers.

Gibson, E. J. (1969). *Principles of perceptual learning and development.* New York: Appleton-Century-Crofts.

Gill, J. T. (1992, October). Development of word knowledge as it relates to reading, spelling, and instruction. *Language Arts, 69*(6), 444–453.

Glazer, J. I. (1986). *Literature for young children.* Columbus, OH: Charles E. Merrill.

Glazer, J. I. (2000). *Literature for young children.* Upper Saddle River, NJ: Prentice Hall.

Glazer, S., & Burke, E. (1994). *An integrated approach to early literacy: Literature to language.* Needham Heights, MA: Allyn and Bacon.

Gleitman, L. (1998, March/April). Research suggests that infants begin learning language at seven months of age. News. *Journal of Early Education and Family Review, 5*(4), 4.

Goffin, S. G. (2000, August). The role of curriculum models in early childhood education. *ERIC Digest,* EDO-PS-00-8.

Goldenberg, C. (2002). Making schools work for low-income families in the 21st century. In S. Neuman & D. Dickinson (Eds.), *Handbook of early literacy research* (pp. 211–241), New York: The Guilford Press.

Goodman, K. S. (1986). *What's whole in whole language.* Portsmouth, NH: Heinemann Educational Publishers.

Goodman, Y. (1985). Kidwatching: Observing children in the classroom. In A. Jaggar & M. T. Smith-Burke (Eds.), *Observing the language learner* (pp. 142–156). Newark, DE: International Reading Association, and Urbana, IL: National Council of Teachers of English (co-publishers).

Goodman, Y. (1990). *How children construct literacy.* Newark, DE: International Reading Association.

Gopnik, A. (1999, December 25). Quoted in K. Corcoran, Babies blossom without gimmicks, psychologist says. *San Jose Mercury News*, pp. 1A, 28A.

Gopnik, A., Meltzoff, A., & Kuhl, P. (1999). *The scientist in the crib: Minds, brains, and how children learn.* New York: William Morrow and Company.

Gordon, A. (1984). *A touch of wonder.* Old Tappan, NJ: Revell.

Gordon, E. (1986, August). Listen to the music! *American Baby, 48*(8), 46, 67–69.

Goswani, U. (2002). Early phonological development and the acquisition of literacy. In S. Neuman & D. Dickinson (Eds.), *Handbook of early literacy research* (pp. 111–125). New York: The Guilford Press.

Gould, B. (2002). Stress and the developing brain. *Head Start Bulletin, 73,* 16–18.

Gowen, J. W. (1995, March). The early development of symbolic play. *Young Children, 50*(3), 75–84.

Grant, G., & Murray, C. (1999). *Teaching in America: The slow revolution.* Cambridge, MA: Harvard University Press.

Grant, R. (1995). Meeting the needs of young second language learners. In E. Garcia & B. McLaughlin (Eds.), *Meeting the challenge of linguistic and cultural diversity in early childhood education.* New York: Teachers College Press.

Graue, E. (1999). Diverse perspectives on kindergarten contexts and practices. In R. Pianta & M. Cox (Eds.), *The transition to kindergarten.* Baltimore: Paul Brookes.

Greenberg, P. (1998, July). Some thoughts about phonics, feelings, Don Quixote, diversity, and democracy: Teaching young children to read, write, and spell. Part I. *Young Children, 53*(4), 72–78.

Greenberg, P. (1998, November). Thinking about goals for grownups and young children while we teach writing, reading, and spelling (and a few thoughts about the 'J' word). Part 3. *Young Children, 53*(6), 31–42.

Greenspan, S. I. (1997). *The growth of the mind and the endangered origins of intelligence.* Reading, MA: Addison-Wesley.

Greenspan, S. I. (1999). *Building healthy minds: The six experiences that create intelligence and emotional growth in babies and young children.* Cambridge, MA: Perseus Books.

Greenspan, S. I. (2001, November/December). Working with the bilingual child who has language delay. *Early Childhood Today, 16*(3), 28–30.

Grey, K. (1996, May). In S. Lapinski (Ed.), Signs of intelligence. *Child, 11*(4), 46–51.

Griffing, P. (1983, January). Encouraging dramatic play in early childhood. *Young Children, 38*(2), 45–51.

Griffith, P., & Olson, M. (1992). Phonemic awareness helps beginning readers break the code. *The Reading Teacher, 45*(5), 516–523.

Gundling, R. (2002, Fall). Promoting early literacy in early childhood programs. *Child Care Bulletin, 27,* 7–8.

Gurian, M., & Ballew, A. C. (2003). *The boys and girls learn differently.* San Francisco: Jossey-Bass.

Gutierrez, K. D. (1992). A comparison of instructional contexts in writing process classrooms with Latino children. *Education and Urban Society, 24*(2), 244–262.

Gutierrez, K. D. (1993). Biliteracy and language-minority child. In B. Spodek & O. Saracho (Eds.), *Language and literacy in early childhood education* (Vol. 4, pp. 210–232). New York: Teachers College Press.

Hale, E. (1997, January 12). Flap over Ebonics clarifies the problem, but not the solution. *The Idaho Statesman,* p. A12.

Halliday, M. A. K. (1973). *Explorations in the functions of language.* London: Edward Arnold.

Halliday, M. A. K. (1979). One child's protolanguage. In M. Bullowa (Ed.), *Before speech* (pp. 171–190). London: Cambridge University Press.

Hand, A., & Nourot, P. (1999). *First class: A guide for early primary education.* Sacramento, CA: California Department of Education.

Harker, J. O., & Green, J. L. (1985). When you get the right answer to the wrong question: Observing and understanding communication in classrooms. In A. Jaggar & M. T. Smith-Burke (Eds.), *Observing the language learner* (pp. 221–231). Newark, DE: International Reading Association, and Urbana, IL: National Council of Teachers of English.

Harris, J. (1990). *Early language development.* London: Routledge.

Harris, T., & Fuqua, J. D. (2000, January). What goes around comes around: Building a community of learners through circle times. *Young Children, 55*(1), 44–47.

Harris, T., & Hodges, R. (Eds.). (1995). *The literacy dictionary: The vocabulary of reading and writing.* Newark, DE: International Reading Association.

Harris, V. J. (1993). From the margin to the center of the curricula: Multicultural children's literature. In B. Spodek & O. Saracho (Eds.), *Language and literacy in early childhood education* (Vol. 4, pp. 123–140). New York: Teachers College Press.

Hartley, E. A. (1991). Through Navaho eyes: Examining differences in giftedness. *Journal of American Indian Education, 31*(1), 53–64.

Haugland, S. W. (1992). Effects of computer software on preschool children's developmental gains. *Journal of Computing in Childhood Education, 2*(2), 17–28.

Haugland, S. W. (1997). *The developmental scale for software.* Cape Girardeau, MO: K.I.D.S. and Computers.

Haugland, S. W. (2000, January). Early childhood classrooms in the 21st century: Using computers to maximize learning. *Young Children, 55*(1), 33–41.

Haugland, S. W., & Wright, J. L. (1997). *Young children and technology: A world of discovery.* Needham Heights, MA: Allyn and Bacon.

Healy, J. M. (1987). *Your child's growing mind.* New York: Doubleday.

Healy, J. M. (1990). *Endangered minds.* New York: Simon & Schuster.

Healy, M. K., & Barr, M. (1992). Language across the curriculum. In J. Flood, J. M. Jensen, D. Lapp, & J. R. Squire (Eds.), *Handbook of research on teaching English language arts* (pp. 820–826). New York: Macmillan.

Heath, A. (1987). *Off the wall: The art of book display.* Littleton, CO: Libraries Unlimited.

Hendrick, J. (Ed.). (1997). *First steps toward teaching the Reggio way.* Upper Saddle River, NJ: Prentice Hall.

Hendrick, J. (1998, November 21). *Thinking about thinking: Fostering mental development in young children in appropriate ways.* Conference presentation at the national conference of the National Association for the Education of Young Children, Toronto, Canada.

Hess, R. D., & Shipman, V. C. (1966). Early experience and the socialization of cognitive modes in children. *Child Development, 28.4,* 221–257.

Hildebrandt, C. (1998, November). Creativity in music and early childhood. *Young Children, 53*(6), 41–53.

Hillerich, R. L. (1976, February). Toward an assessable definition of literacy. *The English Journal, 65,* 29–31.

Hirsch, E. (1987). *Cultural literacy: What every American needs to know.* Boston: Houghton Mifflin.

Hirsch, E. D., Jr., (2004, February 25). Many Americans can read but can't comprehend. *USA Today,* p. 13A.

Hodges, D. (1996). Neuromusical research. In *Handbook of music psychology* (2nd ed.). San Antonio, NM: IMP Press.

Hofferth, S. C. (1998). *Healthy environments, healthy children: Children in families.* Ann Arbor, MI: University of Michigan Institute for Social Research.

Holdaway, D. (1979). *The foundations of literacy.* New York: Ashton Scholastic.

Holdaway, D. (1991). Shared book experience: Teaching reading using favorite books. In C. Kamii, M. Manning, & G. Manning (Eds.), *Early literacy: A constructivist foundation for whole language* (pp. 91–110). Washington, DC: National Education Association of the United States.

Holmes, D. L., & Morrison, F. J. (1979). *The child.* Monterey, CA: Brooks/Cole.

Honig, A. S. (1981, November). What are the needs of infants? *Young Children, 36.5,* 38–41.

Honig, A. S. (1995, July). Singing with infants and toddlers. *Young Children, 50*(5), 71–78.

Honig, A. S. (1999, March). The amazing brain. *Scholastic Early Childhood Today, 13*(6), 17–22.

Honig, W. (1988, October 14). In A. Watson (Ed.), Dick and Jane meet the classics. *San Jose Mercury News,* p. 4L.

Hostetler, A. J. (1988, July). Why baby cries: Data may shush skeptics. *The APA Monitor, 19.7,* 27–32.

Hostetler, M. (2000, January). We help our children create books. *Young Children, 55*(1), 28–32.

Hough, R. A., Nurss, J. R., & Goodson, M. S. (1984). Children in day care: An observational study. *Child Study Journal, 14.1,* 33–41.

Howard, S., Shaughnessy, A., Sanger, D., & Hux, K. (1998, May). Lets talk! Facilitating language in early elementary school classrooms. *Young Children, 53*(3), 34–39.

Howarth, M. (1989, November). Rediscovering the power of fairy tales. *Young Children, 45*(1), 58–59.

Howell, W. G., & Casserly, M. (2004, Summer). Where the rubber meets the road. *Education Next, 4*(3), 25.

Howes, C., Smith, E., & Galinsky, E. (1995). *Florida quality improvement study: Interim report.* New York: Families and Work Institute.

Huck, C. S. (1992, November). Literacy and literature. *Language Arts, 69*(7), 520–526.

Huck, C. S., Hepler, S., & Hickman, J. (1993). *Children's literature in the elementary school* (5th ed.). New York: Holt.

Huey, E. B. (1908). *The psychology and pedagogy of reading.* New York: Macmillan.

Hunt, T., & Renfro, N. (1982). *Puppetry in early childhood education.* Austin, TX: Renfro Studios.

Hunter, T. (2000, May). Some thoughts about sitting still. *Young Children, 55*(3), 29–34.

Hunter, T. (2003, May). What about Mr. Baker? *Young Children, 58*(3), 77.

Hurlock, E. B. (1972). *Child development.* New York: McGraw-Hill.

Hutinger, P. L. (1978, Spring). Language development: It's much more than a kit. *Day Care and Early Education, 5.2,* 44–47.

The Idaho Statesman. (1999, June 9). Poor daycare hurts kids language, math skills, study says. *The Idaho Statesman,* p. 4A.

Ingram, D. (1995). The cultural basis of prosodic modifications to infants and children: A response to Fernald's universalist theory. *Journal of Child Language, 22,* 52–64.

International Reading Association. (2003). *Standards for reading professionals.* Newark, DE: Author.

International Reading Association & The National Association for the Education of Young Children. (1999). *Learning to read and write: Developmentally appropriate practices for young children.* Washington, DC: National Association for the Education of Young Children.

International Visual Literacy Association. (2004). Retrieved July 23, 2004, from http://www.ivla.com

Invernizzi, M. A. (2003). The complex world of one-on-one tutoring. In S. B. Neuman & D. K. Dickinson (Eds.), *Handbook of early literacy research* (pp. 459–470). New York: The Guilford Press.

Itzkoff, S. (1986). *How we learn to read.* New York: Paideia Publishers.

Jacobs, N. L., & Eskridge, B. J. (1999, September). Teacher memories: Support or hindrance to good practice? *Young Children, 54*(5), 64–67.

Jaffe, N. (1992). Music in early childhood. In A. Mitchell & J. David (Eds.), *Explorations with young children* (pp. 215–228). Mt. Rainier, MD: Gryphon House.

Jaggar, A. (1980). Allowing for language differences. In G. S. Pinnell (Ed.), *Discovering language with children* (pp. 25–28). Urbana, IL: National Council of Teachers of English.

Jalongo, M. (1996, January). Teaching young children to become better listeners. *Young Children, 51*(2), 21–26.

James, J. Y., & Kormanski, L. M. (1999, May). Positive intergenerational picture books for young children. *Young Children, 54*(3), 37–43.

Jenkins, E. C. (1973). Multi-ethnic literature: Promise and problems. *Elementary English, 31.6,* 17–26.

Jewell, M. G., & Zintz, M. V. (1986). *Learning to read naturally.* Dubuque, IA: Kendall/Hunt.

Johnson, K. (1987). *Doing words.* Boston, MA: Houghton Mifflin.

Johnston, P., & Rogers, R. (2002). Early literacy development: The case for "informed assessment." In S. Neuman & D. Dickinson (Eds.), *Handbook of early literacy research* (pp. 377–389). New York: The Guilford Press.

Jones, E., & Nimmo, J. (1994). *Emergent curriculum.* Washington, DC: National Association for the Education of Young Children.

Jones, J. (2004, January). Framing the assessment discussion. *Young Children, 59*(1), 14–19.

Jones, R. (1996). *Emerging patterns of literacy. A multidisciplinary perspective.* London: Routledge.

Jusczyk, P. W. (1997, September 26). Quote in P. Recer, Scientists: Word recognition starts in crib. *The Idaho Statesman,* 3A.

Kagan, J. (1971). *Change and continuity.* New York: John Wiley & Sons.

Kaiser Family Foundation Family Survey. (2003). Menlo Park, CA: Kaiser Family Foundation. Retrieved October 26, 2004, from http://www.kff.org

Kamii, C., Manning, M., & Manning, G. (Eds.). (1991). *Early literacy: A constructivist foundation for whole language* (pp. 9–16). Washington, DC: National Education Association of the United States.

Kantrowitz, B. (1997, Spring/Summer). Off to a good start [Special Edition]. *Newsweek,* pp. 5–8.

Kantrowitz, B. (2000, Fall/Winter). 21st century babies. [Special Edition]. *Newsweek,* pp. 4–7.

Kasten, W., Lolli, E., & Vander Wilt, J. (1998). Common roots and threads: Developmentally appropriate practice, whole language, and continuous progress. *Literacy Teaching and Learning, 3*(2), 19–40.

Katz, L., & Chard, S. (1989). *Engaging children's minds: The project approach.* Norwood, NJ: Ablex.

Kay, J. (1996, April 12). Therapy helps stutterers speak out. *The Idaho Statesman,* p. 2D.

Kaye, K. (1979). Thickening thin data: The maternal role in developing communication and language. In M. Bullowa (Ed.), *Before speech* (pp. 191–206). London: Cambridge University Press.

Kelly, M. (1985, September 4). At 4, reading shouldn't be an issue. *San Jose Mercury News,* p. 16E.

Kindler, A. (2002). *Survey of the states' limited English proficient students and available educational programs and services 2000-2001, summary report.* Washington DC: National Clearinghouse for English Language Acquisition.

King, M. L. (1985). Language and language learning for child watchers. In A. Jaggar & M. T. Smith-Burke (Eds.), *Observing the language learner* (pp. 19–38). Newark, DE: International Reading Association, and Urbana, IL: National Council of Teachers of English (co-publishers).

Kirk, E. W. (1998, November). My favorite day is "story day." *Young Children, 53*(6), 44–54.

Kitano, M. (1982, May). Young gifted children: Strategies for preschool teachers. *Young Children, 37.4,* 29–31.

Klaus, M. H., & Klaus, P. H. (1985). *The amazing newborn.* Menlo Park, CA: Addison-Wesley.

Klein, A., & Starkey, P. (2000, February 17). In S. Steffens (Ed.), Preschool years give children the building blocks for learning. *San Jose Mercury News,* p. 1A.

Kletzien, S. B., & Szabo, R. J. (1998, December 5). *Informational text or narrative text? Children's preferences revisited.* Paper presented at the National Reading Conference, Austin, TX.

Kneas, K. M. (1999, March). Finding a place for computers. *Scholastic Early Childhood Today, 13*(6), 38–45.

Koc, K., & Buzzelli, C. A. (2004, January). The moral of the story is . . . : Using children's literature in moral education. *Young Children, 59*(1), 92–96.

Kontos, S., & Wilcox-Herzog, A. (1997, January). Teacher interactions with children: Why are they so important? *Young Children, 52*(4), 4–12.

Koons, K. (1986, May). Puppet plays. *First Teacher, 7.5,* 56–64.

Kotulak, R. (1996). *Inside the brain: Revolutionary discoveries of how the mind works.* Kansas City, MO: Andrews and McMeel.

Kranyik, M. A. (1986, May). Acting without words. *First Teacher, 7.5,* 65–71.

Kupetz, B. N., & Green, E. J. (1997, January). Sharing books with infants and toddlers: Facing the challenges. *Young Children, 52*(2), 22–27.

Lair, J. (1985). *I ain't much baby but I'm all I got.* New York: Fawcett.

Lally, J. R. (1997). Curriculum and lesson planning: A responsive approach. Unpublished manuscript. Sausalito, CA: West Ed.

Lancy, D. F., & Bergin, C. (1992, April 20). *The role of parents in supporting beginning reading.* Paper presented at the annual meeting of the American Research Association, San Francisco.

Landreth, C. (1972). *Preschool learning and teaching.* New York: Harper and Row.

Langer, J. A. (1992). Rethinking literature instruction. In J. A. Langer (Ed.), *Literature instruction* (pp. 35–53). Urbana, IL: National Council of Teachers of English.

Langer, J. A., & Applebee, A. N. (1986). In E. Z. Rothkopt (Ed.), Reading and writing instruction: Toward a theory of teaching and learning. *Review in Education, 13,* 171–194.

Lapinski, S. (1996, May). Signs of intelligence. *Child, 11*(4), 46–51.

Larrick, N. (1965, September 11). The all-white world of children's books. *Saturday Review,* pp. 63–65.

Leads, D. (2003, January 15). . . . four-year-olds ask questions. *Bottom Line, 24*(2), 9.

Lee, L. L. (1970). The relevance of general semantics to development of sentence structure in children's language. In L. Thayer (Ed.), *Communication: General semantics perspectives.* New York: Spartan Books.

Lenneberg, E. H. (1971). The natural history of language. In J. Eloit (Ed.), *Human development and cognitive processes* (pp. 200–225). Toronto: Holt, Rinehart, and Winston.

Lentz, K. A., & Burris, N. A. (1985, January/February). How to make your own books. *Childhood Education, 37.5,* 199–202.

Leu, D. J. (1997, September). Exploring literacy on the Internet. *The Reading Teacher, 51*(1), 62–67.

Lindfors, J. W. (1985). Oral language learning. In A. Jaggar & M. T. Smith-Burke (Eds.), *Observing the young language learner* (pp. 41–56). Newark, DE: International Reading Association, and Urbana, IL: NCTE (co-publishers).

Lloyd-Jones, L. (2002). Relationships as curriculum. *Head Start Bulletin, 73,* 10–12.

Locke, J. (1974). *An essay concerning human understanding.* Oxford, UK: The Clarendon Press.

Love, J. M. (2003). Instrumentation for state readiness assessment: Issues in measuring children's early development and learning. *Assessing the State of State Assessments: Special Report.* Greensboro, NC: The Regional Education Laboratory at SERVE.

Lundberg, I., Frost, J., & Peterson, O. (1988). Effects of an extensive program for stimulating phonological awareness in preschool children. *Reading Research Quarterly, 23,* 264–284.

Lundgren, D., & Morrison, J. W. (2003, May). Involving Spanish-speaking families in early education programs. *Young Children, 58*(3), 88–95.

Lunt, I. (1993). The practice of assessment. In H. Daniels (Ed.), *Charting the agenda: Educational activity after Vygotsky* (pp. 141–162). New York: Routledge.

Lynch, E. W., & Hanson, M. J. (1998). *Developing cross-cultural competence: A guide for working with young children and their families.* Baltimore, MD: Brookes.

Lynch-Brown, C., & Tomlinson, C. (1998). Children's literature past and present: Is there a future? *Peabody Journal of Education, 73*(3), 228–252.

Lyons, C. A. (1999a). Emotions, cognition, and becoming a reader: A message to teachers of struggling learners. *Journal of Early Reading and Writing, 4*(1), 67–87.

Lyons, C. A. (1999b). Letter learning in the early childhood classroom. In I. Fountas & G. S. Pinnell (Eds.), *Voices on word matters: Learning about phonics and spelling in the literacy classroom* (pp. 197–211). Portsmouth, NH: Heinemann.

MacDonald, M. B. (1992). Valuing diversity. In A. Mitchell & J. David (Eds.), *Explorations with young children* (pp. 103–120). Mt. Rainier, MD: Gryphon House.

MacDonald, M. R. (1993). *The storyteller's start-up book: Finding, learning, performing and using folktales.* Little Rock, AR: August House Publishers.

MacDonald, M. R. (1995). *Bookplay: 101 creative themes to share with young children.* New Haven, CT: The Shoe String Press.

MacDonald, M. R. (1996). Quoted in Mooney, B., & Holt, D. *The storyteller's guide.* Little Rock, AR: August House Publishers.

Machado, J. (1989, April 18). Recorded observation notes. Busy Bee Children's Center. Santa Clara, CA.

Machado, J., & Botnarescue, H. (2005). *Student teaching: Early childhood practicum guide.* Clifton Park, NY: Thomson Delmar Learning.

Mallan, K. (1994). "Do it again, Dwayne": Finding out about children as storytellers. In A. Trousdale, C. Woestehoff, & M. Schwartz (Eds.), *Give a listen* (pp. 13–18). Urbana, IL: National Council of Teachers of English.

Marcon, R. A. (1992). Differential effects of three preschool models on inner-city 4-year-olds. *Early Childhood Research Quarterly, 7,* 517–530.

Marcon, R. A. (1999, March). Differential impact of preschool models on development and early learning of inner-city children: A three-cohort study. *Developmental Psychology, 35*(2), 358–375.

Martens, P. A. (1999, Fall/Winter). "Mommy, how do you write 'Sarah'?": The role of name writing in one child's literacy. *Journal of Research in Childhood Education, 14*(1), 5–14

Martinez, M., & Roser, N. (1985). Read it again: The value of repeated readings during storytime. *The Reading Teacher, 38,* 782–786.

Martinez, N., & Johnson, M. (1987, September 22). Read aloud to give kids the picture. *San Jose Mercury News,* p. 4L.

Masataka, N. (1992, June). Pitch characteristics of Japanese maternal speech to infants. *Journal of Child Language, 19*(2), 213.

Masataka, N. (1993). Effects of contingent and non-contingent maternal stimulation on the vocal behavior of three-to-four-month-old Japanese infants. *Journal of Child Language, 20,* 40–57.

Mason, J. M. (1980). When do children begin to read: An exploration of four-year-old children's letter and word reading competencies. *Reading Research Quarterly, 15,* 203–227.

Mason, J. M., Herman, P. A., & Au, K. H. (1992). Children's developing knowledge of word. In J. Flood, J. M. Jensen, D. Lapp, & J. R. Squire (Eds.), *Handbook of research on teaching English language arts* (pp. 721–730). New York: Macmillan.

Mavrogenes, N. A. (1990, May). Helping parents help their children become literate. *Young Children, 45*(4), 4–9.

McCarrier, A., Pinnell, G. S., & Fountas, I. C. (2000). *Interactive writing: How language and literacy come together, K-2.* Portsmouth, NH: Heinemann.

McClelland, M. M., Morrison, F. J., & Holmes, D. L. (2000). Children at risk for early academic problems: The role of learning-related social skills. *Early Childhood Research Quarterly, 15*(3), 307–329.

McCord, S. (1995). *The storybook journey: Pathways to literacy through story and play.* Columbus, OH: Merrill.

McDonald, D. T., & Simons, G. M. (1989). *Musical growth and development.* New York: Schirmer Books.

McGee, L. M. (2003a). Book acting: Storytelling and drama in the early childhood classroom. In D. M. Barone & L. M. Morrow (Eds.), *Literacy and young children: Research-based practices* (pp. 157–172). New York: The Guilford Press.

McGee, L. M. (2003b, Summer). The influence of Early Reading First on High/Scope's preschool reading instruction. *High Scope Resource, 22*(2), 24–25.

McGhee, P. (1979). *Humor: Its origins and development.* San Francisco: Freeman.

McKenzie, M. G. (1985). Classroom contexts for language and literacy. In A. Jaggar & M. T. Smith-Burke (Eds.), *Observing the language learner* (pp. 233–249). Newark, DE: International Reading Association, and Urbana, IL: NCTE (co-publishers).

McLane, J. B., & McNamee, G. D. (1990). *Early literacy.* Cambridge, MA: Harvard University Press.

McMullen, M. B. (1998, May). Thinking before doing. *Young Children, 53*(3), 65–70.

Meers, H. J. (1976). *Helping our children talk.* New York: Longman Group.

Meier, D. R. (2004). *The young child's memory for words.* New York: Teachers College Press.

Miller, J. (1990, November). Three-year-olds in their reading corner. *Young Children, 46*(1), 51–54.

Miller, J. W. (1998). Literacy in the 21st century: Emergent themes. *Peabody Journal of Education, 73*(3 & 4), 1–14.

Miller, K. (1987, August/September). Room arrangement. *Pre-K Today, 2.1*, 28–33.

Miller, P. J., & Mehler, R. A. (1994). The power of personal storytelling in families and kindergartens. In A. H. Dyson & C. Genishi (Eds.), *The need for story: Cultural diversity in classroom and community* (pp. 38–71). Urbana, IL: National Council of Teachers of English.

Miller, S. A. (2001, November/December). Why children like what they like. *Early Childhood Today, 16*(3), 39–40.

Mody, M., Schwartz. R., Gravel, J., & Ruben, R. (1999, October). Speech perception and verbal memory in children with and without histories of otitis media. *Journal of Speech, Language, and Hearing Research, 42*(5), 1069–1077.

Montessori, M. (1967a). *The absorbent mind.* New York: Holt, Rinehart, and Winston.

Montessori, M. (1967b). *The discovery of the child.* New York: Holt, Rinehart, and Winston.

Moon, J. (1996, October). *Focus on the year 2000, CACEI.* Keynote address given at the Fall Study Conference at California State University-Hayward, Walnut Creek, CA.

Mooney, B., & Holt, D. (1996). *The storyteller's guide.* Little Rock, AR: August House Publishing.

Moore, B. (1985). *Words that taste good.* Markham, Ontario: Pembroke.

Morphett, M. V., & Washburne, C. (1931). When should children begin to read? *Elementary School Journal, 31*, 496–508.

Morrow, L. M. (1988). Young children's responses to one-to-one story readings in school settings. *Reading Research Quarterly, 23*, 89–107.

Morrow, L. M. (1989). *Literacy development in the early years. Helping children read and write.* Englewood Cliffs, NJ: Prentice Hall.

Morrow, L. M. (1990). Assessing children's understanding of story through their construction and reconstruction of narrative. In L. Morrow & J. Smith (Eds.), *Assessment for instruction in early literacy* (pp. 408–431). Englewood Cliffs, NJ: Prentice Hall.

Morrow, L. M., & Asbury, E. (2003). Current practices in early childhood literacy development. In L. M. Morrow, L. B. Gambrell, & M. Pressley (Eds.), *Best practices in literacy instruction* (pp. 43–63). New York: The Guilford Press.

Morrow, L. M., Burks, S., & Rand, M. (1992). *Resources in early literacy development.* Newark, DE: International Reading Association.

Morrow, L. M., Tracey, D. H., Woo, D. G., & Pressley, M. (1999). Characteristics of exemplary first grade literacy instruction. *Reading Teacher, 52*, 462–476.

Moustafa, M. (1998). Reconceptualizing phonics instruction. In C. Weaver (Ed.), *Reconsidering a balanced approach to reading* (pp. 380–401). Urbana, IL: National Council of Teachers of English.

Muenchow, S. (2003). A risk management approach to readiness assessment. *Assessing the State of State Assessments: Special Report.* Greensboro, NC: The Regional Education Laboratory at SERVE.

Murphy, J. C. (2003, November). Case studies in African American school success and parenting behaviors. *Young Children, 58*(6), 85–89.

Nash, J. M. (1997, February 3). Fertile minds. *Time, 149*(5), 48–56.

National Assessment of Educational Progress. (1995). *The NAEP reading: A first look—Findings from the National Assessment of Educational Progress.* Washington, DC: U.S. Government Printing Office.

National Association for the Education of Young Children. (1996, January). Position statement: Responding to linguistic and cultural diversity—Recommendations for effective early childhood education. *Young Children, 51*(2), 4–12.

National Association for the Education of Young Children, and the International Reading Association. (1998, July). Learning to read and write: Developmentally appropriate practice for young children. A position statement. *Young Children, 53*(4), 30–46.

National Association for the Education of Young Children and the National Association of Early Childhood Specialists in State Departments of Education. (2003, November). *Early childhood curriculum, assessment, and program evaluation.* Position Statement Summary. Paper presented at National Association for the Education of Young Children Annual Conference. Chicago: Authors.

National Association for Hearing and Speech Action (NAHSA). (1985). *Recognizing communication disorders.* Rockville, MD: NAHSA.

National Association for Hearing and Speech Action (NAHSA). (2000). *What do you hear?* Rockville, MD: NAHSA.

National Council of Teachers of English. (1994). *Emerging literacy* [Brochure]. Urbana, IL: National Council of Teachers of English.

National Reading Panel. (2000). *Teaching children to read: An evidence-based assessment of the scientific research literature on reading and its implications for reading instruction* (NIH Publication No. 00-4769). Washington, DC: National Institute of Child Health and Human Development.

National Reading Panel Report. (2000). *Teaching children to read.* Washington, DC: National Institute of Child Health and Human Development.

National Research Council. (1998). *Preventing reading difficulties in young children.* Washington, DC: National Academy Press.

National Research Council. (2000). *How people learn: Brain, mind, experience and school.* Washington, DC: National Academy Press.

Neergaard, L. (2004, June 8). New guidelines call for vision screening for preschoolers. *The Idaho Statesman.* p. 1.

Nelson, K. (1985). *Making sense: The acquisition of shared meaning.* New York: Academic Press.

Nelson, K., & Shaw, L. (2002). Developing a socially shared symbolic system. In E. Amsel & J. Byrnes (Eds.), *Language, literacy and cognitive development: The development and consequences of symbolic communication* (pp. 27–57). Mahwah, NJ: Erlbaum.

Nelson, M. A. (1972). *Children's literature.* New York: Holt, Rinehart, and Winston.

Neugebauer, O. (1981). *On language.* Boston: Preston Books.

Neuman, S., Copple, C., & Bredekamp, S. (1999). *Learning to read and write: Developmentally appropriate practices for young children.* Washington, DC: National Association for the Education of Young Children.

Neuman, S. B. (1999, November). *Study finds quality book gap for very young children: Children in low income families bear the brunt* [Unpublished study]. Center for the Improvement of Early Reading Achievement.

Neuman, S. B., & Roskos, K. (1990). Influence of literacy enriched play settings on preschoolers' engagement with written language. In S. McCormick & J. Zutell (Eds.), *Literacy theory and research: Analyses from multiple paradigms* (pp. 179–187). Chicago: National Reading Conference.

Neuman, S. B., & Roskos, K. (1992, November 3). Literacy objects as cultural tools: Effects on children's literacy behaviors in play. *Reading Research Quarterly, 27,* 203–225.

Neuman, S. B., & Roskos, K. A. (1993). *Language and literacy learning in the early years: An integrated approach.* New York: Holt, Rinehart and Winston.

New, R. S. (2002). Early literacy and developmentally appropriate practice: Rethinking the paradigm. In S. Neuman & D. Dickinson (Eds.), *Handbook of early literacy research* (pp. 245–262). New York: The Guilford Press.

Newkirk, T. (1989). *More than stories: The range of children's writing.* Portsmouth, NH: Heinemann.

Newson, J. (1979). The growth of shared understandings between infant and caregiver. In M. Bullowa (Ed.), *Before speech* (pp. 207–222). London: Cambridge University Press.

Nichols, R. (1984). Factors in listening comprehension. *Speech Monographs, 15,* 154–163.

Nicolopoulou, A., Scales, B., & Weintraub, J. (1994). Gender differences and symbolic imagination in stories of four-year-olds. In A. H. Dyson & C. Genishi (Eds.), *The need for story* (pp. 102–123). New York: National Council of Teachers of English.

Noori, K. (1996, March). Writing my own script: Pathways to teaching. *Young Children, 51*(3), 17–19.

Norton, D. E. (1983). *Through the eyes of a child.* Columbus, OH: Charles E. Merrill.

Norton, D. E. (1993). *The effective teaching of language arts.* New York: Macmillan.

Ohl, J. (2002, Fall). Linking child care and early literacy: Building the foundation for success. *Child Care Bulletin, 27,* 1–4.

Okagaki, L., & Diamond, K. (2000, May). Responding to cultural and linguistic differences in the beliefs and practices of families with young children. *Young Children, 55*(3), 47–55.

Okagaki, L., & Sternberg, R. (1993). Parental beliefs and children's school performance. *Child Development, 64,* 37–41, 84–93.

Oken-Wright, P. (1988, January). Show-and-tell grows up. *Young Children, 43.2,* 52–63.

O'Leary, C., Newton, J., Lundz, B., Hall, M., O'Connell, K., Raby, C., & Czarnecka, M. (2002, June 1–4). Visual Communication Group. ACM SIGGRAPH Workshop. Snowbird, UT.

Opitz, M. (2000). *Rhymes and reasons: Literature & language play for phonological awareness.* Portsmouth, NH: Heinemann.

O'Rourke, S. (1990). Personal communication, September 1988. In J. M. Healy (Ed.), *Endangered minds: Why children don't think and what we can do about it.* New York: Simon & Schuster.

Ornstein, R., & Sobel, D. (1987). *The healing brain.* New York: Simon & Schuster.

Owens, C. V. (1999, September). Conversational science 101A: Talking it up! *Young Children, 54*(5), 4–9.

Padron, Y. N., Waxman, H. C., & Rivera, H. H. (2002, August). Educating Hispanic students: Effective instructional practices. *Practitioners Brief #5.* Santa Cruz, CA: Center for Research on Education, Diversity and Excellence, University of California.

Paley, V. (1981). *Wally's stories.* Cambridge, MA: Harvard University Press.

Paley, V. (1990). *The boy who would be a helicopter: The use of story telling in the classroom.* Cambridge, MA: Harvard University Press.

Paley, V. (1994). Princess Annabella and the black girls. In A. H. Dyson & C. Genishi (Eds.), *The need for story: Cultural diversity in classroom and community* (pp. 145–154). Urbana, IL: National Council of Teachers of English.

Pan, B. A., & Gleason, J. B. (1997). Semantic development: Learning the meanings of words. In J. Gleason (Ed.), *The development of language* (4th ed., pp. 311–331). Boston: Allyn and Bacon.

Papadaki-D'Onofrio, E. (2003, September/October). Bilingualism/multilingualism and language acquisition theories. *Child Care Information Exchange, 153,* 46–50.

Parents As Teachers. (1986). *Parents As Teachers program planning and implementation guide.* Jefferson City, MO: Missouri Department of Elementary and Secondary Education.

Pellegrini, A., & Galda, L. (1982). The effects of thematic fantasy play training on the development of children's story comprehension. *American Educational Research Journal, 19,* 443–452.

Perry, B. (2000, November/December). How the brain learns best: Easy ways to gain optimal learning in the classroom by activating different parts of the brain. *Instructor, 110*(4), 34–35.

Perry, J. (2000, February 17). In S. Steffens (Ed.), Preschool years give children the building blocks for learning. *San Jose Mercury News,* p. 1A.

Peterson, M. E., & Haines, L. P. (1998). Orthographic analogy training with kindergarten children. In C. Weaver (Ed.), *Reconsidering a balanced approach to reading* (pp. 94–111). Urbana, IL: National Council of Teachers of English.

Peterson, R. W. (1994). School readiness considered from a neuro-cognitive perspective. *Early Education and Development, 5*(2), 19–31.

Piaget, J. (1952). *The language and thought of the child.* London: Routledge and Kegan Paul.

Piaget, J. (1970). *Science of education and the psychology of the child.* New York: Orion.

Piaget, J., & Inheldder, B. (1969). *The psychology of the child.* New York: Basic Books.

Pica, R. (1997, September). Beyond physical development: Why young children need to move. *Young Children, 52*(6), 4–11.

Pick, A. (1986, August). In C. Garcia-Barrio (Ed.), Listen to the music! *American Baby, 48*(8), 46, 67–69.

Pines, M. (1983, November). Can a rock walk? *Psychology Today, 39.11,* 46–50, 52, 54.

Pinnell, G., & Jaggar, A. M. (1992). Oral language: Speaking and listening in the classroom. In J. Flood J. M. Jensen, D. Lapp, & J. R. Squire (Eds.), *Handbook of research in teaching English language arts* (pp. 691–720). New York: Macmillan.

Pinnell, G. S. (1999). Word solving. In I. Fountas & G. S. Pinnell (Eds.), *Voices on word matters: Learning about phonics and spelling in the literacy classroom* (pp. 151–186). Portsmouth, NH: Heinemann.

Poltarnees, W. (1972). *All mirrors are magic mirrors.* New York: The Green Tiger Press.

Poole, C. (1999, March). You've got to hand it to me! *Scholastic Early Childhood Today, 13*(6), 34–39.

Powell, R. E. (1992, September). Goals for language arts program: Toward a democratic vision. *Language Arts, 69,* 342–343.

Pressley, M., Rankin, J. L., & Yokoi, L. (1996). A survey of instructional practices of primary teachers nominated as effective in promoting literacy. *Elementary School Journal, 96,* 363–384.

Putnam, L. (1991, October). Dramatizing nonfiction with emerging readers. *Language Arts, 68*(6), 463–469.

Putnam, L. R. (1994, September). Reading instruction: What do we know that we didn't know thirty years ago? *Language Arts, 71*(5), 362–366.

Quindlen, A. (2001, February 12). Building blocks for every kid. *Newsweek,* p. 68.

Raines, S., & Isbell, R. (1994). *Stories: Children's literature in early education.* Clifton Park, NY: Thomson Delmar Learning.

Rauscher, F. H. (2003, September). Can music instruction affect children's cognitive development? *ERIC Digest,* EDO-PS-03-12.

Raver, C., & Knitzer, J. (2002). *Ready to enter: What research tells policymakers about strategies to promote social and emotional school readiness among three- and four-year-old children.* New York: National Center for Children in Poverty.

Raver, C. C. (2003, July). Young children's emotional development and school readiness. *ERIC Digest,* EDO-PS-03-8.

Raymond, J. (2000, Fall/Winter). Kids, start your engines [Special Edition]. *Newsweek,* 8–11.

Reading Today. (2004, December/2005, January). New report: State are narrowing achievement gaps and raising achievement, but not fast enough. *Reading Today, 22*(3), 4.

Renzulli, J. (1986, October). Interview quote in Alvino, J. Guiding your gifted child. *American Baby, 48*(10), 54, 57–58.

Reznick, J. S. (1996, December 10). In M. Elias (Ed.), Talking doesn't indicate tot's progress study finds. *The Idaho Statesman,* p. D2.

Rhodes, L. K. (1981, February). I can read! Predictable books as resources for reading and writing instruction. *The Reading Teacher, 34,* 511–518.

Riley, J. (1996). *The teaching of reading.* London: Paul Chapman.

Riley, R. (1999, June 9). Poor day care hurts kid's language, math skills, study says. *The Idaho Statesman,* p. 4A.

Rivers, K. (1996, November 24). Once upon a time. *Orlando Sentinel,* Florida Supplement.

Robertson, S. B., & Weismer, S. E. (1999, October). Effects of treatment on linguistic and social skills in toddlers with delayed language development. *Journal of Speech, Language, and Hearing Research, 42,* 1234–1248.

Robisson, H. F. (1983). *Exploring teaching in early childhood education.* Boston: Allyn and Bacon.

Rock, A., Trainor, L., & Addison, T. (1999, March). Distinctive messages in infant-directed lullabies and play sounds. *Developmental Psychology, 35*(2), 527–534.

Rones, N. (2004, August). Listen to this. *Parents,* pp. 167–168.

Roskos, K., & Christie, J. (2001, May). On not pushing too hard: A few cautionary remarks about linking literacy and play. *Young Children, 56*(37), 64–66.

Rothbaum, F., Grauer, A., & Rubin, D. (1997, September). Becoming sexual: Differences between child and adult sexuality. *Young Children, 52*(6), 22–28.

Rouseau, J. J. (1947). L'Emile ou l'education. In O. E. Tellows & N. R. Tarrey (Eds.), *The age of enlightenment.* New York: F. S. Croft.

Rowley, R. (1999, July). A visiting puppet. Caregivers' corner. *Young Children, 54*(4), 21.

Rubin, K. H., & Coplan, R. J. (1998). Social and nonsocial play in childhood: An individual differences perspective. In O. N Saracho & B. Spodek (Eds.), *Multiple perspectives on play in early childhood* (pp. 144–170). Albany: State University of New York Press.

Rubin, R. R., & Fisher, J. J. (1982). *Your preschooler.* New York: Macmillan.

Ruddell, R. B., & Ruddell, M. R. (1995). *Teaching children to read and write: Becoming an influential teacher.* Boston: Allyn and Bacon.

Rusk, R., & Scotland, J. (1979). *Doctrines of the great educators.* New York: St. Martin's Press.

Sachs, J. (1997). Communication development in infancy. In J. Gleason (Ed.), *The development of language* (4th ed., pp. 261–282). Boston: Allyn and Bacon.

Saltz, E., & Johnson, J. (1974). Training for thematic-fantasy play in culturally disadvantaged children. Preliminary results. *Journal of Educational Psychology, 66,* pp. 623–630.

Sanders, N. (1966). *Classroom questions: What kind?* New York: Harper & Row.

Saville-Troike, M. (1978). *A guide to culture in the classroom.* Rosslyn, VA: National Clearinghouse for Bilingual Education.

Sawyer, D. (1969). *The way of the storyteller.* New York: Viking.

Schickedanz, J. A. (1982). The acquisition of written language in young children. In B. Spodek (Ed.), *Handbook of research in early childhood education.* New York: The Free Press.

Schickedanz, J. A. (1986). *More than the ABCs: The early stages of reading and writing.* Washington, DC: National Association for the Education of Young Children.

Schickedanz, J. A. (1989, August/September). What about preschoolers and academics? *Reading Today, 7*(1), 24.

Schickedanz, J. A. (1993). Designing the early childhood classroom environment to facilitate literacy development. In B. Spodek & O. Saracho (Eds.), *Language and literacy in early childhood education* (pp. 141–145). New York: Teachers College Press.

Schickedanz, J. A. (1999). Written language use within the context of young children's symbolic play. *Early Childhood Research Quarterly, 4,* 225–244.

Schickendanz, J. A. (2003). Engaging preschoolers in code learning. In D. M. Barone & L. M. Morrow (Eds.), *Literacy and young children: Research-based practices* (pp. 121–139). New York: The Guilford Press.

Schimmel, N. (1978). *Just enough to make a story.* Berkeley, CA: Sister's Choice Press.

Schmidt, S. (1991). Interview. Busy Bee Children's Center. Santa Clara, CA.

Schnur, J., Lowrey, M. A., & Brazell, W. (1985). *A profile of the precocious reader.* Hattiesburg, MI: University of Southern Mississippi, College of Education and Psychology.

Schomberg, J. (1993, May). Messages of peace. *Book Links, 3*(1), 9–11.

Schrader, C. (1989). Written language use within the context of young children's symbolic play. *Early Childhood Research Quarterly, 4,* 225–244.

Schulz, R. (1999). Stories, readers, and the world beyond books. In L. Reid and J. N. Golub (Eds.), *Classroom practices in teaching English* (pp. 27–34), Urbana, IL: National Council of Teachers of English.

Schwartz, S. (1980, February). The young gifted child. *Early Years, 11.5,* 55–62.

Segal, M. (1987, October). Should superheroes be expelled from preschool? *Pre-K Today, 1.8,* 37–45.

Self, F. (1987, January). Choosing for children under three. *CBC Features, 41.4,* 2–3.

Shanahan, T. (2004, November 12). Laying the groundwork for literacy: The National Early Literacy Panel synthesis for research on early literacy education. Conference presentation. National Association for the Education of Young Children Annual Conference. Anaheim, CA.

Shanahan, T., & Barr, R. (1995). Reading Recovery: An independent evaluation of the effects of early instructional intervention for at-risk learners. *Reading Research Quarterly, 30,* 58–69.

Sheldon, A. (1990, January). Kings are royaler than queens: Language and socialization. *Young Children, 45.2,* 4–9.

Sherwin, A. (1987, Spring). Your baby at 12 months. *The Beginning Years, 11*(7), 27–30.

Shore, R. (1997). *Rethinking the brain.* New York: Families and Work Institute.

Sierra, J., & Kaminski, R. (1989). *Twice upon a time: Stories to tell, retell, act out and write about.* Bronx, NY: The H. W. Wilson Co.

Sigel, I. E. (1982). The relationship between distancing strategies and the child's cognitive behavior. In L. M. Laosa & I. E. Sigel (Eds.), *Families—Research and practice: Vol. 1. Families as learning environments for children* (pp. 47–86). New York: Plenum.

Singhal, J. (1999, March). Tuning in to the musical brain. *Bay Area Parent, 16*(12), 21–23.

Sivulich, S. S. (1977). Strategies for presenting literature. In B.E. Cullinan & C. W. Carmichael (Eds.), *Literature and young children* (pp. 120–129). Urbana, IL: National Council of Teachers of English.

Skarpness, L. R., & Carson, D. K. (1987, December). Correlates of kindergarten adjustment: Temperament and communicative competence. *Early Childhood Research Quarterly, 2.4,* 215–229.

Slavin, R. E., Karweit, N. L., & Wasik, B. A. (1994). *Preventing early school failure: Research, policy, practice.* Boston: Allyn and Bacon.

Sloane, G. L. (1942). *Fun with folk tales.* New York: Dutton.

Slobin, D. I. (1971). *Psycholinguistics.* Glenview, IL: Scott, Foresman.

Smilansky, S. (1968). *The effects of sociodramatic play on disadvantaged preschool children.* New York: Wiley.

Smilansky, S., & Shefatya, L. (1990). *Facilitating play: A medium for promoting cognitive, socio-emotional, and academic development in young children.* Gaithersburg, MD: Psychosocial and Educational Publications.

Smith, M. W. (2001). Children's experiences in preschool. In D. Dickinson & P. Tabors (Eds.), *Beginning literacy with language* (pp. 149–174). Baltimore: Brookes.

Smith-Burke, M. T. (1985). Reading and talking: Learning through interaction. In A. Jaggar & M. T. Smith-Burke (Eds.), *Observing the language learner* (pp. 199–211). Newark, DE: International Reading Association, and Urbana, IL: National Council of Teachers of English (co-publishers).

Snow, C. (2003). Ensuring reading success for African America children. In B. Bowman. (Ed.), *Love to read. Essays in developing and enhancing early literacy skills in African American children.* Washington, DC: National Black Child Development Institute.

Snow, C., Burns, S., & Griffin, P. (Eds.). (1998). *Preventing reading difficulties in young children.* Washington, DC: National Academy Press.

Snow, C., De Blauw, A., & Van Roosmalen, G. (1979). Talking and playing with babies. In M. Bullowa (Ed.), *Before speech* (pp. 269–288). London: Cambridge University Press.

Snow, C. E., & Tabors, P. O. (1993). Language skills that relate to literacy development. In B. Spodek & O. Saracho (Eds.), *Yearbook in early childhood education* (pp. 222–246). New York: Teachers College Press.

Soto, L. D. (1991, January). Understanding bilingual/bicultural young children. *Young Children, 40*(2), 30–36.

Sowers, S. (1982). Early writing development. In R. D. Walshe (Ed.), *Children want to write.* Exeter, NH: Heinemann Books.

Spencer, M. (1987). *How texts teach what readers learn.* Victoria, British Columbia: Abel Press.

Spieker, S. (1987, September 13). Study links tots' smiles. *San Jose Mercury News,* p. 8B.

Spitzer, D. R. (1977). *Concept formation and learning in early childhood.* Columbus, OH: Charles E. Merrill.

Spivak, L. (2000, Fall/Winter). In G. Cowley (Ed.), For the love of language [Special Edition]. *Newsweek,* pp. 12–15.

St. Pierre, R. G., & Layzer, J. I. (1998). Improving the life chances of children in poverty: Assumptions and what we have learned. *Social Policy Report, 12*(4), 1–25.

Stahl, S. A. (1998) Understanding shifts in reading and its instruction. *Peabody Journal of Education, 73*(3 & 4), 31–67.

Stanchfield, J. (1994, September). In L. R. Putnam (Ed.), Reading instruction: What do we know now that we didn't know thirty years ago? *Language Arts, 71*(5), 326–366.

Stauffer, R. C. (1970). *The language experience approach to the teaching of reading.* New York: Harper and Row.

Stewig, J. W. (1977). Encouraging language growth. In B. E. Cullinan & C. W. Carmichael (Eds.), *Literature and young children* (pp. 17–38). Urbana, IL: National Council of Teachers of English.

Stieglitz, M. G. (1972). The visual differential: An experimental study of the relation of varied experiences with visuals to shape discrimination. Unpublished doctoral dissertation, University of Wisconsin.

Stipek, D. (2004, Summer). The new Head Start. *Education Next, 4*(3), 7.

Stoel-Gammon, C. (1997). Phonological development. In J. Gleason (Ed.), *The development of language* (4th ed., pp. 138–201). Boston: Allyn and Bacon.

Stott, F. (2003, November/December). Making standards meaningful: Aligning preschool standards with those established for K-12 can be an important step toward offering equality in early educational experiences. *Early Childhood Today, 18*(3), 19–20.

Strickland, D. (1982, December 4). The last word on the first "R." *New York Daily News,* p. 13F.

Strickland, D. S. (1990, March). Family literacy: Sharing good books. *Young Children, 43*(7), 518–519.

Strickland, D. S. (2003, November). Exemplary practice in organizing skill development in the early literacy classroom. National Association for the Education of Young Children. Annual Conference. Chicago.

Strickland, D. S., & Feeney, J. T. (1992). Development in the elementary school years. In J. Flood, J. M. Jensen, D. Lapp, & J. R. Squire (Eds.), *Handbook of research on teaching the English language arts* (pp. 401–432). New York: Macmillan.

Strickland, D. S., & Morrow, L. M. (1989, January). Interactive experience with storybook reading. *The Reading Teacher, 58*(2), 322–323.

Strickland, D. S., & Morrow, L. M. (1990, January). Sharing big books. *The Reading Teacher, 43*, 342–344.

Strickland, D. S., Shanahan, T., & Escamalia, K. (2004, November 12). Laying the groundwork for literacy: The National Early Literacy Panel synthesis of research on early literacy education. National Association for the Education of Young Children Annual Conference. Anaheim, CA.

Strommen, L. T., & Mates, B. F. (1997, October). What readers do: Young children's ideas about the nature of reading. *The Reading Teacher, 51*(2), 37–42.

Sulzby, E. (1992, April). Research directions: Transitions from emergent to conventional writing. *Language Arts, 69*, 290–297.

Sulzby, E. (1996). Roles of oral and written language as children approach conventional literacy. In C. Pontevecorvo, M. Orsolini, B. Burge, & L. B. Resnick (Eds.), *Children's early text construction* (pp. 25–46). Mahwah, NJ: Lawrence Erlbaum.

Tabors, P. O. (1997). *One child, two languages: A guide for preschool educators of children learning English as a second language.* Baltimore, MD: Paul H. Brookes.

Tabors, P. O. (2002). Language and literacy for all children. *Head Start Bulletin,* (74), 10–14.

Tabors, P. O., & Snow, C. E. (2002). Young bilingual children and early literacy development. In S. B. Neuman & D. K. Dickinson (Eds.), *Handbook of early literacy research* (pp. 159–178). New York: The Guilford Press.

Tao, F., Gamse, B., & Tarr, H. (1998). *National evaluation of the Even Start Family Literacy Program, 1994-1997. Final Report.* Washington, DC: U.S. Department of Education, Planning and Evaluation Service.

Taylor, J. K. (1993, October). *Learning through movement.* Conference presentation, Snake River Association for the Education of Young Children. Twin Falls, ID.

Taylor, R. (2002, March). Helping language grow. *Instructor, III*(6), 25–26.

Teale, W. H. (1995). Introduction. In T. Harris & R. Hodges (Eds.), *The literacy dictionary.* Newark, DE: International Reading Association.

Thernstrom, A., & Thernstrom, B. (2003). *No excuses: Closing the racial gap in learning.* New York: Simon & Schuster.

Thomas, W., & Collier, V. (2002). *A national study of school effectiveness for language minority students' long term academic achievement.* Washington, DC: Center for Research on Education, Diversity and Excellence.

Thompson, N. S. (2000, January). Sylvia Ashton-Warner: Reclaiming personal meaning in literacy teaching. *English Journal, 89*(3), 90–96.

Throne, J. (1988, September). Becoming a kindergarten of readers. *Young Children, 43.6,* 10–16.

Thurber, D. (1988). *Teaching handwriting.* Glenview, IL: Scott, Foresman.

Tizard, B., Rankin, L., Shonic, J., & Cobb, S. (1972). Environmental effects on language development: A study of young children in long-stay residential nurseries. *Child Development, 43.4,* 337–358.

Tokuhama-Espinosa, T. (2001). *Raising multilingual children: Foreign language acquisition and children.* Westport, CT: Bergin & Garvey.

Toppo, G. (2004, July 7). No child left behind has teachers singing protest songs. *USA Today,* p. 9D.

Tough, J. (1977). *Talking and learning: A guide to fostering communication skills in nursery and infant schools.* London: Ward Lock.

Trautman, L. S. (2003, November/December). If your child stutters. *Parent & Child, 11*(3), 64–67.

Trelease, J. (1995). *The new read-aloud handbook.* New York: Penguin Books.

Tronick, E. (1987, May 18). In J. Kunerth (Ed.), Born communicators. *Orlando Sentinel,* p. 3L.

Trousdale, A. M. (1990, February). Interactive storytelling: Scaffolding children's early narratives. *Language Arts, 69*(2), 164–173.

Tunnell, M. O. (1994, December). The double-edged sword: Fantasy and censorship. *Language Arts, 71*(6), 606–611.

U.S. Bureau of the Census. (1995). *The foreign-born population: 1994 current population reports.* Washington, DC: Government Printing Office.

U.S. Department of Education. (1991). *Help your child become a good reader.* Washington, DC: Author.

U.S. Department of Education. (1998). Federal Reading Excellence Act. Washington, DC: U. S. Government Printing Office.

U.S. Department of Education. (2002a). The No Child Left Behind Act. Washington, DC: Author. Retrieved June 17, 2003, from http://www.edgov/nclb/overview

U.S. Department of Education. (2002b). *The No Child Left Behind Act of 2001: Executive Summary.* U.S. Department of Education. Retrieved July 15, 2002, from http://www.ed.gov/nclb/overview/intro/execsumm.html

U.S. Department of Education, National Center for Educational Statistics. (1993). *National Household Education Survey.* Washington, DC: Author.

U.S. Department of Education, Office of Educational Research and Improvement. (1994). *Identifying outstanding talent in American Indian and Alaska Native students.* Washington, DC: Author.

U.S. Department of Health and Human Services, Administration for Children and Families. (2003). *The Head Start leaders guide to positive child outcomes.* Washington, DC: Author.

U.S. Department of Health and Human Services Fatherhood Initiative. (2001). Retrieved June 6, 2002, from http://hhs.fatherhood.hhs.gov/index.shtml

U.S. Department of Health and Human Services. (2003). *The Head Start path to positive child outcomes.* [The Head Start Child Outcomes Framework]. Retrieved May 21, 2004, from http://www.hsnrc.org/CDI/outcontent.cfm

Vardell, S. M. (1994, September). Nonfiction for young children. *Young Children, 49*(6), 40–41.

Venn, E. C., & Jahn, M. D. (2004). *Teaching and learning in the preschool: Using individually appropriate practices in early childhood literacy instruction.* Newark, DE: International Reading Association.

Vernon-Feagans, L., Hammer C., Miccio, A., & Manlove, E. (2003). Early language and literacy skills in low-income African American and Hispanic children. In S. B. Neuman & D. Dickinson (Eds.), *Handbook of early literacy research* (pp. 192–210). New York: The Guilford Press.

Villarruel, F., Imig, D., & Kostelnik, M. (1995). Diverse families. In E. Garcia & B. McLaughlin (Eds.), *Meeting the challenge of linguistic and cultural diversity in early childhood education.* New York: Teachers College Press.

Vygotsky, L. (1986). *Thought and language.* Cambridge, MA: MIT Press.

Vygotsky, L. S. (1978). *Mind and society: The development of higher psychological process.* Cambridge, MA: Harvard University Press.

Vygotsky, L. S. (1980). *Mind in society.* Cambridge, MA: Harvard University Press.

Vygotsky, L. S. (1987). Thinking and speech. In R. W. Rieber & A. S. Carton (Eds.), *The collected works of L. S. Vygotsky* (N. Minick, Trans.). New York: Plenum.

Walmsley, S., & Adams, E. L. (1993, April). Realities of "whole language." *Language Arts, 70*(4), 272–280.

Wardle, F. (1987, November–December). Getting parents involved! *Pre-K Today, 2.3,* 71–75.

Wardle, F. (2003, September/October). Language immersion programs for young children. *Child Care Information Exchange, 153,* 54–57.

Washington, J., & Craig, H. K. (1995, June). In brief. *The Council Chronicle, National Council of Teachers of English, 4*(6), 5.

Weaver, C. (1998a). Introduction. In C. Weaver (Ed.), *Reconsidering a balanced approach to reading* (pp.

19–41). Urbana, IL: National Council of Teachers of English.

Weaver, C. (1998b). *Practicing what we know: Informed reading instruction.* Urbana, IL: National Council of Teachers of English.

Weaver, C. (Ed.). (1998c). *Reconsidering a balanced approach to reading.* Urbana, IL: National Council of Teachers of English.

Weir, M. E., & Eggleston, P. (1975, November/December). Teacher's first words. *Day Care and Early Education, 13.5,* 71–82.

Weiser, M. G. (1982). *Group care and education of infants and toddlers.* St. Louis: Mosby.

Weismann, D. (1970). *The visual arts as human experience.* Englewood Cliffs, NJ: Prentice Hall.

Weiss, C. E., & Lillywhite, H. S. (1981). *Communicative disorders.* St. Louis: Mosby.

Weissbourd, R. (1996). *The vulnerable child.* Reading, MA: Addison-Wesley.

Weitzman, E. (1992). *Learning language and loving it.* Toronto: A Hanen Centre Publication.

Wells, G. (1981). *Learning through interaction: The study of language development.* Cambridge, MA: Cambridge University Press.

Wells, G. (1986). *The meaning makers.* Portsmouth, NH: Heinemann.

Werner, E. E., & Smith, R. S. (1982). *Vulnerable, but invincible.* New York: McGraw-Hill.

West, J., Denton, K., & Germino-Hausken, E. (2000). *America's kindergartners.* Washington, DC: National Center for Educational Statistics.

Weymouth, F. W. (1963). *Visual acuity of children,* A symposium presentation at the National Education Association Conference, Philadelphia.

White, B. L. (1986a). *A person is emerging. Parents As Teachers program planning and implementation guide.* Jefferson City, MO: Missouri Department of Elementary and Secondary Education.

White, B. L. (1986b). *The learning experience. Parents As Teachers program planning and implementation guide.* Jefferson City, MO: Missouri Department of Elementary and Secondary Education.

White, B. L. (1987). *The first three years of life.* Englewood Cliffs, NJ: Prentice Hall.

Whitehurst, C. J., Epstein, J. N., Angell, A. L., Payne, A. C., Crone, D. A., & Fischel, J. E. (1994). Outcomes of emergent literacy intervention in Head Start. *Journal of Educational Psychology, 86,* 542–555.

Williams, K. C. (1997, September). What do you wonder? *Young Children, 52*(6), 78–81.

Wiltz, N. W., & Fein, C. G. (1996, March). Evolution of a narrative curriculum: The contributions of Vivian Gussin Paley. *Young Children, 51*(3), 61–68.

Wingert, P., & Kantrowitz, B. (1997, October 27). Why Andy couldn't read. *Newsweek,* pp. 56–64.

Winn, M. (1981). *Children without childhood.* New York: Pantheon.

Winter, M., & Rouse, J. (1990, February). Fostering intergenerational literacy: The Missouri Parents As Teachers Program. *The Reading Teacher, 43*(6), 382–386.

Wolf, J. (1992, January). Creating music with young children. *Young Children, 47*(2), 56–61.

Wolf, J. (1994, May). Singing with children is a cinch. *Young Children, 49*(4), 20–25.

Wolf, J. (2000, March). Sharing songs with children. *Young Children, 55*(2), 19–31.

Wong-Fillmore, L. (1976). The second time around: Cognitive and social strategies in second language acquisition. Unpublished doctoral dissertation, Stanford University, Stanford, CA.

Wong-Fillmore, L. (1991). When learning a second language means losing the first. *Early Childhood Research Quarterly, 6*(33), 323–346.

Woodward, C., Haskins, G., Schaefer, G., & Smolen, L. (2004, July). Let's talk: A different approach to oral language development. *Young Children, 59*(4), 92–95.

Wylie, R. E., & Durrell, D. (1970). Literacy. *Elementary English, 47,* 787–791.

Yaden, D., Jr., Smolkin, L. B., & Conlon, A. (1989). Preschoolers' questions about pictures, print, convention, and story text. *Reading Research Quarterly, 24*(2), 188–214.

Yairi, E., & Ambrose, N. G. (1999, October). Early childhood stuttering: Persistency and recovery rates. *Journal of Speech, Language and Hearing Research, 42,* 1097–1109.

Yokota, J. (1993, March). Issues in selecting multicultural children's literature. *Language Arts, 70,* 156–167.

Yopp, H. K. (1995, March). Teaching reading: Read-aloud books for developing phonemic awareness: An annotated bibliography. *The Reading Teacher, 48*(6), 538–542.

649